Living Liturgy

Living Liturgy

Spirituality, Celebration, and Catechesis for Sundays and Solemnities

Year C • 2004

Joyce Ann Zimmerman, C.PP.S.
Thomas A. Greisen
Kathleen Harmon, S.N.D. de N.
Thomas L. Leclerc, M.S.

LITURGICAL PRESS
Collegeville, Minnesota

www.litpress.org

Design by Ann Blattner. Art by Barbara Knutson.

ISBN 0-8146-2741-2 [Year C, 2004]

1   2   3   4   5   6   7   8

Library of Congress Cataloging-in-Publication Data

Living liturgy : spirituality, celebration, and catechesis for Sundays
and solemnities : year B, 2000 / Joyce Ann Zimmerman ... [et al.].
      p.   cm.
  Includes bibliographical references.
  ISBN 0-8146-2567-3 (alk. paper)
   1. Church year.   2. Bible—Liturgical use.   3. Catholic Church—
Liturgy.   I. Zimmerman, Joyce Ann, 1945–   .
BV30.L56   1999
264'.02—dc21

99-28091
CIP

CONTENTS

Contributors   vi

Using this Resource   vii

Introduction to Luke's Gospel   ix

Abbreviations   xi

Season of Advent   1

Season of Christmas   21

Ordinary Time I   41

Season of Lent   67

Easter Triduum   99

Season of Easter   111

Ordinary Time II   145

Appendix A   259

Appendix B   290

Appendix C   292

Index of Liturgical Topics   296

Index of Biblical Topics   298

CONTRIBUTORS

Joyce Ann Zimmerman, C.PP.S. is the director of the Institute for Liturgical Ministry in Dayton, Ohio, and is the founding editor and columnist for *Liturgical Ministry*. She is also an adjunct professor of liturgy, liturgical consultant, and frequent facilitator of workshops on liturgy. She has published numerous scholarly and pastoral liturgical works. She holds civil and pontifical doctorates of theology.

Thomas A. Greisen is a priest of the Archdiocese of Omaha, Nebraska, who is presently the director of the Lay Ministry Formation Office for the Archdiocese of Omaha and a spiritual director. He has been the director of spiritual formation for college seminarians and a professor of spirituality. He holds graduate degrees in both theology and spirituality.

Kathleen Harmon, S.N.D. de N. is the music director for programs of the Institute for Liturgical Ministry in Dayton, Ohio, and is the author of the *Music Notes* column for *Liturgical Ministry*. An educator and musician, she facilitates liturgical music workshops and cantor formation programs, teaches private voice lessons, and is a parish liturgy and music director. She holds a graduate degree in music and a doctorate in liturgy.

Thomas L. Leclerc, M.S. is a priest of the Missionaries of La Salette (North American Province). He has been director of theology for his congregation, an associate pastor in parishes in Georgia and Connecticut, has been involved with adult education in the Archdioceses of Atlanta and Boston, and has been a professor of Sacred Scripture. He holds a doctorate of theology in Hebrew Bible/Old Testament.

+ USING THIS RESOURCE

Sunday after Sunday people gather for liturgy. With rare exception, whatever is the scheduled time for a Mass, there it is—presider and ministers are there, environment is appropriate, bread and wine, etc., are out and ready. How many of us have ever wondered how many hours of preparation goes into making all this happen? How many hours does Father spend preparing his homily? How many hours does the sacristan put in cleaning linens? How many hours do the musicians practice? And the list goes on. Yes, many hours go into prayerfully celebrating each Mass. Yet, the most important preparation of all is that of those who gather as assembly. The word "liturgy" comes from two Greek words meaning the "work of the people." The real work isn't so much the participation at Mass itself; the real work of the people is the preparation they put into Mass *before they come on Sunday* and the *way they live Mass* once they've left Church. This Mass preparation aid is planned specifically to help people prepare for and live liturgy.

Living Liturgy: Spirituality, Celebration, and Catechesis for Sundays and Solemnities is designed to help people live a liturgical spirituality (that is, a spirituality or way of living that is rooted in liturgy) which opens their vision to their baptismal identity as the body of Christ and shapes their living according to the rhythm of paschal mystery dying and rising. The paschal mystery is the entire salvific mystery of Jesus Christ—that is, his life, mission, passion, death, resurrection, ascension, sending of the Spirit, and promised second coming—and *our* participation in this mystery. Liturgy both *enacts* in the here and now Christ's mystery as well as sends each one of us forth to *live* this mystery.

This volume is entirely new, although there have been no major format changes this time. We have included with this volume a separate, more lengthy article at the beginning of the book to offer readers a more substantial introduction to Luke's gospel and its use in the Lectionary. Readers will also notice a different format for the questions for reflection for the various liturgical ministers. Rather than questions they are now written as open-ended statements (and written with the first person pronoun) appropriate for reflection whether that is alone or with others in a faith-sharing group. Hopefully, this will open up the discussion to a broader range of possibilities than the questions suggested. Also, we've added an Appendix C which is a Lectionary pronunciation guide, especially helpful for lectors who use *Living Liturgy* to prepare themselves to proclaim well on Sundays.

LITURGY TAKES WORK!

LITURGICAL SPIRITUALITY: PASCHAL MYSTERY LIVING

WHAT'S NEW IN THIS VOLUME

THOSE WHO WOULD BENEFIT BY USING THIS RESOURCE

Clearly, anyone involved directly with liturgical planning and preparation would benefit from using this resource, including **clergy, pastoral ministers, liturgy directors, musicians,** and **liturgy committee members**. *Living Liturgy* also assists those who serve the community in the **visible liturgical ministries** (presiders, deacons, music ministers, hospitality ministers, altar ministers, lectors, eucharistic ministers) because it clearly shows that each ministry deserves not only practical preparation but (even more importantly) spiritual preparation, suggestions for which are a key component of *Living Liturgy*. Further, **catechumens, candidates, and sponsors** could use *Living Liturgy* to support and deepen their liturgical journey within the R.C.I.A. and **members of faith-sharing groups** could use this resource as the focus of weekly prayer and reflection together. **Parents** and **teachers** could improve their ministry by simplifying its content and sharing it with younger members of the liturgical community.

SPIRITUALITY, CELEBRATION, AND CATECHESIS

A threefold dynamic of daily living, prayer, and study determines the basic structure of *Living Liturgy*. The content on the two pages for each Sunday and solemnity under the heading "Spirituality" helps us grasp that our living the paschal mystery is shaped by focusing the word that leads to prayerful reflection on the gospel. The content under "Celebration" suggests models for introductory rites and general intercessions which are derived from the readings and/or liturgical season; also on this page is content that enables the assembly to understand better the responsorial psalm and its relationship to the readings. The content under "Catechesis" leads to a better grasp of elements of liturgy and liturgical music. Rather than a systematic approach to liturgical catechesis, these catechetical points flow from aspects of the readings or the liturgical season and are not intended to be comprehensive; in time, however, much is covered!

UNIQUE FEATURES

Certain unique features mark this resource. First, *Living Liturgy* clearly identifies the paschal mystery as the core of liturgy and our everyday living. Second, *Living Liturgy* takes the gospel as the starting point of liturgical preparation, for there we learn about Jesus' identity and mission and are challenged to take these up as our own. Third, *Living Liturgy* integrates spirituality, celebration, and catechesis. Fourth, it was written by a pastorally-experienced team with expertise in each area. Fifth, *Living Liturgy* includes solemnities since these festivals are so intimately connected to our annual unfolding of the paschal mystery; for those unable to participate in Mass on these days, the material here can still be used for personal prayer and reflection. Sixth, *Living Liturgy* has a simple and consistent format with short and to-the-point sections that aid using only snatches at a time for reflection. And finally, seventh, *Living Liturgy* suggests methods (printed on a handy bookmark card) for how both individuals and groups might use this resource.

LIVE DIVINE MERCY AND COMPASSION!

During this year when we draw so heavily on Luke's gospel, we are immersed in divine mercy and compassion. What better way to live the liturgy than to consciously emulate these expressions of God's love for us! What better way to prepare for celebrating liturgy than being merciful and compassionate as God is toward us! Thus may all of us learn to rejoice more deeply in God our savior.

INTRODUCTION to the Lectionary's Proclamation of the Gospel according to Luke

This liturgical year our scriptural guide to living the paschal mystery is Saint Luke. From the First Sunday of Advent to the Last Sunday of the Year (The Solemnity of Our Lord Jesus Christ the King), the universal Church will walk in the company of Saint Luke whose lively narratives, vivid characters, and poignant scenes unfold the mission, message, and meaning of Jesus, the Savior.

Yet our journey with Luke is not a mini-course in Luke's gospel, that is, the liturgy is not a classroom in which we will study the theology and themes of this year's gospel. To approach the gospel in this way would be a serious misunderstanding of liturgy. The liturgy is not a forum in which to present the gospel; instead, the gospel is placed at the service of the liturgy where we encounter the living Lord Jesus and, through word, ritual, and sacrament, enter more deeply into the pattern of his dying and rising. This introduction will describe, first, some of the characteristics of the gospel so that our proclamation of individual passages will benefit from the context of Luke's work and, second, how the Lectionary (the assigned readings) makes use of the Gospel according to Luke, drawing the worshiping community into deeper union with Jesus.

Luke and his gospel. Luke was an extraordinary writer whose monumental two-volume work (the Gospel and the Acts of the Apostles) fills almost one-quarter of the New Testament. It seems likely that Luke was a Gentile (perhaps a convert to Judaism) who wrote in the mid-eighties. It is possible, though not certain, that he was a companion of St. Paul (Phlm 24; Col 4:14). Luke himself acknowledges that he is not an eyewitness to the ministry of Jesus but he assures readers that he has spoken to eyewitnesses and has carefully examined other written accounts of Jesus' life (Luke 1:1-4).

While we may not know a lot about Luke, most people know a good deal about his gospel. Some of the most cherished stories about Jesus are reported by Luke: the annunciation to Mary, the birth in a manger, the disciples on the road to Emmaus. Some of the New Testament's most memorable characters are found in Luke: the diminutive but resourceful Zacchaeus, the aged and astonished Elizabeth and Zechariah, the hospitable Martha and the attentive Mary. Some of Jesus' most beloved parables—brimming with poignancy and compassion, and universal in their broad religious and humanitarian appeal—are jewels of Luke's gospel: the good Samaritan, the prodigal son, the rich man and poor Lazarus, the Pharisee and the tax collector. The backbone of the Church's daily prayer comes from Luke's gospel: Zechariah's canticle at morning prayer, Mary's *Magnificat* at evening prayer, and Simeon's canticle at night prayer.

His gospel is such a treasure trove of themes that it has invited numerous nicknames, such as "The Gospel of Joy," "The Gospel of the Holy Spirit . . . of Prayer . . . of the Poor," among others. Other obvious themes include warnings against wealth; frequent meals with sinners; the inclusion of women; and concern for tax collectors, lepers, and outcasts. Luke's portrait of Jesus is perhaps the most beloved and easily approachable of all the gospels: Luke's Jesus is the embodiment of divine compassion. Indeed, Luke's portrayal of Jesus is at the heart of his proclamation of the "good news."

Luke advances his understanding of Jesus in two noteworthy ways. One way is in the titles he uses of Jesus. While Luke follows other gospel writers in calling Jesus "Son of God," "Son of Man," and "Messiah," Luke is distinctive among the synoptic gospels in calling Jesus the "Savior" (2:11). Jesus' work as Savior is anticipated in many healing stories in which one is "saved" (7:50/Sunday 11; 8:36, 48, 50; 17:19/Sunday 28; 18:42). Discussion about Jesus as Savior appropriately dominates the crucifixion (23:35, 37, 39). Another favorite title Luke uses of Jesus is "Lord." In the New Testament "Lord" is typically a post-Easter title; its occurrence throughout the Gospel, especially its use by the narrator, serves to present the entire Gospel as an Easter proclamation of faith in Jesus.

A second distinctive feature of Luke's portrayal of Jesus is his presentation of Jesus as compassionate and merciful. Early in the gospel the Canticle of Mary (the *Magnificat*) indicates that God is acting now because "he has remembered his promise of mercy . . .

to Abraham and his descendants for ever" (1:54-55). As the Canticle of Zechariah makes clear, the "tender mercy" of God "promised through the holy prophets of old" and sworn "to our father Abraham" is a promise of "redemption" and a "horn of salvation" (1:68-79). For Luke "mercy" means "salvation." Jesus, born "within the house of David," is the fulfillment of that ancient promise.

This theme of divine mercy/compassion is evident throughout the gospel, from beginning to end. At the outset angels announce to shepherds the Savior's birth; at the close of the gospel Jesus assures the thief who was crucified with him, "today you will be with me in Paradise" (23:43). In between these enactments of salvation Jesus uses the image of a father welcoming the return of the prodigal son to describe the compassion of God (15:11-32/Sunday 24 and Lent 4); in the parable of the good Samaritan (10:25-37/Sunday 15) Jesus urges his disciples to extend to others a similar compassion and mercy. The astounding and confounding compassion of God is announced programmatically by Mary who declares that God "has thrown down the rulers from their thrones but lifted up the lowly; the hungry he has filled with good things; the rich he has sent away empty" (Luke 1:52-53). The ministry of Jesus is the realization of this compassion for the lowly and the poor, the outcast and the sinner.

Jesus' ability to embody such a tender divine compassion is rooted in his profound prayer, an aspect of Jesus' personal life which Luke develops more completely than any other evangelist. Not surprisingly, then, this prayerful Jesus devotes particular attention to instructing his disciples in prayer (the friend at night, 11:5-8/Sunday 17; the persistent widow, 18:1-8/Sunday 29; the Pharisee and the tax collector, 18:9-14/Sunday 30). The inner strength that comes from prayer is showcased in the passion narrative which describes Jesus at prayer no fewer than six times. Luke further shows Jesus ending his life by praying from the cross that his executioners be forgiven—the consummate extension of mercy. Finally, Jesus serenely commends his life into God's hands. Jesus' ministry of mercy and compassion, grounded in his prayer, is the basis of the "good news" that God, in Christ, is fulfilling the ancient promise of mercy to Jews and Gentiles alike.

Luke in the Lectionary. The primary purpose of the Lectionary is to draw people into the liturgical experience of the paschal mystery celebrated in both word and sacrament. Our focus in these brief comments is on the word. As indicated above Mary's *Magnificat* and the Canticle of Zechariah set out some of the major themes Luke develops throughout his gospel: the Canticle of Zechariah highlights the themes of mercy and salvation so central to the gospel while the *Magnificat* announces the pattern of reversal that illuminates both Jesus' teaching and minis-

try to outcasts. As central as these are to the themes and theology of Luke, neither is included in the Sunday readings. Instead the Lectionary will develop these aspects in the ministry of Jesus as aspects of the paschal mystery to be lived rather than as literary themes to be understood and appreciated.

Another example of the Lectionary's distinctive approach is found in the infancy stories. Luke presents the annunciation and birth of Jesus alongside the annunciation and birth of John the Baptist: the two annunciations and two births are presented back-to-back, John's stories first, then those of Jesus. Luke goes to great lengths to show how extraordinary John is and then he shows how Jesus is even greater. This is key to Luke's understanding of Jesus in the history of salvation. Yet the Sunday Lectionary includes none of the stories about John, for the paschal mystery is embodied in Jesus, not in his esteemed forerunner. In Jesus the compassion and mercy of God find their fullest expression.

Though the Lectionary's selection of readings is chosen to unfold the paschal mystery, it does not disregard all the special features of Luke. On the one hand, it is selective in developing some of his favorite themes (mercy, compassion, salvation, prayer) but not others (the passion predictions, the centrality of the Temple). It is careful to include all fourteen parables that only Luke recounts as well as events unique to Luke, e.g., the stories of Martha and Mary (Sunday 16), Zacchaeus (Sunday 31), and the disciples on the road to Emmaus (Easter 3). With only one exception the Lectionary for year C does not repeat any parable that is proclaimed in year A (Matthew) or year B (Mark); and with so many parables found only in Luke, the Lectionary only once gives Luke's version of a parable which is also found in one of the other gospels. All of this is to point out that the Lectionary is conscious of the three-year rotation of gospels, carefully avoiding undue repetition and taking advantage of the distinctive material in each of the three synoptic gospels. Because of the three year architecture of the Lectionary, repeated events or stories can be omitted even if they are central to an individual gospel's structure or theme. On the other hand, by repeating certain stories in each of the three years (e.g., Peter's profession of faith: Sundays 21A, 24B, 12C; the feeding of the five thousand: Sundays 18A, 17B, Body and Blood of Christ, C), the Lectionary draws attention to those passages which are of particular significance to the Church. Which brings us back to an important point: the gospel serves the liturgy, and the liturgy does not serve the gospel. What is paramount is the paschal mystery. Though there may be a variety of ways to approach it, there is only one paschal mystery. The Gospel according to Luke is this year's guide to our entering more deeply into the dying and rising of Jesus.

ABBREVIATIONS

LITURGICAL RESOURCES

BofB   *Book of Blessings*. International Commission on English in the Liturgy. Collegeville: The Liturgical Press, 1989.

EACW   *Environment and Art in Catholic Worship.* In *The Liturgy Documents: A Parish Resource.* 3rd edition. Chicago: Liturgy Training Publications, 1991.

GIRM   *General Instruction of the Roman Missal* (2000).

GNLYC   General Norms for the Liturgical Year and the Calendar. In *The Liturgy Documents.*

ILM   Introduction to the Lectionary for Mass

L   *Lectionary*

NT   New Testament

OT   Old Testament

SC   *Sacrosanctum Concilium.* The Constitution on the Sacred Liturgy. Vatican II. In *The Liturgy Documents.*

MUSICAL RESOURCES

BB   *Breaking Bread.* Portland, OR: Oregon Catholic Press.

CBW3   *Catholic Book of Worship III.* Ottawa, Ontario: Canadian Conference of Catholic Bishops, 1994.

CH   *The Collegeville Hymnal.* Collegeville: The Liturgical Press, 1990.

G   *Gather.* Chicago: GIA Publications, Inc., 1988.

G2   *Gather.* 2nd edition. Chicago: GIA Publications, Inc., 1994.

GC   *Gather Comprehensive.* Chicago: GIA Publications, Inc., 1994.

HG   *Hymns for the Gospels.* Chicago: GIA Publications, Inc., 2001.

LMGM   *Lead Me, Guide Me.* Chicago: GIA Publications, Inc., 1987.

RS   *Ritual Song.* Chicago: GIA Publications, Inc., 1996.

W3   *Worship.* 3rd edition. Chicago: GIA Publications, Inc., 1986.

WC   *We Celebrate.* Schiller Park, IL: World Library Publications, 2001.

GIA   GIA Publications, Inc.

OCP   Oregon Catholic Press

WLP   World Library Publications

Season of Advent

SPIRITUALITY

Gospel

Luke 21:25-28, 34-36; L3C

Jesus said to his disciples:
"There will be signs in the sun,
    the moon, and the stars,
    and on earth nations will be in
        dismay,
    perplexed by the roaring of the
        sea and the waves.
People will die of fright
    in anticipation of what is
        coming upon the world,
    for the powers of the heavens
        will be shaken.
And then they will see the Son of
    Man
    coming in a cloud with power and
        great glory.
But when these signs begin to happen,
    stand erect and raise your heads
    because your redemption is at hand.

"Beware that your hearts do not
        become drowsy
    from carousing and drunkenness
    and the anxieties of daily life,
    and that day catch you by surprise
        like a trap.
For that day will assault everyone
    who lives on the face of the earth.
Be vigilant at all times
    and pray that you have the strength
    to escape the tribulations that are
        imminent
    and to stand before the Son of Man."

Reflecting on the Gospel

The future has always held a fascination for us humans. We keep talismans and do rituals; we may hunt for four-leaf clovers or carry a rabbit's foot or knock on wood for good luck. To ward off bad luck we may avoid walking under ladders and stepping on cracks in the sidewalk or we may stay home on a Friday the 13th. Wouldn't it have been nice if Jesus had simply said (when he warned us of the future events of the end of the world and judgment), "Here, carry this olive seed in your pocket and it will protect you" or, "Add some myrrh to your bath water each night and you will be safe." Instead of such magical notions Jesus gives us a blueprint for *guaranteeing* a certain future for ourselves: we begin our liturgical year by having a glimpse of where the journey takes us.

Jeremiah's prophesying of the Lord's promise of a new world with safety and security for all is fulfilled in the coming of the Son of Man. For some, this will be a time of dismay, perplexity, and fright. For others, it is a time to embrace the coming of the Son of Man with redemption. What is it that puts us in one group or the other? According to Jesus the answer is quite simple: those who are not vigilant belong to the doomed group; those who are vigilant belong to the saved group. The answer may be simple but "being vigilant *at all times*" is quite a challenge and requires that we live with heightened attentiveness to the presence of God.

The gospel charges us to "stand erect and raise [our] heads." The image here is of readiness and anticipation. The challenge is that the Lord's coming isn't something that we take for granted or that we only think about when we end one and begin another liturgical year. Anticipation of the Lord's coming *determines* how we live each day. The readiness *is the anticipation*. The gospel also charges us to "stand before the Son of Man." The image here is of such an intimacy with Jesus that the Son of Man *has already come* for us, is present to us. We do not fear these future calamities because we are already in union with the One who is to come. This intimacy of union with the Divine is born out of our prayer and is the source of our strength. The intimacy *is the prayer and strength*.

We Christians don't need a rabbit's foot or some silly little ritual to ward off future calamities. All we need is daily vigilance, for our redemption is already at hand. Our "talisman" is Christ crucified and our profound, saving ritual is constantly seeking union with Christ who is already the fulfillment of God's promise.

Living the Paschal Mystery

Vigilance for the many comings of Christ in our daily lives involves a dying to self. This means that our focus is not on our own wants and needs but on the Christ who chooses to be intimately present to us. Our prayer for strength might be that Jesus help us see his presence in the people around us. This is pretty easy (with a practical reminder to ourselves) when the other person is pleasant or cooperative or helpful. The dying happens when the other is cranky or not to our liking or threatening. How can we see Christ in the other when the other doesn't conform to our image of Christ? This is the question "anxieties of daily life" raises. The dying comes in growing in our image of who Christ is! The dying comes in forming the habit of seeing Christ in *all* others because Christ came to redeem *all*. The rising comes in constant vigilance, for Christ comes in many ways.

Focusing the Word

Key words and phrases from the gospel: Son of Man coming, redemption is at hand

To the point: The gospel (and the entire season of Advent) proclaims that the Lord comes. The Lord's coming *fulfills* God's promise (first reading), *reveals* God's purpose ("redemption is at hand"; gospel), and *strengthens* us to "stand erect and raise [our] head[s]," readied for the Lord even now in "the anxieties of daily life."

Connecting the Word

to the second reading: Paul commends the Thessalonians for conducting themselves in a manner pleasing to God and exhorts them to "do so even more." Similarly, Advent invites us to consider what we already do that is pleasing to God and to "do so even more."

to culture: Typically, we tend to want things now even knowing that we will pay later, for example, when the bills come in. Advent reverses this "have now, pay later" lifestyle to one in which we conduct ourselves rightly now for the sake of future glory, or in other words, "pay now, have later."

Understanding the Word

Promise/Fulfillment: Luke begins his gospel with a formal introduction that describes his work and the work of others who preceded him as a "narrative of the events that have been fulfilled among us" (1:1). The theme of "fulfillment" is important to Luke as he presents his gospel both to Jewish and Gentile Christians. To his Jewish Christian readers Luke offers assurances that God's word is reliable and that ancient promises made to their ancestors have not been abrogated but instead have been fulfilled. Thus, both Mary and Zechariah in their Canticles indicate that the wondrous deeds signaled in the annunciation to Mary and in the birth of John the Baptist are concrete realizations of past commitments. Mary exclaims that God remembered his mercy "according to his promise to our fathers, to Abraham and to his descendants forever" (1:54-55); Zechariah praises God who "has raised up a horn for our salvation . . . as he promised through the mouth of his holy prophets from of old" (1:69-70). Divine promises and prophetic words are being fulfilled in Jesus.

Luke's Gentile readers face a different but related problem: as Christianity loses ground in the Jewish world and increasingly moves into Gentile territory, it could easily be assumed that God has abandoned the Jews and has newly adopted the Gentiles. (Paul had to argue against this view in his letter to the Romans.) If this were the case, Gentiles might fear that God would also abandon them in the future. Luke goes to great lengths to show that God's plan is orderly (1:3): the offer of salvation began with Jews and when God had fulfilled the divine promises to them, God extended salvation to include Gentiles. Thus, Gentiles can be assured that Jesus' offer of salvation is trustworthy and is a continuation of the divine mercy that began with the Jewish ancestors, "Abraham and his descendants."

In like manner, the words of Jesus in this gospel are trustworthy. Being forewarned, disciples can stand with confident assurance because the coming of the Son of Man is not disaster, but rather is the dawn of their redemption.

ASSEMBLY & FAITH-SHARING GROUPS

- In my daily living I usually anticipate and concern myself with . . . Advent makes me remember to concern myself with . . .
- My heart and faith "become drowsy" when I . . .
- Some of the ways I try to "be vigilant at all times" for Christ's coming are . . .

PRESIDERS

My living and my ministry are an advent, a fulfilling of the Lord's promise (see first reading) when . . .

DEACONS

The "do so even more" (see second reading) to which Advent calls me is . . .

HOSPITALITY MINISTERS

I notice how Christ comes to me in the gathering of the assembly whenever . . .

MUSIC MINISTERS

Leading the music of the assembly is an act of vigilance for Christ's coming when . . . It is a revelation of Christ's coming when . . .

ALTAR MINISTERS

My service at the altar models the vigilance Advent requires whenever I . . .

LECTORS

God's word during Advent awakens the drowsy heart. As God's living word I awaken the drowsiness of others when I . . .

EUCHARISTIC MINISTERS

My life—as Christ's Eucharist for others—reveals Christ's coming when I . . . I nourish and strengthen others until Christ comes in glory whenever I . . .

Model Penitential Rite

Presider: Our God is coming—not just in our anticipation of Christmas as we begin Advent, but at the end of time when Christ will come in great power to judge and save. We pause at the beginning of this celebration to open our hearts in anticipation and ask God to help us be ever vigilant . . . [pause]

Lord Jesus, you are the Son of Man who comes in great power and glory: Lord . . .

Christ Jesus, you bring redemption and peace: Christ . . .

Lord Jesus, you call us to vigilance and prayer: Lord . . .

Appreciating the Responsorial Psalm

Christ challenges us in the gospel for this First Sunday of Advent not to "become drowsy" but to remain "vigilant" while we await his final coming at the end of time. "Pray," he says, "that you have the strength" and this is just what Paul does for us in the second reading ("May the Lord . . . strengthen your hearts"). The final coming of Christ stands in some unknown future but we are to conduct ourselves now with the holiness (second reading) that will enable us to "stand erect" when we at last see him face-to-face (gospel). The verses we sing this Sunday from Psalm 25 are a humble request to be guided by God along the path of righteousness. They are a confident assertion of God's friendship and constancy along the way. They express our prayer that God will indeed keep us strong until the end.

Model General Intercessions

Presider: We pray to a God who is ever attentive to our needs.

Response:

Lord, hear our prayer.

Cantor:

we pray to the Lord,

That all the Church have the strength to live lives reflecting that Christ is already present among us . . . [pause]

That all world leaders have the strength to govern with justice and equity . . . [pause]

That the weak and downhearted have the strength to stand erect and recognize Christ's presence to them . . . [pause]

That each of us here have the strength always to see Christ in each other . . . [pause]

Presider: O God, you come to save us: hear these our prayers of need that we might be ready to meet you when you come. We ask this through Christ our Lord. **Amen.**

OPENING PRAYER
Let us pray
[that we may take Christ's coming seriously]

Pause for silent prayer

All-powerful God,
increase our strength of will for doing good
that Christ may find an eager welcome at his coming
and call us to his side in the kingdom of heaven,
where he lives and reigns with you and the Holy Spirit,
one God, for ever and ever. **Amen.**

FIRST READING
Jer 33:14-16

The days are coming, says the LORD,
when I will fulfill the promise
I made to the house of Israel and Judah.
In those days, in that time,
I will raise up for David a just shoot;
he shall do what is right and just in the land.
In those days Judah shall be safe
and Jerusalem shall dwell secure;
this is what they shall call her:
"The LORD our justice."

RESPONSORIAL PSALM
Ps 25:4-5, 8-9, 10, 14

℟. (1b) To you, O Lord, I lift my soul.

Your ways, O LORD, make known to me;
    teach me your paths,
guide me in your truth and teach me,
    for you are God my savior,
    and for you I wait all the day.

℟. To you, O Lord, I lift my soul.

Good and upright is the LORD;
    thus he shows sinners the way.
He guides the humble to justice,
    and teaches the humble his way.

℟. To you, O Lord, I lift my soul.

All the paths of the LORD are kindness and
    constancy
    toward those who keep his covenant
        and his decrees.
The friendship of the LORD is with those
    who fear him,
    and his covenant, for their instruction.

℟. To you, O Lord, I lift my soul.

SECOND READING
1 Thess 3:12–4:2

Brothers and sisters:
May the Lord make you increase and
    abound in love
    for one another and for all,
    just as we have for you,
    so as to strengthen your hearts,
    to be blameless in holiness before our
        God and Father
    at the coming of our Lord Jesus with all
        his holy ones. Amen.

Finally, brothers and sisters,
    we earnestly ask and exhort you in the
        Lord Jesus that,
    as you received from us
    how you should conduct yourselves to
        please God
    —and as you are conducting
        yourselves—
    you do so even more.
For you know what instructions we gave
    you through the Lord Jesus.

About Liturgy

Advent and redemption: The future is in God's hands and God will bring it to fulfillment. What we do know is the outcome (God comes with redemption) and how we achieve it (through intimacy with Christ). Advent is a special liturgical season which begins with looking to the future, comes to a climax in looking to the past, and bears fruit in the present. Advent is a season when we bring to mind and celebrate the three comings of Christ and redemption.

Christ's first coming (which we celebrate on Christmas) *fulfilled* the Old Testament prophecies that God's Messiah would come to restore all things new. Christ's birth as the incarnate Son fulfilled these promises. Jesus' public ministry showed us how God's new reign would come about: by repenting and believing in the gospel. His death and resurrection assured us that salvation is surely at hand, but it is only at Christ's second coming that the fullness of God's glory and justice will be *revealed.* We find ourselves in an age straddling the first and second comings of Christ, at a time when we need to be *strengthened* now. The third coming of Christ is *now,* when Christ comes, first and foremost, in sacraments but no less through each other. Our Advent vigilance and waiting doesn't just look back to the first coming or forward to the second coming. The first coming bears fruit and the second coming is not frightening to the extent that our vigilance and waiting is in the here and now, recognizing Christ in the many sacramental comings of our everyday lives.

The challenge of Advent and our Christian living is to heighten our expectation of the coming of Christ so that we can be attentive to Christ's presence already among us. Attentive waiting is already a presence that is redemptive.

About Liturgical Music

Cantor preparation: As you sing this psalm refrain you model the posture of the Church during these days of Advent—heads up and eyes lifted for the coming of Christ. Use the refrain every day as part of your personal prayer. At the end of the week reflect on how this has kept you ready for the coming of Christ and helped you spot his arrival.

Songs for the first two weeks of Advent: The songs we sing for the first two Sundays of Advent should focus on Christ's coming in glory at the end of time. Singing songs such as "Soon and Very Soon"; "The King Shall Come"; "Wait for the Lord"; "City of God, Jerusalem"; and "When the Lord in Glory Comes" will pull us into the messianic vision which characterizes the beginning weeks of Advent. Songs such as "O Come, O Come, Emmanuel" need to be reserved for the final two weeks of Advent when the focus shifts to expectation of Christ's coming by incarnation.

Advent service music: One of the most important functions of service music is to mark the liturgical season. The parish needs to have a set reserved for use only during Advent, a setting which draws people into joyful expectation without spilling over into the total exuberance of Easter and expresses quiet waiting without the penitential somberness of Lent. Since Advent and Christmas together form a unified festal season, it would be best to use a setting which can be sung simply during Advent and then embellished with choral and instrumental parts between Christmas and Epiphany.

✝ SPIRITUALITY

Gospel

Luke 3:1-6; L6C

In the fifteenth year of the reign of
   Tiberius Caesar,
   when Pontius Pilate was governor
      of Judea,
   and Herod was tetrarch of Galilee,
   and his brother Philip tetrarch of
      the region of Ituraea and
      Trachonitis,
   and Lysanias was tetrarch of
      Abilene,
   during the high priesthood of
      Annas and Caiaphas,
   the word of God came to John the
      son of Zechariah in the desert.
John went throughout the whole region
   of the Jordan,
   proclaiming a baptism of repentance
      for the forgiveness of sins,
   as it is written in the book of the
      words of the prophet Isaiah:
   *A voice of one crying out in the
      desert:*
   "Prepare the way of the Lord,
      make straight his paths.
   Every valley shall be filled
      and every mountain and hill shall
         be made low.
   The winding roads shall be made
      straight,
      and the rough ways made smooth,
   and all flesh shall see the salvation
      of God."

Reflecting on the Gospel

Homing pigeons are fascinating birds that have long baffled ornithologists. They can be trained to return home swiftly without losing their way from even several thousand miles. It's clear that they don't do this by eyesight; the birds can be blindfolded and they still find their way home. Researchers generally agree that it is probably no one faculty that enables the pigeons to find their home, but a combination of possibilities including "reading" the position of the sun and stars, magnetic fields in the earth, ultraviolet light patterns in the sky or polarized light, or perhaps they are guided by sound waves. However they do it, they are masters at finding home. At this time of liturgical year when we consider the end times and our own true and ultimate home, we might well wonder what leads us just as swiftly and surely there. John the Baptist gives us a pretty clear answer in this Sunday's gospel.

The gospel selection concludes with a concrete description of our true home—of the fullness of the end days when everything "shall be made straight" and "all flesh shall see the salvation of God." How do we arrive swiftly and surely at our true home—to the fullness of these end days? John gives us the answer when he proclaims "a baptism of repentance for the forgiveness of sins." The struggle of this life is with captivity yielding to freedom, sorrow turning to joy, darkness revealing glory, and justice made known through mercy (see first reading). John's call to repentance is our homing pigeon heading us in the right direction to our true home with God.

The salvation of God is progressively revealed in repentance (our work) and forgiveness (God's work). The paths and winding roads of our lives are straightened and the valleys filled and mountains brought low when our lives are characterized by attitudes of repentance. To repent means to change one's mind, one's life; this is how we reach the fullness that is promised and our true home: by increasing our love for one another, discerning "what is of [true] value," and by being "filled with the fruit of righteousness" (see second reading). Our work of repentance is a matter of turning ourselves toward the God who embraces us in mercy and forgiveness and welcomes us home.

Living the Paschal Mystery

Last Sunday's gospel directed our attention to the end times and gave us a glimpse of those times, both in terms of the calamities that will befall those who are not ready as well as the promise of safety and security for those who are vigilant. This Sunday both the gospel and first reading give us a glimpse of the fullness of the end days. Our natural tendency is to want to get to the fullness and bypass the hard work of daily dying to self that is required to reach the glory and joy that is promised.

Let's be honest: it's not just the busyness of Christmas preparations now in full December fury that distract us from our ongoing work of repentance. Every day of the year we tend to be distracted by mountains of work, paths of indecision, valleys of doubt and fear. This would be a good Sunday in Advent to take some special time to reflect on God's forgiveness and mercy and how it is God who gives sure direction to our lives and will eventually bring us home to eternal glory if we are faithful partners in the gospel. Our Advent watchfulness and waiting includes taking time to rest in the security of God's nearness.

Focusing the Word

Key words and phrases from the gospel: the word of God came to John, repentance, forgiveness, all flesh shall see the salvation of God

To the point: Baruch's prophecy of a glorious future was fulfilled when Israel returned from exile (first reading and psalm). John's prophecy of future glory ("all flesh shall see the salvation of God") is fulfilled when we return to God through repentance and forgiveness.

Connecting the Word

to the second reading: Paul's prayer for the Philippians focuses our own Advent prayer: that we bear "partnership for the gospel" and increase our love for one another. And, in this way, we, like John, make known to "all flesh . . . the salvation of God."

to Catholic culture: When we hear the words "repentance" and "forgiveness of sins" some immediately think of confession and the Sacrament of Penance. The gospel points us to repentance and forgiveness as a way of life.

Understanding the Word

Repentance/Forgiveness: Luke uses the technical term "proclaiming" to describe the preaching of John (3:3), Jesus' preaching in the synagogues (4:44), and Jesus' announcing "the good news of the Kingdom of God" (8:1). John's exhortations, then, are more than ordinary preaching: his ministry, like the ministry of Jesus, is a proclamation of the gospel. Moreover, his preparatory ministry fulfills Gabriel's prediction to Zechariah ("he will turn many of the children of Israel to the Lord their God. He will go before [the Lord] in the spirit and power of Elijah"; 1:16-17) and anticipates the ministry of the disciples when the risen Jesus sends them to proclaim "repentance for the forgiveness of sins" (24:47).

John is proclaiming "a baptism of repentance for the forgiveness of sins." Washing in water is both part of traditional Jewish ritual practice (see Leviticus 15) and is generally symbolic of the removal of sin. John's baptism, however, requires that sinners change their ways. Isaiah 1:16-17 is a powerful example of the relationship between washing and a change in behavior: "Wash yourselves clean! Put away your misdeeds from before my eyes; cease doing evil; learn to do good." One is purified by changing behavior. In this way John's baptism symbolizes repentance. In next Sunday's gospel John describes specific concrete changes in the lives of a number of different people. Repentance is real to the extent that it brings about change; such repentance is the precondition for forgiveness.

But baptism is more than an expression of repentance: it is also a ritual enactment of the good news that sin can be taken away. Forgiveness of sins reveals the mercy of God and draws the individual into an experience of salvation. But for baptism to be a saving event, a change of behavior is necessary. John's baptism ritualizes both the repentance of the sinner and God's forgiveness of sin.

Luke understands John's ministry as a fulfillment of the passage from Isaiah which he quotes (Isa 40:3-5a). The future coming of salvation which Isaiah had foreseen is taking place now in the ministry of John and in the coming of Jesus.

ASSEMBLY & FAITH-SHARING GROUPS

- John's call "of repentance for the forgiveness of sins" is real for me in my relationship with . . .

PRESIDERS

During this Advent the "good work" that Christ is completing *in* me is . . . (see second reading); the "good work" that Christ is completing *through* me is . . .

DEACONS

I recognize my ministry as a "partnership for the gospel" (see second reading) when . . .

HOSPITALITY MINISTERS

To insure that my hospitality—at home or at church—goes beyond mere busyness to tending to Christ's coming among us I need to . . .

MUSIC MINISTERS

The music we sing becomes a means of the assembly "preparing the way of the Lord" when . . .

ALTAR MINISTERS

As I consider John's preaching, the really important Advent preparations in my life are about straightening up and smoothing out . . .

LECTORS

The "word of God came to" me when . . . I am God's word coming to others when I . . .

EUCHARISTIC MINISTERS

The Eucharist reveals the "salvation of God" for me as . . .
When I receive Eucharist I am called to enflesh this same salvation for others by . . .

Model Penitential Rite

Presider: Our lives are constantly filled with the ups and downs, the mountains and valleys, of everyday living, challenging us to keep focused on the God who comes to save us. We pause now to recognize God's mercy and forgiveness . . . [pause]

Lord Jesus, you are the light and glory of God: Lord . . .

Christ Jesus, you bring mercy and forgiveness: Christ . . .

Lord Jesus, you sent John to prepare your way by proclaiming repentance: Lord . . .

Appreciating the Responsorial Psalm

Psalm 126 celebrated Israel's return from the exile to Babylon. God intervened and those who had gone forth weeping returned home rejoicing. Over time Israel came to use this psalm any time the community felt endangered or threatened. The remembrance of God's past saving actions became the source of confidence that God would again and always intervene to save them.

Advent is the season when we look as did Jerusalem toward the redemption coming on our behalf from the hand of God (first reading). Truly "the one who began a good work in [us] will . . . complete it" (second reading). Luke tells us this redemption will take place in real history ("In the fifteenth year of . . . when . . .") and that it will demand choices and changes (gospel). This Advent may we recognize what God is doing. May we make the choices and changes redemption requires. May we make Psalm 126 our story and our song.

Model General Intercessions

Presider: Recognizing God's constant care for us, we are confident that God will hear these, our prayers.

Response:

Lord, _____ hear our prayer.

Cantor:

we pray to the Lord,

That the Church be a herald of the presence of God through a fruitful ministry of forgiveness and mercy . . . [pause]

That all peoples of the world repent of sinfulness and turn to their God for forgiveness and mercy . . . [pause]

That political prisoners and those who are imprisoned by their own sinfulness be set free . . . [pause]

That each of us here today take sufficient time to be mindful of what God is asking of us in order to be faithful to the way of salvation . . . [pause]

Presider: Saving God, you are merciful and forgiving: hear these our prayers that one day we might dwell with you in everlasting glory. We ask this through Christ our Lord. **Amen.**

OPENING PRAYER
Let us pray

Pause for silent prayer

God of power and mercy,
open our hearts in welcome.
Remove the things that hinder us from
    receiving Christ with joy,
so that we may share his wisdom
and become one with him
when he comes in glory,
for he lives and reigns with you and the
    Holy Spirit,
one God, for ever and ever. **Amen.**

FIRST READING
Bar 5:1-9

Jerusalem, take off your robe of mourning
    and misery;
    put on the splendor of glory from God
      forever:
wrapped in the cloak of justice from God,
    bear on your head the mitre
    that displays the glory of the eternal
      name.
For God will show all the earth your
    splendor:
    you will be named by God forever
    the peace of justice, the glory of God's
      worship.

Up, Jerusalem! stand upon the heights;
    look to the east and see your children
gathered from the east and the west
    at the word of the Holy One,
    rejoicing that they are remembered by
      God.
Led away on foot by their enemies they
    left you:
    but God will bring them back to you
    borne aloft in glory as on royal thrones.
For God has commanded
    that every lofty mountain be made low,
and that the age-old depths and gorges
    be filled to level ground,
    that Israel may advance secure in the
      glory of God.
The forests and every fragrant kind of
    tree
    have overshadowed Israel at God's
      command;
for God is leading Israel in joy
    by the light of his glory,
    with his mercy and justice for company.

RESPONSORIAL PSALM

Ps 126:1-2, 2-3, 4-5, 6

R̞. (3) The Lord has done great things for us; we are filled with joy.

When the LORD brought back the captives
    of Zion,
  we were like men dreaming.
Then our mouth was filled with laughter,
  and our tongue with rejoicing.

R̞. The Lord has done great things for us; we are filled with joy.

Then they said among the nations,
    "The LORD has done great things for
    them."
The LORD has done great things for us;
  we are glad indeed.

R̞. The Lord has done great things for us; we are filled with joy.

Restore our fortunes, O LORD,
  like the torrents in the southern desert.
Those who sow in tears
  shall reap rejoicing.

R̞. The Lord has done great things for us; we are filled with joy.

Although they go forth weeping,
  carrying the seed to be sown,
they shall come back rejoicing,
  carrying their sheaves.

R̞. The Lord has done great things for us; we are filled with joy.

SECOND READING

Phil 1:4-6, 8-11

Brothers and sisters:
I pray always with joy in my every prayer
    for all of you,
  because of your partnership for the
    gospel
  from the first day until now.
I am confident of this,
  that the one who began a good work in
    you
  will continue to complete it
  until the day of Christ Jesus.
God is my witness,
  how I long for all of you with the
    affection of Christ Jesus.
And this is my prayer:
  that your love may increase ever more
    and more
  in knowledge and every kind of
    perception,
  to discern what is of value,
  so that you may be pure and blameless
    for the day of Christ,
  filled with the fruit of righteousness
  that comes through Jesus Christ
  for the glory and praise of God.

About Liturgy

Advent penance service: Many parishes offer communal penance liturgies at least twice a year, during Advent and Lent. The readings this Sunday remind us that this sacrament is not primarily about lists of sins but about repentance, changing one's heart. Just as with all the sacraments, we repeat the ritual as a way of appropriating the insight of the sacrament, namely, to "take off" the robes of sin and "put on the splendor" of the gospel attitudes of repentance and forgiveness (see first reading).

Penitential rite: Sometimes people claim that they have no need for the Sacrament of Penance because every Sunday Mass begins with a penitential rite. Two points by way of response might be made to such objections. First of all, the penitential rite isn't the same as the Sacrament of Penance and so it doesn't replace the need for this special sacrament of forgiveness and healing in our Christian practice. Second, the "penitential rite" really isn't primarily about the forgiveness of sins as such but is about celebrating God's mercy and offer of salvation that always leads us to praise and thanksgiving.

    Although it is always good to acknowledge our sinfulness and beg for God's mercy, it is telling that the Sacramentary gives us other choices for the introductory rites and it is good pastoral practice to choose carefully among them according to the liturgical season and/or festival. For example, since Lent focuses our attention specifically on the work of being penitential, on the Sundays of Lent the strongest option among the choices for the penitential rite would be to use the *Confiteor* ("I confess to almighty God . . ."). On other Sundays of the year another choice would be more appropriate, especially since every Sunday is a celebration of resurrection, a little Easter (even the Sundays of Lent!). To protect, preserve that sense, it would be pastorally effective to reserve the *Confiteor* for Lent, using form C the rest of the year.

About Liturgical Music

Cantor preparation: Psalm 126 invites the community to take the long view of history. It reminds them that what God has done in the past God will do in the future. In singing it you embody the messianic hope which marks the Church. What or who helps keep this hope alive in yourself? When this hope feels shaken, what or who revives it?

Hymns/Songs: As with the First Sunday of Advent the songs we sing this day need to focus on the final coming of Christ and the completion of redemption at the end of time. Some good examples would be "City of God, Jerusalem" [RS, W3]; The King Shall Come" [most hymnals]; "Lift Up Your Heads, O Mighty Gates" [BB, W3]; "When the King Shall Come Again" [GC, RS, WC, W3]; and "Soon and Very Soon" [BB, G2, LMGM, WC]. One hymn notable for speaking of the hope, expectation, and "earnest looking forward" as well as the "doubt and sorrow" and "gloom and terror" felt as we continue "marching to the promised land" is "Singing Songs of Expectation" [RS]. The *Benedictine Book of Song II* (The Liturgical Press, 1992) and previous editions of BB offer a variation of the text (titled "On Our Journey to the Kingdom") in which each phrase begins on a pick-up beat. The very singing of this text, set to a well-written tune by Tobias Colgan, keeps us moving forward on the journey.

✚ SPIRITUALITY

Gospel

Luke 1:26-38; L689

The angel Gabriel was sent from God
  to a town of Galilee called
    Nazareth,
  to a virgin betrothed to a man
    named Joseph,
  of the house of David,
  and the virgin's name was Mary.
And coming to her, he said,
  "Hail, full of grace! The Lord is
    with you."
But she was greatly troubled at
    what was said
  and pondered what sort of
    greeting this might be.
Then the angel said to her,
  "Do not be afraid, Mary,
  for you have found favor with God.
Behold, you will conceive in your womb
    and bear a son,
  and you shall name him Jesus.
He will be great and will be called Son of
    the Most High,
  and the Lord God will give him the
    throne of David his father,
  and he will rule over the house of
    Jacob forever,
  and of his kingdom there will be no end."
But Mary said to the angel,
  "How can this be,
  since I have no relations with a man?"
And the angel said to her in reply,
  "The Holy Spirit will come upon you,
  and the power of the Most High will
    overshadow you.
Therefore the child to be born
  will be called holy, the Son of God.
And behold, Elizabeth, your relative,
  has also conceived a son in her old age,
  and this is the sixth month for her who
    was called barren;
  for nothing will be impossible for God."
Mary said, "Behold, I am the handmaid of
    the Lord.
May it be done to me according to your
    word."
Then the angel departed from her.

See Appendix A, p. 259, for other readings.

Reflecting on the Gospel

An Aesop's fable titled "The Lioness" tells the story of a great discussion among the animals in the forest about who could produce the largest litter. Some could only shamefacedly boast of a litter of two or three while others could boast of a dozen and sometimes even more than that. Thinking that greatness lay in quantity rather than quality, they decided to ask the lioness how many cubs she bore at a time. "One," she replied, "but that one is a lion!"

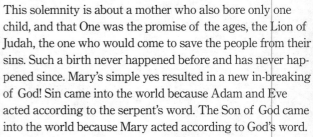

This solemnity is about a mother who also bore only one child, and that One was the promise of the ages, the Lion of Judah, the one who would come to save the people from their sins. Such a birth never happened before and has never happened since. Mary's simple yes resulted in a new in-breaking of God! Sin came into the world because Adam and Eve acted according to the serpent's word. The Son of God came into the world because Mary acted according to God's word.

The quality of Mary's yes goes beyond her being overshadowed by the Holy Spirit and giving birth to the Son of God. Mary's yes is indicative of her faithful cooperation with God's plan of salvation both before and after the birth of Jesus. We might surmise that her yes didn't come all of a sudden out of nowhere. Mary's yes to Gabriel is indicative of how Mary must have lived her daily life from the moment of her own conception—being in tune with God's word, probably through the habit of a virtuous life and union with God through prayer. Her "How can this be?" is less a doubt and more a genuine question seeking the new direction in which God might want her life to unfold. We know from the gospel accounts that after Jesus' birth Mary still questioned about the direction of her life (e.g., at the finding in the Temple), but she always heard the answer as God's word for her as she remained the first disciple of Jesus.

This solemnity challenges us to say yes to whatever challenging word God sends our way and thus we, too, participate in God's ongoing plan of salvation. God's word probably won't come to us in such an extraordinary way as an angel announcing it to us. God's word does come to us in the ordinary people and circumstances of our everyday lives. God's word comes to us at liturgy and when we take personal time to pray. God's word comes to us during times of questioning and doubt as well as during times of great joy and success. God's word comes to us at times of repentance and forgiveness. The challenge is to recognize God's word and respond with a faithful yes.

As Mary bore the Son of God, we are also to bear Christ within us. Our yes to this intimate relationship with the Divine hastens future glory.

Living the Paschal Mystery

We don't know how many children St. Anne, the mother of Mary bore, but we do believe that from the moment of conception Mary was free from sin. This is a privilege accorded her because she bore the Son of God, but it no doubt is also a privilege because she was always open to God's word for her and the direction her life should take. None of us live our lives without sin, but nonetheless we can say yes to God's plan of salvation as Mary did. In our own times of prayer we can question the direction that God wills our lives to take and then we, too, can say, "May it be done to me according to your word." Living the paschal mystery simply means conforming our will to God's. It means saying yes.

Focusing the Word

Key words and phrases from the gospel: Holy Spirit . . . overshadow you, child to be born . . . Son of God, May it be done to me

To the point: Mary participates in God's work of salvation and hastens the coming of future glory in these ways: she was overshadowed by the Holy Spirit, the child born to her is the Son of God, and she said yes—"May it be done to me." We, too, each in our own way, are called to participate in God's work of salvation and hasten the coming of future glory.

Model Penitential Rite

Presider: Mary was conceived without sin and lived blamelessly before God. Her yes to God's will is a model for our own fidelity to God's grace. We pause at the beginning of this celebration to examine our faithfulness to saying yes to God's will . . . [pause]

Lord Jesus, you are called holy, the Son of God: Lord . . .
Christ Jesus, you were conceived in the womb of Mary: Christ . . .
Lord Jesus, you are the savior of the world: Lord . . .

Model General Intercessions

Presider: As surely as God showed favor to Mary, God will favor us and grant us the needs we now name in our prayer.

Response:

Cantor:

That Mary's motherhood be a model for how all members of the Church live their yes to God . . . [pause]

That all peoples of the world share in the salvation of Jesus Christ . . . [pause]

That those who are unable to say yes to God's will be touched by God's word and encouraged to say yes . . . [pause]

That we ourselves might participate in God's plan of salvation through our hearing God's word and saying yes to God's will . . . [pause]

Presider: Saving God, Mary the sinless one conceived and bore your only-begotten Son: hear these our prayers that we might draw closer to you and one day share in your everlasting glory. We ask this through that same Son, Jesus Christ our Lord. **Amen.**

OPENING PRAYER

Let us pray

Pause for silent prayer

Father,
you prepared the Virgin Mary
to be the worthy mother of your Son.
You let her share beforehand
in the salvation Christ would bring by his
     death,
and kept her sinless from the first moment
     of her conception.
Help us by her prayers
to live in your presence without sin.

We ask this through our Lord Jesus Christ,
     your Son,
who lives and reigns with you and the Holy
     Spirit,
one God, for ever and ever. **Amen.**

FOR REFLECTION

• I am more likely to hide from God's invitation like Adam and Eve did (see first reading) when . . .

• I am more likely to respond to God with "May it be done to me" when . . .

• Like Mary, I have been invited to participate in God's plan/work of salvation for others by . . .

✠ SPIRITUALITY

Gospel

Luke 3:10-18; L9C

The crowds asked John the Baptist,
  "What should we do?"
He said to them in reply,
  "Whoever has two cloaks
  should share with the person
    who has none.
And whoever has food should do
    likewise."
Even tax collectors came to be
    baptized and they said to him,
  "Teacher, what should we do?"
He answered them,
  "Stop collecting more than what is
    prescribed."
Soldiers also asked him,
  "And what is it that we should do?"
He told them,
  "Do not practice extortion,
  do not falsely accuse anyone,
  and be satisfied with your wages."
Now the people were filled with
    expectation,
  and all were asking in their hearts
  whether John might be the Christ.
John answered them all, saying,
  "I am baptizing you with water,
  but one mightier than I is coming.
I am not worthy to loosen the thongs of
    his sandals.
He will baptize you with the Holy Spirit
    and fire.
His winnowing fan is in his hand to
    clear his threshing floor
  and to gather the wheat into his barn,
  but the chaff he will burn with
    unquenchable fire."
Exhorting them in many other ways,
  he preached good news to the people.

Reflecting on the Gospel

Small children are prone to ask the question just about any time an adult caring for them is within earshot, but especially so on long, rainy, dreary days: "What should we do?" Mom or dad or the adult in charge might make many suggestions to fill their play time, but generally these suggestions don't interest them because they really are not asking for something to *do*. They are asking, indirectly in their own child's way, for the adult to play with them. Children's self-esteem is enhanced when adults pay attention to them, when adults *relate to them*. Children need this kind of healthy, relational attention. So do adults!

In this Sunday's gospel three groups of people ask John the Baptist, "What should we do?" At first John answers all three groups by outlining, literally, what they should *do:* share, collect only what is appropriate, be satisfied. Looking deeper, each of these answers requires the people to enter into a new and different relationship with those around them, to change their ways. Even in doing what is our lot in life we are to focus not on ourselves but on others and their good.

Whether the people caught the deeper implication at this point or not the gospel doesn't relate. What the gospel does tell us is that John's loaded answers about right living (his effective proclamation of the good news) fill the people "with expectation." Their seeking "the Christ"—that is, the Messiah, the anointed one of God—means that they were seeking a new life. John answers them by using himself as the model for the ultimate answer to the question, "What should we do?" John exhorts them to define their obligations in relation to others, just as John himself defines his role in relation to Jesus. John denies being "the Christ" himself and announces that "one mightier than I is coming." Just like John, our lives are about others.

Further, the explicit question about what we are to do points to our natural desire for finding the ultimate One. We define ourselves not in terms of what we do but who we are in relation to Other and others. The good news that John preached challenges us to relate to Christ and define ourselves in terms of this One who baptizes with "the Holy Spirit and fire."

Living the Paschal Mystery

When we've ordered our lives in the minimal things—fulfilling the requirements of our state in life and job or ministry—then we can seek the greater things, the greater One. Our being baptized in the Holy Spirit means that we already share in divine life. This means that we are enabled to relate to Christ not as One "out there" but as One who is in our midst, one who is near. Relationship to others takes on a whole new meaning because we now enter into a unique relationship with the divine One.

In our daily living we, too, point to the One who is to come first by doing well what is expected of us. Second and more importantly, we point to the One who is to come by being who we have become in Christ: the presence of Christ; we ourselves are to be the "mighty one" for others. Thus because of God's indwelling the doing and being collapse into one: whatever it is we do, we always do so as bearers of Christ because we are "in Christ Jesus" (second reading). For this reason—we are the presence of the risen Christ for each other—nothing we do is small or inconsequential. Everything we do brings the Lord near to those around us.

Focusing the Word
Key words and phrases from the gospel: What should we do?, the Christ, one mightier than I is coming

To the point: In the gospel three groups of people ask the same question, "What should we do?" John exhorts them to define their obligations in relation to others, just as John himself defines his role in relation to Jesus. This is the ultimate goal of Advent and Christian life: to understand and define ourselves in relation to the "one mightier [who] is coming"—"the Christ."

Connecting the Word
to the first and second reading: These two readings open up for us what is at the basis of the good news: "the LORD . . . is in your midst" (first reading) and "The Lord is near" (second reading).

to culture: With so much to do in these hectic, final days before Christmas, we may find ourselves asking, "What should we do?" The gospel pushes us to answer the question on a deeper level than organizing busy holiday preparations.

Understanding the Word
Repentance and relationship with God: John's preaching spells out the details of the "repentance" he proclaimed in last Sunday's gospel. His uncompromising directives to a variety of people require them to repent by changing their behavior towards others. For some it will mean positive action such as sharing surplus goods with those who are in need; for others it will involve stopping corrupt behavior such as extortion, over-charging, and making false accusations. This "other-centered" approach reflects John's own approach to ministry which he understands in terms of his relationship to "the one mightier" than he who "is coming." Knowing that in relation to Jesus he is but a servant gives him his sense of place and purpose in proclaiming the good news. Both his identity and mission are defined in relation to Jesus.

In this John stands in the company of a long line of servants who understood themselves and their mission in terms of their relationship with God. Certainly all the prophets realized that they were messengers of God, a vocation that simultaneously gave them great status and authority but also made of them servants. Their preaching and exhortation made it clear that their words were not their own ("thus says the Lord") and that their authority came from God. Apart from God they were nothing. The same can be said of Abraham and Moses. Abraham, who became the father of a host of nations (Gen 17:4) and was a mediator of blessing to all the nations of the earth (Gen 12:3) nevertheless was one who faithfully and unquestioningly obeyed the commands of God (Gen 12:1; 13:17; 22:2). Abraham could fulfill his mission because he knew that he was the servant of God (Gen 26:24). Moses, who could withstand the mighty Pharaoh and lead a great nation, knew that he was the "intimate friend" of God (Exod 33:12, 17). This relationship with God was the source of his identity and mission. As it happens, this is an apt description of repentance: to order our life and to understand ourselves in terms of our relationship with God.

ASSEMBLY & FAITH-SHARING GROUPS
- After asking John the Baptist, "What should I do?" he said to me . . .
- Usually I define my life and myself according to . . .
- In order to define my life and myself more deeply in relation to Christ I would need to . . .

PRESIDERS
I am aware that "the Lord is near" (second reading) when . . .

DEACONS
I "rejoice in the Lord always" (second reading) when I recall . . .

HOSPITALITY MINISTERS
"Your kindness should be known to all" (second reading). What is known about me through my ministry is . . .

MUSIC MINISTERS
I have experienced God "singing joyfully because of [me]" (first reading) when . . . We have experienced God "in the midst" of our music-making when . . .

ALTAR MINISTERS
When I recollect that I, too, am serving—at the altar, in my daily life—"one mightier than I," then my service becomes . . .

LECTORS
The last time the word of God made me "filled with expectation" and "asking in [my] heart" was . . . I share this power of the Word by . . .

EUCHARISTIC MINISTERS
Knowing that I distribute the Body and Blood of Whom "I am not worthy to loosen the thongs of his sandals" changes me into . . .

Model Penitential Rite

Presider: The gospel for today three times asks, "What should we do?" We pause at the beginning of this celebration and ask the same question of ourselves—in this busy time before Christmas, what is the Lord asking of us? . . . [pause]

Lord Jesus, you are the Christ, the Son of God: Lord . . .

Christ Jesus, you are the mighty One who dwells among us: Christ . . .

Lord Jesus, you baptized us with the Holy Spirit and fire: Lord . . .

Appreciating the Responsorial Psalm

It is easy to see the connection between this Sunday's readings and the verses from Isaiah we sing as the responsorial psalm. The first reading proclaims God "is in your midst." The second reading affirms "the Lord is near." The gospel portrays John the Baptist announcing "one mightier than I" is coming. "Cry out with joy and gladness, for among you is the great and Holy One of Israel," we shout in the psalm refrain.

But all is not joy and gladness in the gospel reading. John challenges his hearers to change their behavior. And he announces that when the Messiah does arrive he will sort the wheat from the chaff and burn what he does not want. Nonetheless, John's audience hears his exhortations as "good news." They hear the call to conversion and the imminence of judgment as heralds of the coming of the Holy One of Israel. They know the promise of renewal (first reading) is about to be fulfilled. Let us with them pray, give thanks, know unsurpassed peace (second reading). And sing for joy.

Model General Intercessions

Presider: God fills us with the expectation that we will encounter the Christ who dwells among us. We pray that we recognize that Christ.

Response:

Lord, hear our prayer.

Cantor:

we pray to the Lord,

That all members of the Church, baptized with the Holy Spirit and fire, point to the Christ who is in our midst . . . [pause]

That all peoples of the world fulfill the obligations of their state in life faithfully . . . [pause]

That the lonely and outcasts be welcomed in our midst . . . [pause]

That each of us define ourselves as those in relationship to Christ our savior . . . [pause]

Presider: Mighty God, you sent John to announce the coming of your Son into the world: hear these our prayers that we might recognize his presence among us today. We ask this through that same Christ our Lord. **Amen.**

ALTERNATIVE OPENING PRAYER
Let us pray

Pause for silent prayer

Father of our Lord Jesus Christ,
ever faithful to your promises
and ever close to your Church:
the earth rejoices in hope of the Savior's
    coming
and looks forward with longing
to his return at the end of time.
Prepare our hearts and remove the
    sadness
that hinders us from feeling the joy and
    hope
which his presence will bestow,
for he is Lord for ever and ever. **Amen.**

FIRST READING
Zeph 3:14-18a

Shout for joy, O daughter Zion!
    Sing joyfully, O Israel!
Be glad and exult with all your heart,
    O daughter Jerusalem!
The LORD has removed the judgment
    against you,
    he has turned away your enemies;
the King of Israel, the LORD, is in your
    midst,
    you have no further misfortune to fear.
On that day, it shall be said to Jerusalem:
    Fear not, O Zion, be not discouraged!
The LORD, your God, is in your midst,
    a mighty savior;
he will rejoice over you with gladness,
    and renew you in his love,
he will sing joyfully because of you,
    as one sings at festivals.

RESPONSORIAL PSALM
Isa 12:2-3, 4, 5-6

R̸. (6) Cry out with joy and gladness: for among you is the great and Holy One of Israel.

God indeed is my savior;
   I am confident and unafraid.
My strength and my courage is the LORD,
   and he has been my savior.
With joy you will draw water
   at the fountain of salvation.

R̸. Cry out with joy and gladness: for among you is the great and Holy One of Israel.

Give thanks to the LORD, acclaim his name;
   among the nations make known his
      deeds,
   proclaim how exalted is his name.

R̸. Cry out with joy and gladness: for among you is the great and Holy One of Israel.

Sing praise to the LORD for his glorious
      achievement;
   let this be known throughout all the
      earth.
Shout with exultation, O city of Zion,
   for great in your midst
   is the Holy One of Israel!

R̸. Cry out with joy and gladness: for among you is the great and Holy One of Israel.

SECOND READING
Phil 4:4-7

Brothers and sisters:
Rejoice in the Lord always.
I shall say it again: rejoice!
Your kindness should be known to all.
The Lord is near.
Have no anxiety at all, but in everything,
   by prayer and petition, with
      thanksgiving,
   make your requests known to God.
Then the peace of God that surpasses all
      understanding
   will guard your hearts and minds in
      Christ Jesus.

About Liturgy

Ministry of the assembly: We hear much these days about the visible liturgical ministries (hospitality ministers, music ministers, altar ministers, lectors, eucharistic ministers). We also know that these ministries require preparation and formation. Rarely do we hear, however, about the ministry of the assembly itself. All these visible ministers, the presiders and deacons, and all the others who are present at any liturgy together make up the *assembly*. We might think that the assembly is just *there* to pray and the visible ministers have all the *doing*. This isn't a very accurate assessment of the role of the assembly. The most important ministry at any liturgy is the *ministry of the assembly*.

To be sure, there is a *doing* on the part of the assembly: standing, sitting, kneeling, singing, responding, acclaiming, professing, etc. Sometimes we might fall into the trap of presuming that this is all the assembly does and this is all there is to participation. The most fruitful role of the assembly *comes out of* the doing. First and foremost the liturgical assembly is the body of Christ gathered around the Head. The assembly, then, makes visible the Church, makes visible Christ. Inherent to the role of the assembly, then, is to be present to one another, to relate to each other as the presence of the risen Christ. This relational ministry of the assembly makes concrete and visible how we live our everyday lives: relating to each other as members of the body of Christ. The ministry of the assembly is to be the body of Christ made visible. Our very being there together to celebrate this most sacred act of praise and thanksgiving to God is, in itself, a kind of preaching the good news. We learn from each other so that we might live what we preach.

About Liturgical Music

Cantor preparation: How does your manner of living announce the presence of the Holy One?

Hymns/Songs: This Sunday the focus of Advent turns from looking toward the return of Christ at the end of time to remembering his coming 2000 years ago. Accordingly, the texts of the songs we sing need to change focus. Appropriate hymns available in most hymnals include "O Come, O Come, Emmanuel"; "On Jordan's Bank"; "Savior of the Nations, Come"; "Come, O Long Expected Jesus"; "People, Look East"; and "Creator of the Stars of Night" (also titled "O Lord Who Made the Stars of Night"). Songs less widely available but also expressing the imminent expectation of the Christ Child's arrival include "Each Winter as You Grow Older" [G1, G2, GC, RS] and "Awake! Awake, and Greet the New Morn" [RS, WC, W3, CBW3; with a change of one word G1, G2, and GC categorize this as a Christmas song, but the text as a whole better serves the final weeks of Advent].

SPIRITUALITY

Gospel

Luke 1:39-45; L12C

Mary set out
  and traveled to the hill country in
      haste
  to a town of Judah,
  where she entered the house of
      Zechariah
  and greeted Elizabeth.
When Elizabeth heard Mary's
      greeting,
  the infant leaped in her womb,
  and Elizabeth, filled with the
      Holy Spirit,
  cried out in a loud voice and
      said,
  Blessed are you among women,
  and blessed is the fruit of your
      womb.
And how does this happen to me,
  that the mother of my Lord should
      come to me?
For at the moment the sound of your
      greeting reached my ears,
  the infant in my womb leaped for joy.
Blessed are you who believed
  that what was spoken to you by the
      Lord
  would be fulfilled."

Reflecting on the Gospel

In this day and age parenting is no easy task! More than one parent has lamented, "When they were under my control things were fine; as soon as they go to school, we lose them." How parents ought to form their children in good values is an open question but all agree that as the children grow there will be frequent clash of wills (the "terrible twos" is all too real!). The desire of parents is that the children grow in their *obedience* so that they learn the family *spirit* and grow into adults who *make known* by the way they live the good values taught them. The gospel this Sunday is the story of Mary's visitation to Elizabeth. Here we have two adult women who, as the story unfolds, exemplify for us the same threefold dynamic parents try to instill in their children: obedience, spirit, make known.

Mary "set[s] out" to visit Elizabeth in obedience to Gabriel's command. Elizabeth, too, is pregnant according to the word of Gabriel, so the meeting of these two women naturally promises something unusual! Mary was overshadowed by the Holy Spirit and the Son of God became incarnate; Elizabeth was "filled with the Holy Spirit" and announced the presence of her Lord. Mary and Elizabeth both receive the Holy Spirit, are obedient ("hear" and respond), and have annunciations (Mary, that she would conceive Jesus; Elizabeth, that her Lord was present).

On this last Sunday before Christmas we are gently led into the depths of the Christmas mystery. Jesus' incarnation was no Hallmark card. Already on this Sunday we are reminded that his life was one of obedience to his Father ("Behold, I come to do your will"; second reading) that meant offering his body for our salvation. Mary and Elizabeth show us the way to *our* being overshadowed by the Spirit, obedient to God's will, and our own living as disciples who announce the nearness of our God. Our entry into Christ is through the Holy Spirit and obedience. We define ourselves in relation to our Lord through obedience. But always our encounter with God leads to annunciation of God's presence.

Obedience, Holy Spirit, annunciation: here is the depth of the Christmas mystery. The beginning of Jesus' life is the beginning of our own new life in Christ.

Living the Paschal Mystery

God's plan of salvation is fulfilled by Christ's obedience to the Father's will. The way the mystery moves from annunciation to fulfillment is by obedience. The same dynamic defines our Christian way of living: we are overshadowed by the Holy Spirit in baptism when, in the midst of the Christian community, the Lord's presence is announced. But our own annunciation only comes to fulfillment when we spend our lives being obedient to God's will.

Think about this: doing God's will is an incarnation and annunciation! The circumstances of our obedience won't be so spectacular as Mary's and Elizabeth's; but our obedience is no less fruitful. In our helping hand, God is present. In our visits to the sick and elderly, God is present. In our disciplining and forming our children, God is present. In all our daily dying to self, God is present. This is incarnation: God is present. This is the depth of the Christmas mystery: our obedience.

Focusing the Word

Key words and phrases from the gospel: Mary; Elizabeth, filled with the Holy Spirit, cried out . . . my Lord; fulfilled

To the point: The Word became flesh when the Holy Spirit overshadowed Mary. This mystery of incarnation is announced when the Holy Spirit fills Elizabeth who recognizes the fruit of Mary's womb as her own Lord. The mystery is fulfilled when Christ obediently offers his "body . . . once for all" (second reading).

Connecting the Word

to the First Sunday of Advent: Advent began with a reading from Jeremiah that the Lord fulfills promises. This Sunday's gospel ends the Sundays of Advent by affirming "that what was spoken to you by the Lord would be fulfilled."

to culture: We tend to think of fulfillment in terms of being personally "filled full." The fulfillment of salvation requires self-emptying; for example, God empties self to send the Son, the Son empties self on the cross.

Understanding the Word

Infancy and passion: Especially so close to Christmas, the second reading from Hebrews is jarring. As we prepare to celebrate the birth of Jesus, the Letter to the Hebrews speaks of his death: "we have been consecrated through the offering of the body of Jesus Christ once for all." This passage begins, however, with two references to his birth: "when Christ came into the world" and "a body you prepared for me." Why did Christ come? Why did he take on a human body? The answer: "I come to do your will." Through obedience to the will of God, Jesus established a new covenant. Obedience is the key: the extent of obedience is demonstrated by his death on the cross. This connection between the birth of Jesus and his obedience unto death is integral to the Christmas festival. In the annunciation Mary responds to the words of Gabriel by saying, "I am the handmaid of the Lord. May it be done to me according to your word" (1:38; this Sunday's gospel acclamation). By obediently submitting to the divine word, she puts her body at the disposal of God: "you will conceive in your womb and bear a son, and you will name him Jesus" (1:31). Submission to God's will makes possible the birth that will lead to salvation. The birth of the Messiah and the death of the Savior are inseparable.

Elizabeth's question to Mary is really a proclamation of faith: "How does this happen to me, that the mother of my Lord should come to me?" The reference to Jesus as "Lord" is an Easter title, indicating that Luke is telling the initial episodes of the gospel in view of the entire story. The resurrection is not a surprise ending: it is where the story really begins and the vantage point from which the gospel is proclaimed. The story of the birth of Jesus cannot be separated from the story of his death. Christ was born for a purpose: "to do your will, O God" (Hebrews 10:7, 9). Birth leads to death as surely as death leads to life.

ASSEMBLY & FAITH-SHARING GROUPS

- The word of the Lord that has been fulfilled for me this Advent is . . .
- My blessing(s) for believing in the Lord's word is (are) . . .
- Like Elizabeth, I am amazed that "my Lord" should come to me. I express and share my joy by . . .

PRESIDERS

Christ demands more than sacrifices or offerings (see second reading). The will of God that Christ is inviting me to *live* now is . . .

DEACONS

My diaconal service helps others to trust and believe in "what was spoken to [them] by the Lord would be fulfilled" by . . .

HOSPITALITY MINISTERS

As Elizabeth welcomed and greeted Mary, she witnessed the presence of the Lord. In my ministry of hospitality I have witnessed *in* others and *to* others the presence of the Lord when . . .

MUSIC MINISTERS

In singing together I have experienced God coming to me when . . . .
I have experienced God coming to the assembly in their singing when . . .

ALTAR MINISTERS

Serving others empties me of . . . so that Christ may be born in me.

LECTORS

When I believe that the word is spoken by the Lord and will be fulfilled, my proclamation and living are like . . .
When I doubt that word, my proclamation and living are like . . .

EUCHARISTIC MINISTERS

Each communicant's *Amen* professes his or her willingness to do God's will and consecrates him or her in Christ (see second reading). My response to such faith is . . .

Model Penitential Rite

Presider: In obedience to the angel Gabriel Mary sets out to visit her cousin Elizabeth who, "filled with the Holy Spirit," announces that her Lord is present. As we prepare for this liturgy let us open our hearts to hear God's word and be attentive to God's presence to us . . . [pause]

  Lord Jesus, you were conceived by the power of the Holy Spirit: Lord . . .

  Christ Jesus, you are the blessed fruit of Mary's womb: Christ . . .

  Lord Jesus, you obediently offered your body on the cross for our salvation: Lord . . .

Appreciating the Responsorial Psalm

Psalm 80 was a lament the whole Israelite community raised at times of national destruction. The community begged God to "look down from heaven" and see their suffering, to "rouse . . . power and come to save" them. The "man of your right hand" prayed for in verse 18 was the king who represented them all. Like many laments this one contained a note of penitence. The people asked to be returned to God ("make us turn to you") so that they would no longer "withdraw" from divine love and presence. Like all laments this one rose on a note of faith: Israel begged God to act in their favor because they believed beyond doubt that God would.

  For us the request that God show us the divine face (refrain) has been answered by the enfleshing of Christ in the womb of Mary (gospel). The request that God save us has been fulfilled by Christ offering his very body that we be consecrated (second reading). What remains for us is the call to believe as did Israel (first reading) and Mary (gospel) that God will continue to come to save us. As we near this year's celebration of the birth of Christ, may we sing with hope and confidence.

Model General Intercessions

Presider: Through obedience the Lord comes and saves. We pray now that we might always do God's will.

Response:

Lord, hear our prayer.

Cantor:

we pray to the Lord,

May all members of the Church, obedient to God's will, always announce the nearness of God . . . [pause]

May all peoples of the world, obedient to God's will, live in peace and justice . . . [pause]

May the poor and needy, obedient to God's will, receive what they need to grow in belief in God's goodness . . . [pause]

May each of us, obedient to God's will, celebrate the Christmas mystery with joyful self-emptying . . . [pause]

Presider: Gracious God, you visit your people in so many ways: hear these our prayers that our lives might always announce your nearness. We ask this through Christ our Lord. **Amen.**

ALTERNATIVE OPENING PRAYER

Let us pray
[as Advent draws to a close for the faith
that opens our lives to the Spirit of God]

Pause for silent prayer

Father, all-powerful God,
your eternal Word took flesh on our earth
when the Virgin Mary placed her life
at the service of your plan.
Lift our minds in watchful hope
to hear the voice which announces his
     glory
and open our minds to receive the Spirit
who prepares us for his coming.

We ask this through Christ our Lord.
  Amen.

FIRST READING
Mic 5:1-4a

Thus says the LORD:
You, Bethlehem-Ephrathah
     too small to be among the clans of
          Judah,
from you shall come forth for me
     one who is to be ruler in Israel;
whose origin is from of old,
     from ancient times.
Therefore the Lord will give them up, until
     the time
     when she who is to give birth has
          borne,
and the rest of his kindred shall return
     to the children of Israel.
He shall stand firm and shepherd his flock
     by the strength of the LORD,
     in the majestic name of the LORD, his
          God;
and they shall remain, for now his
     greatness
     shall reach to the ends of the earth;
     he shall be peace.

RESPONSORIAL PSALM

Ps 80:2-3, 15-16, 18-19

℟. (4) Lord, make us turn to you; let us see your face and we shall be saved.

O shepherd of Israel, hearken,
  from your throne upon the cherubim,
    shine forth.
Rouse your power,
  and come to save us.

℟. Lord, make us turn to you; let us see your face and we shall be saved.

Once again, O LORD of hosts,
  look down from heaven, and see;
take care of this vine,
  and protect what your right hand has
    planted,
  the son of man whom you yourself
    made strong.

℟. Lord, make us turn to you; let us see your face and we shall be saved.

May your help be with the man of your
    right hand,
  with the son of man whom you yourself
    made strong.
Then we will no more withdraw from you;
  give us new life, and we will call upon
    your name.

℟. Lord, make us turn to you; let us see your face and we shall be saved.

SECOND READING

Heb 10:5-10

Brothers and sisters:
When Christ came into the world, he said:
  "Sacrifice and offering you did not
    desire,
  but a body you prepared for me;
  in holocausts and sin offerings you took
    no delight.
  Then I said, 'As is written of me in the
    scroll,
  behold, I come to do your will, O God.'"

First he says, "Sacrifices and offerings,
  holocausts and sin offerings,
  you neither desired nor delighted in."
These are offered according to the law.
Then he says, "Behold, I come to do your
    will."
He takes away the first to establish the
    second.
By this "will," we have been consecrated
  through the offering of the body of
    Jesus Christ once for all.

About Liturgy

Announcing the Christmas mystery: Opportunities for us to announce the Christmas mystery abound. Here are two clusters of possibilities.

First, with respect to the ritual "tangibles." The way we enhance the sacred space for Christmas, the music we choose, the way people who come (especially those who have been away from church for a while) are greeted all beg us to think about how we want to announce the Christmas mystery. Is the focus almost entirely on a Babe who was born long ago? If so, there is the real danger that Christmas will come and go without affecting us and the way we live. Our Christmas preparations and celebrations must lead us to the deeper mystery: Christmas is a salvation feast that reminds us this Babe whose birth we celebrate was obedient even to death on a cross. The mystery of birth always enfolds the mystery of death. Our environment, music, hospitality, etc. all must affect us in such a way that we are led to announce the Christmas mystery as God's presence to humanity so that we are more obedient sons and daughters of God.

Second, with respect to the liturgy itself. Liturgy always makes demands on us: the word proclaimed, the homily's challenge, the creed's demands, the intercession's follow-through, Communion's unity. All preparation for liturgy must open the space for the Spirit to work within the community so that liturgy, truly, transforms us into being better and more fruitful disciples of Christ. The deepest and most lasting joy of Christmas spills beyond the liturgy into making the world a better place to be, a place of peace and good will to all. The liturgy itself must be celebrated in such a way as to lead us to announce in our daily living that we believe with all our hearts that the Lord is come.

About Liturgical Music

Cantor preparation: As you prepare to sing this psalm you might spend some time reflecting on where you see the face of God and where you struggle to see it. Is there any way you need to "turn" toward God so that you might better see?

Hymns/Songs: Herman G. Stuempfle's "The Night Will Soon Be Ending" [found in the collection *Awake Our Heart to Praise!,* ©2000 GIA] combines the sense of hope in the imminent dawn of Christ with the reality of our ongoing struggle with darkness. The opening phrases of each verse express Stuempfle's understanding and his hope. Consider, for example, the progression from verses 1 to 4 to 5: "The night will soon be ending; the dawn cannot be far . . . . Yet nights will still bring sadness and rob our hearts of peace . . . . God dwells with us in darkness and makes the night as day . . . ." This hymn would be a fitting choice for the entrance procession; if the procession is not long enough to accommodate all verses, however, have choir alone sing it as prelude.

A thought-provoking after-Communion hymn as we enter this last week of Advent would be John A. Dalles' "We Blew No Trumpet Blasts to Sound" [found in the collection *Swift Currents and Still Waters,* © 2000 GIA]: "We blew no trumpet blasts . . . . We built no bonfire . . . . We spread no welc'ming canopy . . . . [instead] We hurried through another week, unheeding, and unmoved . . . . Dear God, how unprepared we were to welcome Jesus, then. We pray you, help us not to miss your priceless gift again."

Season of Christmas

✚ SPIRITUALITY

At the Vigil Mass

Gospel

Matt 1:1-25; L13ABC

The book of the genealogy of Jesus Christ,
  the son of David, the son of Abraham.

Abraham became the father of Isaac,
  Isaac the father of Jacob,
  Jacob the father of Judah and his brothers.
Judah became the father of Perez and Zerah,
  whose mother was Tamar.
Perez became the father of Hezron,
  Hezron the father of Ram,
  Ram the father of Amminadab.
Amminadab became the father of Nahshon,
  Nahshon the father of Salmon,
  Salmon the father of Boaz,
  whose mother was Rahab.
Boaz became the father of Obed,
  whose mother was Ruth.
Obed became the father of Jesse,
  Jesse the father of David the king.

David became the father of Solomon,
  whose mother had been the wife of Uriah.
Solomon became the father of Rehoboam,
  Rehoboam the father of Abijah,
  Abijah the father of Asaph.
Asaph became the father of Jehoshaphat,
  Jehoshaphat the father of Joram,
  Joram the father of Uzziah.
Uzziah became the father of Jotham,
  Jotham the father of Ahaz,
  Ahaz the father of Hezekiah.
Hezekiah became the father of Manasseh,
  Manasseh the father of Amos,
  Amos the father of Josiah.
Josiah became the father of Jechoniah and his brothers
  at the time of the Babylonian exile.

Continued in Appendix A, p. 260.

Reflecting on the Gospel

The longer reading of the gospel selection for the Vigil Mass of Christmas includes the genealogy of Jesus and begins with the words "The book of the genealogy of Jesus Christ . . ." In one sense we might interpret "book" as the list of names that is given which is completed with Jesus' birth. In another sense we might interpret "book" as all of Matthew's gospel, in which case the genealogy isn't completed with "Jesus who is called the Christ" but with ourselves who are disciples of Jesus. Christmas is about more than the birth of the Baby in Bethlehem. It includes our espousal relationship with God (see first reading) that is realized when the divine and human are wed at the incarnation. This unprecedented marriage is hinted at in the unusual marriage of Joseph and Mary; it continues to be announced in our own intimate relationship with God. Christmas is a celebration of intimacy and the possibility of a whole new relationship with God, one including delight and rejoicing (see first reading). It is also about the harsh reality of the cost of that intimacy.

The conception and birth of Jesus don't exactly unfold smoothly for those so closely involved. The Vigil gospel gives us a hint at Joseph's anguish—shame, fear, self-control. Although the angel of Joseph's dream assures him, the name the angel told Joseph to give this foster Son must still have left him concerned: Jesus—savior. These unusual circumstances must have kept Joseph guessing about what all this means, pondering them in his heart, as did Mary. Christmas reminds us that the incarnation happened because of the faithful obedience of these two devout people. This solemn feast calls each of us to the same faithful obedience.

Isaiah announced that Israel would "be called by a new name pronounced by the mouth of the LORD" (first reading); when the Son of God is named "savior" each of us is called by a new name as well because the incarnation weds us to divinity in a whole new way. The gospel book takes us to where "savior" leads—to the cross. This is where Christmas ultimately leads.

Living the Paschal Mystery

For all the good news of the incarnation and the joy and peace of this solemn feast, we are ever mindful that Jesus is *savior* who fulfills his mission on the cross. This thought shouldn't dampen our joy during this time of the year. Rather, it should deepen it because it helps us appreciate ever more deeply the implications *for us* of this birth we celebrate.

All the readings for the Vigil Mass are still anticipatory of Jesus' birth. This is even appropriate on Christmas day itself because the readings remind us that we always anticipate the coming of Christ; his coming is never concluded. Concretely, we anticipate the coming of Christ in our own faithful obedience to God's will as we live out our discipleship each and every day. In this sense we celebrate Christmas every day, each time we say yes to God. Our own yes is an incarnation of God's love for us that was so decisively announced on the cross. Our own yes is an announcement of the intimate relationship God desires with each of us. Christmas celebrates the love of God for us expressed in the mightiest deed of salvation: *Emmanuel*—"God is with us."

Focusing the Word

Key words and phrases from the gospel: name him Jesus, save his people from their sins, *Emmanuel . . .* "God is with us."

To the point: Already at his birth the mission of this Child is disclosed by his very name Jesus: "he will save his people from their sins." Isaiah describes sin as being "Forsaken . . . desolate." To describe salvation he uses espousal imagery: to be saved is to enter into an intimate relationship with God. In this sense Jesus is also "*Emmanuel . . .* 'God is with us.'"

Connecting the Word

to the second reading: The birth of Christ does not bring to an end the Advent theme of repentance; even on this solemn feast the second reading reminds us that repentance is a necessary response to his coming.

to culture: As high as cultural expectations for this feast may be—universal good will, peace, joy, etc.—the reality far surpasses these, for in Christ humanity and divinity are wed.

Understanding the Word

The genealogy of Jesus: Just as many people research their "family tree" in order to understand themselves better, Matthew records the genealogy of Jesus to offer an insight into Jesus' identity.

Matthew structures his genealogy into three equal parts covering the patriarchs, the kings, and the "commoners" (we have no further information about most of them). Jesus, descended from all kinds of people, is the savior of all kinds of people. The deliberate ordering of three sets of fourteen generations, neatly dividing Israel's history, testifies to God's careful planning: the coming of the Messiah is not an afterthought. By beginning with Abraham, Matthew is telling us first that Jesus is descendant of the chosen people; but Jesus is also the one through whom the promise made to Abraham would be fulfilled: "All the communities of the earth shall find blessing in you" (Gen 12:3), i.e., Jesus will extend the blessing of salvation to Gentiles and Jews alike. By beginning the second section with David, readers are reminded that Jesus is of the royal house and that God's promise to David is fulfilled: "I will raise up your heir after you, sprung from your loins, and I will make his kingdom firm . . . I will make his royal throne firm forever. I will be a father to him, and he shall be a son to me" (2 Sam 7:12-14).

Somewhat unusual for a patriarchal genealogy, Matthew includes references to four women. Three of the four (Tamar, Rahab, Ruth) were Gentiles, again indicating Gentiles are integral to God's saving plan. Furthermore, all four (the fourth is "the wife of Uriah," namely, Bathsheba) had scandalous sexual experiences: Tamar seduced her father-in-law, Judah (Genesis 38); Rahab was a harlot in Jericho (Joshua 2 and 6); Ruth was a Moabite who secretly slipped into Boaz's bed at night (Ruth 3:4-8); Bathsheba committed adultery with David (2 Sam 11:2-5). Yet even in these scandalous circumstances God was working out the plan of salvation. Mary, too, is in a scandalous situation—pregnant but not by her betrothed husband Joseph (Matt 1:18-19). But God's carefully plotted plan is being realized.

ASSEMBLY & FAITH-SHARING GROUPS
- "This is how the birth of Jesus came about" *in* me . . .
- Jesus' birth was necessary (and is good news) for me because I need him to save me from . . .
- I believe "God is with us" in the life and ministry of Jesus because . . .

PRESIDERS
My ministry reveals to others the Christmas joy of how the Lord delights and rejoices in them (first reading) whenever I . . .

DEACONS
Just like Matthew's genealogy moves in the direction of finding myself as part of God's long salvation history, so too does my diaconal service help others find a place in God's plan by . . .

HOSPITALITY MINISTERS
My ministry announces to the assembly that they are "a glorious crown in the hand of the Lord" (first reading) when I . . .

MUSIC MINISTERS
What seems to help my music-making become a genuine experience of "God with us" is . . .
The music becomes this same experience for the assembly when . . .

ALTAR MINISTERS
The God who has chosen Israel, David, and Jesus has also chosen me (see second reading). This election shapes my serving by . . .

LECTORS
The part of the Christmas mystery about which "I will not be silent . . . will not be quiet" (first reading) is . . .
I am announcing it by . . .

EUCHARISTIC MINISTERS
The gift and miracle of Eucharist is that, like Christmas, divinity weds with humanity. Because of this marriage I see myself as . . . , and I must see others as . . .

Model Penitential Rite

Presider: Today we celebrate the birth of the incarnate Son of God, Jesus our Savior. As we prepare to celebrate this liturgy, may we open our hearts to God's offer of salvation and loving relationship with us as beloved sons and daughters . . . [pause]

> Lord Jesus, you were born of Mary: Lord . . .
>
> Christ Jesus, you are *Emmanuel,* God with us: Christ . . .
>
> Lord Jesus, you are the prince of peace: Lord . . .

Appreciating the Responsorial Psalm

In the first reading for the Christmas Vigil Mass God promises to keep acting until Jerusalem's salvation is completed. In the second reading Paul expounds how God has relentlessly acted throughout history for this salvation. With its lengthy genealogy the gospel grounds progress toward salvation in real human history, among real human beings. Although this salvation has been long in coming, its coming has been, nonetheless, certain thanks to the promise of God given in covenant fidelity (responsorial psalm) and spousal love (first reading). As we celebrate the full celebration of the birth of Christ we stand with generations who looked forward to this day. May we with them and with Joseph receive in ordinary human events the inbreaking of divine miracle. May we with them see and sing of "the goodness of the Lord."

Model General Intercessions

Presider: Let us pray on this Christmas Day that all might share in the joy of the incarnation.

Response:

Lord, hear our prayer.

Cantor:

we pray to the Lord,

For the Church, the beloved spouse of Christ . . . [pause]

For all peoples of the world, the beloved redeemed of God . . . [pause]

For the poor and lonely and for those who are confused and afraid, all the beloved children of God . . . [pause]

For each of us here, the beloved disciples of Jesus . . . [pause]

Presider: O saving God, you sent your only-begotten Son into the world to be our savior: hear these our prayers that we might one day enjoy everlasting glory with you and your incarnate Son, Jesus Christ our Lord. **Amen.**

ALTERNATIVE OPENING PRAYER
(Vigil Mass)
Let us pray

Pause for silent prayer

God of endless ages, Father of all goodness,
we keep vigil for the dawn of salvation
and the birth of your Son.

With gratitude we recall his humanity,
the life he shared with the sons of men.
May the power of his divinity
help us answer his call to forgiveness and life.

We ask this through Christ our Lord.
Amen.

FIRST READING
Isa 62:1-5

For Zion's sake I will not be silent,
    for Jerusalem's sake I will not be quiet,
until her vindication shines forth like the dawn
    and her victory like a burning torch.

Nations shall behold your vindication,
    and all the kings your glory;
you shall be called by a new name
    pronounced by the mouth of the LORD.
You shall be a glorious crown in the hand of the LORD,
    a royal diadem held by your God.
No more shall people call you "Forsaken,"
    or your land "Desolate,"
but you shall be called "My Delight,"
    and your land "Espoused."
For the LORD delights in you
    and makes your land his spouse.
As a young man marries a virgin,
    your Builder shall marry you;
and as a bridegroom rejoices in his bride
    so shall your God rejoice in you.

RESPONSORIAL PSALM
Ps 89:4-5, 16-17, 27, 29

R̶J. (2a) Forever I will sing the goodness of the Lord.

I have made a covenant with my chosen one,
    I have sworn to David my servant:
forever will I confirm your posterity
    and establish your throne for all generations.

R̶J. Forever I will sing the goodness of the Lord.

Blessed the people who know the joyful
shout;
in the light of your countenance, O
LORD, they walk.
At your name they rejoice all the day,
and through your justice they are
exalted.

R⁊. Forever I will sing the goodness of the
Lord.

He shall say of me, "You are my father,
my God, the rock, my savior."
Forever I will maintain my kindness
toward him,
and my covenant with him stands firm.

R⁊. Forever I will sing the goodness of the
Lord.

SECOND READING
Acts 13:16-17, 22-25

When Paul reached Antioch in Pisidia and
entered the synagogue,
he stood up, motioned with his hand,
and said,
"Fellow Israelites and you others who
are God-fearing, listen.
The God of this people Israel chose our
ancestors
and exalted the people during their
sojourn in the land of Egypt.
With uplifted arm he led them out of it.
Then he removed Saul and raised up
David as king;
of him he testified,
'I have found David, son of Jesse, a man
after my own heart;
he will carry out my every wish.'
From this man's descendants God,
according to his promise,
has brought to Israel a savior, Jesus.
John heralded his coming by proclaiming a
baptism of repentance
to all the people of Israel;
and as John was completing his course,
he would say,
'What do you suppose that I am? I am
not he.
Behold, one is coming after me;
I am not worthy to unfasten the sandals
of his feet.'"

About Liturgy

Vigil readings: The Lectionary actually gives four sets of readings for Christmas and, as the rubric note says, any one of the four sets may be used on Christmas Day itself. The first volume of *Living Liturgy* (year B, 2000) gave an overview of all four readings and showed the progression from the anticipation of Jesus' birth to the lofty Christology of the gospel for Mass on Christmas Day. Year C, 2001, we chose to reflect on the readings selected for the Mass at Midnight, for year A, 2002, we used the Mass at Dawn readings, and year B, 2003, we chose to reflect on the readings for the Mass During the Day. Hence, this year we turn to the readings for the Vigil Mass.

Most parishes use the proper readings according to the time a Mass is being celebrated, but homilists tend to preach the same homily on the mystery of the feast at all Masses. This is certainly permitted (see GIRM no. 65), but the different sets of readings help us delve into different facets of the solemnity. The temptation is to stay with the Lucan gospels and miss what the other readings have to offer.

Matthew's genealogy: One of the advantages of reading the longer gospel for the Vigil Mass is that Matthew's genealogy moves us in the direction of finding ourselves as part of this long salvation history. Pastorally, however, reading (and pronouncing) all those names in an engaging and meaningful way is surely challenging. If the homily doesn't explain something of the importance of the genealogy (see *The genealogy of Jesus* under Understanding the Word), then it would be more pastorally helpful to choose the shorter form of the gospel.

About Liturgical Music

Cantor preparation: In this responsorial psalm you sing of the covenant made by God with "my chosen one." Do you recognize yourself as "chosen" by God, as participating in the covenant God made with Israel, David, Mary, and Joseph? Do you recognize the assembly as "chosen"? How might this awareness affect your singing of this psalm and your celebration of Christmas?

Hymn suggestion: The genealogy in the gospel reading grounds the coming of Christ in the human story. Bernadette Gasslein's "In the Darkness Shines the Splendour" [CBW3] uses imagery which does the same: "Bearing ev'ry human story . . . Healing ev'ry human story . . . Gladd'ning ev'ry human story . . . Word made flesh reveals our glory." The hymn would be appropriate during either the presentation of the gifts or for the Communion procession.

Purpose of Communion hymn: One of the purposes of the Communion hymn is to express the joy of being called to the messianic table to feast on the Body and Blood of Jesus and become together the one body of Christ. Hymns appropriate for Communion express praise, thanksgiving, joy in being fed and filled, gratitude for being healed and forgiven, gladness in being one in Christ, etc. GIRM indicates that the Communion song may be seasonal in nature, but it is here that we must be discerning in our choices. For example, while a hymn such as "Away in a Manger" has a gentle style suitable for Communion, its text has an adorational slant which is not appropriate. Furthermore, the text focuses on the infant Jesus rather than on the risen Jesus whom we encounter in the messianic banquet. It is better to save hymns such as this for the presentation of the gifts and use more appropriate texts such as "Good Christian Friends, Rejoice," and "Once in Royal David's City," etc., for Communion.

✠ SPIRITUALITY

Gospel

Luke 2:41-52; L17C

Each year Jesus' parents went to
    Jerusalem for the feast of Passover,
    and when he was twelve years old,
    they went up according to festival
        custom.
After they had completed its days,
        as they were returning,
    the boy Jesus remained behind in
        Jerusalem,
    but his parents did not know it.
Thinking that he was in the
        caravan,
    they journeyed for a day
    and looked for him among their
        relatives and acquaintances,
    but not finding him,
    they returned to Jerusalem to look
        for him.
After three days they found him in the
        temple,
    sitting in the midst of the teachers,
    listening to them and asking them
        questions,
    and all who heard him were astounded
    at his understanding and his answers.
When his parents saw him,
    they were astonished,
    and his mother said to him,
    "Son, why have you done this to us?
Your father and I have been looking for
        you with great anxiety."
And he said to them,
    "Why were you looking for me?
Did you not know that I must be in my
        Father's house?"
But they did not understand what he
        said to them.
He went down with them and came to
        Nazareth,
    and was obedient to them;
    and his mother kept all these things
        in her heart.
And Jesus advanced in wisdom and age
        and favor
    before God and man.

Reflecting on the Gospel

At first glance the gospel for this feast seems to indicate a "crack" in the holy family—Jesus deliberately stays behind in Jerusalem to speak to the teachers in the Temple, causing Mary and Joseph no small amount of consternation. It's as though Jesus chooses this moment to "cut the apron strings." Upon a closer reading the gospel links this story from the childhood of Jesus to the events at the end of his life. Both this Sunday's gospel story and those at the end of Jesus' life take place in Jerusalem, at Passover; both place Jesus teaching in the Temple; and, ultimately, both stress how Jesus submitted his life in obedience—first to his parents and, finally, to his Father.

The point the gospel writer is making in this childhood story about Jesus is that we cannot just see Jesus as a gift from the Father without remembering at the same time that his purpose is to return to the Father on the cross. Jesus was a most sublime gift to us from the Father—what we try to capture in our reflections on the mystery of the incarnation each year at Christmas. But the gift is not ours to keep; Jesus "must be in [his] Father's house," Jesus must return to the Father. This is how the first reading relates to the gospel: just as Hannah realized that Samuel was God's gift to her and had to return him to the Lord, so, too, we see that the very identity of Jesus (and of ourselves as his followers) is a giving away of self (ultimately on the cross). This is what constitutes holiness: returning ourselves to God through self-emptying service. Family is holy whenever it becomes a gift of God that must give itself back to God.

This feast and these readings remind us that being a "holy" family isn't a matter of being obsessively religious and weird. The model the Holy Family gives us is one of self-emptying dedication and service. They teach us that holiness means we are "in [our] Father's house," that is, we somehow manage to form the habit of keeping our eyes turned to God as we go about living our everyday lives with all the demands and distractions. Holiness is a matter of recognizing that we are all one in the Lord who came to save us. Holiness is a matter of seeing our "Jerusalem" and cross in the daily struggle to do God's will. Holiness is a matter of God's "temple" not being a place but a habit of belonging to God. Holiness is a matter of growing "in wisdom and age and favor before God" because, like the Holy Family, our lives are given back to God.

Living the Paschal Mystery

The familiarity of family life can sometimes blind us to see the goodness in each other. This feast reminds us to open our eyes and be "astonished" at the goodness of each other rather than anxious about our own concerns. Families grow in strength when each person in the family—from parents to the smallest child and including anyone extended the hospitality of the family—is treated as one dedicated to God and, therefore, holy.

This is challenging when sometimes all we can see is each other's faults. It takes a great deal of self-emptying to get beyond the normal, everyday annoyances that are part of family life and see others as both gift and consecrated to God as we are. Mary and Joseph were not free from family struggles; after all, they lost Jesus on a trip! But they did not give up until they found him. Neither does God give up on us!

Focusing the Word
Key words and phrases from the gospel: went to Jerusalem, Passover, temple, must be in my Father's house

To the point: The first reading helps us interpret the gospel. The child whom God gives to Hannah is returned to God in the Temple where he becomes God's servant. Jesus, given to Mary and to all humanity in the incarnation, returns to God first in his Passover pilgrimage to the Temple and, ultimately, when he surrenders his life on the cross at Passover. The gift of family which this feast celebrates is more than merely a social unit united by biological and emotional ties, but a community given to each other in life-giving service.

Connecting the Word
to the second reading: By calling us "children of God" the second reading carries baptismal overtones. Our baptism is both a celebration of who we are as a gift from God and a giving back that gift to God in our ongoing Christian living.

to our culture: This feast reminds us that the normal giving-and-receiving within families reflects God's relationship with us.

Understanding the Word
The families of Jesus and Samuel: This Sunday's readings give us the stories of two families distinguished by piety and religious devotion. From these families come two extraordinary children.

Both the first reading and the gospel indicate that worship is a regular part of family life. Hannah and her husband routinely went up to the shrine at Shiloh to worship; this is indicated by the phrases "the next time," "to offer the customary sacrifice," and Hannah's intention to "take [Samuel] to appear before the Lord" once he is old enough. Elkanah, Hannah's husband, makes the pilgrimage to Shiloh, "going up with the rest of his household." On a previous trip, Hannah had prayed earnestly for a son and "God heard" (Hebrew = Samuel) her prayer. Pilgrimage, prayer, dedication to God, and trust in God are marks of this holy family.

Mary and Joseph "each year" made a pilgrimage to Jerusalem for Passover. They "went up according to festival custom" and traveled with "their relatives and acquaintances." Pious observance of the law is part of this family's life (see Luke 2:22-40).

Not contained in this Sunday's readings are the lengthy prayers of praise that the two mothers sing. Hannah sings her canticle (1 Sam 2:1-10) immediately after she leaves her son in the Lord's service; and Mary sings her canticle (*Magnificat,* Luke 1:46-55) during her visitation with Elizabeth.

Samuel is vowed to the Lord's service in the "temple of the Lord in Shiloh" (v. 24) for his entire life. Jesus, too, is a regular at the Temple: he is presented there and dedicated to the Lord (Luke 2:21-24); this Sunday's gospel finds him among the teachers in "my Father's house"; and he will spend his final days in teaching in the temple area (Luke 19–21). Finally, both children grow up under God's blessing: "Now the boy Samuel continued to grow both in stature and in favor with the LORD and with the people" (1 Sam 2:26); "And Jesus increased in wisdom and in years, and in divine and human favor" (Luke 2:52). In these stories holy children come from holy families.

ASSEMBLY & FAITH-SHARING GROUPS
- Even at twelve Jesus' life was shaped and defined by holy places and events—Jerusalem, Passover, the Temple. My family is being shaped into holiness by . . .
- Jesus said, "I must be in my Father's house." Some of the *musts* in my life are . . .
- The ones that are bringing me and my loved ones into "the Father's house" are . . .
- It makes sense to me to speak about and celebrate how family life is holy because . . .

PRESIDERS
I am helping families realize that "we are God's children now" (second reading) by . . .

DEACONS
My ministry enriches my family by . . . My ministry has distracted me from my family when . . .

HOSPITALITY MINISTERS
My hospitality—whether with my family or the parish family—can be an occasion for others to "see [and experience] what love the Father has bestowed on us" (second reading) when I . . .

MUSIC MINISTERS
My music ministry has enabled the assembly to experience themselves as God's holy family when . . .

ALTAR MINISTERS
What my ministry of service has taught me about being a holy family is . . .

LECTORS
Some examples when Jesus' word has astounded me, like the teachers in the Temple, and called me to greater obedience, are . . .

EUCHARISTIC MINISTERS
My *Amen* at Eucharist is a key and privileged time when I rededicate myself to God (see first reading). I see myself faithfully living this *Amen* when . . .

Model Penitential Rite

Presider: We may think that the Holy Family of Jesus, Mary, and Joseph provides an impossible model for us to follow in our own families and homes. What they teach us is simple but demanding: holiness is found in self-giving for the sake of others. Let us prepare ourselves for this liturgy by opening our hearts so that we might become more holy . . . [pause]

Lord Jesus, you were the obedient Son of Mary and Joseph: Lord . . .

Christ Jesus, you show us the way to holiness by your life-giving self-emptying on the cross: Christ . . .

Lord Jesus, you were found in the Temple, in your Father's house: Lord . . .

Appreciating the Responsorial Psalm

On this Feast of the Holy Family our psalm refrain identifies as blessed those who dwell in the house of the Lord. Hannah and Elkanah (first reading), Mary and Joseph (gospel) show us that to dwell in the house of the Lord means to keep God and God's Law as the center of one's life. Both sets of parents are faithful to the cultic demands of the covenant with God. They travel regularly to Jerusalem for the Temple celebrations. They are faithful to prayer—to offering sacrifice, to persisting in petition, to contemplating what of God's ways they do not yet understand. Above all they acknowledge that the offspring given them belong to God, Hannah and Elkanah without hesitation, Mary and Joseph with as yet incomplete understanding.

This solemnity calls us to the same focus: to stay centered on God, faithful to communal worship and personal prayer, and steadfast in granting God first place in the hearts of our children. Thus will we who "are God's children" (second reading) dwell in God's house. And thus can we sing of our blessedness.

Model General Intercessions

Presider: Let us pray that we might truly become more holy.

Response:

Cantor:

For all members of the Church, the family of God, that they may be models of self-giving for the sake of others . . . [pause]

For the peoples of the world, the family of humanity, that they may be just toward one another and bring about lasting peace . . . [pause]

For members of hurting families, much beloved of God, that they may find healing and strength . . . [pause]

For ourselves gathered here, our parish family, that they may be astonished at the gifts and goodness of each other . . . [pause]

Presider: Gracious God, you gave us your Son who enables us to be your children: hear these our prayers that our families may be strengthened in our dedication to you and one day be with you for ever and ever. **Amen.**

OPENING PRAYER

Let us pray

Pause for silent prayer

Father,
help us to live as the holy family,
united in respect and love.
Bring us to the joy and peace of your
    eternal home.

Grant this through our Lord Jesus Christ,
    your Son,
who lives and reigns with you and the
    Holy Spirit,
one God, for ever and ever. **Amen.**

FIRST READING
1 Sam 1:20-22, 24-28

In those days Hannah conceived, and at
    the end of her term bore a son
    whom she called Samuel, since she had
    asked the LORD for him.
The next time her husband Elkanah was
    going up
    with the rest of his household
    to offer the customary sacrifice to the
    LORD and to fulfill his vows,
Hannah did not go, explaining to her
    husband,
"Once the child is weaned,
I will take him to appear before the
    LORD
and to remain there forever;
I will offer him as a perpetual nazirite."

Once Samuel was weaned, Hannah
    brought him up with her,
    along with a three-year-old bull,
    an ephah of flour, and a skin of wine,
    and presented him at the temple of the
    LORD in Shiloh.
After the boy's father had sacrificed the
    young bull,
    Hannah, his mother, approached Eli and
    said:
    "Pardon, my lord!
As you live, my lord,
I am the woman who stood near you
    here, praying to the LORD.
I prayed for this child, and the LORD
    granted my request.
Now I, in turn, give him to the LORD;
    as long as he lives, he shall be dedicated
    to the LORD."
Hannah left Samuel there.

RESPONSORIAL PSALM

Ps 84:2-3, 5-6, 9-10

R̸. (cf. 5a) Blessed are they who dwell in your house, O Lord.

How lovely is your dwelling place, O LORD of hosts!
   My soul yearns and pines for the courts of the LORD.
My heart and my flesh cry out for the living God.

R̸. Blessed are they who dwell in your house, O Lord.

Happy they who dwell in your house!
   Continually they praise you.
Happy the men whose strength you are!
   Their hearts are set upon the pilgrimage.

R̸. Blessed are they who dwell in your house, O Lord.

O LORD of hosts, hear our prayer;
   hearken, O God of Jacob!
O God, behold our shield,
   and look upon the face of your anointed.

R̸. Blessed are they who dwell in your house, O Lord.

SECOND READING

1 John 3:1-2, 21-24

Beloved:
See what love the Father has bestowed on us
   that we may be called the children of God.
And so we are.
The reason the world does not know us
   is that it did not know him.
Beloved, we are God's children now;
   what we shall be has not yet been revealed.
We do know that when it is revealed we
      shall be like him,
   for we shall see him as he is.

Beloved, if our hearts do not condemn us,
   we have confidence in God and receive
      from him whatever we ask,
   because we keep his commandments
      and do what pleases him.
And his commandment is this:
   we should believe in the name of his
      Son, Jesus Christ,
   and love one another just as he
      commanded us.
Those who keep his commandments
      remain in him, and he in them,
   and the way we know that he remains
      in us
   is from the Spirit he gave us.

About Liturgy

Choice of readings: The revised Lectionary on some festivals has provided readings for all three years of the Lectionary cycle. The Feast of the Holy Family is one such festival. In order to plumb the riches of the Lectionary the *Living Liturgy* team has chosen to go with the proper readings; hence, these reflections are based on the readings that may be used for year C.

Strengthening family life: The Church provides us with two celebrations helpful for strengthening family life immediately following our celebration of Christmas. First (and since these are weekday celebrations many may not be aware of them), the liturgical calendar celebrates three special feast days immediately after Christmas: December 26, the Feast of St. Stephen, the first martyr; December 27, the Feast of St. John the Evangelist; December 28, the Feast of the Holy Innocents. All three of these feasts remind us that following Christ has its demands, even to the point of giving one's life in order to remain faithful to our Christian discipleship. Naturally, family life has its demands but none of these exceed our strength if we remember that God has given us the gift of the divine Son who dwells within each of us because of our baptism. Second, the liturgical calendar gives us this Feast of the Holy Family. Although the gospel passages about the Holy Family are scanty, we know that life wasn't easy for Jesus, Mary, and Joseph. They model for us a family life not beyond our reach, but one that is very real: care for each other. We can draw strength and encouragement from the reflections these days offer.

About Liturgical Music

Cantor preparation: The context of the readings suggests the "dwelling place" you sing about in this responsorial psalm is not a building but a way of life. When you sing the refrain for the first time during the Liturgy of the Word, can you look upon the assembly as the "blessed" who are faithful to this way of life? What difference might this make in the way you sing and the manner you gesture?

Hymn suggestion: Delores Dufner's "What Feast of Love" [in *Sing a New Church*, © 1994 OCP] exemplifies a way of introducing an excellent eucharistic text for the Christmas season via use of a traditional text and tune. Using "What Child Is This" Dufner moves from the gift of Jesus in his birth at Bethlehem to his ongoing gift of self in the Eucharist. Because of their long familiarity with the original, any assembly will sing this new hymn with ease. Singing it will also entice them to reflect on the traditional text with deepened insight. Dufner suggests that cantor(s) or choir only sing the first four lines of each verse and the assembly respond with the refrain ("This, this is Christ the King . . ."). Depending on the length of the Communion procession, either sing only Dufner's text (perhaps with instrumental interludes to lengthen it) or sing the traditional text followed with Dufner's eucharistic verses. Unlike the traditional refrain Dufner's refrain changes text with each repetition, so the assembly will need copies in hand.

DECEMBER 28, 2003
THE HOLY FAMILY OF JESUS, MARY, AND JOSEPH

✚ *SPIRITUALITY*

Gospel

Luke 2:16-21; L18ABC

The shepherds went in haste to
    Bethlehem and found Mary and
    Joseph,
  and the infant lying in the manger.
When they saw this,
  they made known the message
  that had been told them about
    this child.
All who heard it were amazed
  by what had been told them by
    the shepherds.
And Mary kept all these things,
  reflecting on them in her heart.
Then the shepherds returned,
  glorifying and praising God
  for all they had heard and seen,
  just as it had been told to them.
When eight days were completed for
    his circumcision,
  he was named Jesus, the name given
    him by the angel
  before he was conceived in the
    womb.

See Appendix A, p. 260, for these readings:

FIRST READING
Num 6:22-27

RESPONSORIAL PSALM
Ps 67:2-3, 5, 6, 8

SECOND READING
Gal 4:4-7

Reflecting on the Gospel

Most parents are so proud of their newborn that they naturally wish to show off their infant. No doubt Mary and Joseph were proud parents, too, and only too willing to show off Jesus to even these stranger-shepherds. Mary and Joseph heard the shepherds' message and rejoiced when the shepherds were "glorifying and praising God." The security and joy of a newborn was tempered by the reality of who this Child was to be—"he was named Jesus," savior.

Jesus' destiny from the moment of his conception was to be savior; Mary's destiny from the moment of her yes response to the angel and as a mother was to give this savior flesh and then let go of her infant so salvation could happen (second reading: "God sent his Son . . . to ransom those under the law").

Because Mary's conception and giving birth happened under such extraordinary circumstances we might think that Mary took all this for granted and that it was easy for her. The central lines to the gospel suggest otherwise: "Mary kept all these things, reflecting on them in her heart." This suggests that Mary's ongoing yes to God wasn't really very easy at all. The only way she continued to be faithful was that she took a contemplative stance: reflecting, pondering, praying. The salvation events the incarnation unleashed are neither easy to understand nor to embrace. Mary shows us the way: fidelity to God's way means we, too, must adopt a contemplative stance before God and the mystery of salvation.

It is important that we have a Marian feast this close to Christmas. It not only gives Mary her just due as the mother of God, it also is a feast that encourages us in our own yes to God. Mary was human, like us. Her need for reflection to align herself with God's plan is a model for our own Christian discipleship. The mystery of the incarnation and salvation is too big to celebrate during one week of the year and too deep for us to grasp easily. Like Mary, we must ponder these things in our hearts so that, as children of God (see second reading), we can continually glorify and praise God for the wonders of salvation.

How kindly God looked upon Mary and bestowed on her blessing and peace (see first reading)! God does the same with us: we are no longer "slaves" to sin but "heirs" to God's very life. The mystery of the incarnation which Mary models for us is that God's life dwells within each of us.

Living the Paschal Mystery

Like Mary, we too must "give flesh" to the Savior, ponder his presence within us, and then let go. This letting go means that we must die to ourselves; God's life within us isn't a "possession" but a blessing so that we are transformed into being bearers of grace for others. Like the shepherds, we too must hear God's message of salvation and then make it known to others. This solemnity so closely following Christmas helps us realize that the joy of Christmas is ongoing only when we ourselves are the incarnation of Christ and are the bearers of his message of good news. We "give flesh" to the Savior in the simple, ordinary demands of our daily living when they are done with a contemplative stance; that is, when they are done because we know ourselves to be the body of Christ and treat all others the same way. Thus is the Word made flesh in our lives.

Focusing the Word

Key words and phrases from the gospel: shepherds, made known the message, Mary . . . reflecting on them in her heart

To the point: The shepherds heard the message of the angels and made it known. Mary, in turn, heard their good news, took it into her heart, and reflected on it. The full meaning of these events is revealed when Jesus "ransom[s] those under the law" and makes us children of God (see second reading).

Model Penitential Rite

Presider: We honor today Mary, the one who bore the Son of God, the savior of the world. This mystery is so great that Mary "kept all these things, reflecting on them in her heart." Let us pause a moment in reflection, becoming aware of God's presence to us and the call to model our lives after Mary's . . . [pause]

Lord Jesus, you are the Son of God and Son of Mary: Lord . . .

Christ Jesus, you are deserving of all glory and praise: Christ . . .

Lord Jesus, you are the Savior of the world: Lord . . .

Model General Intercessions

Presider: God sent the Son to bring us salvation and peace. Let us pray that we and all peoples in our world may be blessed this year.

Response:

Lord, hear our prayer.

Cantor:

we pray to the Lord,

That all members of the Church be people of prayerful contemplation, pondering God's blessings and salvific works . . . [pause]

That all peoples of the world enjoy peace and receive justice during this new year . . . [pause]

That those who are poor and needy find prosperity this year through the generosity of others who ponder God's word . . . [pause]

That each of us during this coming year be bearers of God's presence to all those we meet . . . [pause]

Presider: God of peace and justice, you bless us and are gracious to us beyond measure: hear these our prayers that we might live in peace with you for ever and ever. **Amen.**

OPENING PRAYER

Let us pray

Pause for silent prayer

God our Father,
may we always profit by the prayers
of the Virgin Mother Mary,
for you bring us life and salvation
through Jesus Christ her Son
who lives and reigns with you and the Holy
    Spirit,
one God, for ever and ever. **Amen.**

FOR REFLECTION

- As I celebrate and pray about the Christmas mystery, what continues to amaze me and cause me to glorify and praise God is . . .

- My daily living—among family, neighbors, and coworkers—makes "known the message . . . about this child" whenever I . . .

- If I am to imitate and develop Mary's reflective stance found in the gospel, I must . . .

SPIRITUALITY

Gospel

Matt 2:1-12; L20ABC

When Jesus was born in
    Bethlehem of Judea,
in the days of King Herod,
behold, magi from the east
    arrived in Jerusalem, saying,
"Where is the newborn king of
    the Jews?
We saw his star at its rising
    and have come to do him
    homage."
When King Herod heard this,
    he was greatly troubled,
    and all Jerusalem with him.
Assembling all the chief priests
    and the scribes of the people,
    he inquired of them where the Christ
    was to be born.
They said to him, "In Bethlehem of
    Judea,
for thus it has been written through
    the prophet:
*And you, Bethlehem, land of Judah,
    are by no means least among the
        rulers of Judah;
since from you shall come a ruler,
    who is to shepherd my people
        Israel."*
Then Herod called the magi secretly
    and ascertained from them the time
    of the star's appearance.
He sent them to Bethlehem and said,
    "Go and search diligently for the child.
When you have found him, bring me
    word,
    that I too may go and do him homage."
After their audience with the king they
    set out.
And behold, the star that they had seen
    at its rising preceded them,
    until it came and stopped over the
        place where the child was.
They were overjoyed at seeing the star,
    and on entering the house
    they saw the child with Mary his
        mother.

Continued in Appendix A, p. 261.

Reflecting on the Gospel

An old tale tells about a rich and miserly but foolish man who constantly worried about his many possessions being stolen. So one day he sold everything and bought a lump of pure gold which he buried in his garden. Each day he would go out and dig up his gold, look at it, then bury it again. This went on for many a day until one day a thief happened to be passing by and noticed the wealthy man's odd behavior. Creeping closer, he saw the man bury the gold again. That night the thief came to the garden and stole the gold and so, of course, the next day when the wealthy man dug in his garden, the gold was gone. When the sheriff came to investigate he told the man, "Why don't you just bury a lump of shiny coal and come out at night in the dark to dig it up? You never did anything with your gold anyway, so digging up the coal at night when you can't see the difference will be just the same as digging up the gold during the daylight." The point is, simply *having* is not a value in itself; it's what we *do* with what we have that has value.

The three magi from the east must have been men of means; they traveled a long distance to find the "newborn king of the Jews" and to offer him precious gifts, trusting in only the star's guidance. But they must also have been men who recognized the prior generosity of God, for their initial response in finding the Child was to "do him homage." This was their first and most important gift and helps us appreciate the symbolic meaning of their treasures: giving the gold was a response of sharing their possessions; giving the frankincense was a response of reverence and gratitude for God's gifts to them; giving the myrrh was a response of obedience in following God's revelation in the star (paralleling the obedience of Christ who went to the cross where he was offered wine mixed with myrrh and laid in the tomb with myrrh as one of the burial spices).

Homage is, finally, a gift of self and the most appropriate response of our giving in face of God's giving to us. Homage is an obeisance that gestures a relationship. The magi in this Sunday's gospel model for us the most appropriate response to God's unprecedented generosity to us: gift of self expressed in worship and our own generous deeds.

Living the Paschal Mystery

All gifts given invite a response. Socially, a verbal or written thank you note usually suffices. Simply because God's generosity is so lavish our response must be much more. God has given us great treasure, two of which are mystery so deep: the gift of the only-begotten Son and our being "members of the same body" (see second reading). Our response can be no less than the total gift of ourselves.

"Total gift of ourselves" is one way to describe the paschal mystery. In our baptism we become "coheirs" and "copartners" in Christ, in his death and resurrection. We are copartners, therefore, in Jesus' ministry. To be a disciple means not only to live the gospel, it also means that we will go to our death as Jesus did. "Total gift of ourselves" means that daily we must die to ourselves if we are to remain faithful to our identity with Christ. Why would we choose to respond to God's generosity in such a radical way? Because we know that by dying to ourselves we are "coheirs"—we receive God's life now and the promise of fullness to come.

Focusing the Word

Key words and phrases from the gospel: magi, star, written through the prophet, the child, did him homage, opened their treasures

To the point: Initially on this feast we tend to focus on the gifts the magi give to the newborn Jesus. But, in fact, their gifts are inspired by God's prior generosity: the manifestation of the star, the revelation of Scripture, and, ultimately, God's self-gift in Jesus. This manifestation of God's great generosity requires a response in kind: the gift of ourselves.

Connecting the Word

to the second reading: To be "coheirs [and] members of the same body" of Jesus Christ means that we share his mission: total self-giving.

to culture: Etiquette experts advise us that receiving a gift requires writing a thank you note. The ongoing gift of God in Christ, however, calls us to the ongoing gift of ourselves.

Understanding the Word

The gift of revelation: The story of creation tells us that God set the sun, moon, and stars in the heavens to be, as it were, a map through time measuring days, months, and years (Gen 1:14). The psalmist exclaims, "When I see your heavens . . . the moon and stars that you set in place—What are humans that you are mindful of them? . . . O LORD, our Lord, how awesome is your name through all the earth!" (Ps 8:4-5, 10). The wonder of creation, particularly the heavens, reveals the even greater wonder of humanity. All this, in turn, reveals how awesome is God. It is built into the biblical view of the world that creation reveals to humanity something about God. Such knowledge of God is available to every person. The magi in this Sunday's gospel were particularly interested in celestial phenomena and knew, according to the "science" of their day, that a new star signaled something great. A sign in nature—a star—leads them to Jerusalem.

But God wasn't content to allow humanity merely to deduce something about God from nature. God took more positive steps and made a covenant with Abraham, gave the Law to Moses, and spoke words through the prophets. In short, Sacred Scripture is the record of God's words and deeds and reveals who God is and what God wants of humanity. So when the magi arrive in Jerusalem, they have come as far as nature can lead them. Now they turn to an even more direct source of God's revelation: Scripture.

The gospel sadly reveals how God's word is used in this instance: while it leads the magi to worship "the newborn King of the Jews," the Scriptures are subverted and used by the religious and civil leaders to plot the death of Jesus.

Finally, God imparts yet another gift and is personally revealed in "Emmanuel"—"God with us." The birth of Jesus is the culmination of divine generosity, for in Christ God is fully revealed. Compared to all these divine gifts (nature, Scripture, Jesus) the gifts of the magi (gold, frankincense, myrrh) are merely trinkets.

ASSEMBLY & FAITH-SHARING GROUPS

- The magi's journey began with God's first reaching out to them through the star; my faith journey began with God's first reaching out to me through . . .
- Like the magi, as I face the great mystery of my "newborn king," the treasures I offer him are . . .
- The way I offer homage to the Lord is . . .

PRESIDERS

When Christ's light shines in and through my ministry it looks like . . .

DEACONS

Surprisingly, magi and Gentiles (outsiders) are part of God's plan and "members of the same body" (second reading). I was surprised by God's plan when . . .

HOSPITALITY MINISTERS

My ministry communicates how all are "coheirs, members of the same body, and copartners in the promise in Christ Jesus" (second reading) whenever I . . .

MUSIC MINISTERS

Martin Luther taught that the music we sing in worship is only the return of a gift first given us by God. I/we have experienced music as a gift from God when . . . I/we return that gift to God when . . .

ALTAR MINISTERS

When I see my serving as my doing for God or others, it looks and feels like . . .
When I see my serving as a response to God's always serving me, it looks and feels like . . .

LECTORS

The "chief priests and scribes" could quote the words of the prophet, but they didn't "go and search diligently for the child." My ministry requires that I know God's word not for quoting but for living. The Word I am being challenged to live now is . . .

EUCHARISTIC MINISTERS

As I bring the "newborn King" to the homebound, I am privileged to witness them "open up their treasures" and "do him homage." Their faith has influenced me by . . .

Model Penitential Rite

Presider: The magi followed the star to the newborn King and offered him homage and their treasures. Let us prepare ourselves to offer God homage in this liturgy by examining how well we have followed God's guidance in our own lives . . . [pause]

Lord Jesus, your presence was revealed by the light of a star: Lord . . .

Christ Jesus, you received homage from the magi: Christ . . .

Lord Jesus, you are light for all nations: Lord . . .

Appreciating the Responsorial Psalm

Exegetically, the purpose of Psalm 72 from which this responsorial psalm is taken is to intercede for the king of Israel who represents God. The people ask God to endow the king with divine judgment so that justice may reign, the poor and afflicted be rescued, and peace blossom for all time. Then light will shine from Jerusalem and all peoples will recognize and pay homage to the true King, the Lord God (first reading).

Liturgically, the Lectionary uses these verses from Psalm 72 to identify Christ as the fulfillment of Israel's prayer: this newborn babe is the King *par excellence,* God's justice and mercy in the flesh, come to rescue the poor and bring peace to all nations. Those who "see" recognize who he is (gospel). But the gospel also casts a paschal mystery shadow. We know full well the unexpressed yet hinted conclusion that some, even those deputed to represent God, will seek Christ's death rather than do him homage. Paul tells us the revelation made known in the coming of Christ is complete and universal (second reading). But that all people see this and come to adore yet awaits our choice and needs our prayer. And so we sing this psalm with both jubilation for what has already been given in Christ and longing for what is yet to be recognized and received.

Model General Intercessions

Presider: As always, God continues to be generous to us as we make known our needs.

Response:

Lord, hear our prayer.

Cantor:

we pray to the Lord,

That the Church be generous to those in need as God is generous to us . . . [pause]

That peoples of the world open their treasures so all share equitably in God's good gifts . . . [pause]

That the poor receive abundantly . . . [pause]

That each of us here may offer God homage always and everywhere in response to God's generous gifts to us . . . [pause]

Presider: Generous God, you lavish us with all good things: hear these our prayers that we might one day enjoy with you the fullness of your generosity, life everlasting. We ask this through Christ our Lord. **Amen.**

OPENING PRAYER

Let us pray

Pause for silent prayer

Father,
you revealed your Son to the nations
  by the guidance of a star.
Lead us to your glory in heaven
  by the light of faith.

We ask this through our Lord Jesus Christ,
    your Son,
who lives and reigns with you and the
    Holy Spirit,
one God, for ever and ever. **Amen.**

FIRST READING

Isa 60:1-6

Rise up in splendor, Jerusalem! Your light
    has come,
    the glory of the Lord shines upon you.
See, darkness covers the earth,
    and thick clouds cover the peoples;
but upon you the LORD shines,
    and over you appears his glory.
Nations shall walk by your light,
    and kings by your shining radiance.
Raise your eyes and look about;
    they all gather and come to you:
your sons come from afar,
    and your daughters in the arms of their
        nurses.

Then you shall be radiant at what you see,
    your heart shall throb and overflow,
for the riches of the sea shall be emptied
        out before you,
    the wealth of nations shall be brought
        to you.
Caravans of camels shall fill you,
    dromedaries from Midian and Ephah;
all from Sheba shall come
    bearing gold and frankincense,
    and proclaiming the praises of the LORD.

RESPONSORIAL PSALM
Ps 72:1-2, 7-8, 10-11, 12-13

R̸. (cf. 11) Lord, every nation on earth will adore you.

O God, with your judgment endow the
    king,
    and with your justice, the king's son;
he shall govern your people with justice
    and your afflicted ones with judgment.

R̸. Lord, every nation on earth will adore you.

Justice shall flower in his days,
    and profound peace, till the moon be no
        more.
May he rule from sea to sea,
    and from the River to the ends of the
        earth.

R̸. Lord, every nation on earth will adore you.

The kings of Tarshish and the Isles shall
        offer gifts;
    the kings of Arabia and Seba shall
        bring tribute.
All kings shall pay him homage,
    all nations shall serve him.

R̸. Lord, every nation on earth will adore you.

For he shall rescue the poor when he cries
        out,
    and the afflicted when he has no one to
        help him.
He shall have pity for the lowly and the
        poor;
    the lives of the poor he shall save.

R̸. Lord, every nation on earth will adore you.

SECOND READING
Eph 3:2-3a, 5-6

Brothers and sisters:
You have heard of the stewardship of
        God's grace
    that was given to me for your benefit,
    namely, that the mystery was made
        known to me by revelation.
It was not made known to people in other
        generations
    as it has now been revealed
to his holy apostles and prophets by the
        Spirit:
    that the Gentiles are coheirs, members
        of the same body,
    and copartners in the promise in Christ
        Jesus through the gospel.

About Liturgy

Gift of worship: Each Sunday when the Christian assembly gathers for liturgy many gifts are clearly given to God: the gift of time and talent shown in the various ministries; the gift of money and food goods for those in need and the upkeep of the parish; the gift of ourselves to each other by our presence and full, conscious, and active participation. All of this is good. At the same time we must never forget that we gather on Sunday *in response to* God's prior gifts to us summed up in the Son and our share in divine life. Thus our Sunday celebration most of all ought to be characterized by thankfulness for all God has given us and praise (homage) for this God who chooses to be so intimately present to us.

It is all too easy for our Sunday celebrations to be subtly focused on ourselves. Although we can never be passive at Sunday Mass (and our greeting each other, hospitality, and offerings are an important and indispensable part of the time spent in worship), we must never forget, however, that we are there first and foremost to give God praise and thanksgiving. The purpose of Sunday worship is just that: *worship*. Threaded through the speaking and singing, gestures and postures, relating and responding must be an attitude of awe, reverence, and deep-felt gratitude for God's lavish generosity to us in so many ways. In the end the only lasting gift we can really give God is ourselves in worship and self-emptying service of others.

About Liturgical Music

Cantor preparation: When you sing this responsorial psalm you reveal who Christ is: the justice, peace, and mercy of God in full flesh. You also participate in the Church's prayer that all peoples recognize who Christ is and come to adore him. What might you do this week to help yourself recognize Christ more clearly in your own life and pay him homage?

Hymn suggestion: Although the Christmas season celebrates our jubilation at Christ's birth, the liturgy never lets us stray far from the looming presence of the paschal mystery implications of his birth. Ruth Duck's "O Radiant Christ, Incarnate Word" [in *Dancing in the Universe,* © 1992 GIA] captures both the confidence we feel in the revelation brought by Christ and the struggle we experience with letting that revelation guide human affairs: "Our bartered, busy lives burn dim, too tired to care, too numb to feel . . . Come, shine upon our shadowed world . . . illumine all we say and do . . . lead the peoples to your peace, as stars once lead the way to you." The text is set to a specifically commissioned tune (David Cherwien's RADIANT LIGHT) whose shifts from C major to minor to major aptly express the light-darkness-light shifts in the text itself. As this tune will be unknown to most assemblies, you might have choir only sing the hymn during presentation of the gifts. Otherwise, as Duck suggests, choose a familiar tune such as WAREHAM for the assembly to sing.

SPIRITUALITY

Gospel

Luke 3:15-16, 21-22; L21C

The people were filled with
   expectation,
   and all were asking in their
      hearts
   whether John might be the
      Christ.
John answered them all, saying,
   "I am baptizing you with water,
   but one mightier than I is
      coming.
I am not worthy to loosen the
   thongs of his sandals.
He will baptize you with the Holy
   Spirit and fire."

After all the people had been baptized
   and Jesus also had been baptized and
      was praying,
   heaven was opened and the Holy
      Spirit descended upon him
   in bodily form like a dove.
And a voice came from heaven,
   "You are my beloved Son;
   with you I am well pleased."

Reflecting on the Gospel

"Show and Tell" is generally a popular time in elementary school classrooms and this for at least two reasons. First, education research has revealed that we learn best by concrete, hands-on experiences. When the children can see and touch some object their curiosity is roused, questions come easy, and they are usually eager to run home after school and tell others about the experience. Second, "Show and Tell" is popular because it boosts the self-esteem of the little one in front of the class doing the explaining. Something significant to the child is shared with others and the interest of the classmates encourages the child and makes him or her feel important. "Show and Tell" is a manifestation of good learning technique and the worth of an individual. This Sunday's gospel tells of a kind of "Show and Tell" on the part of both Jesus and us. It manifests who we are and how we have been gifted.

In effect, Jesus' baptism wasn't John's (that is, a baptism of repentance) but the occasion for the revelation of Jesus' identity. Interestingly enough, in Luke's gospel Jesus' identity isn't revealed at the baptism when Jesus came up out of the water (as in Mark and Matthew), but when "Jesus . . . was praying." The manifestation of Jesus' identity as "beloved Son" while he was praying underscores his relationship with the Father and his identity as consistent with that relationship.

As Jesus was baptized by John, so must we be baptized—not just in the waters of repentance but by the Holy Spirit and fire which calls us, too, to give ourselves (see second reading). Thus receiving the Spirit in our own baptism manifests our identity as ones who are saved, renewed, justified, and heirs of eternal life (second reading), that is, those who also share in God's life. Being baptized by fire means that we share in Jesus' mission, including the total gift of ourselves. We come to an appreciation of all this when we, like Jesus, contemplate this mystery of baptism in prayer. As we appreciate more and more who we are (sharers in divinity) and what we are to do (die to ourselves) we gradually come to realize that our lives are one big "show and tell." Who we are manifests God's presence in the very dying we do each day as we conform ourselves to God's will. Like the simple "Show and Tell" time in the classroom, we learn from experiencing and encounter with the Divine through others. In this our own self-esteem is boosted when we realize that *we ourselves* are God's presence for another. The gift far exceeds the cost!

Living the Paschal Mystery

These kind, merciful, and generous gifts of God are manifested to the world when we "live temperately, justly, and devoutly in this age" (second reading). Yes, the gift of divine identity and its attendant call to discipleship does make demands on us. Taking our baptism seriously means that the ritual moment is just the beginning of a lifetime of openness to God's continuing grace "training" us to be faithful to who God has made us to be. Our share in divinity is a gift so gracious that the only response is dying to self. But in the dying is the hope of a share in eternal life because the One whose identity we share has already been raised from the dead. Living the paschal mystery means that while our life manifests dying for the sake of others we also manifest the hope that is sure because God's ultimate gift to us is everlasting life, a promise already fulfilled.

Focusing the Word

Key words and phrases from the gospel: one mightier . . . baptize you with the Holy Spirit and fire, Jesus . . . baptized . . . beloved Son

To the point: The gospel speaks of two baptisms. The first is the event this feast celebrates: the baptism Jesus received. The second is the baptism with the Holy Spirit and fire which we receive. Just as Jesus' baptism revealed him as "beloved Son," our own baptism reveals us as ones who are saved, renewed, justified, and heirs of eternal life (see second reading). In this sense baptism is an epiphany.

Connecting the Word

to Ordinary Time: The whole Christmas season now ended has opened up for us God's many and wondrous gifts to us. We begin Ordinary Time now in the strength of these gifts.

to Catholic culture: Baptism is more than a ritual moment on a specific day; it is a gift of divine life which God continuously sustains with yet more gifts to which we must respond daily.

Understanding the Word

Baptism and identity: John had preached a "baptism of repentance for the forgiveness of sins." Obviously, this would present a problem for Jesus to undergo such a baptism. Luke resolves this problem differently from the other evangelists. In Luke 3:19-20 (omitted from this Sunday's gospel), Luke informs his readers that John had been arrested and imprisoned by Herod. The baptism that Jesus receives is not John's baptism.

In Mark's gospel the story of Jesus begins with his baptism and so that event is a disclosure of his identity. But in Luke's gospel readers have already been told several times who Jesus is. In the annunciation Gabriel tells Mary that the child to be born will be called "Son of the Most High" (1:32) and "the Son of God" (1:36). The child Jesus, when found in the Temple, tells his anxious parents that he is in "my Father's house" (2:49). The voice heard at the baptism, then, is a confirmation of the identity of Jesus: "You are my beloved Son."

Only Luke indicates that God's voice is heard and the Spirit is seen while Jesus is in prayer; later, in the transfiguration, Jesus will once again be deep in prayer when the heavenly voice announces, "This is my chosen Son" (9:35). It is worth noting that it is while the disciples are at prayer that the Holy Spirit descends upon them at Pentecost (Acts 1:14; 2:1-5). Prayer confirms (for Jesus) and discloses (to others) the identity of Jesus. A similar dynamic is at work in the lives of disciples: baptism is a public act by which disciples become children of God (1 John 3:2). The second reading makes the same point with different language: "[God] saved us through the bath of rebirth and renewal by the Holy Spirit, whom he richly poured out on us through Jesus Christ our savior, so that we might . . . become heirs in hope of eternal life" (Titus 3:5-7). Disciples, in imitation of their Master, find in prayer an affirmation of their baptismal identity and undertake their ministry in the power of the Holy Spirit.

ASSEMBLY & FAITH-SHARING GROUPS

- Jesus heard who he was ("beloved Son") when he prayed; I realize and remember who I am in faith when I . . .
- Having been baptized "with the Holy Spirit and fire" means to me . . .
- My daily living manifests what I believe about my baptism whenever I . . .

PRESIDERS

I hold up the assembly's baptismal dignity ("heirs . . . of eternal life"; second reading) whenever I . . .
I also keep before them their baptismal duty ("to live temperately, justly, devoutly in this age"; second reading) whenever I . . .

DEACONS

My ministry is meant to renew the baptismal dignity of others. The people most in need of comfort and of being carried with care (see first reading) are . . .

HOSPITALITY MINISTERS

Genuine hospitality makes "the kindness and generous love of God our savior appear" (second reading). I have received such hospitality at the hands of . . .
I have extended this hospitality to . . .

MUSIC MINISTERS

At its deepest level participation in liturgy is participation in my baptismal identity as body of Christ. I experience my music-making leading the assembly to this level of participation when . . .

ALTAR MINISTERS

Serving is a ministry (and more than a task) when it shapes the person. Examples of how serving is making me more Christ-like are . . .

LECTORS

We have a proverb that says, "Actions speak louder than words." My actions that proclaim the dignity and duty of baptism are . . .

EUCHARISTIC MINISTERS

Just as "a voice came from heaven" and announces Jesus' identity as "beloved Son," so, too, at Eucharist each one of the baptized hears (again) his or her identity as "Body/Blood of Christ." The difference this makes in my life is . . .

Rite of Blessing and Sprinkling Holy Water

Presider: Jesus' identity as beloved Son of God was manifested at his baptism. Through our own baptism we share in this divine identity which is manifested in the good works of our own lives. We bless this water and sprinkle it, and ask God to strengthen us to be faithful disciples of Jesus.

[continue with form B of the blessing of water]

Appreciating the Responsorial Psalm

The verses from Psalm 104 used for this responsorial psalm recite the many ways God's glory is revealed: God generates the heavens, rules water and wind, creates all that roams earth and swims seas, gives all creatures their food in due season, and, above all, continuously sends the Spirit, the breath of life and renewal.

The first and second readings proclaim that in Christ the fullness of God's glory has appeared. His identity is confirmed at his baptism: "You are my beloved Son" who will "baptize . . . with the Holy Spirit and fire" (gospel). The power of God has become fully manifest in Christ who cleanses us from sin and recreates us as a people "eager to do . . . good" (second reading). What better response can we make than "O bless the Lord, my soul"? May this response express our acknowledgment of our baptismal identity and our willingness to enter with Christ into the Ordinary Time journey to which this identity calls us.

Model General Intercessions

Presider: Our baptism confers on us the gift of divine identity and requires of us self-emptying discipleship. We pray for the strength to be faithful.

Response:

Cantor:

May the Church, the body of Christ, faithfully manifest God's graciousness to the world . . . [pause]

May all peoples, children of God, faithfully manifest that God's salvation is for all . . . [pause]

May the poor, beloved of God, receive more abundantly the gifts of this world . . . [pause]

May each of us, the presence of the risen Christ, be faithful to our baptismal commitment . . . [pause]

Presider: Gracious God, you give all good gifts: hear these our prayers that one day we may share in the hope of eternal life. We ask this through Christ our Lord. **Amen.**

OPENING PRAYER

Let us pray

Pause for silent prayer

Almighty, eternal God,
when the Spirit descended upon Jesus
at his baptism in the Jordan,
you revealed him as your own beloved
Son.
Keep us, your children born of water and
the Spirit,
faithful to our calling.

We ask this through our Lord Jesus Christ,
your Son,
who lives and reigns with you and the
Holy Spirit,
one God, for ever and ever. **Amen.**

FIRST READING
Isa 40:1-5, 9-11

Comfort, give comfort to my people,
 says your God.
Speak tenderly to Jerusalem, and proclaim
 to her
 that her service is at an end,
 her guilt is expiated;
indeed, she has received from the hand of
 the LORD
 double for all her sins.

 A voice cries out:
In the desert prepare the way of the LORD!
 Make straight in the wasteland a
 highway for our God!
Every valley shall be filled in,
 every mountain and hill shall be made
 low;
the rugged land shall be made a plain,
 the rough country, a broad valley.
Then the glory of the LORD shall be
 revealed,
 and all people shall see it together;
 for the mouth of the LORD has spoken.

Go up onto a high mountain,
 Zion, herald of glad tidings;
cry out at the top of your voice,
 Jerusalem, herald of good news!
Fear not to cry out
 and say to the cities of Judah:
 Here is your God!
Here comes with power
 the Lord GOD,
 who rules by a strong arm;
here is his reward with him,
 his recompense before him.
Like a shepherd he feeds his flock;
 in his arms he gathers the lambs,
carrying them in his bosom,
 and leading the ewes with care.

RESPONSORIAL PSALM
Ps 104:1b-2, 3-4, 24-25, 27-28, 29-30

R̷. (1) O bless the Lord, my soul.

O LORD, my God, you are great indeed!
 You are clothed with majesty and glory,
robed in light as with a cloak.
 You have spread out the heavens like a
  tent-cloth;

R̷. O bless the Lord, my soul.

You have constructed your palace upon
  the waters.
 You make the clouds your chariot;
you travel on the wings of the wind.
 You make the winds your messengers,
and flaming fire your ministers.

R̷. O bless the Lord, my soul.

How manifold are your works, O LORD!
 In wisdom you have wrought them all—
 the earth is full of your creatures;
the sea also, great and wide,
 in which are schools without number
 of living things both small and great.

R̷. O bless the Lord, my soul.

They look to you to give them food in due
  time.
When you give it to them, they gather it;
 when you open your hand, they are
  filled with good things.

R̷. O bless the Lord, my soul.

If you take away their breath, they perish
  and return to the dust.
When you send forth your spirit, they are
  created,
 and you renew the face of the earth.

R̷. O bless the Lord, my soul.

SECOND READING
Titus 2:11-14; 3:4-7

Beloved:
The grace of God has appeared, saving all
 and training us to reject godless ways
  and worldly desires
 and to live temperately, justly, and
  devoutly in this age,
 as we await the blessed hope,
 the appearance of the glory of our
  great God
 and savior Jesus Christ,
 who gave himself for us to deliver us
  from all lawlessness
 and to cleanse for himself a people as
  his own,
 eager to do what is good.

Continued in Appendix A, p. 261.

About Liturgy

Symbols of baptism: The symbols of the baptismal rite put into focus the primary gift of baptism—a share in divine life which is for us a new identity:

 Water—plunged into the baptismal waters, we are plunged into Christ's death; rising, we share in divine life. Water brings both death (to our old selves) and life (new life in God).

 Chrism—anointed with Chrism, we share in the threefold office of Christ—priest, prophet, ruler. Our being anointed with Chrism is a consecration of ourselves to conform our life to Christ's.

 White garment—clothed in a white garment, we are reminded of our new, resurrected life in Christ. We are to live unstained until we enjoy eternal life with God.

 Lighted candle—enlightened by Christ, we are also to be the light of Christ dispelling sin and darkness in the world. We ourselves are manifestations that in Christ the light of salvation has come into the world.

 Although all of these symbols also imply the demands of discipleship (*water*—dying to self; *Chrism*—conforming ourselves to Christ; *white garment*—living lives worthy of who we are; *lighted candle*—overcoming the darkness of evil) they primarily help us understand who we become in baptism—members of the body of Christ sharing in divine identity. Moreover, greater awareness and appreciation of our identity eases the way for us to be more faithful in our discipleship.

About Liturgical Music

Cantor preparation: The numerous signs of God's glory which you enumerate in these psalm verses are external revelations of the even greater glory God works within us through our baptism in Christ. What might you do this week to renew your awareness of the power and grace of baptism? What might you do to bless God for this power and grace?

Service music for Ordinary Time: The celebration of the Baptism of the Lord is the hinge Sunday marking the changeover from the Christmas season to Ordinary Time. Because the solemnity stands as a turning point and faces both directions, it would be appropriate either to sing the service music used during Christmas season one last time or to begin using your Ordinary Time setting. Some examples of service music suitable for Ordinary Time—that is, settings which are well-written musically and which possess acclamatory energy without being overly festive—are Vermulst's "People's Mass," Owen Alstott's "Heritage Mass," the St. Louis Jesuits Mass, and the Danish Mass.

Hymn suggestion: A hymn text extraordinarily appropriate for this Sunday when we return to Ordinary Time is Herman Stuempfle's "The Hills Are Still, the Darkness Deep" [in *The Word Goes Forth*, ©1993 GIA]. Stuempfle brings us down from the glories of Christmas and plants us firmly in the reality of ordinary life. The song of angels no longer fills the sky but instead a "hungry cry"; shepherds once roused by glorious light have returned to "cold and lonely vigil"; the kings have departed leaving Mary to tend a child in the night. The final verse captures the challenge of Ordinary Time: "O God, when glory fades away And duties fill the night, the day: By grace unseen but present still, Give strength to heart and hand and will." This would make an excellent text for the assembly to sing after Communion as an act of quiet renewal of their baptism and its meaning for daily life.

Ordinary Time I

✛ SPIRITUALITY

Gospel

John 2:1-11; L66C

There was a wedding at Cana in
    Galilee,
  and the mother of Jesus was there.
Jesus and his disciples were also
    invited to the wedding.
When the wine ran short,
  the mother of Jesus said to him,
  "They have no wine."
And Jesus said to her,
  "Woman, how does your concern
    affect me?
My hour has not yet come."
His mother said to the servers,
  "Do whatever he tells you."
Now there were six stone water jars
    there for Jewish ceremonial
    washings,
  each holding twenty to thirty gallons.
Jesus told them,
  "Fill the jars with water."
So they filled them to the brim.
Then he told them,
  "Draw some out now and take it to
    the headwaiter."
So they took it.
And when the headwaiter tasted the
    water that had become wine,
  without knowing where it came from
  —although the servers who had
    drawn the water knew—,
  the headwaiter called the bridegroom
    and said to him,
  "Everyone serves good wine first,
  and then when people have drunk
    freely, an inferior one;
  but you have kept the good wine until
    now."
Jesus did this as the beginning of his
    signs at Cana in Galilee
  and so revealed his glory,
  and his disciples began to believe in
    him.

Reflecting on the Gospel

Probably no other human ritual has as many customs surrounding it as a wedding. Take the average modern North American wedding: engagement ring, invitations, showers, stag parties, attendants, music, flowers, flower girls and ring bearers, giving the bride away, white dress, veil, something old and something new, bouquets and garters, cutting the cake and the couple feeding each other the first piece, a grand wedding feast, beer and wine, decorating the wedding car, honeymoon, carrying the bride over the threshold; it doesn't even stop with this but continues into specified anniversary gifts. Add to the list particular customs of many different cultures, and the customs proliferate at a dizzying pace. In all of this, two things are sure: everyone wants the day to be perfect and the focus is on the couple this day.

For their own time and custom we can well imagine that the couple in this Sunday's gospel probably spent a proportionate amount of time preparing for their own wedding day. We identify with Mary's sensitivity in noticing that the wine was running short (this would surely spoil a perfect day!) and Jesus' sensitivity in keeping the miracle quiet (the focus was on the couple, not him!). This miracle wasn't a big show; the gospel intimates that those who noticed were the disciples with him, and they "came to believe in him." The purpose of the miracle, then, wasn't to save the wedding couple's day or to draw attention to Jesus. The purpose runs deeper: the sign "revealed [Jesus'] glory." The wedding feast was an opportunity for epiphany and belief.

The first reading gives us a hint about why Jesus had to reveal his glory: so that we might "be called by a new name," that is, God's "Delight" and "Espoused." The epiphany of Jesus' glory is a sign of the persistence of God's overtures of love to us—God reveals glory to us in many ways to make sure we catch it—and the depths of God's love, so much that we are espoused to God.

We begin Ordinary Time with calm assurance about how much God loves us. God's epiphanies come through many signs, but all of them are to show forth God's glory and invite us to an espoused relationship so that we, too, share in that glory.

Living the Paschal Mystery

Belief entails a *Who* rather than a *what*. Our own encounters with Jesus (in prayer, through others, in struggling with daily dying) are truly epiphanies of God's glory which also invite *us* to respond to divine Presence with belief. These epiphany signs might come in many ways—through others in a cry for help, in a lonely person's plea for companionship, in the spontaneous laughter of delight, in the beauty of nature. The challenge to us is to see these as revelations of God's glory, as epiphanies of God's love for us, and an opportunity to respond in belief.

Yes, these common, ordinary signs of God's love and glory are all around us. By *responding* to other persons (recognizing them as revelations of God to us) we ourselves also become signs of God's in-breaking, epiphanies for others. We ourselves are the good wine kept until after Jesus' ascension when we take up Jesus' mission as disciples. Living the paschal mystery means that we empty ourselves in order to be filled with the goodness of God's glory.

Focusing the Word

Key words and phrases from the gospel: revealed his glory, began to believe

To the point: The wedding at Cana is yet another epiphany. The purpose of this sign is not simply to provide additional wine for the wedding guests but to reveal Jesus' glory and to draw his disciples to believe. All that Jesus does and everything that God reveals is for the same purpose—that we begin to believe.

Connecting the Word

to the liturgical year: The believing to which the gospel calls us lays a suitable and solid foundation on which the entire liturgical year builds.

to Catholic culture: Few of us ever witness the kind of dramatic signs like that reported in this gospel. Nevertheless, we are called to the same faith response because faith is not in the sign but in the person of Jesus.

Understanding the Word

Signs: John calls the mighty deeds of Jesus "signs." He is very selective in reporting these signs, including only seven in chapters 1:19–12:50 ("The Book of Signs"). Of these, the wedding feast at Cana is the only sign for which there is no comparable story in the other gospels.

In John's gospel signs are ambiguous: they invite but do not compel faith. Often spectators in the crowd are divided in their assessment of Jesus: some see a sign and believe (5:53; 11:45), others see a sign and conclude that Jesus must be destroyed (5:15-16; 11:46-53). Ideally signs lead people to see beyond the wonder of the event (e.g., the water turned into wine) to see instead the revelation of Jesus' glory. And seeing Jesus' glory, people respond by believing in him. Thus, this first of his signs sets up the ideal pattern: a sign manifests Jesus' glory and moves people to believe.

This Sunday's gospel story is the third Sunday in a row in which the gospel has presented some kind of public revelation or manifestation of Jesus. The series began with the Feast of the Epiphany in which Jesus is revealed as the gift of God given for the salvation of Jews and Gentiles alike; last week's gospel of the baptism confirmed Jesus' identity as the Son of God; this Sunday's "miracle" at Cana "revealed his glory." In the Old Testament "glory" refers to God's visible radiance which God manifests instead of an actual visible appearance which would overwhelm people (Exod 33:20). When Jesus "revealed his glory," he gave a "sneak preview" of what will be fully revealed in his death/resurrection/ascension. Ideally the response to this revelation—like the response to all his signs—is that people believe. John expressly states this in the conclusion: "Jesus did many other signs in the presence of [his] disciples that are not written in this book. But these are written that you may [come to] believe that Jesus is the Messiah, the Son of God, and that through this belief you may have life in his name" (20:30-31).

ASSEMBLY & FAITH-SHARING GROUPS

- That Jesus' first sign was at a wedding is part of the message. Its significance for me is . . .
- The fact that Jesus' sign consists of an overgenerous amount of wine means to me . . .
- I extend to those around me that extravagance of Jesus by . . .
- Where I have seen the glory of Jesus that has led me "to begin to believe in him" is . . .

PRESIDERS

I can only give with such abandon as long as I receive first the extravagant glory of Jesus. I receive this . . .
I have given myself extravagantly to . . .

DEACONS

My ministry connects me to so many with countless needs. Like Mary, I trust that Jesus' glory will be revealed as I bring these concerns to him . . .

HOSPITALITY MINISTERS

Jesus changed water into wine, so too can he transform the "Forsaken" into God's "Delight" (first reading) through my ministry of hospitality. As I consider this I am moved to . . .

MUSIC MINISTERS

In my music-making I am a sign that leads others to belief in Jesus when . . .

ALTAR MINISTERS

Jesus' glory is revealed in the self-emptying that my service demands. I see self-emptying as a sharing in Jesus' glory because . . .

LECTORS

There are times when I feel and live as "Forsaken" (see first reading) . . .
That I am God's "Delight" was announced to me through . . .
I announce this to others by . . .

EUCHARISTIC MINISTERS

If water changed to wine can reveal Jesus' glory, how much more can changed hearts reveal it! Those who have been living signs (Eucharist) of Jesus' glory for me are . . .

Model Penitential Rite

Presider: Jesus performed his first public sign at the wedding feast at Cana and re-vealed his glory so that his disciples began to believe. We pause at the beginning of this celebration to reflect on the signs of Jesus' glory in our own lives and to ask God during this liturgy to increase our belief . . . [pause]

Lord Jesus, you turned the water into wine and thus revealed your great power and glory: Lord . . .

Christ Jesus, your disciples came to believe in you: Christ . . .

Lord Jesus, you call us to be believing disciples: Lord . . .

Appreciating the Responsorial Psalm

What marvelous deeds are we proclaiming in this Sunday's responsorial psalm? We at-test to God's saving actions in transforming Jerusalem from "forsaken" and "desolate" to "delight" and "espoused" (first reading). We attest to Christ's action in transforming simple water into choice wine and to the revelation this miracle made about his identity and mission (gospel). And we attest to the change that was wrought in the hearts and minds of the disciples at Cana who let themselves be transformed by this sign from mere onlookers to true believers in the person of Jesus.

In singing this psalm we announce that we, too, have seen the signs and have come to believe in the One sent for the world's salvation. We proclaim our belief in him and invite all nations to join us in praise and worship.

Model General Intercessions

Presider: With great confidence that our prayers will be heard, we make our needs known to our loving and glory-filled God.

Response:

Lord,— hear our prayer.

Cantor:

we pray to the Lord,

That the Church always be an epiphany of God's love and care . . . [pause]

That world leaders always be attentive to the needs of those under their care . . . [pause]

That those in need have their fill . . . [pause]

That each of us here believe in God's love and goodness and manifest these through the way we live generously for others . . . [pause]

Presider: Loving God, your glory is an epiphany of your presence: hear these our prayers that one day we might share forever in that same glory. We ask this through Christ our Lord. **Amen.**

ALTERNATIVE OPENING PRAYER

Let us pray

Pause for silent prayer

Almighty and ever-present Father,
your watchful care reaches from end to
    end
and orders all things in such power
that even the tensions and the tragedies of
    sin
cannot frustrate your loving plans.
Help us to embrace your will,
give us the strength to follow your call,
so that your truth may live in our hearts
and reflect peace to those who believe in
    your love.

We ask this in the name of Jesus the Lord.
    Amen.

FIRST READING

Isa 62:1-5

For Zion's sake I will not be silent,
    for Jerusalem's sake I will not be quiet,
until her vindication shines forth like the
    dawn
    and her victory like a burning torch.

Nations shall behold your vindication,
    and all the kings your glory;
you shall be called by a new name
    pronounced by the mouth of the LORD.
You shall be a glorious crown in the hand
    of the LORD,
    a royal diadem held by your God.
No more shall people call you "Forsaken,"
    or your land "Desolate,"
but you shall be called "My Delight,"
    and your land "Espoused."
For the LORD delights in you
    and makes your land his spouse.
As a young man marries a virgin,
    your Builder shall marry you;
and as a bridegroom rejoices in his bride
    so shall your God rejoice in you.

RESPONSORIAL PSALM

Ps 96:1-2, 2-3, 7-8, 9-10

℟. (3) Proclaim his marvelous deeds to all the nations.

Sing to the LORD a new song;
  sing to the LORD, all you lands.
Sing to the LORD; bless his name.

℟. Proclaim his marvelous deeds to all the nations.

Announce his salvation, day after day.
  Tell his glory among the nations;
among all peoples, his wondrous deeds.

℟. Proclaim his marvelous deeds to all the nations.

Give to the LORD, you families of nations,
  give to the LORD glory and praise;
  give to the LORD the glory due his name!

℟. Proclaim his marvelous deeds to all the nations.

Worship the LORD in holy attire.
  Tremble before him, all the earth;
say among the nations: The LORD is king.
  He governs the peoples with equity.

℟. Proclaim his marvelous deeds to all the nations.

SECOND READING

1 Cor 12:4-11

Brothers and sisters:
There are different kinds of spiritual gifts
    but the same Spirit;
  there are different forms of service but
      the same Lord;
  there are different workings but the
      same God
  who produces all of them in everyone.
To each individual the manifestation of
    the Spirit
  is given for some benefit.
To one is given through the Spirit the
    expression of wisdom;
  to another, the expression of knowledge
      according to the same Spirit;
  to another, faith by the same Spirit;
  to another, gifts of healing by the one
      Spirit;
  to another, mighty deeds;
  to another, prophecy;
  to another, discernment of spirits;
  to another, varieties of tongues;
  to another, interpretation of tongues.
But one and the same Spirit produces all of
    these,
  distributing them individually to each
      person as he wishes.

About Liturgy

Epiphany themes: Year C in the Lectionary cycle is the only one in which the three traditional epiphany themes occur on three consecutive Sundays: epiphany to the magi, Jesus' baptism, and the sign at the wedding feast at Cana. Accordingly, this volume of *Living Liturgy* focused on the notion of epiphany (manifestation, showing forth) on all three Sundays.

Eucharist's epiphanies: Each time we celebrate liturgy God manifests divine Self to us in a number of ways. For example, in the *introductory rites* we are given an opportunity to be aware that God calls us into divine presence and asks us to be attentive to and respond to that epiphany. In the *Liturgy of the Word* God speaks to us—sometimes in terms of promise and fulfillment, sometimes exhorting us to right living, sometimes assuring us with divine love, sometimes challenging us to change our ways—and in the epiphany of word invites a response of a renewed commitment to follow Jesus as disciples. In the *Liturgy of the Eucharist* Christ becomes substantially present to us in the consecrated Bread and Wine and gives his very Body and Blood for our food and drink. This epiphany shows us God's tremendous love for us and God's desire for intimacy; it also shows forth our own dignity as we ourselves are and are becoming the very body of Christ. In the *concluding rite* we are sent forth to be the epiphany of God's presence in our everyday lives.

The Sunday Eucharist is a most sublime epiphany of God. Moreover, through our being transformed by the ritual action we ourselves are reminded over and over again to be the presence of Christ in our world. God loves us so much as to send the Son to be our savior; God trusts us so much as to send us to be the manifestation of God's presence!

About Liturgical Music

Cantor preparation: In every phrase but one of this Sunday's responsorial psalm you command the assembly to "proclaim . . . sing . . . announce . . . give glory . . . worship . . ." In what ways this week can you proclaim, sing, announce, glorify, or worship God?

Selecting seasonal service music, Pt. 1: Just as changes in art and environment cue the assembly about a change in liturgical season, so must the service music assist the parish to enter into the character of each season and into the unfolding rhythms of the liturgical year. For this to happen a parish needs to have a set of service music in place for each season which over time becomes recognizable as part of celebrating that season.

Selecting such seasonal service music must begin by considering the liturgical year, both as a whole and in its individual seasons. Why does the Church follow a liturgical year? What relationship exists between the unfolding seasons and solemnities of the liturgical year and the identity and mission of the Church? Why, in the midst of the busy commercialism of pre-Christmas do we have the four weeks of Advent? Why each year do we enter into the renewal period of Lent prior to the resurrection celebration of the weeks of Easter? What is the purpose of Ordinary Time and what formative influence does it bear on our growth in Christian living?

These questions are worth reflecting over and discussing with music ministers, parish staff, and the parish at large for their answers will form the theological basis for the musical decisions to be made.

JANUARY 18, 2004

SECOND SUNDAY IN ORDINARY TIME

✠ SPIRITUALITY

Gospel

Luke 1:1-4; 4:14-21; L69C

Since many have undertaken to compile
    a narrative of the events
      that have been fulfilled among us,
    just as those who were
        eyewitnesses from the
        beginning
    and ministers of the word have
        handed them down to us,
I too have decided,
    after investigating everything
        accurately anew,
to write it down in an orderly
        sequence for you,
most excellent Theophilus,
so that you may realize the
        certainty of the teachings
you have received.

Jesus returned to Galilee in the power of
    the Spirit,
    and news of him spread throughout
      the whole region.
He taught in their synagogues and was
    praised by all.

He came to Nazareth, where he had
    grown up,
    and went according to his custom
into the synagogue on the sabbath day.
He stood up to read and was handed a
    scroll of the prophet Isaiah.
He unrolled the scroll and found the
    passage where it was written:
    The Spirit of the Lord is upon me,
    because he has anointed me
    to bring glad tidings to the poor.
    He has sent me to proclaim liberty to
      captives
    and recovery of sight to the blind,
    to let the oppressed go free,
    and to proclaim a year acceptable
      to the Lord.
Rolling up the scroll, he handed it back
    to the attendant and sat down,
    and the eyes of all in the synagogue
      looked intently at him.
He said to them,
    "Today this Scripture passage is
      fulfilled in your hearing."

Reflecting on the Gospel

The way one reads aloud to a group is already part of the message. Eye contact, "pregnant" pauses, voice inflection all help the reader to take command of his or her audience and more strongly get the point across. The first reading for this Sunday shows Ezra the priest as a master at effective reading: he stood "on a wooden platform" so that all could see, he opened the scroll deliberately and carefully so that "all the people might see it," he "read plainly" and "interpreted" the Law, and instructed the people to feast for "today is holy."

The people were so moved that they "bowed down and prostrated themselves." The gospel shows Jesus as a master at effective reading: he "stood up to read," "unrolled the scroll," and after he had finished reading the selected passage he "handed [the scroll] back to the attendant and sat down." The gospel goes on to explain that the "eyes of all . . . looked intently at him." We would guess that Jesus introduced here a long, pregnant pause. His next words were hardly what the synagogue people could expect: "Today this Scripture passage is fulfilled in your hearing."

The same intensity with which the people of Nehemiah's time heard the Law proclaimed by Ezra is focused on Jesus in the synagogue ("the eyes of all . . . looked intently at him").

Their intense anticipation is met by Jesus' dramatic assertion that the Scripture passage from Isaiah is fulfilled because the one anointed by the Spirit is Jesus. In the first reading Ezra reads from the book of the Law; in the gospel Jesus *is* the book, the good news. Ezra interprets what he read; in the gospel Jesus himself *is* the interpretation. Ezra's word was an inspiring word that had power and moved the people to worship and praise; Jesus' word is a creative word fulfilled *in him* and continues in the gospel in which *we ourselves* encounter Jesus and are moved to be disciples. The feasting, joy, and new strength on the holy day when Ezra read the Law are now fulfilled in a new order in which the feasting is on Jesus and the strength comes from our sharing in the same Spirit.

Luke begins his gospel by telling "Theophilus" that he wishes to write down an "orderly" and "certain" sequence of the "events that have been fulfilled" in Jesus. Jesus' words later in this gospel suggest to us that writing down the gospel on a scroll has not completed Luke's objective; the gospel is complete only in the lives of those who encounter Jesus, the gospel's fulfillment, throughout the ages. We are still in the time when the scroll has been set aside, when all eyes turn to Jesus, and there is a pregnant pause. Now we—our own lives—fill the meaning of that pregnant pause. We can do so because, like Jesus, in our baptism we also have been anointed with the Spirit.

Living the Paschal Mystery

Living the paschal mystery means that we continually look for the poor, captive, blind, and oppressed among us. We don't have to look very far! "Today this passage has been fulfilled" is now true only when we ourselves respond to those around us who need a nourishing, strengthening, joyful word. This means that God's word isn't something we only hear on Sunday, but becomes a living word in our hearts, inspiring us to be in our very selves living gospels. As we gradually grow into being anointed by the Spirit, we like Jesus are the fulfillment of the Scriptures.

Focusing the Word

Key words and phrases from the gospel: the Spirit of the Lord is upon me, fulfilled in your hearing

To the point: When Jesus quotes Isaiah, "The Spirit of the Lord is upon me," we hear a reference to his baptism and anointing; this is what "is fulfilled in your hearing." Jesus further quotes Isaiah to explain why he has been anointed: to bring "glad tidings to the poor," "liberty to captives," "sight to the blind," freedom for the oppressed. The fulfillment of the first part of the prophecy (his baptism) is a guarantee that his mission will also be fulfilled.

Connecting the Word

to the baptism of the Lord: According to Luke, at Jesus' baptism "the Holy Spirit descended upon him" and this is the prophetic anointing referred to in the passage from Isaiah.

to our baptism: Jesus' bold confidence in his identity as the anointed one invites similar boldness from us who have received the same Spirit in our baptism.

Understanding the Word

Prophecy and fulfillment: More than the other gospel writers Luke approaches his work "historically." He views the time of Jesus as the center point of history: the story of the Old Testament leads to its climax and fulfillment in Jesus and the Acts of the Apostles (also written by Luke) tells the story of the spread of the good news of Jesus. With this in mind Luke makes a distinctive use of the Old Testament.

Luke, like other early Christian writers, makes frequent references to the Old Testament. Matthew in particular made extensive use of Scripture. His references to the Old Testament were most often "proof texts"; that is, events from Jesus' life were clarified by references to the Old Testament to offer "proof" of Jesus' identity and mission. For example, Matthew explains Herod's execution of the infant boys in Bethlehem (Matt 2:18) as a fulfillment of Jeremiah 31:15. The overall effect is somewhat mechanical, a stilted alignment of biblical text and event from Jesus' life.

While Luke also does this, he does far more. On the grandest scale he sees the emergence and growth of the Church, recounted in Acts of the Apostles, as also a fulfillment of prophecy; moreover, words of Jesus in the gospel are fulfilled in Acts. But even in the gospel the whole shape of the story of Jesus, rather than specific events, fits a pattern of fulfillment; e.g., the story of Abraham and Sarah—both too old for children and Sarah barren—is reappropriated in the story of the aged and sterile Elizabeth and Zechariah. When Jesus reads from Isaiah 61:1 and 58:6 in this Sunday's gospel, it can be seen that the first line—"the Spirit of the Lord is upon me"—has been specifically fulfilled in his baptism (Isa 61:1 confirms Luke 3:21-22). But the rest of the passage from Isaiah will be fulfilled broadly in the entire ministry of Jesus. Rather than a point-for-point correspondence the entire ministry is a fulfillment of prophecy. Luke announces as much in the introduction: his gospel is "a narrative of the events that have been fulfilled among us" (1:1).

ASSEMBLY & FAITH-SHARING GROUPS

- The people who have helped me "realize the certainty of the teachings [I] have received" are . . .
- Like Jesus, the Spirit of the Lord has anointed me (at baptism). This anointing is sending me to fulfill . . .
- I am fulfilling Jesus' mission to the poor, captives, blind, and oppressed whenever I . . .

PRESIDERS

Jesus found his mission in the Scriptures. The passage that depicts my life most clearly would be . . .

DEACONS

Just as Ezra had to interpret God's Law (see first reading), so too my life and ministry are meant to be an interpretation and fulfillment of God's word. When people "read" me, the gospel they hear is . . .

HOSPITALITY MINISTERS

". . . rejoicing in the Lord must be [my] strength!" (see first reading). My hospitality is able to strengthen others for rejoicing by . . .

MUSIC MINISTERS

Just as Jesus interpreted the Scriptures for his hearers so must I through my music ministry. I find the music pulls the assembly to the gospel and to Christ when . . . I find myself pulled to the gospel and to Christ when . . .

ALTAR MINISTERS

The ministry of serving is meant to make me a servant. I see how my serving is making me more mindful of the needy because . . .

LECTORS

The people assembled before Ezra were so moved by God's Law that they "prostrated themselves" and "were weeping" (see first reading). My prayerful hearing of God's word is moving me to . . .

EUCHARISTIC MINISTERS

The words "Body/Blood of Christ" announce the Spirit's anointing upon me. My *Amen* implies that I believe this anointing to be fulfilled in my hearing.
I forget this because . . .
I see this as true when . . .

Model Penitential Rite

Presider: Just as Jesus was anointed by the Spirit in his baptism and preached an effective word fulfilled in him, so are we anointed by the Spirit in our own baptism. At the beginning of this celebration let us open ourselves to God's word and pray that it be fulfilled in each of us . . . [pause]

Lord Jesus, the Spirit of the Lord was upon you: Lord . . .

Christ Jesus, you are the fulfillment of God's word: Christ . . .

Lord Jesus, you proclaimed a year acceptable to the Lord: Lord . . .

Appreciating the Responsorial Psalm

The responsorial psalm proclaims that the word of God is perfect, trustworthy, right, and clear. The word of God refreshes the soul, rejoices the heart, and enlightens the eye. In the first reading this word is the Law read by Ezra to the assembled people who weep at its hearing. In the gospel this word from the prophet Isaiah is announced by Jesus to the synagogue gathering who "look intently at him" for its interpretation. His interpretation is a stunner: this word is his very person "fulfilled in your hearing."

Jesus' interpretation takes our understanding of the psalm to a new level. The word of God given in the Law and the prophets expresses God's will for human salvation. Jesus reveals that this will is himself, the Word-will of God in flesh and bone, bringing good news to the poor, restoring sight to the blind, and granting freedom to the oppressed. The Word which is trustworthy and clear, which rejoices the heart and enlightens the eye is the very person of Christ. Such a Word is truly salvation for the world. This is the Word about which we sing.

Model General Intercessions

Presider: In response to Jesus' proclamation of the word, let us pray for the poor, captives, and oppressed among us.

Response:

Lord, —— hear our prayer.

Cantor:

we pray to the Lord,

That all members of the Church respond generously to those who are in need . . . [pause]

That world leaders govern justly and free captives unjustly imprisoned . . . [pause]

That the poor and oppressed have what they need and are freed . . . [pause]

That each of us grow in our realization of being anointed with the Spirit to proclaim an effective word fulfilled in us . . . [pause]

Presider: O God, you desire that all people live in peace and abundance: hear these our prayers that one day we might live in the everlasting joy of eternal life. We ask this through Christ our Lord. **Amen.**

ALTERNATIVE OPENING PRAYER

Let us pray

Pause for silent prayer

Almighty Father,
the love you offer
always exceeds the furthest expression of
     our human longing,
for you are greater than the human heart.
Direct each thought, each effort of our life,
so that the limits of our faults and
     weaknesses
may not obscure the vision of your glory
or keep us from the peace you have
     promised.

We ask this through Christ our Lord.
   Amen.

FIRST READING
Neh 8:2-4a, 5-6, 8-10

Ezra the priest brought the law before the
     assembly,
   which consisted of men, women,
   and those children old enough to
        understand.
Standing at one end of the open place that
     was before the Water Gate,
   he read out of the book from daybreak
        till midday,
   in the presence of the men, the women,
   and those children old enough to
        understand;
   and all the people listened attentively to
        the book of the law.
Ezra the scribe stood on a wooden
     platform
   that had been made for the occasion.
He opened the scroll
   so that all the people might see it
   —for he was standing higher up than
        any of the people—;
   and, as he opened it, all the people rose.
Ezra blessed the LORD, the great God,
   and all the people, their hands raised
        high, answered,
   "Amen, amen!"
Then they bowed down and prostrated
     themselves before the LORD,
   their faces to the ground.
Ezra read plainly from the book of the law
     of God,
   interpreting it so that all could
        understand what was read.
Then Nehemiah, that is, His Excellency,
     and Ezra the priest-scribe
   and the Levites who were instructing
        the people
   said to all the people:
"Today is holy to the LORD your God.

Do not be sad, and do not weep"—
   for all the people were weeping as they
      heard the words of the law.
He said further: "Go, eat rich foods and
      drink sweet drinks,
   and allot portions to those who had
      nothing prepared;
   for today is holy to our LORD.
Do not be saddened this day,
   for rejoicing in the LORD must be your
      strength!"

RESPONSORIAL PSALM
Ps 19:8, 9, 10, 15

R⃥. (cf. John 6:63c) Your words, Lord, are Spirit and life.

The law of the LORD is perfect,
   refreshing the soul;
the decree of the LORD is trustworthy,
   giving wisdom to the simple.

R⃥. Your words, Lord, are Spirit and life.

The precepts of the LORD are right,
   rejoicing the heart;
the command of the LORD is clear,
   enlightening the eye.

R⃥. Your words, Lord, are Spirit and life.

The fear of the LORD is pure,
   enduring forever;
the ordinances of the LORD are true,
   all of them just.

R⃥. Your words, Lord, are Spirit and life.

Let the words of my mouth and the
      thought of my heart
   find favor before you,
O LORD, my rock and my redeemer.

R⃥. Your words, Lord, are Spirit and life.

SECOND READING
1 Cor 12:12-14, 27

Brothers and sisters:
As a body is one though it has many parts,
   and all the parts of the body, though
      many, are one body,
   so also Christ.
For in one Spirit we were all baptized into
      one body,
   whether Jews or Greeks, slaves or free
      persons,
   and we were all given to drink of one
      Spirit.
Now the body is not a single part, but
      many.
You are Christ's body, and individually
      parts of it.

About Liturgy

Eucharistic word and its fulfillment: Each Sunday during the Liturgy of the Word we hear God's word proclaimed. Would that this word so moved us that, like the people of Ezra's time, we would prostrate ourselves before the presence of God! Yet, even when our hearing the word is less enthusiastic God still fulfills it.

The Liturgy of the Word always opens onto the Liturgy of the Eucharist. There is always a pastoral danger that we focus during this part of the Mass only on receiving Communion. Important as that moment is, we cannot neglect the eucharistic prayer. In this narrative we hear the story of God's faithful deeds in bringing about our salvation. Now, with our twenty-twenty hindsight, we are hearing a narrative of salvation *already fulfilled in Christ* and in this are encouraged and strengthened to respond to the word that we have just heard. We come forward in the Communion procession, toward the altar which is a symbol of the messianic banquet, to feast and have our fill at God's table, knowing that God nourishes us to be ourselves the fulfillment of the word in our daily lives.

Coming to Communion without paying due attention to the Liturgy of the Word and the salvation narrative of the eucharistic prayer is like coming late for a banquet meal and missing all the conversation that helps bring the joy and satisfaction to the meal. This gospel challenges us to prepare well for Sunday liturgy—not just to reflect on the readings but also occasionally to read prayerfully the eucharistic prayers so that they are truly *prayers*.

About Liturgical Music

Cantor preparation: The word of God about which you sing in this responsorial psalm is fulfilled in the person of Christ. As you pray the psalm in preparation this week you might substitute the name of Christ for the words "law," "decree,""precept," etc. How does this deepen your personal relationship with Christ? How might this affect your singing of the psalm before the assembly?

Selecting seasonal service music, Pt. 2: Each liturgical season has its unique identity. Advent is directed towards the coming of Christ, both at the fullness of the messianic end-time and in the here-and-now of today. Advent, then, is a season of preparation and expectation, of hope-filled joy, of patient yet confident waiting. Christmas is the celebration of promised fulfillment, of feasting and celebrating repeatedly the birth of redemption. Lent is the season of baptismal renewal and of the prayer, fasting, and almsgiving which mark this recommitment to our Christian identity. Easter is the season of Alleluia, our octave-of-octaves-long *jubilus* in celebration of resurrection when we are forbidden to fast or even to kneel when praying. Ordinary Time is the season of prolonged fidelity, of our ongoing pilgrimage through Christian life which is sometimes quiet and unremarkable and other times turbulent and challenging.

The service music we sing during each liturgical season needs to correlate with and express the purpose and character of that season. Selecting appropriate settings takes time but it is a task necessary for full assembly participation in the formative power of the liturgical year.

✝ SPIRITUALITY

Gospel

Luke 4:21-30; L72C

Jesus began speaking in the synagogue, saying:
"Today this Scripture passage is fulfilled in your hearing."
And all spoke highly of him and were amazed at the gracious words that came from his mouth.
They also asked, "Isn't this the son of Joseph?"
He said to them, "Surely you will quote me this proverb,
'Physician, cure yourself,' and say,
'Do here in your native place the things that we heard were done in Capernaum.'"
And he said, "Amen, I say to you, no prophet is accepted in his own native place.
Indeed, I tell you, there were many widows in Israel in the days of Elijah when the sky was closed for three and a half years and a severe famine spread over the entire land.
It was to none of these that Elijah was sent, but only to a widow in Zarephath in the land of Sidon.
Again, there were many lepers in Israel during the time of Elisha the prophet; yet not one of them was cleansed, but only Naaman the Syrian."
When the people in the synagogue heard this, they were all filled with fury.
They rose up, drove him out of the town, and led him to the brow of the hill on which their town had been built, to hurl him down headlong.
But Jesus passed through the midst of them and went away.

Reflecting on the Gospel

Many of us have experienced the extreme discomfort that comes from literally standing alone on principle. Like Jesus in this Sunday's gospel, we might want to just fade away and escape. Everything about our need for community and acceptance militates against standing alone against a popular current. In this way our values are constantly being challenged; when we have support, it is reasonably easy to stay the course. When we meet opposition, at best we reevaluate our position; at worst we cave. From another perspective, if we never experience opposition we might ask ourselves if we truly stand for anything at all. The gospel challenges us to stand pat on the truth of God's word, to stake our life on it.

Early on in Jesus' public ministry he is standing alone, heads and shoulders above the crowd. The response of the crowd registers increasing resistance—from amazement (at his "gracious words") to skepticism ("Isn't this the son of Joseph?") to fury (they wanted "to hurl him down headlong" from "the brow of the hill"). It would seem that Jesus would have been much smarter to quit while he was ahead—while the crowds were amazed. But, no, he had to push on. He had to challenge the crowd because the good news is always broader than our selective preferences. Yes, salvation would be for Gentiles as well as Jews.

Jesus himself provokes a negative response when he pushes the crowd to want to destroy him by using as examples the prophets Elijah and Elisha who ministered to Gentiles. The demise of the prophets is that they forced choices; the challenge of the gospel is also that it forces choices. The good news isn't always comfortable and often takes us where we would rather not go. The comforting thing about God's word is that we have always had the reassurance that God will protect and deliver us (see first reading). The disturbing thing is that the protection and deliverance don't always come as quickly as we might like or in the way we might like.

Jeremiah ended up in a cistern and some of the prophets were killed; Jesus ended up on the cross. These hardly seem like protection and deliverance! Prophets may be rejected and destroyed, but God's word is always enduring. One symbol of this is that Jesus does escape the crowd in this gospel, demonstrating that, like God's word, the gospel will prevail.

Living the Paschal Mystery

As the crowds doubted who Jesus was because of his simple origins, so will others doubt who we are if we courageously live the gospel. Again, if we never meet doubt or opposition then we must examine how committed to the gospel we are. Most of us aren't called to "professionally" preach the good news. All of us, because of our baptism, are committed to living it. No matter what simple origins we might have, our living the gospel is what must shape our everyday choices. This means, for example, that if the chatter around the coffee machine at work grows uncharitable or coarse, we have the courage to walk away. Another example: if prejudice exists among our friends and acquaintances, we have the courage to extol the dignity of the minority. Dying to oneself means that we place gospel values before any others and are willing to put our lives on the line for them. We might not always concretely experience God's protection and deliverance in the given moment; but we know from Jesus' life that it is there when it really counts—leading us to life everlasting.

Focusing the Word

Key words and phrases from the gospel: amazed at the gracious words, to none of these, filled with fury

To the point: As long as Jesus announces glad tidings, the crowd responds positively. But when Jesus challenges their narrowness with the examples of Elijah's and Elisha's outreach to Gentiles (Sidon and Syria), they grow furious. While the gospel is always good news, it is not always comfortable.

Connecting the Word

to the first reading: There are at least two points of contact between the first reading and the gospel. The first is the presentation of Jeremiah and Jesus as prophets who are rejected. The second is God's promise of protection and deliverance.

to culture: So much of our contemporary culture is based on what is popular, for example, Nielson ratings, political polls, marketing samples, etc. Jesus based his message not on popular reaction but on the truth of God's word.

Understanding the Word

Good news for Gentiles: This Sunday's gospel repeats the last verse of last Sunday's gospel and then continues the episode. It is important to remember that in Luke's gospel we are still reading about the first public preaching of Jesus. He began with a quote from Isaiah which summarizes his entire ministry. After an initial response of enthusiasm the people quickly move to hostile rejection. This episode is reported by Mark and Matthew only much later in the gospel and provides a context for such hostility. But in Luke this is his first public appearance. By Luke including it in the very first episode of Jesus' public ministry he is clearly indicating both the fickleness of the crowd that will dog Jesus' ministry and the rejection that will culminate in his death. Jesus' prophetic words, "no prophet is accepted in his own native place" (4:24) are tragically fulfilled by the end of this passage when his townsfolk "drove him out of the town." (Note, too, how this episode fulfills the prophecy of Simeon in 2:34—"this child is destined for the fall and rise of many in Israel, and to be a sign that will be contradicted.")

Why the hostility? The crowd was enthusiastic enough when Jesus announced the "gracious words" of liberty, recovery, freedom, and a year of favor; they thought these blessings would be theirs, just as this prophet was apparently one of their own. But Jesus, in claiming to be a prophet, refers to two episodes in which Elijah and Elisha performed powerful deeds for the benefit of Gentiles. Readers of the gospel have been told of Jesus' mission of universal salvation: Simeon prophesied that Jesus would be "a light for revelation to the Gentiles" (2:32) and Luke had quoted Isaiah 3:6 to describe John's ministry: "all flesh shall see the salvation of God" (Luke 3:6). But this is the first time anyone in Jesus' audience hears this word. The hometown crowd is angered to hear that Jesus will share their blessings with Gentiles. Apparently, they took this "good news" for others as bad news for themselves.

ASSEMBLY & FAITH-SHARING GROUPS

- Words of Jesus that are amazing and "gracious" to me are . . .
- Words of Jesus that I would rather not hear are . . .
- Words of Jesus that I have staked my life on are . . .

PRESIDERS

It is said, "The gospel comforts the disturbed and disturbs the comfortable." Of these two, I prefer . . . because . . .

DEACONS

Jesus challenged those around him about their narrow view of God and salvation. The views of God and salvation that have been stretched in me because of my experiences in ministry are . . .

HOSPITALITY MINISTERS

Jesus offers Elijah and Elisha as examples that the prophetic outreach extends to *outsiders,* too. My ministry challenges me beyond the familiar to . . .

MUSIC MINISTERS

The music we sing challenges me/the assembly to live the gospel more radically when . . .

ALTAR MINISTERS

Jesus stands faithful to God's word even when the people attempted "to hurl him down headlong."
I give up on self-emptying service when . . .
What encourages my fidelity to God's word is . . .

LECTORS

I heed or dismiss a passage from Scripture based on . . .

EUCHARISTIC MINISTERS

Eucharist is the Food that sustains me during conflicts and assures me, "I am with you to deliver you" (first reading).
I can recall the Eucharist sustaining me in difficult times . . .
I also remember when I was eucharist for another, sustaining them during trials . . .

Model Penitential Rite

Presider: Jesus was sent to announce the good news of salvation to Jews and Gentiles alike. Sometimes this raised amazement in people at his gracious words, sometimes fury because people didn't like what they were hearing. As we prepare to celebrate this liturgy, when has God's word amazed us? When has it angered us? . . . [pause]

Lord Jesus, you spoke gracious words that amazed the crowds: Lord . . .

Christ Jesus, you spoke prophetic words that angered the crowds: Christ . . .

Lord Jesus, you are the Word that endures forever: Lord . . .

Appreciating the Responsorial Psalm

Psalm 71 from which the verses of the responsorial psalm are taken is a lament prayed by a righteous person undergoing persecution. Out of a confidence instilled at birth the psalmist cries for help and sings of hope in God, the "rock of refuge" who will act to rescue. This is the confidence which enables both Jeremiah and Jesus to remain faithful to their identity and mission. Jeremiah faces crushing opposition for speaking God's message to the people (first reading). God responds with full knowledge of the terrible price Jeremiah pays and with promise of deliverance. Jesus delivers words of divine judgment and incurs the wrath of his hearers (gospel). This time he slips away unhurt, but it will not always be so.

Remaining faithful to the mission appointed by God means facing persecution and death. What gives us courage to do so is the sure knowledge that we are known and loved by God who will remain with us and will ultimately deliver us. Such is the knowledge expressed in this psalm. Such was Jesus' knowledge. Such is ours as we sing.

Model General Intercessions

Presider: God promises protection and deliverance to those who call out in need. And so we pray.

Response:

Lord, hear our prayer.

Cantor:

we pray to the Lord,

That all members of the Church have the courage to speak only the truth of God's word . . . [pause]

That leaders of nations speak just, encouraging, peaceful words . . . [pause]

That those who speak harsh and uncharitable words truly hear God's word gently inviting them to change . . . [pause]

That each of us risk being prophets in our own native places . . . [pause]

Presider: Saving God, you are with us through all trials and challenges: hear these our prayers that we might always speak only the truth of your word and live it faithfully so that one day we might enjoy everlasting life with you. We ask this through Christ our Lord. **Amen.**

ALTERNATIVE OPENING PRAYER

Let us pray

Pause for silent prayer

Father in heaven,
from the days of Abraham and Moses
until this gathering of your Church in
    prayer,
you have formed a people in the image of
    your Son.
Bless this people with the gift of your
    kingdom.
May we serve you with our every desire
and show love for one another
even as you have loved us.

Grant this through Christ our Lord.
    Amen.

FIRST READING
Jer 1:4-5, 17-19

The word of the LORD came to me, saying:
    Before I formed you in the womb I knew
        you,
    before you were born I dedicated you,
    a prophet to the nations I appointed
        you.

    But do you gird your loins;
    stand up and tell them
    all that I command you.
    Be not crushed on their account,
    as though I would leave you crushed
        before them;
    for it is I this day
    who have made you a fortified city,
    a pillar of iron, a wall of brass,
    against the whole land:
    against Judah's kings and princes,
    against its priests and people.
    They will fight against you but not
        prevail over you,
    for I am with you to deliver you, says
        the LORD.

RESPONSORIAL PSALM
Ps 71:1-2, 3-4, 5-6, 15, 17

R̸. (cf. 15ab) I will sing of your salvation.

In you, O LORD, I take refuge;
    let me never be put to shame.
In your justice rescue me, and deliver me;
    incline your ear to me, and save me.

R̸. I will sing of your salvation.

Be my rock of refuge,
    a stronghold to give me safety,
    for you are my rock and my fortress.
O my God, rescue me from the hand of the
    wicked.

R̸. I will sing of your salvation.

For you are my hope, O LORD;
  my trust, O God, from my youth.
On you I depend from birth;
  from my mother's womb you are my
    strength.

R℣. I will sing of your salvation.

My mouth shall declare your justice,
  day by day your salvation.
O God, you have taught me from my
    youth,
  and till the present I proclaim your
    wondrous deeds.

R℣. I will sing of your salvation.

SECOND READING
1 Cor 13:4-13

Brothers and sisters:
Love is patient, love is kind.
It is not jealous, it is not pompous,
  it is not inflated, it is not rude,
  it does not seek its own interests,
  it is not quick-tempered, it does not
    brood over injury,
  it does not rejoice over wrongdoing but
    rejoices with the truth.
It bears all things, believes all things,
  hopes all things, endures all things.

Love never fails.
If there are prophecies, they will be
    brought to nothing;
  if tongues, they will cease;
  if knowledge, it will be brought to
    nothing.
For we know partially and we prophesy
    partially,
  but when the perfect comes, the partial
    will pass away.
When I was a child, I used to talk as a
    child,
  think as a child, reason as a child;
  when I became a man, I put aside
    childish things.
At present we see indistinctly, as in a
    mirror,
  but then face to face.
At present I know partially;
  then I shall know fully, as I am fully
    known.
So faith, hope, love remain, these three;
  but the greatest of these is love.

CATECHESIS

About Liturgy

Liturgy of the Word: When we claim that God's word is enduring, we are saying more than the fact that it is proclaimed throughout the world every Saturday evening and Sunday (and weekdays, too!). The mere *saying* or *proclaiming* God's word isn't what makes it enduring; it is *receiving, internalizing,* and *living* God's word that makes it enduring. God's word endures as each of us is transformed, realizing ever more perfectly the spread of God's reign. God's word endures *in us*.

Almost always on Sundays the Lectionary selections include both a prophetic word and a comforting word. First challenge: we must truly hear God's word and not let it simply go over our heads. The best way to *hear* (receive) God's word is not to come to liturgy cold; if this is our first hearing, we probably won't get much out of the Liturgy of the Word. A good spiritual practice for all of us is to read the Scriptures well in advance of Sunday so that we can be thinking about them as we go through our normal everyday routines.

Second challenge: we must hear God's word in terms of how it challenges each of us *personally*. This means that almost every Sunday we will hear something in the word that calls us to change (internalize the word) some behavior or attitude. We must help ourselves get into the habit of truly *listening* for that personal word to us. Let our prayer during the rest of the Mass then be one in which we beg God's help to live this word.

Third challenge: we must let that internalized word help us see what in our personal lives and the world in which we live needs to be addressed (living the word). Sometimes our world is so complex that we don't even recognize the hurts and injustices around us. God's enduring word within us helps us see our world with new eyes—God's eyes. We will no longer be able to take things for granted; we will begin to understand that hearing God's word each Sunday makes demands on us.

About Liturgical Music

Cantor preparation: The confidence of this psalm is perfect counterbalance to the reality of persecution about which the first reading and the gospel speak. If you choose to be faithful to the mission you share with Christ, you will know rejection. But you will also know in an ever-deepening way the intimate presence of the God who guides and protects you. Are you willing to take the risk?

Selecting seasonal service music, Pt. 3: In addition to correlating with the specific character of each liturgical season, the service music should also accord with the principle of progressive solemnity (see the General Instruction of the Liturgy of the Hours no. 273).

The principle of progressive solemnity reminds us that not all liturgical celebrations are equal in importance nor are all the elements of a given celebration of equal priority. Thus, the festal seasons (Advent-Christmas and Lent-Easter) are more important than Ordinary Time. Solemnities such as Christ the King and the Assumption are more important than Ordinary Time Sundays. The eucharistic acclamations are more important musical elements than the Glory to God or the Lamb of God. Applying this principle to the selection of liturgical music means that more festive musical settings will be reserved for the festal seasons and the solemnities.

SPIRITUALITY

Gospel

Luke 5:1-11; L75C

While the crowd was pressing in on Jesus
and listening to the word of God,
he was standing by the Lake of
Gennesaret.
He saw two boats there alongside the
lake;
the fishermen had disembarked and
were washing their nets.
Getting into one of the boats, the
one belonging to Simon,
he asked him to put out a short
distance from the shore.
Then he sat down and taught the
crowds from the boat.
After he had finished speaking, he
said to Simon,
"Put out into deep water and lower
your nets for a catch."
Simon said in reply,
"Master, we have worked hard all
night and have caught nothing,
but at your command I will lower the
nets."
When they had done this, they caught a
great number of fish
and their nets were tearing.
They signaled to their partners in the
other boat
to come to help them.
They came and filled both boats
so that the boats were in danger of
sinking.
When Simon Peter saw this, he fell at
the knees of Jesus and said,
"Depart from me, Lord, for I am a
sinful man."
For astonishment at the catch of fish
they had made seized him
and all those with him,
and likewise James and John, the sons
of Zebedee,
who were partners of Simon.
Jesus said to Simon, "Do not be afraid;
from now on you will be catching men."
When they brought their boats to the
shore,
they left everything and followed him.

Reflecting on the Gospel

The life-affecting and powerful circumstances of God's presence recorded in both the first reading and gospel for this Sunday are, perhaps, not so unusual as we might think. Theophanies (God's self-revelation) don't always mean that door-frames shake, smoke billows, angels fly around, or crowds press in with eagerness at effective preaching. Setting aside these unusual circumstances, this gospel can teach us much about divine presence, God's call, and our response. Isaiah sees God, confesses his sinfulness, is cleansed, and from this can eagerly respond, "Here I am . . . send me!" The gospel unravels a similar call narrative. Simon Peter's addressing Jesus as "Master" indicates that Peter has already had a kind of theophany—possibly just the thrill of this crowd-pleasing rabbi asking to use his boat, possibly Peter had heard Jesus' powerful words before (much has already happened in Luke's gospel before we get to this first call narrative). One more theophany—Jesus' power manifested in the great catch of fish—brings Peter, like Isaiah, to confess his sinfulness. One (and probably a first) response to displays of divine holiness and presence is a sense of sinfulness and unworthiness. But neither story stops with the confession of sinfulness; both stories continue with Isaiah's and Peter's yes responses to God's call.

Theophany or the appearance of God always reveals our own sinfulness, but God's focus is elsewhere—on call and mission. God sees humanity that is created good, persons who can choose to respond to God's call and fulfill the mission God gives. Once cleansed, Isaiah responds eagerly. Once Peter overcomes his fear, he and the others with him "left everything and followed him." God's call and our response transforms us from people overcome with sinfulness to disciples taking up the mission.

One implication of these Scripture passages is that theophany transforms us from sinners to copartners in God's work of salvation. Another is that the focus of our lives changes—in the case of Peter and his companions, from fishermen to "catching men." Yet another implication is that we cannot let our sinfulness paralyze us and keep us from responding to God's call and doing God's work. Finally, God's call isn't only to be prophet or apostle; some, surely, are called to fill these roles. We must not forget that through our baptism each of us is called to be a disciple.

Living the Paschal Mystery

The dynamic of the first reading and gospel is theophany—call. This suggests that in our own lives we must be tuned into God's theophanies for each time God makes divine presence known there is a call to follow.

If we look for shaking door frames, billowing smoke, and large catches of fish we will miss God's theophanies! The gospel invites us to look to the simple manifestations of holiness that indicate the presence of God, for example, in the generosity of so many volunteers, in the faithfulness of husbands and wives, in the unselfishness of pastoral workers, in the uncomplaining suffering of the sick, in the gracious wisdom of the elderly. Our yes response to the call within these theophanies is to imitate these good behaviors and by doing so we extend God's reign. Living the paschal mystery means we respond to God's call—fulfill our baptismal commitment—in these little, everyday things. The astonishing thing about this good news is that we are all made worthy simply because God calls.

Focusing the Word

Key words and phrases from the gospel: I am a sinful man, Do not be afraid, they left everything and followed him

To the point: In responding to God's call personal worthiness is not the issue, for all humanity is sinful. All that matters is the call of God, the mission God gives, and our fidelity to it.

Connecting the Word

to the first reading: In the selection of Isaiah, though the holiness of God overwhelms Isaiah, the nature of God's call always remains as an invitation: "Whom shall I send?"

to culture: Contemporary culture sets up standards of acceptability: body shape, fashions, job performance, etc. The good news is that God calls us precisely as we are and works through our humanity.

Understanding the Word

The call of Simon Peter: In his introduction Luke had promised "to write . . . down in an orderly sequence" (1:3) "a narrative of the events that have been fulfilled among us" (1:1). This Sunday's episode—the call of the first disciples—is a good example of Luke's "orderly sequence." Mark's gospel begins with a telescoped account of John the Baptist's ministry, a very brief report of Jesus' baptism and temptations in the wilderness, and a two verse summary of Jesus' initial preaching. Then, out of the blue, Jesus meets and calls his first disciples in the sixteenth verse of the first chapter! Apart from Jesus' announcement that the Kingdom of God is at hand, he has done no preaching, performed no miracles, expelled no demons; yet when he calls Peter and Andrew, James and John, they drop everything and follow him.

By contrast, Luke carefully prepares the ground for this dramatic call. After an elaborate infancy narrative that explicitly lays out the identity of Jesus, Luke begins with an extended presentation of John's ministry, a more detailed narration of the baptism, a dramatic account of the three temptations in the wilderness, and Jesus' inaugural sermon in the synagogue in Nazareth; then (omitted from the Lectionary) Luke gives us more of Jesus' teaching in Capernaum and several healings (a possessed man, Simon's mother-in-law, and the sick villagers). Only now does Jesus call Simon Peter. By this time the credentials of Jesus have been clearly established and Simon has personally witnessed the healing of his mother-in-law. Further, in Luke's account, there is a miraculous catch of fish—not reported in the other three versions of the call of Simon. Luke provides a record of accomplishment and a factual basis on which Simon and the others can make their response. Luke makes both Jesus' authority and Peter's response something readers can relate to.

The presence of Jesus brings about great transformations: empty nets become overflowing and a man who protested to Jesus, "depart from me!" ends up following him. In this last transformation Jesus' power turns a sinner into a disciple.

ASSEMBLY & FAITH-SHARING GROUPS

• I have encountered the divine Presence in places like . . . and in times of . . .
• When encountering God, like Peter, there were things I realized about myself, like . . ., and there were things asked of me, like . . .

PRESIDERS

C. S. Lewis said the real labor for the Christian is to stay awake. My ministry inspires others to remain awake and witness the divine call by . . .

DEACONS

Peter's call occurred while doing what fishermen do; he sensed mystery in the midst of the ordinary. I invite others to notice mystery in their lives by . . .

HOSPITALITY MINISTERS

One of the roles hospitality plays at liturgy is to embody Jesus' words, "Do not be afraid." I embody this for others by . . .

MUSIC MINISTERS

I experience music-making as an encounter with the Holy whenever . . .
Music-making has called me to conversion when . . .
I experience music-making as a participation in the mission of Christ whenever . . .

ALTAR MINISTERS

Peter became a "catcher of men" because of what is told in the gospel. I became a servant minister because . . .

LECTORS

The disciples didn't just follow Jesus; they "left everything." What I have to leave behind in order to follow him is . . .

EUCHARISTIC MINISTERS

I understand Isaiah's and Peter's confessions; nevertheless, God has used me, too, for the benefit of others by . . .

55

Model Penitential Rite

Presider: Each time God reveals divine holiness to us there is a call to take up the mission of spreading the good news. As we begin this liturgy let us take some time to become aware of how God has been present to us this week and how we have responded to that presence . . . [pause]

Lord Jesus, you preached effectively the word of God: Lord . . .

Christ Jesus, you showed forth your great power: Christ . . .

Lord Jesus, you call followers to preach your gospel: Lord . . .

Appreciating the Responsorial Psalm

Confronted with the Holy both Isaiah (first reading) and Peter (gospel) immediately acknowledge their sinfulness. Their encounter with the holy and their subsequent conversion are not entirely private nor personal events. Rather the experience thrusts them into public mission. Isaiah instantly asks to be sent as prophet; Peter leaves everything to become a "catch[er] of men." A similar narrative unfolds in the verses of Psalm 138 used for the responsorial psalm. The psalmist has cried to God for help and has been rescued. She or he now shouts the story before heaven and earth and "all the kings of the earth" come to glorify God.

Every time we gather for liturgical celebration we, too, encounter the Holy in the person of Christ. We, too, discover our need for conversion and find forgiveness. And we, too, are called to tell the story. May we do so not only in the singing of this psalm but the living of our lives.

Model General Intercessions

Presider: The same power that Jesus manifested in the great catch of fish God will manifest in answering our prayers. So we are encouraged to place our needs before such a generous God.

Response:

Lord,⎯ hear our prayer.

Cantor:

we pray to the Lord,

That the Church may always show forth God's holiness and goodness . . . [pause]

That peoples of the world become holy as the God they worship is holy . . . [pause]

That sinners repent and embrace the presence and holiness of God . . . [pause]

That each of us leave whatever we must to be faithful followers of Jesus . . . [pause]

Presider: God of holiness: you come in many different ways, calling us to be disciples. Hear these our prayers that we might one day share everlasting life with you. We ask this through Christ our Lord. **Amen.**

ALTERNATIVE OPENING PRAYER

Let us pray
[with reverence in the presence of the living God]

Pause for silent prayer

In faith and love we ask you, Father,
to watch over your family gathered here.
In your mercy and loving kindness
no thought of ours is left unguarded,
no tear unheeded, no joy unnoticed.
Through the prayer of Jesus
may the blessings promised to the poor in spirit
lead us to the treasures of your heavenly kingdom.

We ask this in the name of Jesus the Lord.
Amen.

FIRST READING
Isa 6:1-2a, 3-8

In the year King Uzziah died,
I saw the Lord seated on a high and lofty throne,
with the train of his garment filling the temple.
Seraphim were stationed above.

They cried one to the other,
"Holy, holy, holy is the LORD of hosts!
All the earth is filled with his glory!"
At the sound of that cry, the frame of the door shook
and the house was filled with smoke.

Then I said, "Woe is me, I am doomed!
For I am a man of unclean lips,
living among a people of unclean lips;
yet my eyes have seen the King,
the LORD of hosts!"
Then one of the seraphim flew to me,
holding an ember that he had taken
with tongs from the altar.

He touched my mouth with it, and said,
"See, now that this has touched your lips,
your wickedness is removed, your sin purged."

Then I heard the voice of the Lord saying,
"Whom shall I send? Who will go for us?"
"Here I am," I said; "send me!"

RESPONSORIAL PSALM
Ps 138:1-2, 2-3, 4-5, 7-8

R̸. (1c) In the sight of the angels I will sing your praises, Lord.

I will give thanks to you, O LORD, with all my heart,
    for you have heard the words of my mouth;
    in the presence of the angels I will sing your praise;
I will worship at your holy temple
    and give thanks to your name.

R̸. In the sight of the angels I will sing your praises, Lord.

Because of your kindness and your truth;
    for you have made great above all things
    your name and your promise.
When I called, you answered me;
    you built up strength within me.

R̸. In the sight of the angels I will sing your praises, Lord.

All the kings of the earth shall give
    thanks to you, O LORD,
    when they hear the words of your mouth;
and they shall sing of the ways of the LORD:
    "Great is the glory of the LORD."

R̸. In the sight of the angels I will sing your praises, Lord.

Your right hand saves me.
    The LORD will complete what he has done for me;
your kindness, O LORD, endures forever;
    forsake not the work of your hands.

R̸. In the sight of the angels I will sing your praises, Lord.

SECOND READING
1 Cor 15:3-8, 11

Brothers and sisters,
    I handed on to you as of first
        importance what I also received:
    that Christ died for our sins
    in accordance with the Scriptures;
    that he was buried;
    that he was raised on the third day
    in accordance with the Scriptures;
    that he appeared to Cephas, then to the Twelve.
After that, he appeared to more
    than five hundred brothers at once,
    most of whom are still living,
    though some have fallen asleep.
After that he appeared to James,
    then to all the apostles.
Last of all, as to one abnormally born,
    he appeared to me.
Therefore, whether it be I or they,
    so we preach and so you believed.

About Liturgy
"Lord, I am not worthy . . ." At Mass our response to the invitation to Holy Communion includes the words, "Lord, I am not worthy." This Sunday's gospel challenges us to utter these words not simply as a confession of sinfulness or a way to debase our own dignity as daughters and sons of God, but as a simple statement of recognizing our own status as creatures before God's all-powerful and divine holiness. The amazing generosity of Jesus' self-offering of his body and blood for our nourishment and drink is that God doesn't focus on our unworthiness but raises us up to share in divinity. Communion should always be a kind of wake-up call in which we praise and thank God for the call to holiness and also resolve to be faithful to God's mission. Sharing in God's holiness is also sharing in God's mission.

About Liturgical Music
Cantor preparation: In this psalm you tell the whole story of salvation: the cry for help, God's saving response, the proclamation of what God has done. Telling the story is one thing, however, living it another. In what way this week might you call for God's help? In what way might you experience God's response? In what way might you tell others?

Selecting seasonal service music, Pt. 4: Part of implementing the principle of progressive solemnity means making decisions about optional elements and the music that accompanies them. When, for example, will you choose the sprinkling rite? Certainly during the Easter season, but also perhaps during Christmastide. Using the sprinkling rite during both of these festal seasons would highlight their relationship to one another and the music chosen can further highlight the connection of these festal seasons.

When will you sing the penitential rite? The most obvious time is during the season of Lent. Since the most appropriate form of the penitential rite for Lent is the *Confiteor,* you could follow the *Confiteor* with a simple chanted *Kyrie.* During Advent, because of its character as an eschatological season, one might also sing the penitential rite using Form C.

When might you do a prolonged gospel procession? All of the Sundays of the Easter season would be appropriate, as would the Sundays and solemnities of the Christmas season. On Easter and Pentecost you can combine the sequence with the gospel acclamation (originally, sequences were extensions of the Alleluia verse) and extend the procession throughout the body of the church. Music publishers have begun providing such settings for the sequence (for example, WLP's "Let Christians All Their Voices Raise" set to O FILII ET FILIAE).

When might you sing the general intercessions? It is always appropriate to do so as they are a litany, but you may not have the musical or cantorial resources to do so every Sunday. Sing them, then, on the most important days or seasons (e.g., Easter, Christmas, Christ the King, all the Sundays of Eastertime).

✚ SPIRITUALITY

Gospel

Luke 6:17, 20-26; L78C

Jesus came down with the Twelve
and stood on a stretch of level
ground
with a great crowd of his
disciples
and a large number of the
people
from all Judea and Jerusalem
and the coastal region of Tyre
and Sidon.
And raising his eyes toward his
disciples he said:
"Blessed are you who are poor,
for the kingdom of God is yours.
Blessed are you who are now hungry,
for you will be satisfied.
Blessed are you who are now
weeping,
for you will laugh.
Blessed are you when people hate you,
and when they exclude and insult
you,
and denounce your name as evil
on account of the Son of Man.
Rejoice and leap for joy on that day!
Behold, your reward will be great in
heaven.
For their ancestors treated the
prophets in the same way.
But woe to you who are rich,
for you have received your
consolation.
Woe to you who are filled now,
for you will be hungry.
Woe to you who laugh now,
for you will grieve and weep.
Woe to you when all speak well of
you,
for their ancestors treated the false
prophets in this way."

Reflecting on the Gospel

High-ranking government officials, popular movie stars, great sports figures, heros all attract large crowds of people when they are out in public. But often, if we observe closely, their smiles and handshakes and barely uttered words are quite impersonal and rarely make contact with specific individuals. We might notice that the sought-after one is shaking hands with one person but looking at someone else. Even this little bit of contact—impersonal though it often is—satisfies us, tends to make us grow in stature even if only in our eyes. It is a thrill for most of us to have even minimal contact with these people we consider well beyond our simple lifestyle and humble selves. Some interesting details about this Sunday's gospel reveal Jesus to be a very different kind of celebrity.

The opening line of the gospel selection is that "Jesus came down." The implication is that Jesus was up, on a hill or mountain. These are the places for theophanies. Probably Jesus was praying with "the Twelve." Then he came down to "a stretch of level ground" to mingle with the common folk (the missing two verses of this gospel selection say the crowd came to hear him and be healed). He even does the unthinkable for a rabbi of his time; he not only speaks to the Jews, but welcomes the Gentiles (people from "Tyre and Sidon") into his midst as well. Then he raises "his eyes toward his disciples"—no passing glance here. Jesus has eye contact. He is *meeting, encountering* those to whom he speaks. The blessing *is Jesus* who stands on level ground with the poor, hungry, weeping, outcasts. Jesus' presence precipitates change; it's not that the people have to change in order for Jesus to come.

Jesus is an epiphany of God's presence among all those who had been excluded. He aligns himself in such a way with the people that the normal social status is broken—all are on "level ground." In this way Jesus is *living* the kingdom or reign of God which has clearly already begun. Moral right or wrong and choices aren't the only focus of Luke's Beatitudes. Luke also highlights God's prior generosity which inspires presence. The gospel does indicate, however, the decisiveness of choice: blessing or woe (the same choice is given in the first reading from Jeremiah: curse or blessing). There are two paths in life one can follow, and either one is with Jesus or against him. The lure is to be consoled *now,* have our fill *now,* laugh *now,* be respected *now.* Jesus is showing another way: our condition now doesn't matter so long as we trust and hope in the Lord *now* (see first reading). When we choose God, our reward may be deferred, but it is sure: it "will be great in heaven." Blessedness isn't a matter of social status, satisfaction, possessions, respect, etc; it is a matter of keeping our own eyes glued on Jesus.

Living the Paschal Mystery

Most of us live just barely getting by—we never have enough time, enough money, enough energy. We tend to keep our focus on *now* and, to a large extent, this is necessary. The Beatitudes, however, invite another stance. Even in being caught up in the cares of everyday living, we can still keep our eyes on Jesus Christ and what we are really seeking—everlasting glory with him in the time to come. We Christians are not so much *now* people as *future* people. This is why social status, what people think of us, or possessions lead to woes—they turn our eyes from the future glory that awaits us when we keep our eyes on Christ.

Focusing the Word

Key words and phrases from the gospel: level ground, blessed, kingdom of God

To the point: With Jesus those who were social outcasts find a place in the kingdom of God. The good news is that the poor, hungry, weeping, and excluded are "blessed" because Jesus' very presence and ministry among them gathers them into the kingdom of God. The source of blessedness is not social condition but Jesus himself.

Connecting the Word

to last Sunday: Last Sunday both Isaiah and Peter thought that their sinfulness made them unworthy of divine presence. In this gospel those who thought they were beyond blessing discover that Jesus comes to them.

to culture: In every society there are attitudes, language, and behaviors that stigmatize those considered "unworthy." This fact is already a judgment that the kingdom of God has not yet fully taken hold.

Understanding the Word

The Beatitudes in Luke: Luke's "Beatitudes" are part of a longer instruction (6:17-49) sometimes called "The Sermon on the Plain" (as opposed to Matthew's more famous "Sermon on the Mount"). The major theme of this sermon is discipleship: notice that Luke has Jesus addressing "his disciples."

As an instruction on discipleship it is noteworthy that Luke begins with words of blessing rather than a call to action. In Jesus' first sermon (OT 3) he had declared that he has come to "bring good news [NAB = "glad tidings"] to the poor" (4:18). In the Beatitudes Jesus announces the good news that the poor, the hungry, the sorrowful, and the hated are blessed by God. Blessing precedes the demands of discipleship. Earlier both Mary and Zechariah were richly blessed and they raised their voices in praise (1:46-55, 68-79).

When compared to Matthew's version of the Beatitudes certain of Luke's favorite themes become evident. Unlike Matthew who spiritualizes ("the poor in spirit . . . those who hunger and thirst for righteousness"; Matt 5:3, 6), Luke addresses the materially poor. He further emphasizes the material aspect of poverty by adding four "woes" (not found in Matthew's Beatitudes) which announce judgment on the wealthy. But why does God so favor the poor? Because this is how God always acts: "The hungry he has filled with good things; the rich he has sent away empty" (1:53). And so those who have nothing now will inherit the Kingdom. This is unmerited blessing, an offer of mercy, the gift of salvation.

In the second and third Beatitudes Luke's theme of reversal is evident: the hungry will be satisfied, the weeping will laugh. In a sense, these two Beatitudes heighten the scandal of the first, for the condition of the poor will not be reversed: they will not become materially wealthy. On the one hand, this again emphasizes the material aspect of poverty. But more shockingly, it shows the superabundance of God's gift: from poverty to the Kingdom! Jesus will later dramatize this teaching in his famous parable of Lazarus and the Rich Man (Luke 16:19-31). The poor are blessed indeed!

ASSEMBLY & FAITH-SHARING GROUPS

- Jesus' teaching on "level ground" is part of Luke's message. What it signifies to me is . . .
- Jesus' Beatitudes describe a divine reversal. To share in Christ's promise of blessedness I need to reverse in my life . . .
- I have learned that the anguish or misery from riches, consolation, fullness, etc., is . . .

PRESIDERS

What keeps me on "level ground" with those for whom I minister is . . .

DEACONS

It is Jesus' presence to those who are poor, hungry, weeping, insulted, etc., which makes them blessed. As Jesus' minister I am to be a living blessing to others. I need to reach out and be a blessing to . . .

HOSPITALITY MINISTERS

Jesus' Beatitudes describe a divine reversal. My hospitality can effect this reversal when I . . .

MUSIC MINISTERS

I experience Jesus coming to us in blessing in my music-making when . . .
I lead the assembly to blessedness in their music-making when . . .

ALTAR MINISTERS

Self-emptying service is like a Beatitude: it seems lowly and demeaning while it is announced as blessed because Jesus' presence is found in the self-emptying. I experience this as true when . . .

LECTORS

I can proclaim these readings because I know the difference between the two paths depicted in Jeremiah, the psalm, and the Beatitudes. The way I would describe this is . . .

EUCHARISTIC MINISTERS

Even when life is like a "year of drought" (first reading), Jesus' presence—at Eucharist and in others—is blessing to me because . . .

✠ CELEBRATION

Model Penitential Rite

Presider: Jesus came down on level ground to mingle with the crowds, the common people. It is sheer gift that Jesus would come among them. At the beginning of this celebration let us become aware of the gift of Jesus' presence and open ourselves to hear his word and feast at his table . . . [pause]

Lord Jesus, you came down on level ground to be present to the crowd: Lord . . .

Christ Jesus, you promise the kingdom of God to those who follow you: Christ . . .

Lord Jesus, you bring blessing and salvation to all: Lord . . .

Appreciating the Responsorial Psalm

Jewish Wisdom literature portrays two ways of living: as faithful to the Law of God or as unfaithful. The first way brings blessings and fruitfulness, the second waste and destruction. Psalm 1 introduces the entire collection of psalms by deliberately reminding the Israelites of the call to be faithful to the way of God in the midst of all the ups and downs, the losses and deliverances, the laments and thanksgivings which characterize human history (as the ensuing psalms reveal).

In the first reading Jeremiah uses the same imagery as Psalm 1 to make the same point. Those who turn from God will be dry and barren; those who trust in God will be deep-rooted and green. In the gospel Jesus specifies this blessedness and cursedness in concrete but surprising ways. The psalm refrain helps us get to the core: blessed are those who hope in, trust, keep their focus on God. Regardless of appearances these are the ones prospering. In singing this psalm we express our choice to prosper and we celebrate our blessedness.

Model General Intercessions

Presider: We pray now that God might continue to bless us with divine presence and all we need to live in God's reign.

Response:

Lord,—— hear our prayer.

Cantor:

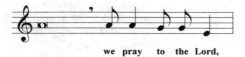

we pray to the Lord,

That the Church may always be the continued blessing of Christ's presence in the world . . . [pause]

That the peoples of the world may all share equally in the abundance with which God has blessed creation . . . [pause]

That the poor, hungry, weeping, and excluded may be the blessed children of God inheriting the fullness of God's kingdom . . . [pause]

That all of us gathered here may always welcome the gift of Christ's presence in the many ways it comes into our lives . . . [pause]

Presider: Gracious God, you bless all who come to you: hear these our prayers that one day we might enjoy the fullness of life with you in heaven. We ask this through Christ our Lord. **Amen.**

OPENING PRAYER

Let us pray

Pause for silent prayer

God our Father,
you have promised to remain for ever
with those who do what is just and right.
Help us to live in your presence.

We ask this through our Lord Jesus Christ,
    your Son,
who lives and reigns with you and the
    Holy Spirit,
one God, for ever and ever. **Amen.**

FIRST READING

Jer 17:5-8

Thus says the LORD:
    Cursed is the one who trusts in human
        beings,
        who seeks his strength in flesh,
        whose heart turns away from the
            LORD.
    He is like a barren bush in the desert
        that enjoys no change of season,
        but stands in a lava waste, a salt and
            empty earth.
    Blessed is the one who trusts in the
        LORD,
        whose hope is the LORD.
    He is like a tree planted beside the
        waters
        that stretches out its roots to the
            stream:
    it fears not the heat when it comes;
        its leaves stay green;
    in the year of drought it shows no
        distress,
        but still bears fruit.

CATECHESIS

RESPONSORIAL PSALM
Ps 1:1-2, 3, 4, 6

R̊. (40:5a) Blessed are they who hope in the Lord.

Blessed the man who follows not
   the counsel of the wicked,
nor walks in the way of sinners,
   nor sits in the company of the insolent,
but delights in the law of the LORD
   and meditates on his law day and night.

R̊. Blessed are they who hope in the Lord.

He is like a tree
   planted near running water,
that yields its fruit in due season,
   and whose leaves never fade.
   Whatever he does, prospers.

R̊. Blessed are they who hope in the Lord.

Not so the wicked, not so;
   they are like chaff which the wind
      drives away.
For the LORD watches over the way of the
   just,
   but the way of the wicked vanishes.

R̊. Blessed are they who hope in the Lord.

SECOND READING
1 Cor 15:12, 16-20

Brothers and sisters:
If Christ is preached as raised from the
   dead,
   how can some among you say there is no
      resurrection of the dead?
If the dead are not raised, neither has
   Christ been raised,
   and if Christ has not been raised, your
      faith is vain;
   you are still in your sins.
Then those who have fallen asleep in
   Christ have perished.
If for this life only we have hoped in
   Christ,
   we are the most pitiable people of all.

But now Christ has been raised from the
   dead,
   the firstfruits of those who have fallen
      asleep.

About Liturgy

Christ's presence in liturgy: The Constitution on the Sacred Liturgy outlines four presences of Christ in liturgical celebration: Christ "is present . . . in the person of his minister . . . in the eucharistic species . . . in the word . . . when the Church prays and sings . . ." (SC no. 7). Our natural tendency is to focus on the sublime and substantial presence of Christ in the eucharistic species, but the Constitution makes clear that this is not the only presence of Christ. Perhaps for too long now we have been neglecting Christ's presence in the word, the presider, and the assembly, yet these presences are also clearly presented in this Sunday's gospel.

We open ourselves to a much broader and richer experience of Christ when we also look for him in the presider, in eating and drinking the consecrated Bread and Wine, in the proclamation of the word, and in the assembled community itself who is the body of Christ being led, challenged, nourished, and offered dignity. Moreover, when we are able to recognize Christ in these other presences at Mass, we have begun to form ourselves to see Christ's presence in the everyday people and circumstances of our lives. In this way we already begin to live the blessedness (and reversals) of which Jesus speaks in this gospel. Liturgy teaches us that Christ is present in many ways.

About Liturgical Music

Cantor preparation: As you prepare to sing this psalm you might reflect on times when you find yourself struggling to stay focused on God. What helps you stay faithful? How during these times do you experience God watching over you?

Selecting seasonal service music, Pt. 5: The following suggestions are not definitive, but are meant simply to exemplify general styles appropriate to different liturgical seasons. Some examples of good Ordinary Time settings are Vermulst's People's Mass, Richard Proulx' A Community Mass, Owen Alstott's Heritage Mass, the St. Louis Jesuits Mass, and the Danish Mass. One might select two settings and switch from one to the other at the point in the gospel readings when Jesus confronts the disciples with the reality of the cross (22nd Sunday in Year A, 24th Sunday in Year B, 21st Sunday in Year C).

For Lent one might select a simple Latin chant setting of the eucharistic acclamations or use the acclamations from David Hurd's English New Plainsong Mass. If not used for Ordinary Time the People's Mass or the Heritage Mass is also an appropriate selection.

For the festive seasons of Christmas and Easter choose the two most musically elaborate settings, ones with high rhythmic energy, full choir parts, and added instrumentation. Use a different one for each season. One could use the same setting for both Advent and Christmas, but hold off on the choir parts and the added instrumentation until Christmas.

Making these selections judiciously may mean separating parts of a full Mass setting. For example, Hurd's New Plainsong Mass includes a Glory to God, which would not be used during Lent. Although there is an aesthetic value to using the entirety of a Mass setting, the demands of a given liturgical season may require choosing only some elements from a setting or combining parts of one setting with parts from another. What should never be submitted to this "cut and paste" approach, however, are the eucharistic acclamations: it is vital that these be related in style and key in order to preserve the unity of the eucharistic prayer.

FEBRUARY 15, 2004

SIXTH SUNDAY IN ORDINARY TIME

✠ SPIRITUALITY

Gospel

Luke 6:27-38; L81C

Jesus said to his disciples:
    "To you who hear I say,
    love your enemies, do good to those
        who hate you,
    bless those who curse you, pray
        for those who mistreat you.
To the person who strikes you on one
        cheek,
    offer the other one as well,
    and from the person who takes
        your cloak,
    do not withhold even your tunic.
Give to everyone who asks of you,
    and from the one who takes what
        is yours do not demand it back.
Do to others as you would have them do
        to you.
For if you love those who love you,
    what credit is that to you?
Even sinners love those who love them.
And if you do good to those who do good
        to you,
    what credit is that to you?
Even sinners do the same.
If you lend money to those from whom
        you expect repayment,
    what credit is that to you?
Even sinners lend to sinners,
    and get back the same amount.
But rather, love your enemies and do
        good to them,
    and lend expecting nothing back;
    then your reward will be great
    and you will be children of the Most
        High,
    for he himself is kind to the
        ungrateful and the wicked.
Be merciful, just as your Father is
        merciful.
"Stop judging and you will not be judged.
Stop condemning and you will not be
        condemned.
Forgive and you will be forgiven.
Give, and gifts will be given to you;
    a good measure, packed together,
        shaken down, and overflowing,
    will be poured into your lap.
For the measure with which you measure
    will in return be measured out to you."

Reflecting on the Gospel

We can be uncompromising and demanding of ourselves when we want to achieve great success. For example, athletes train long hours for months on end to make an Olympic team and then train even more rigorously with their eye on the gold. Artists practice long hours to give a stellar performance and win standing applause and acclaim. Some adults may work eighty- or ninety-hour weeks to gain promotion and increased salary. The demands Jesus puts on us in this Sunday's gospel ought not shock us; we put extraordinary demands on ourselves all the time. Yet, we tend to hear this gospel and figure it is hyperbole—this kind of relating to others isn't normal! No, it's not!

Jesus begins his teaching with, "To you who hear I say." Jesus knew that many would consider his words too extraordinary. Despite all our own discipline to get ahead, the discipline of love essential to experiencing true blessedness ("good measure") sounds like too much. We have here, for those "who hear," the deeper challenge beyond the Beatitudes. Not everyone can hear and live this challenge; this is why it is so difficult to establish God's reign. Jesus lays out the concrete conduct that establishes the kingdom, and it truly is extraordinary in its demands.

We have an example of such extraordinary conduct in the person of David in the first reading who refuses to "harm the LORD's anointed." Moreover, David is the Old Testament foreshadowing of Christ; David embodies in his actions toward Saul what Jesus is asking of his disciples. Twice David says, "I would not harm the LORD's anointed"; David wouldn't kill Saul who had set out to kill him. Jesus preached demanding ethical imperatives and, while some heard, others did kill him, the anointed of God. What Jesus sets before his disciples is nothing less than what he himself has already done in his life.

We have the example of David and Jesus to encourage us to this extraordinary way of discipleship. But there is more: we are able to hear and respond to this extraordinary challenge because "the Most High" has already extended kindness and mercy to us, first in Christ and then through our baptism by which we are "children of the Most High," sharing in divine life. It's as though God practiced the golden rule before the words were on the lips of Jesus. We have already been given the grace ("credit" = *charis,* grace) to love in the way God has loved first.

True, this extraordinary way of relating to others isn't normal! It's divine! God has acted toward us already with extraordinary kindness and mercy, already giving us a full measure of blessedness. Can we afford not to hear?

Living the Paschal Mystery

The very doing of these extraordinary things is the "hearing," and this further enables us to grow in our love and goodness. Our whole life is the "training" for this extraordinary love and goodness. Rather than being overwhelmed by the sweeping demands, we need to take each moment as it comes and recognize in each an opportunity to "hear." For example, instead of doing something half way, we might shave a few minutes off our coffee break and do the task to the very best of our ability. Instead of brushing someone off, we might pause to smile. Instead of expressing our anger inappropriately, we might consider the dignity of the other.

Focusing the Word

Key words and phrases from the gospel: love, do good, the Most High, kind, merciful, measure

To the point: The "measure" of love and goodness that Jesus requires of his hearers is extraordinary. Jesus sets this standard without ambiguity or compromise. This extraordinary requirement is possible and demanded of us because "the Most High" has already extended kindness and mercy to us beyond measure.

Connecting the Word

to the first reading: Despite the fact that King Saul had tried repeatedly to kill David, David did not respond in kind but respected the anointed of God, and this models for us the behavior described for us in the gospel.

to culture: The measure of our ethical behavior is not only determined by social standards, philosophical systems, or public polls, but by Jesus himself.

Understanding the Word

Moral life flows from the Beatitudes: There is a connection between last Sunday's Beatitudes and this Sunday's moral teachings. The last of the Beatitudes had pronounced this blessing: "Blessed are you when people hate you, and when they exclude and insult you, and denounce your name as evil on account of the Son of Man" (6:22). This Sunday's passage begins by prescribing a disciple's response to such abuse: "love your enemies, do good to those who hate you, bless those who curse you, pray for those who mistreat you" (6:27). The two passages are similarly structured and the verbs are perfectly paired: hate/love, exclude/do good, insult/bless, denounce/pray. Clearly such an extraordinary response to abuse is possible only because disciples are blessed: their strength for good comes from God.

The passage continues with four specific examples of a disciple's response to maltreatment from enemies. Then Luke summarizes the teaching to this point by the "Golden Rule": "Do to others as you would have them do to you" (6:31). Matthew, too, has this saying in his Sermon on the Mount (7:12) but later and in a different collection of sayings. Luke's insertion of the saying here strengthens the impact and sharpens the demand: in context, "the others" whom disciples are to treat kindly are enemies and persecutors!

After three questions about conduct toward one's enemies, the benefits of discipleship are declared. First, disciples will receive a great reward; moreover, they will be children of God. As Luke explains, God loves the ungrateful and the wicked (this is why Jesus came!); similarly, God's children should do as their "Father." The implication is clear: in this sermon instructing disciples, the comparison between Father and children parallels the relationship between Master and disciples. In both cases the values of the greater (Father, Master) are the moral norms of the lesser (children, disciples). Ultimately, the Golden Rule is surpassed: more than doing as you would have done, disciples are to do as God would do—"Be merciful as God is merciful." Disciples have been blessed with mercy so they are to act with mercy. Moral life flows from blessing.

ASSEMBLY & FAITH-SHARING GROUPS

- As I try to hear Jesus in the gospel, I am challenged to . . .
- As I try to hear Jesus, I am resisting . . .
- In my life "the measure with which [I] measure" looks like . . .
- If God were to use that same measure with me my life would be . . .

PRESIDERS

Jesus demands of me what God first gives and does to me in "good measure." If this became a standard for shaping my ministry I could see that . . .

DEACONS

My diaconal service is most divine when I extend kindness and mercy (especially) to "the ungrateful and the wicked."
I can recall my failures . . .
For those times it did happen I give thanks to the Source of all "good measure" . . .

HOSPITALITY MINISTERS

My hospitality is a "good measure . . . and overflowing" when . . .
My hospitality is of no greater "credit" than that of other "sinners" when . . .

MUSIC MINISTERS

I experience music ministry as a gift "poured into [my] lap" when . . .
The assembly experiences this gift when . . .

ALTAR MINISTERS

Serving invites self-emptying; it carves one into a "good measure" of love, kindness, mercy, etc.
I can see how this is happening to me . . .

LECTORS

The proverb reads, "Practice what you preach." What I need to practice this week before I can proclaim with integrity is . . .

EUCHARISTIC MINISTERS

Eucharist celebrates Jesus' holding nothing back in giving himself to/for me! When I really comprehend this abundant Gift to me, my life is like . . .

Model Penitential Rite

Presider: We hear in the gospel today what seem like impossible demands for our Christian living: love our enemies and do good to them. We pause at the beginning of this celebration to open ourselves to God's presence so that we can truly hear God's word and share in the blessedness of God's lavish feast given us in full measure . . . [pause]

Lord Jesus, you forgave your enemies: Lord . . .

Christ Jesus, you have shown us kindness and mercy beyond measure: Christ . . .

Lord Jesus, you lavish on us the gift of your very life: Lord . . .

Appreciating the Responsorial Psalm

The first reading narrates the dramatic tale of David's placing mercy for his enemy and faithfulness to God above the self-satisfaction vengeance would have given him. In the gospel Jesus challenges his hearers to love their enemies and do good to those who hate them, calling them to be merciful as God is merciful.

The responsorial psalm fittingly sings about the mercy of this God who does not treat us "according to our sins" but instead acts toward us with compassion. The psalm reminds us that what enables us to comply with the challenging command Jesus issues in this gospel is God's merciful manner toward us. We can grant mercy to one another because God first grants mercy to us. May our singing of this psalm be a joyous celebration of who God is and a commitment to become who we are called to be.

Model General Intercessions

Presider: We now place our needs before a kind and merciful God.

Response:

Lord,⎯⎯ hear our prayer.

Cantor:

we pray to the Lord,

As God is merciful, may all members of the Church show mercy and forgiveness to others . . . [pause]

As God is merciful, may all people forgive their enemies . . . [pause]

As God is merciful, may those steeped in ungraciousness and wickedness know that God is just . . . [pause]

As God is merciful, may we be generous in our giving and quick in our forgiving . . . [pause]

Presider: Gracious and merciful God, you have blessed us in good measure with gifts of life and love: hear these our prayers that we might become more like your Son Jesus in our daily lives. We ask this through that same Son, Jesus Christ our Lord. **Amen.**

OPENING PRAYER

Let us pray
[that God will make us more like Christ, his Son]

Pause for silent prayer

Father,
keep before us the wisdom and love
you have revealed in your Son.
Help us to be like him
in word and deed,
for he lives and reigns with you and the
    Holy Spirit,
one God, for ever and ever. **Amen.**

FIRST READING
1 Sam 26:2, 7-9, 12-13, 22-23

In those days, Saul went down to the
    desert of Ziph
    with three thousand picked men of Israel,
    to search for David in the desert of Ziph.
So David and Abishai went among Saul's
    soldiers by night
    and found Saul lying asleep within the
      barricade,
    with his spear thrust into the ground at
      his head
    and Abner and his men sleeping around
      him.

Abishai whispered to David:
    "God has delivered your enemy into
      your grasp this day.
Let me nail him to the ground with one
      thrust of the spear;
    I will not need a second thrust!"
But David said to Abishai, "Do not harm
    him,
    for who can lay hands on the LORD's
      anointed and remain unpunished?"
So David took the spear and the water jug
    from their place at Saul's head,
    and they got away without anyone's
      seeing or knowing or awakening.
All remained asleep,
    because the LORD had put them into a
      deep slumber.

Going across to an opposite slope,
    David stood on a remote hilltop
    at a great distance from Abner, son of
      Ner, and the troops.
He said: "Here is the king's spear.
Let an attendant come over to get it.
The LORD will reward each man for his
    justice and faithfulness.
Today, though the LORD delivered you into
    my grasp,
    I would not harm the LORD's anointed."

RESPONSORIAL PSALM

Ps 103:1-2, 3-4, 8, 10, 12-13

℞. (8a) The Lord is kind and merciful.

Bless the LORD, O my soul;
  and all my being, bless his holy name.
Bless the LORD, O my soul,
  and forget not all his benefits.

℞. The Lord is kind and merciful.

He pardons all your iniquities,
  heals all your ills.
He redeems your life from destruction,
  crowns you with kindness and
  compassion.

℞. The Lord is kind and merciful.

Merciful and gracious is the LORD,
  slow to anger and abounding in
  kindness.
Not according to our sins does he deal
  with us,
  nor does he requite us according to our
  crimes.

℞. The Lord is kind and merciful.

As far as the east is from the west,
  so far has he put our transgressions
  from us.
As a father has compassion on his
  children,
  so the LORD has compassion on those
  who fear him.

℞. The Lord is kind and merciful.

SECOND READING

1 Cor 15:45-49

Brothers and sisters:
It is written, *The first man, Adam, became
  a living being,*
  the last Adam a life-giving spirit.
But the spiritual was not first;
  rather the natural and then the spiritual.
The first man was from the earth, earthly;
  the second man, from heaven.
As was the earthly one, so also are the
  earthly,
  and as is the heavenly one, so also are
  the heavenly.
Just as we have borne the image of the
  earthly one,
  we shall also bear the image of the
  heavenly one.

About Liturgy

Mass "trains" us: We have formed a good habit over long years of celebrating Mass each Sunday of our lives. Perhaps we've never looked at this hour together each week as a kind of "training" for the demands of living that this Sunday's gospel lays out.

One of the keys for understanding this gospel is to realize that God has already extended such kindness and mercy to us as we are expected to give in return to those we meet. Our Sunday celebration is one sure place where we receive God's extraordinary gifts to us:

Assembly: When we come together we make visible the Church, the body of Christ. In our greeting each other, in the singing and responding and praying we are already doing what Christ asks of us. When inclusivity and hospitality, participation and self-giving are hallmarks of our assembling, we are practicing the love the gospel demands.

God's word: During each Liturgy of the Word God speaks to us a new and fresh word. We are not without sure guidance and heartfelt encouragement as well as demand and challenge—God's word is all these. Listening attentively to the Liturgy of the Word each Sunday is "training" in hearing Jesus' demands of discipleship. We must prepare well and put forth the effort to receive graciously God's word.

Eucharistic prayer: Each Mass the priest prays in the name of all the assembly members the Church's great thanksgiving—the eucharistic prayer. No matter which prayer is prayed on a given Sunday, we hear of God's mighty deeds on our behalf. We are continually reminded of God's goodness, mercy, and love extended to us in the divine deeds of salvation that are recited. What God has already done for us encourages us to go and do likewise with each other.

Communion: At Communion we receive Christ's very Body and Blood for nourishment in our "training." This is surely God's most lavish gift—"a good measure . . . overflowing." God can make demands on the way we disciples live because God has given us the Food and strength to meet those demands.

Concluding rite: At the end of Mass—and the end of our "training"—we are sent forth to live liturgy. Daily life is a kind of "practice" in what we have learned. God has given us every means to succeed at being loving and merciful as God is to us.

About Liturgical Music

Cantor preparation: As you prepare to sing this psalm you might spend some time reflecting on ways you have experienced God's mercy. When have you been forgiven by God? When have you felt the "full measure" of God's compassion? Where in your life right now do you need reassurance of God's mercy?

Selecting seasonal service music, Pt. 6: The following outlines a process that might be followed for selecting appropriate seasonal service music. Begin by selecting a small committee, perhaps one or two members of the choir (or one member from each of the choirs active in the parish), a member of the parish worship commission, and one or two "persons from the pew." Keep the committee small: one wants enough members to generate a mix of input but not so many that one can never reach a decision. Next, lead them in a discussion of the liturgical seasons, their characteristics, and their relationship to the liturgical year as a whole and to the life and identity of the Church (see *Selecting seasonal service music, Pts. 1 and 2,* pp. 45 and 49). Once the committee has developed a good sense of the liturgical year and its rhythms, make a wall chart of the year, mapping the seasons and their service music. Then inventory the present parish repertoire of service music. Evaluate each setting according to its suitability for the different liturgical seasons. As the committee selects what best fits a given season, fill in the chart accordingly. Finally, note the blank spots in the chart and research new repertoire to fill in whatever is missing.

FEBRUARY 22, 2004

SEVENTH SUNDAY IN ORDINARY TIME

Season of Lent

✠ SPIRITUALITY

Gospel   Matt 6:1-6, 16-18; L219

Jesus said to his disciples:
"Take care not to perform righteous deeds
in order that people may see them;
otherwise, you will have no recompense from your heavenly Father.
When you give alms,
do not blow a trumpet before you,
as the hypocrites do in the synagogues and in the streets
to win the praise of others.
Amen, I say to you,
they have received their reward.
But when you give alms,
do not let your left hand know what your right is doing,
so that your almsgiving may be secret.
And your Father who sees in secret will repay you.

"When you pray,
do not be like the hypocrites,
who love to stand and pray in the synagogues and on street corners
so that others may see them.
Amen, I say to you,
they have received their reward.
But when you pray, go to your inner room,
close the door, and pray to your Father in secret.
And your Father who sees in secret will repay you.

"When you fast,
do not look gloomy like the hypocrites.
They neglect their appearance,
so that they may appear to others to be fasting.
Amen, I say to you, they have received their reward.
But when you fast,
anoint your head and wash your face,
so that you may not appear to be fasting,
except to your Father who is hidden.
And your Father who sees what is hidden will repay you."

See Appendix A, p. 261, for other readings.

Reflecting on the Gospel

Ash Wednesday occurs during the middle of the week, a day when we don't usually go to church. Yet this is one day when our churches are almost as full as on Sunday. So many coming to church vouches for the fact that we take Lent seriously, that we recognize ourselves to be sinners, that we desire God's mercy and forgiveness. The gospel sets out more extraordinary standards for discipleship—almsgiving, prayer, and fasting. Probably by the time we get to church many of us have already thought about and chosen our Lenten practices. All this is necessary and good; but it is not enough!

Lent is the time of year the Church sets aside to examine how well we have embraced discipleship. The catechumens will soon become elect and begin their final preparations for baptism; we join with them in their preparation so that we might renew our own baptismal promises at Easter with fervor and renewed commitment. During these next six weeks we discipline ourselves to embrace more adequately the "righteous deeds" of which the gospel speaks and are reminded that these deeds are directed to God and changing ourselves, not to receiving human rewards.

If we examine the three traditional practices of penance that the gospel mentions (almsgiving, prayer, and fasting), we notice that fasting is specifically directed to disciplining ourselves—it directs our attention to the prophet Joel's desire that we "return to the LORD" and to Paul's admonition in the second reading to "be reconciled to God." Part of the discipline of Lent is to set right our relationship with God.

This interior work of personal renewal is not enough, however. We must also set right our relationships with each other. The second prong of our penance, almsgiving, specifically directs our attention to being "ambassadors for Christ." In other words, our Lenten practices include both inward renewal and outward mission for the sake of others. The best way we can assure that our Lenten practices aren't done to receive the reward of another's praise is quietly to reach out to others.

What enables us both to change interiorly (to discipline ourselves to meet the extraordinary personal demands of discipleship) and to move outward toward others in mission? The third prong of our Lenten penance: prayer—our attentiveness to God's presence during which we experience God's graciousness, mercy, kindness, and blessing. Lent might be a good time to pray to God not by using the familiar prayers we usually say, but to pray by taking time to be attentive to God's presence. This is a good time to speak to God from our hearts. Lent is a good time to "rend [our] hearts"—to spill out what within us needs healing and forgiving.

Living the Paschal Mystery

We must take care that we don't live these next six weeks like the other weeks of the year. Now we are in a special kind of "training"—we are redoubling our efforts to learn what gospel living means. If we are to be "reconciled to God" and "ambassadors for Christ" we must make conscious efforts to live now what we will promise and profess at Easter. Extra time faithfully spent in prayer, emptying ourselves through fasting so we hunger for God, being attentive to others—this is how we die to ourselves. Our righteous deeds now will reap the rewards of Easter joy.

Focusing the Word
Key words and phrases from the gospel: perform righteous deeds

To the point: Both Joel and Matthew seem to focus on behaviors—appropriate and typical Lenten concerns. This is necessary, but not enough. The reading from Paul (second reading) describes the desired outcome of our Lenten practices: that we be "reconciled to God" and that we be "ambassadors for Christ." Lent directs us inward to transformation and moves us outward to mission.

[The Penitential Rite is omitted.]

Model General Intercessions
Presider: As we begin this solemn time for charity, prayer, and fasting let us pray that we will persevere and come to Easter renewed in our resolve to be faithful disciples of Christ.

Response:

Cantor:

That all members of the Church enter into this Lenten season with a spirit willing to change and a heart open to God's mercy . . . [pause]

That all peoples of the world work toward reconciliation and forgiveness . . . [pause]

That the hard-hearted may hear God's call to repentance . . . [pause]

That each of us be renewed in our commitment to love and serve God and each other . . . [pause]

Presider: Gracious and merciful God, you hear the prayers of those who call out to you: be near us during Lent so that we might be reconciled to you and be faithful to our mission as disciples. We ask this through Christ our Lord. **Amen.**

OPENING PRAYER
Let us pray

Pause for silent prayer

Lord,
protect us in our struggle against evil.
As we begin the discipline of Lent,
make this day holy by our self-denial.
Grant this through our Lord Jesus Christ,
     your Son,
who lives and reigns with you and the Holy
     Spirit,
one God, for ever and ever. **Amen.**

FOR REFLECTION
- The hypocrisy that can easily sneak into my almsgiving is . . .
  into my prayer is . . .
  into my fasting is . . .
- During this Lent the "righteous deeds" that I need to do *for renewal of myself* are . . .

SPIRITUALITY

Gospel   Luke 4:1-13; L24C

Filled with the Holy Spirit, Jesus
   returned from the Jordan
   and was led by the Spirit into the
      desert for forty days,
   to be tempted by the devil.
He ate nothing during those days,
   and when they were over he was
      hungry.
The devil said to him,
   "If you are the Son of God,
   command this stone to become
      bread."
Jesus answered him,
   "It is written, *One does not live on
      bread alone.*"
Then he took him up and showed him
   all the kingdoms of the world in a
      single instant.
The devil said to him,
   "I shall give to you all this power and
      glory;
   for it has been handed over to me,
   and I may give it to whomever I wish.
All this will be yours, if you worship
      me."
Jesus said to him in reply,
   "It is written:
   *You shall worship the Lord, your God,
      and him alone shall you serve.*"
Then he led him to Jerusalem,
   made him stand on the parapet of the
      temple, and said to him,
   "If you are the Son of God,
   throw yourself down from here, for it
      is written:
   *He will command his angels
      concerning you, to guard you,*
   and:
   *With their hands they will support
      you,
   lest you dash your foot against a
      stone.*"
Jesus said to him in reply,
   "It also says,
   *You shall not put the Lord, your God,
      to the test.*"
When the devil had finished every
   temptation,
   he departed from him for a time.

Reflecting on the Gospel

The wind and the sun were having an argument over which one was the stronger. Along came a traveler and they decided to settle the dispute once and for all. So, they agreed that whichever one could make the traveler take off his coat would be the stronger. The sun hid behind a cloud and let the wind have its chance to prove itself first. So the wind blew an icy blast of air but the harder the wind blew the more tightly did the traveler wrap his coat around himself. The wind blew and blew, but the traveler hung onto his coat. In disgust the wind finally gave up and challenged the sun to try. So the sun came out from behind the cloud and began to shine down on the traveler who felt the sun's genial warmth. As the sun shone warmer and warmer the traveler loosened his coat until finally he took it off altogether. So the sun was right, after all; it was the stronger! This is something like the conflict between the devil and Jesus in the desert. Try as he might by offering every attractive thing—wealth, power, esteem—the devil couldn't prove stronger. The gentle persuasion of prayer and fasting kept Jesus stronger and able to resist temptation.

The desert is a place of isolation and desolation; we have *only* God (the Holy Spirit) to rely on. If we try to overcome temptation by our own power we will be like the traveler—only wrapping the cloak of our own sinfulness more closely around us. But if we remember God's mighty and generous deeds (first reading) and that "the word is near" (second reading) we will be brought closer to God, justified and saved. Then, like both Israel of old and the early Christians, we can profess our faith in word and deed. The response to temptation is the expression of faith.

Not even the Son of God was exempt from being tested! We can expect no less in our own lives. Temptation, then, isn't necessarily a sign of great sinfulness. It is an occasion for showing that our lives are turned to God, for remaining steadfast in the faith that we profess. Lent isn't simply our desert time to overcome temptation. It is also a springtime of renewed relationship to God. It is a time when we are strengthened, with the gentle warmth of God's Spirit leading us, to overcome even temptations to wealth, power, and esteem. Our strength does not lie in force, but in relying on God to be near.

Living the Paschal Mystery

The ritual act of professing our faith is no substitution for *living* it in our daily lives. When we are tested our faith is put to the test, too, and we are faced with a choice of how we live. Lent is a time to examine our choices.

Just as God led Israel to a "land flowing with milk and honey" (first reading), so will God lead us to salvation if we "call on the name of the Lord" (second reading). For us, though, our desert is the demands of everyday living and our salvation is found on the cross. Each day we take up our cross and lay down our life for the sake of others, we are building strength to resist temptation and come to greater faith. Our simple acts of kindness are helping us resist temptation. Our doing well whatever the task at hand helps us resist temptation. Our complimenting another, offering a word of encouragement help us resist temptation.

We don't have to go out into a desert to find temptation! But we do need God's nearness to resist it. And that God has promised us.

Focusing the Word

Key words and phrases from the gospel: led by the Spirit, desert, to be tempted, Son of God

To the point: Jesus was "led by the Spirit into the desert . . . to be tempted." Not even the "Son of God" was exempt from the need for prayer, fasting, and struggling with temptation. Our Lenten imitation of Jesus in prayer, fasting, and resisting temptation strengthens us to follow Jesus by daily taking up our cross and laying down our life.

Connecting the Word

to the first reading: Professing faith involves at least (1) expression in religious rituals (see first reading) and (2) living it daily by resisting temptation.

to religious experience: In daily life people often grow discouraged because they have to face the same temptation over and over again. Being tempted may not mean that we are not growing in our relationship with God or that we are far from God. It is an opportunity to turn more fervently to God.

Understanding the Word

The temptations: Luke organizes the temptations of Jesus to showcase some of the major themes. For Luke the ministry of Jesus fulfills God's promises to Israel. Thus, Luke is very respectful of Jewish traditions, institutions, and Scriptures. For this reason Luke places a special emphasis on the Temple, the visible sign of God's presence to the people. Luke begins the gospel with Zechariah in the Temple (1:8ff); he ends it with the disciples in the Temple praising God (24:52); the only episode from Jesus' youth, and the last story before his appearance as an adult, takes place in the Temple (2:46-52). In this Sunday's episode Luke puts the temptation at the Temple in the third and climactic position (Matthew 4:5-7 has it second). Here, at the Temple in Jerusalem, the devil tempts Jesus to have God preserve him from death. Jesus' refusal to yield to this temptation foreshadows the time when Jesus comes again to Jerusalem to face his death. Then, he will lay down his life rather than throw it away.

Jesus responds to each of the three temptations of the devil using only words from Scripture—he speaks no words of his own to the devil. Jesus quotes—and fulfills—Scripture. This highlights the centrality of God's word. It also attests to the power of Scripture which can be used to resist the power of the devil. Which brings us to the next point.

Before Jesus begins his ministry, he confronts the devil, the most powerful of his adversaries. This confrontation is merely "the first round," as it were. Every time Jesus exorcises demons, heals the sick, and restores the handicapped, he is attacking and subduing the power of the devil. The devil departs "for a time," only to return when he induces Judas to betray Jesus (22:3); similarly, the proceedings that lead to Jesus' death are "the time for the power of darkness" (22:53). These temptations are the first salvo in a struggle that will last throughout the gospel. They reveal Jesus as "the Son of God" (4:3, 9) who demonstrates sonship not in power but in fidelity.

ASSEMBLY & FAITH-SHARING GROUPS

Jesus' temptations are mine, too:

- I have tried to make many possessions *sustain* me (even though they can't), like . . .
- I have *served* countless things besides God, like . . .
- I have *tested* God because I sometimes lack trusting God, like . . .

PRESIDERS

The way I lead and comfort those in the desert of temptation is . . .

DEACONS

Lent is about breaking down sin and building up communion. One way my service can break down the "distinctions between Jew and Greek" within my community is . . .

HOSPITALITY MINISTERS

The grace of hospitality is meant to nurture and support those facing trials and temptations. Some I know who need this now are . . .

MUSIC MINISTERS

Fidelity to prayer and fasting both led Jesus face-to-face with temptation and gave him the strength to resist it (gospel). Sometimes in my very music-making I am tempted to turn from God by . . .
What keeps me faithful to God is . . .

ALTAR MINISTERS

The temptations I face within my ministry are . . .
Relying on God in such times means to me . . .

LECTORS

"The word is near you . . . in your heart" (second reading). The way the written word has helped me experience the Word of God within me is . . .

EUCHARISTIC MINISTERS

Christ's banquet celebrates and affects a world where "there is no distinction . . . the same Lord is Lord of all" (second reading). This Lent I need to live and affect this kind of communion at . . .

Model Penitential Rite

Presider: We hear in the gospel today how the Spirit led Jesus into the desert to be tempted. Most of us don't need to go to a desert to be tempted—we are confronted with it in the ordinary circumstances of our everyday lives. Let us ask God to pardon us for the times we have given in to temptation and to strengthen us in our resolve to believe in and live the gospel . . . [pause]

Confiteor: I confess . . .

Appreciating the Responsorial Psalm

Temptation is never absent from *our* lives just as it was not absent from the life of Jesus who was led by the Spirit directly into its face (gospel). Even when vanquished by Jesus' response, Satan departs only "for a time." The very psalm quoted by Satan as part of the temptation is for Jesus, however, a prayer of unshakable confidence in God who is always present in times of "trouble" (responsorial psalm). The God who forged a people and brought them out of Egypt through the desert to a land of milk and honey (first reading) will not now abandon Christ—or us—in the desert.

As we enter this Lenten period of fasting and prayer we can be certain that as it was with Jesus so it will be with us. Satan will not be idle. The more faithful we are to prayer, fasting, and doing good for others the more will we be tempted simply to give it all up for the sake of easier rewards. The psalm reminds us that when this happens we need only call with Jesus "on the name of the Lord" (second reading) and sing with him our confidence in the God who guards and delivers us.

Model General Intercessions

Presider: We pray for the strength to resist temptation and for an increase in faith.

Response:

Cantor:

That all members of the Church enter into the desert of Lent in fasting and prayer to receive the strength to resist temptation . . . [pause]

That peoples of the world share in the salvation God offers through the death and resurrection of the Son . . . [pause]

That the weak and frightened find courage and strength in the nearness of God . . . [pause]

That each of us enter into Lent with seriousness of purpose and resolve of will to live what we believe . . . [pause]

Presider: Merciful God, you send your Spirit to strengthen us in times of need: hear these our prayers that we will always remain faithful to you and one day enjoy eternal life with you. We ask this through Christ our Savior. **Amen.**

ALTERNATIVE OPENING PRAYER
Let us pray

Pause for silent prayer

Lord our God,
you formed man from the clay of the earth
and breathed into him the spirit of life,
but he turned from your face and sinned.
In this time of repentance
we call out for your mercy.

Bring us back to you
and to the life your Son won for us
by his death on the cross,
for he lives and reigns for ever and ever.
   Amen.

FIRST READING
Deut 26:4-10

Moses spoke to the people, saying:
  "The priest shall receive the basket from you
  and shall set it in front of the altar of the LORD, your God.
Then you shall declare before the LORD, your God,
  'My father was a wandering Aramean
  who went down to Egypt with a small household
  and lived there as an alien.
But there he became a nation
  great, strong, and numerous.
When the Egyptians maltreated and oppressed us,
  imposing hard labor upon us,
  we cried to the LORD, the God of our fathers,
  and he heard our cry
  and saw our affliction, our toil, and our oppression.
He brought us out of Egypt
  with his strong hand and outstretched arm,
  with terrifying power, with signs and wonders;
  and bringing us into this country,
  he gave us this land flowing with milk and honey.
Therefore, I have now brought you the firstfruits
  of the products of the soil
  which you, O LORD, have given me.'
And having set them before the LORD, your God,
  you shall bow down in his presence."

RESPONSORIAL PSALM

Ps 91:1-2, 10-11, 12-13, 14-15

℟. (cf. 15b) Be with me, Lord, when I am
in trouble.

You who dwell in the shelter of the Most
    High,
    who abide in the shadow of the
      Almighty,
say to the LORD, "My refuge and fortress,
    my God in whom I trust."

℟. Be with me, Lord, when I am in trouble.

No evil shall befall you,
    nor shall affliction come near your tent,
for to his angels he has given command
    about you,
    that they guard you in all your ways.

℟. Be with me, Lord, when I am in trouble.

Upon their hands they shall bear you up,
    lest you dash your foot against a stone.
You shall tread upon the asp and the
    viper;
    you shall trample down the lion and the
      dragon.

℟. Be with me, Lord, when I am in trouble.

Because he clings to me, I will deliver him;
    I will set him on high because he
      acknowledges my name.
He shall call upon me, and I will answer
    him;
    I will be with him in distress;
I will deliver him and glorify him.

℟. Be with me, Lord, when I am in trouble.

SECOND READING

Rom 10:8-13

See Appendix A, p. 262.

About Liturgy

Creed and intercessions: The general intercessions we pray at Mass are a kind of practical continuation of the profession of faith already begun in the Creed. The other name for these prayers that conclude the Liturgy of the Word is "Prayers of the Faithful" and this suggests that these prayers, then, are a "profession" of our faithful relationship to God that spills over to faithful relationship with each other.

The format used for the general intercessions in *Living Liturgy* involves the assembly in two ways. First of all, they are short—only giving an *announcement* of a general intention that flows from the readings. The slight pause indicated by the ellipses is time for *each of us to pray with all our hearts*. Thus, the first involvement is in genuine prayer for the needs of the Church, the world, the less fortunate, and our own parish or liturgical community. Second, the general intercessions aren't finished when we respond *Amen* to the presider's concluding collect. In fact, the prayers we pray during Mass are only the beginning of our responsibility to those for whom we pray. In these prayers we also make a commitment to actually die to self—to get involved in helping God's reign become a reality in our world.

First readings during Lent: The Old Testament readings during Lent provide a thumbnail of salvation history and, because they have their own purpose, won't necessarily accord with the gospel. The Lectionary is instructing us in God's ways and mighty deeds in the first reading and asking for a faith response in the gospels.

About Liturgical Music

Cantor preparation: The gospel reading suggests a specific shape to the "trouble" about which you sing in the responsorial psalm: the temptation at the beginning of Lent to abandon fidelity to God when the task is too hard, the time too long, and more alluring prospects offer themselves. In this psalm Christ shares with the assembly his certainty of God's presence and protection, and you are his voice. What might you say to Christ during this week to help you prepare for such a ministry?

Hymn suggestion: Sylvia Dunstan's "From the River to the Desert" [*Hymns for the Gospels,* GIA] narrates in poetic form the story of Christ's temptation in the desert. Following the pattern of the gospel story verses 2 to 4 unfold as a dialogue between Satan and Jesus. Verse 5 is a prayer begging Jesus who "knows our weakness" to plead for us for whom "your grace is all we need." The text is a lengthy one which must be sung in its entirety. It could be sung during the presentation of the gifts if there is sufficient time. Otherwise the choir alone could sing it as a prelude. Have cantor only sing verse 1 to set the scene, antiphonal sections sing verses 2 to 4 to express the dialogue between Satan and Christ, and everyone sing the final verse.

FEBRUARY 29, 2004
FIRST SUNDAY OF LENT

✦ SPIRITUALITY

Gospel

Luke 9:28b-36; L27C

Jesus took Peter, John, and James
   and went up the mountain to pray.
While he was praying his face
      changed in appearance
   and his clothing became
         dazzling white.
And behold, two men were
      conversing with him, Moses
      and Elijah,
   who appeared in glory and spoke
      of his exodus
   that he was going to accomplish
      in Jerusalem.
Peter and his companions had
      been overcome by sleep,
   but becoming fully awake,
   they saw his glory and the two men
      standing with him.
As they were about to part from him,
      Peter said to Jesus,
   "Master, it is good that we are here;
   let us make three tents,
      one for you, one for Moses, and one
      for Elijah."
But he did not know what he was
      saying.
While he was still speaking,
   a cloud came and cast a shadow over
      them,
   and they became frightened when
      they entered the cloud.
Then from the cloud came a voice that
      said,
   "This is my chosen Son; listen to
      him."
After the voice had spoken, Jesus was
      found alone.
They fell silent and did not at that time
   tell anyone what they had seen.

Reflecting on the Gospel

Most of us live far too hectic lives—we are busy from morning to night with work, chauffeuring the kids, cleaning, meals, answering email, and a hundred other things. When we might finally sit down in the evening to relax a little, how often right in the middle of a conversation or a TV program do we doze off? We might wake with a start to someone questioning us, "Aren't you listening?" or find we've lost half the TV program so the ending doesn't make any sense. The apostles in this gospel fall asleep—haven't we all had the experience of falling asleep during prayer?—and wake up to Jesus' transfigured glory. Luke's account leads us to believe that the apostles were asleep during Jesus' conversation with Moses and Elijah about his "exodus"—his passing, his death in Jerusalem. The apostles woke up to Jesus' transfigured glory but missed why Jesus is/will be glorified! Luke's insight is that glory always presupposes embracing passion.

Jesus' transfiguration—in all its glory—cannot erase the stark reality of self-offering. Simply put, glory only comes through embracing the passion. This is the paradox of the paschal mystery: that something as desirable as a share in Jesus' transfigured glory only comes through our embracing something as abhorrent as suffering and death.

Luke's transfiguration account remarks that while Peter is suggesting that they remain in the glory, a cloud overshadowed them and a voice, like at Jesus' baptism, announced Jesus as the chosen Son and gave the injunction, "Listen to him." The only way for us to "remain" in Jesus' glory is to accept the baptismal challenge to recognize Jesus as the beloved Son and to "Listen to him." This means that we take to heart gospel living. This means that daily we die to ourselves. Even in this glorious moment of transfiguration—which gives us encouragement and hope on our Lenten journey—we are reminded that the only way to remain in that glory is to die to self. We have to come off the mountain.

Living the Paschal Mystery

Baptism is our covenant with the Lord. Rather than animal offerings and "smoking fire pot and flaming torch" (first reading), the sign of our covenant with God is water, Chrism, white garment, and lighted candle. Luke's allusions to Jesus' death in Jerusalem prompt an allusion to our being plunged into Jesus' dying and rising in the baptismal waters. We are invited this Sunday to see our baptism in light of the transfiguration.

Baptism isn't simply a ritual we perform, but a covenant with God that we live out the rest of our lives. During Lent as we walk with the elect through their final preparation for baptism we, too, prepare to renew our covenant with God at Easter. This means that we not only already share in God's life and look forward to that day when we will share eternal glory with God, but we also embrace the suffering and death.

Let's face it: constant dying to self gets tiresome! This Sunday we are given a glimpse of glory to help ease away the discouragement of a lifetime of self-emptying. This tells us something about how we might keep Sundays. If each Sunday is a day of rest, a time to be good to ourselves, to do something special that is uplifting, to enter into a moment of glory, we would be better fortified to continue dying to self.

Focusing the Word
Key words and phrases from the gospel: his exodus . . . in Jerusalem, saw his glory

To the point: Only Luke's account of the transfiguration alludes to the passion as part of the revelation of Jesus' glory ("his exodus that he was going to accomplish in Jerusalem"). Thus, without detracting from the glory that is central to the transfiguration, the Lenten context challenges us to embrace the paschal aspect of the suffering that leads to glory.

Connecting the Word
to the next three Sundays: In this transfiguration account Luke embraces themes (glory, exodus, Jerusalem) that are developed over the next three Sundays in the gospels having a common motif of repentance: repent or perish, seek forgiveness and feast, repent and live.

to culture: We tend to have two opposite stances toward pain and suffering: avoid it at all costs/end it as soon as possible or "tough it out." Neither approach is what the paschal mystery implies—embracing pain and suffering (dying to self) is what leads to new life and glory.

Understanding the Word
Transfiguration and passion: Several features of the transfiguration story highlight the glorious aspects of this event: Jesus' changed appearance, his dazzlingly white robes, the presence of Moses and Elijah, the manifestation of Jesus' glory, the cloud of divine presence, the heavenly voice announcing Jesus as the Son of God.

But several features also point to the passion/death/resurrection of Jesus. The Lectionary begins the reading in the middle of verse 28. The omitted half of the verse indicates that this event took place "about eight days after" Peter's confession that Jesus is "the Messiah of God" (9:20). "Eight days" was interpreted by the early Fathers of the Church as a reference to the resurrection: in Jewish reckoning, Saturday (the Sabbath) is the seventh day of the week which makes Sunday the first day of the week or, if counting continuously, the eighth day. The expression "the eighth day" became shorthand for the resurrection. While this usage is not attested in the New Testament, early Christian documents moved in this direction.

Only Luke indicates what Moses and Elijah were talking about: "his exodus that he was going to accomplish [Greek = 'fulfill'] in Jerusalem." The use of the term "exodus" may be a reflex from the reference to Moses, the hero of the Exodus, in which case Jesus is being identified as the long-expected "Prophet like Moses" (Deut 18:15, 18; see also Acts 3:22; 7:37). Or, because of the future reference, "he was going to accomplish in Jerusalem," it possibly refers to his coming death/resurrection/ascension. The immediate reference to "his glory" makes this very likely.

Two more details point this story to the passion. The disciples will once again be found sleeping, next time in Gethsemane (Luke 22:45-46). And finally, the words "this is my chosen Son" reflect the vocabulary of the Servant of the Lord (Isa 42:1), the same Servant who "gives his life as an offering for sin" (Isa 53:10) and whose death "shall justify many" (Isa 53:11). Glory and passion are the two sides of the paschal mystery.

ASSEMBLY & FAITH-SHARING GROUPS
- Luke cannot tell the story of Jesus' transfigured glory without referring to Jesus' exodus (suffering and death in Jerusalem). What is significant about that for me is . . .
- Peter and his companions were sleeping, then became "fully awake." The parts of Lent that wake me up are . . .
- I need to wake up and see . . .

PRESIDERS
While Jesus prayed his appearance changed and he heard (again) who he was as "chosen Son."
What is changing in me this Lent is . . .
What I hear in my prayer is . . .

DEACONS
What I would have to change this Lent before I could encourage others to "be imitators of me" (second reading) is . . .

HOSPITALITY MINISTERS
Hospitality is meant to signify to the assembly its heavenly citizenship (see second reading). The way I try to do that is . . .

MUSIC MINISTERS
I find my ministry transforming me more gloriously into the body of Christ when . . .
The dying to self that makes this transformation possible is . . .

ALTAR MINISTERS
The exodus of serving is self-emptying. For me the glory of serving is . . .

LECTORS
The ministry of lector doesn't just communicate the great stories of faith but also inspires the assembly to "put . . . faith in the Lord" (first reading). The way I try to do that is . . .

EUCHARISTIC MINISTERS
The eucharistic table is my mountain of transfiguration where my lowly body is conformed to Christ's glorified body (see second reading). What I must do to climb this mountain is live my Amen, by . . .

Model Penitential Rite

Presider: In the gospel today we hear about Jesus going up the mountain to be transfigured into glory. We also hear that the road to resurrected glory is to Jerusalem, where death awaits. We pause to reflect on the times when we have run from dying to self and ask God's pardon and mercy . . . [pause]

Confiteor: I confess . . .

Appreciating the Responsorial Psalm

Psalm 27 proclaims that those who seek the Lord will see the Lord. Such confidence enables the faithful to wait for salvation with courage and stoutheartedness. Nonetheless, as the middle verses of the psalm reveal, such confidence does not exempt one from anxiety. Just so must the righteous and obedient Abraham sit through a "terrifying darkness" before hearing God's word of promise (first reading). Just so are Peter, James, and John overcome by darkness and fear after seeing Christ glorified (gospel). Jesus' identity as God's Son has been revealed to them and they can only remain silent about what they have seen.

As we journey through Lent—and through all of Christian life—we, too, have moments of revelation and periods of darkness. There are moments when we see the transfigured Christ and know his glory to be our future (second reading). And there are long periods when, as if asleep (gospel) or in a trance (first reading), we can neither see nor speak but only wait in hope. These verses from Psalm 27 capture both sides of our experience and frame them with faith.

Model General Intercessions

Presider: We pray to the God of glory that we might have the strength to die to self.

Response:

Lord, hear our prayer.

Cantor:

we pray to the Lord,

That the Church might remain awake and praying, embracing dying to self as the road to eternal glory . . . [pause]

That all peoples of the world be open to the salvation and glory that God offers . . . [pause]

That those who cannot see through their suffering to the glory awaiting them be comforted by the nearness of God . . . [pause]

That each of us be faithful in embracing our Lenten practices so that we might glimpse the glory of God on Easter . . . [pause]

Presider: Glorious God, you make known your salvation through the presence of your transfigured Son: hear these our prayers that one day we might share in your eternal glory. We ask this through that same Son, Jesus Christ our Lord. **Amen.**

OPENING PRAYER
Let us pray

Pause for silent prayer

God our Father,
help us to hear your Son.
Enlighten us with your word,
that we may find the way to your glory.

We ask this through our Lord Jesus Christ,
  your Son,
who lives and reigns with you and the
  Holy Spirit,
one God, for ever and ever. **Amen.**

FIRST READING
Gen 15:5-12, 17-18

The Lord God took Abram outside and
  said,
  "Look up at the sky and count the stars,
    if you can.
Just so," he added, "shall your descendants
  be."
Abram put his faith in the LORD,
  who credited it to him as an act of
  righteousness.

He then said to him,
  "I am the LORD who brought you from
    Ur of the Chaldeans
  to give you this land as a possession."
"O Lord GOD," he asked,
  "how am I to know that I shall possess
    it?"
He answered him,
  "Bring me a three-year-old heifer, a
    three-year-old she-goat,
  a three-year-old ram, a turtledove, and a
    young pigeon."
Abram brought him all these, split them in
  two,
  and placed each half opposite the other;
  but the birds he did not cut up.
Birds of prey swooped down on the
  carcasses,
  but Abram stayed with them.
As the sun was about to set, a trance fell
  upon Abram,
  and a deep, terrifying darkness
  enveloped him.

When the sun had set and it was dark,
  there appeared a smoking fire pot and a
    flaming torch,
  which passed between those pieces.
It was on that occasion that the LORD
  made a covenant with Abram,
  saying: "To your descendants I give this
    land,
  from the Wadi of Egypt to the Great
    River, the Euphrates."

RESPONSORIAL PSALM

Ps 27:1, 7-8, 8-9, 13-14

R̸. (1a) The Lord is my light and my salvation.

The LORD is my light and my salvation;
    whom should I fear?
The LORD is my life's refuge;
    of whom should I be afraid?

R̸. The Lord is my light and my salvation.

Hear, O LORD, the sound of my call;
    have pity on me, and answer me.
Of you my heart speaks; you my glance
    seeks.

R̸. The Lord is my light and my salvation.

Your presence, O LORD, I seek.
    Hide not your face from me;
do not in anger repel your servant.
    You are my helper: cast me not off.

R̸. The Lord is my light and my salvation.

I believe that I shall see the bounty of the
    LORD
    in the land of the living.
Wait for the LORD with courage;
    be stouthearted, and wait for the LORD.

R̸. The Lord is my light and my salvation.

SECOND READING

Phil 3:17–4:1

Join with others in being imitators of me,
    brothers and sisters,
    and observe those who thus conduct
        themselves
    according to the model you have in us.
For many, as I have often told you
    and now tell you even in tears,
    conduct themselves as enemies of the
        cross of Christ.
Their end is destruction.
Their God is their stomach;
    their glory is in their "shame."
Their minds are occupied with earthly
    things.
But our citizenship is in heaven,
    and from it we also await a savior, the
        Lord Jesus Christ.
He will change our lowly body
    to conform with his glorified body
    by the power that enables him also
    to bring all things into subjection to
        himself.

Therefore, my brothers and sisters,
    whom I love and long for, my joy and
        crown,
    in this way stand firm in the Lord.

About Liturgy

Parish baptisms: Easter is the preferred time for baptisms, especially for those who have embraced the conversion process of the Rite of Christian Initiation of Adults (R.C.I.A.). In most parishes, however, it is not practical to baptize *only* at Easter, especially the infants. The liturgical renewal has encouraged us to celebrate baptisms occasionally at Sunday Mass when the community is gathered. One reason for this is so that we understand that baptism is a *community* event, not some privatized ritual that is happening to this individual. When the parish gathers weekly to celebrate the Lord's resurrection it is fitting that we share in the reception of this infant or young child into the Church community.

Occasionally celebrating baptism during Sunday Mass also reminds each of us that our own baptisms are ongoing—they are not finished and over with the last prayer of the ritual but continue in our daily dying and rising with Christ. These necessary reminders that we already share in Christ's glory encourage and strengthen us to continue with our daily dying to self.

This being said, there ought not be so many baptisms at the Easter Vigil or during the year at Sunday Mass that we lose sight of the primary purpose of both these liturgical celebrations which is to *enact* the death and resurrection of Jesus. Although baptism, like all sacraments, does make present the paschal mystery in its very enactment, its purpose is primarily initiation, a different emphasis from our weekly and yearly celebration of the paschal mystery. This poses some pastoral challenges that ought to be given careful consideration.

About Liturgical Music

Cantor preparation: As you prepare to sing these verses from Psalm 27, read the entire psalm and spend some time with it in prayer. The psalm is shot through with images of danger and death, all the while maintaining its confidence in God's promise of salvation. As a baptized person the danger you face is the struggle with evil and the death to self this entails (see last Sunday's gospel). How are you being called this Lent to die to yourself? How are you experiencing transformation because of it?

Hymn suggestion: There exists a number of hymns specific to the transfiguration event proclaimed every year on the second Sunday of Lent: "'Tis Good, Lord, to Be Here" [CH, GC, RS, WC, W3]; "Christ upon the Mountain Peak" [W3]; "Jesus, Take Us to the Mountain" [HG]; "Transform Us" [RS]; "From Ashes to the Living Font" [WC]. For this year select one which explicitly relates Christ's transfiguration to his passion and death.

An alternative choice for the entrance procession would be "O Sun of Justice" [RS, W3, CBW3]. The text speaks of the light of Christ dispelling darkness and bringing new life. If the traditional tune (JESU DULCIS MEMORIA) is used, it might be accompanied with simple tone chimes or bells, playing open chords or chord clusters at the places of primary rhythmic impulse.

✠ SPIRITUALITY

Gospel
Luke 13:1-9; L30C

Some people told Jesus about the
  Galileans
    whose blood Pilate had mingled with
      the blood of their sacrifices.
Jesus said to them in reply,
  "Do you think that because these
      Galileans suffered in this way
  they were greater sinners than all
      other Galileans?
By no means!
But I tell you, if you do not repent,
  you will all perish as they did!
Or those eighteen people who were
  killed
    when the tower at Siloam fell on
      them—
    do you think they were more
      guilty
    than everyone else who lived in
      Jerusalem?
By no means!
But I tell you, if you do not repent,
  you will all perish as they did!"

And he told them this parable:
  "There once was a person who had a
      fig tree planted in his orchard,
  and when he came in search of fruit
      on it but found none,
  he said to the gardener,
  'For three years now I have come in
      search of fruit on this fig tree
  but have found none.
So cut it down.
Why should it exhaust the soil?'
He said to him in reply,
  'Sir, leave it for this year also,
  and I shall cultivate the ground
      around it and fertilize it;
  it may bear fruit in the future.
If not you can cut it down.'"

Reflecting on the Gospel

The first part of this Sunday's gospel leaves a lot of room for us to fill in the blanks! We don't know anything about these two tragic events about which the people inform Jesus. Jesus doesn't reply to the people by filling in more information, but rather he uses these probably fairly recent events that are very much on the minds of people as a "teachable moment." First he corrects a popular notion among the people at that time (and possibly more prevalent among us than we would like to admit): tragedies that befall individuals aren't a sign of sin or guilt and the punishment due them; therefore we ought not judge others. Then Jesus seizes this opportunity and uses these events of everyday life to teach the people a very important lesson: repent or perish.

The parable of the non-fruit-bearing fig tree describes the fate of those who do not repent. The parable's "bear fruit or die" is parallel to "repent or perish" in the first part of the gospel. As the second reading reminds us, "standing secure" does not mean that, because God gives us everything needed for our journey toward salvation, we ourselves don't need to "cultivate" and "fertilize" our spiritual lives. We "grumble" our way through life—we judge others, fail to live up to our baptismal commitments, do not heed all the warnings given us. Jesus is quite clear in his message: "bear fruit" or be "cut . . . down."

Living the Paschal Mystery

Suffering for suffering's sake is not what transforms us so that we can bear fruit—the dying that leads to new life is how we bear fruit. The dying that repentance requires forestalls meaningless dying; the dying we do in order to bear fruit is the result of cultivating an attitude of openness to constant transformation; the "fertilizer" is the charity, fasting, and prayer of our Christian penance. Repentance is cultivating the soil so it can bear fruit. Repentance is taking what is dying and coaxing it to life. Repentance is changing one's mind, letting go of the narrowness of our own perception of how life should be and embracing the expansiveness of God's plan for salvation.

Repentance, in terms of changing one's mind, is really conversion. Although repentance and conversion are major Lenten themes (and surely capture the work of preparation for our renewal of baptismal commitment), this isn't something we do only these six weeks out of the year. Lent (dying) and Easter (rising) characterize our Christian living, concretize our baptismal commitment, spell out the paschal mystery. If we wish to bear fruit we must die to ourselves. Interesting paradox: if we don't bear fruit, we die, but we must die to bear fruit. The choice before us is about dying: meaningless dying (selfishness) or fruitful dying (to self for the sake of others).

The gospel parable says for "three years" the owner of the fig tree had been waiting for good fruit. God waits more than three years for us to bear fruit—God waits each and every day of our lives for us to bear fruit. The good news is that God never gives up. God continually cultivates and fertilizes—especially by the ongoing proclamation of God's word and the invitation to God's table. All we need do is respond by dying to self. Then God brings forth new life in us.

Focusing the Word
Key words and phrases from the gospel: if you do not repent, cultivate, fertilize, bear fruit

To the point: Jesus redirects the people from idle speculation about the meaning of the tragic fate of others to the serious work of their own repentance. The parable of the fig tree unfolds the meaning of repentance. The images "cultivate" and "fertilize" speak of the effort required to make the fruitless tree fruitful. This is the work of repentance: to take what is dying and coax it to life.

Connecting the Word
to the second reading: Though God gave the Israelites everything they needed on their journey, most were not pleasing to God. Similarly, God gives us everything we need to bear fruit. But having all we need does not in itself guarantee bearing fruit. We still have our part to do.

to culture: Tragedy survived (for example, a near-fatal auto accident, a heart attack) is often experienced as a "wake-up call." Repentance calls us to the same reappraisal of what is truly important.

Understanding the Word
The barren fig tree: This parable, found only in Luke, is introduced by the report of two strange events which only Luke recounts. The first seems to be an act of political violence committed by Pilate against some Galileans; the second is a freak accident at a tower being built at Siloam which is in Jerusalem. What both stories have in common is that a group of people met a quick, unexpected end. Jesus doesn't address the moral issues—whether their sinfulness made them worthy of such a fate; instead, he seizes a teachable moment and warns his hearers to repent lest they perish "as they did," meaning suddenly and unprepared.

In this context—repent now before disaster overtakes you—Jesus gives this parable of the barren fig tree. The owner has been patient, checking for three years to see if this tree would produce fruit. Now, suddenly and without warning, he announces his decision: "Cut it down!" So far, this is a story that recalls the fiery preaching of John the Baptist: "Produce good fruits as evidence of your repentance . . . Even now the ax lies at the root of the trees. Therefore every tree that does not produce good fruit will be cut down and thrown into the fire" (Luke 3:8-9). But in the ministry of Jesus there is a gift of mercy and unexpected postponement of the judgment: the gardener pleads for one more year. He will take extraordinary steps: fertilizing a fig tree was not common practice. But after this short delay and after these exceptional measures, if there is still no fruit, then judgment will fall. The time is short! This situation is urgent! Repent now!

It is possible that there are veiled references to Jesus' approaching fate. He speaks this parable while he is on his journey to Jerusalem; the references to Pilate and violent death certainly alert readers to Jesus' violent death at the hands of Pilate. Jesus' preaching while on the way to Jerusalem represents that last period of grace during which his hearers may repent. Soon it will be too late.

ASSEMBLY & FAITH-SHARING GROUPS
- When I hear "repent [or] you will all perish" my first response is . . .
- What I understand Jesus is asking of me is . . .
- This Lent how I am cultivating and fertilizing my life is . . .
- The fruit I hope to bear in the future is . . .

PRESIDERS
The gardener (Jesus) defends the fruitless tree and willingly offers to cultivate and fertilize it. In my ministry I have been like this gardener when . . .

DEACONS
The "soul" of my ministry that is exhausted is . . .
Lent is my time to coax it back to life by . . .

HOSPITALITY MINISTERS
Hospitality bears fruit:
–the fruit I have harvested by extending hospitality is . . .
–the fruit I have harvested by receiving hospitality is . . .

MUSIC MINISTERS
In order to bear fruit the hard work (cultivation) my ministry requires is . . .
The repentance (conversion) it requires is . . .

ALTAR MINISTERS
The way serving others cultivates repentance and conversion in myself is . . .

LECTORS
"I have come in search of fruit . . . but have found none."
Where God could say this about me is . . .
This diminished my proclamation because . . .

EUCHARISTIC MINISTERS
The eucharistic banquet is God's nurturing me as "exhausted soul."
Beyond the ritual moment my ministry is about refreshing the infirmed by . . .

Model Penitential Rite

Presider: In today's gospel Jesus lays before us the choice to repent or perish. The choice is clear and we know what we want for ourselves—God's life. Yet, we also know that we make bad choices for ourselves. We pause now to acknowledge our lack of repentance and our sinfulness and ask God to pardon and heal us . . . [pause]

Confiteor: I confess . . .

Appreciating the Responsorial Psalm

God sees the sufferings of the people Israel and "come[s] down to rescue them" (first reading). Thus, says God, am I to be remembered. But the people, traveling from slavery in Egypt to freedom in the promised land, do not remember; they "desire evil things" and are "struck down" (second reading). Thus Jesus' stark command in the gospel: repent or perish, bear fruit or be cut down; and Paul's warning in the First Letter to the Corinthians: do not take salvation for granted.

The responsorial psalm, however, reassures us that God will never renege on the work of salvation. No human fickleness will ever change the behavior of God who "pardons all . . . iniquities." Despite every human recalcitrance, I AM will continue to act to redeem. Even in the gospel reading Jesus grants one more chance before final judgment is rendered. Our part of the bargain is to respond to such fidelity with willingness to be converted and transformed. May our singing about this God whose mercy knows no bounds motivate our repentance and keep us faithful to our Lenten journey.

Model General Intercessions

Presider: We pray to God for all we need to be faithful to the work of conversion, repenting of all that takes us away from God.

Response:

Lord, hear our prayer.

Cantor:

we pray to the Lord,

That the Church be a source of encouragement and strength for those seeking conversion . . . [pause]

That all peoples repent of evil so that God's reign of peace may be established . . . [pause]

That those dead because of sin may repent and be given new life . . . [pause]

That each of us be faithful to the hard work of dying to self so that we might share in God's everlasting life . . . [pause]

Presider: Merciful God, you call sinners to repentance: hear these our prayers that we might change from our sinful ways and receive life everlasting. We ask this through Christ our Lord. **Amen.**

ALTERNATIVE OPENING PRAYER

Let us pray

Pause for silent prayer

God of all compassion, Father of all goodness,
to heal the wounds our sins and selfishness bring upon us
you bid us turn to fasting, prayer, and sharing with our brothers.
We acknowledge our sinfulness, our guilt is ever before us:
when our weakness causes discouragement,
let your compassion fill us with hope
and lead us through a Lent of repentance to the beauty of Easter joy.

Grant this through Christ our Lord.
Amen.

FIRST READING

Exod 3:1-8a, 13-15

Moses was tending the flock of his father-in-law Jethro,
    the priest of Midian.
Leading the flock across the desert, he came to Horeb,
    the mountain of God.
There an angel of the LORD appeared to Moses in fire
    flaming out of a bush.
As he looked on, he was surprised to see that the bush,
    though on fire, was not consumed.
So Moses decided,
"I must go over to look at this remarkable sight,
    and see why the bush is not burned."

When the LORD saw him coming over to look at it more closely,
    God called out to him from the bush,
        "Moses! Moses!"
He answered, "Here I am."
God said, "Come no nearer!
Remove the sandals from your feet,
    for the place where you stand is holy ground.
I am the God of your fathers," he continued,
    "the God of Abraham, the God of Isaac, the God of Jacob."
Moses hid his face, for he was afraid to look at God.
But the LORD said,
"I have witnessed the affliction of my people in Egypt
    and have heard their cry of complaint against their slave drivers,
    so I know well what they are suffering.
Therefore I have come down to rescue them

from the hands of the Egyptians
and lead them out of that land into a
    good and spacious land,
a land flowing with milk and honey."

Moses said to God, "But when I go to the
    Israelites
and say to them, 'The God of your
    fathers has sent me to you,'
if they ask me, 'What is his name?'
    what am I to tell them?"
God replied, "I am who am."
Then he added, "This is what you shall tell
    the Israelites:
I AM sent me to you."

God spoke further to Moses, "Thus shall
    you say to the Israelites:
The LORD, the God of your fathers,
the God of Abraham, the God of Isaac, the
    God of Jacob,
has sent me to you.

"This is my name forever;
    thus am I to be remembered through all
        generations."

RESPONSORIAL PSALM
Ps 103:1-2, 3-4, 6-7, 8, 11

R̸. (8a) The Lord is kind and merciful.

Bless the LORD, O my soul;
    and all my being, bless his holy name.
Bless the LORD, O my soul,
    and forget not all his benefits.

R̸. The Lord is kind and merciful.

He pardons all your iniquities,
    heals all your ills.
He redeems your life from destruction,
    crowns you with kindness and
        compassion.

R̸. The Lord is kind and merciful.

The LORD secures justice
    and the rights of all the oppressed.
He has made known his ways to Moses,
    and his deeds to the children of Israel.

R̸. The Lord is kind and merciful.

Merciful and gracious is the LORD,
    slow to anger and abounding in
        kindness.
For as the heavens are high above the
    earth,
    so surpassing is his kindness toward
        those who fear him.

R̸. The Lord is kind and merciful.

SECOND READING
1 Cor 10:1-6, 10-12

See Appendix A, p. 262.

About Liturgy

Year C Lenten gospels: During year C of the Lectionary three-year cycle a common thread runs through the gospels from the third to the fifth Sundays of Lent—that of repentance. Not only is this an important Lenten theme, but it is an important theme in Luke's gospel as well.

Year A Lenten readings: Year A readings with their baptismal motif may be used at Masses when the Scrutinies are celebrated with the Elect: Exod 17:3-7; Ps 95:1-2, 6-7, 8-9; Rom 5:1-2, 5-8; John 4:5-42 (longer form) or John 4:5-15, 19b-26, 39a, 40-42 (shorter form).

Penitential rite and confession of sins: During Lent we have been suggesting the use of the *Confiteor* (I confess to almighty God . . .) for the penitential rite. If we consider all the helpful choices we have for the introductory rites and use them well, we can establish a rhythm at the beginning of Mass that captures something of the rhythm of Christian living. Using the *Confiteor* during Lent (and on Fridays for daily Mass at other times of the year) reminds us that we are sinners in need of repentance and reconciliation. Acknowledging God's gifts to us in bringing us to salvation and our sometimes refusal (like Israel of old) of those gifts fosters a genuine humility in us.

Using the Rite of Blessing and Sprinkling Holy Water during Easter (and on a few other appropriate Sundays during the year, for example, the Feast of the Baptism of the Lord) reminds us that we are the redeemed body of Christ, plunged into baptismal waters that bring us a share in divine life. Using the *Kyrie* litany of praise during Ordinary Time reminds us that the Lord Jesus has walked the journey before us and showed us the way through death to new life. The rhythm, then, flows among repentance and reconciliation, celebration of divine life, and praise for Jesus' example of dying and rising.

About Liturgical Music

Cantor preparation: While the gospel commands the assembly to repent and the second reading warns them not to take salvation for granted, the responsorial psalm reminds them of God's mercy and compassion. The message, however, is not "do what you will and know you'll be forgiven" but "how can we not be faithful to this God who loves us so much?" How can this message motivate your own repentance? How can it help you remain faithful to the Lenten journey?

Hymn suggestion: The U.S. Bishops' Appendix to GIRM allows for the singing of seasonal hymns for the entrance and Communion processions during Advent, Christmas, Lent, and Easter. During Lent, however, we can inadvertently make the Communion procession a penitential rite if what we sing, be it a hymn or a psalm, speaks only of sinfulness and the need for conversion. The Communion procession is an eschatological moment, a celebration of arriving at the messianic banquet where all is forgiven, all healed, all made one in Christ. The Communion song, then, always needs an element of joy, praise, or thanksgiving. In terms of this Sunday an appropriate Communion song would be one in which the assembly sings both their need for repentance and their praise for God's mercy. For example, "Give Thanks to Our God" [BB] balances the text of Psalm 130—"If you, O Lord, mark our iniquities, Lord, who can stand?"—with the refrain "Give thanks to our God, who is Love, whose mercy endures forever. Give thanks to our God, who is Faithfulness, whose mercy endures forever."

✠ SPIRITUALITY

Gospel

Luke 2:41-51a; L543

Each year Jesus' parents went to
    Jerusalem for the feast of Passover,
  and when he was twelve years old,
  they went up according to festival
    custom.
After they had completed its days, as
    they were returning,
  the boy Jesus remained behind
    in Jerusalem,
  but his parents did not know it.
Thinking that he was in the caravan,
  they journeyed for a day
  and looked for him among their
    relatives and acquaintances,
  but not finding him,
  they returned to Jerusalem to look
    for him.
After three days they found him in the
    temple,
  sitting in the midst of the teachers,
  listening to them and asking them
    questions,
  and all who heard him were astounded
    at his understanding and his answers.
When his parents saw him,
  they were astonished,
  and his mother said to him,
  "Son, why have you done this to us?
  Your father and I have been looking for
    you with great anxiety."
And he said to them,
  "Why were you looking for me?
  Did you not know that I must be in my
    Father's house?"
But they did not understand what he
    said to them.
He went down with them and came to
    Nazareth,
  and was obedient to them.

See Appendix A, p. 262, for other readings.

Reflecting on the Gospel

We have many terms indicating weak persons (for example, "backbone of a jellyfish," "milk toast") and all of them imply that we hold people whom we consider weak in less than high regard. Isn't it interesting that in this gospel, after searching for Jesus, it is *Mary* who speaks to Jesus, not Joseph? On the surface we might ask who wore the pants in that family? Joseph is not prominent in this passage nor, for the most part, in the rest of the gospel. Yet, we celebrate a solemnity in honor of Joseph. The Church is telling us to look deeper.

Joseph is truly no weak person; he was chosen to be the foster father of Jesus and by his very silence teaches us much about the strength needed for our salvation journey. The Scriptures underscore that God is the Father of Jesus ("my Father's house") and the Son of David (see first reading and psalm) and in this seem to minimize the role of Joseph. But hints in the gospel lead us to think of Joseph as playing an active role in salvation history and as a model for our own Christian living.

Since the Holy Family was in Jerusalem for the Passover, we can conclude that they were a devout Jewish family fulfilling their religious obligations. We can imagine that weekly on the Sabbath Jesus would have accompanied Joseph to the synagogue in Nazareth and there learned his religious obligations like every other young Jewish boy. No doubt Joseph's fidelity to Jewish custom instilled in Jesus a desire for "his Father's house." When Jesus returned home with Mary and Joseph to Nazareth and "was obedient to them," we can surmise it was Joseph who taught Jesus the obedience that would prepare him for the more demanding obedience to his Father in heaven, an obedience that led him to Jerusalem and the cross.

Joseph's quiet strength no doubt had a great influence on the religious education of Jesus. By Joseph's willingness to let Jesus acknowledge his rightful claim—Son of David and Son of God—Joseph models for us the very dying to self that is an embodiment of the paschal mystery. Joseph died to self so that Christ's mission could be accomplished. His dying led to the new life that he shares now with his foster Son in life eternal. Joseph is surely deserving of the honor we grant him on this festival.

Living the Paschal Mystery

Joseph models more for us than the dying to self and rising to divine life of the paschal mystery (as significant as that is). He also models that the ordinary way we live our baptismal commitment to enter into the dying and rising of Jesus is through fulfilling faithfully the regular demands of Christian living. Living the paschal mystery means nothing less than being faithful to an everyday yes to God.

The quiet strength of Joseph reminds us that our Christian living doesn't have to be in big, showy ways. Joseph-like Christian living is searching diligently for Jesus in our own lives. This might mean renewing our efforts to be faithful to daily prayer. It might mean seeing Jesus in the person who annoys us by recalling that the other is a member of the body of Christ, too. It might mean that we believe more strongly that we ourselves are the body of Christ so that we can be God's presence to others. Joseph teaches us that dignity isn't in extolling what we do but in quietly knowing who we are—sharers in God's plan of salvation.

Focusing the Word

Key words and phrases from the gospel: your Father and I, my Father's house

To the point: The readings, like Christian tradition, eclipse the role of Joseph by directing our attention to God as the Father of Jesus (gospel) and David as the ancestor of Jesus (first reading); even the psalm refers to "the Son of David." In this way was Joseph an embodiment of the paschal mystery and a pattern for our Christian life: he is diminished so Christ is magnified.

Model Penitential Rite

Presider: We take a day during our Lenten penance to honor St. Joseph, one who was ever faithful to God's plan of salvation. As we prepare to celebrate this liturgy, let us examine our own faithfulness to Christian living . . . [pause]

Lord Jesus, you are the foster Son of Joseph to whom you were obedient: Lord . . .

Christ Jesus, you astounded the teachers in the Temple with your answers: Christ . . .

Lord Jesus, you taught us obedience to your Father in heaven: Lord . . .

Model General Intercessions

Presider: Let us ask St. Joseph to intercede for us that we might always be obedient sons and daughters of our heavenly Father.

Response:

Lord, hear our prayer.

Cantor:

we pray to the Lord,

Through the intercession of St. Joseph, may the Church be a model of Christian dying to self . . . [pause]

Through the intercession of St. Joseph, may world leaders be obedient to God's laws of righteousness and justice . . . [pause]

Through the intercession of St. Joseph, may the weak and lonely find strength and solace in God . . . [pause]

Through the intercession of St. Joseph, may each of us come to new life in God . . . [pause]

Presider: Father in heaven, you are attentive to the needs of your faithful children: through the intercession of St. Joseph hear our prayers that one day we might enjoy everlasting life with you. We ask this through Christ our Lord. **Amen.**

✝ SPIRITUALITY

Gospel

Luke 15:1-3, 11-32; L33C

Tax collectors and sinners were all
   drawing near to listen to Jesus,
but the Pharisees and scribes began
   to complain, saying,
"This man welcomes sinners and
   eats with them."
So to them Jesus addressed this
   parable:
"A man had two sons, and the
   younger son said to his father,
'Father give me the share of your
   estate that should come to me.'
So the father divided the property
   between them.
After a few days, the younger
   son collected all his belongings
and set off to a distant country
where he squandered his inheritance
   on a life of dissipation.
When he had freely spent everything,
   a severe famine struck that country,
and he found himself in dire need.
So he hired himself out to one of the
   local citizens
who sent him to his farm to tend the
   swine.
And he longed to eat his fill of the pods
   on which the swine fed,
but nobody gave him any.
Coming to his senses he thought,
   'How many of my father's hired
      workers
have more than enough food to eat,
but here am I, dying from hunger.
I shall get up and go to my father and I
   shall say to him,
   "Father, I have sinned against heaven
      and against you.
I no longer deserve to be called your
   son;
   treat me as you would treat one of
      your hired workers."'"

Continued in Appendix A, p. 263.

Reflecting on the Gospel

Most young adults chomp at the bit to leave home and get out on their own, thinking this is the way they can do what they want. No more adults in authority telling them what to do—they are quite capable of ordering their own lives. Frequently these young folks find out just how expensive living is, and paying for rent, food, utilities, transportation, etc., isn't as easy as it looks. Some of them, quite chagrined, are forced to move back home to get out of debt and begin again. We can identify with the young man in the gospel who is chomping at the bit to leave home. He is even bold enough to ask for his share of the inheritance! Some of us can even identify with the older brother who gets angry with his father who greets his wayward and broken brother with forgiveness and a feast.

By now, the Fourth Sunday of Lent, perhaps some of us have grown enough to begin to identify with the father who is a model of mercy and reconciliation. It is the father who models for us paschal mystery living. It is the father in the parable who models for us the mercy of our heavenly Father—mercy that not only reconciles but offers a feast.

Once again we see that repentance reveals the dying and rising of the paschal mystery at work. The prodigal son is brought to repentance because he is in dire need; he is "dying from hunger." There is nothing he does to deserve the response of the father except to return. Yet, his decision to repent (turn from death) is met by more than mere sustenance; he is given a feast.

What leads *us* to decide to repent? Like the prodigal son, our "changing our minds" is probably precipitated by some specific catalyst—probably not physical starvation, but possibly some spiritual starvation. The penance of Lent is the external factor that brings us to realize our life is much richer when we turn from our sinful ways and turn to God who gives life.

By contrast, the older brother isn't able to see the generosity in which he already shares ("everything I have is yours"); this generosity just doesn't seem to be enough of a catalyst to bring him to choose the feasting. God has already lavished us with every good thing; what is the catalyst that brings us back, that brings us to choose the feasting?

For all of us, the invitation to repent is always there and we know the conclusion—repentance leads to feasting, dying leads to new life. If forgiveness and feasting is what happened to the younger son, we can be assured that it will happen to us.

Living the Paschal Mystery

Our human tendency is to think we can make a go of life on our own. If we are happy to settle for minimums, some of us can muddle through life reasonably happy. This parable reminds us that God offers us much more. If we choose to die to self ("coming to [our] senses") and return to God, we are greeted with forgiveness and feasting. However, our heavenly Father's Feast isn't a matter of welcoming us back as the sons and daughters we were, but actually transforms us into more perfect sons and daughters sharing in divine life. Our feasting is on much more than a fattened calf; the Feast to which we are invited is nothing less than the Body and Blood of the Son. Repentance is the way we pass from death to life. Repentance is the way we pass from Ash Wednesday ashes to Easter feasting.

Focusing the Word
Key words and phrases from the gospel: life of dissipation, coming to his senses, father . . . embraced him, was dead . . . come to life again

To the point: When the prodigal son "come[s] to his senses" (i.e., repents) he returns home hoping for minimal expectations: a place as servant and enough to eat. Unexpectedly, the merciful father embraces him and offers him much more: acceptance as son and a feast. By repentance we receive much more than our own minimal expectations: we pass from death to life.

Connecting the Word
to second reading: The "ministry of reconciliation" given us by God places us in the role of the merciful father.

to Catholic culture: Often this gospel is used for penance services with a focus on repentance and forgiveness, ending with sacramental absolution. The real end of the parable (and of the sacrament) is new life.

Understanding the Word
Repentance: "Coming to his senses": Repentance, announced so urgently in last Sunday's parable of the barren fig tree, is illustrated more tenderly in this Sunday's familiar story of the "prodigal son." Repentance is presented under a number of images. It is dramatized geographically: sin is going away from home "to a distant country," repentance is returning. It is presented metaphorically in two sets of images: sin is being lost and dead, repentance is being found and coming back to life. Repentance is also described psychologically: it is "coming to his senses."

This last expression, "coming to his senses" (15:17) in Greek is "he came to himself." It implies that the son's disdain for his father's property, his departure from home, his foolish management of the funds, his "life of dissipation," and his employment herding swine (according to the rabbis, a forbidden profession; *b. Baba Qamma* 82b), results in alienation from himself. Today we might say that he'd lost his identity, his sense of self. Moreover, as he himself acknowledges, he no longer deserves to be called his father's son. Cut off from self, father, family, and homeland, his alienation is complete. This is a rather good existential description of sin. But Luke, the storyteller, uses visual images to convey the desperate lad's plight: the measure of how low he has sunk is that even pigs eat better than he!

Thus, when the story informs us that "he came to his senses [= himself]," we are at a dramatic turning point. Though he no longer has any financial, legal, or moral claim on his father, and though he has abandoned his ties of kinship, he realizes that his father is the kind of man who might mercifully hire him as a servant. Sin has effects. It changes relationships. No longer worthy to be a son, "he comes to himself" as a servant. Even in this reduced circumstance, "coming to his senses" holds out the hope of change: repentance and a return to self and home is possible. The measure of the Father's mercy is that he restores his identity as "my son."

ASSEMBLY & FAITH-SHARING GROUPS
- Of the various characters in this gospel, this Lent I am more like . . . because . . .
- The people who regularly help me to "come to my senses" and get my life back on track are . . .
- The people who need this from me this Lent are . . .

PRESIDERS
The father returned to the younger son much more than he expected.
The *more-than-expected* I have received from the Father is . . .
My ministry embodies this prodigal Father when . . .

DEACONS
What I have experienced about being "lost" and "found" helps me serve others in their faith journeys by . . .

HOSPITALITY MINISTERS
The Pharisees and scribes complain about whom Jesus welcomes.
With whom I (we as parish) need to be more inclusive is . . .

MUSIC MINISTERS
My music ministry enables the assembly to feast on God when . . .
I have feasted on God when . . .

ALTAR MINISTERS
My ministry is not only about *serving at* Mass; more significantly, it is about *serving out* the Father's compassion. One to whom I need to *serve out* compassion is . . .

LECTORS
Spirit-filled preparation with the word entails hearing, living, proclaiming.
The word I hear today is . . .
I will have the opportunity to live it when . . .

EUCHARISTIC MINISTERS
The father is the one who goes out to both sons and invites them to the feast. Imitating this compassionate father, the one I need to invite back to the Feast is . . .

Model Penitential Rite

Presider: God is our merciful Father who always welcomes us sinning children back with forgiveness and feasting. To prepare to celebrate this eucharistic feast, let us repent of our sinfulness . . . [pause]

   Confiteor: I confess . . .

Appreciating the Responsorial Psalm

The verses of this responsorial psalm move back and forth between first-person declaration ("I will bless . . ."; "I sought the Lord . . .") and direct address ("Glorify the Lord . . ." ; "Look to him . . ."). This grammatical structure implicates us directly in the psalm and the readings. We are the ones who have tasted the goodness of the Lord and now call upon the lowly to cry for help and be saved. We are the Israelites once enslaved in Egypt who, having survived the terrible desert journey, now feast in the land of God's deliverance (first reading). We are the prodigal son once distant and dissipated who, having crossed the terrain of regret and repentance, now feast at our father's table (gospel). We are the ones who, having become a new creation in Christ (second reading), are now ambassadors of the message: repent, come home, the feast is ready and—oh, so good—it is God.

Model General Intercessions

Presider: Aware of God's mercy and forgiveness, let us pray with confidence to this prodigal Father.

Response:

Lord, hear our prayer.

Cantor:

we pray to the Lord,

That the Church be quick to open her arms to repentant sinners, welcoming them back to the feasting table . . . [pause]

That world leaders govern in such a way that everyone shares in the feast of this good earth's resources . . . [pause]

That sinners come to their senses and ask for God's forgiveness and mercy . . . [pause]

That each of us be ambassadors of reconciliation in our families, among our friends, and in our places of work . . . [pause]

Presider: Merciful God, you forgive sinners and welcome them back to your love and care: hear these our prayers that we might one day be with you at your everlasting banquet table. We ask this through Christ our Lord. **Amen.**

OPENING PRAYER
Let us pray

Pause for silent prayer

Father of peace,
we are joyful in your Word,
your Son Jesus Christ,
who reconciles us to you.
Let us hasten toward Easter
with the eagerness of faith and love.

We ask this through our Lord Jesus Christ,
    your Son,
who lives and reigns with you and the
    Holy Spirit,
one God, for ever and ever. **Amen.**

FIRST READING
Josh 5:9a, 10-12

The LORD said to Joshua,
    "Today I have removed the reproach of
        Egypt from you."

While the Israelites were encamped at
    Gilgal on the plains of Jericho,
    they celebrated the Passover
on the evening of the fourteenth of the
    month.
On the day after the Passover,
    they ate of the produce of the land
    in the form of unleavened cakes and
        parched grain.
On that same day after the Passover,
    on which they ate of the produce of the
        land, the manna ceased.
No longer was there manna for the
    Israelites,
    who that year ate of the yield of the
        land of Canaan.

RESPONSORIAL PSALM

Ps 34:2-3, 4-5, 6-7

R℣. (9a) Taste and see the goodness of the Lord.

I will bless the LORD at all times;
   his praise shall be ever in my mouth.
Let my soul glory in the LORD;
   the lowly will hear me and be glad.

R℣. Taste and see the goodness of the Lord.

Glorify the LORD with me,
   let us together extol his name.
I sought the LORD, and he answered me
   and delivered me from all my fears.

R℣. Taste and see the goodness of the Lord.

Look to him that you may be radiant with
      joy,
   and your faces may not blush with
         shame.
When the poor one called out, the LORD
      heard,
   and from all his distress he saved him.

R℣. Taste and see the goodness of the Lord.

SECOND READING

2 Cor 5:17-21

Brothers and sisters:
Whoever is in Christ is a new creation:
   the old things have passed away;
   behold, new things have come.
And all this is from God,
   who has reconciled us to himself
      through Christ
   and given us the ministry of
      reconciliation,
   namely, God was reconciling the world
      to himself in Christ,
   not counting their trespasses against
      them
   and entrusting to us the message of
      reconciliation.
So we are ambassadors for Christ,
   as if God were appealing through us.
We implore you on behalf of Christ,
   be reconciled to God.
For our sake he made him to be sin who
      did not know sin,
   so that we might become the
         righteousness of God in him.

or, these readings from Year A:

1 Sam 16:1b, 6-7, 10-13a
Ps 23:1-3a, 3b-4, 5, 6
Eph 5:8-14
John 9:1-41

About Liturgy

Sin affects the whole body: As each of us grows in our awareness of being members of the body of Christ, we also grow in our understanding that there is no such thing as a "private" sin. As the prodigal son returned to his merciful father and declared that he had "sinned against heaven and against" his father, so each time we choose the death-dealing blow of sin we affect all other members of the body. There can be many motivations for repentance besides "dying from hunger" and dire necessity. One strong motivation might be our genuine Christian love for one another; if I sin, I weaken the body. At the same time, when I repent and seek reconciliation, I make the body stronger. Repentance and a worthy reception of the Sacrament of Penance help us pass from death to life.

This is about the time in Lent when most parishes offer Lenten communal penance liturgies. Part of our preparation for this wonderful opportunity to repent and be forgiven ought to be a serious consideration of how our sin affects those with whom we live, work, and spend our leisure time. It is too easy simply to go to confession and list one's sins, being assured of God's forgiveness through the sacramental ministry of the ordained priest! Perhaps recognizing how we hurt others and reaching out to seek their forgiveness, too, might be the best deterrent for sin and the most fruitful motivation to repent.

About Liturgical Music

Cantor preparation: In this psalm you call those who have abandoned God or sinned in any way to repent, come home, and feast on God's mercy. When in your own life have you repented, come home, and tasted God's goodness?

Hymn suggestions: As last Sunday the readings this week celebrate the mercy of God which supports human repentance. An excellent Communion hymn would be Robert Kreutz' "Our Daily Bread" [BB, CBW3] with its refrain, "Father, merciful and gracious, give us now our daily bread. You alone, O Lord, sustain us, by you alone are we fed." Choral arrangements can be found in Choral Praise [OCP #8723 and 9093] and in the choir edition of CBW3.

A good entrance hymn would be "Eternal Lord of Love" [CBW3, G1, G2, GC, RS]. The image in the first verse of God watching and leading the Church on its "pilgrim way of Lent" identifies the Church with the Israelites on their journey to the promised land but it is also reminiscent of the journey home of the prodigal son, with the father compassionately watching for his return. To all—the Israelites in the desert, the Church on her Lenten journey, the prodigal son returning home—the conclusion of the first verse beautifully applies, "Moved by your love and toward your presence bent: Far off yet here the goal of all desire."

MARCH 21, 2004
FOURTH SUNDAY OF LENT

✠ SPIRITUALITY

Gospel Luke 1:26-38; L545

The angel Gabriel was sent from God
   to a town of Galilee called Nazareth,
   to a virgin betrothed to a man named
      Joseph,
   of the house of David,
   and the virgin's name was Mary.
And coming to her, he said,
   "Hail, full of grace! The Lord is with
      you."
But she was greatly troubled at what
      was said
   and pondered what sort of
      greeting this might be.
Then the angel said to her,
   "Do not be afraid, Mary,
   for you have found favor with God.
Behold, you will conceive in your
      womb and bear a son,
   and you shall name him
      Jesus.
He will be great and will be called Son
      of the Most High,
   and the Lord God will give him the
      throne of David his father,
   and he will rule over the house of
      Jacob forever,
   and of his kingdom there will be no
      end."
But Mary said to the angel,
   "How can this be,
   since I have no relations with a man?"
And the angel said to her in reply,
   "The Holy Spirit will come upon you,
   and the power of the Most High will
      overshadow you.
Therefore the child to be born
   will be called holy, the Son of God.
And behold, Elizabeth, your relative,
   has also conceived a son in her old age,
   and this is the sixth month for her
      who was called barren;
   for nothing will be impossible for God."
Mary said, "Behold, I am the handmaid
      of the Lord.
May it be done to me according to your
      word."
Then the angel departed from her.

See Appendix A, p. 263, for other readings.

Reflecting on the Gospel

Most of us handle with relative ease the change of plans that infringe on the predictability that keeps our everyday lives running fairly smoothly, or at least gets us through one day after another. Someone may unexpectedly drop in, so we take the time to listen. A neighbor's car may have broken down, so we take the time to chauffeur them to wherever. The family's been saving money for a special vacation but a relative dies and we spend the vacation money to travel to the funeral. We might grumble a bit, but we take such change of plans pretty much in stride. We can hardly imagine the upset the annunciation must have caused Mary! These change of plans weren't so simple; they demanded of her a total dying to self, not knowing where any of this would lead.

The repentance fundamental to a good Lent involves some kind of "change of plans" in our own lives. None of us, however, has been asked to surrender plans, life, and body to God quite in the way Mary did. At the same time we must not downplay the significance of our own successes at repentance and the surrender of plans we offer God. Even in these little, imperfect ways is God conceived in us and Life comes not only to us but also to the whole world. This solemnity which usually comes during Lent is a wonderful gift the Church gives us to encourage us in our fledgling acts of repentance.

Why do we have such a hard time accepting God's coming to us, God's indwelling in us? For some of us the answer to this question might lie in our disbelief in the dignity God offers us as graced sons and daughters ("The Lord is with you"). If we cannot accept the fact of this grace, then we can hardly accept that we are the instruments of life for others. For some of us the answer to this question might lie in a clash of wills—we are not ready to submit to God ("Behold, I am the handmaid of the Lord") and assert our own wills. This kind of refusal to die to self cannot lead to new life. For some of us the answer to this question might lie in God's being a stranger to us because we don't take sufficient time to express in prayer and righteous deeds our relationship to God ("The Holy Spirit [has] come upon [us]"). God doesn't force life on us; if God is largely an unknown to us we cannot grow in relationship, holiness, and life.

Mary's conception of Jesus was a singular privilege that came from her surrendering her plans, her life, and her body to the will of God. The amazingly good news of this solemnity is that God offers us the same Life that God offered Mary. Like Mary, we too must surrender our plans, our lives, and our bodies so that Jesus Christ can become incarnate in the world through us. May it be done to all of us "according to [God's] word."

Living the Paschal Mystery

Mary probably had no idea at any point in her life that two thousand years later people would be celebrating her surrender of self to God's plans. Mary was a simple maiden who, without understanding fully how or why, gave herself over to God. She was overshadowed by "the power of the Most High." The challenge in our own lives is to let God take over our lives, to let God do the work. We don't have to have all the answers to God's plan for us; we just need to say yes, like Mary. Only by dying can we come to new life and help bring that Life to the whole world.

Focusing the Word

Key words and phrases from the gospel: virgin betrothed, you will conceive, Son of God, I am the handmaid

To the point: The annunciation account begins with Mary's life and future already established—she is betrothed and expecting a typical married life. The message of the angel changed all this. Mary surrendered her plans, her life, and her body to the will of God. From this dying, Life comes not only to her but through her to the whole world.

Model Penitential Rite

Presider: Mary surrendered her plans, her life, and her body to God, and Jesus was conceived and born of her who said yes. As we prepare to celebrate this liturgy, let us ask God for the strength to say yes in our own lives . . . [pause]

Lord Jesus, you were conceived by the power of the Holy Spirit: Lord . . .
Christ Jesus, you are holy, the Son of God: Christ . . .
Lord Jesus, you are the Savior who brings life to all: Lord . . .

Model General Intercessions

Presider: Our loving God hears our prayers and grants us our needs.

Response:

Lord, hear our prayer.

Cantor:

we pray to the Lord,

That all members of the Church may surrender their lives to God for the sake of the life of the world . . . [pause]

That everyone in the world might surrender their wills to God so that they can be saved . . . [pause]

That those who cling to selfishness and self-will might surrender themselves to God . . . [pause]

That each of us here may grow in the fullness of life that God offers . . . [pause]

Presider: O saving God, you bring us life in abundance: hear these our prayers that one day we might enjoy life everlasting with you. We ask this through Christ our Lord. **Amen.**

Let us pray
[that we may become more like Christ
who chose to become one of us]
Pause for silent prayer

Almighty Father of our Lord Jesus Christ,
you have revealed the beauty of your power
by exalting the lowly virgin of Nazareth
and making her the mother of our Savior.
May the prayers of this woman
bring Jesus to the waiting world
and fill the void of incompletion
with the presence of her child,
who lives and reigns with you and the Holy
    Spirit,
one God, for ever and ever. **Amen.**

FOR REFLECTION

• The message of the angel Gabriel changed what Mary had planned and expected for her future. Times when my plans/life had to be changed to follow God's ways are . . .

• I have a hard time accepting God's coming to me (that I "have found favor with God"), because . . .

• It is said, "Imitation is the highest form of flattery."
I honor Mary this day by imitating her virtue of . . .

✝ SPIRITUALITY

Gospel

John 8:1-11; L36C

Jesus went to the Mount of Olives.
But early in the morning he arrived
    again in the temple area,
    and all the people started coming
        to him,
    and he sat down and taught
        them.
Then the scribes and the
    Pharisees brought a woman
    who had been caught in adultery
    and made her stand in the
        middle.
They said to him,
    "Teacher, this woman was caught
    in the very act of committing
        adultery.
Now in the law, Moses commanded us
    to stone such women.
So what do you say?"
They said this to test him,
    so that they could have some charge
        to bring against him.
Jesus bent down and began to write on
    the ground with his finger.
But when they continued asking him,
    he straightened up and said to them,
    "Let the one among you who is
        without sin
    be the first to throw a stone at her."
Again he bent down and wrote on the
    ground.
And in response, they went away one
    by one,
    beginning with the elders.
So he was left alone with the woman
    before him.
Then Jesus straightened up and said to
    her,
    "Woman, where are they?
Has no one condemned you?"
She replied, "No one, sir."
Then Jesus said, "Neither do I
    condemn you.
Go, and from now on do not sin any
    more."

Reflecting on the Gospel

An amazing number of vocabulary words name or imply the interconnectedness among us; for example, various familial terms (mother, father, brother, sister, etc.), coworkers, teammates, peer groups, partners, colleagues, associates, etc. The gospel raises a point of interconnectedness that we would seldom consider: we are interconnected by our sinfulness. The gospel story this Sunday begins and concludes with the adulterous woman's sin; sandwiched in between is the real jewel of the gospel: in their experience with the woman, the people gathered in the temple area were changed as well; they, too, had to acknowledge that they were sinners. Jesus establishes a solidarity among the people—they were *all* sinners.

A story that begins with deathly accusation ends with divine mercy. Where the community's condemnation would have led the adulterous woman to death, Jesus' mercy leads her to new life. A story that begins with exposing the sin of an individual ends with exposing the sinfulness of all. Where the community begins with awareness of the woman's sinfulness, they are transformed through encountering Jesus into awareness of their own sinfulness. A story that begins with human testing of the divine ends with divine invitation to repent. Where narrow focus on application of a law is an excuse for testing the fidelity of Jesus to Jewish covenantal law, Jesus reveals a new order in which all are called to repentance and experience of divine mercy. Jesus' desire for us is not death but new life.

Central to this gospel is not simply the adulterous woman nor even the crowd that comes to a new realization of their own sinfulness. At issue is Jesus' own identity as the divine One who calls us to repentance and offers us divine mercy. We are quick to condemn each other; Jesus assures us, "Neither do I condemn you." We need only acknowledge our sinfulness and turn toward God. This is repentance. It rests in divine encounter and results in truth: our sinfulness, God's mercy, promise of new life.

Living the Paschal Mystery

We are interconnected not only in grace (we are all members of the body of Christ) but also in our sinfulness. The gospel reminds us that we encounter Jesus at our own risk: we will be confronted with the truth of our own sinfulness. But also encounter with Jesus brings hope: in the confrontation and invitation to repent Jesus offers new life (see first reading).

We begin the last third of the Lenten season. Even if we haven't been all that faithful to our chosen Lenten practices, it isn't too late now to resolve to open ourselves to encounter with Jesus so that we can approach Easter with a renewed spirit seeking new life. Like the crowd in the gospel, it is often easier for us to focus on the sins of others than on our own weaknesses. When we are closely connected with others—in family, workplace, etc.—they can easily rub us the wrong way. But also like the crowd in the gospel, we can encounter Jesus and face the truth of ourselves. Lent is a time to encounter Jesus, turn from our sinfulness in repentance, and seek divine mercy. The remarkable good news of this gospel is that by facing and repenting of our own sinfulness we establish new relations with those around us. Acknowledgment of our own sins and how we have hurt others builds us into stronger members of Christ's body.

Focusing the Word

Key words and phrases from the gospel: woman . . . caught in adultery, stand in the middle, Jesus, no one condemned you, do not sin any more

To the point: Though the woman is at the center of the crowd, Jesus is at the center of the story: through his ministry the community's awareness of this woman's sin unexpectedly and ironically reveals their own sinfulness. However, Jesus' ministry does not end with awareness of sin. He leads both to repentance: the woman to sin no more and the community to abandon their condemnation of her ("they went away . . . no one condemned you.").

Connecting the Word

to the first reading and psalm: The national transformation that Isaiah prophesies and the psalm celebrates is personalized in the encounter of this one woman with Jesus.

to Catholic culture: We tend to think of sin as a private matter. The interaction between Jesus, the woman, and the townspeople reminds us that sin is a community matter. So is repentance and reconciliation.

Understanding the Word

Isaiah and national restoration: The first reading, from what scholars call "Second Isaiah" (chapters 40–55), was most likely written in the 540s B.C. by an anonymous prophet living in Babylon during the Exile (597–539). His mission was to offer comfort for his dispirited people (40:1-2) and to prepare them to return to their homeland (48:20; 55:12).

This Sunday's passage begins by recalling the greatest of all God's saving deeds: the Exodus when Moses led the people through the Red Sea. In Isaiah's words, "the LORD . . . opens a way in the sea and a path in the mighty waters" (43:16). At that pivotal moment God destroyed the Egyptian army when they drowned in the Sea: "[The LORD] leads out chariots and horsemen, a powerful army / Till they lie prostrate together, never to rise" (43:17). This is the event that revealed the God of creation as the God of salvation without equal; this was the great event memorialized every year, even to the present day, in the Passover. This is the apex of Israel's saving history. Yet the prophet says, "Remember not the events of the past, the things of long ago consider not" (43:18). Why? God is about to do something that makes the past insignificant. God will once again lead the people out of their captivity in a foreign land, but this time by not dividing a sea: instead, God will build a super-highway through the great Arabian desert that separated Judah from Babylonia (more than 500 miles). Of course, in a desert the greatest need is water, so the Lord will put "rivers in the wasteland" (43:20).

This is God acting on behalf of the entire people. The future God has planned for them is to be restored as a people and a nation in the land God had promised to Abraham. Just as Judah's sin was corporate and merited the punishment of the entire people, deliverance is also corporate. The liberation and restoration Isaiah describes on a national scale is an image for what Jesus enacts on a personal scale for the woman caught in adultery.

ASSEMBLY & FAITH-SHARING GROUPS

• What is satisfying to me in pointing out the sins of others is . . .
What helps me stop this and face my own sinfulness is . . .

• I throw rocks at the sins of others whenever I . . .

• When Jesus has said to me, "Neither do I condemn you," I have felt and/or thought . . .
I have shared this kind of mercy . . .

PRESIDERS

Jesus turns rock-throwing condemnation to an invitation to repentance. Times when I have added to the rock throwing are . . . Times when I have turned condemnation to a call for mercy and repentance are . . .

DEACONS

An example of when Jesus used the sins of another to make me face my own sinfulness is . . .

HOSPITALITY MINISTERS

My hospitality—whether at liturgy or at home—is about extending Jesus' mercy ("Neither do I condemn you") whenever I . . .

MUSIC MINISTERS

Times in my ministry when I need the presence of Christ to help me let go of judging another are . . .
Times when I have experienced Jesus' forgiving presence have been. . . .

ALTAR MINISTERS

My serving is fashioning me into deeper solidarity with the disadvantaged— whether needy for food, shelter, or mercy (like the woman)—whenever I . . .

LECTORS

Like the scribes and Pharisees I have used "the law" to test Jesus (God) and to condemn another. What makes me open and vulnerable before "the law" so that it might test and judge me is . . .

EUCHARISTIC MINISTERS

Like the woman in the gospel there are those who are singled out for condemnation in my community. Beyond liturgy I "feed" them Jesus' mercy and communion by . . .

CELEBRATION

Model Penitential Rite
Presider: In today's gospel we hear about a crowd who brings an adulterous woman to Jesus and accuses her of her sin. We also hear how their encounter with Jesus brings them to acknowledge their own sinfulness. As we begin this liturgy let us open ourselves to encounter God's presence and acknowledge our own sinfulness . . . [pause]

Confiteor: I confess . . .

Appreciating the Responsorial Psalm
The first reading from Isaiah recounts God's mighty acts in restoring Israel as a nation after the Babylonian captivity. As Isaiah asserts, this restoration will make the Exodus look as if it were nothing ("Remember not the events of the past . . . I am doing something new!"). The gospel reading recounts God's acting again to do something new in Jesus. Salvation becomes personalized in the adulterous woman whom Jesus does not condemn but grants new life, both physically and spiritually.

Psalm 126 is our "pinch me" response: we are not dreaming, this is really happening. God does constantly revolutionize our expectations by saving in newer, deeper ways. The readings remind us, however, that the challenge is not just to see but to believe. We must let this new righteousness take possession of us (second reading). We must change our ways and let go of our judgments (gospel). Only then can we "forget what lies behind" and look toward the future (second reading). Only then can we know the past about which we sing is just the beginning.

Model General Intercessions
Presider: God continually calls us to repentance; let us pray for divine mercy as we make our needs known.

Response:

Cantor:

For God's mercy, that all members of the Church repent of their sins . . . [pause]

For God's mercy, that all peoples of the world share in salvation . . . [pause]

For God's mercy, that the unrepentant seek forgiveness . . . [pause]

For God's mercy, that each of us encounter Jesus in one another . . . [pause]

Presider: Merciful God, hear these our prayers that we might share in the new life of your Son Jesus Christ our Lord. **Amen.**

ALTERNATIVE OPENING PRAYER
Let us pray

Pause for silent prayer

Father in heaven,
the love of your Son led him to accept the suffering of the cross
that his brothers might glory in new life.
Change our selfishness into self-giving.
Help us to embrace the world you have given us,
that we may transform the darkness of its pain
into the life and joy of Easter.

Grant this through Christ our Lord.
Amen.

FIRST READING
Isa 43:16-21

Thus says the LORD,
who opens a way in the sea
and a path in the mighty waters,
who leads out chariots and horsemen,
a powerful army,
till they lie prostrate together, never to rise,
snuffed out and quenched like a wick.
Remember not the events of the past,
the things of long ago consider not;
see, I am doing something new!
Now it springs forth, do you not perceive it?
In the desert I make a way,
in the wasteland, rivers.
Wild beasts honor me,
jackals and ostriches,
for I put water in the desert
and rivers in the wasteland
for my chosen people to drink,
the people whom I formed for myself,
that they might announce my praise.

RESPONSORIAL PSALM
Ps 126:1-2, 2-3, 4-5, 6

R̸. (3) The Lord has done great things for us; we are filled with joy.

When the LORD brought back the captives of Zion,
we were like men dreaming.
Then our mouth was filled with laughter,
and our tongue with rejoicing.

R̸. The Lord has done great things for us; we are filled with joy.

Then they said among the nations,
"The LORD has done great things for them."
The LORD has done great things for us;
we are glad indeed.

R̸. The Lord has done great things for us; we are filled with joy.

Restore our fortunes, O LORD,
   like the torrents in the southern desert.
Those that sow in tears
   shall reap rejoicing.

R℣. The Lord has done great things for us;
we are filled with joy.

Although they go forth weeping,
   carrying the seed to be sown,
they shall come back rejoicing,
   carrying their sheaves.

R℣. The Lord has done great things for us;
we are filled with joy.

SECOND READING
Phil 3:8-14

Brothers and sisters:
I consider everything as a loss
   because of the supreme good of
      knowing Christ Jesus my Lord.
For his sake I have accepted the loss of all
   things
   and I consider them so much rubbish,
   that I may gain Christ and be found in
      him,
   not having any righteousness of my
      own based on the law
   but that which comes through faith in
      Christ,
   the righteousness from God,
   depending on faith to know him and the
      power of his resurrection
   and the sharing of his sufferings by
      being conformed to his death,
   if somehow I may attain the
      resurrection from the dead.

It is not that I have already taken hold of it
   or have already attained perfect
      maturity,
   but I continue my pursuit in hope that I
      may possess it,
   since I have indeed been taken
      possession of by Christ Jesus.
Brothers and sisters, I for my part
   do not consider myself to have taken
      possession.
Just one thing: forgetting what lies behind
   but straining forward to what lies
      ahead,
   I continue my pursuit toward the goal,
   the prize of God's upward calling, in
      Christ Jesus.

or, these readings from Year A:

Ezek 37:12-14
Ps 130:1-2, 3-4, 5-6, 7-8
Rom 8:8-11
John 11:1-45

About Liturgy

Why communal dimension of sin and repentance? One of the major challenges of the liturgical renewal of the last four decades has been to shift from approaching liturgy as private prayer to liturgy as a communal celebration of the paschal mystery. Although some still lament the passing of liturgy as devotional time, most in the Church today appreciate the communal dimension of liturgy.

One challenge is to see this communal dimension as resting in a common identity that runs far deeper than our doing the same things together. Not since the early period of the Church has there been such an emphasis on our baptismal identity as the body of Christ. Herein rests the communal dimension of liturgy: through baptism we are plunged into the saving death/resurrection mystery of Christ; as the body of Christ we are called embrace that same death and resurrection. Because we share a common identity, everything we do affects the other members of the body. When we do good, we build up the body. Conversely, when we sin we weaken the body. For this reason sin and repentance can never be mere individual acts; our own sinfulness and repentance affect all others in the body.

A second challenge about the communal dimension of sin and repentance is that we must constantly nurture our bonds in the body of Christ in order for us to come to greater realization of how our actions affect others. In other words, our common identity as body of Christ must become so real for us that we not only believe it in our heads but live it every day. One practical way to bring this home to ourselves is that each time we receive Communion and hear "The body of Christ" we hear this acclamation as a statement of our own identity, too, in addition to acknowledging the real presence of Christ in the Eucharist; let our "Amen" be an affirmation of who we are and a promise that we grow in our awareness of solidarity with each other—in both grace and repentance.

About Liturgical Music

Cantor preparation: As you sing this psalm you do not just retell past events, you establish hope for the future. The great things God has already done are as nothing compared to what God is yet to do for you in Christ. In what way this week might you let Christ take possession of you (second reading) so that you can sing of this hope with conviction?

Hymn suggestion: In her hymn collection *Sing a New Church* [OCP] Delores Dufner offers a set of "Gospel Responses for the Sundays of Lent" for each year of the Lectionary cycle. The verses in each set correspond chronologically with the gospel readings of that year. Because this would replace the liturgical response which belongs to the rite, we take issue with her suggestion that the respective verse be sung by the assembly as a response after the proclamation of the gospel, but suggest instead that the verses be sung consecutively as a hymn. The first three verses could be sung for the entrance hymn or during the presentation of the gifts on the 3rd Sunday. The last three verses could be used in the same way on the 5th Sunday. Or all verses could become the Communion hymn on the 5th Sunday, recapping for the community what their Lenten journey has been and setting the stage for its completion in the celebration of Jesus' death and resurrection. Dufner sets the text to the tune ST. THEODULPH whose association with Passion Sunday aptly connects the unfolding weeks of Lent with their climax.

✠ SPIRITUALITY

Gospel at the Procession with Palms

Luke 19:28-40; L37C

Jesus proceeded on his journey up to
    Jerusalem.
As he drew near to Bethphage and
    Bethany
    at the place called the Mount of
      Olives,
he sent two of his disciples.
He said, "Go into the village opposite
    you,
    and as you enter it you will find a
      colt tethered
    on which no one has ever sat.
Untie it and bring it here.
And if anyone should ask you,
    'Why are you untying it?'
    you will answer,
    'The Master has need of it.'"
So those who had been sent went off
    and found everything just as he had
      told them.
And as they were untying the colt, its
    owners said to them,
    "Why are you untying this colt?"
They answered,
    "The Master has need of it."
So they brought it to Jesus,
    threw their cloaks over the colt,
    and helped Jesus to mount.
As he rode along,
    the people were spreading their cloaks
      on the road;
    and now as he was approaching the
      slope of the Mount of Olives,
    the whole multitude of his disciples
    began to praise God aloud with joy
    for all the mighty deeds they had seen.
They proclaimed:
    "Blessed is the king who comes
    in the name of the Lord.
    Peace in heaven
    and glory in the highest."
Some of the Pharisees in the crowd said
    to him,
    "Teacher, rebuke your disciples."
He said in reply,
    "I tell you, if they keep silent,
    the stones will cry out!"

*See Appendix A, pp. 264–266, for
the Gospel at Mass.*

Reflecting on the Readings

This Sunday is unusual for so many reasons: we begin the holiest of Christian weeks; we wear red vestments even before we put away for another year the red-violet ones of Lent; we fill the sparse environment of Lent with fresh greens; we have two gospel proclamations; we carry palms in procession; the atmosphere is charged with both expectation and contradiction, with joy and soberness.

The gospels this Sunday contradict each other in presenting two very different salvific scenes—the same contradiction that fills this entire Holy Week. The gospel proclaimed before the procession with palms exudes ***confidence*** ("And if anyone should ask you, 'Why are you untying [the colt]?' you will answer, 'The Master has need of it.'"), ***exuberance*** ("the whole multitude . . . began to praise God aloud with joy . . ."), allusion to Christmas ***glory*** ("Peace in heaven and glory in the highest"), ***assurance*** that God's plan of salvation will be fulfilled ("I tell you, if [my disciples] keep quiet, even the stones will cry out!"). On the other hand, the passion gospel proclaims ***false confidence*** ("Lord, I am prepared . . . to die with you"), ***reticence*** ("I do not know him."), ***ignominy*** ("flogged . . . crucify him"), ***scorn*** ("He saved others, let him save himself . . ."). This Holy Week we ***rejoice*** on Holy Thursday and are confronted with ***suffering*** and death on Good Friday; we ***await*** on Holy Saturday and ***embrace*** new life on Easter Sunday. It would seem as though just the contradictions alone leave us straining to grasp the meaning of this week.

The first reading from Isaiah challenges us to allow the word to "rouse" us so that we might not rebel and turn back. As we've moved through the Lenten season we've been invited to lay aside more and more; the second reading reminds us that Jesus laid aside his divinity and even his life for our sake. Jesus lays down high standards for us! The proclamation of the readings and gospels is more than the recitation of historical events; it is an invitation and challenge for us to take up our own cross and participate in the dying and rising mystery of Christ. The very contradictions that surrounded Jesus' life are the same contradictions that drive our Christian living. The real pity of this Holy Week would be that we miss the opportunity to empty ourselves, take up our own cross, and follow Jesus through death to new life. The real triumph of this week would be that we are roused to self-emptying, humility, and obedience that confess in our everyday lives and in all our actions that "Jesus Christ is Lord" (second reading) and thereby witness to and glorify God (passion gospel).

Living the Paschal Mystery

For most of us Holy Week unfolds like many other weeks; we still contend with work, school, preparing meals, doing laundry, cranky folks, the usual triumphs and set backs. These readings for Palm Sunday invite us to make this an extraordinary week—a week that concentrates in a few days the ultimate meaning of our whole lives. We must slow ourselves down and make choices so that this week doesn't go by without our taking the time to enter into its meaning. We celebrate in the liturgies what we live every day—all the dying to self that characterizes truly faithful disciples of Jesus. We are invited to move beyond Simon Peter's empty "Lord, I am prepared . . . to die with you" to making this dying the very heart of our living.

Focusing the Word

Key words and phrases from the readings: rouse them; emptied himself; Lord, I am prepared . . . to die with you

To the point: The mission given to the servant in the first reading is to "speak to the weary a word that will rouse them." Thus the Church rouses us:

- this Sunday—to *hear* in the passion account the self-emptying of Jesus' suffering and death;
- this Holy Week—to *celebrate* in the liturgy our participation in Jesus' suffering, death, and resurrection;
- every day of our lives—to *live* in our daily discipleship the self-emptying service of Jesus.

Connecting the Word

to the second reading: The self-emptying of Jesus that is obvious on the cross had its beginning in the incarnation: Jesus did not cling to his "equality with God" but took on our humanity even "to the point of death."

to culture: Our culture freezes heroes in the past by building monuments and museums to their memory. By contrast, we do more than remember the death and resurrection of Jesus: we make these present in our liturgy and life.

Understanding the Word

Jesus in the passion according to Luke: Because Luke's audience is primarily Greek in background, his portrayal of Jesus heightens Greek heroic virtues and values. Consistent with the famous Greek interest in philosophy and wisdom (Greece was home to Socrates, Plato, Aristotle, and others), Jesus has been presented as a wise man and sage teacher.

The ideal of the Greek hero confronting death was embodied by Socrates who, though innocent, was condemned to death; though he could have avoided death by renouncing his teaching, he chose not to; up to the very moment of his death he is shown teaching his disciples; he faces his execution (death by hemlock) with courage and serenity, willingly taking the cup, drinking the poison, lying down and dying peacefully.

Jesus, too, teaches his disciples to the very end, instructing them about discipleship at the last supper (22:25-30); even as he is arrested, his concern is directed to others, healing the man whose ear was cut off (22:51); walking to his crucifixion, he comforts the women of Jerusalem (23:28-31); on the cross, he extends salvation to the "good thief" (23:39-43). During his trial and death Luke emphasizes the innocence of Jesus: Pilate declares his innocence three times (23:4, 14, 22), and Herod, too, finds no guilt (23:15); finally, the centurion at the foot of the cross declares that Jesus was innocent (23:47). In Mark's gospel the words of the centurion instead reveal Jesus as "the Son of God" (Mark 15:39). Luke shifts the focus to Jesus' innocence.

Gone from Luke's account is Jesus' anguished cry, "Why have you abandoned me?" (Mark 15:34). Instead, Jesus prays that God might forgive those who "know not what they do" (Luke 23:34). Mark's report, "Jesus gave a loud cry and breathed his last" (Mark 15:37), makes it sound like a cry of anguish or agony. Luke reports the content of that cry: "Jesus cried out in a loud voice, 'Father, into your hands I commend my spirit'; and when he had said this he breathed his last" (Luke 23:46). Jesus is innocent, courageous, forgiving, serene—a model for disciples.

ASSEMBLY & FAITH-SHARING GROUPS

- While considering the passion of Jesus the word that rouses me is . . . This rousing word challenges me to . . . The part of discipleship that wearies me is . . .
- Jesus "emptied himself" (second reading) in his passion and death. The occasions for my self-emptying are . . .
- To guarantee that I will walk with Jesus during these holy days I need to . . .

PRESIDERS

What is emptied in me while ministering is . . . (see second reading)
What is exalted in me because of this emptying is . . .

DEACONS

When facing another's cross:
I have fled (like the disciples) when . . .
I have denied for self-preservation (like Peter) by . . .
I have aided (like Simon) by . . .

HOSPITALITY MINISTERS

Hospitality is an embodied word that can rouse the weary (see first reading) while they carry their cross. I need to extend such kindness to . . .

MUSIC MINISTERS

Holy Week places a great many extra demands on music ministers' time and energy. Meeting these demands will be a true surrender of self to participation in Jesus' death and resurrection if . . .

ALTAR MINISTERS

The parts of my life and ministry that rouse me to follow Jesus through his passion and death unto new life are . . .

LECTORS

My life praises the *mighty deeds of God* (see the gospel before the procession with palms) whenever I . . .
My life proclaims *crucify him* (passion) whenever I . . .

EUCHARISTIC MINISTERS

Eating at the Banquet transforms me into God's food for others. The weary (first reading) or abandoned (psalm) who need nourishment from me to persevere in faith are . . .

CELEBRATION

Model Penitential Rite *[used only with the Simple Entrance]*
Presider: Let us begin this solemn Holy Week by resolving to enter in these liturgies with fervor, admit our sinfulness, and ask for God's strength and mercy . . . [pause]

Confiteor: I confess . . .

Appreciating the Responsorial Psalm

It is unfortunate that we only have time to sing a few verses of Psalm 22 on this day which initiates our celebration of the core mystery of our faith. Of all the psalms Psalm 22 is one of the most intricately formulated, a masterpiece of poetry and theology. While the psalmist struggles with an increasing sense of abandonment (from "My God, my God, why have you abandoned me," to "all who see me scoff at me," to violent imagery of destruction and death), he or she also experiences a deepening intimacy with God (the One who is far away and does not answer is also the One who has been present "from my mother's womb"). The psalmist pleads with God to save him or her from extreme suffering and violence, then concludes with an unusually lengthy statement of praise (vv. 23-32). Most lament psalms end in praise generally encapsulated in one or two short verses. Here the praise continues for nearly one-third of the text. Furthermore, the psalmist invites an ever-widening circle to join in the praise: from the psalmist's immediate family, to all of Israel, to all nations, to generations yet unborn, to even the dead.

Psalm 22 sheds significant light on our understanding of the passion, both for Christ and for ourselves. God is not distant from the suffering, but very near. And the depth of suffering is the wellspring of the most profound praise. As we enter Holy Week we need to pray the entirety of Psalm 22 so that the few verses given in the Lectionary can carry the text's full meaning and give us the understanding and courage we need.

Model General Intercessions

Presider: Let us pray that we enter into this Holy Week with fervor and unite ourselves with Christ's suffering and death so that we might share in his Easter joy.

Response:

Lord, hear our prayer.

Cantor:

we pray to the Lord,

That all members of the Church always be models of self-emptying disciples . . . [pause]

That all peoples in the world be roused to surrender to charity and justice so that they might enjoy salvation . . . [pause]

That those who are scorned and those who suffer might be comforted by Jesus' passion, death, and resurrection . . . [pause]

That each of us take sufficient time this week to enter fervently into the paschal mystery being celebrated . . . [pause]

Presider: Saving God, you sent your only-begotten Son to save us from our sins: strengthen our resolve to surrender ourselves to your will so that we might be fitting disciples of your Son. We ask this through that same Son, Jesus Christ our Lord. **Amen.**

OPENING PRAYER

Let us pray

Pause for silent prayer

Almighty, ever-living God,
you have given the human race Jesus
    Christ our Savior
as a model of humility.
He fulfilled your will by becoming man
and giving his life on the cross.
Help us to bear witness to you
by following his example of suffering
and make us worthy to share in his
    resurrection.

We ask this through our Lord Jesus Christ,
    your Son,
who lives and reigns with you and the
    Holy Spirit,
one God, for ever and ever. **Amen.**

FIRST READING

Isa 50:4-7

The Lord GOD has given me
    a well-trained tongue,
that I might know how to speak to the
    weary
    a word that will rouse them.
Morning after morning
    he opens my ear that I may hear;
and I have not rebelled,
    have not turned back.
I gave my back to those who beat me,
    my cheeks to those who plucked my
        beard;
my face I did not shield
    from buffets and spitting.

The Lord GOD is my help,
    therefore I am not disgraced;
I have set my face like flint,
    knowing that I shall not be put to
        shame.

RESPONSORIAL PSALM

Ps 22:8-9, 17-18, 19-20, 23-24

℟. (2a) My God, my God, why have you abandoned me?

All who see me scoff at me;
    they mock me with parted lips, they
        wag their heads:
"He relied on the LORD; let him deliver him,
    let him rescue him, if he loves him."

℟. My God, my God, why have you abandoned me?

96

Indeed, many dogs surround me,
    a pack of evildoers closes in upon me;
they have pierced my hands and my feet;
    I can count all my bones.

℞. My God, my God, why have you abandoned me?

They divide my garments among them,
    and for my vesture they cast lots.
But you, O LORD, be not far from me;
    O my help, hasten to aid me.

℞. My God, my God, why have you abandoned me?

I will proclaim your name to my brethren;
    in the midst of the assembly I will
        praise you:
"You who fear the LORD, praise him;
    all you descendants of Jacob, give glory
        to him;
revere him, all you descendants of Israel!"

℞. My God, my God, why have you abandoned me?

SECOND READING
Phil 2:6-11

Christ Jesus, though he was in the form of
    God,
    did not regard equality with God
        something to be grasped.
Rather, he emptied himself,
    taking the form of a slave,
    coming in human likeness;
    and found human in appearance,
    he humbled himself,
    becoming obedient to the point of
        death,
    even death on a cross.
Because of this, God greatly exalted him
    and bestowed on him the name
    which is above every name,
    that at the name of Jesus
    every knee should bend,
    of those in heaven and on earth and
        under the earth,
    and every tongue confess that
    Jesus Christ is Lord,
    to the glory of God the Father.

About Liturgy

". . . sweat became like drops of blood . . ." The only time we hear the story of Jesus at the Mount of Olives is on Palm Sunday with one of the three synoptic passion accounts. This year, in the account from Luke, there is included a provocative detail: "He was in such agony and he prayed so fervently that his sweat became like drops of blood falling on the ground." It is tempting to think that because Jesus was the divine Son of God that the decision to be faithful to God's will even to suffering and death was easy. This scene tells us otherwise. Because it is only one tiny part of the whole passion account, Jesus' agony in the garden can easily be overlooked. Yet, this detail indicates precisely to what extent we must struggle to enter into these Holy Week liturgies—conform ourselves to God's will even if it costs us our very life. Add to this reflection the fact that for Jews blood is the seat of life, and we see how already in the decision to be faithful Jesus' life already was ebbing out. Decision-making is not easy. Decision-making that demands the very self-emptying the passion proclaims is even more difficult. Just as an angel strengthened Jesus to say "not my will but yours be done," so will we be strengthened to make the same commitment of self-sacrifice.

Participation in the passion gospels: Some assembly members claim that they feel more engaged in the gospel reading when they use both senses of hearing and sight, and prefer to read along with the passion account. The issue here isn't more active involvement as it is surrender to the word of God being proclaimed. An example might help: when a young man proposes marriage to his lady love, he doesn't give her a text to read while he speaks his proposal to make sure she pays attention. The quality of his voice, intensity of his eye contact, eagerness of his body language all convey that something important is happening. This is the kind of engagement demanded by the proclamation of the gospel. It is entirely relational—between lector and assembly and between Christ and Christian—rather than an exercise in hearing and reading.

About Liturgical Music

Cantor preparation: To sing this psalm well you must take some time to pray the full text of Psalm 22. You sing not only about Christ's suffering but about his transformation into new life through his suffering and death. You sing about your own transformation as well, for through baptism you have been incorporated into Jesus' death and resurrection. How willing are you to undergo this transformation? How willing are you to invite the assembly to do so?

Procession with palms: Since the procession (or solemn entrance) which opens this Sunday's liturgy is meant to symbolize the assembly's full-bodied willingness to enter into the mystery of the cross and resurrection, it needs to be done with as many assembly participants as possible. Leading the music will take logistical planning especially if the procession begins in a place other than the church. If there is a large choir, they might flank the beginning and end of the procession to support the singing. Or they might divide into smaller groups placed at strategic points among the processors. Another option is to begin with everyone standing in place to sing a well-known Christ the King hymn, then processing in profound silence to the door of the church (or into the body of the church). Process slowly and reflectively, letting each step truly be a choice to move closer to the cross. Processing in silence will take some catechesis of the assembly, but doing it can move them from historical reenactment of Jesus' entry into Jerusalem to actual enactment of their here-and-now choice to walk with Jesus to the cross.

Easter Triduum

✝ SPIRITUALITY

TRIDUUM

"Triduum" comes from two Latin words (*tres* and *dies*) which mean "a space of three days." But since we have four days with special names—Holy Thursday, Good Friday, Holy Saturday, and Easter Sunday—the "three" may be confusing to some. The confusion is eliminated when we understand how the days are reckoned. On all high festival days the Church counts a day in the same way as Jews count days and festivals; that is, from sundown to sundown. Thus, the Triduum consists of *three* twenty-four-hour periods that stretch over four days. The Easter Triduum begins at sundown on Holy Thursday with the Mass of the Lord's Supper and concludes with Easter evening prayer at sundown on Easter Sunday; its high point is the celebration of the Easter Vigil (GNLYC no. 19).

SOLEMN PASCHAL FAST

According to the above calculation, Lent ends at sundown on Holy Thursday; thus, Holy Thursday itself is the last day of Lent. This doesn't mean that our fasting concludes on Holy Thursday, however; the Church has traditionally kept a solemn forty-hour fast from the beginning of the Triduum to when the fast is broken at Communion during the Easter Vigil.

Reflecting on the Triduum

The neighborhood had a number of stray cats on the loose. As cats do, they had multiplied over and over so by now they were down to the "nth" generation. With each subsequent litter they became less domesticated and wilder. At the beginning of Holy Week one of the younger cats had her first litter. She took care of them well until she got hungry; then off she went in search of food. She must have forgotten all about her newborn little ones; in the cold of the night two froze to death without the mother's warm protection and two were crying from hunger. They, too, soon died. This young, wild mother did not know how to take care of her little ones. So they died. Somehow, in the subsequent generations, the instinct to sacrifice her own needs for the little ones—especially the newborn—was lost. And the result was death.

"Sacrifice" is something from which we all tend to recoil. Giving up something we want, delaying our own needs' gratification, inconveniencing ourselves for the sake of others isn't something we naturally do. Since Adam and Eve's fall in the Garden of Paradise, it seems like the God-like tendency to care for others has been "bred" out of us. These next days of entering into Jesus' paschal mystery through the Triduum liturgies and our own everyday living can be a clarion call to us, reminding us that we were created in God's image and that means we love with an unselfish love, we give without counting the cost, we sacrifice without recoiling. These are days in which we relearn the deepest meaning of sacrifice.

In ancient Israel sacrifice was the backbone of the people's religious expression. Sacrifice originated as an act of worship and a way for a people to draw near to God. Although there were both animal and grain offerings, perhaps the most symbolic and telling for us during these days of the Triduum are the animal sacrifices. A pure, unblemished animal would be offered to God. The surrender of a prized, living thing clues us that sacrifice is intimately related to *life*. And here's the twist: the animal sacrifices its life—its dying is an offering to God—so that life might return to the people as a gift from God. Death brings new life. Further, since blood was considered to be the seat of life, the sprinkling of the sacrificed animal's blood upon the people was key: this symbolized the return of life from God to them. Spilling blood made possible receiving blood (life).

All sacrifice, then, required a surrendering of life for the sake of the people. This observation offers a context for interpreting these three days: Jesus surrendered his life for the sake of the people so that we might live. **Holy Thursday/Good Friday:** each time we share in Eucharist we don't have the blood sprinkled upon us but actually take the Blood *within us* for the sake of our own life and, ultimately, for the sake of another; Jesus' own sacrifice of life invites a sacrifice of our own lives. **Holy Saturday:** at the Vigil we hear the story of salvation in the readings—we hear of God's mighty deeds on our behalf, how much God has continually been faithful in offering us life; but before we can open ourselves to this salvific story we prepare ourselves in the quiet and emptiness of the day, surrendering ourselves to God's still call to celebrate the mystery of salvation. **Easter Sunday:** our life of surrender has prepared us to burst with the joy of new life we celebrate with resurrection. We can dare to sing unending alleluias only when we have surrendered to the unending demands of sacrifice—giving our own selves for the sake of others. Jesus is the model.

Living the Paschal Mystery

The young, neighborhood mother cat had lost her instinct for taking care of her newborn. Apparently, the experienced mother cats among the strays didn't teach her life-giving skills. At this time of celebrating Jesus' dying and rising, we are intensely reminded of God's life-giving skills—God's faithful care for us in the self-surrendering sacrifice of Jesus. Jesus did not shirk from what the Father asked of him: model for us the kind of selflessness that leads to life. Jesus teaches us how to bring life to others by the way he brought life to us. Unlike the stray mother cat, Jesus will never abandon us to death; Jesus took death upon *himself* so that we might live. We only need to learn from him.

Few of us are asked to die—literally, physically—for our faith. Yet the paschal mystery tells us over and over again that the only way to live is through death. The spilling of blood in sacrifice to God brings a communion with God which makes us sacred, holy. Through Jesus' sacrifice on the cross we are enabled to share in God's divine life. But this life has its cost, too: we must, like Jesus, be willing to sacrifice for the sake of others.

The kind of dying that brings us new life is sacrifice of self; opportunities present themselves often during our ordinary daily living. Every act of charity is a surrender of self and communion with the other. If we wait for the huge opportunities for self-sacrifice—like being a martyr for our faith and actually, physically dying—we kid ourselves about the meaning of our participation in the paschal mystery. Our own dying to self comes in the routine of our everyday living. Wiping the child's runny nose with a loving pat on the back is surrendering ourselves for the sake of another. Turning off the TV and spending some quality time in conversation with family members is surrendering. Listening to the lonely senior member of our family or community is surrendering. Guiding our young ones in Christian values and holding a steady line when challenged is surrendering. Not giving in to peer group pressure is surrendering. All these and countless other simple ways of surrendering are how we die to self and bring life not only to others but to ourselves as well. All these and countless other simple ways of surrendering are how we participate in Jesus' paschal mystery. This is how the paschal mystery expresses the mystery of our own Christian living.

The real challenge of these days of the paschal Triduum is to see what we celebrate as being characteristic of our daily living. The paschal mystery isn't just something we celebrate in church while commemorating Jesus' suffering, death, and resurrection. The paschal mystery is a way of life for Christians. We might consider these days—which afford us rich liturgies and, hopefully, a bit more time to spend in prayer and contemplation—as focusing what our daily living all year long is really all about. Jesus models for us a life of self-surrendering sacrifice. He also teaches us that the purpose of this sacrifice is communion with God. The paradox is that our communion with God comes through our caring for others.

As we pray and reflect during these days we might come to a deeper realization that sacrifice isn't something from which we need to recoil. Sacrifice is the means for communion with God and a richer and fuller relationship with each other. Sacrifice is a sure way to die to self; it is also a sure way to a joyful life now and everlasting life to come.

ASSEMBLY & FAITH-SHARING GROUPS

- The way I experience sacrifice in my life is . . .
  The way I experience sacrifice in the lives of others is . . .
- I have found sacrifice to be life-giving when . . .
- The way I see my sacrifices uniting me with Jesus is . . .

PRESIDERS

The self-surrendering sacrifice God is asking of me during this Triduum is . . .
What I have learned to be positive, life-giving aspects of sacrifice are . . .

DEACONS

The liturgical roles of these days that demand the most sacrifice from me are . . . because . . .
The ones that are most life-giving for me are . . . because . . .

HOSPITALITY MINISTERS

The kind of sacrificing that hospitality demands is . . .
This is life-giving for me because . . .
It brings new life to others by . . .

MUSIC MINISTERS

The physical demands of good singing model Christian sacrifice by . . .
In my ministry I have been modeling sacrifice to others by . . .

ALTAR MINISTERS

The way I see the relationship between self-sacrifice and effective service of others is . . .

LECTORS

Ways of proclaiming so that others are drawn into Jesus' mystery of dying and rising are . . .
The kind of self-sacrifice this manner of proclamation demands is . . .

EUCHARISTIC MINISTERS

Jesus' giving his Body and Blood for us is a model for our own self-giving. The way I live and model this kind of self-giving is . . .
What is life-giving about this is . . .

✠ SPIRITUALITY

Gospel John 13:1-15; L39ABC

Before the feast of Passover, Jesus
    knew that his hour had come
    to pass from this world to the Father.
He loved his own in the world and he
    loved them to the end.
The devil had already induced Judas,
    son of Simon the Iscariot, to
    hand him over.
So, during supper,
    fully aware that the Father
        had put everything into
        his power
    and that he had come from
        God and was returning to
        God,
    he rose from supper and took
        off his outer garments.
He took a towel and tied it around his
    waist.
Then he poured water into a basin
    and began to wash the disciples' feet
    and dry them with the towel around
        his waist.
He came to Simon Peter, who said to
    him,
    "Master, are you going to wash my
        feet?"
Jesus answered and said to him,
    "What I am doing, you do not
        understand now,
    but you will understand later."
Peter said to him, "You will never wash
    my feet."
Jesus answered him,
    "Unless I wash you, you will have no
        inheritance with me."
Simon Peter said to him,
    "Master, then not only my feet, but
        my hands and head as well."
Jesus said to him,
    "Whoever has bathed has no need
        except to have his feet washed,
        for he is clean all over;
    so you are clean, but not all."
For he knew who would betray him;
    for this reason, he said, "Not all of
        you are clean."

Continued in Appendix A, p. 267.

Reflecting on the Gospel

The verse before the gospel reads: "I give you a new commandment, says the Lord: love one another as I have loved you." Near the beginning of the gospel proclamation we hear: "He loved his own in the world and he loved them to the end." By juxtaposing these verses we see a startling reality: Jesus not only spoke about and commanded love, he *modeled* love. He did so, surely, by giving his all—his very life—on the cross. But on that first Holy Thursday so long ago he showed us two other models. Indeed, toward the end of this holy night's gospel we hear Jesus say: "I have given you a model to follow." The idea here, from the gospel account, isn't simply to clean the feet of folks; the profound message Jesus modeled is that loving is not simply word but must also be deed. Loving is being servant; loving is giving our body and blood for others. These two really are the same thing: the servant gives self to others for their sake.

In John's gospel we don't have an account of the institution of the Eucharist; on this sacred night we read that account as recorded in Paul's First Letter to the Corinthians: "This is my body that is for you . . . This cup . . . is my blood." By giving his Body and Blood as our nourishment—by inviting us even in this life to already share in the messianic banquet—Jesus models for us a most profound servanthood: the sacrifice of his very body and blood. As if he knew this would be too much for us to sacrifice, he showed us another, much more manageable model: stoop and wash the feet of others. No, John doesn't record the institution of the Eucharist; he does record for us its ultimate meaning and demand.

This sacred night, with its ritual of foot-washing, is a profound reminder of what our Christian living is all about. Jesus invites each of us to be washed and, indeed, we have been washed in the waters of baptism. This plunges us into Jesus' mystery. This demands of us that we, too, become servants to all. This demands that we be willing to stoop and wash the feet of others. Love in this gospel is modeled as something eminently practical: no task is too menial for us, no one is too lowly for us. We have been shown by the Master: stoop and wash the feet of others.

Every parent has washed the feet of their little ones. Health care workers have washed the feet of those for whom they provide daily personal care. We all wash our own feet when we take a bath or shower. Washing feet is a common, daily task. Jesus raises it to a new level: washing feet becomes a symbol of love. The simple gesture of Jesus in the gospel reminds us that love knows no bounds, excludes no one, is a gesture of self-sacrifice.

Yes, Jesus loved us to the end. But the end wasn't the cross. The end is the ongoing invitation to stand at the messianic table and be nourished by the Body and Blood of Christ. We come to the table worthily when we do as the Master has done: empty ourselves in self-sacrifice for the good of others. To follow Jesus means to be washed clean in order that we might serve.

Key words and phrases from the gospel: he loved them to the end, unless I wash you, I have given you a model to follow

To the point: If we should be so bold as to receive the very Body and Blood of Christ for our nourishment, then we should be so humble as to be at the loving service of others, to stoop to wash their feet.

About Liturgy: Special Features of the Ritual

Foot-washing is a metaphor and in the ritual ought to be taken as such. Often this ritual is made too literal—"wash one another's feet" means that anyone may come forward because we think that for the foot-washing to be most meaningful everyone must actually be involved (sometimes hands are washed rather than feet so more can be involved). The foot-washing is a metaphor that relates to us how word and deed come together. Rather than a gesture that we apply literally, it is a brief action that captures for us the significance of the gospel: as Jesus modeled self-sacrificing service to the disciples at the Last Supper and commanded that they go and do likewise, so does the presider model self-sacrificing service and in that commands us to go and do likewise. The purpose of the ritual is not found in literalizing it but in receiving its insight that inspires the essence of Christian living for us—self-sacrificing service of others. We miss the point and the power of the ritual when we literalize it.

Model Penitential Rite

Presider: Each time that we gather to celebrate Eucharist, Jesus' great gift of self to us, we experience Jesus' self-sacrificing love for us. Tonight we ritualize Jesus' love in the washing of feet. Let us prepare for this liturgy—and for the celebration of these three days of the paschal Triduum—by remembering that we are washed in the waters of baptism and made daughters and sons of a loving God. Open your hearts to God's love and prepare yourself to hear God's word and be fed at God's table . . . [pause]

> Lord Jesus, you are our Teacher and Master: Lord . . .
> Christ Jesus, you love us so much you give us your Body and Blood as our nourishment: Christ . . .
> Lord Jesus, you model for us love in both word and deed: Lord . . .

Model General Intercessions

Presider: We confidently make our needs known to a loving and self-sacrificing God.

Response:

Cantor:

That all members of the Church follow Jesus in serving others . . . [pause]

That all people of the world share in God's gift of salvation . . . [pause]

That the hungering of the world be fed physically, emotionally, and spiritually . . . [pause]

That all of us here see in the service modeled by Jesus at the Last Supper an invitation to serve others generously . . . [pause]

Presider: Loving God, you sent your son to nourish us and give his life for us: hear these our prayers that we might follow his example and live our lives for others so that one day we might enjoy life with you forever at the messianic banquet of love. We ask this through that same Son, Jesus Christ our Lord. **Amen.**

OPENING PRAYER

Let us pray

Pause for silent prayer

God our Father,
we are gathered here to share in the supper
which your only Son left to his Church to
    reveal his love.
He gave it to us when he was about to die
and commanded us to celebrate it as the
    new and eternal sacrifice.
We pray that in this eucharist
we may find the fullness of love and life.

Grant this through our Lord Jesus Christ,
    your Son,
who lives and reigns with you and the Holy
    Spirit,
one God, for ever and ever. **Amen.**

FOR REFLECTION

- Foot-washing is a metaphor for serving others. This metaphor is made concrete in my daily living whenever I . . .

- How Jesus' life encourages me to sacrifice for others is . . .

- The way serving others (foot-washing) and being nourished at the eucharistic table are connected for me is . . .

✠ SPIRITUALITY

Gospel

John 18:1–19:42; L40ABC

Jesus went out with his disciples across
    the Kidron valley
  to where there was a garden,
  into which he and his disciples
      entered.
Judas his betrayer also knew the
    place,
  because Jesus had often met
      there with his disciples.
So Judas got a band of soldiers and
    guards
  from the chief priests and the
      Pharisees
  and went there with lanterns,
      torches, and weapons.
Jesus, knowing everything that was
    going to happen to him,
  went out and said to them, "Whom
      are you looking for?"
They answered him, "Jesus the
    Nazarene."
He said to them, "I AM."
Judas his betrayer was also with them.
When he said to them, "I AM,"
  they turned away and fell to the
      ground.
So he again asked them,
  "Whom are you looking for?"
They said, "Jesus the Nazarene."
Jesus answered,
  "I told you that I AM.
So if you are looking for me, let these
    men go."
This was to fulfill what he had said,
  "I have not lost any of those you gave
      me."
Then Simon Peter, who had a sword,
    drew it,
  struck the high priest's slave, and cut
      off his right ear.
The slave's name was Malchus.
Jesus said to Peter,
  "Put your sword into its scabbard.
Shall I not drink the cup that the
    Father gave me?"

Continued in Appendix A, pp. 268–270.

Reflecting on the Gospel

The verse before John's passion gospel might not be what we would expect on Good Friday: "Because of this God greatly *exalted* him." Nor is the opening verse from the first reading what we might expect: "See, my servant shall prosper, he shall be raised high and greatly *exalted*." Exalted? Isn't today a day of sadness? Why speak of exaltation?

John's passion account is quite different from those of Matthew, Mark, and Luke. In the three synoptic accounts the focus is on the suffering Jesus, one falsely accused who goes to an undeserved death. We hear from Matthew's gospel the soul-searing cry "My God, My God, why have you forsaken me?" We can identify more easily with this Jesus—the one who suffers, feels abandoned, remains silent before his accusers. The Jesus of John's passion is much more challenging to us. In this gospel Jesus is the one in charge; he chooses his destiny. It almost seems like he is arranging his own death. When the soldiers and guards come to the garden to get Jesus, it is he who goes out to meet them and identifies himself as the one they are looking for. In his conversation with the high priest Jesus is bold, almost accusatory in his answers—so bold, in fact, that he receives a slap from an indignant temple guard. In John Jesus carries the cross *himself*—this is *his* destiny and he chooses to walk to it. Even on the cross Jesus is in charge, attending to unexpected details—he places his mother and his beloved disciple into each other's care. Finally, it is Jesus who announces "It is finished."

Jesus is the paschal victim; it is he who is sacrificed for us and "it was our infirmities that he bore" (first reading). By giving up his own life, Jesus makes it possible for us to receive life. The greatly unexpected turn of this sacrifice is that by dying Jesus was raised to new life. The communion with God made possible by sacrifice is raised to new heights: now the sacrifice is the very Son of God and the life that is returned is God's very own life. This is why Good Friday is called "good" and why it is a day of quiet exaltation: because Jesus showed us that suffering and death is not all there is. Jesus is exalted because "he learned obedience from what he suffered" (second reading), an obedience that took him through death to life.

Good Friday is more than a step to resurrection; it is a day on which we celebrate Jesus' obedience, his kingship, the everlasting establishment of his reign, his side being opened and himself being poured out so that we can be washed in his very blood and water. The real scandal of the cross isn't suffering and death; the real scandal of the cross is that God is victorious in Christ's obedience. Death has no power over God. Jesus, our high priest, has offered himself obediently and willingly and "became the source of salvation for all" (second reading). No wonder this is a "good" Friday. No wonder we quietly burst with exaltation.

Key words and phrases from the gospel: Jesus . . . went out and said to them, "Whom are you looking for?"; "Is this the way you answer the high priest?"; carrying the cross himself; "Woman, behold your son."; "It is finished"

To the point: The cross is an instrument of suffering; it is also the means to exaltation. Even on Good Friday—the day we commemorate Jesus' passion and death—we cannot lose sight of the end: everlasting exaltation.

About Liturgy: Special Features of the Ritual

The Good Friday celebration of the Lord's Passion is unique as liturgies go—it is a curious mix of both liturgical and devotional elements. We are most familiar with and comfortable with the first part of the liturgy, the Liturgy of the Word. However, even this has something a bit unfamiliar to us: the ten solemn general intercessory prayers.

Structure: The structure of these ten prayers is an ancient one consisting of three parts: an announcement of an intention (sung or said by a deacon or cantor), silent time for the assembly to pray, and then a prayer by the presider that "collects" together all the assembly's individual prayers. This is the same format as the general intercessions at Mass: an intention is announced, there is time for prayer or response, and the presider concludes with a collect. Although we don't have ten intercessions and collects, intentions are included in each of four categories—for the Church, the salvation of all people, those in need, the local community (see GIRM nos. 70–71);

Meaning: These prayers are an exercise of our own share in Christ's priesthood; through them we make intercession to God on behalf of the world for salvation (see GIRM no. 69). Moreover, these are more than merely *saying* prayers. As a response to the word we have just heard proclaimed (see GIRM no. 69), they invite each of us to make the spoken word come alive in our own daily living through deeds on behalf of others. In this way our carrying out these intercessions is a kind of proclamation of faith by which we model for others our own obedient willingness to die for the sake of others. Each time, then, that we pray the general intercessions we are uniting ourselves to the meaning of Good Friday: we are to die to ourselves so that others may have more abundant life.

Suggestions for Music

Singing the solemn prayers: Because of their solemnity the Good Friday solemn prayers are meant to be sung using the simple chant given in the Sacramentary and to include short periods of silent prayer after each statement of intention. If it is not possible to sing these intercessions, they should be spoken with solemnity and with time allowed for the appropriate silences.

Music during the veneration of the cross: As the title of this part of the liturgy indicates, what we honor in this procession is not the One crucified but the Cross which embodies the mystery of his—and our—redemptive triumph over sin and death. Because we are not historicizing or reenacting a past event but ritualizing the meaning of this event for our lives here and now, this procession is not one of sorrow or expiation but of gratitude, of triumph, and of quiet and confident acceptance (the very sentiments expressed in the responsorial psalm). The music during this procession needs, then, to sing about the mystery and triumph of the cross rather than about the details of Jesus' suffering and death. This means that hymns such as "Were You There" are not appropriate here but are better reserved for devotional services such as Stations of the Cross. Examples of hymns which would be excellent for use during this procession are: "We Acclaim the Cross of Jesus [WC]; "O Cross of Christ, Immortal Tree" [WC]; and Genevieve Glen's "O Tree of Life, by Running Stream" [in *Take with You Words,* OCP].

Communion hymn: The imagery used in Sylvia Dunstan's "Eternal Intercessor" [in *In Search of Hope and Grace,* GIA] powerfully combines the death of Christ on the cross with his gift of Body and Blood in the Eucharist. If the Communion procession is lengthy, you could sing "O Sacred Head, Surrounded" first, play a brief instrumental interlude, then sing this text which is set to the same tune.

OPENING PRAYER

Let us pray

Pause for silent prayer

Lord,
by shedding his blood for us,
your son, Jesus Christ,
established the paschal mystery.
In your goodness, make us holy
and watch over us always.

We ask this through Christ our Lord.
Amen.

FOR REFLECTION

- The kind of exaltation I have found coming out of suffering is . . .
- A time when I took upon myself the infirmities of another was . . .
  The way it was life-giving for me was . . .
  How it was life-giving for the other was . . .
- I model for others Jesus' obedience as the paschal victim whenever I . . .
  Such obedience gives life to others by . . .

✦ SPIRITUALITY

Gospel

Luke 24:1-12; L41ABC

At daybreak on the first day of the week
    the women who had come from
        Galilee with Jesus
    took the spices they had prepared
        and went to the tomb.
They found the stone rolled away
        from the tomb;
    but when they entered,
    they did not find the body of the
        Lord Jesus.
While they were puzzling over
        this, behold,
    two men in dazzling garments
        appeared to them.
They were terrified and bowed
        their faces to the ground.
They said to them,
    "Why do you seek the living one
        among the dead?
He is not here, but he has been raised.
Remember what he said to you while he
        was still in Galilee,
    that the Son of Man must be handed
        over to sinners
    and be crucified, and rise on the third
        day."
And they remembered his words.
Then they returned from the tomb
    and announced all these things to the
        eleven
    and to all the others.
The women were Mary Magdalene,
    Joanna, and Mary the mother of
        James;
    the others who accompanied them
        also told this to the apostles,
    but their story seemed like nonsense
    and they did not believe them.
But Peter got up and ran to the tomb,
    bent down, and saw the burial cloths
        alone;
    then he went home amazed at what
        had happened.

Readings in Appendix A, pp. 271–276.

Reflecting on the Gospel

The Easter Vigil is the climax of our whole liturgical year. This is the night when we celebrate light, recapitulate the story of salvation, solemnize initiation sacraments and renewal of baptismal promises, ring out our joyous Easter alleluias. This night, of all nights, we celebrate new life. And as we anticipate the proclamation of the Easter gospel—our first hearing this year of the story of resurrection—we enter into Luke's world and experience in our hearts the puzzlement, wonderment, and, yes, maybe even a little of the nonsense that the proclamation announces. This is the night in which we, too, are invited to remember that Jesus would "be crucified, and rise on the third day." Is our own belief any less challenged by this event than those women who took burial spices to the tomb so long ago?

This is the night when the stones of our Lenten penance are rolled away and we are invited to peer into the empty space and see ourselves in "dazzling garments." This is the night when we announce all these things to anyone who will hear—even though sometimes we are still puzzled at the seeming nonsense. This is the night when God surprises humanity yet another time: he who is dead has risen!

This is the night when Jesus passes from death to life. This is the night when we remember that we, too, "were indeed buried with him through baptism into death" (epistle). This is the night when we celebrate that we, too, "live in newness of life." This is the night when we don't "seek the living one among the dead" because our seeking need go no further than our own selves. By Jesus' resurrection we share in God's divinity; we ourselves become the life and presence of the Risen One.

This is the night when sacrifice makes sense. Sacrificial death is for communion with God. This is the night when Christ's sacrifice and our own self-sacrificing surrender come together into one grand celebration of God's gift of Self to us. This is the night—just this one night—when we can ignore the sting of death because life is so abundant.

This is the night when the announcement of salvation cannot be contained. And so this night has its challenge: the new life isn't simply for our own gain, but so that God can renew creation. "Let there be light" God creatively spoke so long ago. This is the night when God speaks again and now the light is the risen Son. And so the challenge of this night is that we, too, bring light to a world still darkened by disbelief and "slavery to sin" (epistle). In the simple smile, helping hand, listening ear do we make resurrection happen. In the kind word, the self-sacrificing surrender to another, the daily dying to self do we make resurrection happen.

The utter amazement of this night is that while we celebrate Jesus' resurrection, we also celebrate our own new life. No wonder our alleluias cannot be contained. He has risen!

Key words and phrases from the gospel: puzzling over this, terrified and bowed, he has been raised, story seemed like nonsense

To the point: After two thousand years, the story of Jesus' resurrection is still as puzzling, terrifying, and seemingly nonsensical to us as it was to those early disciples. The resurrection doesn't call forth understanding; it calls forth belief. We can only be amazed at what God offers to those of us who have chosen to believe and follow Jesus through death to new life.

About Liturgy: *Special Features of the Ritual*

This is the night when liturgy's symbolism is overgenerous. But perhaps the most pervasive symbol is that of light. The liturgy begins in darkness. Then a spark lights the new Easter fire. From this the paschal candle is lit. Three symbols—fire, paschal candle, light. So much meaning.

Fire: Abraham carried the fire for the holocaust he thought would be his only son. The fiery cloud protected the Israelites but God's glance through it caused the Egyptian army's destruction. Fire can be destructive. It can also be our friend bringing warmth and protection. As we pray in the blessing of the new fire, "inflame us with new hope."

Paschal candle: For fifty days the candle will stand in our midst, a symbol of Christ; but at the end of these fifty days we don't put the paschal candle away. It stands near the baptismal font, reminding us that our baptism is an ongoing yes-commitment to God. From this candle will be lit the baptismal candles of those who will be baptized throughout the year. This candle will stand at the head of the coffin of the faithful departed, lighting their way to "the feast of eternal light." The paschal candle speaks eloquently to us of the meaning of our Christian life: that we are to die and rise with Christ each day of our lives.

Light: "Christ our light." Three times we sing this proclamation. Christ our light is among us. Even when sin and doubt overcome us the light remains steady, beckoning us back to Christ who is our life and light. We share the light among us and are reminded that *together* we dispel darkness. Light, then, can be a symbol for community, for our being the one body of Christ. One little light can be a beacon in the darkness; many lights actually push back darkness so that it is overcome. This is why the Church from earliest times celebrated a light service each evening at prayer (notice that the *Exsultet* refers to "our evening sacrifice of praise"): the light draws us together, makes visible the one body of Christ, and dispels darkness. We do in a solemn ritual this night what the Church does every night: we celebrate Christ our light who is among us. We celebrate that through baptism we are this light for the salvation of the world.

Model General Intercessions

Presider: On this joyous night when we celebrate resurrected life, let us ask God to bring light and wholeness to our darkened world.

Response:

Cantor:

That the Church light the way of all people to Christ's salvation . . . [pause]

That Christ's light dispel the darkness of our broken world and bring peace . . . [pause]

That the newly baptized radiate Christ's new life within them and remain faithful to their promises . . . [pause]

That each of us bring new light and life to all those we meet . . . [pause]

Presider: Redeeming God, you raised your Son to new life that we might share in his glory: hear these our prayers that all might be healed and share in the everlasting glory of your eternal life. We ask this through that same risen Son, Jesus Christ our Lord. **Amen.**

OPENING PRAYER

Let us pray

Pause for silent prayer

Lord God,
you have brightened this night
with the radiance of the risen Christ.
Quicken the spirit of sonship in your
 Church;
renew us in mind and body
to give you whole-hearted service.

Grant this through our Lord Jesus Christ,
 your Son,
who lives and reigns with you and the Holy
 Spirit,
one God, for ever and ever. **Amen.**

FOR REFLECTION

- The way I understand resurrection is . . .
 One way I experience resurrection in my
 daily living is . . .

- The light of resurrected life was brought
 to me when . . .
 I am bringing the light of resurrected life
 to . . . when I . . .

- Obstacles to my experiencing new life
 are . . .
 Aids to my experiencing new life are . . .

✠ SPIRITUALITY

Gospel

John 20:1-9; L42ABC

On the first day of the week,
  Mary of Magdala came to the
    tomb early in the morning,
  while it was still dark,
  and saw the stone removed
    from the tomb.
So she ran and went to Simon
  Peter
  and to the other disciple
    whom Jesus loved, and
    told them,
  "They have taken the Lord
    from the tomb,
  and we don't know where they
    put him."
So Peter and the other disciple went out
  and came to the tomb.
They both ran, but the other disciple
  ran faster than Peter
  and arrived at the tomb first;
  he bent down and saw the burial
    cloths there, but did not go in.
When Simon Peter arrived after him,
  he went into the tomb and saw the
    burial cloths there,
  and the cloth that had covered his
    head,
  not with the burial cloths but rolled
    up in a separate place.
Then the other disciple also went in,
  the one who had arrived at the tomb
    first,
  and he saw and believed.
For they did not yet understand the
  Scripture
  that he had to rise from the dead.

or

Luke 24:1-12; L41C

or, at an afternoon or evening Mass

Luke 24:13-35; L46

See Appendix A, pp. 276–278.

Reflecting on the Gospel

Even on this day when the gospel announces the risen Lord, we feel the contradictions that the resurrection mystery arouses—seeing and believing on the one hand, misunderstanding and confusion on the other. This mystery defies all human understanding. These Easter stories tell us that the resurrection isn't something we understand, but believe and live.

We might take our clue to entering into the mystery from the second reading (from 1 Corinthians). Lent has been the time when we cleared out the old yeast (of "malice and wickedness") "so that [we] may become a fresh batch of dough." Like Christ, our "paschal lamb [who] has been sacrificed," we too must be willing to give ourselves up in the self-sacrifice "of sincerity and truth." Inasmuch as we are the dough, we must be willing to allow others to feast on us. When Paul invites the Corinthians, "let us celebrate the feast," it is truly a startling invitation: as Jesus gave his body on the cross and gives his Body and Blood to us as nourishment, so must we do the same. The only way to open ourselves to the new life that God promises through the resurrection of Jesus Christ is to open ourselves to the needs of others in self-sacrifice. If we try to *understand* this resurrection mystery we will miss it. The readings today invite us to *live* the mystery and in the living of self-sacrifice does God give us the new life that Jesus' resurrection offers.

The gospel identifies three characters: Mary of Magdala, Peter, and the "disciple whom Jesus loved." By not naming him, John can function symbolically—all of us are the "disciple whom Jesus loved." Instead of trying to understand we simply "run" to the mystery and embrace it so that we, like John, can enter into it and see and believe. In John's gospel seeing and believing aren't mental exercises but actions that express one's inner disposition. Thus our belief in the resurrection is a matter of self-sacrifice, of allowing others to "feast" on us.

Even on this Easter day when we rejoice in the resurrected life of Jesus we are reminded that resurrection has its cost: self-emptying for the sake of others. The paradox of Christianity is that death and self-sacrifice aren't presented as negatives to avoid but positive stances to embrace because they are the door into resurrected life. We have the next fifty days of celebrating resurrection to help us grasp in our hearts and daily living that when we reach out to others we ourselves are actually living Jesus' resurrected life. We only need take the time to contemplate this mystery and recognize the good with which God blesses us. We need to see beyond the obvious—an empty tomb and the demands of self-emptying—to the glory that God has bestowed through Christ Jesus.

The alleluia that bursts forth with the news of resurrection captures a heartfelt cry that we be willing to identify ourselves with the dying and rising Christ. Let the feast begin!

Key words and phrases from the gospel: we don't know where they put him, saw and believed, did not yet understand, rise from the dead

To the point: Our seeing and believing in Jesus' resurrection is as much a challenge to us today as it was to the disciples who were eye witnesses. The challenge really lies in seeing and believing the resurrection comes through our own lives of self-sacrifice that bring new life to others.

About Liturgy: Special Features of the Ritual

The U.S. bishops have stipulated that at all Masses on Easter the renewal of baptismal promises takes place. This ritual addition highlights that baptism isn't a once-and-for all ceremony but an ongoing way of Christian living—a commitment to allow our own bodies to be the "feast" for others. Renewing at least annually our baptismal promises reminds us that sharing in Christ's Easter glory means that we also share in his death by dying to our own wills in order to follow God's will.

Since sprinkling the people takes place after the renewal of promises, it is best to use Form C of the penitential rite.

Model Penitential Rite

Presider: Happy Easter! "Happy" because Jesus is risen from the dead. "Happy" because we also share in this resurrection life through our lives of good works for the sake of others. After the homily we will all renew our baptismal commitment in which we promise to avoid evil and do good. Let us prepare ourselves for this happy celebration by emptying ourselves before our redeeming God.

Lord Jesus, you are our resurrection and our life: Lord . . .

Christ Jesus, you are our paschal lamb that has been sacrificed for our redemption: Christ . . .

Lord Jesus, you call us to feast at the banquet of love: Lord . . .

Model General Intercessions

Presider: On this Easter day when we celebrate Jesus' resurrection let us pray that this new life may be accepted by all God's children.

Response:

Lord, hear our prayer.

Cantor:

we pray to the Lord,

May all members of the Church express their seeing and believing in the resurrection by self-emptying lives in service of others . . . [pause]

May all leaders of the world's nations lead others to share in the abundance of new life God offers . . . [pause]

May all those in need have their fill of new life . . . [pause]

May each of us here feast at the table of the Lord so that we might be strengthened to bring Jesus' resurrected life to others . . . [pause]

Presider: O redeeming God, you give us all good things: hear these our prayers that one day we might enjoy life everlasting with you, sharing forever in your banquet of love. We ask this through your resurrected Son, our Lord Jesus Christ. **Amen.**

OPENING PRAYER

Let us pray

Pause for silent prayer

God our Father,
by raising Christ your Son
you conquered the power of death
and opened for us the way to eternal life.
Let our celebration today
raise us up and renew our lives
by the Spirit that is within us.

Grant this through our Lord Jesus Christ,
    your Son,
who lives and reigns with you and the Holy
    Spirit,
one God, for ever and ever. **Amen.**

FOR REFLECTION

- During Lent I tried to get rid of the leaven of sinfulness. The way I see those efforts bursting forth into new life is . . .

- The times in my life when I have run to find the resurrected Jesus (like Peter and the other disciple did) are . . .

- "Seeing" and "believing" in Jesus' resurrection means to me . . .
  The way I try to live this mystery is . . .

Season of Easter

✠ SPIRITUALITY

Gospel

John 20:19-31; L45C

On the evening of that first day of the
week,
  when the doors were locked,
    where the disciples were,
  for fear of the Jews,
  Jesus came and stood in their
    midst
  and said to them, "Peace be with
    you."
When he had said this, he showed
  them his hands and his side.
The disciples rejoiced when
  they saw the Lord.
Jesus said to them again,
  "Peace be with you.
As the Father has sent me, so I
  send you."
And when he had said this, he breathed
  on them and said to them,
  "Receive the Holy Spirit.
Whose sins you forgive are forgiven
  them,
  and whose sins you retain are
    retained."

Thomas, called Didymus, one of the
  Twelve,
  was not with them when Jesus came.
So the other disciples said to him, "We
  have seen the Lord."
But he said to them,
  "Unless I see the mark of the nails in
    his hands
  and put my finger into the nailmarks
  and put my hand into his side, I will
    not believe."

Now a week later his disciples were
  again inside
  and Thomas was with them.
Jesus came, although the doors were
  locked,
  and stood in their midst and said,
    "Peace be with you."

Continued in Appendix A, p. 278.

Reflecting on the Gospel

The gospel stresses coming to belief, but it is only at the very last line of this gospel that we hear the goal of belief: so "that . . . you may have life." Moreover, we can even see *how* we receive that life ("he breathed on them . . . the Holy Spirit") and the fruit of that life (peace and forgiveness).

While we are steeped in this natural life, it is difficult for us to come to terms with resurrected life. This was part of Thomas' problem: he was seeking tangible proofs—seeing and touching—to come to belief, but the resurrected life of Jesus is a *new* life that is beyond tangible proofs. Just how broad is the scope of this new life is hinted at by two temporal references in the gospel.

The first temporal reference is teased out of Jesus' *breathing* on the gathered disciples so they would receive the Holy Spirit. This image of breath takes us *backward* to the beginning of time and creation when God "blew into his nostrils the breath of life, and so man became a living being" (Gen 2:7). God's breath brought life to the first creatures and the breath of the Holy Spirit recreates humankind in new, resurrected life. The second temporal reference occurs in the account of Jesus' second appearance to the disciples, which took place "a week later." The Greek text has "after eight days," a clear reference to eschatological time—a look *forward* to the end of time when all will be fulfilled in Christ.

The last line of the second reading recording John's vision outlines the gamut of temporal references as well: "what you have seen"—Jesus' new life; "what is happening"—the Spirit breathes this new life into us; "and what will happen afterwards"—the transformation of the world toward eschatological time and completion. These temporal references remind us that the resurrection brings a whole new order to creation of which peace and forgiveness are but two manifestations.

We know *to what* our belief is directed: to Jesus and new life. We know *how* we receive new life: through Jesus' gift of the Holy Spirit. We know the *fruit* of this new life: peace and forgiveness. For all this, how do we come to belief without seeing? It seems we are back to Thomas' problem. The first reading gives us a hint about how we might get ourselves out of this seeing/believing impasse. We hear how "many signs and wonders were done among the people." We know this is true when Jesus was publicly ministering; but Acts records how the first disciples carried on Jesus' mission. So much so that if even Peter's shadow fell upon the sick or disturbed "they were all cured." The message here is that Jesus' ministry is continued in the disciples. Seeing these works is seeing Jesus. Seeing these works brings us to belief. More importantly, *our doing* what Jesus did brings us to belief. Believing isn't seeing; it's *doing* the good works of Jesus.

Living the Paschal Mystery

Most of us won't cure anyone when our shadow falls upon them. But this doesn't mean that we don't continue the works of Jesus that lead others to believing. Any good we do for others is overshadowing them with the goodness of Jesus. Any good we do brings this same new, resurrected life to others. We are empowered to do so through the Holy Spirit. All we need do is surrender to God's action within us. We have these fifty days of Easter to come to greater belief. We have our whole lifetime to manifest the good works of our belief.

Focusing the Word

Key words and phrases from the gospel: peace, breathed . . . the Holy Spirit, are forgiven, come to believe, have life

To the point: Thomas dramatizes the struggle of the disciples coming to believe. The struggle is important because the stakes are high: "that . . . you may have life." New life comes through Jesus' *gift* of the Holy Spirit; the *fruit* of this new life is peace and forgiveness.

Connecting the Word

to the fifty days of Easter: All of the gospels of these fifty days of Easter are especially directed to helping us come to greater belief and fuller participation in this new Easter life.

to culture: We are a culture that tends to demand and expect tangible proofs, e.g., through electron microscopes and intergalactic telescopes. We are challenged by the gospel to believe without seeing.

Understanding the Word

New life: Holy Spirit, peace, forgiveness: Though the exact expression "new life" does not occur in the New Testament, we frequently use it as a kind of "shorthand" to describe both the kind of life to which Jesus was raised and what believers have because of Jesus. This Sunday's well-known gospel story conveys the idea of "new life" using different images and vocabulary.

Jesus' new life is described by his ability to come to the disciples despite the locked doors. Though the marks of his death are clear, he is alive nevertheless. The risen Jesus greets the disciples with "Peace," fulfilling his promise: "Peace I leave with you; my peace I give to you" (John 14:27). Seeing him, the disciples rejoice, fulfilling another promise of Jesus: "I will see you again, and your hearts will rejoice" (16:22). Finally, Jesus commissions them by sending them into the world, fulfilling yet again another promise he made when speaking to his Father: "As you sent me into the world, so I sent them into the world" (17:18). The reliability of Jesus' word is stressed for a reason, as we shall soon see.

Then the risen Jesus imparts life to them when "he breathed on them" (20:22) and gave them the Holy Spirit. In the story of creation God breathed the breath of life into the clay man to make him a living being (Gen 2:7; the same Greek word *[emphusao]* is used in John 20:22 and the Greek version of Genesis). The disciples, then, are made anew, or are a new creation, infused with the Holy Spirit. The presence of the Spirit is both the sign of, and the power behind, their extraordinary mission: to forgive sins. Sent, as Jesus was sent, the disciples continue his work by forgiving sins. In the same way that all that Jesus had spoken has been proved true, the disciples (and readers!) are assured that the forgiveness of sins is accomplished.

The abundant signs of new life are these: peace, re-creation by the gift of the Holy Spirit, the mission ("sent"), and the forgiveness of sins.

ASSEMBLY & FAITH-SHARING GROUPS

- Where God is calling me to extend the peace of the risen Lord is . . .
- Forgiving another is an experience of Jesus' new life for me and the other. The new life I receive when offering forgiveness is . . . The new life I gain when receiving forgiveness from another is . . .
- A time when I was like Thomas and doubted was . . . The way Jesus responded to my doubt was . . .

PRESIDERS
The way I could respond more Christ-like when others are doubting is . . .

DEACONS
The doing of my ministry has brought me to greater belief because . . .

HOSPITALITY MINISTERS
My hospitality unlocks doubting hearts to believe in the presence and peace of the risen Lord by . . .

MUSIC MINISTERS
Part of "what is happening" (see second reading) is the community's recognition through the liturgical celebration of their identity as resurrected body of Christ. My music ministry helps make this happen when . . .

ALTAR MINISTERS
Genuine service is a "sign and wonder" (first reading) of the resurrection. A way I experienced new life in serving others was . . .

LECTORS
When I am like Thomas and filled with doubt, my proclamation is like . . . and my daily living is like . . .
God's word has resolved my doubt by . . .

EUCHARISTIC MINISTERS
Jesus' breath re-creates us in the Holy Spirit. My ministry and my daily living are about re-creating others in the Spirit by . . .

Rite of Blessing and Sprinkling Holy Water

Presider: Dear friends, this water reminds us of our baptism and our receiving the Holy Spirit. As we ask God to bless it, let us also ask God that we might be faithful disciples, witnessing to Christ's resurrected life among us . . . [pause]

[Continue with Form C of the blessing of water]

Appreciating the Responsorial Psalm

The psalmist in Psalm 118 invites an ever-widening circle to join in praising God for mercy and deliverance. This is our mission as the resurrected body of Christ, to "write down what [we] have seen, and what is happening, and what will happen" (second reading). What has happened and will continue to happen is God's victory over death (second reading), disease (first reading), and sin (gospel). God takes what is flawed, useless, and inconsequential—the rejected stone (psalm), our failing lives (psalm), our diseased bodies (first reading), our doubting hearts (gospel)—and makes them the cornerstone of faith and forgiveness. This is resurrection, done "by the Lord" and "wonderful in our eyes." In singing this psalm we proclaim to the world what we have seen and what we believe.

Model General Intercessions

Presider: Let us place our needs before our God, confident that the One who raised Jesus to new life will give us all we need to share in that life.

Response:

Lord, hear our prayer.

Cantor:

we pray to the Lord,

That the Church may always witness to the presence of the resurrected Christ through a belief expressed in good deeds . . . [pause]

That all peoples of the world may be overshadowed by the Holy Spirit and receive the new life God offers . . . [pause]

That those locked in disbelief may come to belief . . . [pause]

That each of us gathered here may be peace-bearers and be quick to forgive . . . [pause]

Presider: Ever-creating God, you always breathe within us the new life of the Spirit: hear these our prayers that one day we might share that life with you for ever and ever. **Amen.**

OPENING PRAYER

Let us pray

Pause for silent prayer

God of mercy,
you wash away our sins in water,
you give us new birth in the Spirit,
and redeem us in the blood of Christ.
As we celebrate Christ's resurrection
increase our awareness of these blessings,
and renew your gift of life within us.

We ask this through our Lord Jesus Christ,
    your Son,
who lives and reigns with you and the
    Holy Spirit,
one God, for ever and ever. **Amen.**

FIRST READING

Acts 5:12-16

Many signs and wonders were done
    among the people
    at the hands of the apostles.
They were all together in Solomon's
    portico.
None of the others dared to join them, but
    the people esteemed them.
Yet more than ever, believers in the Lord,
    great numbers of men and women,
    were added to them.
Thus they even carried the sick out into
    the streets
    and laid them on cots and mats
    so that when Peter came by,
    at least his shadow might fall on one or
    another of them.
A large number of people from the towns
    in the vicinity of Jerusalem also
    gathered,
    bringing the sick and those disturbed
    by unclean spirits,
    and they were all cured.

RESPONSORIAL PSALM

Ps 118:2-4, 13-15, 22-24

℟. (1) Give thanks to the Lord for he is good, his love is everlasting.
    or:
℟. Alleluia.

Let the house of Israel say,
    "His mercy endures forever."
Let the house of Aaron say,
    "His mercy endures forever."
Let those who fear the LORD say,
    "His mercy endures forever."

℟. Give thanks to the Lord for he is good, his love is everlasting.
    or:
℟. Alleluia.

I was hard pressed and was falling,
 but the LORD helped me.
My strength and my courage is the LORD,
 and he has been my savior.
The joyful shout of victory
 in the tents of the just.

R͂. Give thanks to the Lord for he is good,
his love is everlasting.
 or:
R͂. Alleluia.

The stone which the builders rejected
 has become the cornerstone.
By the LORD has this been done;
 it is wonderful in our eyes.
This is the day the LORD has made;
 let us be glad and rejoice in it.

R͂. Give thanks to the Lord for he is good,
his love is everlasting.
 or:
R͂. Alleluia.

SECOND READING
Rev 1:9-11a, 12-13, 17-19

I, John, your brother, who share with you
 the distress, the kingdom, and the
  endurance we have in Jesus,
 found myself on the island called
  Patmos
 because I proclaimed God's word and
  gave testimony to Jesus.
I was caught up in spirit on the Lord's day
 and heard behind me a voice as loud as
  a trumpet, which said,
 "Write on a scroll what you see."
Then I turned to see whose voice it was
 that spoke to me,
 and when I turned, I saw seven gold
  lampstands
 and in the midst of the lampstands one
  like a son of man,
 wearing an ankle-length robe, with a
  gold sash around his chest.

When I caught sight of him, I fell down at
 his feet as though dead.
He touched me with his right hand and
 said, "Do not be afraid.
I am the first and the last, the one who
 lives.
Once I was dead, but now I am alive
 forever and ever.
I hold the keys to death and the
 netherworld.
Write down, therefore, what you have
 seen,
 and what is happening, and what will
  happen afterwards."

About Liturgy

First reading from Acts and the Easter Lectionary: During these eight Sundays of Easter the first reading deviates from the norm: rather than being taken from the Old Testament it is always taken from the Acts of the Apostles. This first book of the New Testament after the four gospels records for us the reception of Easter faith in the early Christian community. Although these first readings don't accord with the gospels for these Sundays in the usual way—either by a selection with a parallel theme or account, a promise-fulfillment motif, or a contrast—they do in one sense accord with the gospel.

The Easter Lectionary presents eight gospels that form a marvelous progression and whole: the first three Sundays of Easter all present appearance accounts of the resurrected Jesus; the Fourth Sunday of Easter is Good Shepherd Sunday on which we are assured of Jesus' continued care and love; the fifth through seventh Sundays of Easter prepare us to be disciples who receive the Holy Spirit and carry on the ministry of Jesus; the eighth Sunday is Pentecost on which we celebrate the giving and receiving of the Holy Spirit. We move in these eight gospels from celebrating the resurrected Lord to being given the power (the Holy Spirit) to do the works of Jesus.

The selections from the Acts of the Apostles simply record for us how those first Christians received the Spirit and carried on Jesus' mission. We see in this "mini-history" how the new life of Jesus' resurrection re-created these people. These accounts from Acts, then, make concrete what the gospels promise and help us see how we make the resurrection real in our own lives.

About Liturgical Music

Cantor preparation: Many people believe because of the written word (gospel, second reading). Many others believe because of "signs and wonders" worked by apostles (first reading). Still others will believe only if they see for themselves (Thomas). How are you as cantor a sign of belief and an avenue to belief?

Hymn suggestions: The hymns sung during the weeks of Easter are an important means of reinforcing the thematic progression which unfolds in the Lectionary readings (see above). For the first three weeks use hymns which simply exult over Christ's resurrection (most Easter hymns fall into this category). For the fourth Sunday select hymns which speak of Christ's ongoing presence, of his tender nurturance, of his active support as we strive to live out our discipleship (for example, "Sing of One Who Walks Beside Us" [CBW3]). For the last weeks use hymns which endorse our mission to bring resurrected life to all people (for example, "We Know that Christ Is Raised" [CBW3, CH, RS, WC, W3], "Now We Remain" [BB, G1, G2, RS, WC], and "The Paschal Hymn" [CH]).

✠ SPIRITUALITY

Gospel

John 21:1-19; L48C

At that time, Jesus revealed himself
  again to his disciples at the Sea of
  Tiberias.
He revealed himself in this way.
Together were Simon Peter, Thomas
  called Didymus,
  Nathanael from Cana in Galilee,
  Zebedee's sons, and two others
  of his disciples.
Simon Peter said to them, "I am
  going fishing."
They said to him, "We also will
  come with you."
So they went out and got into the
  boat,
  but that night they caught nothing.
When it was already dawn, Jesus was
  standing on the shore;
  but the disciples did not realize that
  it was Jesus.
Jesus said to them, "Children, have you
  caught anything to eat?"
They answered him, "No."
So he said to them, "Cast the net over
  the right side of the boat
  and you will find something."
So they cast it, and were not able to
  pull it in
  because of the number of fish.
So the disciple whom Jesus loved said
  to Peter, "It is the Lord."
When Simon Peter heard that it was
  the Lord,
  he tucked in his garment, for he was
  lightly clad,
  and jumped into the sea.
The other disciples came in the boat,
  for they were not far from shore, only
  about a hundred yards,
  dragging the net with the fish.
When they climbed out on shore,
  they saw a charcoal fire with fish on
  it and bread.

Continued in Appendix A, p. 279.

Reflecting on the Gospel

Love is the subject of many a fairy tale and children's story. One particular Grimm's tale tells of a king and queen who had twelve sons. The king wanted a daughter so much that he told the queen if their thirteenth child should be a daughter all the brothers would be killed so she could inherit the entire kingdom. The mother sent the boys away and, yes, the thirteenth was a girl. One day the princess found out that she had twelve brothers and went deep into the woods looking for them. Upon finding them they all rejoiced and the princess willingly said she would give her life so the brothers could return home. They refused, of course. So she lived happily with them in the woods until a wicked witch turned the twelve brothers into ravens. The princess was distraught so the witch said there was but one way to bring her brothers back: she could neither speak nor laugh for seven years. Meanwhile a wonderful king discovered her and made her his queen. The king's mother, however, (disliking the beautiful new queen) convinced the king that she was evil because she neither spoke nor laughed, not even on their wedding day. So the king ordered her burned at the stake. Just when the fire was lit and the flames came close to burning her, the seven years were up and the brothers swooped down and rescued her. The king was delighted to find that the queen was not evil and they all lived happily ever after.

Twice in the fairy tale the princess willingly offers her life because of her love for her brothers. Such is the stuff of fairy tales. The gospel for this Sunday, however, suggests that such is also the stuff of living the gospel. Following Jesus isn't easy; it means that we must be willing to sacrifice ourselves—even to the point of death—for the sake of our beloved.

Three times does Jesus ask Peter if he loves him and three times Peter responds, "you know that I love you." But Peter is yet to find out that following Jesus always leads to death. The first part of this gospel shows us how we can give such a self-sacrificing love to Jesus.

It would seem as though the disciples are still missing the point of the resurrection and how it changes one's life because Peter and several other disciples revert to what is familiar—they go fishing. On their own they catch nothing. It is only in response to Jesus' command that they cast their nets and pull in a great catch. The eucharistic overtones are clear: we share in the abundance of the fruit of this new resurrected life when we follow Jesus' commands. But we share in new life only if we are willing to share in its cost: following Jesus even to death—dying to self. Heeding Jesus' call and sharing in resurrected life means that our own love must be so great that we feed and care for Jesus' flock, glorify God by dying to self, and all this because we choose to follow Jesus.

Living the Paschal Mystery

Resurrected life has its demands—but Jesus gives us all we need in terms of abundance and nourishment in order to meet those demands. The incredible thing about our God is that God provides us with all we need, beginning with offering us new life. Accepting the abundance that God offers means that by following Jesus we become Jesus' resurrected presence, those who lead others to him. Every day we must take care that our actions announce God's blessings at the same time that they speak of God's goodness and care. Leading others to Jesus doesn't mean doing big things; it means doing the little things well and so reflecting the Life in us.

Focusing the Word

Key words and phrases from the gospel: the number of fish; Come, have breakfast; love; feed; death; glorify God; Follow me

To the point: The two scenes in the gospel capture aspects of the Easter mystery. The first scene of the miraculous catch of fish dramatizes what God gives us—abundance of life in which we share. The second scene of the encounter between Jesus and Peter dramatizes our response—love that overflows into feeding God's flock, dying that glorifies God, and following Jesus that leads to new life.

Connecting the Word

to the first reading: The first reading embodies how the early believers truly responded to Jesus' injunction to follow him: they taught in Jesus' name and, consequently, "suffer[ed] dishonor for the sake of the name."

to culture: We sometimes talk of leaders and followers as if people fall into one of these two groups. In Christ, however, we are both followers and leaders: we follow Christ and this entails that we lead others in the Christian way of life.

Understanding the Word

Being fed and feeding others: This Sunday's gospel has two scenes: the miraculous catch of fish which ends with Jesus feeding the disciples; the questioning of Peter which ends with his being commissioned to feed others. Both episodes have connections with earlier episodes in the Gospel of John.

This episode of feeding with bread and fish recalls Jesus' feeding a crowd of five thousand with five loaves and two fish (John 6). Both events take place near the Lake of Tiberius (6:1; 21:1). In both stories the same Greek words for "bread" and "fish" are used; in both Jesus "took and gave" the food. Both stories stress abundance: in John 6, there were "twelve wicker baskets with fragments" left over (6:13); in John 21 there were so many fish in the net that the disciples could not "pull it in" the boat and so had to drag it to shore. These stories also recall the abundance of wine at Cana. In all three stories the abundance discloses some aspect of the identity of Jesus: at Cana, his glory is revealed (2:11); at the multiplication of the loaves, the people exclaim, "This is truly the prophet" (6:14) whom they want to make "king" (6:15); and at the miraculous catch of fish the beloved disciple announces, "It is the Lord" (21:7). In all the stories Jesus provides for others: he is the source of abundance.

The second half of this Sunday's gospel recalls John 10 in which Jesus describes himself as the Good Shepherd who cares for his sheep. These are the only two episodes that deal with shepherds. Just as last Sunday's gospel shows Jesus sending the disciples as he himself had been sent, in this gospel Jesus commands Peter to do as he himself has done: to care for the sheep. As Jesus lays down his life for the sheep (10:11), so Peter would also glorify God by his death (21:19).

The similarities between the pre- and post-Resurrection stories remind us that it is the same Jesus at work in both and that the entire gospel is told from the perspective of Easter faith.

ASSEMBLY & FAITH-SHARING GROUPS

- My net has been filled by the risen Lord with . . .
  What I have learned about God through such abundance is . . .
- How I have responded to God's abundance to me is . . .
- At this point in my life following Jesus means to me . . .

PRESIDERS

The way my ministry dramatizes the abundance God gives us is . . .
The way my ministry models our response to God's generous giving is . . .

DEACONS

My ministry is about tending Jesus' sheep. When I do it out of obligation my service is like . . .
When I do it out of love my service is like . . .

HOSPITALITY MINISTERS

Hospitality is concerned with feeding and tending Jesus' flock. The dying to self that this demands is . . .
The glory I experience while generously tending to others is . . .

MUSIC MINISTERS

Even after his resurrection Jesus continued to lead, nourish, and challenge the disciples to love and follow him (gospel). Jesus leads, nourishes, challenges me in my ministry by . . .
I lead, nourish, and challenge the assembly through my ministry by . . .

ALTAR MINISTERS

The fullness that I have witnessed from Jesus that has led me to serving others is . . .

LECTORS

The apostles rejoiced because they suffered dishonor for the sake of Jesus' name (first reading). What I have been willing to do "for the sake of the name" is . . .
What I have been unwilling to do "for the sake of the name" is . . .

EUCHARISTIC MINISTERS

The way I feed and tend to God's flock (my family and my parish) is . . .

Rite of Blessing and Sprinkling Holy Water

Presider: Dear friends, this water reminds us of our baptism. Through baptismal water we are washed clean of our sinfulness and made children of God who follow Jesus. As we bless and sprinkle this water let us ask God to strengthen us so that we might live the abundance of resurrected life through tending God's beloved. . . . [pause]

[Continue with Form C of the blessing of water]

Appreciating the Responsorial Psalm

Although probably written before the Babylonian Exile, the superscription or "title" given Psalm 30—"a song for the dedication of the temple" (cf. New American Bible)—indicates that it came to be used at Chanukah, the annual festival commemorating the reconsecration of the Temple after it had been desecrated by the Seleucid army. The psalm is a song of thanksgiving to God for restoration after destruction.

What is the restoration we celebrate this Sunday? Most obviously Jesus' resurrection from death. But also Peter's restoration to loving relationship with Jesus after his denial of him before the passion (gospel). Once fearful of speaking up in Jesus' name, Peter now rejoices in the very suffering which doing so will bring him (first reading). With joy he joins the crowds in heaven who cry out in praise of the "Lamb that was slain" (second reading). In singing Psalm 30 we make Peter's restoration our restoration. We celebrate that we, too, have been "brought up from the netherworld" of sin, infidelity, and fear of death to a new life of courageous witness to the power of Jesus' resurrection.

Model General Intercessions

Presider: One way we tend God's flock is through prayer. And so let us pray for the needs of the Church and our world.

Response:

Lord, hear our prayer.

Cantor:

we pray to the Lord,

That the Church might always feed the hungry and tend those in need with love . . . [pause]

That all peoples of the world share equitably in the abundance God offers everyone . . . [pause]

That all laborers share in the fruitful abundance of their work . . . [pause]

That each of us here respond to the abundance of Easter new life through following Jesus more closely by dying to self . . . [pause]

Presider: Tender and loving God, you offer us abundance of new life: hear these our prayers that one day we might share in your everlasting life. We ask this through your resurrected Son, Jesus Christ our Lord. **Amen.**

Let us pray

Pause for silent prayer

Father in heaven, author of all truth,
a people once in darkness has listened to
your Word
and followed your Son as he rose from the
tomb.
Hear the prayer of this newborn people
and strengthen your Church to answer
your call.
May we rise and come forth into the light
of day
to stand in your presence until eternity
dawns.

We ask this through Christ our Lord.
Amen.

FIRST READING
Acts 5:27-32, 40b-41

When the captain and the court officers
had brought the apostles in
and made them stand before the
Sanhedrin,
the high priest questioned them,
"We gave you strict orders, did we not,
to stop teaching in that name?
Yet you have filled Jerusalem with your
teaching
and want to bring this man's blood
upon us."
But Peter and the apostles said in reply,
"We must obey God rather than men.
The God of our ancestors raised Jesus,
though you had him killed by hanging
him on a tree.
God exalted him at his right hand as
leader and savior
to grant Israel repentance and
forgiveness of sins.
We are witnesses of these things,
as is the Holy Spirit whom God has
given to those who obey him."

The Sanhedrin ordered the apostles
to stop speaking in the name of Jesus,
and dismissed them.
So they left the presence of the Sanhedrin,
rejoicing that they had been found
worthy
to suffer dishonor for the sake of the
name.

RESPONSORIAL PSALM
Ps 30:2, 4, 5-6, 11-12, 13

℟. (2a) I will praise you, Lord, for you
have rescued me.
or:
℟. Alleluia.

I will extol you, O LORD, for you drew me clear
  and did not let my enemies rejoice over me.
O LORD, you brought me up from the netherworld;
  you preserved me from among those going down into the pit.

R℣. I will praise you, Lord, for you have rescued me.
  or:
R℣. Alleluia.

Sing praise to the LORD, you his faithful ones,
  and give thanks to his holy name.
For his anger lasts but a moment;
  a lifetime, his good will.
At nightfall, weeping enters in,
  but with the dawn, rejoicing.

R℣. I will praise you, Lord, for you have rescued me.
  or:
R℣. Alleluia.

Hear, O LORD, and have pity on me;
  O LORD, be my helper.
You changed my mourning into dancing;
  O LORD, my God, forever will I give you thanks.

R℣. I will praise you, Lord, for you have rescued me.
  or:
R℣. Alleluia.

SECOND READING
Rev 5:11-14

I, John, looked and heard the voices of many angels
  who surrounded the throne
  and the living creatures and the elders.
They were countless in number, and they cried out in a loud voice:
  "Worthy is the Lamb that was slain
    to receive power and riches, wisdom and strength,
    honor and glory and blessing."
Then I heard every creature in heaven and on earth
  and under the earth and in the sea,
  everything in the universe, cry out:
  "To the one who sits on the throne and to the Lamb
    be blessing and honor, glory and might,
    forever and ever."
The four living creatures answered, "Amen,"
  and the elders fell down and worshiped.

About Liturgy

Eucharist is God's gift asking for a response: Each time we share in the eucharistic banquet we are invited to be aware of God's gracious gifts to us. The gift of Eucharist is already a share in Christ's resurrected life. By eating and drinking Christ's very Body and Blood we are transformed into being more perfect members of the body of Christ. This means that we follow Christ more perfectly as we are more identified with him—follow him even to death. Thus, the gift of Eucharist requires of us a response in kind. Jesus' gift of self to us means that we respond with the gift of self to others.

Far from a privatized action, Eucharist is the action of the whole Church through which we share in God's abundant life and are called to bring that life to others. Inherent in Eucharist is a call to charity and just actions on behalf of the whole world. One way to evaluate the quality of our eucharistic celebrations is not by simply focusing on the elements of the rite itself (as important as that task is!) but by focusing on how Christ's life is lived in the community. If the liturgical assembly doesn't become more loving, more charitable, more just by their weekly share in God's abundance, then clearly those celebrations are not doing what they are supposed to do. Suitable questions to ask by way of evaluation: How do we visibly love one another more? How are we making a difference in our neighborhoods, city, nation, world? Do we relate the general intercessions as prayers that extend beyond the celebration of Eucharist and demand a commitment of life from us?

About Liturgical Music

Cantor preparation: In singing this responsorial psalm you not only celebrate deliverance from death but also accept the mission of proclaiming what God has done. The apostles accepted this mission knowing full well what it would cost (first reading). What is the cost to you? What is the reward?

Maintaining Easter festivity: One of the challenges of the Easter season is maintaining the musical festivity for seven weeks. Often the choir and other music ministers are exhausted from the Triduum alone. The Triduum is the climax of the liturgical year and needs to be celebrated as such. But how to do that without letting the rest of the season become like Haydn's Farewell Symphony where the musicians gradually slip out until only two violinists are left to finish? The answer lies in how one plans the year as a whole.

When beginning musical planning for the year start with the Triduum and Easter season. Plan backwards from this high point and utilize rehearsals throughout the whole year to prepare the choir for it. A second suggestion is to work over time toward a festive Easter repertory the choir can sing every year. Choose music that is aesthetically and liturgically substantial so that it will not tire and concentrate on helping the choir sing it better each year. This does not mean that the music director will never introduce new music, but that he or she will do so more judiciously and with the long view in mind.

SPIRITUALITY

Gospel

John 10:27-30; L51C

Jesus said:
"My sheep hear my voice;
  I know them, and they follow me.
I give them eternal life, and they
    shall never perish.
No one can take them out of
    my hand.
My Father, who has given
    them to me, is greater than
    all,
  and no one can take them out of
    the Father's hand.
The Father and I are one."

Reflecting on the Gospel

Hands are strong symbols. Two clasped hands are the logo for the United Way. A child walking hand-in-hand with an adult is sometimes featured on commercials for Hallmark cards. A child who falls and receives a bump or scratch runs to embracing hands for comfort. Anyone who has sat with a very ill or dying person knows how important the touch of a hand is—a loving caress, a gentle stroke, the massage of soothing cream. Massage therapy is a respected alternative medical practice. All of these images and countless others remind us that hands are a symbol for connectedness, care, reassurance, hope. Hands are a powerful symbol because we humans have a basic need for interrelationships.

Simply the traditional name for this Sunday—Good Shepherd Sunday—prompts us to reflect on Jesus' care and assurance. We know the shepherd stories, for example, the good shepherd looks for the one lost sheep, is the protecting gate for the sheepfold. This very brief gospel reiterates this same caring message with the words, "No one can take them out of my hand." At the same time that this particular gospel speaks about Jesus, it also speaks about (and to) us: we are to hear the voice of the Good Shepherd and follow him.

By juxtaposing hearing and following, the gospel intimates that hearing Jesus is already following him. We follow first by listening. The call to follow is a call to faithful obedience (the root word for obedience means "to hear"). In other words, hearing Jesus—heeding his voice—is already an act of following. Heeding Jesus' voice is already our own participation in proclaiming the gospel. But probably most importantly, hearing Jesus' voice is already our participation in eternal life. Last Sunday we reflected on following Jesus that leads to new, resurrected life; this Sunday the following takes us another step: following Jesus leads to eternal life. Ultimately this is the reassurance and care that Jesus offers: by hearing Jesus' voice and following him we will not perish but already share in Jesus' eternal life. No better care than this could Jesus offer!

Living the Paschal Mystery

Most of our reflections on the paschal mystery revolve around reminders that being plunged into the dying and rising mystery of Christ through our baptism means we must die to self if we wish to share in Jesus' eternal life. We look for ordinary opportunities in our daily living to die to self and thus transform what appears to be ordinary, human actions into extensions of the ministry of the Good Shepherd himself. For example, comforting the sick and dying isn't simply a caring human action; in the context of our baptismal commitment it is an expression of Jesus' love for us and the dignity of the other as member of the body of Christ.

This is true and surely the heart of the mystery. This Sunday, however, we might turn this around and rest a bit in what the Good Shepherd offers us when we live the paschal mystery: eternal life, the assurance that we will never perish. For all our efforts at dying to self, they do not equal the gift of self that Jesus gives us. Sometimes we are so caught up in the effort of dying that we do forget that new life is already within us and among us. This is a good Sunday to bask in Jesus' care and protection, listen to his voice calling us to his loving, embracing hands, and rejoice in the goodness showered upon us who are faithful to his call. This, too, is living the paschal mystery.

Focusing the Word

Key words and phrases from the gospel: hear my voice, I know them, follow me, I give them eternal life, my hand

To the point: Disciples "hear [Jesus'] voice" and "follow" him. The gospel reminds us what Jesus does for faithful disciples: he knows us, he gives us eternal life, he keeps us in his hand. This is the kind of shepherd whom we follow—One who gives far more than he demands.

Connecting the Word

to the first reading: The gospel promise that no one will be taken out of Jesus' or the Father's hand is fulfilled in the first reading. Despite "violent abuse" and "persecution," Paul and Barnabas are kept safe and are "filled with joy and the Holy Spirit."

to culture: As consumers we love a bargain—we want to get as much as we can for as little payment as possible. In this light eternal life is the greatest bargain of all—all it costs is our very lives.

Understanding the Word

Jesus and the Father are one: Throughout his gospel John carefully coordinates certain events in the life of Jesus with particular Jewish feasts, e.g., both the multiplication of the loaves (John 6) and the death of Jesus, who is the Lamb of God (John 1:36), take place at Passover. John sets chapters 7–9 during the Feast of Tabernacles (Booths). Two major symbols of this festival were the lighting of four lampstands and the ceremonial drawing of water at Siloam. In chapter 9 Jesus declares "I am the light of the world" (9:5) and he sends the blind man to the waters of Siloam (9:7).

This Sunday's passage unfolds during the Feast of Dedication (10:22) which today we know as *Hanukkah*. It commemorates the victory of the Jews, led by the Maccabees, over Antiochus Epiphanes in 164 B.C. That evil ruler had made the practice of Judaism illegal and punishable by death. In the Holy of Holies of the Temple he set up a pagan altar to offer sacrifice to the Greek god Zeus Olympios. The Jews rebelled, defeated their enemies, purified the Temple, and rededicated it on the 25 of Chislev, 164 B.C.

For Jews the Temple is the visible sign of the presence of God in their midst. There is no holier place. The worship of God alone is the greatest commandment and idolatry is the worst sin. The desecration of the Temple was a grievous offense and its rededication a cause of great joy. God could dwell among the people again.

Against this background Jesus in this gospel claims, "I and the Father are one" (10:30). According to John the Temple's function as a visible sign of God's presence is taken over by Jesus. To see God, one need not go to the Temple; as Jesus tells Philip, "Whoever has seen me has seen the Father" (14:9). This identity between Jesus and the Father is suggested in another way in this gospel. The protection Jesus provides for his sheep is the same protection the Father provides: "no one can take [the sheep] out of my/the Father's hand" (10:28/29).

ASSEMBLY & FAITH-SHARING GROUPS
- The places and ways I hear Jesus' voice are . . .
- Where Jesus my good Shepherd is asking me to follow him is . . .
- When I hear Jesus say, "No one can take them out of my hand," my first response is . . .

PRESIDERS
"No one can take them out of my hand." In ministry when I touch another I am trying to say to them . . .
When I allow another to touch me I receive . . .

DEACONS
My prayer is alive when the biblical text becomes the voice of Jesus that I hear and follow. The voice is saying to me . . . Where I must follow is . . .

HOSPITALITY MINISTERS
Consider: My hospitality mediates to the assembly that the good Shepherd "know[s] them" when . . .

MUSIC MINISTERS
In ministering together music ministers experience themselves as God's people whenever . . .
I know I am being shepherded by Christ when . . .

ALTAR MINISTERS
Consider: When I hear his voice to follow him, I am moved to serve his sheep. When I ignore his voice I end up serving myself because . . .

LECTORS
God's word can be ignored and contradicted (Paul's opponents) or welcomed (Gentile community; see first reading). I work at welcoming God's word by . . .

EUCHARISTIC MINISTERS
Our eucharistic banquet celebrates our good Shepherd's giving us eternal life. I am extending this gift to others by . . .

Rite of Blessing and Sprinkling Holy Water

Presider: Dear friends, these waters remind us of our baptism and the privilege of following Jesus. As we bless these waters and ourselves, let us open our hearts to the Good Shepherd who cares for us and prepare ourselves to hear and follow him . . . [pause]

[Continue with Form C of the blessing of water]

Appreciating the Responsorial Psalm

Psalm 100 is part of a set (Pss 93, 95–100) which celebrates God's sovereignty over all things. Peoples of the ancient Near East acclaimed a god powerful because of specific acts, the greatest of which was creation. The Israelites believed their God acted not only to create the world but also to create them as a people. All forces inimical to Israel as a community—from natural disasters to human enemies—quelled before the power of God, who arranged all events in the cosmos to support Israel's coming together as a people.

In Christ God has shown the ultimate creative power by overcoming death with resurrection. Out of this act God has formed a new people beyond the boundaries of the community of Israel (first reading), a people "no one could count, from every nation, race, people, and tongue" (second reading). No hostility or persecution can prevail against this people for they are held in God's hand (gospel). In singing Psalm 100 we are recognizing who we are because of Christ's death and resurrection: a people created by God, protected by God, and shepherded by God to eternal life.

Model General Intercessions

Presider: Our loving God shepherds us with care and protection and so we are confident that these needs we place before God will be heard.

Response:

Lord, hear our prayer.

Cantor:

we pray to the Lord,

That all members of the Church hear the voice of the Good Shepherd and follow him in doing good for others . . . [pause]

That leaders of the world's nations shepherd their people with the justice and care that leads to peace and well-being . . . [pause]

That those who are perishing through sickness, depression, or hopelessness might know the care and nearness of the Good Shepherd . . . [pause]

That each one of us here might shepherd others faithfully to the eternal life that Jesus offers all of us . . . [pause]

Presider: Loving God, you shepherd your people with unfailing care: hear these our prayers that one day we might all enjoy eternal life with you. We ask this through our Good Shepherd and Savior, Jesus Christ our Lord. **Amen.**

OPENING PRAYER

Let us pray

Pause for silent prayer

Almighty and everlasting God,
give us new strength
from the courage of Christ our shepherd,
and lead us to join the saints in heaven,
where he lives and reigns with you and the
    Holy Spirit,
one God, for ever and ever. **Amen.**

FIRST READING
Acts 13:14, 43-52

Paul and Barnabas continued on from
    Perga
    and reached Antioch in Pisidia.
On the sabbath they entered the
    synagogue and took their seats.
Many Jews and worshipers who were
    converts to Judaism
    followed Paul and Barnabas, who spoke
      to them
    and urged them to remain faithful to the
      grace of God.

On the following sabbath almost the whole
    city gathered
    to hear the word of the Lord.
When the Jews saw the crowds, they were
    filled with jealousy
    and with violent abuse contradicted
      what Paul said.
Both Paul and Barnabas spoke out boldly
    and said,
    "It was necessary that the word of God
      be spoken to you first,
    but since you reject it
    and condemn yourselves as unworthy of
      eternal life,
    we now turn to the Gentiles.
For so the Lord has commanded us,
    I have made you a light to the Gentiles,
    that you may be an instrument of
      salvation
    to the ends of the earth."

The Gentiles were delighted when they
    heard this
    and glorified the word of the Lord.
All who were destined for eternal life came
    to believe,
    and the word of the Lord continued to
      spread
    through the whole region.

The Jews, however, incited the women of
prominence who were worshipers
and the leading men of the city,
stirred up a persecution against Paul
and Barnabas,
and expelled them from their territory.
So they shook the dust from their feet in
protest against them,
and went to Iconium.
The disciples were filled with joy and the
Holy Spirit.

RESPONSORIAL PSALM
Ps 100:1-2, 3, 5

R℣. (3c) We are his people, the sheep of his
flock.
or:
R℣. Alleluia.

Sing joyfully to the LORD, all you lands;
serve the LORD with gladness;
come before him with joyful song.

R℣. We are his people, the sheep of his
flock.
or:
R℣. Alleluia.

Know that the LORD is God;
he made us, his we are;
his people, the flock he tends.

R℣. We are his people, the sheep of his
flock.
or:
R℣. Alleluia.

The LORD is good:
his kindness endures forever,
and his faithfulness, to all generations.

R℣. We are his people, the sheep of his
flock.
or:
R℣. Alleluia.

SECOND READING
Rev 7:9, 14b-17

See Appendix A, p. 279.

About Liturgy
Hinge Sunday in Easter Lectionary: Traditionally known as "Good Shepherd
Sunday," this Fourth Sunday of Easter (on the previous liturgical calendar Good Shepherd Sunday was the second Sunday after Easter) is something of a hinge Sunday. On
the one hand, the image of a loving, caring shepherd bids us look back to the first
three Sundays of Easter on which the gospels all record appearance accounts of Jesus;
these Sundays assure us that Jesus is alive and continues to be present to us, teach us,
and care for us. On the other hand, the image of a loving, caring shepherd bids us look
forward to the next three Sundays and Pentecost; Jesus prepares us to be disciples by
"knowing" us. No matter what demands our discipleship makes on us (at least the demand of dying to self), we are assured on this Sunday (as on all Sundays) that Jesus
will never let us "perish." Such reassurance gives the hope and courage we need to be
faithful to Jesus' call to follow.

Hands as sacramental symbol: Because the hands are such a powerful gesture, it
ought come as no surprise to us that hands are used as a symbol in all of our Catholic
sacraments. Four of the sacraments (baptism, confirmation, Sacrament of the Sick,
Holy Orders) expressly call for an imposition of the hands that includes actual physical touch. The other three sacraments (Eucharist, penance, marriage) use extended
hands (and, sometimes, in face-to-face confession the confessor might actually touch
the head of the penitent during absolution). This latter gesture of extended hands usually signifies an *epiklesis* which means calling down the Holy Spirit in blessing and/or
consecration. In all cases the symbolic gesture with hands conveys the intimacy with
which God chooses to be connected with us.

About Liturgical Music
Cantor preparation: The "know[ing]" spoken of in the second strophe of the responsorial psalm refers to "hearing" and "following" the shepherd. What do you hear Christ
saying? Where is he asking you to follow? What gives you confidence to respond?

Hymn suggestion: Jesus already began calling the Church to mission in last Sunday's gospel ("Feed my lambs"). In the coming weeks this call to mission will become
even more intense. This week's readings couch the hardships of the mission with the
Shepherd's promise of protection. The hymn "I Know that My Redeemer Lives" [BB,
CH, LMGM, WC, W3] is particularly appropriate, especially if the assembly sings the
verse, "Christ lives to silence all my fears; He lives to wipe away my tears; Christ lives
to calm my troubled heart; He lives all blessings to impart." Not all hymnals include
this verse but a cantor could interpolate it between other verses sung by the assembly.
In this case, the song might work best as a hymn of praise
after Communion. It would be good to vary the manner
in which the other verses are sung. For example, re-
serve the SATB voicing for the verses with the
strongest texts and sing the gentlest texts a
cappella. Let the text be the guide.

+ SPIRITUALITY

Gospel

John 13:31-33a, 34-35; L54C

When Judas had left them, Jesus said,
  "Now is the Son of Man glorified, and God is glorified in him.
If God is glorified in him,
  God will also glorify him in himself,
  and God will glorify him at once.
My children, I will be with you only a little while longer.
I give you a new commandment: love one another.
As I have loved you, so you also should love one another.
This is how all will know that you are my disciples,
  if you have love for one another."

Reflecting on the Gospel

Some plays and movies use flashbacks as a literary technique to help tell the story, fill in details that are helpful for viewers to understand the unfolding tale, and/or remind viewers of previous incidents. The gospel this Sunday functions in the Lectionary as something of a flashback for us. The gospel's context is Jesus' farewell discourse to his disciples at the Lord's Supper—an event that took place *before* Jesus' suffering, death, and resurrection. Now we read this gospel *after* those events and hear Jesus' words in a new light because of those events.

Judas left the Supper to betray Jesus who at this point surmised more than the disciples about the events of the next few days. Yet in this context Jesus still speaks of glory. In hindsight we know that Jesus is glorified by being crucified (an important theme of John's passion narrative) because the crucifixion leads to new life. Here is the first twist of the gospel: Judas thinks that things end in death when, in reality, the death ends in life. Death simultaneously reveals Jesus' glory and the full measure of his love for us: Jesus is willing to suffer and die not only so that he might live, but that all of us might share in that same glory and new life.

This flashback also helps us understand more clearly Jesus' final command to his disciples: "love one another." First, Jesus doesn't ask of us anything that he himself hasn't already done to the fullest: the Good Friday-Easter events portray for us the extent of Jesus' love for us—he will lay down his very life so that we might have a share in that same life. As disciples we are commanded to love as the Master; if our love is to imitate his, then our love must also include the willingness to lay down our lives for others. The kind of love that Jesus commands leads to self-emptying dying to self. Herein is the second twist of the gospel: Jesus was betrayed by Judas; we, through self-sacrifice, "betray" ourselves. That is, we die to our old selves in order to take up new life in Jesus.

Glory and love are promised to us—but we share in them only if we take up Jesus' mission. As the gospel says, Jesus was with the disciples only a little longer; through our own self-sacrificing love we continue his mission of love whereby God is glorified. Loving one another, then, isn't just a nice idea filled out by a flashback of a pleasant meal with friends and supporters. Loving one another is how we are disciples.

Living the Paschal Mystery

The gospels tell us over and over in ever so many ways that love means self-sacrifice. We only live the paschal mystery when our own lives emulate the love of Jesus: giving one's all for the sake of another. In many human ways we already do this and could think of no other way to act: most parents sacrifice plenty for their children; we readily respond to others' tragedies with gifts of money and service; we reach out to the perfect stranger on the street who is in need. In so many ways we already act out of the love that Jesus commands in this gospel. Perhaps this gospel flashback reminds us that we need only do the everyday things we are already doing with a new context: we share in Jesus' mission when we love. On the other hand, if an examination of our lives suggests that perhaps we are not so self-sacrificing as Jesus, then this gospel is an invitation to love more completely. What is at stake is a share in Jesus' everlasting life and glory. This is worth loving for!

Focusing the Word

Key words and phrases from the gospel: Judas had left, glorified, love one another

To the point: Jesus knows that Judas is leaving to betray him; nevertheless, Jesus announces that he is about to be glorified. Jesus' death simultaneously reveals his glory and the full measure of his love. Disciples share in Jesus' death and glory when they fulfill his command: "As I have loved you, so you also should love one another."

Connecting the Word

to the second reading: The "new heaven and a new earth" come about by fulfilling a new commandment: loving in the measure that Jesus loved.

to human experience: In the crisis of betrayal Jesus revealed the extent of his love. Similarly, in the crises of our own everyday lives the extent of our own love is revealed.

Understanding the Word

The Book of Glory: John's gospel is usually divided into two main sections: The Book of Signs (1:19–12:5; see Sunday 2) and the Book of Glory (13:1–20:31). In turn the Book of Glory begins with The Last Discourse of Jesus, i.e., the final speech which he makes to his disciples during a rather protracted Last Supper (13:1–17:26). This gospel, then, is from the beginning of the Book of Glory and the beginning of the Last Discourse.

The theme of "glory" which gives its name to this entire section of the gospel is stressed in the first two verses of this Sunday's gospel. The context is crucial: as the text indicates, Judas, the betrayer, has just left the Last Supper table. John tells us that "Satan had entered him" (13:27) and that when Judas left, "It was night" (13:30). The betrayal is the work of Satan, the triumph of darkness. But only apparently, for at that exact moment Jesus announces that the Son of Man is glorified! For John the death of Jesus is his moment of victory: "when I am lifted up from the earth [i.e., on the cross], I will draw everyone to myself" (12:32). Thus the Book of Glory will come to an end when Jesus has accomplished his mission by dying, rising, and ascending. This is another meaning of being "lifted up"—to ascend to heaven (20:17).

For Jesus "to be glorified" means two different but related things. First, it is to receive praise or honor from God; this is the only honor worth anything, for "glory" received from humans is worthless (5:41; 7:18). Second, "glory" in the Old Testament is a visible manifestation of the invisible God—his radiant presence. Jesus, the Word made flesh (1:14), is the visible presence of God or the glory of God incarnate. "To be glorified" is to reveal the presence of God at work in him: "God is glorified in him" (13:31). The moment of ultimate glorification, and the climax of "The Book of Glory," is the death-resurrection-ascension of Jesus. The betrayal sets glorification into motion.

Rite of Blessing and Sprinkling Holy Water

Presider: Dear friends, this water reminds us of our baptism through which we are plunged into the life and ministry of Jesus. Let us use it to call us to the kind of self-sacrificing love for which Jesus is the perfect example . . . [pause]

[Continue with Form C of the blessing of water]

Appreciating the Responsorial Psalm

Paul and Barnabas are highly energetic and immensely successful in their mission to the Gentiles. All this they credit to God working in them (first reading). John relays his vision of a new heaven and new earth, God working to "make all things new" (second reading). Jesus speaks of his glorification, God's final work to complete the mission for which he was sent (gospel). In the responsorial psalm we command these works and more to give God thanks and to proclaim the power of God's might and the splendor of God's kingdom to all peoples. One work remains: that we who are God's people love one another as Jesus has loved us (gospel). This, too, will be God's work and the one which will most definitively declare who God is and who we are because of God. May our surrender to this new and final commandment be the praise we sing.

Model General Intercessions

Presider: God is love and commands us to the same love. Let us pray for the strength to take up this awesome mission.

Response:

Lord, hear our prayer.

Cantor:

we pray to the Lord,

That the Church always be a model of self-sacrificing love in the world . . . [pause]

That all peoples of the world share in the glory of God through loving one another . . . [pause]

That the unloved and those who lack dignity be helped to share in God's love and glory . . . [pause]

That each of us love to the fullest extent that we have been loved by Jesus . . . [pause]

Presider: Loving God, you hear our prayers and grant our needs. Help us to take up your Son's command to love so that our world might reflect your glory. We ask this through that same Son, Jesus Christ our Lord. **Amen.**

OPENING PRAYER

Let us pray

Pause for silent prayer

God our Father,
look upon us with love.
You redeem us and make us your children
    in Christ.
Give us true freedom
and bring us to the inheritance you
    promised.
We ask this through our Lord Jesus Christ,
    your Son,
who lives and reigns with you and the
    Holy Spirit,
one God, for ever and ever. **Amen.**

FIRST READING

Acts 14:21-27

After Paul and Barnabas had proclaimed
    the good news to that city
and made a considerable number of
    disciples,
    they returned to Lystra and to Iconium
        and to Antioch.
They strengthened the spirits of the
    disciples
    and exhorted them to persevere in the
        faith, saying,
    "It is necessary for us to undergo many
        hardships
    to enter the kingdom of God."
They appointed elders for them in each
    church and,
    with prayer and fasting, commended
        them to the Lord
    in whom they had put their faith.
Then they traveled through Pisidia and
    reached Pamphylia.
After proclaiming the word at Perga they
    went down to Attalia.
From there they sailed to Antioch,
    where they had been commended to the
        grace of God
    for the work they had now
        accomplished.
And when they arrived, they called the
    church together
    and reported what God had done with
        them
    and how he had opened the door of
        faith to the Gentiles.

RESPONSORIAL PSALM

Ps 145:8-9, 10-11, 12-13

R̷. (cf. 1) I will praise your name forever,
my king and my God.
    or:
R̷. Alleluia.

The LORD is gracious and merciful,
    slow to anger and of great kindness.
The LORD is good to all
    and compassionate toward all his
        works.

R℣. I will praise your name forever, my
king and my God.
    or:
R℣. Alleluia.

Let all your works give you thanks, O
    LORD,
    and let your faithful ones bless you.
Let them discourse of the glory of your
        kingdom
    and speak of your might.

R℣. I will praise your name forever, my
king and my God.
    or:
R℣. Alleluia.

Let them make known your might to the
        children of Adam,
    and the glorious splendor of your
        kingdom.
Your kingdom is a kingdom for all ages,
    and your dominion endures through all
        generations.

R℣. I will praise your name forever, my
king and my God.
    or:
R℣. Alleluia.

SECOND READING
Rev 21:1-5a

Then I, John, saw a new heaven and a new
        earth.
The former heaven and the former earth
        had passed away,
    and the sea was no more.
I also saw the holy city, a new Jerusalem,
        coming down out of heaven from God,
        prepared as a bride adorned for her
        husband.
I heard a loud voice from the throne
        saying,
    "Behold, God's dwelling is with the
        human race.
He will dwell with them and they will be
        his people
    and God himself will always be with
        them as their God.
He will wipe every tear from their eyes,
    and there shall be no more death or
        mourning, wailing or pain,
    for the old order has passed away."

The One who sat on the throne said,
    "Behold, I make all things new."

About Liturgy

Mother's Day: This second Sunday of May is traditionally observed as Mother's Day. Although it would be very inappropriate to focus the liturgy on mothers, two ritual elements are always appropriate.

1. The following model intercession based on the gospel might be used as a fifth intercession: That all mothers' self-sacrificing love enable them to shine with the glory of God and receive strength from it . . . [pause]. Three other model intercessions are given in BofB chapter 55, no. 1727.

2. In BofB chapter 55, no. 1728, a prayer over the people is given and may replace the prayer over the people given in the Sacramentary for the Fifth Sunday of Easter.

Intercessions for the dead at Mass: The categories given in GIRM no. 70 (for the Church, world, needy, ourselves) do not include a specific intention praying for the dead, although the same paragraph does allow for other intentions to fit special occasions such as weddings and funerals. As modeled in the *Book of Blessings,* it surely would be appropriate to include an intention on Mother's Day for deceased mothers.

This does raise a question about whether it is good pastoral practice to have an intention for the deceased always at Sunday Mass. The four categories listed would suggest not; this, because the Church provides another time for praying for the dead (at Evening Prayer as part of the intercessions). Perhaps a pastorally sensitive balance might be to include an intercession for the dead when a parishioner has died but on other Sundays to omit it (with the obvious caveat that in larger parishes or parishes with a larger elderly population someone might die almost every week).

About Liturgical Music

Cantor preparation: Your singing of this responsorial psalm needs to invite the assembly to see themselves as a work of God, a new creation, giving praise. What might you do this week to help yourself see them in this way? to see yourself in this way? How is this way of seeing a living out of Jesus' commandment to love one another as he has loved us?

Hymn suggestions: An excellent hymn for the entrance procession or for the sprinkling rite this Sunday would be "We Know that Christ Is Raised and Dies No More" [CBW3, CH, RS, WC, W3]. The text speaks of sharing by water in Jesus' death and new life. Especially apropos is verse 4, "A new creation comes to life and grows As Christ's new body takes on flesh and blood. The universe restored and whole will sing." Another hymn which speaks of the new creation ushered in by Christ's resurrection is "Christ Is Risen! Shout Hosanna!" [G2, G3]. The text is full of the Scriptural allusions and poetic imagery characteristic of Brian Wren's work. The catchy and upbeat tune would make the hymn work well either for the entrance procession or as a song of praise after Communion.

SPIRITUALITY

Gospel

John 14:23-29; L57C

Jesus said to his disciples:
"Whoever loves me will keep
my word,
and my Father will love him,
and we will come to him and
make our dwelling with
him.
Whoever does not love me does
not keep my words;
yet the word you hear is not
mine
but that of the Father who
sent me.

"I have told you this while I am with
you.
The Advocate, the Holy Spirit,
whom the Father will send in my
name,
will teach you everything
and remind you of all that I told you.
Peace I leave with you; my peace I give
to you.
Not as the world gives do I give it to
you.
Do not let your hearts be troubled or
afraid.
You heard me tell you,
'I am going away and I will come
back to you.'
If you loved me,
you would rejoice that I am going to
the Father;
for the Father is greater than I.
And now I have told you this before it
happens,
so that when it happens you may
believe."

Reflecting on the Gospel

It seems hard enough for most of us to have the integrity to keep our own word and promises faithfully. Lo and behold in this gospel Jesus takes this one step further: "Whoever loves me will keep *my* word . . ." If we have difficulty keeping our own word, how in the world can we be successful in keeping *Jesus'* word? Last week Jesus commanded us to love one another as he loves us, and we saw the context of this love in terms of self-sacrifice. Now in this gospel we see the context of the love as keeping Jesus' word; this is surely a new and far more difficult way of talking about commandment. But Jesus promises an indwelling God to strengthen and guide us.

When does God dwell among us? The gospel is clear in its answer to this question: when we love, keep Jesus' word, and believe. Rather than three tasks, let us think about loving, keeping Jesus' word, and believing as three descriptions of the same action. Let's put it this way: loving means self-sacrifice; keeping Jesus' word means self-sacrifice; believing means self-sacrifice. In other words all three of these behests of Jesus revolve around the same idea: we simply hand ourselves over to Jesus. The only way God dwells among us is to let go of ourselves and hand ourselves over. On our own we would not be able to succeed; the good news is that we are not alone but God dwells within us and gives us all we need to be faithful.

What does God bring when he dwells among us? The difficult behests of the first part of the gospel are softened by the second part of the gospel. God gives us the Holy Spirit, peace, and untroubled and unafraid hearts; these enable us to have the strength and courage to fulfill the commands of the gospel. The good news is that what we desire by keeping Jesus' commandments—new life—is already given us so that we can keep those very commandments. We already have what we desire: God's dwelling within us that is already a share in resurrected life.

Having said this, there is still one issue to address: what is Jesus' word that we are to keep? Within the context of these last two Sundays, we would suppose that Jesus' word is the commandment to love. As we said above, loving, keeping Jesus' word, and believing are really three expressions of how we answer Jesus' call to follow him. We need say more, though: our Christian understanding of love rests precisely in the breadth of self-sacrifice we are willing to offer. Keeping Jesus' word ultimately means that we make all of the gospel our own. This is surely no small task! But the rewards are not small, either: God's indwelling that brings us new life.

Living the Paschal Mystery

Living the paschal mystery is as demanding as loving with the same self-sacrifice as Jesus and as easy as responding to God's indwelling as an intimate Friend who is always with us, never forsakes us, and at all times is there for us with care and strength. These Sundays before Pentecost when we celebrate the gift of the Spirit are so important for our daily Christian living: they remind us that as disciples we never have to feel like the whole task of living the gospel falls on our shoulders alone. God is always present, dwelling within us, to give us the strength we need to be faithful to Jesus' commands. Only in this way can our everyday lives be fruitful, can we keep Jesus' word as our own word.

Focusing the Word

Key words and phrases from the gospel: keep my word, love, make our dwelling, Holy Spirit, peace, not . . . afraid, believe

To the point: The radiant vision of God's dwelling among us (see second reading) is realized when disciples take up the practical way of life Jesus commands in the gospel: to love, keep his word, believe. To take up this daunting way of life Jesus sends his Spirit, gives his peace, and removes our fears.

Connecting the Word

to the unfolding of the Easter mystery: We begin the Easter season with accounts of Jesus' resurrected presence among his disciples. As the season nears its end we discover Jesus' resurrected presence within us through the indwelling of the Spirit.

to Catholic experience: For forty years since the Second Vatican Council we have heard that the Church is the people of God. How easy it still is to think of God's dwelling place as a church building and how difficult to remember God's dwelling is found among the people who follow Jesus!

Understanding the Word

The New Jerusalem: The scene described in the second reading takes place after the world has been destroyed and evil utterly vanquished. There is now a "new heaven and a new earth" (21:1). Next, the visionary John sees "Jerusalem coming down out of heaven from God." This city, like the new heaven and earth, is entirely the work of God. In the new age, God is the absolute origin of all things.

Our reading omits the city's massive dimensions—a perfect cube over nine miles in each direction! It has multiple gates, signifying easy access; the twelve gates represent the twelve tribes of Israel, while the twelve courses of stone that form its foundation are inscribed with the names of the twelve apostles. The structure, then, represents the people of God in their fullness—yet the city is not identified with the people.

The visionary expresses some surprise at not seeing a Temple—and this is indeed remarkable. Every city in the ancient world had at least one temple. For Israel its single Temple, matching its belief in one God, was the sign on earth of God's presence among them (see Easter 4). It was a visible sign of the invisible God, the nexus between heaven and earth, the meeting place for God and humanity. It had graded areas of holiness corresponding to the holiness of individuals. Moving outward from the center: the Holy of Holies accessible only to the High Priest, then the Holy Place for priests, then the Court of (Israelite) Men, then the Court of Women, and finally, furthest away, the Court of Gentiles. Access to God was closely guarded. *But,* in this City, there is no Temple! Why? The "Lord God almighty and the Lamb" dwell there with unrestricted access for everyone. Whereas in the old city the Temple represented God's presence, now God's actual presence replaces the Temple. The radiance of the divine presence also replaces sun and moon: there is no more darkness. This vision fulfills the promise of Jesus in the gospel: Jesus and God will dwell with those who keep Jesus' words.

ASSEMBLY & FAITH-SHARING GROUPS

- This Easter the word of Jesus that I am being called to keep is . . .
- When I am aware that God dwells with me, my daily living is like . . .
- I need the Holy Spirit as an advocate because . . .

PRESIDERS

To me the connection between Jesus' word during the week and proclaiming that word on Sunday is . . .

DEACONS

Sometimes when I preach I realize the word is "not mine but that of the Father who sent me." Sometimes when I preach it seems to be just me. The difference between the two—for me, for the assembly—is . . .

HOSPITALITY MINISTERS

". . . we will come to him and make our dwelling with him." I help God's people be ready for God's dwelling among them by . . .

MUSIC MINISTERS

Sometimes in my music ministry I need to be more aware of God's dwelling within me because . . .
I need to be more aware of God's dwelling with the assembly because . . .

ALTAR MINISTERS

My serving others prepares me for the Holy Spirit ("whom the Father will send") by . . .

LECTORS

When I approach the text and only worry about enunciation, my preparation is like . . .
When I approach the text recalling that it is the Father's word sent to us (see the gospel), my preparation is like . . .

EUCHARISTIC MINISTERS

Jesus' eucharistic Presence instills in us a peace so that our hearts need not be troubled or afraid. I am becoming that kind of presence for others when I . . .

Rite of Blessing and Sprinkling Holy Water

Presider: Dear friends, in the waters of baptism we were plunged into the paschal mystery of Jesus Christ. As we bless and sprinkle this water now may it help us to keep Jesus' word and live in peace with unafraid and untroubled hearts . . . [pause]

[Continue with Form C of the blessing of water]

Appreciating the Responsorial Psalm

Psalm 67 begins with part of the Blessing of Aaron (Num 6:24-26). In *The Lord's Song in a Foreign Land: The Psalms as Prayer* (The Liturgical Press, 1998) Thomas Peter Wahl points out that for the Israelite community blessings were different from intercessory prayer in times of need or danger and were given at turning points in life such as weddings, deaths, and certain religious ceremonies. What is the turning point on this Sixth Sunday of Easter? For the early Church the decision to eliminate certain identifying Jewish practices as requirements for entrance into the community was a huge shift (first reading). The understanding that Jerusalem was not a place on earth but a heavenly dwelling and that the Temple was not a building but the very person of God was a radically new conceptualization (second reading). Love of Christ and fidelity to his word meant acceptance of a markedly new way of living (gospel).

Psalm 67 can be seen as our acknowledgment that the resurrection of Christ (and this Easter season) have brought our lives to a turning point. We are no longer who we were. Our understanding of salvation is more extensive, our concept of God broader, and our need to change deeper. May God bless us.

Model General Intercessions

Presider: God always makes demands on us to live the gospel faithfully and gives us the means to be able to live as Jesus did. Let us pray for others and ourselves.

Response:

Lord, hear our prayer.

Cantor:

we pray to the Lord,

That the Church always be the visible presence of God's love for the world . . . [pause]

That government leaders be faithful in keeping God's word so that there may be peace and justice for all . . . [pause]

That those who are frightened and troubled may find peace in the loving concern of others . . . [pause]

That each of us here become more deeply aware of God's indwelling and make that presence known to others we meet . . . [pause]

Presider: Loving God, you dwell within us and enable us to keep your word: hear these our prayers that we might always be faithful disciples of your Son and one day dwell forever with you and the Holy Spirit, one God, for ever and ever. **Amen.**

OPENING PRAYER

Let us pray

Pause for silent prayer

Ever-living God,
help us to celebrate our joy
in the resurrection of the Lord
and to express in our lives
the love we celebrate.

Grant this through our Lord Jesus Christ,
    your Son,
who lives and reigns with you and the
    Holy Spirit,
one God, for ever and ever. **Amen.**

FIRST READING

Acts 15:1-2, 22-29

Some who had come down from Judea were
    instructing the brothers,
    "Unless you are circumcised according
        to the Mosaic practice,
    you cannot be saved."
Because there arose no little dissension
    and debate
    by Paul and Barnabas with them,
    it was decided that Paul, Barnabas, and
        some of the others
    should go up to Jerusalem to the
        apostles and elders
    about this question.

The apostles and elders, in agreement
    with the whole church,
    decided to choose representatives
    and to send them to Antioch with Paul
        and Barnabas.
The ones chosen were Judas, who was
        called Barsabbas,
    and Silas, leaders among the brothers.
This is the letter delivered by them:

"The apostles and the elders, your brothers,
    to the brothers in Antioch, Syria, and
        Cilicia
    of Gentile origin: greetings.
Since we have heard that some of our
        number
    who went out without any mandate
        from us
    have upset you with their teachings
    and disturbed your peace of mind,
    we have with one accord decided to
        choose representatives
    and to send them to you along with our
        beloved Barnabas and Paul,
    who have dedicated their lives to the
        name of our Lord Jesus Christ.

So we are sending Judas and Silas
who will also convey this same message
by word of mouth:
'It is the decision of the Holy Spirit and
of us
not to place on you any burden beyond
these necessities,
namely, to abstain from meat sacrificed
to idols,
from blood, from meats of strangled
animals,
and from unlawful marriage.
If you keep free of these,
you will be doing what is right. Farewell.'"

RESPONSORIAL PSALM

Ps 67:2-3, 5, 6, 8

℟. (4) O God, let all the nations praise you!
or:
℟. Alleluia.

May God have pity on us and bless us;
may he let his face shine upon us.
So may your way be known upon earth;
among all nations, your salvation.

℟. O God, let all the nations praise you!
or:
℟. Alleluia.

May the nations be glad and exult
because you rule the peoples in equity;
the nations on the earth you guide.

℟. O God, let all the nations praise you!
or:
℟. Alleluia.

May the peoples praise you, O God;
may all the peoples praise you!
May God bless us,
and may all the ends of the earth fear
him!

℟. O God, let all the nations praise you!
or:
℟. Alleluia.

SECOND READING

Rev 21:10-14, 22-23

See Appendix A, p. 279.

About Liturgy

God's indwelling: Divine indwelling has been part of our Catholic doctrine from the very beginning. In particular, the sacraments of initiation celebrate a divine love that is so great that God chooses to live within us and among us. In baptism we are plunged into the paschal mystery of Christ, dying to self so that we might rise to new life in Christ. We are sealed in baptism with the gift of the Holy Spirit and strengthened in confirmation to live this new life. In Eucharist we are nourished by Christ's Body and Blood and by eating and drinking so sublime a Food we become what we eat—the body of Christ in whom God dwells in glory.

The challenge, of course, is that these sacraments remain not simply actions we go through but become dynamic ways of living. This is one reason why we celebrate liturgy each Sunday—so that we remember Jesus' words and deeds. One practice that might help us make this practical in our daily living—and over the years see real spiritual growth in ourselves—is to make sure we take one thought that leads to particular action in our daily living from each Sunday celebration. A question to ask might be, How, this week, might I express to others that God dwells within me; how does this week's gospel challenge me to live?

Another practice might be to pay closer attention each time the Church in her liturgy calls the Holy Spirit down upon the gifts we offer and upon ourselves. This is called an *epiklesis* and is usually accompanied by an extension of the presider's hands. Even the closing blessing at Mass, while not formally an *epiklesis,* has the same meaning: God's blessing enables us to live this mystery.

About Liturgical Music

Cantor preparation: Understanding that a blessing often marks a turning point in one's life casts this responsorial psalm in a whole new light. In singing it you are praying for what needs to come because of what has already happened. What has happened to the assembly because of Christ's resurrection? to you? What is the assembly being called to? What are you being called to?

Hymn suggestions: "For Your Gift of God the Spirit" [HG] combines thanksgiving for the gift of the Spirit with proclamation about what this Spirit does within us—stirs life, interprets Scripture, gives strength to conquer evil, etc. Verse 3 is particularly relevant to this gospel: "He, himself the living Author, Wakes to life the sacred Word, Reads with us its holy pages And reveals our risen Lord . . ." The final verse is a petition that God give this Spirit full sway in our hearts. HG suggests HYMN TO JOY as the tune, making this a strong processional hymn which would work well for the entrance. The hymn could also be used during the presentation of the gifts provided this be long enough to accommodate all the verses. As a third option the hymn would make a wonderful after-Communion song of praise for the assembly.

A hymn directly connected to the second reading is "I Want to Walk as a Child of the Light" [G1, G2, RS, WC, W3]. The refrain concludes with "The Lamb is the light of the city of God. Shine in my heart, Lord Jesus." The song could be used at either the preparation of the gifts or after Communion. Or an SATB arrangement could be used as a chorale prelude [GIA #G-2786; WC Choral Companion].

SPIRITUALITY

Gospel

Luke 24:46-53; L58C

Jesus said to his disciples:
"Thus it is written that the Christ
would suffer
and rise from the dead on the
third day
and that repentance, for the
forgiveness of sins,
would be preached in his name
to all the nations, beginning
from Jerusalem.
You are witnesses of these things.
And behold I am sending the
promise of my Father upon
you;
but stay in the city
until you are clothed with power from
on high."

Then he led them out as far as
Bethany,
raised his hands, and blessed them.
As he blessed them he parted from
them
and was taken up to heaven.
They did him homage
and then returned to Jerusalem with
great joy,
and they were continually in the
temple praising God.

Reflecting on the Gospel

The first reading and gospel are unusual on this solemnity in that both give an account of the ascension and both intimate that the focus isn't on ascension but on what God has already accomplished through Jesus' death and resurrection. The first reading speaks of the fruits of the paschal mystery in terms of God's kingdom; the gospel spells out characteristics of this new presence of God's reign concretely in terms of repentance and forgiveness of sins. Further, in both proclamations Jesus admonishes the disciples to be "witnesses of these things." Surprisingly, the gospel indicates *two very different* ways we witness.

First, and what we might expect, our witness is by *acting*—preaching and teaching the paschal events and all that Jesus himself had preached and taught. But second—and the surprise, perhaps—is that after experiencing Jesus' ascension the disciples "did him homage" and "were continually in the temple praising God." In other words, witnessing to Jesus isn't simply through acts of preaching and teaching his message of repentance and forgiveness of sins. Witnessing is also giving *homage and praise;* worship of God is itself an act of witness! Discipleship, then, is both witness to repentance and forgiveness of sins (carried out through preaching, teaching, etc.) and following Jesus to heaven (see second reading from the Letter to the Hebrews: "we have confidence of entrance into the sanctuary"). Jesus opened a new way to the eternal sanctuary—by our own participation in his paschal sacrifice (witnessing by actions and worship) we will share in Jesus' eternal glory where we will give constant praise and thanksgiving for all God has accomplished in Christ Jesus.

"All good things come to those who wait," says the adage. The courage and insight to witness to Jesus didn't come immediately to the disciples. Both the first reading and gospel relate to us that Jesus admonished the disciples to wait for the gift of the Holy Spirit. The Holy Spirit is the "power from on high" with which we are consecrated to witness. We can't set out on the witnessing that characterizes the life of Jesus' disciples until we receive the Holy Spirit. This ensures us that our work isn't ours but Christ's. Ultimately we witness not simply to events but to a Person—Jesus Christ, the risen One.

Living the Paschal Mystery

Sometimes we Christians can get so caught up in the *doing* that we forget simply taking time to *be* with our God offering homage and praise is also an important part of our Christian witness. Taking time to pray each day, to be alone with God, is as important to our Christian witness (even if no one sees us praying!), as actually doing Christian acts. Taking care with our Sunday worship in everything from preparing for Sunday Mass (for example, reflecting on the readings the week before), dressing differently from how we dress for work or leisure, or taking time to rest on Sunday can all be acts of witnessing to Christ.

It's a challenge to keep some balance in our lives between the demands of our everyday activities and our desire to give God homage and praise. When things get hectic the first temptation is to skip prayer time because that seems to have the least immediate results for us. Our deadlines and schedules don't change, but it seems prayer time can be dispensable. In fact, cheating on our prayer over time can radically affect everything we do. Christian witnessing means God is our focus.

Focusing the Word

Key words and phrases from the gospel: suffer, rise, witnesses, homage, praising God

To the point: In Luke's gospel the focus of the ascension is not so much on what the disciples are sent to do but on what God has already accomplished through Christ's suffering, death, and rising. The disciples respond in two ways: (1) they become witnesses to all they have experienced and (2) they offer him homage and go to the Temple where they continually praise God—itself an act of witness.

Connecting the Word

to the Easter season: The Easter season highlights what God has accomplished in Christ and is an opportunity for us to enter into this experience. Witness flows from experience.

to culture: In our legal system we know the importance of eyewitnesses; hearsay is not admissible. Similarly, credible Christian witness cannot be hearsay but must be based on personal experience.

Understanding the Word

Major themes conclude Luke's gospel: In the conclusion of his gospel Luke recaps some of his favorite themes. Luke had begun by calling his gospel "a narrative of the events that have been fulfilled among us" (1:1); he concludes by having Jesus indicate that his suffering, death, and resurrection have fulfilled God's plan, as "it is written" (see Advent 1 and OT 3). The fulfillment of past promises proves the reliability of his predictions for the future, namely, the preaching of the gospel to all nations and the coming of the Holy Spirit ("the promise of my Father").

Similarly, the ministry of John the Baptist began with his "proclaiming a baptism of repentance for the forgiveness of sins" (Luke 3:3). Jesus continued this theme of John's preaching ("I have not come to call the righteous to repentance but sinners"; 5:32) and now he sends his disciples to preach "repentance for the forgiveness of sins" (24:47; see Advent 2 and 3).

The disciples' mission will proceed orderly: it will begin in Jerusalem and extend to all nations. This reflects Luke's assurance that the promises of God to the Jews have not been abandoned but fulfilled; and once fulfilled, the good news of salvation can reach out to others as well.

As Jesus departs, he imparts blessing. Luke stresses this by using the word twice in verses 51 and 52: Jesus "raised his hands, and blessed them. As he blessed them . . ." Jesus had begun his great Sermon on the Plain with words of blessing: "Blessed are you who are poor . . ." (6:20; see OT 6). The mission the disciples are about to undertake begins with their having been blessed.

Finally, the disciples return to Jerusalem in great joy—joy being one of Luke's major themes (he uses the word "joy" eleven times and "rejoice" thirteen times; see "Introduction to Luke"). In Jerusalem they are in the Temple constantly praising God. (For the importance of the Temple in Luke's gospel, see Holy Family and Easter 6.) All these themes testify to God's actions; the disciples are now sent as witness to this good news.

Rite of Blessing and Sprinkling Holy Water

Presider: Dear friends, this water will be blessed and sprinkled to remind us that we have been "sprinkled clean from an evil conscience" and "washed in pure water." Let us renew ourselves in our resolve to resist evil and witness to Jesus . . . [pause]

[Continue with Form C of the blessing of water]

Appreciating the Responsorial Psalm

Psalm 47 was an enthronement psalm used when the Ark of the Covenant was carried in procession into the Temple. It celebrated God's sovereignty over all heaven and earth. The song contains verses (omitted from this responsorial psalm) which express Israel's belief that choosing them as a special people was part of God's plan for establishing kingship over all nations. Verses 4-5, for example, acclaim, "He brings peoples under us, nations under our feet . . ."

Knowing the full text of this psalm brings its use on this solemnity into fuller perspective. The psalm is not just about the historical ascension of Jesus to the throne of God but includes our participation in his ascendancy. We, too, "have confidence of entrance into the sanctuary" (second reading). Though we do not know the time of the kingdom's coming, we do witness to its presence (first reading). We have been blessed by Christ to tell of it (gospel). By Jesus' ascension all humanity is raised to the glory of God. When we sing Psalm 47 on this solemnity this is what we witness to, celebrate, and proclaim.

Model General Intercessions

Presider: Let us pray that we might be faithful witnesses to God's mighty deeds among us.

Response:

Lord, hear our prayer.

Cantor:

we pray to the Lord,

That the Church always be a living witness to the praise and thanksgiving that is God's due . . . [pause]

That all peoples of the world come to the fullness of glory that God offers in Christ Jesus . . . [pause]

That those who lack courage or strength to do what is right in following God's ways be open to the coming of the Spirit . . . [pause]

That each of us continually praise God through our readiness to repent and forgive . . . [pause]

Presider: Good and gracious God, your Son Jesus ascended into heaven so that we might receive the Holy Spirit: help us to be true witnesses of all you have done for us in that same Christ Jesus, our Lord. **Amen.**

ALTERNATIVE OPENING PRAYER
Let us pray

Pause for silent prayer

Father in heaven,
our minds were prepared for the coming of
        your kingdom
when you took Christ beyond our sight
so that we might seek him in his glory.

May we follow where he has led
and find our hope in his glory,
for he is Lord for ever. **Amen.**

FIRST READING
Acts 1:1-11

In the first book, Theophilus,
    I dealt with all that Jesus did and taught
    until the day he was taken up,
    after giving instructions through the
        Holy Spirit
    to the apostles whom he had chosen.
He presented himself alive to them
    by many proofs after he had suffered,
    appearing to them during forty days
    and speaking about the kingdom of
        God.
While meeting with them,
    he enjoined them not to depart from
        Jerusalem,
    but to wait for "the promise of the
        Father
    about which you have heard me speak;
    for John baptized with water,
    but in a few days you will be baptized
        with the Holy Spirit."

When they had gathered together they
        asked him,
    "Lord, are you at this time going to
        restore the kingdom to Israel?"
He answered them, "It is not for you to
        know the times or seasons
    that the Father has established by his
        own authority.
But you will receive power when the Holy
        Spirit comes upon you,
    and you will be my witnesses in
        Jerusalem,
    throughout Judea and Samaria,
    and to the ends of the earth."
When he had said this, as they were
        looking on,
    he was lifted up, and a cloud took him
        from their sight.

While they were looking intently at the
    sky as he was going,
    suddenly two men dressed in white
        garments stood beside them.
They said, "Men of Galilee,
    why are you standing there looking at
        the sky?
This Jesus who has been taken up from
    you into heaven
    will return in the same way as you have
        seen him going into heaven."

RESPONSORIAL PSALM

Ps 47:2-3, 6-7, 8-9

R℣. (6) God mounts his throne to shouts of
joy: a blare of trumpets for the Lord.
    or:
R℣. Alleluia.

All you peoples, clap your hands,
    shout to God with cries of gladness,
for the LORD, the Most High, the awesome,
    is the great king over all the earth.

R℣. God mounts his throne to shouts of
joy: a blare of trumpets for the Lord.
    or:
R℣. Alleluia.

God mounts his throne amid shouts of joy;
    the LORD, amid trumpet blasts.
Sing praise to God, sing praise;
    sing praise to our king, sing praise.

R℣. God mounts his throne to shouts of
joy: a blare of trumpets for the Lord.
    or:
R℣. Alleluia.

For king of all the earth is God;
    sing hymns of praise.
God reigns over the nations,
    God sits upon his holy throne.

R℣. God mounts his throne to shouts of
joy: a blare of trumpets for the Lord.
    or:
R℣. Alleluia.

SECOND READING

Eph 1:17-23

or

Heb 9:24-28; 10:19-23

See Appendix A, p. 280.

About Liturgy

Choice of second reading for Ascension: Since the second reading from Ephesians is the only option given for year A, we suggest that reading be reserved for year A and the reading from the Letter to the Hebrews be chosen for this year C.

Silences during Mass: Several times during Mass it is appropriate to pause in silence. Two times in particular help us to experience homage and praise as witnessing to Christ.

First, both the Rite of Blessing and Sprinkling Holy Water and the Penitential Rite call for a brief period of silence and reflection. This time allows us to make the transition from our busy lives into God's presence, consciously surrender ourselves to God's action within us, and call to mind anything that we have done that keeps us from giving ourselves over in heartfelt worship of God. Although this time is brief (and in some cases so brief as to be nonexistent!) it is mightily important; this opens the door for our participation in the rest of Mass. We take much time to prepare for important events in our lives; surely this brief time is no less important!

Second, after Communion there may be a brief period of silence. Since we have just shared in eating and drinking the Body and Blood of Christ, this is time afforded us to appreciate more fully what we have shared and think about how we might be a better presence of the Body and Blood of Christ to others in our daily living. We might consider one specific way during the coming week when we will consciously be the presence of the risen Christ for someone else.

About Liturgical Music

Cantor preparation: On the surface you can interpret this psalm as a celebration of the historical event of Jesus' ascension. But it is about far more than that. The psalm is about the complete victory of the whole body of Christ over the forces of sin and death. Who sits on the "holy throne"? The Church does. This assembly does. You do. As you prepare to sing this psalm you need to reflect on this fuller understanding so that you can move the assembly (and yourself) beyond historicizing over Jesus' life and mission to participation in it.

Hymn suggestions: Hymns celebrating the ascension are designated in every hymnal. Look for ones which connect Jesus' ascension with the elevation of all humanity. Some Easter hymns do this; for example, "Up from the Earth" [G2, RS]. Its style and energy suit it best either for the entrance procession or for a song of praise after Communion.

Another possibility for an assembly song after Communion would be a hymn praying for the descent of the Holy Spirit. For example, quietly singing the Taizé "Veni, Sancte Spiritus" with its suggested shifts in dynamic levels and harmonizations would be an effective way to enter into the prayer and expectancy of the Church as she awaits the day of Pentecost. Although in general it is appropriate for the assembly to stand for the hymn after Communion, the meditative nature and purpose of this song suggest it would be better to be seated, then to stand for the prayer after Communion. And, as always when singing a post-Communion hymn, it is preferable to omit a recessional hymn and go immediately to an instrumental postlude.

✠ SPIRITUALITY

Gospel

John 17:20-26; L61C

Lifting up his eyes to heaven, Jesus
    prayed, saying:
  "Holy Father, I pray not only for
    them,
  but also for those who will believe
    in me through their word,
  so that they may all be one,
  as you, Father, are in me and
    I in you,
  that they also may be in us,
  that the world may believe
    that you sent me.
And I have given them the
    glory you gave me,
  so that they may be one, as we are
    one,
  I in them and you in me,
  that they may be brought to
    perfection as one,
  that the world may know that you
    sent me,
  and that you loved them even as you
    loved me.
Father, they are your gift to me.
I wish that where I am they also may
    be with me,
  that they may see my glory that you
    gave me,
  because you loved me before the
    foundation of the world.
Righteous Father, the world also does
    not know you,
  but I know you, and they know that
    you sent me.
I made known to them your name and I
    will make it known,
  that the love with which you loved me
    may be in them and I in them."

Reflecting on the Gospel

The Little Prince is a classic work by French author Antoine De Saint-Exupery that tells the tale of a little prince from a far-off world who comes to earth searching for happiness. He finally chances upon a wise fox who teaches him about friendship. When the Little Prince is about ready to return to his own planet the fox says goodbye by giving him a secret: "It is only with the heart that one can see rightly; what is essential is invisible to the eye." For all the time Jesus has spent with his disciples and, no doubt, he had many an intimate moment, perhaps the one recorded in this Sunday's gospel is the most telling. Jesus is preparing to say goodbye to his own disciples and he lets them through his prayer see intimately into his own heart. The "secret" Jesus reveals is how much he loves us and that he desires for us the same unity and glory that he and the Father share.

The honesty and vulnerability of prayer is that we see ourselves for who we are; in this gospel we see Jesus for who he is—One who, the night of his arrest and just before his passion and death, is not thinking about himself but is focused on his beloved disciples and, even beyond that present moment, to thinking about all those who "will believe in him through [the disciples'] word." In this prayer of Jesus we hear what is really in Jesus' heart: his love for us and his desire for us to share in his glory and unity.

God's glory isn't something so far removed from us that we will only share in it at the end times. Jesus' prayer teaches us that in the unity we share as the one body of Christ we already participate in Jesus' glory. This, because by surrendering to being the one body of Christ we are already united with the Trinity in all their glory. Jesus' prayer reminds us that being a disciple means that we already share in Jesus' glory. Whether we are faithful disciples even to giving our lives for Christ (see the first reading in which Stephen "saw the glory of God" before he was stoned to death) or whether we are faithful disciples who plod along being faithful witnesses to Christ in the ordinary circumstances of life, the result is the same: we are the Father's gift to Jesus and share in his glory.

In this intimate prayer of Jesus before his suffering and death we see clearly how much Jesus sustains us in our discipleship. Our peek into what is deepest in Jesus' heart encourages us that the gift of the Spirit that we receive helps us see who we are as the one body of Christ: those whose lives are spent in self-sacrificing surrender for the sake of others. The glory lies in imitating Jesus where we learn that passion and death lead to resurrected life.

Living the Paschal Mystery

Most often when we think of living the paschal mystery we think in terms of the concrete self-surrendering acts we undertake in order to live the dying and rising mystery of Christ. The gospel for this Sunday affords us an opportunity to reflect on a completely different kind of self-surrender—that of giving ourselves over to God in the intimacy of prayer. Just as Jesus' prayer reveals us as sharing in Jesus' glory and unity with the Father, so will our own prayer reveal both our union with God and our union with each other. As Jesus was prompted in his prayer to look not to himself but to the well-being of his disciples, so does our prayer draw us out of ourselves toward God and concern for others. Thus, prayer itself is a kind of self-sacrificing surrender for others.

Focusing the Word

Key words and phrases from the gospel: Jesus prayed, may all be one, give them the glory, gift to me

To the point: Prayer reveals the deepest desire of our hearts and our truest selves. As Jesus prays in this gospel we learn what is deepest in his heart—he loves us as God's gift to him and he desires for us the same unity and glory that he and the Father share.

Connecting the Word

to Pentecost: The sending of the Spirit is not just the answer to Jesus' prayer but the work of the Spirit brings the prayer to completion.

to religious experience: Praying aloud is not only an expression of intimacy with God; it is also an occasion of intimacy among those who hear. The intimacy of shared prayer fosters the very unity Jesus and the Father desire for us.

Understanding the Word

Jesus' high priestly prayer: As discussed earlier (Easter 5), John 13–20 is called the Book of Glory and within that is Jesus' Last Discourse (13–17) which he give to his disciples after the washing of the feet during the Last Supper. That Discourse concludes with a formal prayer by Jesus for his disciples; this is called the High Priestly Prayer (ch. 17), a title which highlights Jesus' role as an intercessor. We read from this prayer each year on the Seventh Sunday of Easter. Over the three year Lectionary cycle we read the entire prayer.

Jesus prays for eight specific things, indicated by the language, "so that . . ." or simply "that . . ." (vv. 21a, 21b, 22b [3 times], 23a, 23b, 24a, 24b). Three times Jesus prays explicitly that the disciples may "be one" and twice he prays either that the disciples "may be in us" or "may be with me." Why this focus on unity? The community's unity shows forth the unity of the Father and the Son ("I am in the Father and the Father is in me," 14:10; see also 10:38; 14:20). The quality of the community's life together is an act of witness, a proclamation to the world of the very nature of God and the intimacy that Jesus uniquely shares with God. What is implied is that division in the community distorts the community's witness to God and impedes the world's believing in Jesus.

The community's oneness is not its own work: it comes from participating in the life of God. God's relationship with Jesus is the source of the community's oneness. The oneness of the community does more than witness to the nature of God. Through the witness and preaching of the disciples the world will come to "believe" (v. 21) and to "know" (vv. 23, 25) "that you sent me" (vv. 21, 23, 25).

Jesus, priest and intercessor, prays for his disciples—us. He prays that we may be as deeply united in Jesus as he is in his Father. This is the source of unity and the content of Christian witness.

ASSEMBLY & FAITH-SHARING GROUPS
- As I listen to Jesus' prayer for me, what is most comforting to me is . . .
- One thing I need to change in order to conform my life more closely to Jesus' prayer is . . .
- What Jesus' prayer for unity and glory means to me is . . .

PRESIDERS
Generally when I look upon the people in my care I see them as . . .
When I recall that they are God's "gift to me," my ministry looks like . . .

DEACONS
Reconciliation leads to the unity for which Jesus prays. Where reconciliation is most needed—in my personal life and ministry—is . . .

HOSPITALITY MINISTERS
Where I could incite oneness among those who are alienated (in my family or parish) is . . .

MUSIC MINISTERS
Music is a powerful agent of unity. I find my liturgical music-making leads me—and the assembly—to union with Christ and one another when . . .
What gets in the way of my union with others is . . .

ALTAR MINISTERS
My serving others is part of the completion of Jesus' prayer because . . .

LECTORS
God's name was made known to me by . . .
I have made his name known to . . . by . . .

EUCHARISTIC MINISTERS
"I pray . . . that they may all be one." Ritually I distribute Communion. I am effecting communion in my daily life by . . .

Rite of Blessing and Sprinkling Holy Water

Presider: Dear friends, we become the Father's gift to Jesus in our baptism when we become members of the one body of Christ. We bless and sprinkle this water as a reminder of our share in the glory and unity of Jesus with his Father and the Holy Spirit . . . [pause]

[Continue with Form C of the blessing of water]

Appreciating the Responsorial Psalm

The responsorial psalm seems a strange follow-up to the recounting of Stephen's martyrdom until we read the entirety of Psalm 97 and discover its parallels with Stephen's story. Psalm 97 begins with a theophany (vv. 1-6) which concludes with the acclamation that "all peoples see [God's] glory." The psalm describes two responses to this epiphany of God's glory. False gods and those who worship them fall down in fear and defeat (v. 7) and believers faithful to God rejoice (v. 8). Verse 10 states that God guards the lives of these faithful ones and delivers them from the hand of the wicked.

In the account from Acts we have a theophany—Stephen sees the glory of God and of Christ in heaven—and the reaction of an unbelieving crowd. We also have a deliverance, for in freely giving his spirit over to Christ and in forgiving his killers, Stephen was glorified. His death was his resurrection. Stephen had seen the glory given him by Christ (gospel) and cried out, "Come" (second reading). In singing this psalm we acclaim that we, too, have seen the glory and that we, too, can stake our lives on it.

Model General Intercessions

Presider: Let us unite our prayer with Jesus' prayer for us, asking God for what we need to share in God's glory.

Response:

Lord,   hear   our prayer.

Cantor:

we pray to the Lord,

That all members of the Church celebrate liturgy with the same self-sacrificing intention as Jesus prayed . . . [pause]

That all peoples of the world share in a bond of unity that brings peace and justice for all . . . [pause]

That those who find it difficult to pray or don't take time to pray learn to enjoy the intimacy with God that prayer offers . . . [pause]

That each one of us always pray with the same intimacy and fervor as Jesus . . . [pause]

Presider: Glorious God, you invite us to share in your unity: hear these our prayers that we might one day share in your everlasting glory. We ask this through Christ our risen Savior. **Amen.**

OPENING PRAYER

Let us pray

Pause for silent prayer

Father,
help us keep in mind that Christ our Savior
lives with you in glory
and promised to remain with us until the end of time.

We ask this through our Lord Jesus Christ, your Son,
who lives and reigns with you and the Holy Spirit,
one God, for ever and ever. **Amen.**

FIRST READING

Acts 7:55-60

Stephen, filled with the Holy Spirit,
    looked up intently to heaven and saw the glory of God
    and Jesus standing at the right hand of God,
    and Stephen said, "Behold, I see the heavens opened
    and the Son of Man standing at the right hand of God."
But they cried out in a loud voice,
    covered their ears, and rushed upon him together.
They threw him out of the city, and began to stone him.
The witnesses laid down their cloaks
    at the feet of a young man named Saul.
As they were stoning Stephen, he called out,
    "Lord Jesus, receive my spirit."
Then he fell to his knees and cried out in a loud voice,
    "Lord, do not hold this sin against them";
    and when he said this, he fell asleep.

RESPONSORIAL PSALM

Ps 97:1-2, 6-7, 9

℟. (1a and 9a) The Lord is king, the most high over all the earth.
  or:
℟. Alleluia.

The LORD is king; let the earth rejoice;
    let the many islands be glad.
Justice and judgment are the foundation of
        his throne.

℟. The Lord is king, the most high over all the earth.
  or:
℟. Alleluia.

The heavens proclaim his justice,
    and all peoples see his glory.
All gods are prostrate before him.

℟. The Lord is king, the most high over all the earth.
  or:
℟. Alleluia.

You, O LORD, are the Most High over all
        the earth,
    exalted far above all gods.

℟. The Lord is king, the most high over all the earth.
  or:
℟. Alleluia.

SECOND READING

Rev 22:12-14, 16-17, 20

I, John, heard a voice saying to me:
    "Behold, I am coming soon.
I bring with me the recompense I will give
        to each
    according to his deeds.
I am the Alpha and the Omega, the first
        and the last,
    the beginning and the end."

Blessed are they who wash their robes
    so as to have the right to the tree of life
    and enter the city through its gates.

"I, Jesus, sent my angel to give you this
        testimony for the churches.
I am the root and offspring of David,
    the bright morning star."

The Spirit and the bride say, "Come."
Let the hearer say, "Come."
Let the one who thirsts come forward,
    and the one who wants it receive the gift
        of life-giving water.

The one who gives this testimony says,
    "Yes, I am coming soon."
Amen! Come, Lord Jesus!

About Liturgy

The intimacy of prayer: We are comfortable praying together the traditional prayers such as litanies or the rosary, but it is seldom that we are comfortable praying aloud spontaneously when others can hear us. Even people who belong to shared prayer groups and have much practice in this kind of prayer can find it unsettling. It makes us quite vulnerable! Yet one of the most precious gifts we can give to each other is a share in our prayer life.

This kind of shared prayer when we pour out our hearts to God and allow others to witness it is a wonderful gift of love to others. It says that we trust them and desire the same kind of unity with them that we have with God. Shared prayer together between husband and wife and among family members, among parish staff, at parish meetings, etc., can all promote a new kind of tolerance for one another so the differences we naturally have with each other seem less divisive.

Prayer as the gift of the elder members of the community: One of the most priceless gifts the elder members of our parish communities can give to the parish is the gift of prayer. Generally when we retire we have a bit more time on our hands. What better way to spend this time for the good of others than to pray for those in need! In a real way elder parish members can make up what is "lacking" in the prayer life of the busier members of the parish. This is another way we can witness to the unity of the one body of Christ: all our prayers together help build up the body.

About Liturgical Music

Cantor preparation: It would be easy to skim over this responsorial psalm as a generic text about the glory of God and sing it perhaps in only a perfunctory way. But the context of Stephen's martyrdom for bearing witness to the glory of God and Jesus' prayer that we be one with him and the Father invites a much deeper interpretation. To see truly the glory of God means to discover the mystery of your own glory. To become truly one with Christ means to accept that such glorification can come only through death. To sing these verses is, like Stephen then, to lay down your life in surrender and belief. You sing no simple song.

Hymn suggestion: Modeling her cycle of gospel responses for the Sundays of Lent (see "Hymn suggestion," p. 93) Delores Dufner provides similar "Gospel Responses for the Easter Season" [in *Sing a New Church,* OCP]. The verses in each set correspond chronologically with the gospel readings for each year of the Lectionary cycle. Dufner intends them to be used as sung responses to the gospel proclamation, but as this would replace the liturgical response which belongs to the rite, they are best sung instead as a hymn. From the third Sunday on appropriate sequences of verses could be sung for the entrance hymn or during the presentation of the gifts. This Sunday and again on Pentecost all the verses could be sung as the Communion hymn, recapping our gospel journey with Christ through the Easter season. Set to the familiar SURGIT IN HAEC DIES with alleluia refrain, the verses could be sung by cantor or choir alone with assembly joining in on the refrain.

✝ SPIRITUALITY

Gospel

John 14:15-16, 23b-26; L63C

Jesus said to his disciples:
  "If you love me, you will keep
    my commandments.
  And I will ask the Father,
    and he will give you another
      Advocate to be with you
      always.

"Whoever loves me will keep my
    word,
  and my Father will love him,
  and we will come to him and
    make our dwelling with him.
Those who do not love me do not
    keep my words;
  yet the word you hear is not
    mine
  but that of the Father who sent me.

"I have told you this while I am with you.
The Advocate, the Holy Spirit whom
    the Father will send in my name,
  will teach you everything
  and remind you of all that I told you."

or John 20:19-23

On the evening of that first day of the
    week,
  when the doors were locked, where
      the disciples were,
  for fear of the Jews,
  Jesus came and stood in their midst
  and said to them, "Peace be with you."
When he had said this, he showed them
    his hands and his side.
The disciples rejoiced when they saw
    the Lord.
Jesus said to them again, "Peace be
    with you.
As the Father has sent me, so I send
    you."
And when he had said this, he breathed
    on them and said to them,
  "Receive the Holy Spirit.
Whose sins you forgive are forgiven
    them,
  and whose sins you retain are
    retained."

Reflecting on the Gospel

Once upon a time a small village nestled at the base of a giant mountain. The villagers were happy in its shadow; it afforded protection from the hot sun and provided runoff rain that watered their fields and provided for them in abundance. One day the mountain began to rumble. Then it began to shake. Then it began to spit some smoke. Some of the villagers ran for fear of their lives. Other villagers came nearer to see what the mountain would produce; they were unafraid because the mountain had always been good to them before. Finally the mountain gave one great quake, a fissure opened up, and out flew a river of precious gems and gold. They used the gold to make their village even more beautiful, they sold the gems to buy seed for larger crops, and they lived happily ever after because they had had the courage not to flee.

Like the villagers above, the disciples had waited out the disheartening and no doubt frightening events of Jesus' arrest, suffering, and death. The first reading from Acts begins by relating similar catastrophic events as our story: a "strong driving wind" that "filled the entire house" where the disciples were and tongues of fire. These events, too, bring great fruit to the disciples' lives: "they were all filled with the Holy Spirit." Jesus' promise in the gospel to send an Advocate that would continue to teach them (gospel) and "enable them to proclaim" (first reading) had become a reality. But the sending of the Spirit has an even more astounding effect.

Throughout salvation history we hear of God's predilection for God's chosen people. The Old Testament events of God's love expressed in creation, in establishing covenants with humanity, and through sending prophets are wonderful events in themselves. Even surpassing these is God's sending the incarnate Word to dwell among us, to teach us, to heal us. We would think we've reached the top of the mountain! But, no, God still has one more gift to give: God sends the Spirit who *dwells within us*. This Indwelling is the resurrected life within us by which we are made children of God and heirs whereby we are glorified along with Christ.

God can give us no greater gift than a share in God's very life. This is what we celebrate on this solemnity of Pentecost—God dwells within us, giving us a share in divine life. Moreover, since we all share in the same life, the Spirit is the bond of unity among us. Pentecost is a celebration of both the gift of the Spirit and the effects of that gift—we are sharers in the one body of Christ who take up Jesus' mission to preach the good news of salvation.

Living the Paschal Mystery

By this indwelling of the Holy Spirit we ourselves become advocates of God's presence for others. This gift of the Spirit, then, makes its demands on us. We must monitor the way we live so that others truly see us as advocates of God's presence bringing new life.

This new life that we share with others might be so simple as a reassuring touch or helping hand. It might be so great as making a sacrifice of time to join the parish choir or volunteer for some task that needs to be done for the good of all. At any rate living the paschal mystery means that we bask in the good gift of God's life that the Spirit brings. Living the paschal mystery means also that this good gift has its cost—we still must die to ourselves in order to be the true presence of Christ for others.

Focusing the Word

Key words and phrases from the gospel: another Advocate, we will . . . make our dwelling

To the point: Pentecost culminates our fifty-day Easter celebration of salvation. The story of our salvation recounts the untiring gift of God's self to humanity—in creation, in covenant, in prophetic word, in the incarnate Word, and in the gift of the Spirit. In our receiving the Holy Spirit to dwell *with us* the story continues: we become "joint heirs with Christ" (second reading), advocates of God's presence.

Connecting the Word

to Christmas: Pentecost is like a second Christmas. At Christmas God's Word was made flesh to dwell among us as Advocate of God. At Pentecost God's Spirit is sent in Jesus' name to dwell within us as another Advocate of God.

to culture: In our world the most important and wealthy people live in the best places, for example, royalty in palaces, movie stars in mansions. Wondrously, our God dwells within *us*!

Understanding the Word

Pentecost as fitting conclusion to the fifty-day celebration of Easter: Throughout this festive time we have reflected on the extraordinary gift that God has given us: eternal life through the life, death, resurrection, and ascension of Jesus. Like an advertisement on TV that is too good to be true: "Wait! There's more!"

The gospel from John's account of Jesus' Last Supper Discourse highlights the gifts already given and those yet to come. Jesus urges the disciples to pray for "another Advocate to be with you always" (14:16). This means that God has already sent one Advocate—Jesus (1 John 2:1). Like a true advocate (this term refers to a legal defender) who helps, defends, and pleads a cause, Jesus has interceded for his disciples (see "Jesus' High Priestly Prayer," Easter 7). Reading this solemnity's gospel from an Easter perspective, we know that this first Advocate held nothing back, not even his life. But now that he has ascended, God will send yet another Advocate and this time the Advocate will remain for ever. "The Father who sent me" (14:24) will also "send [the Holy Spirit] in my name" (14:26).

Jesus assures his disciples that, far from leaving them, the Father and he will come to loving disciples and make their dwelling with them. John began the gospel with this assertion: "The Word became flesh and dwelt among us" (1:14). Though the time of that historical dwelling among us has come to an end, in a more wondrous way Jesus and the Father—through the gift of the Spirit—will dwell with disciples "always."

The Spirit is a truly lavish gift. Already John has told us that the Spirit will be our Advocate; the Spirit will also bring the presence of the Father and the Son to abide with disciples always. The Spirit does more. In the absence of the great Teacher/Rabbi (a frequent title for Jesus in John's gospel), the Spirit will continue to teach disciples by reminding them of the words and teachings of Jesus. The Spirit continues the presence and the work of Jesus.

ASSEMBLY & FAITH-SHARING GROUPS

- The "good news" to me about there even being a Pentecost is . . .
- The way I experience God's indwelling is . . .
- In receiving the Spirit we become advocates of God's presence. What that means to me is . . .
  This requires that I . . .

PRESIDERS

My ministry inspires the assembly to claim their dignity and role as advocates of God's presence in the world by . . .

DEACONS

What my ministry has taught me about the working and indwelling of the Spirit is . . . What my family life has taught me about the working and indwelling of the Spirit is . . .

HOSPITALITY MINISTERS

Everyone who gathers is a child of God, an heir with Christ (see second reading). The kind of hospitality that necessitates is . . .

MUSIC MINISTERS

Some things the Spirit has taught me through my ministry have been . . . Some things which the Spirit needs to remind me of are . . .

ALTAR MINISTERS

Consider: Whenever I serve or aid another, I am an advocate of God's presence to them.

LECTORS

Where I need the Holy Spirit to enable me to *live* a better proclamation is . . .

EUCHARISTIC MINISTERS

The way I witness to others that they are children of God (see second reading) is . . .

Rite of Blessing and Sprinkling Holy Water

Presider: Dear friends, this water reminds us of our baptism when we first received the new life of the Holy Spirit. On this Pentecost Sunday when we celebrate the gift of the coming of the Spirit we once again bless this water and sprinkle it upon ourselves to remind us that God dwells within us and we must always be faithful to the gift we have been given . . . [pause]

[*Continue with Form C of the blessing of water*]

Appreciating the Responsorial Psalm

Psalm 104 is a masterful hymn praising God for the creation of the cosmos. It unfolds in a seven-part structure paralleling the creation account in Genesis 1. In Hebrew thought the cause of creation is God's breath or spirit *(ruach)*. Take breath away and creatures die; give them breath/spirit and they live (vv. 29-30).

In the first reading this breath of God comes like a "strong driving wind" which enables the disciples to witness to "the mighty acts of God." In the second reading this breath comes as a "spirit of adoption" making us sons and daughters of God. In the gospel this breath comes as Advocate sent in Jesus' name to teach us all things. This is the Spirit we ask God to send us in the responsorial psalm: the power pushing us forward in mission, the love which is God's very life within us, and the spokesperson reminding us of all that Jesus has taught. Truly a breath that will re-create the universe!

Model General Intercessions

Presider: Today we celebrate the gift of the Spirit. Let us pray fervently that we be a fitting dwelling place for God.

Response:

Lord, hear our prayer.

Cantor:

we pray to the Lord,

That all members of the Church be faithful advocates of God's presence to the world . . . [pause]

That world leaders be advocates of peace and justice for all people . . . [pause]

That all those in need receive from the abundance of God's gift of creation . . . [pause]

That each one of us here listen to the Spirit who dwells within us and faithfully proclaim Jesus' good news of salvation . . . [pause]

Presider: Saving God, you send your Spirit to dwell within us and make us your children: hear these our prayers that we might always be fitting dwelling places and bring your presence to all we meet. We ask this through your Son, Jesus Christ the risen Lord. **Amen.**

ALTERNATIVE OPENING PRAYER
Let us pray

Pause for silent prayer

Father of light, from whom every good
   gift comes,
send your Spirit into our lives with the
   power of a mighty wind,
and by the flame of your wisdom
open the horizons of our minds.
Loosen our tongues to sing your praise
in words beyond the power of speech,
for without your Spirit
man could never raise his voice in words
   of peace
or announce the truth that Jesus is Lord,
who lives and reigns with you and the
   Holy Spirit,
one God for ever and ever. **Amen.**

FIRST READING
Acts 2:1-11

When the time for Pentecost was fulfilled,
   they were all in one place together.
And suddenly there came from the sky
   a noise like a strong driving wind,
   and it filled the entire house in which
      they were.
Then there appeared to them tongues as of
      fire,
   which parted and came to rest on each
      one of them.
And they were all filled with the Holy
      Spirit
   and began to speak in different tongues,
   as the Spirit enabled them to proclaim.
Now there were devout Jews from every
      nation under heaven staying in
      Jerusalem.
At this sound, they gathered in a large
      crowd,
   but they were confused
   because each one heard them speaking
      in his own language.
They were astounded, and in amazement
      they asked,
   "Are not all these people who are
      speaking Galileans?
Then how does each of us hear them in
      his native language?
We are Parthians, Medes, and Elamites,
   inhabitants of Mesopotamia, Judea and
      Cappadocia,
   Pontus and Asia, Phrygia and
      Pamphylia,
   Egypt and the districts of Libya near
      Cyrene,
   as well as travelers from Rome,
   both Jews and converts to Judaism,
      Cretans and Arabs,
   yet we hear them speaking in our own
      tongues
   of the mighty acts of God."

RESPONSORIAL PSALM
Ps 104:1, 24, 29-30, 31, 34

℟. (cf. 30) Lord, send out your Spirit, and renew the face of the earth.
   or:
℟. Alleluia.

Bless the LORD, O my soul!
   O LORD, my God, you are great indeed!
How manifold are your works, O LORD!
   The earth is full of your creatures.

℟. Lord, send out your Spirit, and renew the face of the earth.
   or:
℟. Alleluia.

If you take away their breath, they perish
   and return to their dust.
When you send forth your spirit, they are
      created,
   and you renew the face of the earth.

℟. Lord, send out your Spirit, and renew the face of the earth.
   or:
℟. Alleluia.

May the glory of the LORD endure forever;
   may the LORD be glad in his works!
Pleasing to him be my theme;
   I will be glad in the LORD.

℟. Lord, send out your Spirit, and renew the face of the earth.
   or:
℟. Alleluia.

SECOND READING 1 Cor 12:3b-7, 12-13

Brothers and sisters:
No one can say, "Jesus is Lord," except by
      the Holy Spirit.
There are different kinds of spiritual gifts
      but the same Spirit;
   there are different forms of service but
      the same Lord;
   there are different workings but the
      same God
   who produces all of them in everyone.
To each individual the manifestation of
      the Spirit
   is given for some benefit.

As a body is one though it has many parts,
   and all the parts of the body, though
      many, are one body,
   so also Christ.
For in one Spirit we were all baptized into
      one body,
   whether Jews or Greeks, slaves or free
      persons,
   and we were all given to drink of one
      Spirit.

OR

SECOND READING Rom 8:8-17

See Appendix A, p. 280.

SEQUENCE

See Appendix A, p. 280.

About Liturgy

Pentecost readings: For all three years given in the Lectionary, the first reading from Acts relating the Pentecost account and the responsorial psalm are the same. For years B and C two choices are given for the second reading and gospel, but the first of those choices are proper for year A. Therefore, we suggest that the second reading and gospel proper for the respective year be used. This maximizes the use of Sacred Scripture on these great feasts.

The gospel given for year C is similar to the gospel proclaimed just two weeks ago on the Sixth Sunday of Easter but with different verses. These different verses and the Pentecost context suggest that our interpretation be different from that two weeks ago. We stressed God's dwelling on both the Sixth Sunday of Easter and on Pentecost, but with a bit different twist: on Easter 6 we focused on the tasks of discipleship; on Pentecost we focus on *being* God's presence.

Pentecost—birthday of the Church? We have customarily interpreted Pentecost as the birthday of the Church. We must take care that we don't trivialize this (for example, using birthday cakes, singing happy birthday). The more demanding effect of the birth of the Church through the coming of the Spirit who dwells in us and makes us one is that through the indwelling of the Spirit we become the missionary presence of Christ—*we ourselves* are advocates of God's plan of salvation. Any "birthing" that happens is our own making present for others of God's life.

About Liturgical Music

Cantor preparation: You pray in this responsorial psalm for renewal—the renewal of your knowledge of Christ (gospel), the renewal of your sense of identity as children of God (second reading), and the renewal of your commitment to mission (first reading). How during these past weeks of Easter celebration have you felt renewed in Christ? How have you seen the parish community become renewed?

Singing the sequence: In the Middle Ages myriads of sequences were added to the liturgy to expand on and explain the meaning of certain feasts and celebrations. Today only four remain: the obligatory ones on Easter and Pentecost and optional ones on The Body and Blood of Christ and Our Lady of Sorrows. Most often the sequences were attached to the gospel acclamation (hence, why the Easter one concludes with "Amen. Alleluia"). One can conjecture, then, that the sequences accompanied extended gospel processions.

To honor its original purpose as well as to demonstrate the centrality of the gospel in the life of the Church, this solemnity's sequence needs to be sung as part of an extended gospel procession using incense and moving among the people, ending with a shout of alleluia at the ambo. Musical settings already exist in which cantor(s) or choir sing the verses and the assembly joins in on the alleluia refrain. "Come, Holy Spirit, on Us Shine" [WC] uses the familiar tune O FILII ET FILIAE. "O Holy Spirit, by Whose Breath" is a different though closely related text. WC sets this to LASST UNS ERFREUEN giving it a built-in alleluia refrain. RS and W3 use another tune, but one could use LASST UNS ERFREUEN since it will be well known to the assembly. The energy of this setting makes it the most acclamatory. A complete score is available (WLP #2610).

Appropriate posture during the procession is to stand just as we do for the gospel acclamation every Sunday.

Ordinary Time II

SPIRITUALITY

Gospel

John 16:12-15; L166C

Jesus said to his disciples:
"I have much more to tell you,
    but you cannot bear it
    now.
But when he comes, the Spirit
    of truth,
    he will guide you to all truth.
He will not speak on his own,
    but he will speak what he
    hears,
    and will declare to you the
    things that are coming.
He will glorify me,
    because he will take from what is
    mine and declare it to you.
Everything that the Father has is mine;
    for this reason I told you that he will
    take from what is mine
    and declare it to you."

Reflecting on the Gospel

Anyone who has little children or has worked with them knows that they are not very good secret keepers. Primary teachers often relate how they know far more about family secrets than they ought! Tell a child a secret and it's bound to be told, probably to the very next person the child meets. We can't keep good things inside us. Besides, telling a secret to another tends to bond the two together in a unique kind of relationship.

The gospels never show us a laughing or joking Jesus. The beginning of this Sunday's gospel comes close, however. Jesus tells his disciples, "I have much more to tell you." If we would permit ourselves to be a bit mirthful, we might translate this something like, "Aha, I have a secret and I'm not going to tell you!" Jesus says we "cannot bear it now." Good grief! As if bearing all that Jesus has already taught in his public ministry is easy! What is this secret? Interestingly enough, Jesus does tell his disciples he is sending the Spirit who gives us what the Father in heaven has and in this God will be glorified. The secret? That God and God's glory dwells in us through the Holy Spirit!

God's "telling" is first in creation and then in the incarnate Word. What we cannot bear is further revelation of who God is. Yet in the Spirit's coming and indwelling we actually do have a greater revelation of God—the God-within-us. The readings for this solemnity attempt to describe the majesty of God in terms of creation which is tangible and all around us, in terms of the glorified Jesus who lived among us, and the Holy Spirit who is poured forth in our hearts. God's glory or presence is found in both creation and humanity!

Although Jesus has told us this much about God and how God loves us so much that we actually share God's glory through divine indwelling, there is still much more to tell—there is an overflow of the mystery and majesty of God. The "much more to tell" isn't so much more of a revelation of who God is as our own opening up to God's presence to us and our participation in it. Practically speaking, this means that we share in God's creating, redeeming, and indwelling activity. This means that the way we respond to God's tremendous offer of divine presence is an act of creation in itself, saves all the world, and furthers God's presence in that world. The overflowing majesty of God is that God loves us so much as to share the divine Self with us.

The majesty of the Trinity defies any intellectual unraveling of the mystery. An intellectual exercise is not what God reveals to us nor asks of us. God gives triune Self to us simply so that we can experience God's glory. Our endurance, proven character, and hope all rest in God's love given us in the Spirit. We only need faith to "gain access" (see second reading).

Living the Paschal Mystery

As difficult as it is to grasp the mystery of God's triune majesty, it is even more difficult to grasp that God loves us enough to share divine life and glory with us. Living the paschal mystery means that we are faithful witnesses to the God within. Sometimes rather than witnessing through doing good works, we need to witness simply by appreciating ourselves and others for the wonderful gift of God's presence that we are. The readings this week challenge us to become more deeply aware of God's presence in creation, in Jesus, and in ourselves. Then allow that awareness to overflow in thanksgiving and praise that gives God glory.

Focusing the Word
Key words and phrases from the gospel: Jesus, Spirit, glorify, Father

To the point: The majesty of God is revealed in creation (first reading and psalm), the glorified Jesus (gospel), and the Holy Spirit who is poured forth in our hearts (second reading). Through faith (second reading) we share in the glory of this creating, redeeming, and indwelling God. This festival celebrates both the majesty of God and our participation in God's life.

Connecting the Word
to Ordinary Time: This mystery of God is so great that we "cannot bear it now" fully. One of the tasks of Ordinary Time and, indeed, of our lives is appreciating this mystery and how we participate in it.

to religious experience: The dogma of the Trinity poses a great intellectual challenge. Religious commitment, however, is not based on unraveling this mystery but in our being transformed by the love of this triune God.

Understanding the Word
Faith: The Solemnity of the Most Holy Trinity is a doctrinal feast, that is, it does not commemorate an event in the life of Christ (his baptism, transfiguration, resurrection, ascension, etc.) but celebrates a teaching of the Church. In one sense the mystery of the Trinity is more than we can bear (John 16:12); unable to comprehend it, we assent to this teaching in faith. "Faith" here refers to an activity of the mind. The second reading from Paul's letter to the Romans considers faith from a different perspective.

For Paul faith begins with hearing the gospel, the good news that "while we were still sinners Christ died for us" (Rom 5:8) and this same Christ "was raised for our justification" (Rom 4:24). When one hears this good news, one accepts the lordship of Jesus and dedicates oneself wholly and entirely to Jesus Christ. This personal relationship with, and dedication to, Jesus Christ is "faith." It is personal, it is vital, it is entire. Such a commitment to the person of Jesus has astonishing results: it leads to salvation/justification. Elsewhere Paul says, "if you confess with your mouth that Jesus is Lord and believe in your heart that God raised him from the dead, you will be saved" (Rom 10:9).

In this solemnity's second reading the opening line summarizes Paul's teaching to this point in Romans: "we have been justified by faith." To be "justified" is to be put right with God; the first and most obvious result of being justified is that "we have peace with God." Though faith is our response, this peace comes, not from our response, but "through our Lord Jesus Christ." Salvation is entirely Christ's work. Christ's work, in turn, is the fulfillment of the Father's plan (Eph 1:1; 3:11). By faith we have access to this grace, that is, it is an unmerited gift. Such an unexpected, unmerited, and otherwise unobtainable gift (salvation/justification) gives hope of attaining "the glory of God." In the meantime endurance in the life of faith is made possible "through the Holy Spirit that has been given us."

ASSEMBLY & FAITH-SHARING GROUPS
- I generally conceive of God as . . .
- The significance for me of believing in God as triune is . . .
- The way my prayer and living is influenced by my belief in God as triune is . . .

PRESIDERS
The way my ministry embodies God's majesty (see first reading) for others is . . . The way I mediate God's closeness (see second reading) to God's people is . . .

DEACONS
While marveling at creation (see first reading, psalm) and pondering Jesus' ministry I have learned that God is . . .

HOSPITALITY MINISTERS
My hospitality is a pouring of God's love into another's heart (see second reading) when I . . .

MUSIC MINISTERS
My collaboration with others in the ministry of music reveals the grace and love of God by . . .

ALTAR MINISTERS
My service highlights God's majesty by . . .

LECTORS
The Spirit does "not speak on his own but he will speak what he hears." What I hear in these readings is . . . What I must speak—by word and deed—to others is . . .

EUCHARISTIC MINISTERS
I carry out my ministry in a way that respects both God's majesty and intimacy among us by . . .

Model Penitential Rite

Presider: This Sunday when we celebrate the glory of our triune God, we also remember that God has shared divine life with us. At the beginning of this liturgy let us prepare ourselves to receive this new life of God . . . [pause]

Lord Jesus, you are the glory of the Father: Lord . . .

Christ Jesus, you sent the Spirit of truth to dwell within us: Christ . . .

Lord Jesus, you teach us the good news of salvation: Lord . . .

Appreciating the Responsorial Psalm

The wisdom about which the first reading speaks is often interpreted as a figure of Christ. Preexisting forerunner, Christ participated in creation and danced for God's delight. Poured forth by God to play on the earth, he in turn found "delight in the human race." Thus it is through him we are given access to our own grace and glory (second reading).

But such glory is too much for us to bear (gospel). With all that has already been revealed through creation and incarnation the whole truth of who we are in God's sight is yet beyond imagining. For the whole truth is that God holds back nothing, pouring the very force of divine life—God's own love—"into our hearts" (second reading). For all its touting of our dignity the responsorial psalm in fact understates the truth. We have not been created only "little less than the angels" but very like unto God. This the Spirit does, this the Spirit declares, and this the Spirit enables us to bear (second reading and gospel). Truly, we have much to sing about this Trinity who dances, who delights, and who divinizes.

Model General Intercessions

Presider: With confidence let us pray to our triune God for our needs and for those of our Church and world.

Response:

Lord, hear our prayer.

Cantor:

we pray to the Lord,

That each member of the Church rejoice in being God's presence in the world . . . [pause]

That all people faithfully participate in God's life through acts of charity and justice that bring peace . . . [pause]

That those in need have confidence in God's nearness and generosity . . . [pause]

That each of us reflect the glory of God's presence within us in all our deeds . . . [pause]

Presider: Creating, redeeming, and indwelling God, you are filled with majesty and glory: hear these our prayers that one day we might share your glory for ever and ever. **Amen.**

ALTERNATIVE OPENING PRAYER
Let us pray

Pause for silent prayer

God, we praise you:
Father all-powerful, Christ Lord and
    Savior, Spirit of love.
You reveal yourself in the depths of our
    being,
drawing us to share in your life and your
    love.
One God, three Persons,
be near to the people formed in your image,
close to the world your love brings to life.

We ask this, Father, Son, and Holy Spirit,
one God, true and living, for ever and ever.
    Amen.

FIRST READING
Prov 8:22-31

Thus says the wisdom of God:
"The LORD possessed me, the beginning of
    his ways,
    the forerunner of his prodigies of long
        ago;
from of old I was poured forth,
    at the first, before the earth.
When there were no depths I was brought
    forth,
    when there were no fountains or springs
        of water;
before the mountains were settled into
    place,
    before the hills, I was brought forth;
while as yet the earth and fields were not
    made,
    nor the first clods of the world.

"When the Lord established the heavens
    I was there,
    when he marked out the vault over the
        face of the deep;
when he made firm the skies above,
    when he fixed fast the foundations of
        the earth;
when he set for the sea its limit,
    so that the waters should not transgress
        his command;
then was I beside him as his craftsman,
    and I was his delight day by day,
playing before him all the while,
    playing on the surface of his earth;
    and I found delight in the human race."

RESPONSORIAL PSALM
Ps 8:4-5, 6-7, 8-9

R̸. (2a) O Lord, our God, how wonderful your name in all the earth!

When I behold your heavens, the work of your fingers,
  the moon and the stars which you set in place—
what is man that you should be mindful of him,
  or the son of man that you should care for him?

R̸. O Lord, our God, how wonderful your name in all the earth!

You have made him little less than the angels,
  and crowned him with glory and honor.
You have given him rule over the works of your hands,
  putting all things under his feet:

R̸. O Lord, our God, how wonderful your name in all the earth!

All sheep and oxen,
  yes, and the beasts of the field,
the birds of the air, the fishes of the sea,
  and whatever swims the paths of the seas.

R̸. O Lord, our God, how wonderful your name in all the earth!

SECOND READING
Rom 5:1-5

Brothers and sisters:
Therefore, since we have been justified by faith,
  we have peace with God through our Lord Jesus Christ,
  through whom we have gained access by faith
to this grace in which we stand,
  and we boast in hope of the glory of God.
Not only that, but we even boast of our afflictions,
  knowing that affliction produces endurance,
  and endurance, proven character,
  and proven character, hope,
  and hope does not disappoint,
  because the love of God has been poured out into our hearts
  through the Holy Spirit that has been given to us.

About Liturgy

Making the sign of the cross: Because we sign ourselves in the form of a cross, this traditional Catholic gesture is probably more readily connected with Christ and his paschal mystery than with the mystery of the Trinity. Yet the words of the gesture— In the name of the Father, and of the Son, and of the Holy Spirit—clearly connect this gesture with the whole triune mystery of God.

We begin and end each Mass with the sign of the cross. When we make it at the beginning of Mass, we are prompted to remember that this celebration is God's invitation to be in God's triune presence. Mass isn't *our* celebration but God's gift of self to us in which we are transformed into being more perfect images of the body of Christ. It is well that we make this sign slowly and deliberately at the beginning of Mass and ask God to help us to surrender ourselves to this great mystery of God's presence to us.

When we are blessed and sent forth at the end of Mass, we are prompted to remember that we are dismissed to be God's presence to all those we meet in the ordinary circumstances of our daily lives. By signing ourselves with the cross in blessing we also make a commitment to live in such a way that others might see the goodness in us that is God's presence. Further, this signing and blessing remind us that in our ordinary actions we are to carry on the work of our triune God; that is, to re-create our world in newness of life, to redeem our world from the evil that besets it, and to bring God's glory and holiness to all we meet. Thus through the indwelling God we participate in God's loving work on behalf of all.

About Liturgical Music

Cantor preparation: This responsorial psalm is not so much about our greatness as human beings as about the beneficence of God who treats us with unimaginable dignity and grace. How this week might you treat those whom you meet with this same dignity and grace—at home? at work? on the street? How is such behavior an act of glorifying the Trinity?

Hymn suggestions: Two hymns which connect well with this year's Trinity Sunday readings are "How Wonderful the Three-in-One" [G2, WC, RS] and "May God's Love Be Fixed Above You" [HG]. The former captures very well the imagery of the first reading: "How wonderful the Three-in-One, Whose energies of dancing light Are undivided, pure and good, Communing love in shared delight. Before the flow of dawn and dark, Creation's lover dreamed of earth, And with a caring deep and wise, All things conceived and brought to birth." Since the tune will most likely be unfamiliar to the assembly, the choir might sing the hymn as a prelude or during the preparation of the gifts with the assembly joining in on the last verse.

The second hymn is an extended blessing asking that God's love be "fixed above you . . . advance before you . . . be close beside you . . . remain upon you." The suggested tune (LAUDA ANIMA) is well-known and perfect for the text. This hymn would make an excellent song after Communion through which the assembly could express their prayer for one another as they reenter Ordinary Time in the grace of the Trinity.

JUNE 6, 2004
THE SOLEMNITY OF THE MOST HOLY TRINITY

SPIRITUALITY

Gospel

Luke 9:11b-17; L169C

Jesus spoke to the crowds about
    the kingdom of God,
  and he healed those who needed
    to be cured.
As the day was drawing to a close,
  the Twelve approached him and
    said,
  "Dismiss the crowd
  so that they can go to the
    surrounding villages and farms
  and find lodging and provisions;
  for we are in a deserted place here."
He said to them, "Give them some food
    yourselves."
They replied, "Five loaves and two fish
    are all we have,
  unless we ourselves go and buy food
    for all these people."
Now the men there numbered about
    five thousand.
Then he said to his disciples,
  "Have them sit down in groups of
    about fifty."
They did so and made them all sit
    down.
Then taking the five loaves and the two
    fish,
  and looking up to heaven,
  he said the blessing over them, broke
    them,
  and gave them to the disciples to set
    before the crowd.
They all ate and were satisfied.
And when the leftover fragments were
    picked up,
  they filled twelve wicker baskets.

Reflecting on the Gospel

There is perhaps no more heart-wrenching sight than the malnourished and starving. We receive pamphlets in the mail, see images on TV, bring nonperishable food staples to church to offer during the presentation of gifts. These sights demand a response from us. We know there is food in abundance; we know we are a nation that generally overeats. We know that often the world hunger problem is tied into politics. We know all these facts. And so when we celebrate this particular feast and hear these particular readings we are once more prodded to respond. Our own share in God's abundant gifts to us demands those gifts spill out for those in need. But the plight of the needy extends beyond food and our response must extend beyond providing food, because this festival is about more than even the sublime gift of Eucharist. This festival is about "the kingdom of God."

The gospel opens with an important scene-setting line: "Jesus spoke to the crowds about the kingdom of God, and he healed those who needed to be cured." The context of the abundance—even excess—of Jesus' feeding the crowd with bread and fish is the in-breaking of God's kingdom. We see this concretely in Jesus' healing. This context reminds us that when we eat and drink Jesus' Body and Blood then we ourselves are an in-breaking of God's kingdom. Eucharist is more than a personal nourishment; it is about establishing God's kingdom. Jesus *spoke* to the crowds about the kingdom of God and then put it into action by healing and providing in abundance.

The Twelve still haven't quite got this message. They approach Jesus with the instruction to "dismiss the crowd"; this is clearly a practical response to a practical situation—a hungry, tired, large crowd. At first Jesus answers on a practical level: "Give them some food yourselves." The gospel moves from the practical, tangible level to the mystery of God's abundance and excess; the gospel moves from our being in control to surrendering ourselves so that God provides all we need. Herein is the real good news, the truth of God's kingdom: on our own we will always lack; surrender ourselves to God and let God act and we will have all we need in abundance.

This solemnity looks back to the Last Supper (see second reading), helps us see the in-breaking of God's kingdom (gospel), and draws us to await the fullness of that kingdom when the Lord comes (second reading). We celebrate God's graciousness to us—a gift of abundance—and we choose to participate in the coming of the kingdom by our passing on of his abundance.

Living the Paschal Mystery

The first reading relates the priest Melchizedek's bringing out gifts of bread and wine and blessing Abram. The last line of the reading records Abram's response: "Then Abram gave him a tenth of everything." Like Abram, we've been given many gifts, surely not least being the Eucharist. Our response, like Abram, must be to tithe ourselves, to share those gifts with others. We proclaim the death of the Lord when we are the "body that is for [others]." Death is in giving of ourselves. If we dare to share in the sublime gift of Jesus' Body and Blood, then we must also dare to die to ourselves and share our own abundance with others. Gift demands response. Sublime gift demands ultimate response— dying to ourselves so that we might share eucharistic life with the world.

Focusing the Word
Key words and phrases from the gospel: Jesus spoke, kingdom of God, healed, were satisfied

To the point: Jesus not only "spoke to the crowds about the kingdom of God," he also gave them an experience of the kingdom by healing the sick and providing food in abundance, even excess. Every celebration of the Body and Blood looks back to the Last Supper (second reading), is an in-breaking of God's kingdom here and now, and draws us to await the fullness of that kingdom when the Lord comes.

Connecting the Word
to Trinity Sunday: Part of the good news of Trinity Sunday was our participation in the mystery of God's life. This Solemnity of the Most Holy Body and Blood of Christ celebrates this participation in concrete form: we eat the Bread and drink the Wine of Christ's very presence.

to Catholic experience: We tend to narrow our consideration of the Eucharist to the sacramental elements of Bread and Wine. Eucharist is more.

Understanding the Word
The kingdom and feeding the 5000: To understand better the miraculous feeding of the 5000, it is helpful to look at the larger context in this section of Luke's gospel. Chapter 9 begins when Jesus commissions the Twelve, giving them authority, sending them "to proclaim the kingdom of God," and to heal the sick (9:1-2). After they go out, Luke reports Herod's curiosity about Jesus: "who is this about whom I hear such things?" (9:9). Then the Twelve return and Jesus once again "spoke to the crowds about the kingdom of God" (9:11). This is where this solemnity's gospel begins. The feeding of the 5000, then, is both a partial answer to Herod's question about the identity of Jesus and is another way in which Jesus, the Teacher, explains the Kingdom. Just as the Twelve went out to heal and to preach the kingdom (9:1-2), Jesus, too, preaches the kingdom and heals the sick (9:11). Healing is an enactment of the teaching; the visible sign that the kingdom is indeed being established is that demons are cast out (9:1) and illness is cured. The two aspects go together: evil diminishes life and enslaves people; God's reign restores life and liberates them from evil. Healing is the wholeness and liberation *(shalom)* that God's merciful rule brings.

The context of the kingdom heightens the significance of the miraculous feeding. In the Beatitudes Jesus had promised the poor "the kingdom of God is yours" and said to the hungry "you will be satisfied" (6:21-22; at the end of the feeding, "they were satisfied," 9:17). In the Kingdom the poor are gathered in and hunger is satisfied. Moreover, there is a superabundance of food, a sign of the heavenly banquet (see 13:23-30). Again, this action fulfills another of Jesus' sayings: "give and it will be given to you" (6:38).

While the gospel and this solemnity clearly point to the eucharistic aspects of the miracle (he took, blessed, broke, and gave the bread; 9:16; compare 22:19), the context—preaching, healing, feeding, abundance—indicates that in Jesus' ministry, the kingdom of God is being established.

ASSEMBLY & FAITH-SHARING GROUPS
- What is most important to me about the Eucharist is . . .
- Where Jesus could say to me, "Give them some food yourselves," is . . .
- Where God has satisfied me with abundance is . . .
  My response to such abundance has been . . . my response should be . . .

PRESIDERS
I am willing to offer my simple "five loaves and two fish" to the vast crowd of human need because . . .

DEACONS
A time when I was abundantly satisfied for serving others was . . .

HOSPITALITY MINISTERS
The occasions when I am tempted to "dismiss" the needs of others are . . .
Where I have witnessed to God's abundance through my welcome care is . . .

MUSIC MINISTERS
My ministry of music is a gift of self that feeds others when . . .

ALTAR MINISTERS
In serving others I am "proclaiming the death of the Lord until he comes" because . . .

LECTORS
Proclamation is one way I hand on what I received from the Lord (see second reading). My daily living is another way when I . . .

EUCHARISTIC MINISTERS
Luke connects Jesus' healing others to the feeding of the thousands. The way I connect my Communion ministry to the needy is . . .

Model Penitential Rite

Presider: Today we celebrate God's gracious gift of abundance to us, not only in giving us the gift of Christ's Body and Blood for our nourishment but for establishing God's reign in our world. Let us open ourselves to this great mystery and prepare to receive the abundance from our God . . . [pause]

    Lord Jesus, you preached the presence of God's reign: Lord . . .

    Christ Jesus, you fed the crowd with an abundance of bread and fish: Christ . . .

    Lord Jesus, you nourish us with your Body and Blood: Lord . . .

Appreciating the Responsorial Psalm

Psalm 110 was a royal psalm used at the coronation ceremony of a king descended from the line of David. The text promised the king a place of honor next to God, victory over enemies, and a priestly role before the people. In the first reading Melchizedek, "a priest of God Most High," gives food, drink, and blessing to Abram. In the gospel Jesus heals those in need and feeds the starving crowd, creating an amazing abundance out of a meager supply. In the second reading Paul reminds us that the food and drink Jesus gives us is his very Body and Blood. In singing this psalm we recognize what Jesus does and who Jesus is. He is the one victorious over all that impedes fullness of life. He is the one who feeds us with his very self. He is the completion of the Davidic line and a "priest forever, in the line of Melchizedek."

Model General Intercessions

Presider: Our God is gracious and gives us all we need in abundance. We are encouraged to make our needs known to such a good God.

Response:

Cantor:

That the Church celebrate Eucharist ever more fervently as a gift of God and a sign of the presence of God's reign . . . [pause]

That all peoples share in the abundance of the world's resources and conserve them for future generations . . . [pause]

That the hungry be fed to satisfaction so the quality of their life might improve . . . [pause]

That each of us here always be generous with the gifts God has given us and recognize this as our participation in establishing God's reign . . . [pause]

Presider: Gracious God, you give us all good things in abundance: hear our prayers that we might receive the gifts you have given us and in turn share them with others. We ask this through Christ our Lord. **Amen.**

ALTERNATIVE OPENING PRAYER

Let us pray

Pause for silent prayer

Lord Jesus Christ,
we worship you living among us
in the sacrament of your body and blood.
May we offer to our Father in heaven
a solemn pledge of undivided love.
May we offer to our brothers and sisters
a life poured out in loving service of that
    kingdom
where you live with the Father and the
    Holy Spirit,
one God, for ever and ever. **Amen.**

FIRST READING
Gen 14:18-20

In those days, Melchizedek, king of Salem,
    brought out bread and wine,
    and being a priest of God Most High,
    he blessed Abram with these words:
"Blessed be Abram by God Most High,
    the creator of heaven and earth;
    and blessed be God Most High,
    who delivered your foes into your
      hand."
Then Abram gave him a tenth of
    everything.

RESPONSORIAL PSALM

Ps 110:1, 2, 3, 4

℟. (4b) You are a priest forever, in the line of Melchizedek.

The LORD said to my Lord: "Sit at my right hand
   till I make your enemies your footstool."

℟. You are a priest forever, in the line of Melchizedek.

The scepter of your power the LORD will stretch forth from Zion:
   "Rule in the midst of your enemies."

℟. You are a priest forever, in the line of Melchizedek.

"Yours is princely power in the day of your birth, in holy splendor;
   before the daystar, like the dew, I have begotten you."

℟. You are a priest forever, in the line of Melchizedek.

The LORD has sworn, and he will not repent:
   "You are a priest forever, according to the order of Melchizedek."

℟. You are a priest forever, in the line of Melchizedek.

SECOND READING

1 Cor 11:23-26

Brothers and sisters:
I received from the Lord what I also handed on to you,
   that the Lord Jesus, on the night he was handed over,
   took bread, and, after he had given thanks,
   broke it and said, "This is my body that is for you.
Do this in remembrance of me."
In the same way also the cup, after supper, saying,
   "This cup is the new covenant in my blood.
Do this, as often as you drink it, in remembrance of me."
For as often as you eat this bread and drink the cup,
   you proclaim the death of the Lord until he comes.

SEQUENCE

See Appendix A, p. 281.

About Liturgy

Drinking from the cup: When we speak about the "fullness of the sign" that drinking from the cup brings, we are not speaking about whether or not we receive the "whole" Christ under the species of the consecrated Bread. Of course, we do. Insisting on the "fullness of the sign" is a response to Jesus' command to eat *and drink*. Jesus gave us his Body *and* he poured out his Blood. We participate more fully in this mystery of what Jesus has done by consuming both his Body and his Blood. Jesus himself understood this when he invited the disciples at the Last Supper to "take and eat" and "take and drink" (see Matt 26:26-29; Mark 14:22-25; Luke 28:17-20) as did Paul when he taught "For as often as you eat this bread and drink this cup, you proclaim the death of the Lord until he comes" (1 Cor 11:26).

Our reception of Communion, then, is more than consuming his Body and Blood; it is *participation in the mystery of his death and resurrection*. We eat his Body and drink his Blood as sign that, nourished by him, we are now able to lay down our own bodies and pour out our own blood so that salvation comes to others. Drinking from the cup is a response to Jesus' command as well as a concrete sign of Jesus' shedding (giving) his Blood for us and our participation in this great mystery.

Breadth of the eucharistic mystery: We rightly think of the Eucharist as God's gift of nourishment for us when we share in the Body and Blood of the Lord and recognize this as a sublime gift that Jesus has left us. The readings for this solemnity also help us think of the eucharistic mystery in even broader terms. First, by sharing in the Body and Blood of Christ we are *transformed* into being more perfect members of the body of Christ. Thus, sharing in Eucharist is our way of growing more deeply into our own baptismal identity. Second, the eucharistic mystery includes continually establishing God's reign which is evidenced by healing, reconciling, and feeding others. Third, the eucharistic mystery calls forth from us practical, everyday actions by which we ourselves help establish God's reign by dying to ourselves for the sake of others. Fourth, the eucharistic mystery demands a response and so we tithe the gifts given to us for the sake of others less fortunate. In a real sense the eucharistic mystery begins at Mass, is expressed during Communion, and extends to our everyday lives when we live its self-sacrificing demand-response.

About Liturgical Music

Cantor preparation: The psalm you sing this Sunday acclaims the power and priesthood of Christ, both most evident to us in the gift of his Body and Blood for food. What might you do this week to affirm your personal faith in Jesus and express your gratitude for what he does in giving us the Eucharist?

Hymn suggestions: Eucharistic hymns which express our participation in Jesus' feeding of the hungry would be especially appropriate this Sunday. Marty Haugen's litanic "Bread to Share" [RS] is appropriately uplifting with its repetition of "You have plenty to share, you have plenty of bread to share." Thomas Porter's "Let Us Be Bread" [G2, RS] uses the refrain, "Let us be bread, broken and shared, life for the world. Let us be wine, love freely poured. Let us be one in the Lord." Delores Dufner's "We Come with Joy" [HG] combines narration of the story of Jesus' feeding the crowd with the call that we do likewise, "For Christ will bless our bit of bread, The loaves our hands provide, Till empty baskets overflow And all are satisfied." This last suggestion could be sung during the presentation of the gifts, during the Communion procession, or as a post-Communion hymn.

JUNE 13, 2004

THE SOLEMNITY OF THE MOST HOLY BODY AND BLOOD OF CHRIST

✝ SPIRITUALITY

Gospel

Luke 15:3-7; L172C

Jesus addressed this parable to the
    Pharisees and scribes:
"What man among you having a
    hundred sheep and losing one
    of them
    would not leave the ninety-nine
        in the desert
    and go after the lost one until
        he finds it?
And when he does find it,
    he sets it on his shoulders with
        great joy
    and, upon his arrival home,
    he calls together his friends and
        neighbors and says to them,
    'Rejoice with me because I have
        found my lost sheep.'
I tell you, in just the same way
    there will be more joy in heaven over
        one sinner who repents
    than over ninety-nine righteous
        people
    who have no need of repentance.'"

See Appendix A, p. 282, for these readings:

FIRST READING
Ezek 34:11-16

RESPONSORIAL PSALM
Ps 23:1-3a, 3b-4, 5, 6

SECOND READING
Rom 5:5b-11

Reflecting on the Gospel

At face value this parable makes no common sense in two ways. First, who would jeopardize ninety-nine possessions in order to save one possession worth no more than any one of the ninety-nine? Second, calling together "friends and neighbors" to rejoice suggests that the man threw a party to celebrate finding one sheep and probably spent many more times the value of the sheep wining and dining his friends. That makes no sense at all! And that is exactly the point of the parable.

The gospel story is really about God's kingdom in which nothing God does makes sense by our human standards. The gospel invites us to begin thinking—and acting—like God! This festival honoring the sacred heart of Jesus reminds us of God's tremendous love and care for us. It reminds us that God's heart is large enough to welcome the stranger and tender enough to search out the lost and stray. This is the "stuff" of God's kingdom: one is worth as much as the ninety-nine.

God's kingdom is evidenced by God's rescue, care, our being led rightly, rest, healing (first reading), inpouring of the Holy Spirit, being loved, justified, saved, reconciled (second reading), being found and celebrating repentance (gospel). All of this goes beyond how we humans would normally measure out our actions. This festival of the Sacred Heart of Jesus helps us bridge the Easter season and Ordinary Time. During Easter we celebrated the new life given us in Christ. We celebrated the coming of the kingdom established by Jesus' dying and rising. We celebrated how we share in God's glory. So, we have just completed fifty days when we considered in depth how we are given all the gifts we need—especially the Holy Spirit—to measure our actions by divine standards. At the same time we are in Ordinary Time, the Church's time to walk with Jesus through a gospel and learn what discipleship demands of us. So, we are still learning how to act with Jesus' heart. We are still establishing God's reign in an imperfect and sometimes cruel world. Most of all, this festival reminds us that we ourselves are still to be counted among the lost, among those whom Jesus is persistent to search after, caring enough to forgive, and loving enough to embrace with joy.

Living the Paschal Mystery

Jesus' image of the persistent sheep owner who leaves ninety-nine to find the one lost sheep is a model for paschal mystery living. We often speak of dying to self. One way to die to self is to search out the "one" among the "ninety-nine." Who among us is lonely? Reach out to that person. Is someone being neglected because of age, religion, social status, economic status? Reach out to that person. Do the physically or mentally challenged leave us uncomfortable? Find out enough about them that we can be comfortable and then reach out with a friendly word or gesture.

If we open our eyes and look we will no doubt discover many among us who seem isolated and alone. Emulating the sacred, tender heart of Jesus means that we make room in our own hearts for everyone, not just those who are naturally close to us or with whom we are most comfortable. This doesn't mean that we don't have a justified predilection for our family and friends. It does mean that we are willing to break out of our usual family, work, and social groups to be present to those who seem alone or lost. Dying to self can mean caring enough to have room in our own hearts for all who come.

Focusing the Word
Key words and phrases from the gospel: one, ninety-nine, until he finds it

To the point: In the gospel we hear a parable about the utter newness of the in-breaking of God's kingdom: one is worth as much as ninety-nine. This persistent love of the shepherd seeking out the lost captures an aspect of this festival.

Model Penitential Rite
Presider: Jesus is persistent in searching out the lost and tenderly gathers them close to his sacred heart. We pause at the beginning of this liturgy to see how we have strayed from Jesus' embrace and open ourselves to his loving presence . . . [pause]

Lord Jesus, you persist in seeking out the lost: Lord . . .

Christ Jesus, your pierced heart announces to us your great love: Christ . . .

Lord Jesus, you teach us that God's reign is upon us: Lord . . .

Model General Intercessions
Presider: Let us confidently commend our needs to the heart of a loving and caring God.

Response:

Lord, hear our prayer.

Cantor:

we pray to the Lord,

That the Church be the visible presence of Jesus' loving heart . . . [pause]

That government leaders lead rightly and persist in securing peace for their people . . . [pause]

That the lost and forsaken find comfort in Jesus' sacred heart . . . [pause]

That each one of us have the courage to reach out to one lonely person . . . [pause]

Presider: Loving and caring God, the sacred heart of your Son Jesus embraces the lost and those who have strayed: hear these our prayers that we might rest everlastingly in your loving embrace. We make our prayer through that same Son, Jesus Christ our Lord. **Amen.**

ALTERNATIVE OPENING PRAYER
Let us pray

Pause for silent prayer

Father,
we honor the heart of your Son
broken by man's cruelty,
yet symbol of love's triumph,
pledge of all that man is called to be.

Teach us to see Christ in the lives we touch,
to offer him living worship
by love-filled service to our brothers and
    sisters.

We ask this through Christ our Lord.
    Amen.

FOR REFLECTION
- The most striking thing in this parable to me is . . .
  What this parable teaches me about the "sacred heart" of Jesus is . . .

- "God proves his love for us" (second reading). The experience that convinced me of this was . . .

- I can emulate the sacred heart of Jesus by making room in my heart for . . .

✠ SPIRITUALITY

Gospel

Luke 9:18-24; L96C

Once when Jesus was praying in
solitude,
  and the disciples were with him,
  he asked them, "Who do the
    crowds say that I am?"
They said in reply, "John the
    Baptist;
  others, Elijah;
  still others, 'One of the ancient
    prophets has arisen.'"
Then he said to them, "But who
  do you say that I am?"
Peter said in reply, "The Christ
  of God."
He rebuked them
  and directed them not to tell this to
    anyone.

He said, "The Son of Man must suffer
  greatly
  and be rejected by the elders, the
    chief priests, and the scribes,
  and be killed and on the third day be
    raised."

Then he said to all,
  "If anyone wishes to come after me,
    he must deny himself
  and take up his cross daily and follow
    me.
For whoever wishes to save his life will
  lose it,
  but whoever loses his life for my sake
    will save it."

Reflecting on the Gospel

Although we've been in Ordinary Time since Pentecost, the solemnities of the past two Sundays have taken our minds off the task during this long but important time of the liturgical year. It is only by chance that we resume our Sunday Ordinary Time readings with this particular gospel. It is quite fitting. The gospel lays out for us quite explicitly the task of true disciples as well as the task of Ordinary Time—be as self-surrendering as the Master. Jesus' suffering and death is very much tied to who he is. Peter's confession of Jesus' identity is couched in the context of passion imagery.

The very progression in the gospel opens up its meaning for us. Jesus "was *praying* in solitude." While our own prayer is directed toward God and experiencing God's presence, Jesus' prayer is unique—while experiencing God, Jesus experiences self as divine. In the prayer Jesus' connection with Divinity is a connection with who he is as the Son of God. Jesus' prayer, then, not only opens up God's identity, it also opens up *Jesus'* identity. By thus being in touch with who he is, Jesus is in touch with his ultimate *mission*—to "suffer greatly," "be rejected," "be killed," and "be raised." This mission is an extension of who Jesus is—Savior. We usually think of Jesus' mission as teaching and preaching, healing and working miracles, and so it was. But underlying these activities is the ultimate one—his suffering, death, and resurrection. So it is with us.

Because through baptism we share in Jesus' identity and mission—we are plunged into the waters of baptism, dying to self and rising to new life in Christ and thus are made members of the body of Christ—a similar thing happens to us in prayer as happened in Jesus' prayer. By opening ourselves to divine Presence, we are actually opening ourselves to our own identity and mission as well. This is why prayer is so very important for the Christian: it is an encounter with God that reassures us of who we are (members of Christ's body) and gives us the strength to deny ourselves, take up our daily cross, and lose ourselves in Jesus. Following Jesus has its cost. The riddle is true: we save our lives by losing them. We know this is true because Jesus showed us the way.

Living the Paschal Mystery

The first reading from the prophet Zechariah mentions "a fountain to purify from sin and uncleanness." For us Christians we naturally think of the baptismal font that purifies and cleanses us. Two points might be made.

First, these waters of baptism don't flow just once. The ritual is an action that aptly describes an ongoing sacramental reality in our lives: we are constantly being washed clean. One way to do this, of course, is through confessing our sins either in prayer itself or in sacramental confession. We sometimes forget, though, that good works also cleanse us of our sins! So, the denying self and carrying our daily cross mentioned in the gospel are cleansing activities that lead us to forgiveness and new life.

Second, baptismal purification is also tied into our Christian identity. We are not only freed from sin but are made members of Christ's body. As such, we might expect to happen to us the same things that happened to Jesus. To be practical, that means that when we live our baptismal promises we can expect to be misunderstood, ridiculed, shunned, etc. Paschal mystery living has its demands (dying to self) and rewards (new life).

Focusing the Word

Key words and phrases from the gospel: The Christ of God, suffer greatly, killed, raised, come after me

To the point: Peter calls Jesus "the Christ," a title which refers to the anointed one of the royal house of David. But Jesus' identity as the Christ cannot be separated from his suffering, dying, and rising. Neither can our identity as Christian be separated from denying ourselves, taking up our cross daily, and losing our lives in order to save them. As the Master, so the disciples.

Connecting the Word

to the first reading: Zechariah's prophecy not only describes the royal dimensions of the house of David but also the suffering and death that sometimes came to the king.

to religious experience: Luke shows a real pastoral sensitivity and a pragmatic wisdom in describing the challenge of discipleship not as an occasional commitment but as a "daily" taking up of the cross.

Understanding the Word

"They shall look on him whom they have pierced": In the entire three-year Sunday Lectionary cycle we read from the book of the prophet Zechariah only twice. This is due in part to the fact that this book is tremendously difficult to interpret. The brief and edited selection that makes up this Sunday's first reading is no exception. However, by pairing this reading with the gospel the Lectionary clarifies the difficulty.

The two references to the "house of David" (12:8; 13:1), the profound grief over "him whom they have pierced" (v. 10), and a death on the plain of Megiddo (v. 11), have been taken by some as clues to the mysterious identity of the one who has been pierced. Josiah (640–609 B.C.) of the House of David was one of Judah's greatest kings. Josiah ordered a religious reform, purifying Jerusalem of all traces of foreign religions and of idols (see 2 Kings 23:19-25). Many, including Jeremiah, saw these religious reforms as the beginning of a new era. Unfortunately, in 609 B.C., King Josiah was killed in a battle against the Egyptians on the plain of Megiddo (see 2 Chron 35:20-23). According to this account in Chronicles, "all Judah and Jerusalem mourned him. Jeremiah also composed a lamentation over Josiah, which is recited to this day by all the male and female singers in their lamentations over Josiah" (vv. 24-25). Zechariah prophesies that "on that day" (some unspecified day in the future) the people will again mourn bitterly, but this time their grief will be because of sin. In response God will open a purifying fountain to cleanse them "from sin and uncleanness" (Zech 13:1).

The Lectionary clarifies the uncertainty in Zechariah by taking the passage as a reference to the death of Christ: Jesus, a descendant of the royal house of David, fulfills this prophecy. In this Sunday's gospel Jesus predicts for his disciples that he will "suffer greatly . . . and be killed." At his death Jesus is pierced (John 19:37 explicitly quotes Zech 12:10 at the crucifixion) and Jesus is deeply mourned (Luke 23:27-28, 49). His death purifies people from sin.

ASSEMBLY & FAITH-SHARING GROUPS
- What my prayer tells me about Jesus is . . .
- The cross that faces me in my life is . . . What I must "deny" in order to take it up is . . .
- "Whoever loses his life for my sake will save it." The way I learned that this is true is . . .

PRESIDERS
Occasions when I am tempted to "save" my life (and end up "losing it") are . . .
What enables me to finally "deny" self is . . .

DEACONS
As I serve others what I "lose" is . . . what is "saved" in me is . . .

HOSPITALITY MINISTERS
My hospitality fortifies others while they are carrying their crosses when I . . .

MUSIC MINISTERS
Singing is one way the assembly expresses its thirsting for God. I help them satisfy this thirst when I . . .
In order for them to find their satisfaction in God I must die to myself by . . .

ALTAR MINISTERS
As Christ's "anointed" serving others is not what I do but who I am. What this means to me is . . .

LECTORS
The readings direct me to "look on him whom they have pierced" (first reading). I direct others to "look on him" whenever . . .

EUCHARISTIC MINISTERS
We recognize Jesus in the Body and Blood. The way I recognize Jesus in denying self and taking up the cross is . . .

Model Penitential Rite

Presider: Jesus invites us to follow him, but also warns us that discipleship has its cost: we must deny ourselves and take up our daily cross. During this liturgy let us ask God to strengthen us on our demanding Christian journey . . . [pause]

Lord Jesus, you are the Christ of God: Lord . . .

Christ Jesus, you suffered greatly, were rejected, killed, and raised on the third day: Christ . . .

Lord Jesus, you are the Savior of the world: Lord . . .

Appreciating the Responsorial Psalm

In the first reading God pours onto the people a "spirit of grace and petition." Their prayer moves them to acknowledge their sinfulness, mourn what they have done, and receive purification. The gospel also relates a moment of prayer, one in which Jesus leads the disciples to acknowledge who he is and to accept the suffering that he, and they with him, must undergo.

The responsorial psalm reminds us that prayer—thirsting for God—is the fountainhead of redemption. On the one hand, prayer is a gift from God (first reading). On the other, it is a choice on our part (gospel). Always it is a relationship that reveals both who God is and who we are. Prayer teaches us that we are souls in need of divine nourishment (psalm), sinners in need of repentance and purification (first reading), and disciples called to acknowledge Christ and carry the cross (gospel). Prayer also teaches us that God is our greatest good and ultimate satisfaction, that God acts to bring us to repentance, and that God in Christ takes up the cross ahead of us. May we know for whom we thirst, and may we drink deeply and be transformed.

Model General Intercessions

Presider: God demands of Jesus' disciples great things. With God's help we can be faithful to this call to follow Jesus. And so we pray.

Response:

Lord, hear our prayer.

Cantor:

we pray to the Lord,

For the Church, the body of Christ, called to deny themselves, take up their cross, and follow Jesus . . . [pause]

For all peoples of the world, called to lose their lives for the sake of others . . . [pause]

For all those in need, saved by Jesus' death and resurrection . . . [pause]

For ourselves, strengthened in the bonds of community with one another to be faithful disciples of Jesus . . . [pause]

Presider: Gracious God, you strengthen those who call to you in need: hear these our prayers that one day we might enjoy everlasting life with you and your Son Jesus Christ with the Holy Spirit, one God, for ever and ever. **Amen.**

OPENING PRAYER

Let us pray

Pause for silent prayer

Father,
guide and protector of your people,
grant us an unfailing respect for your name,
and keep us always in your love.

Grant this through our Lord Jesus Christ,
    your Son,
who lives and reigns with you and the
    Holy Spirit,
one God, for ever and ever. **Amen.**

FIRST READING
Zech 12:10-11; 13:1

Thus says the LORD:
    I will pour out on the house of David
    and on the inhabitants of Jerusalem
    a spirit of grace and petition;
    and they shall look on him whom they
        have pierced,
    and they shall mourn for him as one
        mourns for an only son,
    and they shall grieve over him as one
        grieves over a firstborn.

On that day the mourning in Jerusalem
    shall be as great
    as the mourning of Hadadrimmon in
        the plain of Megiddo.

On that day there shall be open to the
    house of David
    and to the inhabitants of Jerusalem,
    a fountain to purify from sin and
        uncleanness.

RESPONSORIAL PSALM
Ps 63:2, 3-4, 5-6, 8-9

R℣. (2b) My soul is thirsting for you, O Lord my God.

O God, you are my God whom I seek;
    for you my flesh pines and my soul thirsts
    like the earth, parched, lifeless and without water.

R℣. My soul is thirsting for you, O Lord my God.

Thus have I gazed toward you in the sanctuary
    to see your power and your glory,
for your kindness is a greater good than life;
    my lips shall glorify you.

R℣. My soul is thirsting for you, O Lord my God.

Thus will I bless you while I live;
    lifting up my hands, I will call upon your name.
As with the riches of a banquet shall my soul be satisfied,
    and with exultant lips my mouth shall praise you.

R℣. My soul is thirsting for you, O Lord my God.

You are my help,
    and in the shadow of your wings I shout for joy.
My soul clings fast to you;
    your right hand upholds me.

R℣. My soul is thirsting for you, O Lord my God.

SECOND READING
Gal 3:26-29

Brothers and sisters:
Through faith you are all children of God
    in Christ Jesus.
For all of you who were baptized into Christ
    have clothed yourselves with Christ.
There is neither Jew nor Greek,
    there is neither slave nor free person,
    there is not male and female;
    for you are all one in Christ Jesus.
And if you belong to Christ,
    then you are Abraham's descendant,
    heirs according to the promise.

About Liturgy

Father's Day: The Mass of the Sunday is to be respected even if this Sunday is Father's Day. An intercession might be added to the general intercessions (see BofB no. 1732) and a blessing for the fathers given in place of the prayer over the people for the Sunday (see BofB no. 1733).

The Cross: The cross has been a Christian symbol of self-denial, self-sacrifice, redemption, and identity with Christ from the very beginning of Christianity. It is probably the primary symbol of Christianity other than the sacramental elements themselves. The cross leads processions (GIRM nos. 117, 119, and 122) and is venerated with incense (GIRM nos. 49 and 277) as are the altar and paschal candle. A cross with a corpus is to be on or near the altar during Mass (GIRM nos. 117 and 308) which helps us relate the sacrifice of the Mass to the sacrifice of Calvary.

In the Eastern Church the custom has been to use a cross rather than a crucifix (a cross with a corpus), often studded with jewels or richly decorated. Sometimes an image of Christ the high priest may be used. The cross in this context celebrates Christ's victory over death and sin and is a symbol of triumph. In the Western Church the custom has been to use a crucifix with an image of the dying or dead Jesus. The cross in this context reminds us of Jesus' self-sacrificing love demonstrated through his passion and death.

About Liturgical Music

Cantor preparation: In the context of this Sunday's readings this responsorial psalm is a courageous, and confident, prayer to make. Jesus pours out his thirst for God as he seeks the reassurance he needs to bear the suffering and death incumbent upon him (gospel). You lead the assembly in joining Jesus in this prayer and the commitment it implies. Do you accept where thirsting for God will ultimately lead you? Do you believe that only carrying the cross will bring ultimate satisfaction?

Selecting seasonal service music, Pt. 7: (See pp. 45, 49, 53, 57, 61, 65 for Parts 1–6.) The process of determining a year-long cycle of seasonal settings may take some years to achieve. Once existing repertoire is earmarked for specific seasons, the task of researching and selecting settings for those seasons for which the parish has no appropriate music, and then of teaching that new repertoire, will take time. Be realistic with the parish and the planning or worship committee. Set goals one small, achievable step at a time.

In terms of the liturgy committee be careful and avoid being overwhelmed with the immensity of the project. The task might be subdivided, letting one group select eucharistic acclamations and another decide about settings of the Glory to God and the Lamb of God. Or the work might be divided seasonally, assigning each season to a different subcommittee. It will also be helpful if the music director makes some prior judgments about available musical settings. Remove from consideration settings which are not appropriate musically, liturgically, or pastorally. This will facilitate the work of the committee(s), and help them more easily accomplish their goals.

JUNE 20, 2004
TWELFTH SUNDAY IN ORDINARY TIME

SPIRITUALITY

Gospel
Luke 1:57-66, 80; L587

When the time arrived for Elizabeth to
    have her child
    she gave birth to a son.
Her neighbors and relatives heard
    that the Lord had shown his
        great mercy toward her,
    and they rejoiced with her.
When they came on the
        eighth day to circumcise
        the child,
    they were going to call him Zechariah
        after his father,
    but his mother said in reply,
    "No. He will be called John."
But they answered her,
    "There is no one among your
        relatives who has this name."
So they made signs, asking his father
    what he wished him to be called.
He asked for a tablet and wrote, "John
    is his name,"
    and all were amazed.
Immediately his mouth was opened, his
    tongue freed,
    and he spoke blessing God.
Then fear came upon all their neighbors,
    and all these matters were discussed
        throughout the hill country of Judea.
All who heard these things took them
        to heart, saying,
    "What, then, will this child be?"
For surely the hand of the Lord was
        with him.

The child grew and became strong in
        spirit,
    and he was in the desert until the day
        of his manifestation to Israel.

See Appendix A, p. 283, for these readings:

FIRST READING
Isa 49:1-6

RESPONSORIAL PSALM
Ps 139:1-3, 13-14, 14-15

SECOND READING
Acts 13:22-26

Reflecting on the Gospel
A car parked in the doctors' parking lot at a hospital had the license plate "Stork 1." It doesn't take a rocket scientist to figure out that it must have been a car belonging to an obstetrician! No doubt this doctor is happy to announce that he is in a profession that almost always is filled with pleasant outcomes and welcomes new life. Conception and birth are usually causes for great joy and wonder, today as well as in the society at the time of John the Baptist's birth. Perhaps even more so in John's time, for progeny was a sign of God's favor and was how people immortalized themselves.

Zechariah and Elizabeth had been barren and now they have a son. God has blessed them and "shown great mercy" toward them. So much of the circumstances surrounding this son's birth, however, announced that he was a blessing even beyond what one might expect or hope for. John's birth was even further cause for wonder—not just for the miracle of birth, but for what this birth means. Something new was happening. But the people were not prepared for exactly how new these events were: John would be the precursor of the One who would be Savior.

John's whole life and ministry were defined in terms of Jesus the messiah. The real amazement of the story of John's conception and birth is that God uses mere humans in his plan of salvation as much as sending the only-begotten Son. John's very birth was an announcement that God continues to be involved in the affairs of humankind to bring us to salvation. John was a light for Jesus so that Jesus could be "a light to the nations" (first reading). This ought to dispel any fears or doubts that our own actions are meaningless. Just as John was the precursor of Jesus, so are we. As John "became strong in spirit" and remained "in the desert" until he was ready to preach and point to Jesus, so must we. As John preached repentance, so ought we. John, then, is a model for how we who are baptized into Christ might live our lives. Like John, we too were given our name "from [our] mother's womb" (see first reading). From all time God planned that we would share in divine life. From all time God intended that we would be saved. We rejoice on this day celebrating John's birth because this birth brought God's plan one step closer to fulfillment. We rejoice also because we, too, participate in God's plan of salvation.

Something new is happening—God continues Christ's saving work through us. We are both precursor and the presence of Christ in the world. Never before has this happened, even in John's time. We announce Jesus and *are* the presence of the risen Christ. No wonder we are amazed. No wonder we rejoice. As with John, so with us: "For surely the hand of the Lord [is] with [us]."

Living the Paschal Mystery
Just as John's whole life and ministry were defined in terms of Jesus, so must ours be. Like John we are not "worthy to unfasten the sandals of his feet," but at the same time we truly are the feet and hands and heart of Jesus in our world today. Paschal mystery living means that our own actions and way of living must be so radically new—so radically different—that people are moved to ask of us, "What, then, is this person?" This doesn't mean that we leave all and go out into a desert. It does mean that we allow ourselves to grow "strong in the spirit" and live as those who have been baptized into Christ the Savior.

Focusing the Word

Key words and phrases from the gospel: she gave birth to a son; all were amazed; What, then, will this child be?

To the point: John's birth was cause for great wonder—something new surely was happening. Though the people asked, "What, then, will this child be?" we know that John became the forerunner of the One who would be Savior. This solemnity invites us both to reflect on God's plan and to rejoice that "this word of salvation has been sent" (second reading).

Model Penitential Rite

Presider: John the Baptist preached a baptism of repentance and also was the forerunner of our Lord. As we begin this liturgy let us open ourselves to the Lord announcing his presence to us . . . [pause]

    Lord Jesus, you are the Savior of the world: Lord . . .

    Christ Jesus, John announced your presence as the Messiah: Christ . . .

    Lord Jesus, you are the word of salvation who dwells among us: Lord . . .

Model General Intercessions

Presider: From the beginning of creation God has desired all humanity to be saved. We are confident that such a loving God will hear our prayers and answer our needs.

Response:

Lord, hear our prayer.

Cantor:

we pray to the Lord,

That each member of the Church point to the presence of Christ in our world as did John the Baptist . . . [pause]

That leaders of nations be agents of righteousness and peace . . . [pause]

That those who are in need receive from God what they ask . . . [pause]

That each one of us be faithful to our own mission to make known Christ in the world . . . [pause]

Presider: Saving God, you hear the prayers of your humble people: grant us what we need so that one day we might share everlasting life with you. We ask this through Christ our Lord. **Amen.**

✚ SPIRITUALITY

Gospel
Luke 9:51-62; L99C

When the days for Jesus' being taken
     up were fulfilled,
  he resolutely determined to journey
     to Jerusalem,
  and he sent messengers ahead of
     him.
On the way they entered a
     Samaritan village
  to prepare for his reception
     there,
  but they would not welcome
     him
  because the destination of
     his journey was
     Jerusalem.
When the disciples James and
     John saw this they asked,
  "Lord, do you want us to call
     down fire from heaven
  to consume them?"
Jesus turned and rebuked them, and
     they journeyed to another village.

As they were proceeding on their
     journey someone said to him,
  "I will follow you wherever you go."
Jesus answered him,
  "Foxes have dens and birds of the
     sky have nests,
  but the Son of Man has nowhere to
     rest his head."

And to another he said, "Follow me."
But he replied, "Lord, let me go first
     and bury my father."
But he answered him, "Let the dead
     bury their dead.
But you, go and proclaim the kingdom
     of God."
And another said, "I will follow you,
     Lord,
  but first let me say farewell to my
     family at home."
To him Jesus said, "No one who sets a
     hand to the plow
  and looks to what was left behind is
     fit for the kingdom of God."

Reflecting on the Gospel

Pilgrimages to well-known destinations are something familiar to all of us. Today devout Jews might visit the Western Wall in Jerusalem; devout Muslims try to visit Mecca at least once before they die; Catholics might make a pilgrimage to Rome or to Lourdes. In the nonreligious realm Disneyland or Disney World, Acapulco, Hawaii, or one of the Caribbean islands might be a favorite destination. In all of these cases the goal of the journey is something desirable and is the motivation for the journey. We usually undertake a journey because we have some good in mind. The gospel for this Sunday is about a journey, too, but the end isn't something anyone would choose. The end is Jerusalem and Jesus was "resolutely determined" to get there. Although the gospel seems to be predominantly about following Jesus and our response to that invitation, we cannot forget that at the center of all this is Jerusalem and the kingdom of God. Clearly, following Jesus leads to Jerusalem and death. Equally clearly, this is the only way to establish God's kingdom.

Jesus' invitation to follow him receives mixed responses. Some try to dissuade Jesus himself from his journey and won't even hear his message ("because the destination of his journey was Jerusalem"). Others seem to make an eager response ("I will follow you wherever you go") but are naive about where the journey leads. Still others make excuses and don't even try to follow Jesus. Each response suggests that people have some sense of what the cost of following Jesus is. At issue is that obedience in following Jesus leads to death.

Our own decision to follow Jesus has implications. For ourselves, the implications lie in terms of our dying to ourselves. For humankind, the implications lie in the fact that our choices truly affect the establishment of God's kingdom here and now. This last point is rather startling; it is easier for us to think of Jesus as Savior of the world and the one who brings about God's reign. It is much more difficult for each of us to grasp that our own actions also bring salvation to others and help establish God's reign. Following Jesus to Jerusalem, then, isn't simply about a personal response to a divine invitation; it is the way God's reign is established.

The challenge of this gospel is for us to be as resolutely determined to accept the dying to self that is necessary for establishing God's reign as Jesus was resolutely determined to go to his own suffering and death. We can be neither naive nor self-excusing. To be "fit for the kingdom of God" we must keep our eyes on Jesus and the destiny.

Living the Paschal Mystery

The context for this Sunday's gospel is that Jesus is "resolutely determined" to go to Jerusalem and this sets the tone for the next months of Ordinary Time for us. On our own journey to the end of the liturgical year (hardly on our minds at this point in June!) we, too, must be resolute about hearing the gospel faithfully and following Jesus, even when that means we, too, are going to "Jerusalem," which symbolizes the ongoing dying to self that is what living the paschal mystery really is.

We hear the gospel faithfully when that gospel is lived in our everyday circumstances. Hearing is more than words going into our ears; it demands of us resolute action. The gospels often are challenging. This one challenges us to go to Jerusalem with Jesus, furthering God's reign.

Focusing the Word

Key words and phrases from the gospel: journey to Jerusalem, follow me, kingdom of God

To the point: The gospel clearly directs our attention to following Jesus. While Luke describes the various responses, motives, and excuses of those who would follow Jesus, we must not ignore Luke's context, indicated at the beginning and end of the episode: Jesus is resolutely going to Jerusalem to fulfill his mission, to die and rise, to establish the kingdom of God.

Connecting the Word

to the first reading: In order to answer Elijah's invitation to succeed him as prophet, Elisha must first relinquish his former way of life ("die") symbolized by the destruction of his plowing equipment and oxen.

to culture: Every journey has its purpose, for example, business, pleasure, refuge, diversion, etc. The Christian journey has a singular purpose—the kingdom of God—about which we must be resolute.

Understanding the Word

Journey to Jerusalem (Part 1): On the occasion of the Transfiguration (9:28-37; Lent 2) Luke told us that Jesus, Moses, and Elijah "spoke of his exodus that he was going to accomplish ['fulfill'] in Jerusalem" (9:31). We discussed how this was a reference to Jesus' approaching death/resurrection/ascension. This Sunday's gospel passage, just a few verses later, tells us that Jesus "resolutely determined to journey to Jerusalem." The Greek expression is, "he firmly set his face to Jerusalem." This passage in Luke's gospel is significant in two ways.

Structurally, this passage introduces a large block of material (9:51–18:14) sometimes called "the great Lukan insertion" or "the big interpolation." Contained in these chapters is much material found only in Luke: several parables, some episodes that take place at meals, controversies, and so on.

Theologically, Luke introduces the theme of the "journey to Jerusalem." Luke divides Jesus' ministry into three parts: the ministry in Galilee (4:14–9:50), the journey to Jerusalem (9:51–19:27), and the ministry in Jerusalem (19:28–21:38). The "journey" section, which begins in this Sunday's gospel and culminates when Jesus arrives in Jerusalem on "Palm Sunday" (19:28), is the middle and longest section of Luke's account of Jesus' ministry. In these chapters Luke refers to Jesus' traveling some eight times, keeping the destination in front of the eyes of his readers.

Without overstating the case, there is a sense in which Luke uses geography in a theological way, that is, the journey becomes a metaphor for discipleship. This Sunday's episode begins with Jesus headed to Jerusalem where he will accomplish his mission (as he will later say, "it is impossible that a prophet should die outside of Jerusalem"; Luke 13:33). The word "journey" is repeated in verses 53 and 55; then the discussion turns to what it means to "follow" Jesus (vv. 57, 59, 61). Just as the passage begins with Jesus firmly setting his face toward Jerusalem, it concludes with the warning that no one who "looks to what was left behind is fit for the kingdom of God" (9:62). The journey of discipleship leads in one direction—to Jerusalem.

ASSEMBLY & FAITH-SHARING GROUPS

Jesus "resolutely determined to journey to Jerusalem."

- To me what this entails is . . .
- In general my life is headed toward . . .
- Ways that I am already "following" Jesus to Jerusalem are . . .
- One thing I could alter in order to journey to Jerusalem with Jesus more closely is . . .

PRESIDERS

I see the "kingdom of God" being established in my very journeying to Jerusalem because . . .

DEACONS

The circumstances that characterize my journey to Jerusalem are . . .
What helps me journey faithfully is . . .

HOSPITALITY MINISTERS

Hospitality is not a haven *from* the journey but reassurance for those *on* the journey. The way I live/minister this for others is . . .

MUSIC MINISTERS

In order to follow Jesus in music ministry some things I have to abandon are . . .
The "inheritance" I am given in return is . . .

ALTAR MINISTERS

The way I am assisting others on their journey to Jerusalem is . . .

LECTORS

Pondering Elijah with Elisha (see first reading)—the way I heard God's invitation to follow Jesus was . . .
What I have "left" to follow him is . . .

EUCHARISTIC MINISTERS

The way even the eucharistic banquet directs me toward Jerusalem is . . .

CELEBRATION

Model Penitential Rite

Presider: The gospel invites us today to follow Jesus on his journey to Jerusalem where Jesus suffers, dies, and rises. Let us open ourselves during this liturgy to God's guiding light and ask for the strength to be faithful to God on our Christian journey . . . [pause]

Lord Jesus, you were resolutely determined to journey to Jerusalem: Lord . . .

Christ Jesus, you call followers to proclaim the good news: Christ . . .

Lord Jesus, you proclaimed the kingdom of God: Lord . . .

Appreciating the Responsorial Psalm

Confronted with the urgency of God's call, Elisha abandoned everything and followed Elijah without hesitation, leaving no possessions intact, not stopping even to bid his parents goodbye (first reading). Similarly, the gospel reveals how radically pressing the journey to Jerusalem is for Jesus. Jesus waits for nothing and no one, wastes no time on those unable to receive him, and cuts no slack for those who hesitate to follow him. For Jesus the urgency of the kingdom overrides everything else.

The responsorial psalm reveals what it is that enables Jesus and Elisha so radically to abandon all for the sake of the kingdom. They can relinquish everything, even what seems necessary for a safe and happy life (home and homeland, family and possessions), because they know they possess the very person of God (psalm refrain). They abandon all because they have been given even more. In this gospel Jesus asks us to make the same choice. Full of divine promise and presence, the psalm gives us the motivation to say yes. May it become our journey-to-Jerusalem song.

Model General Intercessions

Presider: We need strength on our Christian journey and so we make our needs known to God.

Response:

Lord, hear our prayer.

Cantor:

we pray to the Lord,

That all members of the Church resolutely follow Jesus in lives of self-sacrificing love . . . [pause]

That leaders of nations lead their people to justice and peace . . . [pause]

That those who falter on the journey of life might be guided in God's ways . . . [pause]

That each of us further God's reign by being faithful to the gospel's demands of self-sacrifice for the good of others . . . [pause]

Presider: Gracious God, you desire that your reign of justice and peace be established throughout the world: hear these our prayers that one day we might enjoy everlasting life in the kingdom of heaven. We ask this through Christ our Lord. **Amen.**

OPENING PRAYER

Let us pray

Pause for silent prayer

Father,
you call your children
to walk in the light of Christ.
Free us from darkness
and keep us in the radiance of your truth.

We ask this through our Lord Jesus Christ,
  your Son,
who lives and reigns with you and the
  Holy Spirit,
one God, for ever and ever. **Amen.**

FIRST READING
1 Kgs 19:16b, 19-21

The LORD said to Elijah:
  "You shall anoint Elisha, son of
    Shaphat of Abel-meholah,
  as prophet to succeed you."

Elijah set out and came upon Elisha, son
    of Shaphat,
  as he was plowing with twelve yoke of
    oxen;
  he was following the twelfth.
Elijah went over to him and threw his
    cloak over him.
Elisha left the oxen, ran after Elijah,
    and said,
  "Please, let me kiss my father and
    mother goodbye,
  and I will follow you."
Elijah answered, "Go back!
Have I done anything to you?"
Elisha left him and, taking the yoke of
    oxen, slaughtered them;
  he used the plowing equipment for fuel
    to boil their flesh,
  and gave it to his people to eat.
Then Elisha left and followed Elijah as his
    attendant.

RESPONSORIAL PSALM

Ps 16:1-2, 5, 7-8, 9-10, 11

R̸. (cf. 5a) You are my inheritance, O Lord.

Keep me, O God, for in you I take refuge;
   I say to the LORD, "My LORD are you.
O Lord, my allotted portion and my cup,
   you it is who hold fast my lot."

R̸. You are my inheritance, O Lord.

I bless the LORD who counsels me;
   even in the night my heart exhorts me.
I set the LORD ever before me;
   with him at my right hand I shall not be
     disturbed.

R̸. You are my inheritance, O Lord.

Therefore my heart is glad and my soul
   rejoices,
   my body, too, abides in confidence
because you will not abandon my soul to
   the netherworld,
   nor will you suffer your faithful one to
     undergo corruption.

R̸. You are my inheritance, O Lord.

You will show me the path to life,
   fullness of joys in your presence,
   the delights at your right hand forever.

SECOND READING

Gal 5:1, 13-18

Brothers and sisters:
For freedom Christ set us free;
   so stand firm and do not submit again
     to the yoke of slavery.

For you were called for freedom, brothers
   and sisters.
But do not use this freedom
   as an opportunity for the flesh;
   rather, serve one another through love.
For the whole law is fulfilled in one
   statement,
   namely, *You shall love your neighbor as*
     yourself.
But if you go on biting and devouring one
   another,
   beware that you are not consumed by
     one another.

I say, then: live by the Spirit
   and you will certainly not gratify the
     desire of the flesh.
For the flesh has desires against the Spirit,
   and the Spirit against the flesh;
   these are opposed to each other,
   so that you may not do what you want.
But if you are guided by the Spirit, you are
   not under the law.

About Liturgy

Processions at Mass: Processions are like mini-journeys—they lead us from one place to another. They always have a goal. During Mass there are actually four processions, each with its own goal. Although the General Instruction of the Roman Missal refers to the four processions (see GIRM nos. 44, 47, 73, 86, 119, 133), it gives no explanation or theology for them. The following comments may help fill in this lacuna.

   1. Entrance procession. This procession at the beginning of Mass is symbolic of the gathering of all the people into a unity for a common purpose of worship and transformation. The entrance procession symbolizes our journey from being individual *members* of the body of Christ to *being* the body of Christ gathered around the one Head, Christ made visible in the Church.

   2. Gospel procession. The procession with the gospel book (usually from the altar to the ambo) is an opportunity for the assembly to acclaim the presence of Christ in the proclaimed word. It also is a symbolic expression of their journey from *hearing* God's word to putting it into practice.

   3. Procession with the gifts. The procession and presentation of the gifts symbolize the gift of ourselves presented to God for transformation into being more perfect members of the body of Christ just as the bread and wine are transformed into being the real Presence of Christ. As the gifts are placed on the altar we place ourselves on the altar and offer ourselves with Christ in sacrifice. It is symbolic of the ongoing journey of self-sacrifice that characterizes Christian living.

   4. Communion procession. The Communion procession symbolizes our journey to the messianic table, that heavenly banquet in which we already share by partaking in Jesus' Body and Blood at Communion and also which we will forever share when we die and go to heaven. This procession most clearly proclaims what it means when the Communion lines actually move forward toward the altar.

About Liturgical Music

Cantor preparation: Your singing of this psalm testifies that you have come to know that the reward of discipleship is far more valuable than its cost. Because you have chosen to follow Jesus, you have been given God's very self as your "portion" and "lot." How have you come to know this? Who has shown you? How this week might you give God thanks for this knowledge and these tutors?

Selecting seasonal service music, Pt. 8: In the parish, the introduction of new service music needs to be sensitively paced. Learning one new setting a year is a major achievement for most assemblies. This means that some less appropriate music will have to stay in place for a time while the whole process of selecting and establishing a year-round repertoire of seasonal service music unfolds. But what is important is that the music director know where he or she is going and what steps are to be taken—slow but sure—to get there.

   Regarding the music director: be patient with the size of the task and with the educational efforts it requires of you. Keep the goal in front of you and think long term. In the meantime, enjoy the process as it unfolds. You will be teaching the parish a great deal about the liturgical year and the importance of its rhythms; you will be collaborating with a number of parish members in establishing a solid parish repertoire of service music; you will be fulfilling the most important aspect of your ministry as a liturgical musician: leading the assembly into the paschal mystery through the mystery of music.

JUNE 27, 2004
THIRTEENTH SUNDAY
IN ORDINARY TIME

SPIRITUALITY

Gospel
Matt 16:13-19; L591

When Jesus went into the region of
    Caesarea Philippi
  he asked his disciples,
    "Who do people say that the Son of
      Man is?"
They replied, "Some say John the
    Baptist, others Elijah,
  still others Jeremiah or one of the
    prophets."
He said to them, "But who do you
    say that I am?"
Simon Peter said in reply,
  "You are the Christ, the Son of
    the living God."
Jesus said to him in reply,
  "Blessed are you, Simon son
    of Jonah.
For flesh and blood has not
    revealed this to you, but my
    heavenly Father.
And so I say to you, you are Peter,
    and upon this rock I will build my
    church,
    and the gates of the netherworld
      shall not prevail against it.
I will give you the keys to the kingdom
    of heaven.
Whatever you bind on earth shall be
    bound in heaven;
  and whatever you loose on earth
      shall be loosed in heaven."

See Appendix A, p. 284, for these readings:

FIRST READING
Acts 12:1-11

RESPONSORIAL PSALM
Ps 34:2-3, 4-5, 6-7, 8-9

SECOND READING
2 Tim 4:6-8, 17-18

Reflecting on the Gospel

All three readings for this solemnity record rather unusual events that, we would think, place Peter and Paul far and above the rest of us average Christians. The first reading makes a big point about the number of guards surrounding Peter in prison; an angel comes and leads him away. In the second reading Paul is "rescued from the lion's mouth" so that he might complete his mission to the Gentiles. The gospel tells about the disciples' misunderstanding of who Jesus is; it is Peter who, through revelation, grasps Jesus' true identity. If John the Baptist was cause for wonder and amazement, how much more it would seem are Peter and Paul! Yet, interestingly enough, these readings are not about Peter and Paul's successful moments but about times when they are weak or in danger and need God's help.

This solemnity not only honors these two greatest saints (these are the only two apostles who have a festival with the rank of solemnity on our liturgical calendar) but the readings unquestionably direct our attention to God and what God is accomplishing through them—the establishment of Jesus' Church. The first reading's context is "the feast of Unleavened Bread" or "Passover." Peter is to be brought to trial after the festival; he is rescued the night before trial. Clearly there is a parallel with Jesus' own arrest and coming to trial; Jesus suffers and dies while Peter's demise is delayed until he has completed his apostolic work of being instrumental in establishing the Church. Paul is nearing the end of his apostolic mission and readily acknowledges that he has "competed well" and "finished the race" because "the Lord stood by me and gave me strength." Both apostles were successful because they surrendered to God's action within them and made clear that their mission was not their own but Christ's. The gospel reminds us that we can't come to any true sense of who Jesus is or be successful in our own efforts to carry on Jesus' mission except through the hand of God.

Both of these great apostles "kept the faith." And this is what they share with us. We, too, have been given the same faith in Christ Jesus as Peter and Paul. Because of this we can be as extraordinary as they were. All we need do is surrender ourselves like they did to the mystery of God's actions on behalf of the Church. We honor Peter and Paul as the two apostles upon whom the universal mission of the Church rests; this feast challenges us to accept that this same mission is continued in our own efforts to be faithful to Jesus' gospel. Yes, Peter and Paul are amazing and cause for wonder. Because we share in their same mission to make Christ known in the world, so can our efforts be amazing and cause for wonder. Like these apostles, we need only acknowledge that Jesus is the Christ and resolve to follow him wherever he leads. We are the Church. We are the manifestation of God's mighty acts of salvation.

Living the Paschal Mystery

Being great apostles of Christ isn't a matter of doing great things; it is a matter of keeping faith in Christ Jesus. By recognizing ourselves as Church—the body of Christ—all of our actions are truly God's actions on behalf of the Church. It is through us that the proclamation of the good news of Jesus' death and resurrection is being completed. And, like these two great apostles, the Lord will give us strength to carry on the mission, will rescue us from evil, and bring us safely "to his heavenly kingdom."

Focusing the Word

Key words and phrases from the gospel: You are the Christ, revealed
. . . to you, build my church

To the point: While this festival is about two great apostles of Jesus, the
readings direct us to God's actions on behalf of the Church which Jesus founds.
In the gospel it is God's revelation that brings Peter to insight about who Jesus
really is. In the first and second readings it is God's power that rescues both
Peter and Paul from death.

Model Penitential Rite

Presider: We honor today Saints Peter and Paul because they were faithful to
preaching the gospel and cooperating with Christ in establishing his Church.
Let us prepare ourselves to celebrate this liturgy by surrendering ourselves to
God's action within us so that we, too, can be faithful disciples . . . [pause]

> Lord Jesus, you are the Christ: Lord . . .
>
> Christ Jesus, you are the Son of the living God: Christ . . .
>
> Lord Jesus, you build your Church upon your faithful disciples: Lord . . .

Model General Intercessions

Presider: Let us pray that Christ's Church will always prevail against evil and
bring us all to everlasting life.

Response:

Cantor:

That all members of the Church may be models of faithful discipleship like
Peter and Paul . . . [pause]

That all leaders of the world's nations guide their people in righteousness . . .
[pause]

That those who are imprisoned unjustly might be freed and those who are
justly imprisoned might retain their dignity . . . [pause]

That each of us take up our own role in establishing Christ's Church . . .
[pause]

Presider: Caring God, you strengthen all faithful disciples to carry on Christ's
mission of establishing your kingdom: hear our prayers that one day we might
also receive a "crown of righteousness." We pray through the intercession of
Saints Peter and Paul and ask this through Jesus Christ our Lord. **Amen.**

OPENING PRAYER

Let us pray

Pause for silent prayer

Lord our God,
encourage us through the prayers of Saints
    Peter and Paul.
May the apostles who strengthened the
    faith of the infant Church
help us on our way of salvation.

We ask this through our Lord Jesus Christ,
    your Son,
who lives and reigns with you and the Holy
    Spirit,
one God, for ever and ever. **Amen.**

FOR REFLECTION

- As I ponder the lives of Peter and Paul
  some things I can learn from them are . . .

- Like Peter, an example of where Christ is
  building his Church through me is . . .

- Like Paul, a time when "the Lord stood
  by me and gave me strength" (second
  reading) was . . .

✠ SPIRITUALITY

Gospel
Luke 10:1-12, 17-20; L102C

At that time the Lord appointed
    seventy-two others
  whom he sent ahead of him in
    pairs
  to every town and place he
    intended to visit.
He said to them,
  "The harvest is abundant but
    the laborers are few;
  so ask the master of the
    harvest
  to send out laborers for his
    harvest.
Go on your way;
  behold, I am sending you like
    lambs among wolves.
Carry no money bag, no sack,
    no sandals;
  and greet no one along the way.
Into whatever house you enter, first say,
  'Peace to this household.'
If a peaceful person lives there,
  your peace will rest on him;
  but if not, it will return to you.
Stay in the same house and eat and
    drink what is offered to you,
  for the laborer deserves his payment.
Do not move about from one house to
    another.
Whatever town you enter and they
    welcome you,
  eat what is set before you,
  cure the sick in it and say to them,
  'The kingdom of God is at hand for
    you.'
Whatever town you enter and they do
    not receive you,
  go out into the streets and say,
  'The dust of your town that clings to
    our feet,
  even that we shake off against you.'
Yet know this: the kingdom of God is at
    hand.
I tell you,
  it will be more tolerable for Sodom on
    that day than for that town."

Continued in Appendix A, p. 284.

Reflecting on the Gospel

When presidents are no longer in office, they are still addressed as "Mr. President." When ambassadors leave their post, they are still called "Mr. Ambassador." When queens are replaced by daughters or daughters-in-law, they are still called the "queen mother." Some positions in life are not simply term offices; somehow we have a sense that the respect that is due continues even when the individual functions in another capacity. The office itself it tied into the person him- or herself and actually changes who they are. One cannot put off being president or ambassador or queen. In this Sunday's gospel the disciples are "sent ahead" of Jesus, not so much with a mission to do as to be ambassadors for Jesus. The respect and honor that are due Jesus are extended also to Jesus' disciples and this is how God's kingdom is "at hand." Three related issues are posed in the gospel.

First, when God's kingdom is present there is peace, healing, and demons are allayed. The point here is that these wonderful deeds manifest that the kingdom is present because Jesus is present. This leads to the second point, which is this: in the very presence of the disciples who are ambassadors for Jesus the kingdom is present. In other words, the kingdom is present when Jesus is present. Although the kingdom is manifested in external good works, its manifestation is first through the very presence of Christ and the persons who are sent by him. Finally, third, the kingdom is resolutely being realized whether it is accepted or rejected. God will prevail in establishing the reign of righteousness whether we humans accept it or not.

When Jesus is with the disciples they are like John the Baptist—the precursors of Jesus sent ahead to prepare his way. When Jesus is gone (as in our own times) disciples are like Jesus himself and must preach and heal. The gospel doesn't set up an opposition between being and doing but shows us how the mission is connected to being sent by Jesus as ambassadors of his presence. We do everything because we are disciples of Jesus and act in his name.

Living the Paschal Mystery

In our own times we are not so conscious of personified evil as in the time of Jesus. Demons represent a worldview; God's kingdom breaks in on this evil and establishes a new world order in which evil's grasp is broken. The establishment of God's reign is already an in-breaking of the final glory that will be ours—our "names are [already] written in heaven." References to the abundance of the end times are captured in the "harvest" metaphor Jesus uses. Jesus looks at the harvest and sees abundance, fulfillment. Some of this abundance and fulfillment is surely realized in our own taking up of Jesus' mission to bring peace, heal, and dispel evil. The challenge of the gospel is that we don't get so lost in doing Jesus' mission that we forget being disciples—ambassadors—of Christ is in itself already an in-breaking of God's reign. It is in Christ's presence through us that peace and joy are spread.

Living the paschal mystery means believing in what God has made us—ambassadors of Christ, members of his body. It means that we are as satisfied with the presence we bring as we are with the good that we can do. Mission is being sent to *be* Christ for others. Only when we act out of our identity can anything we do help establish God's reign.

Focusing the Word

Key words and phrases from the gospel: I am sending you, peace, cure the sick, kingdom of God is at hand

To the point: When peace prevails, healing takes place, and "demons are subject," the kingdom of God becomes manifest. This kingdom of God is "at hand" in the very ministry of Jesus and the disciples he sends forth. Whether accepted or rejected, God's kingdom is resolutely being realized.

Connecting the Word

to the first reading: Isaiah's prophecy of the future is very positive: there will be comfort, rejoicing, abundance, prosperity. This prophecy is fulfilled in the ministry of Jesus and his disciples: "the harvest is abundant."

to culture: Doomsday preachers today are predominantly negative, seeing the manifestation of evil as signs of the end times. Jesus' (and Isaiah's) language of abundance reminds us that God is bringing about a kingdom where abundance manifests God's care and beneficence.

Understanding the Word

The Kingdom of God: Jesus sends the seventy-two disciples as he had earlier sent the Twelve (9:1-6; see the Solemnity of the Body and Blood of Christ). After giving instructions Jesus tells them what to say: "the kingdom of God is at hand." In Luke's theology the kingdom of God marks a new age. Jesus said, "The law and the prophets lasted until John; but from then on the kingdom of God is proclaimed" (16:16). Consistent with Luke's view of an orderly unfolding of salvation history (Advent 1, OT 3), John the Baptist brought to a completion the former age. With Jesus' coming the new age of the kingdom has begun.

Jesus describes two scenarios: one in which those to whom the disciples preach "welcome you," the other in which "they do not receive you." In both cases the disciples announce, "the kingdom of God is at hand" (vv. 9, 11). For each the kingdom means something different. For those who are peaceable, who welcome the disciples, and give them something to "eat and drink," the kingdom is manifest when the disciples "cure the sick." Thus, hospitality, table fellowship, and the healing of disease are all signs that the kingdom of God is truly "at hand for you." The gracious mercy of God has taken hold: "the kingdom of God is among you" (17:21). Such tokens as fellowship and restored health are pledges of the kingdom in its fullness. The first reading from Isaiah uses different imagery to convey the sense of God's rule over the people: mourning is replaced by rejoicing, there shall be abundance, prosperity, comfort, and people flourish like the grass.

However, the refusal to receive the disciples and their proclamation results in judgment: shaking the dust off their sandals is a traditional sign of disavowal and disowning. On the one hand, refusal brings judgment; the weight of judgment will be greater than that leveled against the notoriously sinful city of Sodom—its destruction was total! On the other hand, refusal does not prevent or impede the kingdom. Its coming is assured, its establishment is not in doubt.

ASSEMBLY & FAITH-SHARING GROUPS

- Jesus' saying "the kingdom of God is at hand" means to me . . .
- Jesus is sending me to announce/establish the kingdom in my daily life. Some of my obstacles are . . .
- Ways that I am manifesting the kingdom's presence for others are . . .

PRESIDERS

How my ministry is the way my name is being "written in heaven" is . . .

DEACONS

My daily life and ministry embodies God's care for the "nurslings" (see first reading) whenever I . . .

HOSPITALITY MINISTERS

Genuine hospitality manifests God's kingdom at hand because . . .

MUSIC MINISTERS

What helps my music ministry announce the presence of the kingdom within the assembly is . . .
What impedes this mission is . . .

ALTAR MINISTERS

My serving makes "the Lord's power . . . known" (first reading) to others because . . .

LECTORS

The Word makes known to me "the Lord's power" (first reading). The way I proclaim that power—in liturgy and in daily living—is . . .

EUCHARISTIC MINISTERS

The eucharistic banquet manifests God's abundance (see first reading). I have experienced this abundance when . . .
I extend it toward others when . . .

Model Penitential Rite

Presider: Jesus sends out the disciples to be ambassadors of his presence. In our baptism we were made members of the body of Christ. Let us prepare to celebrate this liturgy by opening ourselves to God's presence and God's desire to transform us into more perfect ambassadors of Christ . . . [pause]

Lord Jesus, your presence brings peace and healing: Lord . . .

Christ Jesus, your presence dispels evil: Christ . . .

Lord Jesus, your power is given us to further God's reign: Lord . . .

Appreciating the Responsorial Psalm

In these verses from Psalm 66 the psalmist calls the entire earth to come and see the marvelous works of the Lord and to shout praises for this God who has wrought such "tremendous . . . deeds!" In the first reading it is the Lord who calls the people to rejoice over marvelous deeds done on behalf of Jerusalem. In her arms the people will be fed and comforted and will discover how God has acted to save and restore. In the gospel Jesus sends his disciples out to proclaim the same message: God is acting to save, the kingdom is at hand. Some will welcome this message, others will reject it. But regardless the response, the coming of the kingdom of God will not be thwarted; Satan will fall from the sky.

Like the disciples we, too, face successes and failures as we go about the mission of announcing the good news of the kingdom. But we can "cry out . . . with joy" (psalm refrain) for we know that the power of God to overcome evil is indomitable; the kingdom will prevail. Furthermore, we who are its ambassadors already have our "names written there" (gospel).

Model General Intercessions

Presider: Being ambassadors of Christ is no small mission. Let us pray for the grace to be faithful disciples.

Response:

Lord, hear our prayer.

Cantor:

we pray to the Lord,

That all members of the Church be faithful ambassadors of Christ's presence . . . [pause]

That our nation share generously its abundance with its own needy and those of all the world . . . [pause]

That the sick and those needing healing of any kind be touched by the presence of Christ . . . [pause]

That each of us rejoice because God's kingdom is being realized through our being the presence of Christ for others . . . [pause]

Presider: God of abundance, you give us all good things in order that your kingdom may be firmly established: hear these our prayers that one day we might share in your everlasting kingdom of heaven. We pray through Jesus Christ our Lord. **Amen.**

ALTERNATIVE OPENING PRAYER

Let us pray

Pause for silent prayer

Father,
in the rising of your Son
death gives birth to new life.
The sufferings he endured restored hope
    to a fallen world.
Let sin never ensnare us
with empty promises of passing joy.
Make us one with you always,
so that our joy may be holy,
and our love may give life.

We ask this through Christ our Lord.
    Amen.

FIRST READING
Isa 66:10-14c

Thus says the LORD:
Rejoice with Jerusalem and be glad
    because of her,
  all you who love her;
exult, exult with her,
  all you who were mourning over her!
Oh, that you may suck fully
  of the milk of her comfort,
that you may nurse with delight
  at her abundant breasts!
    For thus says the LORD:
Lo, I will spread prosperity over Jerusalem
    like a river,
  and the wealth of the nations like an
      overflowing torrent.
As nurslings, you shall be carried in her
    arms,
  and fondled in her lap;
as a mother comforts her child,
  so will I comfort you;
  in Jerusalem you shall find your comfort.

When you see this, your heart shall rejoice
  and your bodies flourish like the grass;
the LORD's power shall be known to his
  servants.

RESPONSORIAL PSALM

Ps 66:1-3, 4-5, 6-7, 16, 20

℟. (1) Let all the earth cry out to God with joy.

Shout joyfully to God, all the earth,
    sing praise to the glory of his name;
    proclaim his glorious praise.
Say to God, "How tremendous are your
    deeds!"

℟. Let all the earth cry out to God with joy.

"Let all on earth worship and sing praise
    to you,
    sing praise to your name!"
Come and see the works of God,
    his tremendous deeds among the
        children of Adam.

℟. Let all the earth cry out to God with joy.

He has changed the sea into dry land;
    through the river they passed on foot.
Therefore let us rejoice in him.
    He rules by his might forever.

℟. Let all the earth cry out to God with joy.

Hear now, all you who fear God,
    while I declare what he has done for me.
Blessed be God who refused me not
    my prayer or his kindness!

℟. Let all the earth cry out to God with joy.

SECOND READING

Gal 6:14-18

Brothers and sisters:
May I never boast except in the cross of
    our Lord Jesus Christ,
    through which the world has been
        crucified to me,
    and I to the world.
For neither does circumcision mean
    anything, nor does uncircumcision,
    but only a new creation.
Peace and mercy be to all who follow this
    rule
    and to the Israel of God.

From now on, let no one make troubles for
    me;
    for I bear the marks of Jesus on my body.

The grace of our Lord Jesus Christ be
    with your spirit,
    brothers and sisters. Amen.

About Liturgy

Choosing the longer or shorter form of a reading: Sometimes the Lectionary offers a longer or shorter form of a reading and which to use is left to the pastoral discretion of liturgy planners. It is not good to assume that the shorter reading is always best; often it is the longer reading which fills out and completes an important message of the Liturgy of the Word. In the longer form of the gospel for this Sunday, for example, leaving out the last part (as the shorter form does) would omit that we must act in Jesus' name (not on our own), Jesus gives us the power to be successful, and our names are already "written in heaven" which lends an eschatological note. When would one use the shorter form? Some pastoral situations (for example, in a children's Liturgy of the Word) might demand simpler readings. Or when the specific point that is being developed in the homily and carried through the general intercessions does not need the extra Scripture verses. The point is, choices must be made deliberately, carefully, and with good reason.

July 4th: This Sunday is July 4th and there is always a pastoral temptation on such days to blend the Sunday liturgy with the national holiday. Good liturgical planning would enable the Sunday liturgy to take precedence but still acknowledge the holiday. For example, the second petition in the model general intercessions takes into consideration the holiday. Some comments might be made in the presider's introduction. There is a proper Mass for July 4th given in the U.S. Sacramentary, but it may not replace the proper Mass for this Sunday.

About Liturgical Music

Cantor preparation: In this Sunday's gospel Jesus sends the disciples on mission to announce his coming. Your singing of the responsorial psalm is part of that mission for it is a hymn of praise telling of God's saving deeds. Where have you experienced these deeds in your own life? in the lives of others? How have you announced them to the world?

Hymn suggestion: Because of its origins as "Battle Hymn of the Republic," the hymn "Mine Eyes Have Seen the Glory" is often considered more a patriotic song than a religious hymn. But its text heralds more than national victory over enemies (in this case the Union army over the Confederacy). On a deeper, eschatological level the text celebrates the ultimate victory of the kingdom of God over all opposing forces. Furthermore, the fourth verse lays down the ultimate challenge of discipleship: that we give our lives that this kingdom come. In light of its theology this hymn connects well, then, with this Sunday's gospel and would make an appropriate recessional song. The hymn needs to be used cautiously, however. An assembly that does not grasp its eschatological meaning will sing it only as a patriotic hymn celebrating July 4. It is important that they understand this hymn is not a battle cry for national victory in war but a testimony that the kingdom of God will triumph no matter what forces vie against it. To this end it might be wise to run a blurb in the bulletin explaining the hymn's deeper religious meaning and its connection with this Sunday's gospel.

SPIRITUALITY

Gospel
Luke 10:25-37; L105C

There was a scholar of the law who
    stood up to test Jesus and said,
"Teacher, what must I do to
    inherit eternal life?"
Jesus said to him, "What is
    written in the law?
How do you read it?"
He said in reply,
    You shall love the Lord, your
        God,
    with all your heart,
    with all your being,
    with all your strength,
    and with all your mind,
    and your neighbor as
        yourself.
He replied to him, "You have
    answered correctly;
do this and you will live."

But because he wished to justify
    himself, he said to Jesus,
"And who is my neighbor?"
Jesus replied,
    "A man fell victim to robbers
as he went down from Jerusalem to
    Jericho.
They stripped and beat him and went
    off leaving him half-dead.
A priest happened to be going down
    that road,
    but when he saw him, he passed by
        on the opposite side.
Likewise a Levite came to the place,
    and when he saw him, he passed by
        on the opposite side.
But a Samaritan traveler who came
    upon him
was moved with compassion at the
    sight.

Continued in Appendix A, p. 284.

Reflecting on the Gospel

We have a mindset today that keeping or breaking a law doesn't really make any difference so long as one doesn't get caught. Avoiding punishment is the name of the game and choosing to break laws is about getting what we want—whether it involves shoplifting, running a red light, or cheating on our income tax. All too many of us live lives that revolve around personal gain, and that all too often at the expense of another. At first glance the gospel this Sunday is about keeping the two great commandments. By answering the lawyer's question with a parable Jesus shows us a broader issue, that of giving up personal gain for the good of another.

In the gospel the lawyer approaches Jesus to "test" him with the question about eternal life. The issue here isn't whether we have life or not—Jesus wishes us to have life—but on how we gain that life. The lawyer knows that the two great commandments of love of God and love of neighbor sum up the whole law and prophets. One only needs to live that love. The lawyer focuses on himself and refuses to see the broader issue.

Jesus doesn't directly answer the question about "who is [one's] neighbor" because he knows the scholar has the law written within him (see first reading: "command . . . already in your mouths and in your hearts; you have only to carry it out"). Instead Jesus responds to the lawyer's question with a parable that illustrates how keeping the law isn't a matter of focusing on details and right or wrong or personal gain but is a matter of right relationships with one's neighbor as exhibited by acting with compassion and mercy. The lawyer's first question about inheriting eternal life has to do with his own gain. The episode and parable unfold not in terms of personal gain but in terms of compassion and mercy toward another.

Ironically, the way we inherit eternal life is by dying to self for the sake of another. The Samaritan in the parable isn't moved to help the stricken traveler because of the law but because he was a person of compassion and mercy. This is the law written within our hearts—not details about keeping specific laws but a general regard for the other that arises out of genuine care for the other. Moreover, this way of keeping the law is yet another manifestation of God's reign being realized. It is an in-breaking of a new order, a new way of relating to each other: personal gain is set aside in favor of the good of another.

Living the Paschal Mystery

Our reflection on this Sunday's gospel isn't really setting up an opposition between keeping the law and doing good for others. Probably in our society and Church today we need to become more aware of the value of keeping laws. Our reflection does alert us to the fact that keeping laws alone isn't enough. All our actions are directed to the good of others and the furthering of God's kingdom. Keeping laws promotes good order in any community; doing good for others promotes right relationships in those same communities.

Law is something external to us, rather easily measured. Mercy and compassion are internal to us and can be measured only in terms of the good we actually do for others. Laws are internalized when they are kept for the sake of others. We are to do as the Samaritan in the parable: let the law of mercy and compassion gain for us eternal life.

Focusing the Word
Key words and phrases from the gospel: inherit eternal life, moved with compassion, Go and do likewise

To the point: The gospel episode begins with the lawyer's concern about his own gain ("inherit eternal life"). However, Jesus redirects the lawyer from self-concern to compassion and mercy toward another in need. Ironically, the way to inherit eternal life is by dying to self for the sake of another.

Connecting the Word
to the first reading: Moses' words that the law is "already in your mouths and in your hearts" is proved true by the lawyer who readily quotes the law. Jesus, echoing Moses, urges the lawyer to do what he already knows.

to culture: In our legal culture we are very aware of law and know that it cannot legislate love or compassion. Yet these are the foundation of God's law.

Understanding the Word
Love and law: At the center of the discussion between Jesus and the lawyer is a law that requires "love." We might ask: how can "love" be required by law? How does one legislate "love"? The law commanding love of God quoted by the lawyer is the *"Shema"* from Deuteronomy 6:4-5. The *"Shema"* (= "Hear, O Israel . . .") is the core affirmation of Israelite faith and is recited twice a day by devout Jews. The book of Deuteronomy, in its final form, is presented as a covenant. In turn, a "covenant" is a standard ancient Near Eastern contractual agreement between individuals or kingdoms. The main element of all such covenants is found in the requirements that the greater party imposes on the lesser. In this analogy all the laws contained in Deuteronomy are the require-ments of the covenant. Because the covenant has made Israel God's own people, the lawyer rightly speaks of "inheriting" the blessings God had earlier promised. The blessing described in Deuteronomy for "doing" the law will be life in the promised land: ". . . observe all the commandments I enjoin on you today, that you may live and increase" (Deut 8:1). Jesus echoes this command when he says to the lawyer, "Do this and you will live" (Luke 10:28).

It was a standard feature of ancient covenants that the one imposing the stipulations would command his servant to love him. The subjects of the Assyrian king Assurbanipal are commanded, "You will love Assurbanipal as yourselves"; in another text the subjects reply, ". . . the king of Assyria, our lord, we will love." In these contexts "love" means loyalty; in turn, loyalty is expressed in obedience. This kind of "love" can be legislated for it requires a certain kind of behavior, not an emotional response of affection towards an-other. The connection between "love" and "obedience" is clearly in Jesus' mind when he says, "If you love me, you will keep my commandments" (John 14:15). "Love" is not an emotion; it is something one does: "what must I do?" (10:25), "do this and you will live" (10:28), "go and do likewise" (10:37).

**ASSEMBLY &
FAITH-SHARING GROUPS**
- What I like and dislike about Jesus' reply to "who is my neighbor?" is . . .
- I understand treating another "with mercy" to mean . . .
- In light of this parable, I (or my parish) must "go and do" . . .

PRESIDERS
Times when I have tried to "test" Jesus or "justify" myself to him were . . .
The way Jesus responded to me was . . .
What that teaches me about ministry is . . .

DEACONS
The Samaritan was "moved" not by the Law but by compassion. In my ministry I am moved by . . .

HOSPITALITY MINISTERS
Times when my hospitality was merely a formality are . . .
The difference in my hospitality when I em-body compassion is . . .

MUSIC MINISTERS
The mercy which music ministry calls forth from me is . . .
The life God grants me through this minis-try is . . .

ALTAR MINISTERS
Serving others is forming me into a "good Samaritan" because . . .

LECTORS
The word that is "very near" me and that Jesus is asking me to "carry" out (first read-ing) is . . .

EUCHARISTIC MINISTERS
Looking at my daily life, my answer to "who is my neighbor?" has been . . .
The one to whom I need to extend mercy before coming to the altar is . . .

Model Penitential Rite

Presider: The gospel today raises the question of how we inherit eternal life and concludes with a focus on the Good Samaritan's compassion and mercy. Let us prepare ourselves to celebrate this liturgy by opening ourselves up to God's mercy . . . [pause]

Lord Jesus, you desire eternal life for us: Lord . . .

Christ Jesus, you teach us how to live compassionately and with mercy: Christ . . .

Lord Jesus, you show us the way of self-sacrificing love: Lord . . .

Appreciating the Responsorial Psalm

At first glance the verses of Psalm 69 used for this responsorial psalm seem unrelated to either the first reading or the gospel. But further reflection reveals a rich and rewarding connection.

In the first reading Moses counsels the people that the commandments are not beyond them but within them. In the gospel Jesus teaches that the commandments to love God and neighbor are not hazy but clear and applicable: to love God means to love the immediate neighbor in need. Psalm 69 reminds us that whenever we have been in need God has responded without hesitation. We know God's law of love because we have experienced God's loving us—directly and personally. And we know who is the neighbor in need because we have been that neighbor. It is this knowledge which fills our hearts and inspires us to act compassionately toward others. Psalm 69 grounds our ability to love in the One who has first loved us.

Model General Intercessions

Presider: Our God is compassionate and merciful and so surely hears the prayers of those who cry out in need.

Response:

Lord, hear our prayer.

Cantor:

we pray to the Lord,

That all members of the Church model love of God and neighbor . . . [pause]

That peoples of the world act with compassion and mercy . . . [pause]

That those who are stricken down and in need be helped with compassion and mercy . . . [pause]

That we here assembled inherit eternal life because of our concern for others . . . [pause]

Presider: Compassionate and merciful God, you hear the prayers of those who cry out to you: hear us today that one day we might enjoy our eternal inheritance with you in everlasting joy. We ask this through Christ our Lord. **Amen.**

OPENING PRAYER

Let us pray

Pause for silent prayer

God our Father,
your light of truth
guides us to the way of Christ.
May all who follow him
reject what is contrary to the gospel.

We ask this through our Lord Jesus Christ,
    your Son,
who lives and reigns with you and the
    Holy Spirit,
one God, for ever and ever. **Amen.**

FIRST READING
Deut 30:10-14

Moses said to the people:
    "If only you would heed the voice of the
        LORD, your God,
    and keep his commandments and statutes
    that are written in this book of the law,
    when you return to the LORD, your God,
    with all your heart and all your soul.

"For this command that I enjoin on you
        today
    is not too mysterious and remote for you.
It is not up in the sky, that you should say,
    'Who will go up in the sky to get it for us
    and tell us of it, that we may carry it out?'
Nor is it across the sea, that you should say,
    'Who will cross the sea to get it for us
    and tell us of it, that we may carry it out?'
No, it is something very near to you,
    already in your mouths and in your
        hearts;
    you have only to carry it out."

RESPONSORIAL PSALM
Ps 69:14, 17, 30-31, 33-34, 36, 37

R̸. (cf. 33) Turn to the Lord in your need,
and you will live.

I pray to you, O LORD,
    for the time of your favor, O God!
In your great kindness answer me
    with your constant help.
Answer me, O LORD, for bounteous is your
        kindness:
    in your great mercy turn toward me.

R̸. Turn to the Lord in your need, and you
will live.

I am afflicted and in pain;
    let your saving help, O God, protect me.
I will praise the name of God in song,
    and I will glorify him with
        thanksgiving.

R̸. Turn to the Lord in your need, and you
will live.

"See, you lowly ones, and be glad;
   you who seek God, may your hearts
      revive!
For the LORD hears the poor,
   and his own who are in bonds he spurns
      not."

R̸. Turn to the Lord in your need, and you
will live.

For God will save Zion
   and rebuild the cities of Judah.
The descendants of his servants shall
      inherit it,
   and those who love his name shall
      inhabit it.

R̸. Turn to the Lord in your need, and you
will live.

OR

RESPONSORIAL PSALM
Ps 19:8, 9, 10, 11

See Appendix A, p. 285.

SECOND READING
Col 1:15-20

Christ Jesus is the image of the invisible
   God,
   the firstborn of all creation.
For in him were created all things in
      heaven and on earth,
   the visible and the invisible,
   whether thrones or dominions or
      principalities or powers;
   all things were created through him and
      for him.
He is before all things,
   and in him all things hold together.
He is the head of the body, the church.
He is the beginning, the firstborn from the
      dead,
   that in all things he himself might be
      preeminent.
For in him all the fullness was pleased to
      dwell,
   and through him to reconcile all things
      for him,
   making peace by the blood of his cross
   through him, whether those on earth or
      those in heaven.

About Liturgy

Choice of responsorial psalm: The Lectionary gives us two choices for a responsorial psalm and which one is chosen for use would depend upon the approach taken for interpreting the Scripture selections. The verses selected from Psalm 69 are a better choice for the approach we have taken in these reflections because they focus on God's mercy as a model for our own mercy. The verses selected from Psalm 19 focus more on the preciousness of the law itself and how the law brings life.

Liturgical law: enslavement or freedom? Some liturgists, liturgy committees, and segments of the Church get so caught up in keeping every detail of liturgical law that the celebration of liturgy is robbed of any concern for another. Liturgical laws are supposed to ensure that liturgy remains the liturgy of the whole Church and not just an idiosyncratic ritual of a few. We are careful to pay attention to liturgical laws but equally careful that our liturgies unfold as prayer and worship, as making present the paschal mystery, as celebrations of God's word and sacrament that transform us into being better members of Christ's body who live with compassion and mercy towards all. If our adherence to liturgical law does not aid in this transformation, then we have missed its point.

About Liturgical Music

Cantor preparation: In the responsorial psalm you exhort the assembly to turn to God in their need. In this you are a beacon of hope, for you reveal they are saved not because of their strength but because of God's mercy. They have only to ask and God will respond with the gift of life. In what ways do you turn to God when you are in need? In what ways has God responded?

Preludes and postludes: The principle of progressive solemnity suggests that the Sunday Eucharist should be celebrated in such a way that it emerges as clearly more important than weekday eucharistic celebrations. One way of marking this significance is to frame the celebration with a musical prelude and postlude. These musical elements unify the celebration as a whole. The prelude helps the gathering assembly ready themselves for the liturgy. The postlude adds a festive note to their leave-taking. Ideally the prelude connects thematically with the liturgical season or is musically related to the entrance hymn. Likewise the postlude relates to the liturgical season; it can be based on the hymn of praise after Communion or the recessional hymn, or can simply be a generic piece appropriate to the conclusion of Mass.

   Preludes and postludes can be instrumental or choral. The minutes right before Mass begins are often the best time for the choir to sing a piece related to the season or day. When the assembly sings a hymn of praise after Communion and the recessional hymn is then omitted, the choir can sing a festive postlude. For instrumental preludes and postludes numerous resources for organ and piano pieces based on hymn tunes and related to liturgical seasons can be found in every major music publishing catalogue.

SPIRITUALITY

Gospel

Luke 10:38-42; L108C

Jesus entered a village
   where a woman whose name
      was Martha welcomed
      him.
She had a sister named Mary
   who sat beside the Lord at his
      feet listening to him
      speak.
Martha, burdened with much
     serving, came to him and
     said,
  "Lord, do you not care
that my sister has left me by
      myself to do the serving?
Tell her to help me."
The Lord said to her in reply,
  "Martha, Martha, you are anxious
     and worried about many things.
There is need of only one thing.
Mary has chosen the better part
  and it will not be taken from her."

Reflecting on the Gospel

Single-parent families or those who live alone and have invited guests in for dinner can easily identify with the dilemma of this Sunday's gospel account. With guests, the one adult is torn between preparing the refreshments and meal and being attentive to the guests. One quickly learns that it is impossible to do both. While preparing this, the host is either shouting at the guests from the kitchen or is neglecting preparations to be in the living room. It's awkward at best and frustrating at worst. Martha and Mary have Jesus as a guest. They seem to have done the practical thing: Martha does the food preparations while Mary entertains the guest. Martha can't understand why Mary can't pitch in and help at a critical time. Martha wants Mary to be like her. Jesus surprises us in that he wants Martha to be like Mary.

The gospel is about hosts and guest and hospitality but Jesus puts an unparalleled twist on the notion of hospitality. Martha's "hospitality" was made edgy because of her becoming burdened with the cooking and serving. Martha is settling to be a servant where Jesus is looking for disciples. Mary's hospitality was gracious because she focused her attention on Jesus: "sat beside the Lord at his feet listening to him." The surprise is that Jesus affirms that the "better part" is to sit and listen—both metaphors for discipleship. The "better part" is to be disciple!

Even in the first reading from Genesis at first glance it seems like Abraham is caught in the same dilemma as Martha—he appears busy about feeding and making comfortable the three guests who appear from nowhere. Abraham is careful about many details of hospitality: water is brought, they are invited to rest, they are fed the finest he can produce from his stocks. Moreover, he "waited on them under the tree while they ate." All Abraham's actions are really directed toward attentiveness to the guests. This attentiveness is a kind of "listening" to them. In this sense Abraham is a disciple of the three guests and his hospitality is repaid by God's sending new life to Abraham and Sarah.

A welcoming hospitality implies an "at-homeness" and belonging that parallels the unique relationship of disciple to master. As with Abraham and Sarah, this kind of discipleship hospitality always brings new life. The "better part" Jesus promises is not just being disciple but it is also sharing in the new life that Jesus offers. This is better than all the finest food in the world that can be prepared and served!

Living the Paschal Mystery

Before we can carry on the mission of Jesus as disciples we must become disciples by sitting at the feet of Jesus listening to him. In our time today we can hardly invite Jesus over for dinner. But there are ways that Jesus is present to us if we take the time to be present to him.

We usually address living the paschal mystery in terms of how we die to ourselves in our everyday living. This gospel suggests a radically different—and complementary—way of living the paschal mystery: taking the time to listen to Jesus. Practically speaking, this means being attentive to the proclamation of the Scriptures (especially the gospel) during Mass. It means taking the time to be with Jesus in prayer—not just saying prayers, but being quiet and listening to how Jesus speaks to our hearts. There is truly a great deal of self-sacrificing in letting go of our busyness in order to listen to Jesus!

Focusing the Word

Key words and phrases from the gospel: welcomed him, sat . . . at his feet, listening to him, better part

To the point: The gospel is about hospitality, but it is about more. Martha is anxious about her hospitality and perturbed that Mary is not helping. In contrast Mary, sitting at the feet of Jesus listening to him, has taken the posture of a disciple and is affirmed in this by Jesus. The "better part" is to be disciple.

Connecting the Word

to the first reading: Both the first reading and the gospel speak of hospitality. In these stories the hospitality of the hosts is overwhelmed by the generosity of the guests: Abraham and Sarah receive the gift of a son; Mary is affirmed in her stance as disciple.

to biblical culture: In a patriarchal society women were not expected to be in a disciple relationship to a male master. Luke's inclusion of this story is typical of his concern to provide a place for women in his community.

Understanding the Word

Discipleship: sitting at his feet: The Lectionary omits the first half of verse 38: "As they continued on the journey. . . ." On Sunday 13 we discussed the journey as a metaphor for discipleship, i.e., following Jesus, even to Jerusalem. This Sunday's episode in the gospel highlights another aspect of discipleship. Mary "sat beside the Lord at his feet listening to him speak" (v. 39). The Greek here is more specific: Mary "listened to his word." Luke has earlier implied that the word of Jesus is comparable to the word of God (4:36; 7:7; 8:11-15). Mary, then, is listening to "his word." Moreover, Mary's posture indicates what is happening in this scene. "To sit at the feet" is the posture of a disciple. In Acts 22:3, Paul explains his rigorous Jewish background: "At the feet of Gamaliel I was educated strictly in our ancestral law." Any action at the feet of another recognizes the authority of that person (see Luke 7:38; 8:35, 41; 17:16; Acts 4:35, 37; 5:2; 22:3). Disciples are those who are silent and listen to a Master; the Master instructs, the disciple learns.

In a patriarchal society it is very unusual for a woman to be in the place of a disciple. Yet Mary has presumed to take this traditionally male place and Jesus, in violation of expected custom, not only accepts her but declares that she "has chosen the better part." In this Mary models for disciples the essential attitude of attentiveness: "blessed are those who hear the word of God and keep it" (Luke 11:28). Not only do those who are instructed by his word become disciples, they are his family: "My mother and my brothers are those who hear the word of God and act on it" (Luke 8:21).

Martha acknowledges Jesus as the Master by addressing him as "Lord" (v. 40). But then she presumes to give him instructions, "Tell her to help me" (v. 40)! In her eagerness to serve at table she has neglected his word—something the apostles will explicitly refuse to do (see Acts 6:2-4). To follow Jesus, disciples must listen "at his feet."

ASSEMBLY & FAITH-SHARING GROUPS

- When entertaining guests I am more like Martha or Mary . . . because . . .
- When attending to my relationship with God, I am more like Martha or Mary . . . because . . .
- I understand the "better part" chosen by Mary to mean . . .
  For me to embrace this teaching of Jesus more deeply I need to . . .

PRESIDERS

Disciples are to sit before the feet of Jesus before carrying on his mission. When I recall this, my ministry is like . . . my personal life is like . . .

DEACONS

My reason for being "burdened with much serving" is . . .
The "one thing" that Jesus is asking of me is . . .

HOSPITALITY MINISTERS

The benefits of sitting and listening at Jesus' feet before getting "burdened with [the] much serving" of hospitality are . . .

MUSIC MINISTERS

My music ministry helps the assembly welcome Christ when . . .
Sometimes my ministry interferes with their welcoming Christ when . . .

ALTAR MINISTERS

While tending to the "many things" necessary in serving others, the way I keep in mind the Guest for whom I serve is . . .

LECTORS

If my preparation with God's word emulated Abraham's attentive hospitality, my living and proclamation would be greatly enriched because . . .

EUCHARISTIC MINISTERS

At Eucharist Christ is the Host, Guest, and Food.
  I go to the Host anticipating . . .
  I prepare for the Guest by . . .
  The Food nourishes me for . . .

Model Penitential Rite

Presider: Jesus is a guest in the home of Martha and Mary; the gospel scene probably comes close to what happens in some of our homes today—who is going to do the work and who is going to sit. Jesus tells us that the "better part" is to be disciple and listen to him. Let us open our hearts to hear God's word today and celebrate God's love at the table of the Lord . . . [pause]

Lord Jesus, you are guest in our hearts: Lord . . .

Christ Jesus, you teach us when we listen to you: Christ . . .

Lord Jesus, you call disciples to be your presence in the world: Lord . . .

Appreciating the Responsorial Psalm

Psalm 15 was part of a ritual followed whenever a person wished to gain admittance to the Temple. Because the Temple was God's dwelling one could not enter without permission. Instead the person was questioned at the gate by a priest who would ask, "Who, Lord, may dwell in your tent?" (v. 1 of the psalm, omitted in the Lectionary). The person then answered by reciting the subsequent verses of Psalm 15: one who does justice, thinks truth, slanders not, etc. The ritual expressed Israel's understanding that entrance into God's dwelling place required right living.

In the first reading Abraham stands as type of the right living which grants entrance into the divine presence. He receives strangers with hospitality and is blessed for it. That he responds so immediately to their needs, however, indicates he was already living "in the presence of the Lord" (psalm refrain). Such was the consistent orientation of his life. This is the orientation to which the psalm calls us and to which Jesus calls us when he rebukes Martha in the gospel. May our central desire be to live in the presence of God and may that Presence be the source of our right living.

Model General Intercessions

Presider: God always welcomes us and hears our prayers. Let us pray for the needs of our Church and world.

Response:

Lord, hear our prayer.

Cantor:

we pray to the Lord,

That all members of the Church take up their discipleship and listen to Jesus . . . [pause]

That all peoples of the world share in the hospitality of God's generosity . . . [pause]

That those who are burdened with the cares of life might take time to be attentive to God's presence . . . [pause]

That each of us here model in our lives that we have chosen the better part of being a disciple of Jesus . . . [pause]

Presider: Gracious God, you serve your people with unfailing generosity: hear our prayers that we might enjoy the hospitality of everlasting life with you. We ask this through Christ our Lord. **Amen.**

ALTERNATIVE OPENING PRAYER

Let us pray

Pause for silent prayer

Father,
let the gift of your life
continue to grow in us,
drawing us from death to faith, hope, and
love.
Keep us alive in Christ Jesus.
Keep us watchful in prayer
and true to his teaching
till your glory is revealed in us.

Grant this through Christ our Lord.
Amen.

FIRST READING
Gen 18:1-10a

The LORD appeared to Abraham by the
terebinth of Mamre,
as he sat in the entrance of his tent,
while the day was growing hot.
Looking up, Abraham saw three men
standing nearby.
When he saw them, he ran from the
entrance of the tent to greet them;
and bowing to the ground, he said:
"Sir, if I may ask you this favor,
please do not go on past your servant.
Let some water be brought, that you may
bathe your feet,
and then rest yourselves under the tree.
Now that you have come this close to your
servant,
let me bring you a little food, that you
may refresh yourselves;
and afterward you may go on your way."
The men replied, "Very well, do as you
have said."

Abraham hastened into the tent and told
Sarah,
"Quick, three measures of fine flour!
Knead it and make rolls."
He ran to the herd, picked out a tender,
choice steer,
and gave it to a servant, who quickly
prepared it.
Then Abraham got some curds and milk,
as well as the steer that had been
prepared,
and set these before the three men;
and he waited on them under the tree
while they ate.

They asked Abraham, "Where is your
wife Sarah?"
He replied, "There in the tent."
One of them said, "I will surely return to
you about this time next year,
and Sarah will then have a son."

RESPONSORIAL PSALM

Ps 15:2-3, 3-4, 5

R/. (1a) He who does justice will live in the presence of the Lord.

One who walks blamelessly and does justice;
  who thinks the truth in his heart
  and slanders not with his tongue.

R/. He who does justice will live in the presence of the Lord.

Who harms not his fellow man,
  nor takes up a reproach against his neighbor;
by whom the reprobate is despised,
  while he honors those who fear the LORD.

R/. He who does justice will live in the presence of the Lord.

Who lends not his money at usury
  and accepts no bribe against the innocent.
One who does these things
  shall never be disturbed.

R/. He who does justice will live in the presence of the Lord.

SECOND READING

Col 1:24-28

Brothers and sisters:
Now I rejoice in my sufferings for your sake,
  and in my flesh I am filling up
  what is lacking in the afflictions of Christ
  on behalf of his body, which is the church,
  of which I am a minister
  in accordance with God's stewardship given to me
  to bring to completion for you the word of God,
  the mystery hidden from ages and from generations past.
But now it has been manifested to his holy ones,
  to whom God chose to make known the riches of the glory
  of this mystery among the Gentiles;
  it is Christ in you, the hope for glory.
It is he whom we proclaim,
  admonishing everyone and teaching everyone with all wisdom,
  that we may present everyone perfect in Christ.

About Liturgy

Hospitality ministers: Most parishes and liturgical communities have hospitality ministers—whether they are called that or greeters or ushers or some combination of all those. Although we Catholics could certainly take some lessons in church hospitality from our Protestant brothers and sisters (it is only in recent church renovations that we are providing for such simple human necessities as bathrooms and cloak rooms!), we must also take care that our hospitality ministry doesn't limit what the gospel for this Sunday implies.

Hospitality at church is far more than a pleasant greeting and welcome (although surely these are important aspects of the ministry). Hospitality ministers must understand themselves first of all as disciples and, like Mary in the gospel, must assume in their lives and ministry a listening stance toward Jesus. The ministry points to Christ's presence in the community, emphasizes all are welcome because all are members of the body of Christ, and helps the assembling church members to prepare to *listen* to Jesus speak to their hearts during the liturgy. Hospitality ministry is more than a practical convenience or a social nicety; it is an expression of Jesus' ministry that recognizes the other's dignity as member of the body of Christ.

About Liturgical Music

Cantor preparation: In preparing to sing this responsorial psalm, spend some time reflecting on how you choose to live in the presence of God and how that choice shapes your manner of living. When and how do you take time to be with God? How, in concrete ways, do you let God's presence challenge your living?

Role of the responsorial psalm, Pt 1: Years ago Jean-Pierre Prévost (then professor of Old Testament and Hebrew at St. Paul University, Ottawa) suggested that the role of the responsorial psalm in the Liturgy of the Word was to act as bridge between the first reading and the gospel. This image of bridge conveys a sense of both movement and connectedness, and accords with the principle that the climax of the Liturgy of the Word is the gospel for which the preceding elements prepare us (see the Introduction to the Lectionary for Mass no. 13).

The movement aspect of the bridge metaphor implies that we begin the Liturgy of the Word in one place and cross over to another. There is a journey here. The connectedness aspect of the metaphor indicates that the beginning and ending of this journey are related. The starting point and the ending point form opposing shorelines. What we cross over in between varies; sometimes it is moving water, sometimes it is a valley bursting with grain, and sometimes it is a dry gulch or even a frighteningly deep canyon.

The crossing over is not a journey through time from the Old Testament to the New Testament but a journey of transformation. We begin the Liturgy of the Word standing on the threshold of a new moment of encounter with the word of God and we cross over to a new level of self-understanding as body of Christ. The structural element that carries us from one way of being to another is the responsorial psalm.

JULY 18, 2004
SIXTEENTH SUNDAY IN ORDINARY TIME

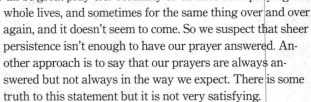

✠ SPIRITUALITY

Gospel
Luke 11:1-13; L111C

Jesus was praying in a certain place,
        and when he had finished,
    one of his disciples said to him,
    "Lord, teach us to pray just as
        John taught his disciples."
He said to them, "When you pray,
        say:
    Father, hallowed be your name,
    your kingdom come.
    Give us each day our daily
        bread
    and forgive us our sins
    for we ourselves forgive
        everyone in debt to us,
    and do not subject us to the
        final test."

And he said to them, "Suppose
        one of you has a friend
    to whom he goes at midnight and
        says,
    'Friend, lend me three loaves of
        bread,
    for a friend of mine has arrived at
        my house from a journey
    and I have nothing to offer him,'
    and he says in reply from within,
    'Do not bother me; the door has
        already been locked
    and my children and I are already in
        bed.
I cannot get up to give you anything.'
I tell you,
    if he does not get up to give the
        visitor the loaves
    because of their friendship,
    he will get up to give him whatever
        he needs
    because of his persistence.

Continued in Appendix A, p. 285.

Reflecting on the Gospel

At first glance the gospel seems quite explicit and simple, and the first reading tends to support this approach to interpretation of this Sunday's readings: the obvious implication of the gospel is that our prayer is answered when we persistently ask. Just think: if persistence alone were all that we need to have our prayers answered, if persistence alone guaranteed we would get what we want, we would probably all be great pray-ers! Yet many of us have been praying our whole lives, and sometimes for the same thing over and over again, and it doesn't seem to come. So we suspect that sheer persistence isn't enough to have our prayer answered. Another approach is to say that our prayers are always answered but not always in the way we expect. There is some truth to this statement but it is not very satisfying.

The two examples that Jesus uses (neighborly friendship and father-son kinship) reveal that what is always granted through prayer is deeper relationship with God and others. Persistence in prayer is linked to friendship and kinship; friendship has its limits and the neighbor in the gospel requires persistence in order to get a response to his request for bread. Jesus teaches us that in prayer God is our "Father" and just as a parent's love for children is unlimited, so is God's love and care for us unlimited. Jesus further teaches that prayer unfolds in the context of a special relationship—"Our Father"— not a kinship relationship as we know it in terms of kinship or progeny but rather "Father" is a metaphor used to describe our unique, intimate relationship with God. This relationship inspires in us the confidence ("how much more . . .") to pray with "persistence" and the realization that what we pray for is not so important as the fact that we address God in such intimate terms. The prayer always deepens our relationship with God and this is already an answer to what we need.

Moreover, the unique relationship established between God and us in prayer is described in terms of the Father giving us the Holy Spirit if we ask. Without the Spirit's indwelling we would not be able to call God our Father. If there is anything at all that should keep us persistent in prayer it is praying for the gift of the Holy Spirit. If there is anything at all that we can be assured will be answered in prayer, it is receiving the gift of the Holy Spirit. With this gift all else we ask for is implicitly given because with the indwelling of the Holy Spirit we already share in God's life and abundance. We already have everything we could possibly need.

Living the Paschal Mystery

If we all persisted in praying for the gift of the indwelling Spirit, were faithful in sharing the abundance of God's life and gifts that the Spirit brings, and held as primary our relationship with God, then our prayer for our needs would probably be different. There is nothing wrong with praying for specific needs; after all, we do it every Mass at the general intercessions, not to mention our own prayers of petition. This gospel challenges us to go beyond specific needs and get the larger picture; a focus on the gift of the indwelling Spirit is already God's answer to all our prayers. What inspires confidence in us is not whether God gives us what we ask for in prayer; our confidence comes from the Spirit who dwells within and establishes a most intimate relationship between God and us—shared life.

Focusing the Word

Key words and phrases from the gospel: teach us to pray, friendship, persistence, Father, Holy Spirit

To the point: When the metaphor of friendship is applied to prayer, persistence will obtain what friendship will not. When the metaphor of parent-child is applied to prayer, God will provide more than what we need merely to survive ("fish" or "egg"). Our "Father" will give us the Holy Spirit. This is the gift disciples are to ask for and seek with confident persistence.

Connecting the Word

to the first reading: Abraham's persistence may not have obtained the ultimate deliverance of Sodom and Gomorrah, but it did reveal to Abraham God's compassion in withholding judgment and his justice in executing it.

to religious experience: We often use prayer as an opportunity to tell God what we need. It is also an opportunity in which God can reveal to us who God is (Father).

Understanding the Word

Prayer: asking confidently: The disciples, seeing Jesus at prayer again (so far: 5:16; 6:12; 9:18, 28), ask Jesus to teach them as John taught his disciples. Two points are noteworthy. First, prayer is placed in the context of discipleship: no understanding of discipleship is complete without prayer. Second, Jesus is likened to John whom the people acknowledge as a prophet (20:6); communication with God is a prophet's specialty.

After teaching the Lord's Prayer Jesus provides two parables illustrating aspects of prayer. The first parable uses friendship as a point of comparison. The Old Testament has many stories, proverbs, and aphorisms about friendship. The first parable seems to illustrate Proverbs 3:28, "Say not to your neighbor, 'Go, and come again, tomorrow I will give,' when you can give at once." Responsiveness is not only the conduct of a wise and virtuous person, it is a demand Jewish and Greek society places on its members. The point of the first parable is in its last line which seems to emphasize persistence. But the Greek word there always means "shamelessness." Unfortunately, the grammar makes it difficult to determine who is shameless—the petitioner or the sleeping neighbor. Apart from the grammar both characters would be subject to shame. For a person not to provide food for an unexpected traveler would bring unbearable shame; far better to risk the ire of a wakened neighbor than to be shamed for not providing "bread"! Similarly, for the neighbor who is wakened from sleep: it would be better to be inconvenienced and to waken his entire household than to have it become known that he did not provide for a needy neighbor and friend. Applied to prayer, the parable says something about both the petitioner and the provider. Just as the petitioner is bold and confident enough to ask his neighbor, so can disciples be bold and confident to ask God for their "daily bread." Conversely, if even a neighbor knows enough to respond when need is made known, so too will God open to those who knock and give to those who ask.

ASSEMBLY & FAITH-SHARING GROUPS

- Every prayer reveals something about the One to whom one prays, the pray-er, and the relationship between them. Jesus' Our Father reveals God as . . .
It discloses my deepest self as . . .
It characterizes my relationship with God as . . .
- That which is most comforting about praying is . . . most difficult is . . .
- For me the challenge in trying to *live* the Our Father is . . .
- The part "persistence" plays in my spiritual life is . . .

PRESIDERS

Like Abraham (see first reading) my ministry is a persistent intercession for the benefit of others when I . . .

DEACONS

My ministry manifests the "how much more" of God by . . .

HOSPITALITY MINISTERS

My hospitality creates an environment conducive for prayer when I . . .

MUSIC MINISTERS

My music ministry helps me pray by . . .
My music ministry is prayer when . . .

ALTAR MINISTERS

My serving others is prayer when . . .
My service aids the prayer of others by . . .

LECTORS

The fruit of remaining persistent with God's word is . . .
The way my proclamation shares that fruit with the assembly is . . .

EUCHARISTIC MINISTERS

The ways I give "daily bread" to my family, neighbors, co-workers, the infirmed, etc., are . . .

Model Penitential Rite

Presider: In today's gospel the disciples ask Jesus to teach them to pray. Let us surrender ourselves to God so that we can truly pray during this liturgy and open our hearts to a God who gives us all good things . . . [pause]

Lord Jesus, you called God Abba, Father: Lord . . .

Christ Jesus, you teach us to ask for the gift of the Holy Spirit: Christ . . .

Lord Jesus, you frequently turned to God in prayer: Lord . . .

Appreciating the Responsorial Psalm

In the gospel Jesus responds on several levels to the disciples' request that he show them how to pray: he teaches them the Our Father; he encourages them to be persistent; he subtly suggests what it is they are to pray for (the gift of the Holy Spirit); and he calls them to ground their prayer in the goodness of God who is their Father. The first reading gives us a dramatic example of such prayer. Abraham persists in his petition. He remains humble yet audacious, speaking to God directly and forcefully. Finally, what he prays for is righteous judgment and protection of the innocent. On the divine side the story reveals that God waits for such prayer. God stands directly in front of Abraham and invites the conversation. God listens each time Abraham speaks and grants his request. Clearly this is a God who desires salvation and who seeks human collaboration in bringing it about.

The responsorial psalm confirms that what grounds confidence in prayer is the nature of God who is great in kindness and true to every promise. God will answer when we call; God will complete the work of salvation begun in us. We need have no hesitation to petition such a God. We have only to carefully discern for what it is we ask.

Model General Intercessions

Presider: Jesus taught us to ask God for our needs and so we confidently pray for the Church and our world.

Response:

Lord, hear our prayer.

Cantor:

we pray to the Lord,

That the Church be an example of persistent prayer for the indwelling of the Holy Spirit . . . [pause]

That leaders of nations respond favorably to the needs of their people . . . [pause]

That those who lack food and shelter may receive these basic needs for a good life . . . [pause]

That each one of us deepen our relationship with God through regular times of prayer . . . [pause]

Presider: O good God, you give us all we need to come to everlasting happiness: hear these our prayers that we might be a sign of your blessings to all we meet. We ask this through Christ our Lord. **Amen.**

OPENING PRAYER

Let us pray

Pause for silent prayer

God our Father and protector,
without you nothing is holy,
nothing has value.
Guide us to everlasting life
by helping us to use wisely
the blessings you have given to the world.

We ask this through our Lord Jesus Christ,
  your Son,
who lives and reigns with you and the
  Holy Spirit,
one God, for ever and ever. **Amen.**

FIRST READING

Gen 18:20-32

In those days, the LORD said: "The outcry
    against Sodom and Gomorrah is so
    great,
  and their sin so grave,
  that I must go down and see whether or
    not their actions
  fully correspond to the cry against them
    that comes to me.
I mean to find out."

While Abraham's visitors walked on
    farther toward Sodom,
  the LORD remained standing before
    Abraham.
Then Abraham drew nearer and said:
  "Will you sweep away the innocent with
    the guilty?
Suppose there were fifty innocent people
    in the city;
  would you wipe out the place, rather
    than spare it
  for the sake of the fifty innocent people
    within it?
Far be it from you to do such a thing,
  to make the innocent die with the guilty
  so that the innocent and the guilty
    would be treated alike!
Should not the judge of all the world act
    with justice?"
The LORD replied,
  "If I find fifty innocent people in the
    city of Sodom,
  I will spare the whole place for their sake."
Abraham spoke up again:
  "See how I am presuming to speak to
    my Lord,
  though I am but dust and ashes!
What if there are five less than fifty
    innocent people?
Will you destroy the whole city because of
    those five?"
He answered, "I will not destroy it, if I find
    forty-five there."
But Abraham persisted, saying, "What if
    only forty are found there?"

He replied, "I will forbear doing it for the sake of the forty."
Then Abraham said, "Let not my Lord grow impatient if I go on.
What if only thirty are found there?"
He replied, "I will forbear doing it if I can find but thirty there."
Still Abraham went on,
"Since I have thus dared to speak to my Lord,
what if there are no more than twenty?"
The LORD answered, "I will not destroy it, for the sake of the twenty."
But he still persisted:
"Please, let not my Lord grow angry if I speak up this last time.
What if there are at least ten there?"
He replied, "For the sake of those ten, I will not destroy it."

RESPONSORIAL PSALM
Ps 138:1-2, 2-3, 6-7, 7-8

R̸. (3a) Lord, on the day I called for help, you answered me.

I will give thanks to you, O LORD, with all my heart,
    for you have heard the words of my mouth;
    in the presence of the angels I will sing your praise;
I will worship at your holy temple
    and give thanks to your name.

R̸. Lord, on the day I called for help, you answered me.

Because of your kindness and your truth;
    for you have made great above all things
    your name and your promise.
When I called you answered me;
    you built up strength within me.

R̸. Lord, on the day I called for help, you answered me.

The LORD is exalted, yet the lowly he sees,
    and the proud he knows from afar.
Though I walk amid distress, you preserve me;
    against the anger of my enemies you raise your hand.

R̸. Lord, on the day I called for help, you answered me.

Your right hand saves me.
    The LORD will complete what he has done for me;
    your kindness, O LORD, endures forever;
    forsake not the work of your hands.

R̸. Lord, on the day I called for help, you answered me.

SECOND READING
Col 2:12-14

See Appendix A, p. 285.

About Liturgy

Liturgy as prayer: We call liturgy a celebration, a ritual act, the communal worship of the people. We process during liturgy, sing, acclaim, proclaim. Liturgy is filled with many different kinds of activities. This Sunday's gospel challenges us to consider whether we approach liturgy as *prayer*. True, we pray the Our Father just before Communion, that prayer that Jesus taught us and we hear about in this Sunday's gospel. Since this is the prayer that Jesus taught, we rightly think of its preeminence. At the same time we cannot forget that *all* of liturgy is prayer from the beginning Sign of the Cross to the concluding blessing. A prayerful attitude should mark how we celebrate liturgy.

Why is it important to insist that liturgy is prayer? An attitude of prayer keeps us focused on the relationship with God that we share. It helps us realize that we don't celebrate liturgy because of any power we have but because God invites us and gives us the Spirit who enables us to respond with praise and thanksgiving.

True, different kinds of prayer mark our liturgies. Sometimes we say prayers together such as at the responsorial psalm and the Our Father. Sometimes we are given silent time in which to pour our hearts out to God very personally in prayer such as after the readings and after Communion. Sometimes we actively listen as another voices our prayer such as during the presidential prayers (opening prayer, prayer over the gifts, prayer after Communion) and the eucharistic prayer. Surely our acclaiming and hymn singing is also prayer. But for all these (and other) types of prayer present during Mass, the real challenge is that the *whole Mass* is *one prayer* of the one body of Christ.

About Liturgical Music

Cantor preparation: When you sing the responsorial psalm what the assembly hears more than the beauty of your voice is the sound of your praying. Ask Christ this week to teach you how to pray the psalm.

Role of the responsorial psalm, Pt. 2: How does the responsorial psalm act as bridge between the first reading and the gospel? How does the psalm help us surrender to the transformation the gospel calls for? Part of what happens is that the movement within the psalm text itself—its internal changes of mood, focus, content, and metaphor—parallel the movement meant to take place within us as we respond to the word of God. There is an integral relationship between the process of transformation and conversion within the heart, mind, and behavior of the original psalmist as he or she was responding to the actions of God, and the change which takes place within us as we pray that psalm within the context of this Liturgy of the Word. One of the implications here is that the role of the cantor is very important. The cantor personally embodies the transformation embedded in the psalm and calls us to that transformation. This is no small task, and certainly one that involves far more than the singing of a nice song.

Each week "Appreciating the Responsorial Psalm" (found on the facing page) explores the relationship between the psalm and the readings of the day. Sometimes the connection is obvious, other times it is not so clear, but it is always there. Identifying this connection and reflecting on it deepens our appreciation of the role of the psalm. Only then can we sing it with understanding and surrender to its transformative power.

✝ SPIRITUALITY

Gospel

Luke 12:13-21; L114C

Someone in the crowd said to
    Jesus,
    "Teacher, tell my brother to
        share the inheritance
        with me."
He replied to him,
    "Friend, who appointed me as
        your judge and
        arbitrator?"
Then he said to the crowd,
    "Take care to guard against
        all greed,
    for though one may be rich,
    one's life does not consist of
        possessions."

Then he told them a parable.
"There was a rich man whose land
        produced a bountiful harvest.
He asked himself, 'What shall I do,
    for I do not have space to store my
        harvest?'
And he said, 'This is what I shall do:
    I shall tear down my barns and build
        larger ones.
There I shall store all my grain and
        other goods
    and I shall say to myself, "Now as for
        you,
    you have so many good things stored
        up for many years,
    rest, eat, drink, be merry!"'
But God said to him,
    'You fool, this night your life will be
        demanded of you;
    and the things you have prepared, to
        whom will they belong?'
Thus will it be for all who store up
        treasure for themselves
    but are not rich in what matters to
        God."

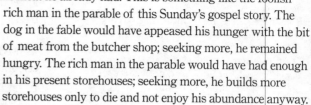

Reflecting on the Gospel

In ancient Greece Aesop told the fable about the dog and his reflection. It seems one day a very hungry dog stole a piece of meat from a butcher shop and was on his way to a safe place to enjoy his fare. As he was crossing a bridge over a clear stream he looked down and saw his reflection in the water. Thinking that it was another dog with more meat, he opened his jaws to snatch the meat, only to lose in the stream the meat he already had. This is something like the foolish rich man in the parable of this Sunday's gospel story. The dog in the fable would have appeased his hunger with the bit of meat from the butcher shop; seeking more, he remained hungry. The rich man in the parable would have had enough in his present storehouses; seeking more, he builds more storehouses only to die and not enjoy his abundance anyway.

We work hard for what we think is important to us, but we may end up with nothing because we have missed the whole point: life. We tend to think we can provide for our own future, but the gospel reminds us that the future is God's. Both the first reading and gospel speak of inheritance this Sunday; what we struggle all our lives to learn is that life does not consist of possessions nor our perceived security, but of being possessed by God. Our true inheritance is not more possessions nor security but life with God. The real reversal of the gospel is that neither we ourselves nor anything we have is really our own. We belong to God and God can demand an accounting of us at any time. The only security we truly possess is a loving relationship with God.

Even with all our Christian living and reflection, we still struggle with what God truly offers us—not more possessions, but eternal life. The gospel challenges us to make all of our work directed to a quality of life that has as its basis growing in our relationship with God. Even our possessions and how we use them have this end—to bring us to right relationship with God so that in the end we possess what really counts—God's life. The irony is that when we are truly possessed by God—are in right relationship with God—then when we see our own reflection (and see God in that reflection) we can let go. But when we let go of what we have, we gain everything—life with God.

Living the Paschal Mystery

If most of us take some time to think about things, we would have to admit that the pressures of our everyday living tend to be our main focus. We are all concerned about calendars and schedules, bills and getting ahead, sickness and health. Our lives tend to be so busy that our immediate goal is to get through another day. What would happen if we would truly take some time to think about what possesses us?

It takes conscious effort to reverse the questions and ask, To whom do our possessions belong? To whom do *we* belong? In some sense these are questions about priorities and putting God truly at the center of our lives. The answers must be more than an intellectual commitment to grow in our relationship with God and have God as our center. We must stop building larger storage barns and begin changing the way we live so that our priorities are evident. Practically speaking, this probably means settling for fewer possessions. But with God at the center, we really gain everything—eternal life.

Focusing the Word

Key words and phrases from the gospel: inheritance, possessions, myself, your life will be demanded

To the point: The rich man is a fool not simply because he seeks to gain more possessions but because he thinks his life is his own. Life is God's gift; it is God's to demand. The gospel raises the question, To whom do our possessions belong? The more important question, however, is, To whom do *we* belong?

Connecting the Word

to the first reading: The first reading expresses the wisdom that the rich man in the gospel lacks. Qoheleth recognizes the vanity of acquiring more and more.

to culture: The rich man's reality is everyone's dream: to have everything we need. Prudently providing for our future is responsible planning. The gospel's challenge, however, is that the future is not made secure by possessions but is secured in God alone.

Understanding the Word

Wealth and riches: In the entire three-year Sunday Lectionary cycle, we read from the book of Ecclesiastes only on this Sunday. The main point of this passage is this: after a long life of hard and skilled labor, people must leave their property "to another who has not labored over it" (Eccl 2:21). In the gospel Jesus illustrates this point with a parable. The rich man stores his harvest (his "nest egg") to provide for his future. But sudden death robs him of his future and God tauntingly asks, ". . . the things you have prepared, to whom will they belong?" (Luke 12:20).

While both readings consider the storing up of wealth for the future to be pointless, they do so for different reasons. The Book of Ecclesiastes presents itself as the learned reflections of wise King Solomon (see Eccl 1:1). As a youth "Solomon" sets out to discover what brings happiness to people in their brief life under the sun (see 1:12-14). He systematically examines many different pursuits thought to bring happiness but dismisses each of them: equally useless are fame (1:11), wisdom (1:17-18), pleasure (2:1-3), great accomplishments (2:4-6), wealth (2:7-10), and hard work (2:11). He concludes the best one can hope for is to enjoy the life that is given now: "Go, eat your bread with joy and drink your wine with a merry heart, because it is now that God favors your works" (9:7; also 2:24; 3:13; 5:17; 8:15). For "Solomon," the accumulation of wealth, like all human pursuits, is ultimately pointless for everything ends in death (there was as yet no belief in an afterlife; see 3:19-21).

Jesus also discounts the accumulation of wealth but for a different reason. The rich man thinks that riches will guarantee his future. But Jesus teaches that "one's life does not consist of possessions" (Luke 12:15). It's not that possessions are not valuable. Rather, there is something more valuable: life. As the parable makes clear, life is God's to give and to take away. It is best, then, to value what is most precious: life with God who alone secures our future.

ASSEMBLY & FAITH-SHARING GROUPS

- Where I am often tempted to build "larger barns" is . . .
  At such times trusting in God to me means . . .
- If I knew that "this night [my] life would be demanded of [me]" I would . . .
- Jesus' words, "are not rich in what matters to God," means to me . . .
  Where my richness (or poverty) in what matters to God is demonstrated is . . .

PRESIDERS

Pursuing and possessing things is vanity (see first reading). I experience the good news of God pursuing and possessing me, however, when . . .

DEACONS

Where greed shows its face in my life/ministry is . . .
I am reminded to remain "rich in what matters to God" by . . .

HOSPITALITY MINISTERS

The way my hospitality furthers the assembly's preparation to hear God's voice (psalm response) is . . .

MUSIC MINISTERS

My music ministry focuses me on "what matters to God" by . . .
Sometimes I struggle with keeping this focus because . . .

ALTAR MINISTERS

Serving is "toil and anxiety of heart" (first reading) when I . . .
Serving embodies what it means to be "rich in what matters to God" when I . . .

LECTORS

The folly and vanity (see first reading) within my daily living is . . .
The wisdom gained when I "number [my] days aright" (psalm) is . . .

EUCHARISTIC MINISTERS

The way my daily living/ministry preaches that "one's life does not consist of possessions" is . . .

Model Penitential Rite

Presider: To whom do our possessions belong? To whom does our life belong? These are the difficult questions Jesus raises in today's gospel. We place ourselves in God's presence at the beginning of this liturgy and give ourselves over to being transformed by God into God's prized treasure . . . [pause]

Lord Jesus, you teach us to love God with all our hearts: Lord . . .

Christ Jesus, you are the Treasure who lives within us: Christ . . .

Lord Jesus, you call us to be rich in what matters to God: Lord . . .

Appreciating the Responsorial Psalm

Psalm 90, from which this responsorial psalm is taken, contrasts the stability and steadfastness of God with the uncertainty and transience of human life. The verses used in the Lectionary express Israel's prayer that God teach them true assessment of their life and work. As the reading from Ecclesiastes indicates, they already realize hard work and physical possessions give no sure value. What is worth possessing is the kind and gracious care of God (psalm). Jesus affirms this stance when he challenges his hearers to turn from evaluating their worth based on physical possessions to evaluating it based on being "rich in what matters to God" (gospel).

It is significant that the psalm refrain is taken not from Psalm 90 but from Psalm 95, a psalm which refers to the infidelity of Israel's ancestors during their desert exodus from slavery to the promised land. No matter how much God gave them (water, manna), they constantly whined that they did not have enough. The Lectionary's choice of this refrain is acknowledgment that reckoning our days and assessing our worth in God's terms is always a challenge. May this be the work God prospers in us.

Model General Intercessions

Presider: Let us pray that we might always be in loving relationship with God and gain what is most valuable—eternal life.

Response:

Cantor:

That all members of the Church grow in their loving relationship with God, keeping God at the center of their lives . . . [pause]

That all peoples of the world be open to God's offer of salvation . . . [pause]

That those who devalue life through violence might respect life as God's precious gift to us . . . [pause]

That each of us gathered here grow in our willingness to be possessed by God . . . [pause]

Presider: Loving God, life is your most precious gift to us: hear these our prayers that one day we might all enjoy everlasting life with you. We ask this through Jesus Christ our Lord. **Amen.**

Fill us at daybreak with your kindness,
    that we may shout for joy and gladness
        all our days.
And may the gracious care of the LORD
    our God be ours;
    prosper the work of our hands for us!
    Prosper the work of our hands!

R̸. If today you hear his voice, harden not your hearts.

SECOND READING

Col 3:1-5, 9-11

Brothers and sisters:
If you were raised with Christ, seek what
    is above,
    where Christ is seated at the right hand
        of God.
Think of what is above, not of what is on
    earth.
For you have died,
    and your life is hidden with Christ in God.
When Christ your life appears,
    then you too will appear with him in
        glory.

Put to death, then, the parts of you that
    are earthly:
    immorality, impurity, passion, evil desire,
    and the greed that is idolatry.
Stop lying to one another,
    since you have taken off the old self
        with its practices
    and have put on the new self,
    which is being renewed, for knowledge,
    in the image of its creator.
Here there is not Greek and Jew,
    circumcision and uncircumcision,
    barbarian, Scythian, slave, free;
    but Christ is all and in all.

About Liturgy

Liturgy's true focus: Just as with our everyday lives, it is also easy to lose sight of the true focus of liturgy itself. Without realizing it we can get so completely caught up in the *doing* of liturgy that subtly we put ourselves at the center. For example, we can be so concerned about hospitality that we forget this isn't a simple gathering of the folks but an assembly gathered to hear God's call to be in divine presence. Or we can be so caught up in doing good music that we forget the music's purpose is to draw us into the ritual action to be transformed into being more perfect members of Christ's body, the Church. Or we can be so caught up in our own need for private prayer time that we can easily forget that at liturgy we surrender ourselves and our own needs in order to be an assembly called to God's presence.

Each Sunday it would be a good practice if each assembly member examined *why* he or she comes to celebrate liturgy. Ultimately we come to respond to God's call and to give praise and thanks for God's tremendous gifts of life and Godself to us. At each liturgy committee/commission meeting it would be a good practice to ask what exactly is the parish's focus of liturgy. What are the subtle ways we place ourselves and our own needs at the center? How faithful are we to the Church's practice of liturgy that draws us into God's presence for transformation?

About Liturgical Music

Cantor preparation: The refrain for this responsorial psalm is particularly challenging. Sometimes when you hear God's voice, your heart hardens. When do you experience this happening for yourself? How does God help you hear in spite of your resistance?

Role of the responsorial psalm, Pt. 3: The primary transformation taking place in us as we respond to the Liturgy of the Word is deeper surrender to the paschal mystery. The word issues a prophetic challenge that we be true to the ideal which stands before us in the gospel, the person of Christ. The word reminds us that we are the body of Christ and our mission is to heal the sick, feed the hungry, clothe the naked, and forgive those who injure us. The word confronts us with how far we fall short of that ideal and reassures us that God forgives this failure and continues to call us forward. What we hear in the proclamation of Scripture, then, is a continuously fresh presentation of the reality of God's faithfulness and of the ideal of faithfulness to which we are summoned in response.

When we sing the responsorial psalm we express our surrender to the paschal mystery in song and voice. The cantor leads the surrender, embodying it in breath and melody and mirroring through gesture the dialogue which is taking place between Christ and his assembled Church. When we the assembly respond, we sacramentalize our assent, that is, we make our surrender audibly, visibly, physically apparent. In other words, we are doing far more in the responsorial psalm than merely singing a song. We are saying yes to the ideal that is being placed before us and that ideal is not a set of directives but a living, breathing relationship to a Person who is calling us to die to self and promising us eternal life.

✠ SPIRITUALITY

Gospel
Luke 12:32-48; L117C

Jesus said to his disciples:
"Do not be afraid any longer, little
** flock,**
** for your Father is pleased to give you**
**   the kingdom.**
Sell your belongings and give
** alms.**
Provide money bags for yourselves
**   that do not wear out,**
** an inexhaustible treasure in**
**   heaven**
** that no thief can reach nor moth**
**   destroy.**
For where your treasure is, there
** also will your heart be.**

"Gird your loins and light your
** lamps**
** and be like servants who await their**
**   master's return from a wedding,**
** ready to open immediately when he**
**   comes and knocks.**
Blessed are those servants
** whom the master finds vigilant on his**
**   arrival.**
Amen, I say to you, he will gird
** himself,**
** have them recline at table, and**
**   proceed to wait on them.**
And should he come in the second or
**   third watch**
** and find them prepared in this way,**
** blessed are those servants.**
Be sure of this:
** if the master of the house had**
**   known the hour**
** when the thief was coming,**
** he would not have let his house be**
**   broken into.**
You also must be prepared, for at an
**   hour you do not expect,**
** the Son of Man will come."**

Continued in Appendix A, p. 285.

Reflecting on the Gospel

When we think of the word "treasure" we often imagine treasure chests filled with gold and precious jewels. We use this word to refer to something very valuable or our most prized possession. It might not always be something objectively worth much. For example, most children have their treasures—sometimes it's just a pretty stone they found but it has no real value. We "treasure" friendships and keepsakes, values and good deeds done for us. "Treasure" is a word that can be used in many contexts and with many meanings. The gospel this Sunday is a good example of treasure as a metaphor—different contexts and many rich meanings. The longer form of the gospel unfolds in three parts; the first part describes the context, the second is a parable, and the third is Jesus' explanation of the parable. Each part unfolds a deeper meaning of "treasure" for us.

The first few lines of this gospel set the context and refer to treasure as "inexhaustible," secure ("no thief can reach"), and incorruptible ("nor moth destroy"). This description is of treasure understood as the kingdom God gives. Interestingly, the way to possess this treasure is *not* by possessing, but by giving away ("Sell your belongings and give alms"). By not having and refocusing our hearts on God's kingdom do we become rich. This hints at what Jesus unfolds in the parable—that the treasure isn't possessing *things* but in being vigilant for the *master*, that is, Jesus himself. In other words, our inexhaustible, secure, incorruptible treasure is Jesus whom the Father gives as gift to us. The parable challenges us to think not of things but of Person as our truest treasure. Finally, in the third part of the gospel Jesus teaches the disciples (and us) how we might have this Treasure—by dispossessing ourselves of unnecessary focus on things, by being vigilant for the presence of our Treasure, and by being faithful disciples. To have our hearts where our treasure is means to "act in accord with [Jesus'] will." This is our ultimate dispossession—to give up our own wills and conform them to Jesus.

If we are preoccupied by possessions, schedules, work, sports, etc., our heart is already filled with exhaustible, insecure, and corruptible matters. The challenge of this gospel is to redirect our hearts to what is our true treasure, Jesus, and then be faithful disciples. The gift is great. Our Treasure is Jesus.

Living the Paschal Mystery

The final line of this gospel is most demanding and directly applicable to our daily paschal mystery living: "Much will be required of the person entrusted with much, and still more will be demanded of the person entrusted with more." We've been entrusted with much: furthering Jesus' mission of bringing the good news of salvation to all as his disciples. We have been entrusted with *even more:* we are not simply servants, but because of our baptism and being plunged into the paschal mystery we become members of the body of Christ. Our faithfulness is measured by even more than doing God's will; it is measured by our *being* the presence of the risen Christ for all those we meet.

The parallel the gospel offers is between possessions or Person. The real surprise of the gospel is that we ourselves, in our daily paschal mystery living of dying to ourselves for the sake of others, become more perfectly that presence of the very Master for whom we are vigilant. We ourselves are treasure, too, when we are faithful disciples.

Focusing the Word

Key words and phrases from the gospel: Father is pleased to give, treasure, will your heart be, vigilant, Son of Man, faithful

To the point: Our hearts will be where our treasure is: possessions we acquire or the gift God gives. If Jesus is our treasure, we will be vigilant for his arrival and faithful to his demands.

Connecting the Word

to the first reading: To the Hebrews, "the night of the passover was known beforehand" and so they maintained their fidelity. We who do not know the hour of the Lord's return are still called to the same fidelity.

to culture: The word "treasure" usually refers to our most valued possession. By sending the Son of Man to us God reveals where God's heart is.

Understanding the Word

The Son of Man and the Kingdom of God: This Sunday's gospel is made up of three distinct units: the first verse is actually the conclusion of 12:22-32; the next two verses (vv. 33-34) are independent sayings about poverty and wealth. Then two parables introduce new themes: vigilance and fidelity. But the Lectionary combines these passages in a new way.

Using the image of a master returning either from a wedding (12:35-40) or from some other journey (12:42-48), Jesus instructs his disciples about the coming of "the Son of Man" (12:40). The Lectionary uses the two parables to illustrate the opening verses in which Jesus assures his disciples that God will bless them with a "treasure" that is inexhaustible, secure in heaven, and immune from destruction (12:33). In the Lectionary context the treasure which God gives is another metaphor for the "kingdom." The kingdom for which disciples are to pray (11:2) and seek (12:31) is the kingdom which God "is pleased to give *[didomi]* you" (12:32). Thus when Jesus says, "much will be required of the person entrusted *[didomi]* with much" (12:48), we have already been told that disciples have been entrusted with the Kingdom (the same Greek word *[didomi]* is translated as "give" in verse 32 and as "entrusted" in verse 48). How great, then, are the Master's expectations when the treasure is so great.

The combination of these two themes—the kingdom and the coming of the Son of Man—recalls another crucial passage, namely, Daniel 7:13-14. In this important passage one "like a Son of Man" comes before God and is given *[didomi]* the kingdom. As the parables make clear, disciples await the coming of the Son of Man. Each of the two parables highlights different aspects of the disciples' waiting. The first parable urges vigilance so as not to be caught off-guard. The second parable demands faithfulness so as to be busy about the duties which have been assigned. Vigilance is rewarded by being served by the Master at table; fidelity in service is rewarded with greater authority, but infidelity is severely punished.

ASSEMBLY & FAITH-SHARING GROUPS

• My treasure and heart are with . . .
 The way my treasure is related to God's kingdom is . . .

• To be vigilant until the "master's return" means to me . . .

• Ways that I am preparing for the master's return are . . .

PRESIDERS

" . . . your Father is pleased to give you the kingdom." I am being given the kingdom by . . .
My life *and* ministry extend this gift to others by . . .

DEACONS

My life and ministry is a living proclamation. What it teaches others about *treasure* is . . .
What it teaches others about *vigilance* is . . .

HOSPITALITY MINISTERS

Good hospitality requires a vigilant posture; what my ministry has taught me about being ready for Christ's Second Coming is . . .

MUSIC MINISTERS

Through my music ministry I have come to treasure Christ more fully because . . .
My ministry sometimes interferes with my treasuring Christ because . . .

ALTAR MINISTERS

By serving others I am becoming a "faithful and prudent steward" because . . .

LECTORS

An example when another's life pointed me to "treasure in heaven" is . . .
My life is directing others to heavenly treasure by . . .

EUCHARISTIC MINISTERS

Eucharist signifies and embodies God's "inexhaustible treasure in heaven" for me. The way I experience this is . . .
I share this with others by . . .

Model Penitential Rite

Presider: The gospel today reminds us that where our treasure is, our heart is. We pause now at the beginning of this liturgy to draw our hearts to God's presence and open ourselves to God's love and grace . . . [pause]

Lord Jesus, you bless your disciples with love and care: Lord . . .

Christ Jesus, you call us to be vigilant for your coming: Christ . . .

Lord Jesus, you are the gift of God to us and our most valued Treasure: Lord . . .

Appreciating the Responsorial Psalm

Jesus tells us in this Sunday's gospel that where our treasure is there will be our heart. Along this very line the responsorial psalm says something remarkable about God: we are God's treasure, chosen as "his own inheritance." And where God's treasure is, God's heart will be.

This is the reason why we can wait with hope and "sure knowledge" for the deliverance promised us, whether we know the hour of its arrival (first reading) or not (gospel). God has chosen us and already given us the kingdom (gospel). Our response is to keep our eyes turned toward the God whose eyes are fixed upon us (psalm) by being faithful servants who fulfill the Lord's will in season and out (gospel). We are but returning the gift.

Model General Intercessions

Presider: Let us pray that our hearts might be conformed to the Treasure God gives us, Jesus.

Response:

Lord, hear our prayer.

Cantor:

we pray to the Lord,

That all members of the Church be vigilant in doing God's will and remain always faithful disciples . . . [pause]

That leaders of the world's nations be faithful in executing the responsibilities entrusted to them . . . [pause]

That the poor be comforted in possessing the great Treasure of Jesus' nearness and care . . . [pause]

That each of us grow in turning our hearts to our greatest Treasure, Jesus . . . [pause]

Presider: Loving God, you give us the gift of your divine Son and ask us to be faithful to his gospel: hear these our prayers that one day we might enjoy lasting treasure with you in heaven. We ask this through that same Son, Jesus Christ our Lord. **Amen.**

ALTERNATIVE OPENING PRAYER

Let us pray

Pause for silent prayer

Father,
we come, reborn in the Spirit,
to celebrate our sonship in the Lord Jesus
    Christ.
Touch our hearts,
help them grow toward the life you have
    promised.
Touch our lives,
make them signs of your love for all men.

Grant this through Christ our Lord.
    Amen.

FIRST READING

Wis 18:6-9

The night of the passover was known
    beforehand to our fathers,
    that, with sure knowledge of the oaths
        in which they put their faith,
    they might have courage.
Your people awaited the salvation of the
    just
    and the destruction of their foes.
For when you punished our adversaries,
    in this you glorified us whom you had
        summoned.
For in secret the holy children of the good
    were offering sacrifice
    and putting into effect with one accord
        the divine institution.

RESPONSORIAL PSALM
Ps 33:1, 12, 18-19, 20-22

R℣. (12b) Blessed the people the Lord has chosen to be his own.

Exult, you just, in the LORD;
    praise from the upright is fitting.
Blessed the nation whose God is the LORD,
    the people he has chosen for his own
        inheritance.

R℣. Blessed the people the Lord has chosen to be his own.

See, the eyes of the Lord are upon those
        who fear him,
    upon those who hope for his kindness,
to deliver them from death
    and preserve them in spite of famine.

R℣. Blessed the people the Lord has chosen to be his own.

Our soul waits for the LORD,
    who is our help and our shield.
May your kindness, O LORD, be upon us
    who have put our hope in you.

R℣. Blessed the people the Lord has chosen to be his own.

SECOND READING
Heb 11:1-2, 8-12

Brothers and sisters:
Faith is the realization of what is hoped for
    and evidence of things not seen.
Because of it the ancients were well attested.

By faith Abraham obeyed when he was
        called to go out to a place
    that he was to receive as an inheritance;
    he went out, not knowing where he was
        to go.
By faith he sojourned in the promised land
    as in a foreign country,
    dwelling in tents with Isaac and Jacob,
        heirs of the same promise;
    for he was looking forward to the city
        with foundations,
    whose architect and maker is God.
By faith he received power to generate,
    even though he was past the normal age
    —and Sarah herself was sterile—
    for he thought that the one who had
        made the promise was trustworthy.
So it was that there came forth from one
        man,
    himself as good as dead,
    descendants as numerous as the stars in
        the sky
    and as countless as the sands on the
        seashore.

About Liturgy

Stewardship, faithfulness, and liturgy: Many parishes next month (September) have various stewardship activities. Often this includes filling out a form indicating monetary gifts to the parish as well as how one will contribute time and expertise during the next year. Our reflections on the gospel for this Sunday raise some issues about stewardship. Our hearts can be displaced in many ways, and if our hearts are displaced then we may lose sight of our true Treasure, Jesus.

For the good management of a parish, of course there must be monetary and time donations. This is part of the "faithfulness" of good disciples. At the same time we must always caution ourselves that we don't become so involved in *doing* that we neglect the way we encounter our Treasure in good celebration of liturgy. Our hearts must always be tuned into the praise and thanksgiving that is liturgy.

It is easy to be distracted during liturgy by the demands of *doing* ministry. Vigilance for our truest Treasure means that we always must bring ourselves back to full, conscious, and active participation in the liturgy that makes present the greatest gift God has given us—Jesus. Celebration of good liturgy makes demands on our energy (it takes more energy to make sure that our minds remain focused on the celebration) and calls us to vigilance (how God is transforming each of us into being richer members of the body of Christ). Ultimately the most important stewardship is not the money or time we donate but surrendering ourselves to being transformed.

About Liturgical Music

Cantor preparation: Preparing to sing the responsorial psalm means more than learning new words and music. Far more, it means preparing yourself for the coming of Christ in the Liturgy of the Word. No matter how many times you have sung a particular psalm, no matter how many times you have heard the proclamation of a particular gospel, there is always a new coming of Christ. How might this hope affect your manner of preparing the psalm?

Selecting musical settings of the responsorial psalm, Pt. 1: Although the responsorial psalm is not proclamation as such, it is a scriptural text bearing direct relationship to the readings of the day. For this reason the text as given in the Lectionary is preferable over a paraphrased version. While it is true that even the translations in the Lectionary are paraphrases to some extent—since adapting concepts from one language to another always requires adjustments—there is a huge difference between a translation that is exegetically based and a paraphrase that is determined by the requirements of a melodic line. There are many highly paraphrased psalm texts available which are poetically beautiful and musically uplifting, but these function more appropriately at other times in the liturgy (for example, during the Communion procession). The issue here is not the quality of the music but the capability of the setting to enable the psalm to fulfill its liturgical role.

A second principle in selecting a psalm setting is that the text of the psalm must predominate over the music. If the music is so elaborate or so thickly woven chorally or instrumentally that the text cannot be readily heard and understood, then the setting interferes with the functioning of the psalm. This is not to say that the setting cannot be rhythmically or harmonically complex, but only that the complexity should not overshadow the clarity of the words. Often people leave the Sunday Eucharist humming the melody of the psalm refrain. But do they also know what psalm was sung, and how that psalm was related to the readings of the day?

AUGUST 8, 2004
NINETEENTH SUNDAY IN ORDINARY TIME

✝ SPIRITUALITY

Gospel
Luke 1:39-56; L622

Mary set out
and traveled to the hill
country in haste
to a town of Judah,
where she entered the house
of Zechariah
and greeted Elizabeth.
When Elizabeth heard Mary's
greeting,
the infant leaped in her womb,
and Elizabeth, filled with the
Holy Spirit,
cried out in a loud voice and
said,
"Blessed are you among
women,
and blessed is the fruit of
your womb.
And how does this happen to me,
that the mother of my Lord should
come to me?
For at the moment the sound of your
greeting reached my ears,
the infant in my womb leaped for joy.
Blessed are you who believed
that what was spoken to you by the
Lord
would be fulfilled."

And Mary said:
"My soul proclaims the greatness of
the Lord;
my spirit rejoices in God my Savior
for he has looked upon his lowly
servant.
From this day all generations will
call me blessed:
the Almighty has done great things
for me,
and holy is his name.
He has mercy on those who fear him
in every generation.
He has shown the strength of his arm,
and has scattered the proud in
their conceit.

Continued in Appendix A, p. 286.

Reflecting on the Gospel

Even before the dawn of feminism and rising consciousness about the dignity of women, great women have done great things and history has been kind to their memory. We have, for example, Esther, Ruth, and Judith from the Old Testament; pagan societies had goddesses as well as gods; Troy had Helen and France had Joan; Constantine had Helena and Augustine had Monica; Florence Nightingale, Dorothy Day, and Mother Teresa have all left their indelible marks. It is no surprise, then, that we also find a great woman remembered along with the founding events of Christianity. Mary is remembered because she was the first disciple to whom God did great things, lifting her up from among the lowly. Mary belongs so completely to God that even her body is at God's disposal.

The gospel opens with Elizabeth's being "filled with the Holy Spirit" and recognizing and responding to Mary's blessedness. Yet Elizabeth misunderstands and locates these "great things" with Mary. Mary herself redirects Elizabeth's (and our) attention to God. It is God who does great things because God has promised mercy. The great thing Mary does is say *yes* to being an instrument of God's promise. The great thing about Jesus is that he *is* the promise. The great thing for us is that we *receive* that promise.

Jesus' birth ushers in a new age of promise which is manifested in *Magnificat's* reversals: the conceited are scattered, the mighty are cast down, the lowly are lifted up, the hungry are filled, the rich are sent away empty. In her *Magnificat* Mary already announces the new age to come which is established through faithful discipleship. God's kingdom of the new age is brought to completion when all are gathered into a sharing in eternal life. Mary's assumption—this festival—is a sign of the completion already coming about. This is why we might think of Mary's assumption as a festival of mercy: Mary "returned to her home" when she completed her mission of being an instrument of God's promise, a home which is to be with God for all eternity. The assumption is a sign of God's mercy being fulfilled. It is also a sign that our true home is with God.

Living the Paschal Mystery

Mary remained with Elizabeth "about three months." Mary remains with the Church (with us) always, to be a sign of God's promises fulfilled. Her discipleship continues in that she is a sign of hope and mercy. So it is with us. One way our own discipleship is expressed is through our being a sign of God's mercy.

Mercy in the gospel is shown not only in the forgiveness of sins but also in the fulfillment of promises. Therefore, one important aspect of discipleship is to live in such a way as to witness to God's promise of mercy being fulfilled. Practically speaking, this means that we carry ourselves with dignity and bestow that same dignity on others. No one is beneath us or too "lowly" or insignificant to deserve our attention and respect. This is easier said than done!

Dying to self means treating the other as one deserving and receiving God's mercy. First of all, this means that we don't judge others. Our judgments of each other are usually much more unkind that God's merciful judgment of us! This also means that we are careful never to speak negatively of others. Diminishing another surely doesn't raise them up and ultimately diminishes even ourselves. Finally, paschal mystery living means that we treat the other as one blessed by God.

Focusing the Word

Key words and phrases from the gospel: lowly servant, great things, lifted up, promise of mercy

To the point: This solemnity celebrates the "great things" God has done for Mary. God, who has "lifted up" his "lowly servant" Mary, lifts up all the lowly not only because they are faithful but because God is faithful to the promise of divine mercy. Assumption celebrates the mercy of God.

Connecting the Word

to the second reading: The second reading rehearses the entire history of God's promise of mercy: death came through Adam; life came through Christ. Mary's assumption foreshadows the destiny of all "those who belong to Christ."

to culture: In our news-dominated culture we tend to view events historically. In this approach the assumption celebrates what happened to Mary in the past. Liturgy does more than recall a past event; it draws us into divine mystery where that event is present now.

Understanding the Word

Mercy: Luke's great manifesto of divine mercy is found in the first chapter of his gospel in two programmatic prayers, Mary's *Magnificat* (1:46-55) and Zechariah's *Benedictus* (1:68-79). These prayers set forth many of Luke's favorite themes: God's preference for the poor and lowly, the fulfillment of divine promises and prophetic predictions, deliverance and salvation, and the reversal of fortunes. A prominent theme in both texts is the celebration of God's mercy.

The first mention of mercy in Luke's gospel is 1:50, "He has mercy on those who fear him in every generation" (literally, "from generation to generation"); this, in turn, paraphrases the Greek version of Psalm 103:17, "The mercy of the Lord is from generation to generation upon those who fear him." This verse celebrates not a singular act of divine compassion but a perpetual stance taken by God toward those who acknowledge God's sovereignty. Mary stands in the line of those faithful Israelites who, reverencing God, are blessed with mercy.

Luke 1:54-55 reads, God "has come to the help of his servant Israel for he has remembered his promise of mercy." This is a paraphrase of Psalm 98:3, "He has remembered his steadfast love and faithfulness to the house of Israel." Again, God's action is on behalf of all Israel, the people called and designated as God's servant (see Isa 41:8-9). By ending with a reference to the "promise he made to our fathers, to Abraham and his children forever" (see Gen 12:1-3), Luke extends this divine mercy beyond Israel to all nations on earth. This is an overarching theme of Luke-Acts: salvation for all.

In context, Mary's prayer interprets the history of God's mercy as coming to fulfillment now in the wondrous birth of this still more wondrous child who has been called "Son of the Most High" (1:32) and "the Son of God" (1:35). "Mercy" cannot be separated from God's saving plan: salvation is the concrete realization of divine mercy. In turn, the salvation promised of old will be realized by the birth of Jesus who is hailed as "savior . . . Messiah and Lord" (2:11).

**ASSEMBLY &
FAITH-SHARING GROUPS**

- Mary's blessedness is completed by God in her assumption to heaven. What I need completed within me by God is . . .

- Elizabeth realizes Mary is blessed because she believed in "what was spoken" to her. Believing has blessed my life by . . .

- Mary recognizes the source of her blessedness as "the Almighty." I am reminded that God is the source of my blessedness when . . . A way I direct others to God as the source of blessedness is . . .

PRESIDERS
A way my ministry participates in fulfilling God's "promise of mercy" (see the *Magnificat*) is . . .

DEACONS
A way my service points others to heaven as a Christian's "final goal" (see opening prayer) is . . .

HOSPITALITY MINISTERS
Elizabeth experiences being blessed in welcoming Mary. A blessing for me whenever I welcome another is . . .

MUSIC MINISTERS
My music ministry sings of the mercy of God and the blessedness of Mary by . . . It sings of the blessedness of the assembly when . . .

ALTAR MINISTERS
When I serve others as a response to the "great things" God has done my service looks like . . .

LECTORS
"God's temple . . . was opened, and the ark . . . could be seen" (first reading). Praying God's word has opened within me . . . Praying God's word has allowed me to see . . .

EUCHARISTIC MINISTERS
Like Mary the Eucharist makes me into an instrument of God's promise of mercy for others. I witness this whenever . . .

Model Penitential Rite

Presider: Today we celebrate the assumption of Mary into heaven. The promise of God's divine mercy is fulfilled as Mary joins her divine Son in everlasting glory. Let us pause and prepare ourselves to celebrate these great mysteries and ask God's help in being faithful as Mary was faithful . . . [pause]

Lord Jesus, your mother Mary is blessed among all women: Lord . . .

Christ Jesus, you are the Promise of God's mercy: Christ . . .

Lord Jesus, you are God our Savior: Lord . . .

Appreciating the Responsorial Psalm

Psalm 45 is a nuptial psalm used by the Israelites in the wedding ceremony between their king and his bride. The people call her to forget her family and homeland and embrace a more glorious relationship. She chooses to do so, but not alone: with "gladness and joy" an entire retinue follows.

By accepting her role in the incarnation Mary chose to embody the cosmic struggle between the forces of evil and the saving power of God (first reading). Blessed is she for believing in the power and promise of God even when these seemed hidden from view (gospel). Blessed is she for not clinging to past and present and venturing in hope into an unseen future. Now the victory of Christ over sin and death is completed in her (second reading) and God celebrates her beauty (psalm). In her the lowly have been lifted up and the hungering satisfied with salvation (gospel). In her humanity has been wedded to God. And we belong to the retinue.

Model General Intercessions

Presider: Let us pray for faithfulness and God's mercy.

Response:

Cantor:

That the Church remain a faithful witness to God's promise of mercy for all . . . [pause]

That those in leadership positions be imitators of God's mercy so all may have justice and peace . . . [pause]

That the lowly be lifted up, the hungry be fed, and the poor have dignity . . . [pause]

That each one of us model our lives after Mary's faithfulness . . . [pause]

Presider: Merciful God, you called Mary to be the mother of your divine Son: hear these our prayers that through her intercession we might one day also live in glory with you. We ask this through the divine Son, Christ our Lord. **Amen.**

OPENING PRAYER

Let us pray

Pause for silent prayer

All-powerful and ever-living God,
you raised the sinless Virgin Mary, mother
 of your Son,
body and soul to the glory of heaven.
May we see heaven as our final goal
and come to share her glory.

We ask this through our Lord Jesus Christ,
 your Son,
who lives and reigns with you and the
 Holy Spirit,
one God, for ever and ever. **Amen.**

FIRST READING

Rev 11:19a; 12:1-6a, 10ab

God's temple in heaven was opened,
 and the ark of his covenant could be
  seen in the temple.

A great sign appeared in the sky, a woman
  clothed with the sun,
 with the moon beneath her feet,
 and on her head a crown of twelve stars.
She was with child and wailed aloud in
  pain as she labored to give birth.
Then another sign appeared in the sky;
 it was a huge red dragon, with seven
  heads and ten horns,
 and on its heads were seven diadems.
Its tail swept away a third of the stars in
  the sky
 and hurled them down to the earth.
Then the dragon stood before the woman
  about to give birth,
 to devour her child when she gave birth.
She gave birth to a son, a male child,
  destined to rule all the nations with an
  iron rod.
Her child was caught up to God and his
  throne.
The woman herself fled into the desert
 where she had a place prepared by God.

Then I heard a loud voice in heaven say:
 "Now have salvation and power come,
  and the kingdom of our God
  and the authority of his Anointed
  One."

RESPONSORIAL PSALM

Ps 45:10, 11, 12, 16

℞. (10bc) The queen stands at your right hand, arrayed in gold.

The queen takes her place at your right
    hand in gold of Ophir.

℞. The queen stands at your right hand,
arrayed in gold.

Hear, O daughter, and see; turn your ear,
    forget your people and your father's
        house.

℞. The queen stands at your right hand,
arrayed in gold.

So shall the king desire your beauty;
    for he is your lord.

℞. The queen stands at your right hand,
arrayed in gold.

They are borne in with gladness and joy;
    they enter the palace of the king.

℞. The queen stands at your right hand,
arrayed in gold.

SECOND READING

1 Cor 15:20-27

Brothers and sisters:
Christ has been raised from the dead,
    the firstfruits of those who have fallen
        asleep.
For since death came through man,
    the resurrection of the dead came also
        through man.
For just as in Adam all die,
    so too in Christ shall all be brought to
        life,
    but each one in proper order:
    Christ the firstfruits;
    then, at his coming, those who belong to
        Christ;
    then comes the end,
    when he hands over the kingdom to his
        God and Father,
    when he has destroyed every sovereignty
    and every authority and power.
For he must reign until he has put all his
    enemies under his feet.
The last enemy to be destroyed is death,
    for "he subjected everything under his
        feet."

About Liturgy

Sundays and solemnities: When August 15 falls on a Sunday, as it does this year, the celebration of the Solemnity of the Assumption of the Blessed Virgin Mary replaces the Sunday in Ordinary Time. There are fewer than a score of solemnities celebrated during our liturgical year; the small number testifies that these are our major festivals, carefully chosen because they celebrate an event in the salvific mission of Jesus or celebrate someone who was key in unfolding those events. This is one way that the liturgical calendar continually keeps before us major aspects of the paschal mystery. We celebrate a Marian festival, but since it falls on Sunday it is also a happy reminder that any celebration of the saints is always a celebration of Christ.

Each Sunday is a celebration of resurrection—a "little Easter." On this first day of the week the whole Church celebrates redemption; this is why we have a *Sunday* Mass obligation—it is the Church's way to underscore that Sunday is a salvation feast. When we have the coincidence of a saint's feast and Sunday, it is a kind of "double reminder" that salvation in Christ is such a great gift from God we need at least a weekly, communal celebration.

This Sunday we also celebrate Jesus' first, faithful disciple—his mother Mary. Its falling on a Sunday is a "double reminder" that God's mighty deeds toward Mary always redound to her Son. Mary's assumption witnesses to God's bringing to completion the work of salvation; Mary's assumption into heaven is a promise to all of us that this is where our own fidelity leads. Each Sunday our celebration at Mass is a remembrance of God's fidelity to the promise of salvation that one day we, too, will dwell in God's everlasting kingdom of heaven.

About Liturgical Music

Cantor preparation: As you sing this responsorial psalm you celebrate your own entrance into heaven, for the entire Church is borne with Mary into God's kingdom. How can you prepare yourself to sing such promise and glory? How can you imitate Mary more fully in her choice to cooperate with God's plan for salvation?

Hymn suggestions: A very appropriate hymn of praise after Communion would be the *Magnificat*. Many settings exist, but one paraphrase which gives fresh insight into the text is Rory Cooney's "Canticle of the Turning" [G2, RS]. Choir or cantor(s) could sing the verses with the assembly joining in on the refrain. The refrain is set to a simple, easily learned SAB arrangement. Its energetic Irish melody and the intriguing metaphor which unifies the text ("the world is about to turn") make this setting especially appealing. A second fresh paraphrase is Alan Hommerding and Steven Warner's "My Soul Flies Free" [WC; WLP octavo #007220]. Choir or cantor(s) could sing the verses with the assembly singing the refrain.

✠ SPIRITUALITY

Gospel
Luke 13:22-30; L123C

Jesus passed through towns and
villages,
   teaching as he went and
      making his way to
      Jerusalem.
Someone asked him,
   "Lord, will only a few people
      be saved?"
He answered them,
   "Strive to enter through the
      narrow gate,
   for many, I tell you, will
      attempt to enter
   but will not be strong enough.
After the master of the house
   has arisen and locked the
      door,
   then will you stand outside knocking
      and saying,
   'Lord, open the door for us.'
He will say to you in reply,
   'I do not know where you are from.'
And you will say,
   'We ate and drank in your company
      and you taught in our streets.'
Then he will say to you,
   'I do not know where you are from.
   Depart from me, all you evildoers!'
And there will be wailing and grinding
   of teeth
   when you see Abraham, Isaac, and
      Jacob
   and all the prophets in the kingdom
      of God
   and you yourselves cast out.
And people will come from the east and
   the west
   and from the north and the south
   and will recline at table in the
      kingdom of God.
For behold, some are last who will be
   first,
   and some are first who will be last."

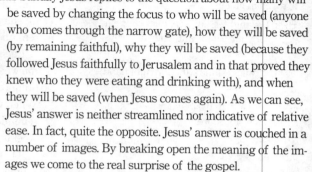

Reflecting on the Gospel

The shortest distance between two points is a straight line. Take the path of least resistance. In these and other ways we try to capture how we achieve goals without putting out any more effort than is necessary. All our modern conveniences are geared toward accomplishing life's tasks in the easiest way possible and in the least amount of time. We like our life streamlined and relatively effortless. In the gospel this Sunday Jesus replies to the question about how many will be saved by changing the focus to who will be saved (anyone who comes through the narrow gate), how they will be saved (by remaining faithful), why they will be saved (because they followed Jesus faithfully to Jerusalem and in that proved they knew who they were eating and drinking with), and when they will be saved (when Jesus comes again). As we can see, Jesus' answer is neither streamlined nor indicative of relative ease. In fact, quite the opposite. Jesus' answer is couched in a number of images. By breaking open the meaning of the images we come to the real surprise of the gospel.

Let's consider the images first. *Making his way to Jerusalem*—Jesus is being faithful to his own mission; by going to Jerusalem he fulfills his Father's will even when that means he must suffer and die. *Narrow gate*—we might see Jesus himself as the gate (compare John 10:7 where Jesus is described as the gate); we are saved by identifying ourselves with Jesus and this includes going to Jerusalem with him even when that means we, too, must die to ourselves. *Strong enough*—strength here isn't the physical strength to push open a literal door but the spiritual strength to remain faithful to our call to discipleship and follow Jesus to Jerusalem. *Locked . . . door*—one day Jesus will return and gather all the faithful to himself; this day of judgment must find us faithful because then the door will be shut. *I do not know where you are from*—discipleship of Jesus demands more than being in Jesus' company (e.g., prayer and celebrating liturgy); it means we must take up the mission of Jesus to die and rise, that is, we must be on the way to Jerusalem.

Putting these images together, it becomes clear that what limits the scope of salvation is not God's reach (which is to east, west, north, and south—that is, salvation is offered to all people) but *our response*. We do not gain eternal salvation by walking in a straight line or by taking the path of least resistance. We gain eternal salvation, rather, by the difficult and demanding path of following Jesus on his way to Jerusalem; we do this by dying to self and being faithful disciples. The surprise of the gospel is that all are offered salvation but this isn't enough. We must also know Jesus well enough to be faithful in following him to Jerusalem.

Living the Paschal Mystery

We all claim to know Jesus; after all, we are for the most part faithful church-goers who weekly eat and drink in his company. This gospel warns us that this isn't enough. There is an urgency about our paschal mystery living; we don't have forever to make up our minds to respond to God's offer of salvation. Each day we must take up our own cross, die to self, and live for the sake of others. This is how we enter through the narrow gate and how we get to know Jesus intimately enough to receive salvation: we must *live and act like Jesus*. Becoming least is a metaphor for dying to self; this is what Jesus asks: that the first become the last. Yes, what limits the scope of salvation is not God's reach but our response.

Focusing the Word

Key words and phrases from the gospel: making his way to Jerusalem, strive to enter through the narrow gate, strong enough, locked . . . door

To the point: Jesus was asked about how many would be saved. He addresses, instead, the urgency of responding to the opportunity for salvation. On the one hand, the "narrow gate" is open now but it will not remain so indefinitely. On the other hand, it is not enough to eat and drink with Jesus but we must follow him on "his way to Jerusalem."

Connecting the Word

to the first reading: Though the gospel seems to place limits on the opportunity for salvation, the first reading reinforces salvation's wide reach: from east, west, north, south.

to Catholic culture: For some a traditional view of God as threatening hellfire and brimstone has given way to a "warm and fuzzy" view of God always overlooking human wrongdoing. The gospel holds in tension the all-inclusive mercy of God who nevertheless enacts judgment.

Understanding the Word

The narrow door: The first verse of the gospel reminds us that Jesus is "making his way to Jerusalem" (see Sunday 13 for "the journey"). The goal in view is the accomplishment of Jesus' mission: salvation through his dying and rising.

To gain access to salvation, one must enter through the narrow door. (The Lectionary unfortunately alternates between "gate" and "door" in v. 24 but it is the same word in Greek, *thura*.) While salvation is made available to all, not all will enter. The door is narrow: one must "strive" to enter. The Greek word for "strive" *(agonizomai)* is a word used for strenuous effort in athletic competition (see 1 Cor 9:25; 1 Tim 6:12; 2 Tim 4:7). Though many compete in various games, winners are few in proportion to competitors. "Striving" to enter through the narrow door implies both effort on the part of those seeking salvation and a judgment that not all will achieve their goal.

But the narrowness of the door is not the only obstacle: time is also critical. An hour will come when "the master of the house has arisen and locked the door." We earlier encountered a door that was closed and locked: in the parable of the unexpected night visitor, the unprepared host goes to his neighbor and knocks on the door to ask for bread (Luke 11:5-8; see OT Sunday 17). On that occasion Jesus instructed his disciples to "knock and the door will be opened for you" (11:9). The situation is different in this gospel. The opportunity to enter is not indefinite. Once the door is closed—once the end has come and judgment is pronounced—it is too late. A decision on the part of those who wish to enter is required *now*.

The protest of those who are locked out points again to the seriousness of effort required of those seeking salvation. It is not enough to have been casually acquainted with Jesus: "We ate and drank in your company and you taught in our streets" (13:26). Those who wish to gain entrance must follow him to Jerusalem.

**ASSEMBLY &
FAITH-SHARING GROUPS**

- To be like Jesus and make my "way to Jerusalem" means to me . . .
- The people and/or practices that enable me to "strive to enter through the narrow gate" are . . .
- This gospel holds in tension the all-inclusive mercy of God who nevertheless enacts judgment. The way I understand and balance God's mercy with God's judgment is . . .

PRESIDERS
The door of salvation is open now! My ministry communicates this invitation and its urgency by . . .

DEACONS
My Christian living goes beyond mere familiarity with Jesus ("we ate and drank in your company") to following him to Jerusalem because . . .

HOSPITALITY MINISTERS
My hospitality embodies God's all-inclusive invitation to enter God's kingdom by . . .

MUSIC MINISTERS
My music ministry is one way I "eat and drink in Jesus' company" because . . .
It is also a way I accept the challenge to follow him to Jerusalem because . . .

ALTAR MINISTERS
The way my service goes beyond attending to vessels and rubrics to supporting others on the way to Jerusalem is . . .

LECTORS
Praying the word faithfully transforms one into a "sign" that draws others to "come and see [God's] glory" (first reading). One way this is happening to me is . . .

EUCHARISTIC MINISTERS
The way I am God's food that aids and encourages others to strive through the narrow gate is . . .

Model Penitential Rite

Presider: The gospel today invites us to get to know Jesus not only by hearing his word and eating and drinking at his banquet table, but also by following him to Jerusalem. We must be faithful disciples who take up our own daily cross of self-sacrifice for the sake of others. Let us ask God for the grace to be faithful . . . [pause]

Lord Jesus, you give us the strength to be faithful disciples: Lord . . .

Christ Jesus, you invite all into the kingdom of God: Christ . . .

Lord Jesus, you teach us to take up our cross daily: Lord . . .

Appreciating the Responsorial Psalm

Jesus challenges us in this Sunday's gospel with the harsh reality that not everyone will be admitted to the kingdom of God (gospel). His message, however, is for those who have heard the good news of salvation, not for those who have "never heard of [God's] name, or seen [God's] glory" (first reading). To these God will send messengers to tell them the good news and gather them to the holy dwelling, Jerusalem. For those who have already heard, radical demands are in place (Jesus has been spelling these out in previous Sundays' gospels). And the responsorial psalm gives yet another command: we are to be the messengers who spread the good news of God's salvation to all the world. The psalm reminds us that we are a necessary part of God's plan of salvation for all. It also suggests that we cannot recline at God's table if we have not invited everyone else to be there with us.

Model General Intercessions

Presider: Let us place our needs before God, so that we might have the strength to be faithful disciples of Jesus.

Response:

Lord, hear our prayer.

Cantor:

we pray to the Lord,

That members of the Church may follow Jesus faithfully . . . [pause]

That world leaders may open the doors of justice and peace . . . [pause]

That those in need may have their fill of this world's abundance . . . [pause]

That all of us may respond to God's call to follow Jesus in dying to self . . . [pause]

Presider: Loving God, you offer salvation to all who come to you: hear these our prayers that one day we might enter through the narrow gate into sharing your everlasting glory. We ask this through Jesus Christ our Lord. **Amen.**

OPENING PRAYER

Let us pray

Pause for silent prayer

Father,
help us to seek the values
that will bring us lasting joy in this
    changing world.
In our desire for what you promise
make us one in mind and heart.

Grant this through our Lord Jesus Christ,
    your Son,
who lives and reigns with you and the
    Holy Spirit,
one God, for ever and ever. **Amen.**

FIRST READING
Isa 66:18-21

Thus says the LORD:
I know their works and their thoughts,
and I come to gather nations of every
    language;
    they shall come and see my glory.
I will set a sign among them;
    from them I will send fugitives to the
        nations:
    to Tarshish, Put and Lud, Mosoch,
        Tubal and Javan,
    to the distant coastlands
    that have never heard of my fame, or
        seen my glory;
    and they shall proclaim my glory
        among the nations.
They shall bring all your brothers and
        sisters from all the nations
    as an offering to the LORD,
    on horses and in chariots, in carts, upon
        mules and dromedaries,
    to Jerusalem, my holy mountain, says
        the LORD,
    just as the Israelites bring their offering
    to the house of the LORD in clean vessels.
Some of these I will take as priests and
    Levites, says the LORD.

RESPONSORIAL PSALM

Ps 117:1, 2

R̶⁷. (Mark 16:15) Go out to all the world and tell the good news.
    or:
R̶⁷. Alleluia.

Praise the LORD, all you nations;
    glorify him, all you peoples!

R̶⁷. Go out to all the world and tell the good news.
    or:
R̶⁷. Alleluia.

For steadfast is his kindness toward us,
    and the fidelity of the LORD endures
        forever.

R̶⁷. Go out to all the world and tell the good news.
    or:
R̶⁷. Alleluia.

SECOND READING

Heb 12:5-7, 11-13

Brothers and sisters,
You have forgotten the exhortation
    addressed to you as children:
    "My son, do not disdain the discipline of
        the Lord
    or lose heart when reproved by him;
    for whom the Lord loves, he disciplines;
    he scourges every son he
        acknowledges."
Endure your trials as "discipline";
    God treats you as sons.
For what "son" is there whom his father
    does not discipline?
At the time,
    all discipline seems a cause not for joy
        but for pain,
    yet later it brings the peaceful fruit of
        righteousness
    to those who are trained by it.

So strengthen your drooping hands and
    your weak knees.
Make straight paths for your feet,
    that what is lame may not be disjointed
        but healed.

About Liturgy

Prefaces: The preface is the first part of the eucharistic prayer. The dialogue before the preface proper begins is one of the oldest of all liturgical texts. The dialogue invites the assembly to prayer, but much more elaborately than the usual "Let us pray" that begins the opening prayer and prayer after Communion. First of all, the invitation to pray the eucharistic prayer is truly a dialogue between presider and assembly. The dialogue unfolds in three parts: greeting ("The Lord be with you"), command to a specific prayer sentiment or stance ("Lift up your hearts"), and an invitation to pray in a particular way ("Let us give thanks to the Lord our God"). The eucharistic prayer is our great thanksgiving to God for the work of salvation.

The body of the preface then unfolds as an act of thanksgiving and praise and includes reasons why we have these sentiments toward God. Often the preface includes mention of God as creator, usually of Jesus as redeemer, and sometimes of the Holy Spirit as sanctifier. When the preface is proper to a feast it often includes themes pertinent to the feast which raise in us cause for praise and thanks.

Originally the Latin word which we translate as preface (*praefatio*) meant "proclamation" and was sometimes ascribed to the whole eucharistic prayer. Our English translation can get in the way here; rather than being merely "preliminary" (like the preface in a book) which can be skipped over or discarded, the preface to the eucharistic prayer is the first invitation and reason to give God praise and thanks.

About Liturgical Music

Cantor preparation: In singing this psalm you command the assembly to tell the world the good news of salvation. Who in your life is especially in need of hearing this news? How do you tell them?

Changing service music: Because Jesus clearly makes the turn toward Jerusalem in this Sunday's gospel this would be an appropriate Sunday to switch to another Ordinary Time setting of service music. Changing this music is one way to express the choice to turn with Jesus and accept the challenge of disciple to walk with him toward the ultimate fulfillment of his mission in passion, death, and resurrection.

Selecting musical settings of the responsorial psalm, Pt. 2: A third principle which guides the selection of musical settings of the responsorial psalm is that the psalm must never overshadow the readings themselves. If the setting is so long or so embellished that the assembly continues mentally humming the refrain during the subsequent readings, then the psalm has overreached its place. We must keep in mind that the psalm is meant to lead to the readings, not to itself. Unfortunately, the problem which often exists is not that the psalm setting is too elaborate, but the proclamation of the readings is too weak. The need here, then, is not to tone down the psalm but to improve the proclamation.

This is not to say that we never use an elaborate musical setting of a responsorial psalm. This is more than appropriate on solemnities like Christmas, Easter, Christ the King, etc. On these occasions highly embellished musical settings with perhaps more than one cantor or the choir as a whole singing the verses in harmony and with solo instrument(s) added communicate the high festivity of the day in contrast with the less festive periods of the year. These solemnities call for more elaborate music. But highly ornamented psalm settings lose their festive capability if they are used on a regular basis, Sunday after Sunday.

✠ SPIRITUALITY

Gospel   Luke 14:1, 7-14; L126C

On a sabbath Jesus went to dine
  at the home of one of the leading
      Pharisees,
  and the people there were
      observing him carefully.

He told a parable to those who had
      been invited,
  noticing how they were choosing
      the places of honor at the
      table.
"When you are invited by someone
      to a wedding banquet,
  do not recline at table in the place
      of honor.
A more distinguished guest than you
      may have been invited by him,
  and the host who invited both of
      you may approach you and say,
  'Give your place to this man,'
  and then you would proceed with
      embarrassment
  to take the lowest place.
Rather, when you are invited,
  go and take the lowest place
  so that when the host comes to you he
      may say,
  'My friend, move up to a higher
      position.'
Then you will enjoy the esteem of your
      companions at the table.
For everyone who exalts himself will be
      humbled,
  but the one who humbles himself will
      be exalted."
Then he said to the host who invited him,
  "When you hold a lunch or a dinner,
  do not invite your friends or your
      brothers
  or your relatives or your wealthy
      neighbors,
  in case they may invite you back and
      you have repayment.
Rather, when you hold a banquet,
  invite the poor, the crippled, the lame,
      the blind;
  blessed indeed will you be because of
      their inability to repay you.
For you will be repaid at the resurrection
      of the righteous."

Reflecting on the Gospel

Let's face it: most of us don't "dine"—at least not very often! So the circumstances of this Sunday's gospel, taken literally, don't tend to faze us much. As "hosts" our invitations are inclined to be with close family and friends and, generally, pretty informal affairs—backyard barbecues or potluck buffets. Our dining room tables—if we have one at all—probably aren't very large so there wouldn't be defined "lowest" or "higher" places. One approach to interpreting this gospel is to see it as an extended metaphor and not take it literally. An interpretive clue is humility. From the point of view of being guest, humility is knowing one's place; from the point of view of being host, humility is knowing whom to invite (to be in relation with). The two parables prod us to see both of these as aspects of authentic Christian self-understanding.

The first parable about wedding guests invites us to reflect on humility as knowing ourselves in relation to others. The "wedding banquet" imagery of the gospel is eschatological imagery; that is, we might think of God as the host and the wedding banquet as the Lord's heavenly banquet. We are all invited to the banquet (offered salvation); but we must remember that it is *God who invites*. Our own relation to God is poor; we cannot choose our own place in heaven. God invites us to this exalted position. God raises us up! Humility is recognizing that by God's choosing us we are raised up to share in divine riches and bestowed the great dignity of sharing in God's life. If this is how God relates to us, then this is how the disciple relates to others. As God has bestowed dignity on us, so do we shower others with dignity.

The second parable about hosts invites us to reflect on humility in terms of how we wish God to relate to us. We know we are poor (a metaphor for sinners). God doesn't extend invitation to the banquet only to those who seem worthy, but extends the invitation to all who would respond. No one is excluded from the banquet. Neither should we exclude others from our own attention and ministrations. If we wish God to invite us who are poor to the divine banquet, then we also extend ourselves to all others regardless of social, economic, religious, or sexual status or orientation.

Jesus' instruction on how to be a gracious host (invite the poor and disadvantaged) comes only after his instruction on how to be a good guest (humble oneself by recognizing one's own poverty). Before disciples can be hosts to the poor and disadvantaged they must humbly recognize themselves as those who have received a place of honor at God's banquet table. First, God receives us, honors us, and nourishes us. Only by being so enriched and strengthened with such marvelous Food can we, in turn, be in such relationship with others. Even the grace to exclude no one is a gracious gift of God.

Living the Paschal Mystery

Humility isn't a matter of beating our breast or putting ourselves down. Humility is recognizing that we are gifted, enriched, and nourished by God and then reaching out to others in the same way. If we wish God to raise us up ("repaid at the resurrection of the righteous") then we must live our lives raising others up.

Each Sunday we are invited to God's banquet table. We ourselves are nourished at the same time that we are called to share the abundance of God's life by reaching out to others in need. We eat and drink in order to be gracious to others. This is the most profound humility!

Focusing the Word
Key words and phrases from the gospel: banquet, lowest place, invite the poor, repaid at the resurrection

To the point: For both guest and host a banquet is not an occasion for self-promotion but an opportunity to acknowledge humbly one's rightful role: the guest—to take the "lowest place"; the host—to disregard the wealthy in favor of the poor. Ironically, such humility brings exaltation—"the resurrection of the righteous" on the last day.

Connecting the Word
to the first reading: The first reading depicts different people—for example, the great, the sage, the sinner—and what humility requires of them. The gospel adds guests and hosts to this list. No matter who we are, humility is a part of authentic discipleship.

to culture: We live in a society in which self-image, self-esteem, ego strength, positive self-regard, etc., have been exaggerated and made ends in themselves. Some tend to see humility as negative and ego-damaging. Humility, however, is necessary for authentic Christian self-understanding.

Understanding the Word
Meals and table fellowship: It is often remarked that Jesus eats his way through the gospel of Luke: Jesus is at table no fewer than nine times; Jesus discusses eating on at least three other occasions; and eating is featured prominently in at least four of his parables.

In both Greek and Jewish cultures meals were significant ritual events governed by rules of etiquette and guests were seated "each in the order of his dignity" (1QSa 2:16*). In Roman and Greek cultures meals were social events that allowed both the host and guest to vaunt their social status and parade their dignity. Inviting guests from the "A List" enhanced one's social standing and reputation. The "humility" that Jesus counsels would be unthinkable!

In Jewish tradition the festive meal became a symbol of the Age to Come when the righteous would be gathered in God's kingdom to enjoy the banquet of the Messiah (Isa 25:6-8). That eschatological (or "end-time") perspective is evident in this Sunday's meal stories when Jesus twice points to end-time reversals: the exalted will be humbled and the humble will be exalted (14:11), and those who are not repaid now "will be repaid at the resurrection of the righteous" (14:14).

Luke's themes of universal salvation and compassion for "the poor" (Luke's generic term for all the socially marginalized) are highlighted in the instruction Jesus gives to those who hold a feast. Those to be invited as honored guests are "the poor, the crippled, the lame, the blind" (14:13). The last three of this group are specifically excluded from the Jewish priesthood (Lev 21:17-21). This exclusion of undesirables is taken even further in the community at Qumran. In the end-time battle, no one "who is lame, or blind, or cripple . . . shall march out to war" with the righteous (1QM 7:4*). And membership in the congregation excludes those who are "paralyzed . . . or lame, or blind, or deaf, or dumb . . . or old and tottery" (1QSa 2:5-8*). This vision of the elect is highly selective and exclusive. By contrast, Jesus welcomes the marginalized. Jesus' meals with them foreshadow the banquet of the Messiah on the last day.

*[*abbreviations from Dead Sea Scroll documents: 1QSa = "Rule of the Community: Appendix A"; 1QM = "War Scroll"]*

**ASSEMBLY &
FAITH-SHARING GROUPS**
- To be humble means to me . . .
  A time when I acted/lived humbly was . . .
- Occasions when I am prompted toward self-exaltation are . . .
- The way Jesus' words "invite the poor, the crippled, the lame, the blind" apply to me is . . .

PRESIDERS
Ministry humbles me when . . .
Ministry exalts me when . . .

DEACONS
The blessing I receive (even now) whenever I minister to those who are unable to repay me is . . .

HOSPITALITY MINISTERS
What is humbling—that is, realizing my rightful place in life and sensing the dignity of others—about hospitality is . . .

MUSIC MINISTERS
Sometimes music ministry leads me to grab for first place among the assembly. When I do this Jesus calls me to humility by . . .

ALTAR MINISTERS
A time when serving others was an occasion of growth in humility was . . .

LECTORS
Practice for proclamation includes more than pronouncing the words in a meaningful way; it necessitates living the Word's meaning. An occasion where I could better "conduct [my] affairs with humility" this week would be . . .

EUCHARISTIC MINISTERS
How I understand the Eucharist modeling humility—that is, my rightful role and responsibility within the body of Christ—is . . .

Model Penitential Rite

Presider: Each Sunday we gather here to share in God's banquet, being fed by God's word and Christ's Body and Blood. Let us prepare ourselves for this banquet by humbling ourselves before our generous God . . . [pause]

Lord Jesus, you raise us up to share in your heavenly banquet: Lord . . .

Christ Jesus, you are the host who excludes no one: Christ . . .

Lord Jesus, you teach us humility and dignity: Lord . . .

Appreciating the Responsorial Psalm

This Sunday's gospel tells us that the people were "observing [Jesus] carefully." The responsorial psalm invites us to the same observation of God, for the psalm shows God "[making] a home for the poor." When Jesus in the gospel advises us to invite to our table "the poor, the crippled, the lame, the blind," he is challenging us to model what we see God doing. And when we do so we experience a remarkable reversal in our own position. Choosing to give up the first place so that room be made for the poor and needy exalts us. Our humility "finds favor with God" (first reading). Even more, we become like God. Our singing of this psalm is our prayer that we see the goodness of God toward the needy and act likewise.

Model General Intercessions

Presider: Let us pray for all those in need, excluding no one from our prayers.

Response:

Lord, hear our prayer.

Cantor:

we pray to the Lord,

For all members of the Church to be conscious of the dignity of all people . . . [pause]

For all world leaders to provide for those under their guidance with care and dignity . . . [pause]

For the poor and disadvantaged to be equitably included in the world's abundance . . . [pause]

For each of us to humble ourselves before our God who exalts us . . . [pause]

Presider: Gracious God, you provide us with all we need: hear these our prayers that each of your children may one day share at your heavenly banquet. We ask this through Christ our Lord. **Amen.**

OPENING PRAYER

Let us pray

Pause for silent prayer

Almighty God,
every good thing comes from you.
Fill our hearts with love for you,
increase our faith,
and by your constant care
protect the good you have given us.

We ask this through our Lord Jesus Christ,
    your Son,
who lives and reigns with you and the
    Holy Spirit,
one God, for ever and ever. **Amen.**

FIRST READING

Sir 3:17-18, 20, 28-29

My child, conduct your affairs with
    humility,
    and you will be loved more than a giver
        of gifts.
Humble yourself the more, the greater you
    are,
    and you will find favor with God.
What is too sublime for you, seek not,
    into things beyond your strength search
        not.
The mind of a sage appreciates proverbs,
    and an attentive ear is the joy of the wise.
Water quenches a flaming fire,
    and alms atone for sins.

RESPONSORIAL PSALM

Ps 68:4-5, 6-7, 10-11

R℣. (cf. 11b) God, in your goodness, you have made a home for the poor.

The just rejoice and exult before God;
   they are glad and rejoice.
Sing to God, chant praise to his name;
   whose name is the Lord.

R℣. God, in your goodness, you have made a home for the poor.

The father of orphans and the defender of
      widows
   is God in his holy dwelling.
God gives a home to the forsaken;
   he leads forth prisoners to prosperity.

R℣. God, in your goodness, you have made a home for the poor.

A bountiful rain you showered down, O
      God, upon your inheritance;
   you restored the land when it languished;
your flock settled in it;
   in your goodness, O God, you provided
      it for the needy.

R℣. God, in your goodness, you have made a home for the poor.

SECOND READING

Heb 12:18-19, 22-24a

Brothers and sisters:
You have not approached that which could
      be touched
   and a blazing fire and gloomy darkness
   and storm and a trumpet blast
   and a voice speaking words such that
         those who heard
   begged that no message be further
         addressed to them.
No, you have approached Mount Zion
   and the city of the living God, the
         heavenly Jerusalem,
   and countless angels in festal gathering,
   and the assembly of the firstborn
         enrolled in heaven,
   and God the judge of all,
   and the spirits of the just made perfect,
   and Jesus, the mediator of a new
         covenant,
   and the sprinkled blood that speaks
         more eloquently than that of Abel.

About Liturgy

Eschatological turning point in Luke's gospel: Toward the end of the liturgical year—as our sequential reading of a synoptic gospel brings events closer to Jerusalem and Jesus' passion and death—we begin to pick up parousia (Jesus' second coming) and eschatological themes. Often this begins toward the end of October or early November and culminates in the great eschatological festival, the Solemnity of Christ the King. This year, however, themes that we would ordinarily be dealing with later in the liturgical year already show up in late August. This is because of the structure of Luke's gospel, about one third of which focuses on Jesus' journey to Jerusalem. The prevailing journey theme is a reminder that our whole Christian life is a journey to our final union with Jesus in eschatological glory.

About Liturgical Music

Cantor preparation: This psalm praises God for goodness to the poor and needy. Only those who recognize themselves among the poor and needy can see what God is doing to lift them up. How are you poor and needy? How is God lifting you up by inviting you to the banquet of Jesus' Body and Blood? How do you offer God praise for this great gift? How do you invite others to join you at this table?

Helping the assembly sing the responsorial psalm, Pt. 1: The most essential aid for helping an assembly sing the responsorial psalm is that the musical setting be easily singable, both for the cantor and the assembly. This norm will be relative to the abilities of the cantor(s) and the assembly. What is the singing level of this assembly? How used to singing the responsorial psalm are they? If watching and listening to a cantor is new to them, simpler musical settings may be better to begin with.

For an assembly not yet accustomed to singing the responsorial psalm the Sunday Lectionary offers seasonal psalm refrains and common seasonal psalms which may be used in place of the psalm assigned for the day (see nos. 173–174). One of the spin-offs of this approach is that over time the people will learn to look at the cantor rather than a line of music in the hymnal or missalette. The same principle applies here as with the proclamation of Scripture. The goal is to lead the assembly to look at and listen to the cantor rather than to follow along in a book. In this way the singing of the responsorial psalm becomes the active dialogue it is meant to be.

A final means of leading the assembly to fuller participation in the responsorial psalm is to print the upcoming Sunday psalm refrain in the same spot in the bulletin each week. This "spotlight" could include an invitation to make the refrain a prayer mantra throughout the week. It could also include one or two sentences about the relationship of the psalm to the readings of the day (see "Appreciating the Responsorial Psalm" in this volume for ideas).

AUGUST 29, 2004
TWENTY-SECOND SUNDAY IN ORDINARY TIME

✝ SPIRITUALITY

Gospel
Luke 14:25-33; L129C

Great crowds were traveling with
    Jesus,
    and he turned and addressed them,
    "If anyone comes to me without
        hating his father and mother,
    wife and children, brothers and
        sisters,
    and even his own life,
    he cannot be my disciple.
Whoever does not carry his
    own cross and come after me
    cannot be my disciple.
Which of you wishing to
    construct a tower
    does not first sit down and
        calculate the cost
    to see if there is enough for its
        completion?
Otherwise, after laying the foundation
    and finding himself unable to finish
        the work
    the onlookers should laugh at him
        and say,
    'This one began to build but did not
        have the resources to finish.'
Or what king marching into battle
    would not first sit down
    and decide whether with ten
        thousand troops
    he can successfully oppose another
        king
    advancing upon him with twenty
        thousand troops?
But if not, while he is still far away,
    he will send a delegation to ask for
        peace terms.
In the same way,
    anyone of you who does not renounce
        all his possessions
    cannot be my disciple."

Reflecting on the Gospel

A legend from the early thirteenth century tells the story about the city of Hamelin in northern Germany which had a plague of rats. A man called the Pied Piper appeared in the town promising to rid the townspeople of their rats. They agreed with the Piper on a sum for payment. So the Piper began playing his music, marching through the town. All the mice and rats followed him through the town and down to the river where they all drowned. But when he returned to collect his fee, the townspeople refused to pay him and the Piper left quite angry. A year later he returned to the town. This time when he began to play his music all the children followed him out of town and into the hills where they were never seen again. The townspeople could hardly have calculated the cost of their trickery. The Piper had a magnetic draw; the cost of following him was high.

In the gospel for this Sunday "great crowds were traveling with Jesus." We might presume that Jesus' deeds must have spread far and wide for many were following him. Jesus doesn't trick us—he lays out clearly the great cost of following him. The gospel lays out three demands and unless we meet those demands we "cannot be [Jesus'] disciple."

First, we must hate father and mother. Obviously, Jesus doesn't mean this literally (over and over again Jesus tells us that we must love even our enemies). This hyperbole is a way for Jesus to stress that even family relationships (where we first receive life and preserve it) and our very own lives must not take precedence over following him. Why is the cost of discipleship so high that we even give our lives? Because we emulate Jesus, who gave his life. No less can be true for disciples. Second, we must carry our cross. This means the daily discipline of self-sacrifice for the sake of others. To follow Jesus means to take up the cross. Third, we must "renounce all . . . possessions." Again, this command must be taken in context. We must forego any thing or conduct that causes us to question discipleship or swerve from the path of following Jesus.

In human situations we calculate the cost of finishing a difficult or expensive task. In three different ways in this gospel does Jesus try to help us calculate the cost of discipleship—it demands everything we are and everything we have. Jesus intends no surprises for those who choose discipleship; here's the fine print: we have to die if we wish to follow Jesus.

The cost of discipleship seems disproportionately high to anything we could want or value as humans. And this is the point: following Jesus to Jerusalem doesn't lead to anything human. It leads to death, to be sure. But it is only through death that we receive divine life. This far outweighs the cost.

Living the Paschal Mystery

The amazing thing is that we *know* the cost of discipleship, yet we spend our whole lives trying to figure it out! We know that we must hand our lives over to Jesus, we know that we are given wisdom and the Holy Spirit to be faithful (see the first reading) yet, like the children of Hamelin, we aren't quite sure where the journey leads. We just follow.

It would be nice to say that we shouldn't start what we can't finish. If we calculate the cost or have undue concern for what others think, or weigh the risks of discipleship, we probably would not begin the journey to follow. We do begin discipleship at baptism. The challenge, then, is not to look at the cost but keep our eyes on Jesus who leads. In Jesus death always leads to new life. This is worth the cost.

Focusing the Word

Key words and phrases from the gospel: hating . . . father and mother, cannot be my disciple, carry . . . own cross, calculate the cost, renounce all

To the point: Jesus bluntly challenges the crowd to take up the demands of discipleship with eyes wide open. Disciples must put Jesus ahead of their families and even their own lives, carry their cross, and renounce all they have. What could be worth so high a cost? Why would anyone make such a choice? Although this gospel episode does not directly answer these questions, we know the answers—don't we?

Connecting the Word

to the first reading: Calculating the cost of buildings and military campaigns are earthly things that we can "grasp . . . with difficulty." The weighty decisions related to as discipleship are possible because God sends us wisdom and the Holy Spirit.

to culture: Anyone who has ever built anything knows that he or she can count on cost overruns. So, too, can we with discipleship.

Understanding the Word

Cost of discipleship: In the parable immediately preceding this Sunday's gospel (14:15-24, omitted from the Lectionary), guests were invited to a banquet three times, and three times they sent excuses. In this gospel, as "great crowds were traveling with Jesus," he turns and three times admonishes them that they "cannot be my disciple" (14:26, 27, 33) unless certain conditions are met. In view of the journey and its destination (see OT Sunday 13), it is imperative that those who wish to follow Jesus "calculate the cost" (14:28).

The costs are indeed staggering. The first and third admonitions require a would-be disciple to leave something behind: "father and mother, wife and children, brothers and sisters, and even his own life" (14:26), as well as "all his possessions" (14:33). The second admonition requires a positive action: to "carry his own cross and come after me" (14:27). Earlier Jesus had indicated the ongoing nature of this task when he said, "If anyone wishes to come after me, he must deny himself and take up his cross *daily* and follow me" (9:23). This is not for the faint of heart nor the impulsive. To illustrate Jesus offers two brief parables.

Both parables feature individuals about to undertake a project: the first is a worker building a tower and the second is a king preparing for war. Whether commoner or royalty, foresight and prudence are required; the ability to see the project through determines whether it should be undertaken. So, too, would-be disciples must subordinate all other competing claims to the overriding demands of following Jesus. Nothing—not family, possessions, or even one's life—is more urgent than fidelity to Jesus.

In a sense the parables apply positively to God and Jesus: God undertook the plan of salvation with full resolve to carry it out even at the cost of the beloved Son's life (Rom 8:32); Jesus, too, "resolutely determined to journey to Jerusalem" (9:51) to lay down his life. Neither God nor Jesus asks of disciples anything they themselves were not prepared to do.

ASSEMBLY & FAITH-SHARING GROUPS

- When I hear Jesus demanding that I place him ahead of family and my own self, I understand Jesus is asking me to . . .
- An example of when I placed someone or something ahead of my discipleship was . . . ; the cost for this was . . .
- The reason(s) I am paying the high cost of discipleship is (are) . . .

PRESIDERS

My preaching helps others understand the cost of discipleship by . . .
My ministry encourages others to bring their discipleship to completion by . . .

DEACONS

Discipleship requires one to place Jesus ahead of family, self, and possessions. Where this is difficult for me is . . .
What makes this possible for me is . . .

HOSPITALITY MINISTERS

My hospitality embodies God's "refuge" for the people (see psalm) while they carry their crosses by . . .

MUSIC MINISTERS

Even in my music ministry what I find myself holding back from Christ is . . .
What helps me give everything over is . . .

ALTAR MINISTERS

What gets renounced in me in order to serve others faithfully is . . .

LECTORS

Humanity's "deliberations" are "timid" and "unsure" (first reading).
God's word brings wisdom and straightness to my path by . . .
I share this in my ministry when . . .

EUCHARISTIC MINISTERS

Eucharist reveals the cost of discipleship by . . .
Eucharist inspires and nourishes me to pay the price until completion because . . .

Model Penitential Rite

Presider: The cost of discipleship is high, as we hear in today's gospel: we must lose our lives, carry our crosses, and renounce our possessions. Jesus speaks strong words to help us understand the reality of following him. Let us pray for wisdom and the Holy Spirit to help us be faithful on our journey . . . [pause]

Lord Jesus, you gave your life for our salvation: Lord . . .

Christ Jesus, you carried the cross of our infirmities: Christ . . .

Lord Jesus, you give us the Spirit of wisdom and strength: Lord . . .

Appreciating the Responsorial Psalm

The first reading reminds us of a truth with which we are already familiar: "the deliberations of mortals are timid and unsure." But Jesus challenges us in the gospel to be neither timid nor unsure when deliberating the cost of discipleship. It is total. Relationships must be abandoned, possessions must be renounced, the cross must be carried. The responsorial psalm promises, however, that we will not be left with only our own meager strength. God will grant us "wisdom" and will "prosper the work of our hands." God will give us both the wisdom to calculate the cost and the courage to pay it (first reading). God knows the all-encompassing cost of discipleship and will be with us when we need strength, support, encouragement, and mercy. In singing this psalm we profess our confidence in God who knows even better than we do what will be exacted of us and who has promised to see us through.

Model General Intercessions

Presider: Let us pray that we might be faithful disciples, even when the cost seems too high.

Response:

Lord, hear our prayer.

Cantor:

we pray to the Lord,

That all members of the Church follow Jesus faithfully through death to life . . . [pause]

That all people of the world find salvation in God . . . [pause]

That those burdened with the cares of life find comfort in Jesus . . . [pause]

That each of us finish faithfully the work which Jesus has entrusted to us . . . [pause]

Presider: God of demands and promises, you offer us new life in Christ: hear these our prayers that we might remain faithful to the demands of discipleship and one day enjoy the promise of glory with you. We ask this through Christ our Lord. **Amen.**

OPENING PRAYER

Let us pray

Pause for silent prayer

God our Father,
you redeem us
and make us your children in Christ.
Look upon us,
give us true freedom
and bring us to the inheritance you
    promised.

Grant this through our Lord Jesus Christ,
    your Son,
who lives and reigns with you and the
    Holy Spirit,
one God, for ever and ever. **Amen.**

FIRST READING

Wis 9:13-18b

Who can know God's counsel,
    or who can conceive what the LORD
        intends?
For the deliberations of mortals are timid,
    and unsure are our plans.
For the corruptible body burdens the soul
    and the earthen shelter weighs down
        the mind that has many concerns.
And scarce do we guess the things on
        earth,
    and what is within our grasp we find
        with difficulty;
    but when things are in heaven, who can
        search them out?
Or who ever knew your counsel, except
        you had given wisdom
    and sent your holy spirit from on high?
And thus were the paths of those on earth
        made straight.

RESPONSORIAL PSALM

Ps 90:3-4, 5-6, 12-13, 14, 17

R̸. (1) In every age, O Lord, you have been our refuge.

You turn man back to dust,
    saying, "Return, O children of men."
For a thousand years in your sight
    are as yesterday, now that it is past,
    or as a watch of the night.

R̸. In every age, O Lord, you have been our refuge.

You make an end of them in their sleep;
   the next morning they are like the
      changing grass,
which at dawn springs up anew,
   but by evening wilts and fades.

R⁊. In every age, O Lord, you have been
our refuge.

Teach us to number our days aright,
   that we may gain wisdom of heart.
Return, O LORD! How long?
   Have pity on your servants!

R⁊. In every age, O Lord, you have been
our refuge.

Fill us at daybreak with your kindness,
   that we may shout for joy and gladness
      all our days.
And may the gracious care of the LORD
     our God be ours;
   prosper the work of our hands for us!
   Prosper the work of our hands!

R⁊. In every age, O Lord, you have been
our refuge.

SECOND READING
Phlm 9-10, 12-17

I, Paul, an old man,
   and now also a prisoner for Christ Jesus,
   urge you on behalf of my child Onesimus,
   whose father I have become in my
      imprisonment;
I am sending him, that is, my own heart,
   back to you.
I should have liked to retain him for myself,
   so that he might serve me on your behalf
   in my imprisonment for the gospel,
   but I did not want to do anything
      without your consent,
   so that the good you do might not be
      forced but voluntary.
Perhaps this is why he was away from you
   for a while,
   that you might have him back forever,
   no longer as a slave
   but more than a slave, a brother,
   beloved especially to me, but even more
      so to you,
   as a man and in the Lord.
So if you regard me as a partner, welcome
   him as you would me.

About Liturgy

Intercessory prayer: When we read gospels such as this Sunday's we could easily become discouraged at the demands of faithful discipleship. Although Jesus speaks in metaphors, he also is making clear to us that following him will cost us dearly. One way we gain the strength to be faithful is through prayer—for ourselves and for other disciples.

Usually when we think of intercessory or petitionary prayer we think of the specific prayer requests of our own that we send to God or for which others have asked us to pray—perhaps for a sick family member, or success in the search for employment, or a friend who is suffering from depression. This kind of prayer is good and helps us connect with the everyday concerns of all of us. In the liturgy, however, most often the intercessory prayer is more general—both in intention and for the persons we pray. This more general intercessory prayer helps us realize that we are all disciples together on the road to Jerusalem and one strength we receive is the prayer we have for each other. None of us is ever forgotten in our need.

After the general intercessions which conclude the Liturgy of the Word, intercessory prayer continues within the very heart of our great prayer of praise and thanksgiving, the eucharistic prayer. By continuing our intercessory prayer here we are reminded that the ultimate praise and thanksgiving we can give God is the gift of our very lives in discipleship. Furthermore, when we are faithful disciples the Church is fruitful in its mission. As we pray for the pope, bishops, ministers, and all God's people we ought to be mindful of the seriousness of the task at hand. Our prayer is that we might not count the cost but look to the fruits of our faithfulness.

About Liturgical Music

Cantor preparation: The cost of following Christ is radical but in this psalm you remind the assembly they have more than themselves to depend upon: their discipleship will prosper because God underwrites it. You sing realistically of both the tenuousness of human strength and the steadfastness of God. May your singing give the assembly courage.

Helping the assembly sing the responsorial psalm, Pt. 2: If the practice of singing the responsorial psalm is new for a parish, the most important starting point is having a confident and competent cantor. This may mean using the same cantor every week at a given Mass for several months while other cantors are in training. The goal is to allow the assembly time to become comfortable and secure with responding to a cantor and this is easier to do when the cantor in front of them is both familiar and competent. The goal is not to have as many people as possible involved in the ministry of cantor but to lead the assembly toward their participation in the singing of the psalm.

For the cantor's part, whether the assembly is novice or veteran with singing the responsorial psalm, it is important that the cantor be attentive to them. The cantor must make it obvious that his or her attention is focused on the assembly and their prayer rather than caught up with self. This means that one of the criteria for selecting cantors must be the quality of other-centeredness. Vocal competency and audience poise are only surface aspects of the ministry. The heart of the ministry is the ability to give self over to God and to others.

SEPTEMBER 5, 2004
TWENTY-THIRD SUNDAY IN ORDINARY TIME

✚ SPIRITUALITY

Gospel
Luke 15:1-32; L132C

Tax collectors and sinners were all
    drawing near to listen to Jesus,
  but the Pharisees and scribes
      began to complain, saying,
  "This man welcomes sinners
      and eats with them."
So to them he addressed this
    parable.
"What man among you having a
    hundred sheep and losing one
    of them
  would not leave the ninety-nine
    in the desert
  and go after the lost one until he
    finds it?
And when he does find it,
  he sets it on his shoulders with
    great joy
  and, upon his arrival home,
  he calls together his friends and
    neighbors and says to them,
  'Rejoice with me because I have
    found my lost sheep.'
I tell you, in just the same way
  there will be more joy in heaven over
    one sinner who repents
  than over ninety-nine righteous people
  who have no need of repentance.

"Or what woman having ten coins and
    losing one
  would not light a lamp and sweep the
    house,
  searching carefully until she finds it?
And when she does find it,
  she calls together her friends and
    neighbors
  and says to them,
  'Rejoice with me because I have
    found the coin that I lost.'
In just the same way, I tell you,
  there will be rejoicing among the
    angels of God
  over one sinner who repents."

Continued in Appendix A, p. 286.

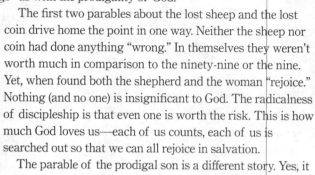

Reflecting on the Gospel

An old Peanuts cartoon pictures Lucy with her arms around Snoopy; both have contented smiles on their faces. The caption reads: "A hug is better than all the theology in the world." It's almost as though Jesus knew that a hug is better than talking about important issues. The gospel for this Sunday presents us three parables about compassion. Instead of defining compassion, Jesus tells stories. Jesus "hugs" us with the prodigality of God.

The first two parables about the lost sheep and the lost coin drive home the point in one way. Neither the sheep nor coin had done anything "wrong." In themselves they weren't worth much in comparison to the ninety-nine or the nine. Yet, when found both the shepherd and the woman "rejoice." Nothing (and no one) is insignificant to God. The radicalness of discipleship is that even one is worth the risk. This is how much God loves us—each of us counts, each of us is searched out so that we can all rejoice in salvation.

The parable of the prodigal son is a different story. Yes, it is also about the prodigality of God. But in this parable the son has done something wrong—demanded inheritance, squandered it, sinned against his father. When he returns to his father's house, the younger son doesn't deserve such lavish behavior on the part of the prodigal father. Yet the father is just that—prodigal, lavish in his love and compassion for this lost son. The father is a faithful disciple because he relents from punishing his son. The elder brother, on the other hand, is an example of one who does not choose discipleship—he refuses to enter the house and celebrate. He refuses to risk the cost of discipleship in order to gain the compassion and love that spill over in feasting.

No calculating person would risk ninety-nine or nine for one or have a feast for one who has squandered so much. But God does not act like us calculating humans—God always acts with the utmost compassion and love. This is why we would choose to be a disciple and follow Jesus no matter what the cost— God is so prodigal with us. Jesus is compassionate to tax collectors and sinners, which is another example of the cost of discipleship and of the prodigality of God. God desires that no one be lost. For this we rejoice and feast.

Living the Paschal Mystery

If God is so compassionate and loving with us, then as faithful disciples of Jesus we must risk being so compassionate and loving with others. First of all, this means that we don't judge whether the other is worth our compassion and love. God shows us that all are—even outcasts and sinners. Second, we don't earn compassion and love. Since it is a free gift of God to us, it is a gift we freely give to others. We don't wait until someone wrongs us to show compassion and love—we offer these gifts simply because the other is a beloved of God.

It's much easier for us to be compassionate and loving when the end situation is better for us. For example, we might forgive a family member some wrongdoing because we want peace in the family. It is far more risky to be compassionate when there is no immediate gain for us in sight. As disciples we are called to be compassionate simply because this is the way Jesus was. Living the paschal mystery means that we feast well and often because we realize that God "hugs" us with compassion and love without calculating whether we deserve it or not.

Focusing the Word

Key words and phrases from the gospel: welcomes sinners, I have found, Rejoice

To the point: Jesus uses three images to dramatize the compassion and love of God: the shepherd, the woman, the father. Whether the loss is small (one sheep, one coin) or great (a son!), each person rejoices in recovering what was lost. The least significant in this world (tax collectors and sinners) are worthy of a diligent search and of great rejoicing.

Connecting the Word

to the first reading: Israel is shown to be a "depraved" and "stiff-necked" people. Though the people deserve punishment, Moses appeals to God's compassion and God relents from punishing Israel.

to culture: In our society we are comfortable with giving people what they deserve, for example, just wage, job promotion, etc. In these readings God doesn't give what people deserve (punishment for Israel and the prodigal son) and does give what the people don't deserve (compassion and feasting).

Understanding the Word

Scribes and Pharisees: The parable of the prodigal son, along with its two companion parables of the lost sheep and the lost coin, are addressed to "the Pharisees and scribes." The occasion is another of Jesus' meals with "tax collectors and sinners" whom Jesus welcomes.

In Luke, as in all the gospels, opposition against Jesus coalesces around the Pharisees and scribes who are often paired (Luke 5:21, 30; 6:7; 11:53; 15:2). According to the Jewish historian Josephus (37–100 A.D.), Pharisees were regarded as the "most accurate interpreters of the Law" and were distinguished from other Jewish groups such as the Sadducees by their also observing the "traditions of the fathers" (see Matt 15:2; Mark 7:3, 5, 8, 13)—prescriptions not found in the Law of Moses. The Pharisees were particularly zealous about the laws of ritual purity and tithing. They regarded as "sinners" all who violated the commandments, moral laws, and the laws of purity. Though Pharisees were not priests or part of the official religious establishment, the esteem they enjoyed among the people and their expertise in religious and legal matters gave them great popular authority.

Closely associated with the Pharisees are the scribes. Skilled in both reading and writing, they were professional interpreters of the Law; indeed, Luke seems to use "scribe" and "lawyer" interchangeably (compare Luke 10:25 and Mark 12:28; see also Luke 7:30; 11:45). Their skill and ability in matters of the Law made them natural allies of the Pharisees who shared their interest in zealous legal observance.

Particularly irksome to the Pharisees was Jesus' associating with the unclean, thereby becoming unclean himself. At the very least this demonstrated Jesus' disregard of the laws of purity. Moreover, Jesus' meals with the unclean were sacrilegious because blessings would be pronounced over the food. Invoking the name of God among the unclean and the unrepentant was scandalous.

As we read the gospels we should be careful not to place all scribes and Pharisees in the role of villains and enemies (see Luke 13:31). Their presentation is shaped by Christian interests at that time to assign responsibility for the death of Jesus.

ASSEMBLY & FAITH-SHARING GROUPS

- When I draw "near to listen to Jesus" (like the tax collectors and sinners) my life is like . . .
- When I "complain" about God's ways (like the Pharisees and scribes) my life is like . . .
- What usually brings me to my "senses" (like the prodigal son) and calls me to return home to God is . . .

PRESIDERS

I am like the father with . . .
I am like the prodigal son with . . .
I am like the older brother with . . .

DEACONS

Like the shepherd and woman, my ministry embodies God's diligent search for the lost by . . .

HOSPITALITY MINISTERS

My experience of God's prodigal love for me during my waywardness shapes my care and concern for others by . . .

MUSIC MINISTERS

One way that my music ministry celebrates that all are welcome at God's banquet table is . . .

ALTAR MINISTERS

When I am like the father my service is like . . .
When I am like the prodigal son my service is like . . .
When I am like the older brother my service is like . . .

LECTORS

God's compassion is greater than the depravity of the stiff-necked people of God (first reading). Where I have witnessed this compassion of God is . . .
Where I am extending this compassion toward another is . . .

EUCHARISTIC MINISTERS

In my parish those who need to experience being found by Jesus are . . .
My ministry embodies Jesus' compassion for them by . . .

209

Model Penitential Rite

Presider: Whenever we are lost or faltering on our Christian journey, our prodigal God is there to bestow on us compassion and love. As we prepare ourselves to celebrate this liturgy, let us open our hearts to such a lavish God . . . [pause]

Lord Jesus, you are compassionate and loving: Lord . . .

Christ Jesus, you invite us to feast at your table: Christ . . .

Lord Jesus, you raise us to new life: Lord . . .

Appreciating the Responsorial Psalm

In his choice to welcome and eat with sinners Jesus reveals the deep mercy at the very heart of God (gospel). Faced with Israel's infidelity and depravity God is nonetheless easily dissuaded from wreaking just punishment (first reading). The injured father gives no thought to punishing the prodigal son but instead throws him a banquet (gospel). Jesus' parables and his actions reveal the orientation of God who desires the restoration of what is lost and who rejoices over the return of even one sinner.

Our role in this reconciliation is revealed in the behavior of the prodigal son who makes the decision to return to his father. The responsorial psalm plays the same role. In the psalm we turn toward God, admit our sinfulness, and beg for restoration. The amazing thing is that once we make the decision to return, the rest of the work of restoration is done by God who washes away our guilt and re-creates our heart. In singing this psalm, then, we enter into the mercy of God. We discover we have a place at the banquet table. We come home, and God rejoices.

Model General Intercessions

Presider: Let us make known to our prodigal God our needs, confident that they will be answered with compassion and love.

Response:

Lord, hear our prayer.

Cantor:

we pray to the Lord,

That the Church be quick to search out the lost with compassion and love . . . [pause]

That all peoples of the world be brought to the feast of God's lavish table . . . [pause]

That the poor and outcasts find their home in the loving embrace of God . . . [pause]

That each of us rejoice that God has called us to be disciples, no matter what the cost . . . [pause]

Presider: Compassionate and loving God, you are ever faithful to your promise of salvation: hear these our prayers that one day we might feast at your everlasting banquet table. We ask this through Christ our Lord. **Amen.**

OPENING PRAYER

Let us pray

Pause for silent prayer

Almighty God,
our creator and guide,
may we serve you with all our heart
and know your forgiveness in our lives.

We ask this through our Lord Jesus Christ,
    your Son,
who lives and reigns with you and the
    Holy Spirit,
one God, for ever and ever. **Amen.**

FIRST READING
Exod 32:7-11, 13-14

The LORD said to Moses,
    "Go down at once to your people,
    whom you brought out of the land of
        Egypt,
    for they have become depraved.
They have soon turned aside from the way
        I pointed out to them,
    making for themselves a molten calf
        and worshiping it,
    sacrificing to it and crying out,
    'This is your God, O Israel,
    who brought you out of the land of
        Egypt!'
I see how stiff-necked this people is,"
        continued the LORD to Moses.
"Let me alone, then,
    that my wrath may blaze up against
        them to consume them.
Then I will make of you a great nation."

But Moses implored the LORD, his God,
        saying,
    "Why, O LORD, should your wrath blaze
        up against your own people,
    whom you brought out of the land of
        Egypt
    with such great power and with so
        strong a hand?
Remember your servants Abraham, Isaac,
        and Israel,
    and how you swore to them by your
        own self, saying,
    'I will make your descendants as
        numerous as the stars in the sky;
    and all this land that I promised,
    I will give your descendants as their
        perpetual heritage.'"
So the LORD relented in the punishment
    he had threatened to inflict on his
        people.

RESPONSORIAL PSALM

Ps 51:3-4, 12-13, 17, 19

R̶. (Luke 15:18) I will rise and go to my father.

Have mercy on me, O God, in your goodness;
   in the greatness of your compassion
      wipe out my offense.
Thoroughly wash me from my guilt
   and of my sin cleanse me.

R̶. I will rise and go to my father.

A clean heart create for me, O God,
   and a steadfast spirit renew within me.
Cast me not out from your presence,
   and your holy spirit take not from me.

R̶. I will rise and go to my father.

O LORD, open my lips,
   and my mouth shall proclaim your praise.
My sacrifice, O God, is a contrite spirit;
   a heart contrite and humbled, O God,
      you will not spurn.

R̶. I will rise and go to my father.

SECOND READING

1 Tim 1:12-17

Beloved:
I am grateful to him who has strengthened
      me, Christ Jesus our Lord,
   because he considered me trustworthy
      in appointing me to the ministry.
I was once a blasphemer and a persecutor
      and arrogant,
   but I have been mercifully treated
      because I acted out of ignorance in my
         unbelief.
Indeed, the grace of our Lord has been
      abundant,
   along with the faith and love that are in
         Christ Jesus.
This saying is trustworthy and deserves
      full acceptance:
   Christ Jesus came into the world to save
      sinners.
Of these I am the foremost.
But for that reason I was mercifully treated,
   so that in me, as the foremost,
   Christ Jesus might display all his
      patience as an example
   for those who would come to believe in
      him for everlasting life.
To the king of ages, incorruptible,
   invisible, the only God,
   honor and glory forever and ever. Amen.

About Liturgy

God's prodigality in liturgy: There can be no more concrete expression of God's lavish compassion and love for us than in the celebration of liturgy's sacred mysteries, especially the Eucharist. God's prodigality takes many special symbolic forms during Mass. Here are some examples.

1. *Incensation.* Some parishes still use incense for the great festivals. It is telling that not only are the altar, crucifix, paschal candle, gospel book, and presider incensed during Mass, but also the assembly. The incense embraces *all* members of the assembly, witnessing to their dignity as presences of the risen Christ.

2. *Gifts for the poor.* It is always acceptable and to be encouraged to bring gifts for the poor to be offered along with the bread and wine. These food staples and monetary gifts are concrete expressions of the solidarity we have in the body of Christ with all others as well as a concrete way that we can share God's lavish gifts to us with others who are less fortunate.

3. *Intercessions.* Always at Mass there are a number of instances where we are invited to pray for others—after the "Let us pray" invitations, during the general intercessions, at the prayers for the living and dead during the eucharistic prayer, during the Our Father, in the quiet meditation time after Communion (just to name a few of the obvious and communal times for intercessory prayer). Our prayer for each other is an aspect of discipleship and one way we express the worth of all others.

4. *Sign of peace.* The sign of peace is an embrace given in compassion and love. GIRM no. 82 specifies that the sign of peace is offered to those nearby. It doesn't say to family members and friends, but to those nearby. We don't judge whether the person is sinner or saint, wealthy or poor, lost or found—we simply offer this gift of peace because God has first given it to us. The dignity of the sign indicates the dignity of both the giver and receiver.

5. *Communion.* God invites us to the messianic banquet where we rejoice and feast on the very Body and Blood of God's only-begotten Son. There is no discrimination in how the line is formed and who may come; indeed, eucharistic ministers are not to judge who may receive Communion but simply offer it to all those who come. Especially important is the sign of the one bread and the one cup, for in the body of Christ we are all beloved in God's eyes.

About Liturgical Music

Cantor preparation: Singing these verses from Psalm 51 is an act of public confession, for you stand before the assembly and admit sinfulness. But even more importantly you confess the mercy of God who never spurns a contrite and humbled heart. As you prepare to sing this psalm, what forgiveness might you ask of God so that you will know this mercy?

Helping the cantor, Pt. 1: What a skillful cantor may sing well, a less trained or less experienced one may not sing so well. This means that psalm settings ought to be chosen with specific cantors in mind and adaptations made if necessary. For example, a given psalm refrain could be combined with two different settings of the verses, one simple, the other more challenging.

It is a mistake to assume, however, that psalm tones (such as the Gelineau ones, for example) are easier to sing. Their simplicity is deceptive. Because they are text driven rather than melody driven, they are in fact more demanding, requiring greater preparation of the text and greater self-effacement on the part of the cantor who must step aside to let the text (rather than personal vocal prowess) shine. What can appear to be the easiest setting can in fact be the most challenging.

SEPTEMBER 12, 2004
TWENTY-FOURTH SUNDAY IN ORDINARY TIME

+ SPIRITUALITY

Gospel

Luke 16:1-13; L135C

Jesus said to his disciples,
   "A rich man had a steward
   who was reported to him for
      squandering his property.
He summoned him and said,
   'What is this I hear about you?
Prepare a full account of your
      stewardship,
   because you can no longer be
      my steward.'
The steward said to himself,
   'What shall I do,
   now that my master is taking
      the position of steward away
      from me?
I am not strong enough to dig and I am
      ashamed to beg.
I know what I shall do so that,
   when I am removed from the
      stewardship,
   they may welcome me into their
      homes.'
He called in his master's debtors one
   by one.
To the first he said,
   'How much do you owe my master?'
He replied, 'One hundred measures of
      olive oil.'
He said to him, 'Here is your
      promissory note.
Sit down and quickly write one for
      fifty.'
Then to another the steward said, 'And
      you, how much do you owe?'
He replied, 'One hundred kors of
      wheat.'
The steward said to him, 'Here is your
      promissory note;
   write one for eighty.'
And the master commended that
      dishonest steward for acting
      prudently.

Continued in Appendix A, p. 287.

Reflecting on the Gospel

How is our scramble to put dinner on the table every night connected with investing in eternal life? This is no easy question! Most of us keep putting one foot in front of the other and barely manage to get through the days and weeks. We are so over scheduled that we seldom think about anything more than the task at hand. We may have some long-range goal about retirement and its security and that getting ahead and securing our future is prudent and responsible. The gospel adds that all of this is to be in view of eternal life.

This doesn't mean that we spend our whole lives making "deposits" on our eternal life so that we can "cash in" at death. In the last analysis this is selfish and exactly the opposite of how we are to live. Prudent decisiveness that this gospel recommends means, first of all, that we take our identity as disciples of Christ so seriously that it defines how we live. Prudent decisiveness means, second, that in face of God and eternal reward, nothing of this world is more valuable. Third, prudent decisiveness means that we recognize that all our choices in daily living are really choices for eternal life (or eternal condemnation) and so there is an urgency about the choices we make. We cannot afford to wait to the end to think about the end.

We must handle the things of this world and our daily actions in relation to what is eternal. This means that there can be no split between our spiritual/religious lives (for example, going to Mass on Sunday) and our daily living. Christianity is better expressed as a *way of life* than as practices to be fulfilled. Finally, then, prudent decisiveness about our future means that "religion" is an expression of our relationship to God that is shown in the simple choices of our daily living. To put it simply, prudent decisiveness about our future means that God is truly at the center of our lives.

Living the Paschal Mystery

Although we tend to be a throw-away society that squanders freely our resources, we also are squanderers in another sense that has far more serious consequences. When it comes to paschal mystery living, we often squander opportunities to gain "true wealth." The thrust of the gospel is that we act prudently in this life in order to "be welcomed into eternal dwellings." Prudence demands that we not squander opportunities to be charitable and just toward others. Prudence demands that we not squander opportunities to die to self. Prudence demands that we not squander opportunities to be trustworthy with the ministry of discipleship which we take on each time we say yes to our baptismal commitment.

Most of us are serious about our paschal mystery living. We honestly try to live good lives. When opportunities present themselves to act in a Christian way, most of us respond appropriately most of the time. This gospel challenges us to take this one step further. Paschal mystery living isn't simply a matter of *surrendering* to the self-sacrificing possibilities that come our way usually in the normal course of daily living. With an eye to the future, we must also *surrender* ourselves to actually *searching out* opportunities to live the paschal mystery. There is such an urgency about discipleship and proclaiming the good news of salvation that we cannot be passive in any way. Just as Jesus did all he needed to do to make his message known, even when that led to Jerusalem and the cross, so must we be as proactive in our own discipleship.

Focusing the Word

Key words and phrases from the gospel: What shall I do? commended . . . for acting prudently, welcomed into eternal dwellings

To the point: Jesus does not commend the steward's dishonesty; he commends his prudence in responding quickly to the crisis of his future. Disciples should be as decisive in conducting their own daily affairs, for what is at stake is not security in this world but eternal life. So we are to treat everything of this world in relation to what is of ultimate worth.

Connecting the Word

to the first reading: Amos' condemnation of the dishonest merchants reinforces the notion that the dishonesty of the steward in the gospel is not being upheld as honorable.

to culture: Some decisions and moments in our life do not have an urgency about them so we can procrastinate without serious consequences. Other decisions and moments have an urgency that requires decisiveness. Discipleship is always urgent.

Understanding the Word

Act now to avoid crisis: After addressing the "Pharisees and scribes" in last Sunday's gospel, Jesus now teaches his disciples once again. The subject matter is the proper use of wealth. This troublesome parable about the dishonest steward looks both forward and backward. It starts the same way as next Sunday's parable about Lazarus, "There was a rich man" (Luke 16:1, 19), and in many details looks back both to the parables of the rich fool (12:13-21; Sunday 18) and to the prodigal son (15:11-32; Sunday 24) who, like the steward in this Sunday's gospel, "squandered" his possessions (15:13; 16:1).

The parables of the rich fool and the dishonest steward find someone in a situation requiring action. The rich man with bountiful harvest and the steward both ask themselves the same question: "What shall I do?" (12:17; 16:3). Each answers his own question: the rich man says, "this is what I shall do . . ." (12:18), while the steward says, "I know what I shall do . . ." (16:4). What is surprising is that while the rich man's plan to build a larger storehouse seems reasonable, God calls him a "fool" and demands of him his life "this night" (12:20), but the dishonest steward is commended by his master (literally, "lord/*kurios*") "for acting prudently" (16:8). The folly of the rich man was to think that his bountiful harvest would guarantee a future of comfort and pleasure.

By contrast the steward recognized his situation as a crisis that required immediate and decisive action. With his employment and security about to end, he put his master's debtors in the position of owing him (the steward) a favor: this *quid pro quo* obligation which the debtors would be honor-bound to repay guaranteed the steward's future survival. The parable doesn't comment on the morality of the steward's actions, only his decisiveness in recognizing a crisis and acting immediately to avert disaster. This is the skill "the children of light" must learn from "the children of this world." This recalls the sayings about the narrow door (13:22-30; Sunday 21): act now before it is too late.

ASSEMBLY & FAITH-SHARING GROUPS

- If Jesus were to say to me, "Prepare a full account of your stewardship," my response would be . . .
- The steward acted decisively and prudently at a critical moment. For a disciple each moment in every day is critical because . . .
  What it means to be decisive and prudent at every moment of my life is . . .
- I am demonstrating trustworthiness for "true wealth" by . . .

PRESIDERS

I am serving mammon whenever I . . .
I am serving God whenever I . . .
The impact each has on my ministry is . . .

DEACONS

My ministry embodies "the Lord who lifts up the poor" (psalm) whenever I . . .

HOSPITALITY MINISTERS

My care and concern embodies for others— whether at church or at home—their being "welcomed into eternal dwellings" whenever I . . .

MUSIC MINISTERS

Sometimes in my music ministry I find myself divided between more than one master. I know God is my master when . . .
I know God is not my master when . . .

ALTAR MINISTERS

Consider: When faced with the question, "How much do you owe my master?" a faithful disciple's answer is: a lifetime of serving others.

LECTORS

The way my daily living is an assurance to the poor that the Lord will never forget an injustice against them (see first reading) is by . . .

EUCHARISTIC MINISTERS

Where God is inviting and challenging me to "lift up the poor" (psalm) as a way of distributing the body of Christ is . . .

Model Penitential Rite

Presider: The gospel today reminds us that all our actions must be in relation to the eternal life for which we strive. At the beginning of this liturgy we pause and ask God to be present to us and to help us respond with decisiveness to the call to be faithful disciples . . . [pause]

Lord Jesus, you became poor and lived among us so that we might gain the rich reward of eternal life: Lord . . .

Christ Jesus, you live in eternal glory: Christ . . .

Lord Jesus, you call us as disciples to serve God with singleness of mind and commitment of heart: Lord . . .

Appreciating the Responsorial Psalm

The connection of the responsorial psalm to the first reading is obvious. In the first reading God swears never to forget an injustice done to the poor. In the psalm God redresses such wrongs and raises the poor from dust to nobility. The relationship of the psalm to the gospel, however, is not so clear. Both the first reading and the gospel relate incidences of unjust and dishonest behavior pursued for the sake of personal gain. The intimation is that these stories exemplify the choice to serve mammon rather than God. Yet while Jesus condemns dishonest behavior, he commends the dishonest steward for pursuing it.

What Jesus invites, however, is not emulation of the behavior but emulation of the shrewdness which motivates it. We are to act in service of what is true and just. The role of the psalm, then, becomes clear. Our real model of behavior is God who redresses wrongs and raises up the poor. In praying this psalm we are singing the praises of the One whom we wish to be like. We are choosing our Master.

Model General Intercessions

Presider: Let us ask for God's help that we might be decisive in our commitment to be faithful disciples of Jesus.

Response:

Lord, hear our prayer.

Cantor:

we pray to the Lord,

That the Church always act prudently in relationships with others . . . [pause]

That all people of the world act prudently so they gain eternal life . . . [pause]

That those who are dying be comforted by the nearness of a loving God . . . [pause]

That each of us may always be honest in our relationships so that we might faithfully lead others to the richness of eternal life . . . [pause]

Presider: Merciful God, you hear the prayers of those who call out to you: help us to be prudent about the affairs of this life so that we might enjoy the richness of your eternal glory. We ask this through Christ our Lord. **Amen.**

OPENING PRAYER

Let us pray

Pause for silent prayer

Father,
guide us, as you guide creation
according to your law of love.
May we love one another
and come to perfection
in the eternal life prepared for us.

Grant this through our Lord Jesus Christ,
　　your Son,
who lives and reigns with you and the
　　Holy Spirit,
one God, for ever and ever. **Amen.**

FIRST READING

Amos 8:4-7

Hear this, you who trample upon the needy
　　and destroy the poor of the land!
"When will the new moon be over," you ask,
　　"that we may sell our grain,
　　and the sabbath, that we may display
　　　　the wheat?
We will diminish the ephah,
　　add to the shekel,
　　and fix our scales for cheating!
We will buy the lowly for silver,
　　and the poor for a pair of sandals;
　　even the refuse of the wheat we will sell!"
The LORD has sworn by the pride of Jacob:
　　Never will I forget a thing they have done!

RESPONSORIAL PSALM

Ps 113:1-2, 4-6, 7-8

R℣. (cf. 1a, 7b) Praise the Lord, who lifts up the poor.
  or:
R℣. Alleluia.

Praise, you servants of the LORD,
  praise the name of the LORD.
Blessed be the name of the LORD
  both now and forever.

R℣. Praise the Lord, who lifts up the poor.
  or:
R℣. Alleluia.

High above all nations is the LORD;
  above the heavens is his glory.
Who is like the LORD, our God, who is
    enthroned on high
  and looks upon the heavens and the
    earth below?

R℣. Praise the Lord, who lifts up the poor.
  or:
R℣. Alleluia.

He raises up the lowly from the dust;
  from the dunghill he lifts up the poor
to seat them with princes,
  with the princes of his own people.

R℣. Praise the Lord, who lifts up the poor.
  or:
R℣. Alleluia.

SECOND READING

1 Tim 2:1-8

Beloved:
First of all, I ask that supplications,
    prayers,
  petitions, and thanksgivings be offered
    for everyone,
  for kings and for all in authority,
  that we may lead a quiet and tranquil life
    in all devotion and dignity.
This is good and pleasing to God our savior,
  who wills everyone to be saved
  and to come to knowledge of the truth.
    For there is one God.
    There is also one mediator between God
        and men, the man Christ Jesus,
      who gave himself as ransom for all.
This was the testimony at the proper time.
For this I was appointed preacher and
    apostle
  —I am speaking the truth, I am not
    lying—,
  teacher of the Gentiles in faith and truth.

It is my wish, then, that in every place the
    men should pray,
  lifting up holy hands, without anger
    or argument.

About Liturgy

Praying always: One way to thwart compartmentalizing our religion is to develop a habit of praying always (see, for example, 1 Thess 5:17). Even if our liturgical prayer is very rich and satisfying—and this is the goal of every parish—we also need our own personal, devotional prayer to complement liturgical prayer. If the only time of the week we think about God is during Sunday Mass, it will be quite difficult, if not impossible, to grasp that our daily decisions are really expressions of our commitment to be disciples of Jesus.

Since Vatican II there has been something of a negative attitude about devotional prayer. Some of this derives from the historical fact that in the past not all devotions were good ones. The Constitution on the Sacred Liturgy gives criteria for good devotional prayer: it should help to draw us into the various liturgical seasons, lead us to a better celebration of liturgy, help us to live liturgy in our daily lives (no. 13). One sure way to accomplish this is to prepare for liturgy ahead of Sunday, especially by reflecting on the readings. Perhaps one might take the response to the psalm and make that a kind of mantra that is recited throughout the week, especially when difficult decisions come our way. If we are singers we might even sing it when we are driving somewhere or while we are doing work at home. It might begin and end our meals.

Meals—these could be another way of praying always. We might turn our meals into a prayer. This doesn't mean that we recite prayers during mealtime! If we remember that prayer is lovingly talking with God and being open to God's divine presence to us, and also remember that because of baptism we are members of the body of Christ, then loving relationships among ourselves are a kind of prayer. First of all, families might have to make a concerted effort to eat at least one or two meals together during the week. Then during the meal there might be conscious sharing about each person's successes and failures, about how members of the family are trying to live the gospel, about the good each one sees in the other. At first this might seem awkward and uncomfortable, especially if family members haven't shared in this way before. With time, each family will find what works best for them. Over time, members will see how more and more of their daily lives is lived with an eye to God.

About Liturgical Music

Cantor preparation: In singing this psalm you invite the assembly to praise God for acting on behalf of the poor and oppressed. By implication you also invite them to imitate God in their own manner of acting. In what ways do you choose God as your Master and guide? In what ways do you struggle with this choice? How might Christ help you?

Helping the cantor, Pt. 2: It is important that all cantors, the skillful as well as the less skillful, be formed to prepare the singing of the psalm in the context of the readings. Even before looking at the psalm, cantors must read the gospel and the first reading and spend some time reflecting on and praying over them. Then cantors look at the text of the psalm and see how it is connected to the readings. They might read "Appreciating the Responsorial Psalm" and "Cantor preparation" in this volume and try to live the suggested cantor spirituality during the week prior to singing the psalm at liturgy.

A cantor who has a sense of how the psalm is connected to the readings and to his or her daily living will have a better sense of how to sing it. The cantor will realize that his or her singing is actually a dialogue with God which mirrors the dialogue going on between God and the assembly in the Liturgy of the Word. A dimension emerges that is deeper than the music alone, that is nothing less than the working of God leading the cantor to surrender to the paschal mystery. It is this which the assembly hears, and this to which they respond.

SEPTEMBER 19, 2004
TWENTY-FIFTH SUNDAY
IN ORDINARY TIME

✠ SPIRITUALITY

Gospel
Luke 16:19-31; L138C

Jesus said to the Pharisees:
  "There was a rich man who
      dressed in purple garments
      and fine linen
  and dined sumptuously each
      day.
And lying at his door was a poor
      man named Lazarus, covered
      with sores,
  who would gladly have eaten
      his fill of the scraps
  that fell from the rich man's
      table.
Dogs even used to come and lick
      his sores.
When the poor man died,
  he was carried away by angels to the
      bosom of Abraham.
The rich man also died and was buried,
  and from the netherworld, where he
      was in torment,
  he raised his eyes and saw Abraham
      far off
  and Lazarus at his side.
And he cried out, 'Father Abraham,
      have pity on me.
Send Lazarus to dip the tip of his
      finger in water and cool my tongue,
  for I am suffering torment in these
      flames.'
Abraham replied,
  'My child, remember that you
      received
  what was good during your lifetime
  while Lazarus likewise received what
      was bad;
  but now he is comforted here,
      whereas you are tormented.
Moreover, between us and you a great
      chasm is established
  to prevent anyone from crossing who
      might wish to go
  from our side to yours or from your
      side to ours.'

Continued in Appendix A, p. 287.

Reflecting on the Gospel

We often hear remarks like, "You're hearing me but not really *listening* to me." This Sunday's gospel is the third parable we've had about a rich man. The real issue in this gospel is that he's *not listening*. One aspect of the urgency of discipleship is to *listen* to what might persuade us to live according to God's will—we have God's word, divine Law, and tradition to guide us toward concern for others. The issue is to see beyond our own needs and self-centeredness to being roused out of our complacency to be in right relationship with others.

Jesus addresses this parable specifically to the Pharisees. This is telling. The Pharisees were the "professional" teachers in Jesus' time. They knew the Law and what is demanded in order to be faithful to the covenant with each other. However, they have become complacent in neglecting what they *know*—Moses and the prophets have urged Israel to care for the poor and needy. Jesus had come with the same message; they weren't listening to him, either. Had the Pharisees had an attitude of *listening,* they would have been open to Jesus. Without this openness, even rising "from the dead" would not persuade.

The rich man in the parable doesn't do anything wrong in terms of keeping the Law or not. He is merely using to his advantage the good things that had come his way in life. However, there is more to law than keeping statutes. The basic commandment is to love God and neighbor. Neglecting hungry Lazarus is as serious as breaking a law. There is such a scriptural insistence on taking care of the poor and needy because when *all* have their fill of the good gifts of God it is a sign of God's care and presence, the in-breaking of God's reign where no one will be in need. When we neglect to care for those in need we actually delay the coming of God's kingdom. Listening to God's word, then, has a double edge: we not only learn how to live but we also further God's kingdom when we respond appropriately to what we hear.

There is a great "chasm" between selfishness and self-surrender, between evil and good, between the lost and saved. This chasm is a metaphor for *listening* to God's word and allowing ourselves to be guided by its demands. The time to respond decisively to God and others is *now;* after death it is too late.

Living the Paschal Mystery

There is no need to be frightened about eternal life if we daily allow God's word to guide us in our responses to others. This message parallels what was presented in last Sunday's gospel—there is an urgency about discipleship. Last Sunday the urgency was depicted in terms of acting prudently; this Sunday the urgency is about listening. In both ways do we prepare for eternal life.

God's word comes to us in more ways than the proclamations at Sunday Mass or taking time to read the Bible—as important as both of those are. God's word also comes to us through others. It can be presented as someone in need. God's word might come in some challenge to our self-centeredness or values. It might come through another's encouragement. In all these ways and countless others we are invited to *listen*. Listening is part of the decisiveness of discipleship.

Focusing the Word

Key words and phrases from the gospel: lying at his door, died, great chasm . . . to prevent . . . crossing

To the point: This is yet another parable about the urgency of discipleship. The time to respond decisively to God and others is now. After death it is too late.

Connecting the Word

to the first reading: Jesus references Moses and the prophets as the basis for acting decisively. This Sunday's reading from Amos is an example of such prophecy.

to Catholic culture: In the *Confiteor* (sometimes used during the penitential rite at Mass) we confess both what we "have done" and what we "have failed to do." Both the first reading and gospel depict consequences of the failure to act.

Understanding the Word

Rich and poor: In the parable of Lazarus and the rich man, Luke returns to one of his major themes: the blessing of poverty and the danger of wealth. This powerful parable dramatizes Mary's words in 1:52-53—"He has cast down the mighty from their thrones and has lifted up the lowly. He has filled the hungry with good things and the rich he has sent away empty." It also fleshes out the contrast of "beatitude and woe" found in the Sermon on the Plain: "Blessed are you who are poor, for the kingdom of God is yours. Blessed are you who are now hungry, for you will be satisfied. . . . But woe to you who are rich, for you have received your consolation. . . . Woe to you who are filled now, for you will be hungry" (6:20-21, 24-25). Though Jesus had instructed the wealthy to invite "the poor, the crippled, the lame, the blind" (14:13; Sunday 22), here is poor Lazarus literally sitting on the doorstep of the self-indulgent rich man and yet given not even a scrap.

Jesus himself announced the theme of blessings for the poor in his first sermon: "The Spirit of the Lord is upon me, because he has anointed me to bring glad tidings to the poor" (4:18; Sunday 3). Luke has warned repeatedly of the dangers of wealth: "Take care to guard against all greed, for though one may be rich, one's life does not consist of possessions" (12:15; Sunday 18) and illustrated that warning with the parable of the rich fool (12:16-21; Sunday 18). He is explicit when he warns, "How hard it is for those who have wealth to enter the kingdom of God" (18:24). This Sunday's parable is an illustration of an earlier saying: the word of God is like seed which can be "choked by the anxieties and riches and pleasures of life, and [which] fail to produce mature fruit" (8:14). This parable puts readers in the place of the rich man's brothers: we have Moses, the prophets, and the teaching of One raised from the dead. This is true wealth.

**ASSEMBLY &
FAITH-SHARING GROUPS**

- The rich man did not heed the warnings from "Moses and the prophets." What makes me face the demanding truth of God's word is . . .
- A Lazarus to whom I need to respond is . . .
- After death Lazarus' and the rich man's quality of life were reversed. Something that needs to be reversed in my life is . . .

PRESIDERS

Amos condemns the complacent for not heeding the suffering within the tribe of Joseph (see first reading). My ministry awakens others to the suffering of the disadvantaged by . . .

DEACONS

The quality of my listening to "Moses and the prophets" is . . .
The last time it has persuaded me to a change of lifestyle is . . .

HOSPITALITY MINISTERS

The rich man loved his brothers enough to wish to warn them of his plight; but his love did not include tending to Lazarus' lying at the door. The boundaries to my love and hospitality are . . .

MUSIC MINISTERS

My music ministry helps me listen better to God's word because . . .
What in my ministry can interfere with this listening is . . .

ALTAR MINISTERS

The last time I served for a Lazarus was . . .
What this taught me about serving at the altar was . . .

LECTORS

An example of God's word shattering my neglect of the needs of others is . . .

EUCHARISTIC MINISTERS

Besides distributing Communion I am an instrument of communion. I am extending communion to the disadvantaged by . . .

Model Penitential Rite

Presider: After death it is too late to respond to the many opportunities presented to us to be faithful disciples. Let us open ourselves to God's presence and prepare to listen to God's word, that we might respond to others generously . . . [pause]

> Lord Jesus, you teach us by your word of truth: Lord . . .
>
> Christ Jesus, you were raised from the dead: Christ . . .
>
> Lord Jesus, you feed us with the Bread of life: Lord . . .

Appreciating the Responsorial Psalm

Both the first reading and the gospel relate stories of indifference to human suffering. In the first reading the complacent revel in wine and music while society collapses around them. In the gospel the rich man gorges himself while the beggar dies of hunger at his gate. Had they heeded Moses and the prophets (gospel) they would have lived differently and secured a different future for themselves. The responsorial psalm relates a contrasting story. In the psalm God secures justice for the oppressed, feeds the hungry, raises up the poor, and cares for those in need.

In a sense the psalm is our message from Moses and the prophets. By praising God for never being indifferent to human suffering the psalm challenges us to act likewise. We have been sent the message, then; it is for us to hear and heed. May our singing of this psalm be a sign that we have heard and have chosen to heed. And may we reign with God forever (psalm).

Model General Intercessions

Presider: Let us pray that we might be unselfish in our response to others.

Response:

Lord, hear our prayer.

Cantor:

we pray to the Lord,

That the Church proclaim boldly and listen attentively to God's word . . . [pause]

That all peoples of the world listen attentively to their Scriptures so that there can be peace and justice for all . . . [pause]

That the poor and hungry have their fill of the fruits of this earth . . . [pause]

That each one of us listen to God's word and be decisive in our actions toward others . . . [pause]

Presider: Merciful God, you send your word of truth to lead us to everlasting life: hear these our prayers that we might become more faithful disciples of your Son who lives and reigns with you and the Holy Spirit, one God for ever and ever. **Amen.**

OPENING PRAYER

Let us pray

Pause for silent prayer

Father,
you show your almighty power
in your mercy and forgiveness.
Continue to fill us with your gifts of love.
Help us to hurry toward the eternal life
    you promise
and come to share in the joys of your
    kingdom.

Grant this through our Lord Jesus Christ,
    your Son,
who lives and reigns with you and the
    Holy Spirit,
one God, for ever and ever. **Amen.**

FIRST READING

Amos 6:1a, 4-7

Thus says the LORD, the God of hosts:
Woe to the complacent in Zion!
Lying upon beds of ivory,
    stretched comfortably on their couches,
they eat lambs taken from the flock,
    and calves from the stall!
Improvising to the music of the harp,
    like David, they devise their own
        accompaniment.
They drink wine from bowls
    and anoint themselves with the best oils;
    yet they are not made ill by the collapse
        of Joseph!
Therefore, now they shall be the first to go
    into exile,
    and their wanton revelry shall be done
        away with.

RESPONSORIAL PSALM
Ps 146:7, 8-9, 9-10

℞. (1b) Praise the Lord, my soul!
   or:
℞. Alleluia.

Blessed is he who keeps faith forever,
   secures justice for the oppressed,
   gives food to the hungry.
The LORD sets captives free.

℞. Praise the Lord, my soul!
   or:
℞. Alleluia.

The LORD gives sight to the blind.
   The LORD raises up those who were
      bowed down;
the LORD loves the just.
   The LORD protects strangers.

℞. Praise the Lord, my soul!
   or:
℞. Alleluia.

The fatherless and the widow he sustains,
   but the way of the wicked he thwarts.
The LORD shall reign forever;
   your God, O Zion, through all
      generations. Alleluia.

℞. Praise the Lord, my soul!
   or:
℞. Alleluia.

SECOND READING
1 Tim 6:11-16

But you, man of God, pursue righteousness,
   devotion, faith, love, patience, and
      gentleness.
Compete well for the faith.
Lay hold of eternal life, to which you were
   called
   when you made the noble confession in
      the presence of many witnesses.
I charge you before God, who gives life to
   all things,
   and before Christ Jesus,
who gave testimony under Pontius
      Pilate for the noble confession,
to keep the commandment without stain
   or reproach
   until the appearance of our Lord Jesus
      Christ
   that the blessed and only ruler
   will make manifest at the proper time,
the King of kings and Lord of lords,
who alone has immortality, who dwells
   in unapproachable light,
and whom no human being has seen or
   can see.
To him be honor and eternal power. Amen.

About Liturgy

Purple and Advent: This gospel's description of the rich man has him "dressed in purple garments and fine linen." The mention of the color isn't simply a nice detail about a man whose favorite color was purple. Purple dye was very expensive at that time and only the wealthy could afford it. Purple clothing, then, proclaimed a status in society. Because purple was also frequently associated with emperors and kings, it also became a color associated with Jesus (see Mark 15:17 and John 19:2 where Jesus is clothed in a purple cloak during his scourging in mockery). When we celebrate Jesus as King (which we will do on the Thirty-fourth Sunday in Ordinary Time, the Solemnity of Christ the King) we recall Jesus' victory and reign of glory. Purple, then, is a liturgical color that reminds us of eschatological glory and the end times when Jesus will come again to reign forever.

We make the distinction between royal purple (blue-purple) and violet purple (red-purple). We use the royal purple during Advent because it is a season that celebrates Jesus' victory and eternal reign. Already in these gospels from Luke our attention is turned toward the end times and Jesus' eschatological victory.

About Liturgical Music

Cantor preparation: As with last Sunday's psalm this psalm holds God up as the model of behavior for faithful disciples. The Church is called to act on behalf of the poor and suffering just as God does. In singing this psalm you invite the assembly to respond to this call. In what ways are you responding? In what ways do you need to grow in response?

Holy, holy, holy: Sometimes referred to as the *Sanctus* from the Latin, this acclamation which concludes the preface echoes the worship of the angels in the Book of the Prophet Isaiah (see Isaiah 6:3). As mentioned last week, the preface itself recounts God's marvelous deeds; how fitting, then, to conclude this recitation with a magnificent song of praise—which, indeed, characterizes the whole eucharistic prayer—whereby we join our worship to all the heavenly choirs.

Beginning in the Middle Ages bells were rung during the Holy, Holy, Holy reminiscent of Psalm 150 (and others) in which all instruments sounded to raise joyful music praising God. GIRM no. 150 mentions that, "A little before the consecration, a minister may ring a bell as a signal to the faithful." This "signal" was a medieval invention at a time when the people were not singing the *Sanctus* nor participating directly in the liturgy. If bells are used today, it would seem more appropriate to locate them at the Holy, Holy, Holy and make it a true acclamation of joy and praise. This is reminiscent of the joyful ringing of bells during the *Gloria* on Holy Thursday and Holy Saturday.

Very early on the "Blessed is he who comes . . ." (see Ps 118:25-26; Matt 21:9) was added to the first phrase, reminding us that God's glory is fully manifested not even in the wonders of creation itself but in the coming of Jesus Christ to dwell among us. Further, the phrase "who comes" is in the present tense, reminding us that Jesus is always coming to us (be careful about narrowing this phrase's meaning down to refer to the consecration). The word "hosanna" is a rendition of the Hebrew "LORD, grant salvation" (Ps 118:25); singing it at the end of the two phrases of the Holy, Holy, Holy expresses our praise and thanksgiving for the salvation God offers us.

✚ SPIRITUALITY

Gospel

Luke 17:5-10; L141C

The apostles said to the Lord,
    "Increase our faith."
The Lord replied,
    "If you have faith the size of a
        mustard seed,
    you would say to this mulberry
        tree,
    'Be uprooted and planted in the
        sea,' and it would obey you.

"Who among you would say to
    your servant
    who has just come in from
        plowing or tending sheep in
        the field,
    'Come here immediately and take
        your place at table'?
Would he not rather say to him,
    'Prepare something for me to eat.
Put on your apron and wait on me while
    I eat and drink.
You may eat and drink when I am
    finished'?
Is he grateful to that servant because
    he did what was commanded?
So should it be with you.
When you have done all you have been
    commanded,
    say, 'We are unprofitable servants;
    we have done what we were obliged
        to do.'"

Reflecting on the Gospel

When the youngsters come home from school, they are often tired and head right to the kitchen for a snack. When we adults come home from work we reach for a cold drink and just want to put our feet up and relax. There is the popular image of the father of the family coming home from work and the well-trained family dog bringing him his slippers and newspaper. After a full day's work we wish to rest. We figure we've earned it. We can identify with the servant in the gospel—after working all day in the field of course he's hungry and wishes to rest. Yet the master makes even more demands on him.

The apostles' request of Jesus to "increase [their] faith" is made in the face of the seemingly impossible demands of discipleship. The issue is to take what we have—whether little or great—and *act*. This Sunday is the capstone of all these past Sundays' parables that keep bringing us back to the decisiveness and urgency of discipleship. This Sunday we see faith as our decisiveness expressed in urgent action. Jesus uses two examples in the gospel to bring home his point.

If we wait until we think we have enough faith, we will never act. In the first example about the mulberry tree, Jesus is saying that even a little faith is enough to move this tree. At issue isn't the *amount* of faith—the apostles have enough—but we must use what we have. The surprise is that by using our little bit of faith it is increased. By acting we deepen our faith. The very work of discipleship, then, increases our faith. If all one needs is faith the size of a mustard seed, then the demands of discipleship aren't beyond anyone. This is the great encouragement of the gospel. We have enough to be faithful disciples.

In the second example Jesus illustrates what the faithful disciple looks like. The servant has been laboring all day in the field, but more is yet to be done. The work of disciples is never completed. At issue here is that by continuing to trudge on with the hard work at hand we are also responding to the urgent decisiveness of discipleship. Discipleship is never-ending. To be disciple means to be servant. Here faith means faithfulness, that is, faithfulness in service.

Putting the two examples together, serving at table is as great as moving trees! Faithfulness is doing all we have been commanded. "Faith-filledness" is *acting* decisively. The faithful and faith-filled disciple is the one who doesn't wait for enough faith but continues to respond to the everyday and never-ending demands of discipleship. The Master demands our service. And then gives us the faith to perform it well.

Living the Paschal Mystery

When we think of people of great faith, we often mention people like Ghandi or Mother Teresa. These were great religious leaders who obviously had great faith and accomplished great things. We make a mistake, however, if we identify faith only with great things. Jesus reminds us in this gospel that our everyday actions, performed in loving service, are expressions of our faith.

The faith-filled person puts in an honest day's work. That person is gracious to those with whom he or she comes in contact. That person is ready to reach out and help another, even beyond one's own work load. The faith-filled person sees Jesus in the other and responds to the situation with Jesus' love and care. Faith is faithfulness in action.

Focusing the Word

Key words and phrases from the gospel: Increase our faith, mustard seed, Put on your apron

To the point: The apostles' request that Jesus "increase [their] faith" is made in response to the seemingly impossible demands of discipleship. Jesus does not grant their request; *abundant* faith is not required for discipleship. Even a little bit of faith is sufficient to do great things.

Connecting the Word

to the first reading: Whereas Jesus describes the obligations that faith entails, Habakkuk describes the goal: "the just one . . . shall live."

to religious experience: We sometimes think people of faith are those who do great things for God and Church. Faith is as readily expressed in acts of everyday service.

Understanding the Word

Faith and obedience: The apostles' earnest plea, "Increase our faith" (17:5) is made in response to Jesus' command in the preceding verse to forgive others even "seven times in one day" (17:4). Such a seemingly impossible task surely requires greater faith than the apostles presently have. The very nature of their request indicates that faith is something that can grow and increase: it is not a static property or attribute. Moreover, such growth comes in answer to prayer and is something the Lord accomplishes in disciples. The powerful effects of faith are made evident several times in Luke's gospel. On four occasions Jesus acknowledges dramatic healings with the repeated phrase, "Your faith has saved you" (7:50; 8:48; 17:19; 18:24). The double meaning of the expression should not be lost: while in the context of a miraculous cure being "saved" refers to healing; readers know that being "saved" has far broader implications. The importance of faith is thereby heightened.

Jesus' reply to his disciples is a stinging rebuke. In effect he says, "More faith? If you had any faith at all—faith as puny as a tiny mustard seed—you could do great things!" But doing great things is not the point, as the parable goes on to explain. What is required is merely doing what is expected. A servant's job is to do what the master commands, namely, both the field work as well as serving at table. Similarly, disciples who are servants of the Lord must do what they are commanded, even forgiving others seven times a day. Though this may seem extraordinary, it is in fact merely required.

Doing what is required is stressed three times: the servant must do "what was commanded" (17:9), disciples must do what they "were obliged to do" (17:10), and the mulberry tree, when commanded to be uprooted and transplanted "would obey you" (17:6). Jesus thus instructs disciples that "faith" is expressed in obedience. Earlier we saw obedience as an expression of love (Luke 12:25-37; Sunday 15); the teaching of Jesus expands now to see obedience as an expression of faith.

ASSEMBLY & FAITH-SHARING GROUPS

- Times when I plead to God for an increase of faith are . . .
- The circumstances where I am regularly required to "put my apron on" after a long day and continue serving is . . . My faith is increased here because . . .
- Doing "what we were obliged to do" increases my faith because . . .

PRESIDERS

The loudest and most effective homily is how one lives. I model acting on mustard seed-sized faith for my community by . . . I model serving others in my community by . . .

DEACONS

The way my ministry writes down God's vision upon the hearts of his people (see first reading) is . . .

HOSPITALITY MINISTERS

Extending hospitality to others has increased my faith when . . . Consider how extending hospitality to another may increase his or her faith.

MUSIC MINISTERS

The discipleship I expect of myself in music ministry is . . . The discipleship God expects is . . .

ALTAR MINISTERS

Acting with the faith one has increases it. An example of where I recognize my faith increased by serving others is . . .

LECTORS

My life sustains others while they "wait" for God's vision for us and trust that "it will not be late" (first reading) by . . .

EUCHARISTIC MINISTERS

Distributing the Eucharist increases my faith because . . .

Model Penitential Rite

Presider: As we begin this liturgy let us pray for the faith to remain decisive in our following Jesus. We open ourselves to God's presence so that we can hear God's word and be nourished at God's table . . . [pause]

Lord Jesus, your word remains forever: Lord . . .

Christ Jesus, you call us to be faithful disciples: Christ . . .

Lord Jesus, you invite us to a place at your banquet table: Lord . . .

Appreciating the Responsorial Psalm

When the disciples ask Jesus to increase their faith, his answer seems unrelated to their request (gospel). The first reading, however, puts his answer in context. To have faith means to maintain hope in God's promise despite the long delay in its fulfillment (first reading). To have faith means to keep working at the task of discipleship even when we think that surely the task has been completed (gospel).

The responsorial psalm adds the dimension that having faith means to keep trudging on the journey to the Promised Land even when the going is rough and the goal far off. The first two strophes of the psalm have us arriving at the goal with joyful song. The final strophe, however, reminds us we are still on the journey and that the temptation to give up faith and quit the task—as did many Israelites in the desert—is real. May we not harden our hearts when God calls us to keep moving. May we keep working and keep maintaining faith.

Model General Intercessions

Presider: We make our needs known to our faithful God, confident that God hears our prayers.

Response:

Lord, hear our prayer.

Cantor:

we pray to the Lord,

That all members of the Church express their faith in service of others . . . [pause]

That all people of the world be led to salvation . . . [pause]

That those of little faith increase their faith by loving service of others . . . [pause]

That each of us model great faith by performing our daily tasks well . . . [pause]

Presider: Gracious God, you give us the strength and faith to be diligent disciples: hear these our prayers that one day we might live with you forever. We ask this through Christ our Lord. **Amen.**

ALTERNATIVE OPENING PRAYER

Let us pray
[before the face of God in trusting faith]

Pause for silent prayer

Almighty and eternal God,
Father of the world to come,
your goodness is beyond what our spirit
    can touch
and your strength is more than the mind
    can bear.
Lead us to seek beyond our reach
and give us the courage to stand before
    your truth.
We ask this through Christ our Lord.
    Amen.

FIRST READING
Hab 1:2-3; 2:2-4

How long, O LORD? I cry for help
    but you do not listen!
I cry out to you, "Violence!"
    but you do not intervene.
Why do you let me see ruin;
    why must I look at misery?
Destruction and violence are before me;
    there is strife, and clamorous discord.
Then the LORD answered me and said:
    Write down the vision clearly upon the
        tablets,
    so that one can read it readily.
For the vision still has its time,
    presses on to fulfillment, and will not
        disappoint;
if it delays, wait for it,
    it will surely come, it will not be late.
The rash one has no integrity;
    but the just one, because of his faith,
        shall live.

RESPONSORIAL PSALM

Ps 95:1-2, 6-7, 8-9

R⁊. (8) If today you hear his voice, harden not your hearts.

Come, let us sing joyfully to the LORD;
    let us acclaim the Rock of our salvation.
Let us come into his presence with
        thanksgiving;
    let us joyfully sing psalms to him.

R⁊. If today you hear his voice, harden not your hearts.

Come, let us bow down in worship;
    let us kneel before the LORD who made us.
For he is our God,
    and we are the people he shepherds, the
        flock he guides.

R⁊. If today you hear his voice, harden not your hearts.

Oh, that today you would hear his voice:
    "Harden not your hearts as at Meribah,
    as in the day of Massah in the desert,
where your fathers tempted me;
    they tested me though they had seen my
        works."

R⁊. If today you hear his voice, harden not your hearts.

SECOND READING

2 Tim 1:6-8, 13-14

Beloved:
I remind you to stir into flame
    the gift of God that you have through
        the imposition of my hands.
For God did not give us a spirit of
        cowardice
    but rather of power and love and
        self-control.
So do not be ashamed of your testimony
        to our Lord,
    nor of me, a prisoner for his sake;
    but bear your share of hardship for the
        gospel
    with the strength that comes from God.

Take as your norm the sound words that
        you heard from me,
    in the faith and love that are in Christ
        Jesus.
Guard this rich trust with the help of the
        Holy Spirit
    that dwells within us.

About Liturgy

Ministry as service: We usually think of service in terms of doing for others. A very special kind of "doing for others" is the ministry each of us undertakes at any given liturgy. The General Instruction of the Roman Missal states in number 95: "In the celebration of Mass the faithful are a holy people, a chosen people, a royal priesthood: they give thanks to God and offer the Victim not only through the hands of the priest but also together with him and learn to offer themselves. They should endeavor to make this clear by their deep sense of reverence for God and their charity toward brothers and sisters who share with them in the celebration." There is a direct link between our ministry at liturgy and our service of each other.

The most important ministry at Mass is that of the assembly. This means, first, that all present have an active, decisive ministry. To be assembly means to surrender ourselves to God's presence and in that surrender we become Church made visible. Our very act of surrender, then, is an expression of faith. This is made concrete in the common responses, gestures, postures, and singing. Faith is also made concrete in the active listening to God's word proclaimed, in heartfelt giving of praise and thanks during the eucharistic prayer, in genuine gift of self to others in the sign of peace, and in walking together in procession to God's banquet table where we are nourished for the demands of discipleship.

Each of the specific, visible ministries at liturgy (presider, deacon, hospitality ministers, altar ministers, musicians, lectors, eucharistic ministers) is, of course, also an opportunity to express faith through service. But we must never forget that the most important ministry is to surrender to being Church made visible. This is the most demanding service because it requires us to lose ourselves in something bigger than ourselves. This is how faith the size of the mustard seed can move mulberry trees—we are not alone, but our service is always with the other members of the body of Christ.

About Liturgical Music

Cantor preparation: The harsh shift between the beginning of this responsorial psalm and its conclusion only makes sense when you acknowledge how easy it is to give up on the task of faithful discipleship. In the refrain you call the assembly to remain faithful despite setbacks and hardships. Where in your own life do you struggle with these setbacks and hardships? What do you hear God saying to you at these times? What helps you respond with faith?

Hymn suggestions: Fred Pratt Green's "The Church of Christ in Every Age" [RS, WC, W3] fits the parable in this Sunday's gospel when it calls the "servant Church" to rise and carry on the task of salvation because "We have no mission but to serve In full obedience to our Lord." The hymn would work well for the entrance procession. A song which captures the hope we maintain despite the sufferings and struggles of life (see first reading) is "Eye Has Not Seen" [BB, CBW3, G1, G2, GC, RS, WC] which would work well for the presentation of the gifts or the Communion procession. Finally, "The Love of the Lord" [RS, G1, G2, GC] speaks of hope grounded in the life and love of the Lord (refrain) and of faith as our greatest possession (v. 4). This song could be used during the presentation of the gifts, the Communion procession, or could be sung as a choir prelude.

OCTOBER 3, 2004
TWENTY-SEVENTH SUNDAY
IN ORDINARY TIME

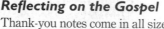

✠ SPIRITUALITY

Gospel

Luke 17:11-19; L144C

As Jesus continued his journey to
    Jerusalem,
  he traveled through Samaria and
    Galilee.
As he was entering a village, ten
    lepers met him.
They stood at a distance from him
    and raised their voices,
    saying,
  "Jesus, Master! Have pity on
    us!"
And when he saw them, he said,
  "Go show yourselves to the
    priests."
As they were going they were cleansed.
And one of them, realizing he had been
    healed,
  returned, glorifying God in a loud
    voice;
  and he fell at the feet of Jesus and
    thanked him.
He was a Samaritan.
Jesus said in reply,
  "Ten were cleansed, were they not?
Where are the other nine?
Has none but this foreigner returned to
    give thanks to God?"
Then he said to him, "Stand up and go;
  your faith has saved you."

Reflecting on the Gospel

Thank-you notes come in all sizes, shapes, and colors. Sometimes there is a nice verse so that we don't even have to write much to the person whom we might owe gratitude for a gift or a nice evening out or a special favor performed. Email has made it even easier for some of us to say thanks—a few words and the click of the mouse and thanks has been rendered. This Sunday's gospel focuses on rendering thanks. However, the gospel's portrayal of gratitude isn't as easy as signing one's name to a card or a click of the mouse.

The gratitude of the gospel points to "glorifying God" which is actually a commitment of life. Gratitude is an expression of discipleship and a sign of God's reign.

This Sunday we shift from parables about the urgency and decisiveness of discipleship to a healing miracle. The healing puts into action those things that make God's reign manifest. The context for these past Sundays' parables on faith and discipleship moves us beyond the tendency to interpret "your faith has saved you" in this Sunday's episode in terms of the healing of the leper. Instead, faith is the simple but profound act of the leper's returning "to give thanks to God," a recognition that God has acted in Christ and this leads to salvation. Both the first reading for this Sunday and the gospel present a foreign leper who asks for healing, obeys what is commanded, experiences healing, and then worships God. The distinctive element is found in the gospel where encounter with Jesus leads to the declaration, "your faith has saved you." Salvation is not freedom from disease but relationship with Christ.

The phrase "your faith has saved you" occurs four times in Luke's gospel (7:50; 8:48; 17:19; 18:42). The faith that saves is the recognition that God acts in many ways on our behalf to bring us salvation. These healing stories anticipate the actions of Jesus as Savior in Jerusalem.

Living the Paschal Mystery

The leper was healed while "Jesus continued his journey to Jerusalem." This is what happens to us when by paschal mystery living we walk with Jesus to Jerusalem: on the way we are healed of our infirmities. We are healed each time we come to Eucharist to give praise and thanks to God and in this act of worship we become more perfect members of the body of Christ. We are healed each time we put others ahead of ourselves and in these simple acts we strengthen our faith. We are healed each time we pause a few seconds to "give thanks to God" for the many blessings of each day because by giving thanks to *God* we acknowledge that God has acted in Christ. Gratitude is an expression of paschal mystery living because by giving thanks we acknowledge our own indebtedness—we are poor and everything we are and are becoming is because God has raised us up.

God gives us so much (salvation) and asks so little of us in return (thankfulness). This is but another reminder that our relationship to God isn't between equals—God's gifts are lavish, far more than anything we could earn or accomplish on our own. This is why paschal mystery living makes such good sense. By living Jesus' dying and rising in our own simple everyday tasks we render God the greatest thanks and worship because our lives become like that of the divine Son. Our thanks is manifestation of God's salvation.

Focusing the Word

Key words and phrases from the gospel: fell at the feet of Jesus, your faith has saved you

To the point: Both the first reading and gospel present a foreign leper who asks for healing, obeys what is commanded, experiences healing, and worships God. The distinctive element is found in the gospel where an encounter with Jesus leads to the declaration, "your faith has saved you." Salvation is not freedom from disease but relationship with Christ.

Connecting the Word

to Eucharist: Catholic worship is defined by Eucharist which means "to give thanks." The fundamental stance of the believer before God is one of gratitude.

to culture: Expressing gratitude is more than a simple social grace; it deepens the relationship between giver and receiver. For the Christian, giving thanks to God reinforces our most important relationship.

Understanding the Word

Journey to Jerusalem (Part 2): This Sunday's gospel begins with two geographical notices. First, Luke indicates that "Jesus continued his journey to Jerusalem" (17:11; see Sunday 13); we will return to the significance of this in a moment. Second, "he traveled through Samaria and Galilee." The Greek text reads, "he traveled through the region between Samaria and Galilee." Many Bibles translate it as "along the border between Samaria and Galilee" (e.g., NIV; NJB has "borderlands"). Quite literally, the lepers whom Jesus encounters there are marginalized, pushed to the edge; they are in "no man's land." While this is true of all lepers, it is particularly true of one of them, later identified as a Samaritan. He is an outcast among outcasts. But just as "the Good Samaritan" became a model of compassion and service (10:30-37; Sunday 15), the Samaritan in this gospel is a model of faith and gratitude.

Jesus is journeying to Jerusalem. In the narrative the apostles, disciples, and crowd have receded to the background. Luke is focusing on Jesus. Just as his journey will end in Jerusalem, this episode ends with Jesus pronouncing that the Samaritan leper has been saved (17:19). The ultimate end of this journey is salvation.

Jerusalem is the city where the Savior accomplishes his mission of salvation. Luke, who has promised his readers an orderly narrative (1:3), prepares for this climax with a presentation of Jesus' ministry in three stages: it begins in Galilee (4:14–9:50), moves south to Samaria (9:51–17:10), and attains its goal in Judea and Jerusalem (17:11–21:38). The events of Jesus' passion and resurrection occupy chapters 23–24. Acts of the Apostles tells the story of the preaching of the gospel which retraces in reverse order this same route: it begins in Jerusalem (Acts 1–7), moves out to Judea and Samaria (Acts 8), reaches Galilee (Acts 9), and will not stop till it reaches the "ends of the earth" (Acts 1:8) which, in this geographical scheme, is Rome (Acts 23:11; 28:14). This Sunday's episode begins the third and final part of Jesus' "exodus that he was going to accomplish in Jerusalem" (9:20; Lent 2).

Model Penitential Rite

Presider: As we prepare ourselves to glorify and give thanks to God during this liturgy, let us open ourselves to God's healing presence . . . [pause]

Lord Jesus, you have pity on those who cry to you for help: Lord . . .

Christ Jesus, you heal us of all our infirmities: Christ . . .

Lord Jesus, you praise our faith and offer us salvation: Lord . . .

Appreciating the Responsorial Psalm

Psalm 93 from which this responsorial psalm is taken is about the completion of God's salvific plan for Israel. All the forces which threaten God's chosen people—depicted in various psalms as enemy nations, roaring seas, evildoers, famine, disease, etc.—have been put to rout by God. The whole world sees what God has done for Israel and rejoices.

The healing stories in the first reading and gospel are concrete dramatizations of God's saving deeds as well as of the faith responses these deeds engender. Surprisingly it is foreigners (Namaan, the Samaritan leper, the entire world in the psalm) who acknowledge what God has done and members of the chosen people (the other nine lepers) who do not. Together the psalm and readings challenge us, then, to examine our faith response to God. As Church do we take salvation for granted or do we see the salvation God is rendering and offer thanks with worship and faith-filled discipleship? As Church do we take for granted the world's praise of God for saving deeds or do we lead the chorus? Our choice is an expression of faith and it is faith, Jesus tells us, which brings salvation (gospel).

Model General Intercessions

Presider: Let us make our needs known to our healing God.

Response:

Cantor:

That all members of the Church express their faith in loving service of others . . . [pause]

That all peoples of the world be open to God's offer of salvation . . . [pause]

That the sick be healed and strengthened in God . . . [pause]

That we always come to God with hearts filled with gratitude . . . [pause]

Presider: Gracious God, you are worthy of all glory and gratitude: hear these our prayers that we might one day enjoy eternal life with you. We ask this through Christ our Lord. **Amen.**

ALTERNATIVE OPENING PRAYER
Let us pray

Pause for silent prayer

Father in heaven,
the hand of your loving kindness
powerfully yet gently guides all the
moments of our day.
Go before us in our pilgrimage of life,
anticipate our needs and prevent our
falling.
Send your Spirit to unite us in faith,
that sharing in your service,
we may rejoice in your presence.

We ask this through Christ our Lord.
Amen.

FIRST READING
2 Kgs 5:14-17

Naaman went down and plunged into the
Jordan seven times
at the word of Elisha, the man of God.
His flesh became again like the flesh of a
little child,
and he was clean of his leprosy.

Naaman returned with his whole retinue
to the man of God.
On his arrival he stood before Elisha and
said,
"Now I know that there is no God in all
the earth,
except in Israel.
Please accept a gift from your servant."

Elisha replied, "As the LORD lives whom
I serve, I will not take it";
and despite Naaman's urging, he still
refused.
Naaman said: "If you will not accept,
please let me, your servant, have two
mule-loads of earth,
for I will no longer offer holocaust or
sacrifice
to any other god except to the LORD."

RESPONSORIAL PSALM

Ps 98:1, 2-3, 3-4

R. (cf. 2b) The Lord has revealed to the nations his saving power.

Sing to the LORD a new song,
    for he has done wondrous deeds;
his right hand has won victory for him,
    his holy arm.

R. The Lord has revealed to the nations his saving power.

The LORD has made his salvation known:
    in the sight of the nations he has
        revealed his justice.
He has remembered his kindness and his
    faithfulness
    toward the house of Israel.

R. The Lord has revealed to the nations his saving power.

All the ends of the earth have seen
    the salvation by our God.
Sing joyfully to the LORD, all you lands:
    break into song; sing praise.

R. The Lord has revealed to the nations his saving power.

SECOND READING

2 Tim 2:8-13

Beloved:
Remember Jesus Christ, raised from the
    dead, a descendant of David:
    such is my gospel, for which I am
        suffering,
    even to the point of chains, like a
        criminal.
But the word of God is not chained.
Therefore, I bear with everything for the
    sake of those who are chosen,
    so that they too may obtain the
        salvation that is in Christ Jesus,
    together with eternal glory.
This saying is trustworthy:
    If we have died with him
        we shall also live with him;
    if we persevere
        we shall also reign with him.
    But if we deny him
        he will deny us.
    If we are unfaithful
        he remains faithful,
        for he cannot deny himself.

About Liturgy

Eucharist—faithfulness and thankfulness: Eucharist defines Catholic worship and even Christians themselves because in Christ, God has given us the most profound gift of sharing in divine life. Our only response can be faithfulness and thankfulness.

Faithfulness. The divine gift of Eucharist calls us to be faithful in its celebration. For most of us there are Sundays when it is more of a hassle to get ourselves (and family) to Mass than we would wish to bother with. Faithfulness means that we still put out the effort. Sometimes going to Sunday Mass is the pure respite from a too-busy schedule and this is some time for quiet and peace. Faithfulness means that we rejoice in God's most gracious gift and make every effort to participate fully, actively, and consciously. Faithful celebration, in turn, strengthens us for faithful discipleship. The Word and Food of Eucharist is a continual renewal of God's presence that, because we are not alone, enables us to respond to the urgency of discipleship with decisiveness.

Thankfulness. Gratitude in face of God's great gifts to us is a recognition of indebtedness that can only be adequately expressed in worship. Each celebration of Eucharist is a profound acknowledgment that all we have is from God and that even still God gives us more. Without an attitude of thankfulness we cannot continually open up the capacity within ourselves to receive God's gifts. Thankfulness, then, is more than saying "thanks." It is opening ourselves to God by worship and self-surrender.

Eucharist defines Catholic worship and Christian living because this is the only way we can adequately express what God desires of us—salvation in Christ. Eucharist not only changes the bread and wine into the Body and Blood of Christ, it changes us into the body and blood of Christ. This is how we are saved—by being transformed.

About Liturgical Music

Cantor preparation: In this responsorial psalm you proclaim God's saving deeds and invite the assembly to acknowledge and give thanks for them. As preparation for singing this psalm you might look each day for an example of salvation and consciously give God thanks for it.

Hymn suggestion: This might be a good Sunday for the assembly to sing a hymn of praise and thanksgiving after Communion. For example, Marty Haugen's setting of Psalm 136 in *Psalms for the Church Year,* Volume 2 [GIA G-3261] has the people responding energetically to a cantor's litany of God's saving deeds. The choir harmonization adds dimension, and the use of percussion instruments would also add intensity. The Presbyterian publication *The Psalter—Psalms and Canticles for Singing* [Louisville: Westminster/John Knox Press, 1993] has reprinted the Gelineau setting of Psalm 136 with a suggestion for an amended, inclusive language refrain. The SATB arrangement is not difficult, but the syncopations which give it life require sure-footedness on the part of the choir.

✠ SPIRITUALITY

Gospel

Luke 18:1-8; L147C

Jesus told his disciples a parable about the necessity for them to pray always without becoming weary.
He said, "There was a judge in a certain town
who neither feared God nor respected any human being.
And a widow in that town used to come to him and say,
'Render a just decision for me against my adversary.'
For a long time the judge was unwilling, but eventually he thought,
'While it is true that I neither fear God nor respect any human being,
because this widow keeps bothering me
I shall deliver a just decision for her lest she finally come and strike me.'"
The Lord said, "Pay attention to what the dishonest judge says.
Will not God then secure the rights of his chosen ones
who call out to him day and night?
Will he be slow to answer them?
I tell you, he will see to it that justice is done for them speedily.
But when the Son of Man comes, will he find faith on earth?"

Reflecting on the Gospel

Both weariness and persistence are things we can all relate and connect to with little difficulty. Sometimes when we are most weary it's simply persistence in getting the task finished, ending the workday, or keeping a goal in mind that gets us through. Persistence. Tenacity. Stubbornness. Stick-to-itiveness. Doggedness. We have lots of words that express how we manage to accomplish what we want even when we think we are beyond the limits of exhaustion or patience. In this Sunday's gospel it is the widow's persistence ("keeps bothering me") that eventually wins her justice. Jesus tells the parable in order to instruct the disciples on praying always. But the parable has other layers of meaning.

With respect to God: The judge renders a just decision because the persistent widow threatens violence. God needs no threat to act justly toward us because God always hears our prayers. The judge acts out of character in giving justice to the widow; he only responds to the widow because of her persistence. God acts in character in giving justice to those who persist in asking because we have faith. If this unjust judge does good for the widow because of her persistence, how much more good will God do for us because of our faith! Because God is just and concerned for the rights of the downtrodden, persistent prayer always leads to justice.

With respect to prayer: In the first reading Aaron and Hur support Moses' arms when he grows weary. The widow was supported only by her own persistence and conviction about her right to justice; she was upheld by her belief that God is the just one and will make justice happen. It ought to be encouraging to us that we are supported in prayer by our faith community. Because of our Christian community we are never alone. Others can provide support but ultimately faith must come from within us, sustaining us and encouraging us in persistence. The very persistence is a kind of relationship, is a kind of prayer.

With respect to faith: Faith is expressed in actions. Last Sunday the gospel gave us the example of giving thanks as faith in action. This Sunday the gospel intimates that persistence in prayer is faith in action.

With respect to Jesus' coming: The legal language of judge, judgment, and justice bring to mind Jesus' promise of his coming again to bring final judgment to all his "chosen ones" who have remained faithful. One way to prepare for this second coming is to be persistent in prayer. Our faith grows through persistence in prayer because through prayer we build a stronger relationship with God. When Jesus comes again, "will he find faith on earth?" Yes, if we are persistent in praying "always without becoming weary." It seems persistence in prayer is a small price to pay for salvation and everlasting glory!

Living the Paschal Mystery

For many, setting aside any definite time for prayer during the day may seem all but impossible, especially if we are talking about ten or fifteen uninterrupted minutes. Persistence in praying always might need to take the form in our lives of developing the habit of being aware of God's abiding presence and blessings even in our busyness. It might mean that we learn to catch little moments for prayer (like we sometimes are able to catch moments for catnaps)—while driving to pick up the youngsters or waiting in a checkout line. The place and manner of prayer aren't nearly so important as the fact that we pray—always and without ceasing.

Focusing the Word

Key words and phrases from the gospel: pray always, justice is done, when the Son of Man comes, faith

To the point: The parable is dominated by legal language: the setting is a court, the complaint is injustice, and the remedy is a just judgment. Such language always directs our attention to the final judgment "when the Son of Man comes" to deliver justice for "his chosen ones." Until "the Son of Man comes" we must be persistent in prayer and constant in faith.

Connecting the Word

to the first reading: Sometimes we, in fact, grow weary in prayer. Like Moses, what sustains us in such times is other members of the faith community.

to religious experience: All of us at times experience dryness in prayer and the temptation is to give up on prayer. At these times we need to remember that the very persistence is a kind of prayer.

Understanding the Word

The persistent widow: The parable of the widow and the unjust judge recalls the parable of the neighbor in need (11:5-8; Sunday 17). Both parables feature someone in need who turns to another for help; when help is denied, the petitioner persists until answered. In both cases the one in a position to help—the judge who has power to give justice and the neighbor who has bread to share—perceives the petitioner as one who is "bothering me" (11:7; 18:5) and is finally moved solely by persistence. Then Jesus makes the point that if even these people who give begrudgingly give nevertheless, how much more will God give to those who ask (11:13) and hasten to secure the rights of God's chosen ones (18:7). In both cases the presentation of God is tied to the nature of the petitioner's need. In the first case people need the Holy Spirit more than the body needs bread: God, the giver of both, will respond to earnest need. God is presented as the divine parent ("Father in heaven," 11:13) and benefactor. In the second case the widow is in need of justice; God is the champion of the oppressed, the defender of justice, the one who will "secure the rights" of widows and those in distress.

In interpreting this parable on its own terms, that is, without Luke's introduction (18:1), we may focus on either the judge or on the widow. The unjust judge serves as a foil for the God of Israel whom the Scriptures celebrate as the "Father of the fatherless, the defender of widows" (Ps 68:6) and as a "God of justice" (Isa 30:18; Sir 35:12). Before such a God who speedily "secures the rights of his chosen ones" (18:7), petitioners may come with supreme confidence that they will be heard and vindicated. To focus on the widow is to move in the direction of Luke's introduction: this is a parable about the "necessity . . . to pray always without becoming weary." In this the widow of the parable is like Anna, another widow who prays "day and night" (2:37; 18:17).

**ASSEMBLY &
FAITH-SHARING GROUPS**

- Jesus' teaching to "pray always without becoming weary" means to me . . .
  The wearisome part of praying for me is . . .
  What keeps me persistent with praying is . . .
- The way I reconcile Jesus' parable that God will render justice speedily with current world events of injustice is . . .

PRESIDERS
The faith Jesus finds on earth when he hears my prayer is . . . when he observes my ministry is . . . when he watches my daily life is . . .

DEACONS
Ministry is part of God's answer to the plea for justice; the way my ministry "secures the rights of [God's] chosen ones" is . . .

HOSPITALITY MINISTERS
Like Aaron and Hur (first reading), my ministry supports the weary, persistent prayers of others by . . .

MUSIC MINISTERS
My music ministry becomes a way of "praying always" when I . . .
My music ministry helps the assembly remain in prayer when I . . .

ALTAR MINISTERS
When God observes my serving others, God is finding "faith on earth" because . . .

LECTORS
God's word supports me in my weariness for justice by . . .
The way my proclamation shares this with the assembly is . . .

EUCHARISTIC MINISTERS
Like Jesus' parable Eucharist itself connects prayer with securing justice.
I aid others to persist in prayer by . . .
The way I am an instrument of justice (at my parish, in my neighborhood) is . . .

Model Penitential Rite

Presider: The widow in today's gospel who is persistent until she receives a just judgment is an example to us of how we ought to be persistent in our prayer so that when Jesus comes again we might also receive a just judgment. As we prepare for this liturgy, let us open ourselves to God's presence so that we might pray with open and receiving hearts . . . [pause]

> Lord Jesus, you teach us to pray always: Lord . . .
>
> Christ Jesus, you are the just judge: Christ . . .
>
> Lord Jesus, you will come to gather your faithful ones into glory: Lord . . .

Appreciating the Responsorial Psalm

Psalm 121, used in its entirety for this Sunday's responsorial psalm, is a pilgrimage song. Having journeyed to Jerusalem for festival, the Israelites must now travel back home. They see the mountains which surround them as a threat—the hideout of thieves and enemies, the home of wild animals. The psalm is a prayer of confidence in God's protection, perhaps said in blessing over them by the Temple priest as the pilgrims began their journey home. What undergirds the psalm is surety about God who will always answer the prayer of those who have been faithful to the covenant and the cry of those who call for justice (gospel). For our part we must persist in prayer even when we have lost the strength for it (first reading, gospel). Such is the faithfulness the Son of Man hopes to find on his return (gospel). Psalm 121 indicates we can count on the faithfulness of God. May our praying of it indicate God can count on our faithfulness in return.

Model General Intercessions

Presider: Let us be persistent in our prayer, asking God to answer us with justice and mercy.

Response:

Lord, hear our prayer.

Cantor:

we pray to the Lord,

That all members of the Church hear the pleas of others for help and answer with justice and mercy . . . [pause]

That all peoples of the world have faith that leads to eternal life . . . [pause]

That the downtrodden and those treated unjustly may receive justice . . . [pause]

That each of us pray always, growing in our relationship with God and with each other . . . [pause]

Presider: Just and merciful God, you hear the prayers of those who cry out to you: grant our needs and bring us to be with you one day in everlasting glory. We ask this through Christ our Lord. **Amen.**

ALTERNATIVE OPENING PRAYER

Let us pray
[to the Lord who bends close to hear our
    prayer]

Pause for silent prayer

Lord our God, Father of all,
you guard us under the shadow of your
    wings
and search into the depth of our hearts.
Remove the blindness that cannot know you
and relieve the fear that would hide us
    from your sight.

We ask this through Christ our Lord.
    Amen.

FIRST READING
Exod 17:8-13

In those days, Amalek came and waged
    war against Israel.
Moses, therefore, said to Joshua,
    "Pick out certain men,
    and tomorrow go out and engage
        Amalek in battle.
I will be standing on top of the hill
    with the staff of God in my hand."
So Joshua did as Moses told him:
    he engaged Amalek in battle
    after Moses had climbed to the top of the
        hill with Aaron and Hur.
As long as Moses kept his hands raised up,
    Israel had the better of the fight,
    but when he let his hands rest,
    Amalek had the better of the fight.
Moses' hands, however, grew tired;
    so they put a rock in place for him to sit
        on.
Meanwhile Aaron and Hur supported his
    hands,
    one on one side and one on the other,
    so that his hands remained steady till
        sunset.
And Joshua mowed down Amalek and his
    people
    with the edge of the sword.

RESPONSORIAL PSALM
Ps 121:1-2, 3-4, 5-6, 7-8

℟. (cf. 2) Our help is from the Lord, who made heaven and earth.

I lift up my eyes toward the mountains;
    whence shall help come to me?
My help is from the LORD,
    who made heaven and earth.

℟. Our help is from the Lord, who made heaven and earth.

May he not suffer your foot to slip;
    may he slumber not who guards you:
indeed he neither slumbers nor sleeps,
    the guardian of Israel.

R℣. Our help is from the Lord, who made
heaven and earth.

The LORD is your guardian; the LORD is
    your shade;
    he is beside you at your right hand.
The sun shall not harm you by day,
    nor the moon by night.

R℣. Our help is from the Lord, who made
heaven and earth.

The LORD will guard you from all evil;
    he will guard your life.
The LORD will guard your coming and
    your going,
    both now and forever.

R℣. Our help is from the Lord, who made
heaven and earth.

SECOND READING
2 Tim 3:14–4:2

Beloved:
Remain faithful to what you have learned
    and believed,
    because you know from whom you
        learned it,
    and that from infancy you have known
        the sacred Scriptures,
    which are capable of giving you
        wisdom for salvation
    through faith in Christ Jesus.
All Scripture is inspired by God
    and is useful for teaching, for refutation,
        for correction,
    and for training in righteousness,
    so that one who belongs to God may be
        competent,
    equipped for every good work.

I charge you in the presence of God and of
    Christ Jesus,
    who will judge the living and the dead,
    and by his appearing and his kingly
        power:
    proclaim the word;
    be persistent whether it is convenient or
        inconvenient;
    convince, reprimand, encourage through
        all patience and teaching.

About Liturgy

Liturgy as prayer: Of course we all understand that liturgy is prayer. There are a number of indicators within the liturgy itself. For example, before the opening prayer and at the post-Communion prayer the presider specifically invites us to pray: "Let us pray." The heart of the Liturgy of the Eucharist is called the eucharistic *prayer*. The general intercessions are alternately called the *prayer* of the faithful. We pray together the Our Father, probably one of the first prayers we learned as children. How is it, though, that liturgy is more than just a stringing together of prayers? How is the liturgy itself a single, seamless prayer?

One part of the answer lies in the fact that in the liturgy we come into God's presence. God *calls* us to worship and to be an assembly before the Lord. Liturgy is the pre-eminent place for encountering God and making present the paschal mystery. Liturgy as prayer, then, helps us to understand that prayer is *encounter* with God and a response to being called into divine presence. Praying is more than saying words; it is personal encounter with the Divine which characterizes every moment of liturgy.

Another part of the answer to our question lies in the fact that in the liturgy we pray as *one body,* the body of Christ. By praying with one voice, we lift up a single prayer to God. Because we are this community, the liturgical prayer doesn't depend on any one individual's ability to pray or not during a particular liturgy. It is as though we are holding each other up and enabling one another strength and persistence in prayer. The constant repetition of liturgy throughout the world is a constant reminder of the persistence of the prayer of the body of Christ.

Another consideration for understanding liturgy as a single, seamless prayer is that the liturgy has an invariable structure. Individual elements may change and vary somewhat from liturgy to liturgy, but the essential structure is the same. This invariability enables us to surrender to the action and in that surrender both encounter with God and visibility of the Church as the body of Christ become possible.

Finally, and perhaps most importantly, the overall sentiments of liturgy are praise and thanksgiving. With these attitudes we glorify God and offer our worship. All the individual prayer—yes, even the petitionary prayer—redounds to praise and thanksgiving. All prayer converges on our acknowledging God's splendor and being grateful for the gift of divine presence.

About Liturgical Music

Cantor preparation: When you sing this responsorial psalm, you are like the Temple priest blessing the people as they begin their journey homeward. The people are the body of Christ, the journey that of faithful discipleship, the homeland God's kingdom. May you assure the assembly of God's presence and protection on the way. And may you persist in your prayer for them.

Hymn suggestions: "O God Our Help in Ages Past" parallels the content of the responsorial psalm and affirms the faith which inspires persistence in prayer. The hymn would be appropriate for entrance or the presentation of the gifts. Another traditional hymn similar in meaning but very different in musical style is "Praise to the Lord, the Almighty" which praises God for keeping us safe, sustaining us, attending us with goodness and mercy. This hymn would be excellent for the entrance procession. Two hymns which ask God to teach us how to pray are "Lord, Teach Us How to Pray" and "Eternal Spirit of the Living Christ," both found in HG. Either would be appropriate during presentation of the gifts. Finally, quiet repetitions of the Taizé "O Lord, Hear My Prayer" could be an appropriate choral prelude, with choir and assembly singing together.

OCTOBER 17, 2004
TWENTY-NINTH SUNDAY
IN ORDINARY TIME

SPIRITUALITY

Gospel

Luke 18:9-14; L150C

Jesus addressed this parable
to those who were convinced
of their own
righteousness
and despised everyone else.
"Two people went up to the
temple area to pray;
one was a Pharisee and the
other was a tax collector.
The Pharisee took up his
position and spoke this
prayer to himself,
'O God, I thank you that I am
not like the rest of
humanity—greedy,
dishonest, adulterous—or even
like this tax collector.
I fast twice a week, and I pay tithes on
my whole income.'
But the tax collector stood off at a
distance
and would not even raise his eyes to
heaven
but beat his breast and prayed,
'O God, be merciful to me a sinner.'
I tell you, the latter went home
justified, not the former;
for whoever exalts himself will be
humbled,
and the one who humbles himself
will be exalted."

Reflecting on the Gospel

A familiar saying warns us that pride goes before the fall. Aesop tells the fable of two roosters who were fighting fiercely to see who would be the barnyard champion. Finally one was defeated and went to hide behind the barn in shame. The victor flew atop the house and crowed loudly so everyone would know about his victory. Then a hawk swooped down, clutched him in his talons, and carried him off for dinner. Whereby the defeated rooster came out from behind the barn and took possession of the barnyard. The gospel this Sunday isn't about two roosters fighting, but about a Pharisee and a tax collector praying. Jesus warns us that pride goes before the fall.

It seems that the Pharisee was righteous and his boast before God was true: he does exemplary things (fasting and paying tithes), even more than is expected. His prayer, however, while addressed to God in thankfulness, is actually filled with himself and his own boast. He "took up his position," presumably one where he will be seen and recognized. The Pharisee praises himself in his prayer rather than God. He does not acknowledge who God is but, rather, he simply exalts himself. Clearly, good works alone don't justify us. We must turn to the prayer of the tax collector to learn what does justify us.

The tax collector would hardly be numbered among the righteous—tax collectors were hated and known for their unscrupulous practices. They lined their own pockets at others' expense. Yet, it is the tax collector who "stood off at a distance and would not even raise his eyes to heaven," a posture indicating he recognized his sinfulness and unworthiness before God. His prayer, too, is addressed to God, but in his prayer he says something true about God (who is merciful) and himself (who is a sinner). The tax collector's prayer allows God to be God and show mercy. The tax collector's prayer reveals both an understanding of God and the desire to be in right relation with God. The tax collector stands afar off, but his prayer draws him near to God.

Justification is knowing who God is and what our relationship to God is. It is addressing God as God and letting God be God. It is acknowledging humbly who we are before God: sinners in need of mercy. The exaltation at the end of time is determined by whether we are justified, that is, humble and in right relationship to God. Good works alone don't justify us—it is right relationship with God. Humility in the face of our all-holy and merciful God brings exaltation.

Living the Paschal Mystery

In practice, probably most of us are like neither the Pharisee nor the tax collector. So both can teach us something. The Pharisee can teach us that religious practices are important, but not enough. They must always be performed in humility and with the goal of deepening our relationship with God. The tax collector can teach us that God doesn't offer salvation only to the perfect, but to those who acknowledge their sinfulness and cry out for God's mercy. At the same time, some of us are so busy beating our breasts about our sinfulness that even this can be a form of pride. Like the tax collector, we must let God be God and receive the mercy offered. Though sinners, God exalts those who are in right relationship. Rather than focus unduly on our own sinfulness, we need to turn to God and ask for mercy.

Focusing the Word

Key words and phrases from the gospel: Be merciful to me a sinner, justified, exalted

To the point: In this parable prayer reveals the true character of the Pharisee and tax collector. The tax collector stands honestly before the all-holy God confessing his sinfulness and need for God's mercy. Such humility expresses a right relation to God which is justification. For the believer there is no greater exaltation.

Connecting the Word

to last Sunday: The two Sundays together offer a balanced approach to prayer: on the one hand, be persistent; on the other hand, be humble.

to religious experience: The hope the gospel offers is that justification comes not to the perfect but to those who acknowledge their need for God's mercy.

Understanding the Word

Humility and prayer: Once again Luke's introduction tells the reader how to interpret the parable. Last Sunday's parable of the widow and the unjust judge was about the need to "pray always" (18:1). Similarly, the parable of the Pharisee and the tax collector is addressed to "those who were convinced of their own righteousness and despised everyone else" (18:9). Though it is traditional to interpret this as a parable about prayer, Luke offers it as a teaching about humility. Thus the moral is stated explicitly: "everyone who exalts himself will be humbled, and the one who humbles himself will be exalted" (18:14; also 14:11, Sunday 22). Again, Luke uses a parable to illustrate a theme: "He has cast down the mighty from their thrones and has lifted up the lowly" (1:52). The Pharisee is humbled, the tax collector is exalted.

The reading from Sirach, together with the responsorial psalm, invites the interpreter of the parable to consider humility as an essential aspect of prayer, thus combining the two themes. Chapter 35 of Sirach (from which this Sunday's first reading is taken) compares moral life and worship in the Temple: "To keep the law is a great oblation, and he who observes the commandments sacrifices a peace offering" (35:1). In other words, religious practice cannot be separated from one's way of life. In this, at least, the Pharisee is correct in avoiding greed, dishonesty, and adultery (Luke 18:11). But this self-made man needs nothing from God; there is nothing asked, nothing for God to grant.

But when the needy call out (especially for what God alone can grant: mercy) then God "will not delay" (Sir 35:18). God attends to "the weak . . . the oppressed . . . the orphan . . . the widow . . . the lowly." God responds to their "cry . . . wail . . . complaint . . . petition . . . prayer." Indeed, God "judges justly and affirms the right." In many ways this passage eloquently summarizes last Sunday's gospel as well. Taken together the two parables highlight a particularly Lukan theme: God's care for the "poor." Their need—expressed simply and poignantly by the prayer of the tax collector—moves the compassionate God of justice to "lift up the lowly."

ASSEMBLY & FAITH-SHARING GROUPS

- When I am "convinced of [my] own righteousness," what ends up humbling me is . . .
- My prayer might better model the tax collector's prayer by . . .
- To go "home justified" means to me . . .

PRESIDERS

The occasions for self-exaltation within my ministry are . . .
What keeps me standing alongside the humble tax collector is . . .

DEACONS

Consider in what ways Sirach's words aptly characterize the mission of diaconal service.

HOSPITALITY MINISTERS

Welcome, care, and concern can convey that "I am . . . like the rest of humanity." This sends me home "justified" (i.e., in right relationship) with God and others because . . .

MUSIC MINISTERS

Times when I find myself focusing on myself rather than on God in my music ministry are . . .
What helps me turn my focus back to God is . . .

ALTAR MINISTERS

What is humbling about serving others is . . .
What is exalted when serving others is . . .

LECTORS

For the lowly and those seeking mercy, the words of Sirach are filled with great hope and comfort. The way I (in my life, through my ministry) can extend this to others is . . .

EUCHARISTIC MINISTERS

The Pharisee became self-inflated by his good deeds of prayer, fasting, and tithing. The good, holy act of Eucharist keeps me humble because . . .

Model Penitential Rite

Presider: We hear in today's gospel that our prayer must be humble, asking God for mercy. Let us pause and open our hearts to God's mercy in humility, that we might be truly transformed by this liturgy . . . [pause]

Lord Jesus, you hear the cry of the poor: Lord . . .

Christ Jesus, you confront evildoers with their pride: Christ . . .

Lord Jesus, you redeem those who take refuge in you: Lord . . .

Appreciating the Responsorial Psalm

God hears the prayer not of the self-righteous (gospel) but of those "crushed in spirit" (responsorial psalm). It is not that God who "knows no favorites" (first reading) is closed to the rich; rather it is that the self-satisfied are closed to God. Because the Pharisee is so full of himself he keeps God at a distance (gospel). When the tax collector, on the other hand, begs for mercy he allows God to draw close. In this Sunday's responsorial psalm we identify ourselves with the poor, the brokenhearted, the lowly. We acknowledge our true relationship with God—that of dependency, of humility, of need for mercy. We allow God to come close, and we are justified (gospel).

Model General Intercessions

Presider: Let us pray with humility to our merciful God for our needs.

Response:

Lord, hear our prayer.

Cantor:

we pray to the Lord,

That all members of the Church acknowledge their sinfulness and praise God for divine mercy . . . [pause]

That all peoples of the world be in right relationship with their God and justified . . . [pause]

That the proud be humbled and the humble be exalted . . . [pause]

That each of us be convinced of God's righteousness and love others as witnesses of God's mercy . . . [pause]

Presider: Merciful God, you hear the cry of the poor: hear these our prayers that one day we might be exalted with you forever. We ask this through Christ our Lord. **Amen.**

ALTERNATIVE OPENING PRAYER
Let us pray
[in humble hope for salvation]

Pause for silent prayer

Praised be you, God and Father of our
    Lord Jesus Christ.
There is no power for good
which does not come from your covenant,
and no promise to hope in,
that your love has not offered.
Strengthen our faith to accept your
    covenant
and give us the love to carry out your
    command.
We ask this through Christ our Lord.
    Amen.

FIRST READING
Sir 35:12-14, 16-18

The LORD is a God of justice,
    who knows no favorites.
Though not unduly partial toward the
    weak,
    yet he hears the cry of the oppressed.
The Lord is not deaf to the wail of the
    orphan,
    nor to the widow when she pours out
        her complaint.
The one who serves God willingly is heard;
    his petition reaches the heavens.
The prayer of the lowly pierces the clouds;
    it does not rest till it reaches its goal,
nor will it withdraw till the Most High
    responds,
    judges justly and affirms the right,
and the LORD will not delay.

RESPONSORIAL PSALM

Ps 34:2-3, 17-18, 19, 23

R̸. (7a) The Lord hears the cry of the poor.

I will bless the LORD at all times;
   his praise shall be ever in my mouth.
Let my soul glory in the LORD;
   the lowly will hear me and be glad.

R̸. The Lord hears the cry of the poor.

The LORD confronts the evildoers,
   to destroy remembrance of them from
     the earth.
When the just cry out, the LORD hears
   them,
   and from all their distress he rescues
   them.

R̸. The Lord hears the cry of the poor.

The LORD is close to the brokenhearted;
   and those who are crushed in spirit he
     saves.
The LORD redeems the lives of his servants;
   no one incurs guilt who takes refuge in
   him.

R̸. The Lord hears the cry of the poor.

SECOND READING

2 Tim 4:6-8, 16-18

Beloved:
I am already being poured out like a
   libation,
   and the time of my departure is at hand.
I have competed well; I have finished the
   race;
   I have kept the faith.
From now on the crown of righteousness
   awaits me,
   which the Lord, the just judge,
   will award to me on that day, and not
     only to me,
   but to all who have longed for his
     appearance.

At my first defense no one appeared on
   my behalf,
   but everyone deserted me.
May it not be held against them!
But the Lord stood by me and gave me
   strength,
   so that through me the proclamation
     might be completed
   and all the Gentiles might hear it.
And I was rescued from the lion's mouth.
The Lord will rescue me from every evil
   threat
   and will bring me safe to his heavenly
     kingdom.
To him be glory forever and ever. Amen.

About Liturgy

Lamb of God: The revised Roman Rite of Vatican II has three occurrences of "Lamb of God": at the *Gloria,* during the fraction rite, and at the *Ecce Agnus Dei* immediately preceding the Communion procession.

Gloria. The first use of this phrase in this great hymn of praise is redemptive in character, requesting that the Lamb of God "take away the sin of the world" followed by the response "have mercy on us." The second invocation acclaims the Lamb's victorious place at the right hand of the Father followed by the response "hear our prayer," reminding us of Christ's ever-constant intercession on our behalf. The entire third part of the hymn is a litany of attributes of Christ, concluding with a trinitarian formula.

Fraction Rite. In the Eastern Church the breaking of the bread is a symbol of the Lord's passion and death, and it is no surprise to find the Greek fathers using *arnion,* lamb, to refer to the eucharistic bread. In the Western Church, however, the Latin fathers referred to the eucharistic bread as *hostia,* the sacrificial gift. These two complementary images merge in the West when the Lamb of God found its way into the Roman liturgy by late seventh century as a litany sung during the fraction rite, repeated as many times as needed until the fraction was completed. When, during the eleventh-twelfth centuries the Roman rite required unleavened bread, the fraction rite lost its meaning and the Lamb of God was reduced to three invocations. Later, it was separated from the (much reduced) fraction rite and accompanied the kiss of peace; hence, the final ending "grant us peace." Another variation was introduced during *Requium* Masses where the responses were changed from "have mercy on us" to "give [us] rest" and from "grant us peace" to "give [us] eternal rest." This latter invocation is now suppressed but it reminds us of God's desire to raise us up in exaltation at the end of time.

Ecce Agnus Dei. The third use of "Lamb of God" during the eucharistic liturgy occurs immediately before the Communion procession begins. The presider raises the bread and cup and says, "This is the Lamb of God who takes away the sins of the world. Happy are those who are called to his supper." This formula clearly addresses Christ in the Eucharist and identifies Eucharist as a sacrificial offering. The *"ecce,"* behold, of the earlier sixteenth-century formula has been changed to a demonstrative adjective, "this," quite in keeping with our contemporary Communion practice of not gazing in spiritual communion but really partaking in Christ our passover sacrifice. By thus partaking we are already being exalted and enjoying the abundance of God's holy table.

About Liturgical Music

Cantor preparation: In singing this responsorial psalm you encourage the assembly in their prayer. You assure them that when they come to God crushed and broken their prayer is at its best. As part of your preparation you might spend some time this week reflecting on your own prayer and your own sense of neediness before God.

Hymn suggestions: When consecutive gospel readings are as clearly interrelated as are the ones for this Sunday and last Sunday, repeating a hymn helps support the connection. Repeating either "Lord, Teach Us How to Pray" [HG] or "Eternal Spirit of the Living Christ" [HG] during the presentation of the gifts would be appropriate. Likewise, repeating quiet repetitions of the Taizé "O Lord, Hear My Prayer" as a choral prelude, with choir and assembly singing together, would be good.

✠ SPIRITUALITY

Gospel

Luke 19:1-10; L153C

At that time, Jesus came to Jericho
and intended to pass through
the town.
Now a man there named Zacchaeus,
who was a chief tax collector and
also a wealthy man,
was seeking to see who Jesus
was;
but he could not see him because
of the crowd,
for he was short in stature.
So he ran ahead and climbed a
sycamore tree in order to
see Jesus,
who was about to pass that way.
When he reached the place, Jesus
looked up and said,
"Zacchaeus, come down quickly,
for today I must stay at your house."
And he came down quickly and
received him with joy.
When they all saw this, they began to
grumble, saying,
"He has gone to stay at the house of
a sinner."
But Zacchaeus stood there and said to
the Lord,
"Behold, half of my possessions,
Lord, I shall give to the poor,
and if I have extorted anything from
anyone
I shall repay it four times over."
And Jesus said to him,
"Today salvation has come to this
house
because this man too is a descendant
of Abraham.
For the Son of Man has come to seek
and to save what was lost."

Reflecting on the Gospel

Zacchaeus finds himself up the proverbial tree—both physically and meta-phorically. As *chief* tax collector and wealthy, he would have been hated by the people of Jericho. Zacchaeus is the last person Luke's gospel mentions before Jesus enters Jerusalem—it is as though Luke saves the worst for last in order to make his point: "For the Son of Man has come to seek and to save what was lost." This last sentence of this Sunday's gospel selection could be a summary of Luke's entire gospel, and it surely is an important point of this Sunday's gospel. If even for this sinner "salvation has come," then who would ever be excluded?

For all Zacchaeus' efforts actively to seek out Jesus, he only manages to climb a tree and "*see* Jesus." Then Jesus stops and *seeks* Zacchaeus ("Jesus looked up . . . I must stay at your house"). An encounter occurs between Jesus and Zacchaeus and the latter is *changed*. He sets his rela-tions right with other people after his encounter with Jesus who comes as guest in his house. Jesus himself is salvation; he came to the house and Zacchaeus changes, putting his affairs in order *vis-à-vis* other people. The outcome of Zacchaeus' encounter with Jesus shows us that salvation requires right relationship with each other, a prerequisite for right relationship with God.

In this gospel episode we see a third aspect of prayer (the other two aspects we met the previous two Sundays: persistence and humility), namely, creativity, innovation, or invention in diligently seeking out God. Prayer is also action: putting our house in order so that we might receive Jesus as our guest, who is salvation. Because Zacchaeus is tax collector, wealthy, and sinner we see that salvation is offered to everyone—no one is excluded (see first reading). But more is needed: we must put our own "house" in order. Now we can answer our question above, who would ever be excluded from salvation? Those who would not seek Jesus or change when they encounter him. All sinners are *invited* to salvation—in this sense no one is excluded. But salvation isn't a throw-away gift; salvation is ours when we are in right relation with God, which entails being in right relation with each other.

Living the Paschal Mystery

Most of us don't have to be so creative or go to the extreme of climbing a tree to encounter Jesus. However, this gospel forewarns us that we ought not be complacent in our spiritual lives. We go to Mass every Sunday and encounter Jesus; we might think this is sufficient. Zacchaeus reminds us that we must also always be willing to change and grow, be vigilant about our relationships with others, for these are barometers of our relationship with God.

Creativity in seeking Jesus might mean that we are innovative in our personal prayer life rather than continually reciting the prayers we might have learned long ago. What prayers might better meet our spiritual needs now so that we can grow in our relationships? It might mean that we keep certain days of the year (perhaps the days of the Triduum or some days during Advent) as a "mini-retreat" in order to diligently seek Jesus and a better relationship with him. It might mean that we don't wait for people to come to us and ask for help but that we notice others' needs and offer to help before they ask. In these and countless other ways we encounter Jesus—and in this salvation comes to our house, too.

Focusing the Word

Key words and phrases from the gospel: tax collector, wealthy, sinner, salvation has come

To the point: In this episode Zacchaeus is the epitome of the despised person—*chief* tax collector, wealthy, and a sinner. And yet he is the one person in the crowd to whom Jesus offers salvation. If even for this sinner "salvation has come," then who would ever be excluded?

Connecting the Word

to the previous two Sundays: The story of Zacchaeus recaps the previous two parables on prayer. Zacchaeus is persistent in seeking out Jesus and, in Jesus' presence, he acknowledges his sin.

to culture: We tend to paint people into a corner by labeling them. Rather than label people, we need to give them room to change.

Understanding the Word

Zacchaeus and tax collectors: Tax collectors were hated for two reasons. First, they were collaborators with the occupying Roman Empire, employed to extract taxes from the Jews; these taxes were over and above the tithe (10%) that Jews owed to the Temple. Second, the way the tax system worked lent itself to abuse. Tax collectors were hired by Roman officials; the yearly tax for an area was assessed and the tax collector paid it up front out of his own pocket. The Romans, money in hand, left it to the devices of the tax collector to make back his money with a profit—gained through over-charging, cheating, interest, or other means. Tax collectors, understandably, gained a reputation for dishonesty. Early Rabbinic writings considered tax collecting a despised trade and associated tax collectors with robbers and murderers; the NT also lists them with other "sinners" (Matt 11:19; Mark 2:15-16; Luke 15:1). Zacchaeus, as chief tax collector, had many tax collectors working for him, adding another layer of employees eager to take their cut. Zacchaeus is thus an embodiment of the outcast and the estranged, or, to use the language of this story, "the lost" (19:10).

Jesus' meeting with Zacchaeus, his last encounter with sinners before he enters Jerusalem, summarizes his ministry to this point and replays some earlier themes. Once again the episode begins by drawing attention to Jesus' journey and it ends with Jesus announcing salvation (see Luke 17:11-19; Sunday 28). The metaphor of finding the lost recalls the parable of the prodigal son in which the father rejoices that his son who "was lost . . . has been found" (15:32; Sunday 24). This episode also recaps the two previous parables. Like the persistent widow, Zacchaeus persists in seeking out Jesus (19:3-4); and like the tax collector in the previous parable, he acknowledges his sin and announces the restitution he repays for extortion committed in the line of business. Such persistence and repentance end with this sinner being saved: this lost child of Abraham has been found—the very reason for which "the Son of Man has come."

Model Penitential Rite

Presider: In today's gospel episode Zacchaeus climbs a tree in order to see Jesus. We ask ourselves at the beginning of this liturgy how far we would go in seeking Jesus. Let us open our hearts to Jesus' seeking us and changing us . . . [pause]

Lord Jesus, you seek the lost: Lord . . .

Christ Jesus, you grant salvation to all those who come to you: Christ . . .

Lord Jesus, you are gracious and merciful: Lord . . .

Appreciating the Responsorial Psalm

Psalm 145 is an acrostic hymn, meaning that each verse begins with a successive letter of the Hebrew alphabet. Consequently, the psalm does not develop any theme in depth but simply offers God general praise. The verses chosen for this Sunday praise God for showing mercy and compassion rather than anger, and for lifting up those who have fallen. The reading from Wisdom confirms this attitude of God when it proclaims that the Lord "overlooks people's sins" and gently coaxes offenders back to right living. Clearly God prefers reconciliation to condemnation.

In his encounter with Zacchaeus Jesus is the living embodiment of this orientation of God (gospel). Jesus has come to "seek and to save what was lost." Zacchaeus recognizes his errant ways and transforms his behavior. In singing this psalm we are the living embodiment of Zacchaeus' response. We recognize ourselves as sinners and shout praise to the One who comes to save us.

Model General Intercessions

Presider: Let us make our needs known to the God who seeks us and saves us.

Response:

Lord, hear our prayer.

Cantor:

we pray to the Lord,

That each member of the Church be creative in seeking encounters with Jesus and never tire of searching for God . . . [pause]

That each person of the world have the room to change and enter into a deeper relationship with their God . . . [pause]

That the lost be found and those who seek God encounter the richness and grace of divine presence . . . [pause]

That each of us here open our hearts to receive Jesus as our guest . . . [pause]

Presider: Saving God, you exclude no one from your grace and blessings: hear these our prayers that one day we might share everlasting life with you. We ask this through Christ our Lord. **Amen.**

Let us pray

Pause for silent prayer

Father in heaven, God of power and Lord of mercy,
from whose fullness we have received,
direct our steps in everyday efforts.
May the changing moods of the human heart
and the limits which our failings impose on hope
never blind us to you, source of every good.
Faith gives us the promise of peace
and makes known the demands of love.
Remove the selfishness that blurs the vision of faith.

Grant this through Christ our Lord.
Amen.

FIRST READING

Wis 11:22–12:2

Before the LORD the whole universe is as a grain from a balance
 or a drop of morning dew come down upon the earth.
But you have mercy on all, because you can do all things;
 and you overlook people's sins that they may repent.
For you love all things that are
 and loathe nothing that you have made;
 for what you hated, you would not have fashioned.
And how could a thing remain, unless you willed it;
 or be preserved, had it not been called forth by you?
But you spare all things, because they are yours,
 O LORD and lover of souls,
 for your imperishable spirit is in all things!
Therefore you rebuke offenders little by little,
 warn them and remind them of the sins they are committing,
 that they may abandon their wickedness and believe in you, O LORD!

RESPONSORIAL PSALM

Ps 145:1-2, 8-9, 10-11, 13, 14

℟. (cf. 1) I will praise your name forever, my king and my God.

I will extol you, O my God and King,
    and I will bless your name forever and
        ever.
Every day will I bless you,
    and I will praise your name forever and
        ever.

R℣. I will praise your name forever, my
king and my God.

The LORD is gracious and merciful,
    slow to anger and of great kindness.
The LORD is good to all
    and compassionate toward all his
        works.

R℣. I will praise your name forever, my
king and my God.

Let all your works give you thanks, O LORD,
    and let your faithful ones bless you.
Let them discourse of the glory of your
        kingdom
    and speak of your might.

R℣. I will praise your name forever, my
king and my God.

The LORD is faithful in all his words
    and holy in all his works.
The LORD lifts up all who are falling
    and raises up all who are bowed down.

R℣. I will praise your name forever, my
king and my God.

SECOND READING
2 Thess 1:11–2:2

Brothers and sisters:
We always pray for you,
    that our God may make you worthy of
        his calling
    and powerfully bring to fulfillment
        every good purpose
    and every effort of faith,
    that the name of our Lord Jesus may be
        glorified in you,
    and you in him,
    in accord with the grace of our God and
        Lord Jesus Christ.

We ask you, brothers and sisters,
    with regard to the coming of our Lord
        Jesus Christ
    and our assembling with him,
    not to be shaken out of your minds
        suddenly, or to be alarmed
    either by a "spirit," or by an oral
        statement,
    or by a letter allegedly from us
    to the effect that the day of the Lord is
        at hand.

About Liturgy

Change and liturgy: Change is generally a good thing—it indicates growth and desire for new directions and accomplishments. Even change in liturgy is good because the need for change is a witness that the liturgical assembly has grown deeper in their relationship with God and each other. Change is a fact of life and of liturgy! Change is good and necessary. But too much change too often in liturgy can actually work against fruitful liturgy.

After change (especially something rather major) we must give ourselves time to "settle in" and make the change a natural part of the rhythm of our ritual celebrations. If we are always adjusting to something new it is very difficult to internalize the fruits of liturgy. We must give ourselves time to "settle in," not in the sense of becoming complacent or resting easy (liturgy is always hard work) or getting sloppy, but in the sense of having the luxury of fine-tuning what changes we have introduced. As we grow in familiarity with our rituals we are free to enter more deeply into the liturgical mystery itself.

While change is necessary and good for the rhythm of our liturgies, novelty and innovation (especially for their own sakes or just to hold people's interest) generally work against good liturgy. We must always remember that liturgy is given an essential ritual structure that has been tested through the centuries of tradition and this structure must be respected. It ensures that we are maximizing liturgy's purpose to make present the paschal mystery and that we are celebrating with the whole Church.

About Liturgical Music

Cantor preparation: Psalm 145 praises God for all that God does, but in the context of the first reading and gospel the praise is particularly for God's mercy to sinners. For what have you been shown this mercy? How have you praised God for it?

Change and liturgical music: The same principles given above about the pace of change in liturgical ritual apply to changes in liturgical music but with some further comments that are specifically musical. First, we must always remember that music stands in a secondary, supporting role. Its purpose is to enable the assembly to surrender to the liturgical ritual. When we change the music too much or too often, we divert the assembly's energies from the ritual demands. We sidetrack the liturgy. When we change the music for its own sake we give it a position that doesn't belong to it by making it primary. Again, we sidetrack the liturgy.

Second, the demands of the ritual are intense and repetition and consistency in the music are meant to ease the task of surrender. For the average assembly this means introducing three new songs or hymns in a year's time is enough. In a year when a new setting of the Mass is being introduced, that alone is sufficient. Any change in service music or introduction of a new song must be related to the goal of enabling deeper participation in the rite, not to the mistaken goal of keeping people "entertained."

Honoring these principles takes discipline. New music should be introduced to support the assembly's liturgical and musical growth. But it is their growth (and the demands of the rite) which must dictate the changes, not the desire for novelty.

SPIRITUALITY

Gospel

Matt 5:1-12a; L667

When Jesus saw the crowds, he went
    up the mountain,
  and after he had sat down, his
    disciples came to him.
He began to teach them, saying:
  "Blessed are the poor in spirit,
    for theirs is the kingdom of
     heaven.
  Blessed are they who mourn,
    for they will be comforted.
  Blessed are the meek,
    for they will inherit the land.
  Blessed are they who hunger
    and thirst for
     righteousness,
    for they will be satisfied.
  Blessed are the merciful,
    for they will be shown mercy.
  Blessed are the clean of heart,
    for they will see God.
  Blessed are the peacemakers,
    for they will be called children of
     God.
  Blessed are they who are persecuted
    for the sake of righteousness,
    for theirs is the kingdom of
     heaven.
  Blessed are you when they insult you
    and persecute you
    and utter every kind of evil against
     you falsely because of me.
  Rejoice and be glad,
    for your reward will be great in
     heaven."

See Appendix A, p. 287, for these readings:

FIRST READING
Rev 7:2-4, 9-14

RESPONSORIAL PSALM
Ps 24:1-2, 3-4, 5-6

SECOND READING
1 John 3:1-3

Reflecting on the Gospel

The baptismal imagery in the first two readings and gospel for this solemnity is abundant and striking. The saints whom we honor today remind us that baptism changes our identity and conforms us to Christ. This is why we can be hopeful that we, too, one day will share in Christ's everlasting glory along with all the angels and saints. Each of the images bears hope and promise in a little different way.

New identity: Perhaps the most telling image is that baptism initiates in us a new identity. Both the gospel and second reading name that identity as "children of God." This identity implies a new and intimate relationship with God, one that we can only capture by using familial terms. As "children of God" we are blood relatives, so to speak. Indeed, as the first reading says, we have been washed "in the blood of the Lamb." The most telling mark of being children of God is that we are "blessed." When we look at the Beatitudes we notice that each result of our blessed status takes us to final glory, which the saints now enjoy. God's kingdom includes comfort, rightful inheritance (heaven), satisfaction (at the messianic banquet), mercy (salvation), seeing God, great reward. This solemnity is a reminder and promise that through our baptism we already share—albeit in a limited way—in the glory of the saints whom we honor.

Put the seal on the foreheads: In baptism we were anointed with holy Chrism on the head in the sign of the cross. This anointing seals our baptism and confers on us the threefold office of prophet, king, and priest. This threefold office enables us to speak and guide in Jesus' name and also offer worship "before the throne" of God. Whenever we worship God we join with all the angels and saints in this singular activity of praise and thanksgiving. The seal of the cross on our heads is a mark of hope—we know to whom we belong and to whom we are going.

White robes: In our baptism we are clothed with the white robe of purity and innocence that symbolizes the new life we have received in Christ. Our baptismal challenge is to keep these robes pure white, that is, to be faithful to our baptismal vows of renouncing evil and putting on Christ. We are "clean of heart" when we are faithful to these vows. The hope we express by "wearing" our white robes is that one day we will be numbered among the multitude giving praise forever to God.

The saints themselves: Perhaps the most striking baptismal imagery of all is the saints themselves whom we honor. They stand out as models who have been faithful to their baptismal commitment and give us courage and strength that we, too, can be faithful. We know some of the saints (those who have been canonized) by name. There are countless others (our deceased relatives and friends among them) whom we know by name in a different way. This multitude of faithful followers of Christ beckon us to hear what Jesus teaches in this gospel: "Blessed are [you] . . . your reward will be great in heaven."

Living the Paschal Mystery

At first glance the Beatitudes seem an impossible blueprint for Christian living and expression of our baptismal commitment; most of us aren't near at all to the ideal that they express. But nine times is the word "blessed" addressed to us. When our blessedness is our focus, then fidelity to our baptismal commitment is no ideal, but becomes a way of expressing who we are in Christ—blessed.

Focusing the Word
Key words and phrases from the gospel: Blessed, children of God, great in heaven

To the point: Baptism initiates a new identity: blessed (gospel) and children of God (gospel and second reading). The saints we honor today are those who have "washed their robes and made them white in the blood of the lamb" (first reading), that is, they have been faithful to their baptismal vows and now enjoy a "reward" that is "great in heaven."

Model Rite of Blessing and Sprinkling Holy Water
Presider: Dear friends, this water reminds us of our baptism when we were blessed by God and made children of God. May we remain faithful to our baptismal promises as were the saints whom we honor today . . . [pause]

[Continue with Form A or B of the blessing of water]

Model General Intercessions
Presider: The God who conferred on us the identity to be children of God will surely hear our prayers. And so we make our needs known to God.

Response:

Lord, hear our prayer.

Cantor:

we pray to the Lord,

That all baptized people remain faithful to their promises and keep their lives pure and spotless . . . [pause]

That all God-fearing people of the world express their blessedness in loving service to others . . . [pause]

That the poor be cared for, those who mourn be comforted, those who are hungry be filled . . . [pause]

That each of us who has been sealed with the sign of the cross witness faithfully to Jesus' love and mercy . . . [pause]

Presider: Loving God, you receive the praise of the angels and saints who are with you in everlasting glory: through their intercession hear these our prayers that one day we might share in that same everlasting glory. We pray through the Lamb, Jesus Christ our Lord. **Amen.**

FOR REFLECTION
* The Beatitude that is most comforting to me is . . .
The one that is most challenging to me is . . .
* I understand a Christian's new identity in baptism as "children of God" to mean . . . Whenever I recall this identity (for me and others) it shapes my relationships with others by . . .
* The impact the saints have on my faith life is . . .

SPIRITUALITY

Gospel
John 17:24-26; L1016.18

Jesus raised his eyes to heaven and said:
"Father, those whom you gave me are your gift to me.
I wish that where I am they also may be with me,
that they may see my glory that you gave me,
because you loved me before the foundation of the world.
Righteous Father, the world also does not know you,
but I know you, and they know that you sent me.
I made known to them your name and I will make it known,
that the love with which you loved me may be in them and I in them."

See Appendix A, p. 288, for these readings:

FIRST READING
Job 19:1, 23-27a; L1011.2

RESPONSORIAL PSALM
Ps 143:1-2, 5-6, 7ab and 8ab, 10; L1013.10

SECOND READING
Rom 8:31b-35, 37-39; L1014.5

Reflecting on the Gospel

At certain points in the year we are given opportunities to remember those who have died, for example, on Memorial Day, Veterans Day, 9/11, anniversaries, birthdays, etc. By so remembering, these loved ones are never really gone from us. It was over two millennia ago that Jesus uttered his cry to be saved from the cup of suffering he faced. He was not saved from his hour of suffering and death; for this he was glorified by his Father and for this we remember him daily. Neither is Jesus really gone from us. Those who serve and follow Jesus are promised that the Father will honor them as Jesus was honored—by sharing in everlasting glory.

We must keep in mind on this festival that we are celebrating, in a real sense, another All Saints day. These souls that we commemorate today are not damned in hell; they have remained faithful to their baptismal promises and so also have the promise of eternal glory. It has been a long tradition of the Church, however, to recognize that some who die are not immediately admitted to the great company of the blessed before God because of the damage sin did to their relationship with God. No doubt our scriptural image of purifying fires (how we have come to image the soul's time in purgatory) has roused our piety and prompted us to pray for the poor souls. Since about the eleventh century the pious faithful have marked this day by attending Mass and making special visits to the Blessed Sacrament and to cemeteries; these were favored ways of keeping this commemoration.

In addition to the purifying benefits of such prayers for the faithful departed, there may be benefits for ourselves as well. Certainly, remembering our departed loved ones in our prayers is an admirable way for us to keep them close to us. We might even suggest that praying for the dead (and to the dead) is an important part of the grieving process—just as we grew in our relationships with our loved ones during their lifetime, so do we continue to deepen our love for them as we remember them in prayer after their death. Praying for the dead reminds us that death isn't an end but a beginning of a new life. Our prayers can be a concrete expression of our belief in everlasting life.

Like Job in the first reading, we must be "consumed with longing" to "see God." The only thing that can "separate us from the love of Christ" (second reading) and sharing in his glory is to refuse to follow Jesus into his death. Our deceased loved ones are awaiting the fullness of glory with Jesus. This festival reminds us to be faithful in our own call to follow Jesus so that one day we will share in his glory. It's not death that is the worst of things; it's being separated from Jesus that is the worst thing.

Living the Paschal Mystery

Following Jesus means being willing to enter into his death; this is the only way to share in Jesus' eternal glory. Although November 2 and all of the month of November have been the Church's time for commemorating the faithful departed, we would do well to remember the deceased throughout the year because they are constant reminders that death leads to life. It might be good practice in our paschal mystery living to keep Fridays not only as days of penance, but also regularly to pray on this day for the faithful departed. This is a kind of service, too—that we never forget those who have touched our lives and whom we have loved and who have loved us.

Focusing the Word

Key words and phrases from the gospel: they are your gift to me, I . . . be in them

To the point: This festival is both comforting and reassuring. We have been given as a gift to Jesus who will keep us. Those who follow Jesus into death follow him into new life. As Jesus is glorified, so will they be.

Model Penitential Rite

Presider: As we pray today for those who have died faithful to Christ but must await sharing fully in Christ's glory, let us resolve to follow Jesus by dying to self in service of others . . . [pause]

Lord Jesus, you make your Father's name known: Lord . . .

Christ Jesus, you live forever in heavenly glory: Christ . . .

Lord Jesus, you call us to be your servant-followers: Lord . . .

Model General Intercessions

Presider: Let us ask God to be merciful to the faithful departed and give us the strength to follow Jesus into his death and resurrection.

Response:

Lord, hear our prayer.

Cantor:

we pray to the Lord,

That all members of the Church follow Jesus faithfully to death and into glory . . . [pause]

That all people of the world know and follow God's laws so that they might enjoy salvation . . . [pause]

That the faithful departed soon enjoy everlasting glory . . . [pause]

That each of us act righteously in following Jesus into everlasting glory . . . [pause]

Presider: Glorious God, you call us from death into eternal life: hear these our prayers that the faithful departed might have eternal rest and we might be faithful in following your Son. We ask this through that same Son, our Lord Jesus Christ. **Amen.**

OPENING PRAYER

Let us pray

Pause for silent prayer

Merciful Father,
hear our prayers and console us.
As we renew our faith in your Son,
whom you raised from the dead,
strengthen our hope that all our departed
    brothers and sisters
will share in his resurrection,
who lives and reigns with you and the
    Holy Spirit,
one God, for ever and ever. **Amen.**

FOR REFLECTION

- What is comforting to me about praying for the dead is . . .
- God's promise of eternal life and glory consoles me in my grief because . . .
- The way God's promise of eternal glory inspires me and shapes my daily living is . . .
- What I need to have purified in my life prior to seeing God face to face is . . .

SPIRITUALITY

Gospel
Luke 20:27-38; L156C

Some Sadducees, those who deny that
there is a resurrection,
came forward and put this question
to Jesus, saying,
"Teacher, Moses wrote for us,
If someone's brother dies
leaving a wife but no child,
his brother must take the wife
and raise up descendants for
his brother.
Now there were seven brothers;
the first married a woman but
died childless.
Then the second and the third
married her,
and likewise all the seven died
childless.
Finally the woman also died.
Now at the resurrection whose wife will
that woman be?
For all seven had been married to her."
Jesus said to them,
"The children of this age marry and
remarry;
but those who are deemed worthy to
attain to the coming age
and to the resurrection of the dead
neither marry nor are given in
marriage.
They can no longer die,
for they are like angels;
and they are the children of God
because they are the ones who will
rise.
That the dead will rise
even Moses made known in the
passage about the bush,
when he called out 'Lord,'
the God of Abraham, the God of
Isaac, and the God of Jacob;
and he is not God of the dead, but of
the living,
for to him all are alive."

Reflecting on the Gospel
It's interesting that important days in our history have *names,* for example, Pearl Harbor Day, D Day, Thanksgiving Day. Very few observances are named by the *date* on which they happened. Fourth of July is one such day, when we celebrate the independence of our country. 9/11 is another when we celebrate the heroic values of so many who gave their lives trying to save others in New York, Washington, D.C., and Shanksville, Pennsylvania. We admire those people who have such absolute convictions in their beliefs that they will undergo anything at all to live them out. We hear of missionaries who sacrifice everything to bring the message of Christ to others. Suicide (homicide) bombers have such conviction that they sacrifice their life for their cause. We *do* sacrifice our lives and this either *inspires* people or *repulses* people. The different responses are significant. In some cases good formation and zeal lead heros to sacrifice their life and this inspires us; in other cases indoctrination and fanaticism take over and this repulses us. The issue isn't really about sacrificing one's life but about fidelity to the truth of God's ways.

The gospel isn't really about marriage, but about resurrection and the categorically new life it brings. The first reading isn't so much about martyrdom as it is about the resolute convictions of the brothers to keep God's laws, couched in the absolute hope for resurrection. Particularly the first reading spells out the conviction and zeal that are essential to face adversity and remain faithful to God. The covenant with God is so important that even marriage—as important as this is—is nothing compared to what is coming.

Resurrection is much more than simply a theological issue worthy of debate. Resurrection is a way of living with surety and hope. Resurrection is surety about eternal life because we have remained faithful to our relationship with a living God. The basis for our belief in resurrection is *hope.* Although hope always has a future orientation about it, when we have confidence in God's grace to bring about change in us, when we have patience with ourselves while that change comes about, we already have something of the future in the present—we already are living this new, resurrected life when we remain in faithful relationship with God. The relationship to be celebrated in resurrected life isn't marriage but the relationship of being "children of God" in an everlasting relationship with the living God.

With the promise of resurrected life, the suffering we face now seems nothing in comparison. In order for this to be really true for us, we must have zeal for God and God's ways such that it is a way of life for us. God is a God of the living. This is the core of our hope.

Living the Paschal Mystery
Paschal mystery living means that we live this life so that it is infused with the life that is to come. The dying part of the mystery always reminds us that suffering and death pale in comparison to the categorically new life that God offers us in Christ.

When we live our Christian life, like the brothers in the first reading we will meet with controversy. In fact, controversy may be a sign of integrity since truly living the gospel always precipitates conflict. This doesn't mean that we go out looking for controversy; it does mean that when controversy happens because of the authenticity of our Christian living, we see through the controversy with hope for eternal life.

Focusing the Word
Key words and phrases from the gospel: resurrection, children of God, God . . . of the living

To the point: The conflicts in the first reading and gospel provide the context for discussing resurrection. For the brothers in the first reading resurrection is the bedrock of their hope and the source of their fidelity to the living God; for the Sadducees in the gospel resurrection is a theological issue worthy of debate. Jesus' response to the Sadducees moves us from speculation about resurrection to surety about resurrection as relationship with the living God.

Connecting the Word
to the liturgical year: The end of the liturgical year directs our attention to the end of time with a cluster of festivals (All Saints, All Souls, Christ the King) and with readings such as this Sunday's about the resurrection of the dead.

to culture: The death of a loved one is one of the few occasions when our thoughts consciously turn to afterlife. The readings this Sunday posit that our hope in resurrection is a way of life.

Understanding the Word
Resurrection: Belief in an afterlife arose very late in the Old Testament, and even in New Testament times such a belief was not universal. The Sadducees in this Sunday's gospel reject the notion of survival beyond death. The traditional view maintained that the human person is identified with the physical body which is animated by the breath of God (Gen 2:7; "breath" does not mean "soul"). Death is final: "When you take away their breath, they perish and return to the dust from which they came" (Ps 104:29). The only thing that survives death is a person's name. Thus, one's only shot at "immortality" is a son who bears the father's name. Therefore, Deuteronomy 25:5-6 provided for "levirate marriage": if a man died without a son, the deceased man's brother was required to marry the widow; the first son born of that union was considered the dead man's son who bore his name and inherited his property.

"Resurrection of the body" as the way to survive death is a logical consequence of Jewish belief. For Jews the human body is identified with the person; thus, if a person were to live beyond death the body must be restored: hence, resurrection of the body. By contrast Greeks believed that a person is made of body and soul. The soul was immortal and was trapped in the body until death when it was freed and lived on. Both the Jewish and Greek solutions to the problem of death and immortality are found in the Bible.

The Sadducees propose to Jesus an extreme case: the pattern of childlessness and death is repeated seven times. If there were a resurrection of the dead, would the wife have seven husbands in the afterlife? They thought the very absurdity of the situation proved the foolishness of the belief. Jesus dismissed the Sadducees' argument. Because resurrection means life, there is no need for sons to carry on the family name. With no need for sons, there was no need for marriage in the Age to Come. The absurdity of multiple marriages doesn't disprove resurrection; resurrection makes remarriage unnecessary.

ASSEMBLY & FAITH-SHARING GROUPS
- Jesus quotes Moses to validate his claim in the resurrection of the dead. I believe in the resurrection because . . .
- The difference my belief in the resurrection makes in my daily life is . . .
- The way I am preparing myself for the resurrection is . . .

PRESIDERS
My ministry embodies the hope and courage of the resurrection for those facing difficulties by . . .

DEACONS
In ministry the minister not only gives but also receives. The last time I marveled at the hope and courage of another's faith (first reading) was . . .
The way that has changed me is . . .

HOSPITALITY MINISTERS
My ministry reminds the assembly that in Christ we are "like angels . . . children of God" by . . .

MUSIC MINISTERS
One way my music ministry strengthens my hope in the resurrection is . . .
One way it strengthens my relationship with the living God is . . .

ALTAR MINISTERS
Consider: The brothers' hope in the resurrection (first reading) afforded them the courage to die. So, too, my hope in the resurrection enables me to die to self in Christian service.

LECTORS
One cannot help but be inspired while praying the first reading. My life/faith inspires others to gospel values by . . .

EUCHARISTIC MINISTERS
In the Eucharist each person participates in the resurrection and becomes "like angels . . . children of God." My life and ministry share this good news with others by . . .

Model Penitential Rite

Presider: We are invited in today's gospel to consider resurrection to new life as the bedrock of our Christian hope and the witness to our relationship with the living God. As we prepare ourselves for this liturgy, let us pause and welcome the living God into our midst and surrender to God's action in us . . . [pause]

Lord Jesus, you will appear in glory: Lord . . .

Christ Jesus, you answer those who call upon you: Christ . . .

Lord Jesus, you are the God of the living: Lord . . .

Appreciating the Responsorial Psalm

On this Sunday when the Church begins to focus on the end times and the Second Coming of Christ, both the first reading and the gospel speak directly of God's promise to raise the just to new life after death. The martyred brothers in the first reading remain faithful to the covenant even to death for they believe that the Giver of life and limb will never take back what has been bestowed. Jesus in the gospel asserts "the dead will rise" for God is "God of the living."

Like the brothers, Jesus knows that he will be put to death for remaining faithful to the call of God. In the responsorial psalm we align ourselves with these brothers and Jesus. We state our hope: on "waking" we shall find ourselves in the presence of God. And we make our commitment: we will remain "steadfast in [the] path" of discipleship. As we celebrate this Eucharist and sing this psalm we look to the glory of Christ to come and know that we shall share that glory as we have shared its price.

Model General Intercessions

Presider: We pray to our living God, confident that God hears the prayer of us who have been called to be God's children.

Response:

Lord,   hear   our   prayer.

Cantor:

we pray   to   the Lord,

That the Church be a bedrock of hope for those who seek a better life . . . [pause]

That all people of the world live the conviction of their faith in God and one day enjoy everlasting life . . . [pause]

That those who are suffering and dying for their convictions may be comforted by the living God . . . [pause]

That each of us be truly alive in Christ and live fully our baptismal promises . . . [pause]

Presider: Saving God, you are the God of the living: hear these our prayers that one day we might enjoy everlasting life with you. We ask this through Christ our Lord. **Amen.**

OPENING PRAYER

Let us pray

Pause for silent prayer

God of power and mercy,
protect us from all harm.
Give us freedom of spirit
and health in mind and body
to do your work on earth.

We ask this through our Lord Jesus Christ,
  your Son,
who lives and reigns with you and the
  Holy Spirit,
one God, for ever and ever. **Amen.**

FIRST READING
2 Macc 7:1-2, 9-14

It happened that seven brothers with their
  mother were arrested
    and tortured with whips and scourges
      by the king,
    to force them to eat pork in violation of
      God's law.
One of the brothers, speaking for the
  others, said:
    "What do you expect to achieve by
      questioning us?
We are ready to die rather than transgress
  the laws of our ancestors."

At the point of death he said:
  "You accursed fiend, you are depriving
    us of this present life,
  but the King of the world will raise us
    up to live again forever.
It is for his laws that we are dying."

After him the third suffered their cruel
  sport.
He put out his tongue at once when told to
  do so,
  and bravely held out his hands, as he
    spoke these noble words:
  "It was from Heaven that I received
    these;
  for the sake of his laws I disdain them;
  from him I hope to receive them again."
Even the king and his attendants
    marveled at the young man's courage,
  because he regarded his sufferings as
    nothing.

After he had died,
  they tortured and maltreated the fourth
    brother in the same way.
When he was near death, he said,
  "It is my choice to die at the hands of men
    with the hope God gives of being raised
      up by him;
  but for you, there will be no resurrection
    to life."

RESPONSORIAL PSALM
Ps 17:1, 5-6, 8, 15

R⁄. (15b) Lord, when your glory appears,
my joy will be full.

Hear, O LORD, a just suit;
   attend to my outcry;
      hearken to my prayer from lips without
         deceit.

R⁄. Lord, when your glory appears, my joy
will be full.

My steps have been steadfast in your
      paths,
   my feet have not faltered.
I call upon you, for you will answer me,
      O God;
      incline your ear to me; hear my word.

R⁄. Lord, when your glory appears, my joy
will be full.

Keep me as the apple of your eye,
   hide me in the shadow of your wings.
But I in justice shall behold your face;
   on waking I shall be content in your
      presence.

R⁄. Lord, when your glory appears, my joy
will be full.

SECOND READING
2 Thess 2:16–3:5

Brothers and sisters:
May our Lord Jesus Christ himself and
      God our Father,
   who has loved us and given us
         everlasting encouragement
   and good hope through his grace,
   encourage your hearts and strengthen
         them in every good deed and word.

Finally, brothers and sisters, pray for us,
   so that the word of the Lord may speed
         forward and be glorified,
   as it did among you,
   and that we may be delivered from
         perverse and wicked people,
   for not all have faith.
But the Lord is faithful;
   he will strengthen you and guard you
         from the evil one.
We are confident of you in the Lord that
      what we instruct you,
   you are doing and will continue to do.
May the Lord direct your hearts to the love
      of God
   and to the endurance of Christ.

About Liturgy

Resurrection of the dead: Easter, of course, is the prime time of the year when we think about Jesus' resurrection from the dead. The end of the liturgical year, when the liturgy invites us to look to the *parousia* or Christ's Second Coming, is another time when we think of resurrection and this time as it also applies to ourselves. Our own hope in resurrection, naturally, is based on Jesus' being raised from the dead to new life. To put this another way (and perhaps make it a bit more concrete and easy to grasp): in his resurrection Jesus was taken into eternity by his Father. Resurrection, then, is less a mystery and more a statement of belief that what happened to Jesus will happen to his faithful disciples as well—we will be with God in eternal glory.

Each time we recite a creed we include a statement of our belief in the resurrection from the dead. This is a doctrine that we Christians have held since apostolic times. Moreover, it is more than belief that the soul will live forever; we also believe that at the general resurrection at Christ's second coming somehow our bodies will also be united with our souls. Just as Jesus' glorified body was different from his body before the resurrection (he could go through doors, was not immediately recognized, etc.), so will our glorified bodies be different from these, our earthly bodies.

In the past the Church disallowed cremation in view of the resurrection of the body. Now the Church allows cremation so long as it isn't chosen out of disbelief in the resurrection of the body. Under all circumstances the Church wants to preserve dignity for our earthly bodies since they have been created by God and are holy.

About Liturgical Music

Cantor preparation: In this responsorial psalm you proclaim your faith in God's promise of eternal life and your choice to remain faithful to discipleship no matter what its costs. No small thing considering the cost will be your life. In singing this psalm you stand before the assembly as a model of surrender and of hope. No small thing. What conversation might you have with Christ this week to give you courage and strengthen your hope?

Hymn suggestions: The readings and psalm this Sunday speak of hope in the resurrection but also of the challenge to be faithful to the demands of discipleship. "A Multitude Comes from the East and the West" [W3] speaks of many who will join Abraham, Isaac, and Jacob (gospel) at the "feast of salvation" and receive the crown of victory. The text with its lovely e-minor tune would work well during the presentation of the gifts. Both "We Shall Rise Again" [G1, G2, GC, RS] and "We Will Rise Again" [BB, G2] speak of the weariness and dangers which accompany discipleship and the certainty we hold in God's promise of resurrection. These verse-refrain songs would work well during the Communion procession. "Want to Go to Heaven When I Die" [LMGM] sings of longing and of hope to join those loved ones who have preceded us to resurrected glory. This song would work well either as a choral prelude or as an assembly song of praise after Communion.

NOVEMBER 7, 2004
THIRTY-SECOND SUNDAY
IN ORDINARY TIME

SPIRITUALITY

Gospel
Luke 21:5-19; L159C

While some people were speaking about

    how the temple was adorned with costly stones and votive offerings,

Jesus said, "All that you see here—

the days will come when there will not be left

a stone upon another stone that will not be thrown down."

Then they asked him,

"Teacher, when will this happen?

And what sign will there be when all these things are about to happen?"

He answered,

"See that you not be deceived,

for many will come in my name, saying,

'I am he,' and 'The time has come.'

Do not follow them!

When you hear of wars and insurrections,

do not be terrified; for such things must happen first,

but it will not immediately be the end."

Then he said to them,

"Nation will rise against nation, and kingdom against kingdom.

There will be powerful earthquakes, famines, and plagues

from place to place;

and awesome sights and mighty signs will come from the sky.

Continued in Appendix A, p. 288.

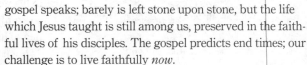

Reflecting on the Gospel

Archaeology teaches us that things last (they tell stories for people living far into the future) and that all things come to an end. Painstakingly do historians of ancient cultures sift through sand and earth to tease out artifacts, outlines of buildings, sometimes even preserved bodies that give us insight into past peoples and cultures long after these have ceased to exist. The Wailing Wall is all that is left of the splendid Temple in Jerusalem of which this Sunday's gospel speaks; barely is left stone upon stone, but the life which Jesus taught is still among us, preserved in the faithful lives of his disciples. The gospel predicts end times; our challenge is to live faithfully *now*.

Jesus lists signs of the end times such as wars, insurrection, earthquakes, famine, plagues, etc. Sometimes we see billboards along the side of the road with the message "The time is now" which shows a clock with the minute hand a few minutes before twelve. This tends to place these events solely in the future and most of us simply dismiss them. The point is that these events are neither singular nor merely future. These events are the context and backdrop for our daily discipleship.

We need not fear these normal, cosmic events as frightening and disheartening as they may be. Jesus admonishes that these signs are now and so the future is "now." The condition for our life and our not having fear of the end times is to fear God's name and live by Jesus' name now. As disciples we must never lose the perseverance to face these tribulations and bring about a better world in which all might live in peace. Only when final peace is attained will the end truly be here. Until then, we live as Jesus taught us.

We might ask, then, what will be so different at the end times? In one sense every day is already the beginning of the end time. The signs we observe of human calamities bid us to give testimony to all that Jesus taught us. We must live faithfully *now*. By our perseverance in giving testimony in Jesus' name do we secure everlasting life. Every day is an opportunity to live discipleship fully and confidently.

If we are able to look to the end time without fear, it is because we live in constant preparedness for Jesus' coming. We follow Jesus (rather than others who might lead us astray) and give testimony to his message of salvation. This is how we actually hasten the coming of the end. For when all is said and done, unity with Jesus now is the only thing that guarantees unity with Jesus for all eternity.

Living the Paschal Mystery

The signs of the end time alert us to the fact that our striving to be faithful disciples has *cosmic* proportions. Living the paschal mystery doesn't just have consequences for ourselves but for all others. When we break out of a chronological understanding of time (that is, time as duration with past, present, and future) and break into God's eternal time (time without duration in which everything just *is*) we can begin to understand how even the little acts of kindness and self-sacrifice we perform each day affect all that is.

This is a sobering thought: the way we care for the children, are honest at the workplace, take leisure time to care for ourselves affects our whole world and everyone in it. This is the privilege of discipleship: we can make a difference!

Focusing the Word

Key words and phrases from the gospel: not immediately . . . the end, testimony, my name, perseverance

To the point: The signs of the end times that Jesus lists (wars, insurrection, earthquakes, famine, plagues, etc.) describe human history as it has *always* been. In this sense, then, every day is already the end time and there is nothing extraordinary about these events. Rather, they are the normal context for daily Christian living. The challenge is to persevere in testifying to Jesus' name by the manner in which we live.

Connecting the Word

to the first reading: The first reading reinforces why disciples persevere in giving testimony: "there will arise the sun of justice with its healing rays."

to culture: The general populace thinks of the end time in terms of cosmic, catastrophic events that are yet to come. Consequently, we think the end time concerns future generations, not us. The truth, however, is that the end time is *now*.

Understanding the Word

The day is coming: Both the prophet Malachi and Jesus speak of "the day that is coming" (Mal 3:19) or the days that "will come" (Luke 21: 6). Jewish prophetic thought had first envisioned "the day of the Lord" as a day when God would deliver Israel from their enemies. Thus it was a day of light, joy, and victory for Israel but darkness, mourning, and judgment for their enemies. However, beginning with Amos, prophets turned the tables and warned of God's coming against Israel in judgment. "The day of the Lord" or "that day" was shorthand for impending judgment and disaster. Gradually that fateful day kept getting deferred to an indefinite future and the scope of judgment was broadened: God would come against all the ungodly, the wicked, and the unrighteous.

With the emergence of apocalyptic thought all of reality was placed in opposing camps: the cosmos was divided between the material world and the spiritual world; time was divided between this age and the age to come; people were divided between the righteous and the wicked. In this "either/or" world such diametrically opposed forces would eventually face each other in an all-out war when God's final judgment will be enacted. On "that day" nature itself will erupt into cataclysm with "earthquakes, famines, and plagues" (Luke 21:11). In addition there will be wars and insurrections (21:9), persecution and imprisonment (21:12), betrayal and death (21:16). Yet despite all this Jesus instructs his hearers, "do not be terrified" (21:9). Why not?

Part of this end-day (apocalyptic) worldview is the profound conviction that the world and its history are in God's hand. Though the present may seem "out of control" and the future may seem bleak and uncertain, everything is unfolding according to God's plan. What is unknown to us is known to God; what is devastating to us is part of God's controlled judgment. Beyond destruction is salvation. The image in Malachi is clearer. After the consuming fire comes in a destroying judgment against the wicked, "the sun of justice with its healing rays" will arise over the righteous (Mal 3:20).

**ASSEMBLY &
FAITH-SHARING GROUPS**

• Whenever I "hear of wars and insurrections . . ." my response is . . .

• The kind of testimony that Jesus is challenging me to live is . . .

• When Jesus says "by your perseverance you will secure your lives," I understand him to mean . . .

PRESIDERS

With such an apocalyptic pericope, the way I help others move beyond calculations and terror to persistent testimony of Jesus' name is . . .

DEACONS

To those troubled and burdened, my ministry embodies "the sun of justice with its healing rays" (first reading) by . . .

HOSPITALITY MINISTERS

Consider: My hospitality directs the disparate individuals to gather in Jesus' name; the assembly once gathered manifests Christ's presence and who they are as his body.

MUSIC MINISTERS

My music ministry helps me hope in the coming of the Lord because . . .
It calls me to persevere in discipleship by . . .

ALTAR MINISTERS

Consider: My ministry announces to the assembly the means by which they are to persevere and "secure [their] lives"—to die to self in serving one another.

LECTORS

" . . . I myself shall give you a wisdom . . ." An example of the wisdom I have been given through prayerful attention to God's word is . . .

EUCHARISTIC MINISTERS

Just as the Eucharist nourishes me with strength, courage, and hope to persevere during difficult times, my ministry nourishes others to persevere by . . .

Model Penitential Rite

Presider: The gospel invites us today not to look to cosmic signs for the end of the world such as wars, earthquakes, and famine, but to look to the faithfulness of our own discipleship. As we begin this liturgy we pause to open ourselves to God's word and to be nourished at God's table so that we might teach faithfully in Jesus' name . . . [pause]

Lord Jesus, you come to rule the earth with justice: Lord . . .

Christ Jesus, you call us to teach in your name: Christ . . .

Lord Jesus, you give us strength and perseverance to secure eternal life: Lord . . .

Appreciating the Responsorial Psalm

The day is coming, says the Lord, when the faithful will see justice (first reading). But "before this happens," Jesus tells us, we will experience the destruction wrought by natural disasters and human will; we will suffer persecution for being disciples; we will be called to testify to the vision we have been granted in him (gospel). And our perseverance will gain us life.

We find the source of our perseverance in the words of the responsorial psalm: the Lord will come to rule the world with justice. This declaration is the hope that sustains us, the vision of the future we see now with the eyes of faith. It is the assurance that gives us courage to continue in discipleship knowing we face persecution, even death. It is the faith to which we testify before the world. As we sing this psalm may we feel the presence of Christ filling us with his wisdom, his courage, and his faithfulness.

Model General Intercessions

Presider: Teaching in Jesus' name as faithful disciples is a daunting ministry. Let us pray for strength and perseverance.

Response:

Lord, hear our prayer.

Cantor:

we pray to the Lord,

That the Church may persevere in faithful discipleship . . . [pause]

That the world may live in peace and justice . . . [pause]

That the poor, sick, and needy may receive all they need . . . [pause]

That we may live by Jesus' name . . . [pause]

Presider: Wondrous God, you created the heavens and earth as a sign of your love for us: hear these our prayers and strengthen us in our perseverance so that one day we might live forever with you and your Son, our Lord Jesus Christ. **Amen.**

Let us pray

Pause for silent prayer

Father of all that is good,
keep us faithful in serving you,
for to serve you is our lasting joy.

We ask this through our Lord Jesus Christ,
   your Son,
who lives and reigns with you and the Holy
   Spirit,
one God, for ever and ever. **Amen.**

FIRST READING
Mal 3:19-20a

Lo, the day is coming, blazing like an oven,
   when all the proud and all evildoers will
      be stubble,
and the day that is coming will set them
      on fire,
   leaving them neither root nor branch,
   says the LORD of hosts.
But for you who fear my name, there will
      arise
   the sun of justice with its healing rays.

RESPONSORIAL PSALM
Ps 98:5-6, 7-8, 9

R℣. (cf. 9) The Lord comes to rule the earth with justice.

Sing praise to the LORD with the harp,
   with the harp and melodious song.
With trumpets and the sound of the horn
   sing joyfully before the King, the LORD.

R℣. The Lord comes to rule the earth with justice.

Let the sea and what fills it resound,
   the world and those who dwell in it;
let the rivers clap their hands,
   the mountains shout with them for joy.

R℣. The Lord comes to rule the earth with justice.

Before the LORD, for he comes,
   for he comes to rule the earth;
he will rule the world with justice
   and the peoples with equity.

R℣. The Lord comes to rule the earth with justice.

SECOND READING
2 Thess 3:7-12

Brothers and sisters:
You know how one must imitate us.
For we did not act in a disorderly way
   among you,
   nor did we eat food received free from
     anyone.
On the contrary, in toil and drudgery,
   night and day
   we worked, so as not to burden any of
     you.
Not that we do not have the right.
Rather, we wanted to present ourselves as
   a model for you,
   so that you might imitate us.
In fact, when we were with you,
   we instructed you that if anyone was
     unwilling to work,
   neither should that one eat.
We hear that some are conducting
     themselves among you in a disorderly
     way,
   by not keeping busy but minding the
     business of others.
Such people we instruct and urge in the
     Lord Jesus Christ to work quietly
   and to eat their own food.

About Liturgy

Ministry of the assembly: When we speak about cosmic dimensions of our discipleship (as in the Reflecting on the Gospel and Living the Paschal Mystery), it seems a bit too much for us to grasp. A reflection on the ministry of the assembly might help us make this more concrete.

When we think of "liturgical ministries" we usually think of the visible ministries, for example, hospitality ministers, lectors, altar ministers, etc. We can easily lose sight of an important ministry that has no "assignment sheet": the ministry of the assembly, a ministry we all share each time we gather. The basic ministry of the assembly is to make visible the Church, members united with Head. What a privilege! Just by our very gathering to "do this in memory of me," we manifest the whole Church! This is how we can begin to grasp the cosmic dimension of our discipleship: we are never acting alone, but always as *Church.*

Jesus promised that where two or three are gathered *in his name,* he is present. What is key here is not just the gathering, but the gathering *in his name.* When we gather as liturgical assembly, we unite the various members of Christ's body with the Head. The very idea of gathering, then, is an expression of who we are: the body of Christ. All ministry is from the body to the body.

When we absent ourselves from the assembly without good reason, we make a difference in how the body is manifested. In other words, coming together for liturgical prayer is far more than fulfilling obligation. The liturgical assembly bids us to surrender ourselves to something—Someone—larger than ourselves. This generous self-giving is the first step in faithful discipleship and is what Church is really all about. It is necessary in order for Church to be concretely and most assuredly visible. It is necessary if the body of Christ is to be built up, to come to full stature. Our presence isn't a luxury, to be given when it's convenient or when we feel like it or when we have nothing better to do. Our presence is indispensable, for we are all members of the Church, the one body. When the membership of the liturgical assembly is diminished, the body is diminished. Our presence makes a difference. It is the first expression of faithful discipleship. It is a concrete expression of the cosmic dimension of faithful discipleship—Jesus' kingdom is present through the whole world throughout all times because we (all of us) gather.

About Liturgical Music

Cantor preparation: When you sing this responsorial psalm, you stand before the assembly testifying to a vision of the future in which God reigns with justice. Do you believe in this future? Are you looking for it? Will you stake your life on it?

Hymn suggestions: "In the Day of the Lord" [BB] is an energetic verse-refrain song whose meter shifts from 4/4 to 6/8 and adds rhythmic interest in just the right places. This would make an excellent entrance song. The Advent song "Now Is the Time Approaching" [WC] speaks of the end of war and strife in the kingdom of the Prince of Peace. Its final verse is especially applicable to this Sunday: "O long expected dawning, Come with your cheering ray! Yet shall the morning brighten, The shadows flee away. O sweet anticipation! It cheers the watchers on, To pray and hope and labor, Till dark of night be gone." This would make an excellent post-Communion or recessional hymn. Another Advent song fitting this Sunday is "City of God, Jerusalem" [RS, W3]. The canonic repetition of the melody in the bass line intensifies the hymn's forward movement and the chromatic rise in the final phrase captures the hope of the Church. This would work well as a post-Communion or a recessional hymn.

NOVEMBER 14, 2004
THIRTY-THIRD SUNDAY
IN ORDINARY TIME

✠ SPIRITUALITY

Gospel

Luke 23:35-43; L162C

The rulers sneered at Jesus and said,
   "He saved others, let him save
      himself
   if he is the chosen one, the
      Christ of God."
Even the soldiers jeered at him.
As they approached to offer him
      wine they called out,
   "If you are King of the Jews,
      save yourself."
Above him there was an
      inscription that read,
   "This is the King of the Jews."

Now one of the criminals hanging there
      reviled Jesus, saying,
   "Are you not the Christ?
Save yourself and us."
The other, however, rebuking him, said
      in reply,
   "Have you no fear of God,
   for you are subject to the same
      condemnation?
And indeed, we have been condemned
      justly,
   for the sentence we received
      corresponds to our crimes,
   but this man has done nothing
      criminal."
Then he said,
   "Jesus, remember me when you come
      into your kingdom."
He replied to him,
   "Amen, I say to you,
   today you will be with me in
      Paradise."

Reflecting on the Gospel

There was a group of pond frogs who lived a happy, carefree life; the secluded pond had no predators and the frogs multiplied and did well. One day they decided they needed a king to rule over them. So they petitioned Zeus for a king. Knowing how well off the frogs were, Zeus threw a huge log into the pond intending to trick the frogs into thinking this was their king. At first the frogs were frightened by the power of the huge splash and ran for cover. When the log just floated lazily and seemed no threat, the frogs grew bolder and eventually came to the log, crawled all over it, and discovered that it was harmless and doing nothing. So they petitioned Zeus again, this time asking for a real king that would truly rule over them. In exasperation Zeus sent a stork who proceeded to gobble up the frogs one by one. When only a few were left, the frogs petitioned Zeus yet a third time, now to remove their stork-king. Zeus replied, "You wanted a ruler-king, now you have one."

On this last Sunday of the liturgical year we celebrate Christ's kingship. The notion of "king" sometimes conjures up images of power and abuse, undue wealth and self-serving rule. The gospel for this solemnity gives us a very different picture. Here we have a King who has no power and wealth; his throne is a cross and his rule is suffering and death. The rulers and soldiers sneered and jeered. What a tame, powerless King! Would we be like the thief crucified with Jesus who wishes Jesus to abuse power to save himself and them? Or would we be like the thief crucified with Jesus who recognizes his own sinfulness and Jesus' goodness? Jesus demonstrates his kingship not by saving himself but by saving others. Jesus demonstrates his kingship not by power but by loving reassurance that Paradise awaits faithful disciples.

Although Jesus' kingdom is established from the very beginning of creation (see second reading) and through the Davidic kingship (see the first reading), his reign is not one of power but of mercy, not one of abuse but of salvation, not one of self-service but of self-sacrifice. The irony of this festival is that exaltation comes from abasement; by not saving himself Jesus saved others. Christ demonstrates his exaltation not in power but through self-sacrifice. He demonstrates his kingship not by saving himself but by saving others. The reign of God is at hand not in power but in mercy. Such a King the world has never seen. The cross is where we least expect a king to be. This is where we least want to be. Yet this is how God's kingdom is established and where our discipleship begins. Only by beginning here, on the cross, can our discipleship end like the good thief's, hearing Jesus say to us, "Amen, I say to you, today you will be with me in Paradise."

Living the Paschal Mystery

The good thief asked, "Jesus, remember me when you come into your kingdom." This solemnity celebrates Christ as King, his kingdom has come. *We* are living in God's kingdom *now*. But we are called not to simply pay homage to our exalted King, but to do as he did. This means that each day we must live in self-sacrifice because only through the cross is God's reign at hand. Living the paschal mystery means living the cross. Just as the cross was the means to Jesus' exaltation, so is the cross the means to our own entry into Paradise. When self-sacrifice seems to swallow us up and we are tempted to choose a self-serving attitude, all we need do is remember that the cross is the door to Paradise. The only way.

Focusing the Word

Key words and phrases from the gospel: saved others, King, with me in Paradise

To the point: Salvation of the world is so far-reaching that it fittingly requires one who is King of all creation. Where does Christ our King accomplish this? On a cross. How does he do this? Ironically, by refusing to save himself he saves others. Christ our Savior King triumphs in death—and thus is exalted forever.

Connecting the Word

to the readings: Jesus' kingship is established from the beginning of creation (see second reading), anticipated in the Davidic kingship (see first reading), and fully revealed on the cross (gospel).

to culture: We admire people who give themselves for others, for example, Dorothy Day, Mother Teresa, Mahatma Ghandi, Martin Luther King, Jr. We are not called only to admire Jesus; we are called to do as he did.

Understanding the Word

Jesus as Savior: Much that had been anticipated in the birth stories of Jesus comes now to tragic and glorious fulfillment on the cross. Gabriel had promised Mary that her child would inherit "the throne of David his father, and he will rule over the house of Jacob" (1:32-33); so fittingly the cross proclaims that he is "the King of the Jews" (23:38). The angels had announced to the shepherds, "a *savior* has been born for you who is Messiah [Christ] and Lord" (2:11); on the cross three times his power to save is tested (23:35, 37, 39) and he is addressed as Messiah (= "Christ" in 23:35, 39). This last title, "the Christ of God," was the one by which Peter acknowledged Jesus (9:20; 23:35). On the cross there are even reminiscences of the devil's temptation of Jesus in the wilderness when he twice challenged Jesus, "If you are the Son of God, do such and such" (4:3, 9); at the cross the soldiers challenge him, "If you are King of the Jews, save yourself" (23:37). The birth stories and temptations have been narrated carefully with the cross always in view. In just the same way the ministry of Jesus to save sinners comes ironically to fulfillment on the cross.

The rulers rightly (though only in ridicule) affirm that "he saved others" (23:35); and indeed he has (6:9; 7:3, 50; 8:36, 48, 50; 17:19; 18:42). Jesus had himself summarized the meaning of his ministry when he announced to Zacchaeus, "For the Son of Man has come to seek and to save what was lost" (19:10). But Jesus had also said, "Whoever seeks to preserve his life will lose it, but whoever loses it will save it" (17:33). To accede to the rulers' taunt to "save himself" (23:35) would mean that he would have lost himself and failed in his mission. So, true to his own teaching, he loses his life and thereby does he "save [him]self and us" (23:39). And, anticipating the salvation he extends to the world, the Savior-King promises Paradise to the repentant thief.

ASSEMBLY & FAITH-SHARING GROUPS

- If I were an author of the Lectionary, the gospel I would select for this solemnity would be . . . because . . .
- What this gospel teaches me about Jesus' kingship is . . .
- What this gospel implies to me about being Jesus' disciple is . . .
- For me to say that Christ is my king means . . .

PRESIDERS

Over the past liturgical year my ministry has helped the assembly realize their "inheritance [as] the holy ones in light" (second reading) by . . .

DEACONS

Jesus' kingship demanded that he be emptied unto death on a cross.
Times when my diaconal service required self-emptying were . . .
The glory I have found in such moments is . . .

HOSPITALITY MINISTERS

Consider: The ministry of hospitality is meant to reveal to the assembly their dignity won by Christ on the cross—a sharing "in the inheritance of the holy ones in light" (second reading).

MUSIC MINISTERS

Through my music ministry I have not "saved" myself but, like Christ, I have given myself for others. I feel remembered by Christ for this and called into his kingdom when . . .

ALTAR MINISTERS

Consider: Jesus shows himself as king and savior by giving his life away for the sake of others. My self-emptying service, then, is a manifestation of this Christ the King.

LECTORS

The word I proclaim declares Christ as king. The life I live proclaims . . . as king because . . .

EUCHARISTIC MINISTERS

Eucharist celebrates one's being "transferred . . . to the kingdom of [God's] beloved Son" (second reading). My daily life has witnessed this to . . . by . . .

253

Model Penitential Rite

Presider: Today's gospel has Jesus hanging on the cross, yet it is our festival to honor him as our saving King. The cross is where we least expect a king to be; this is where we least want to be. As we prepare ourselves to celebrate well these sacred mysteries, let us ask Christ our King strengthen us in our resolve to live a life of self-sacrifice for the sake of others . . . [pause]

Lord Jesus, you are King of all creation: Lord . . .

Christ Jesus, your reign is one of peace and justice: Christ . . .

Lord Jesus, you promise your faithful disciples they will be with you in Paradise:
  Lord . . .

Appreciating the Responsorial Psalm

Israelites arriving at the gates of Jerusalem for annual worship sang Psalm 122. It was a song of great joy, for entering Jerusalem meant encountering God. It meant celebrating membership in God's people. It meant reaffirming who they were and who God was for them. On this Solemnity of Christ the King we, too, celebrate who we are and who God is for us. We are the people forgiven by God through Christ's redeeming death (second reading). We are the very "bone and flesh" (first reading) of Christ, members of the body of which he is the head (second reading). We are the ones remembered by Christ and called to his kingdom (gospel). Let us enter with rejoicing!

Model General Intercessions

Presider: Let us confidently make known our needs to Christ our King who invites us into Paradise.

Response:

Cantor:

That all members of the Church remain faithful disciples through lives of self-sacrifice . . . [pause]

That all peoples of the world come into God's kingdom and live in peace and justice . . . [pause]

That all missionaries and anyone suffering because of their faithful discipleship be strengthened and encouraged by the promise of being with Jesus in Paradise . . . [pause]

That each one of us celebrate in joy this festival in honor of Christ our King . . . [pause]

Presider: O God who reigns over all creation, you bring only goodness and peace: hear these our prayers that one day we might be with you in Paradise. We ask this through Our Lord Jesus Christ our King who lives and reigns with you and the Holy Spirit, one God, for ever and ever. **Amen.**

ALTERNATIVE OPENING PRAYER

Let us pray

Pause for silent prayer

Father all-powerful, God of love,
you have raised our Lord Jesus Christ from
    death to life,
resplendent in glory as King of creation.
Open our hearts,
free all the world to rejoice in his peace,
to glory in his justice, to live in his love.
Bring all mankind together in Jesus Christ
    your Son,
whose kingdom is with you and the Holy
    Spirit,
one God, for ever and ever. **Amen.**

FIRST READING

2 Sam 5:1-3

In those days, all the tribes of Israel came
    to David in Hebron and said:
  "Here we are, your bone and your flesh.
In days past, when Saul was our king,
  it was you who led the Israelites out and
    brought them back.
And the LORD said to you,
  'You shall shepherd my people Israel
  and shall be commander of Israel.'"
When all the elders of Israel came to
    David in Hebron,
  King David made an agreement with
    them there before the LORD,
  and they anointed him king of Israel.

RESPONSORIAL PSALM

Ps 122:1-2, 3-4, 4-5

R̶̸. (cf. 1) Let us go rejoicing to the house of
the Lord.

I rejoiced because they said to me,
  "We will go up to the house of the
    LORD."
And now we have set foot
  within your gates, O Jerusalem.

R̶̸. Let us go rejoicing to the house of the
Lord.

Jerusalem, built as a city
  with compact unity.
To it the tribes go up,
  the tribes of the LORD.

R̴. Let us go rejoicing to the house of the
Lord.

According to the decree for Israel,
  to give thanks to the name of the LORD.
In it are set up judgment seats,
  seats for the house of David.

R̴. Let us go rejoicing to the house of the
Lord.

SECOND READING
Col 1:12-20

Brothers and sisters:
Let us give thanks to the Father,
  who has made you fit to share
  in the inheritance of the holy ones in light.
He delivered us from the power of darkness
  and transferred us to the kingdom of
    his beloved Son,
  in whom we have redemption, the
    forgiveness of sins.
He is the image of the invisible God,
  the firstborn of all creation.
For in him were created all things in
    heaven and on earth,
  the visible and the invisible,
  whether thrones or dominions or
    principalities or powers;
  all things were created through him
    and for him.
He is before all things,
  and in him all things hold together.
He is the head of the body, the church.
He is the beginning, the firstborn from
    the dead,
  that in all things he himself might be
    preeminent.
For in him all the fullness was pleased
    to dwell,
  and through him to reconcile all
    things for him,
  making peace by the blood of his
    cross
  through him, whether those on earth
    or those in heaven.

About Liturgy

Discipleship and victory: For months now we have been traveling with Jesus through the proclamation of Luke's gospel. This festival of Christ the King is the last Sunday and culmination of the whole liturgical year. Next Sunday we begin Advent and thus begin again yet another paschal mystery journey through a liturgical year. This annual celebration reminds us that the difficulties of discipleship are always rewarded by the joy of victory. The cross leads to resurrection. As we embrace the cross in our own journey of discipleship each day we are spurred on to faithfulness by remembering that it all culminates in this victory.

Each year we begin and end the same journey. Why is not this cyclic pattern of our liturgical celebrations tedious? The answer lies in our taking the time to recognize our own growth in discipleship and our personal relationship with Jesus our King during this past year. Since judgment is one of the themes of the end times, it might be good to take some time this week to judge our own growth and preparedness to enter Paradise with Jesus. Without such self-reflection we run the risk of every liturgical year simply being like all others. Endings and beginnings always give us an opportunity to assess growth and recommit ourselves to faithful discipleship. True, the cross is not something we would naturally choose for ourselves. But the end of this liturgical year and the beginning of the new one when we encounter our victorious Christ is exactly what we need in order to be faithful to the disciple's life of self-sacrifice for the sake of others.

About Liturgical Music

Cantor preparation: In singing this responsorial psalm you invite the assembly to enter the kingdom of God. They have journeyed through all of Ordinary Time. They have struggled, they have been faithful. Bring them in with joy.

Liturgical music and growth in discipleship: The Solemnity of Christ the King is also a good time to assess how we have grown this past year in and through liturgical music. How through our music have we more clearly become the body of Christ given for the redemption of the world?

For assembly members: How have we grown in singing well together, that is, with willing heart and full voice? How have we grown in listening to each other as we sing, in becoming one body rather than individuals singing "our own thing"?

For cantors and choir members: How have we grown in focusing on Christ rather than making ourselves the "star" of the liturgy? How have we grown in treating each other as members of the one body of Christ? How have we grown in unselfishness because of the disciplines required for our ministry?

For music directors: How have we grown in our understanding of the role of music in liturgy? How have we stayed faithful to keeping liturgy central and music secondary and supporting? How have we grown through this ministry in our relationship with Christ and in our ability to see the assembly as body of Christ? How have we helped cantors and choir members grow in these ways?

NOVEMBER 21, 2004
THE SOLEMNITY OF OUR LORD
JESUS CHRIST THE KING

✠ SPIRITUALITY

Gospel

Luke 17:11-19; L947.6

As Jesus continued his journey to
　　Jerusalem,
　he traveled through Samaria and
　　Galilee.
As he was entering a village, ten
　　lepers met him.
They stood at a distance from
　　him and raised their
　　voices, saying,
　"Jesus, Master! Have pity on
　　us!"
And when he saw them, he said,
　"Go show yourselves to the
　　priests."
As they were going they were cleansed.
And one of them, realizing he had been
　　healed,
　returned, glorifying God in a loud
　　voice;
　and he fell at the feet of Jesus and
　　thanked him.
He was a Samaritan.
Jesus said in reply,
　"Ten were cleansed, were they not?
Where are the other nine?
Has none but this foreigner returned to
　　give thanks to God?"
Then he said to him, "Stand up and go;
　your faith has saved you."

See Appendix A, p. 289, for the following suggested readings; other readings may be selected from the Appendix to the Lectionary (for Thanksgiving Day).

FIRST READING
Sir 50:22-24; L943.2

RESPONSORIAL PSALM
Ps 113:1-2, 3-4, 5-6, 7-8; L945.2

SECOND READING
1 Cor 1:3-9; L944.1

Reflecting on the Gospel

This is an interesting day: even though it is a civic holiday it has a proper Mass in our U.S. Sacramentary. We have a strong sense that on a day when we celebrate the abundances of our country and its blessings we naturally want to turn to God. This holiday takes many of us back to our immigrant roots and the native Americans who helped our ancestors survive the difficult times of adjusting to this new land. Their grateful response to graciousness and hospitality came out of the religious ground that brought them to this new land in the first place. Deep down we were—and still are—a religious people. We have a natural sense that generosity can be properly repaid only by turning to the One who is all and gives all, just as the leper in the gospel returns to Jesus to give thanks. Our national holiday is, at root, our national holyday. Oh, how liturgical is this day!

Let us remember: Passover took place in the month when the kids and lambs were born. God sent manna and quail and water in the desert. The promised land was flowing with milk and honey. Jewish Pentecost included loaves of bread baked from the wheat of the new crop. Jewish *Sukkot* or feast of booths is an autumn festival celebrating the grape harvest. In fact, the origin of these three great Jewish pilgrimage feasts (so named because every Jewish male twelve years or older was obliged to make pilgrimage to Jerusalem for at least one of these feasts each year) of Passover, Pentecost, and Booths was agricultural.

Ah, and what happens because of the incarnation? We celebrate in our liturgy not only the fruit of the earth (food gifts for the poor have been part of the eucharistic offering from earliest times and are still always appropriate offerings along with the bread and wine) but also the Fruit of heaven—for now our humble gifts (the work of our hands and fruit of the earth) are transformed into the exalted Gift of God's own Son, given to us for our nourishment.

Eucharist and thanksgiving: This is an appropriate time of the year to give thanks for the fruit of the earth and all God's blessings: care, joy, peace (first reading); knowledge of Christ, God's keeping us firm, God's faithfulness, God's calling us to fellowship with Christ (second reading); healing, faith (gospel). This we can understand and take up as our grateful response to such a giving and gracious God. The Samaritan leper in the gospel reminds us, however, that the deepest expression of our thankfulness is worship and our most sublime act of worship is Eucharist. The whole celebration of Eucharist is an offering of praise and thanks to God for all God's gifts, especially for the Fruit of heaven, the Body and Blood of our Lord Jesus Christ.

Living the Paschal Mystery

Each celebration of Eucharist is a reminder that we don't wait until the fourth Thursday of November to give thanks to God for all God has given us, but the very life of Christians is one of putting on the habit of thankfulness. God forbid that Jesus would ever address to us, "Where are the other nine?" As we die to ourselves and come to new life in living daily the paschal mystery, we are brought to a stance of gratitude before our God. Even if our own personal circumstances don't seem to leave much room for thankfulness (hurt or broken relationships, economic hard times, etc.), today and every day we celebrate Eucharist. We are given plenty reason to give thanks: God has given us Jesus Christ and life in him!

Focusing the Word

Key words and phrases from the gospel: realizing, returned, glorified
God, thanked him

To the point: The civil observance of Thanksgiving Day calls us to gratitude
for such things as abundant crops, natural resources, and civil liberties. Our liturgical observance of this day calls us to recognize the origin of all our blessings. The healed leper's return to Jesus takes the act of thanksgiving to its
deepest expression—the worship of God.

Model Penitential Rite

Presider: No matter what our own personal circumstances are, we come together today to celebrate God's many blessings and gifts to us. Let us pause at
the beginning of this celebration of Eucharist and open our hearts in gratitude
to God for this most precious gift—that of Jesus' very word and Body and
Blood . . . [pause]

Lord Jesus, you are worthy of all glory and honor: Lord . . .

Christ Jesus, you receive our heartfelt thanksgiving: Christ . . .

Lord Jesus, you call us to communion with you: Lord . . .

Model General Intercessions

Presider: God has blessed us with abundance. We are confident that God will
hear our prayers and continue to bless us with all we need.

Response:

Lord, hear our prayer.

Cantor:

we pray to the Lord,

That all members of the Church raise grateful hearts always and everywhere
for God's abundant blessings . . . [pause]

That all peoples of the world share equitably in the abundant fruits of this
earth . . . [pause]

That the poor be raised up, the hungry be fed, and the persecuted be freed . . .
[pause]

That each of us share the gifts we have—whether small or great—with those
less fortunate as a sign of our gratitude to God for all the blessings bestowed
on us . . . [pause]

Presider: Gracious God, you give us abundant gifts and most especially your
own Son, Jesus Christ; hear these our prayers that all might share in your goodness and come to everlasting life. We ask this through that same Son, our Lord
Jesus Christ. **Amen.**

OPENING PRAYER

Let us pray
[that our gratitude to God may bear fruit in
    loving service to our fellow men and
    women]

Pause for silent prayer

Father all-powerful,
your gifts of love are countless
and your goodness is infinite.
On Thanksgiving Day we come before you
with gratitude for your kindness:
open our hearts to concern for our fellow
    men and women,
so that we may share your gifts in loving
    service.

We ask this through our Lord Jesus Christ,
    your Son,
who lives and reigns with you and the Holy
    Spirit,
one God, for ever and ever. **Amen.**

FOR REFLECTION

- The spiritual work of this holiday, like
  the Samaritan leper, is threefold: realizing,
  returning, and thanking. Of these three
  the one I do most naturally and regularly
  is . . .
  The one I often neglect is . . .

- What I am doing to foster a habit of
  thankfulness in myself is . . .

- Of the many gifts I have received, the ones
  that lead me to worship God are . . .

Readings *(continued)*

The Immaculate Conception of the Blessed Virgin Mary, *December 8, 2003*

FIRST READING
Gen 3:9-15, 20

After the man, Adam, had eaten of the tree,
    the LORD God called to the man and asked
       him, "Where are you?"
He answered, "I heard you in the garden;
    but I was afraid, because I was naked,
    so I hid myself."
Then he asked, "Who told you that you were
    naked?
You have eaten, then,
    from the tree of which I had forbidden you
      to eat!"
The man replied, "The woman whom you put
    here with me—
    she gave me fruit from the tree, and so I ate
    it."
The LORD God then asked the woman,
    "Why did you do such a thing?"
The woman answered, "The serpent tricked
    me into it, so I ate it."

Then the LORD God said to the serpent:
    "Because you have done this, you shall be
      banned
      from all the animals
      and from all the wild creatures;
    on your belly shall you crawl,
      and dirt shall you eat
      all the days of your life.
    I will put enmity between you and the
      woman,
      and between your offspring and hers;

he will strike at your head,
    while you strike at his heel."
The man called his wife Eve,
    because she became the mother of all the
    living.

RESPONSORIAL PSALM
Ps 98:1, 2-3, 3-4

R̸. (1a) Sing to the Lord a new song, for he
has done marvelous deeds.

Sing to the LORD a new song,
    for he has done wondrous deeds;
his right hand has won victory for him,
    his holy arm.

R̸. Sing to the Lord a new song, for he has
done marvelous deeds.

The LORD has made his salvation known:
    in the sight of the nations he has revealed
      his justice.
He has remembered his kindness and his
    faithfulness
    toward the house of Israel.

R̸. Sing to the Lord a new song, for he has
done marvelous deeds.

All the ends of the earth have seen
    the salvation by our God.
Sing joyfully to the LORD, all you lands;
    break into song; sing praise.

R̸. Sing to the Lord a new song, for he has
done marvelous deeds.

SECOND READING
Eph 1:3-6, 11-12

Brothers and sisters:
Blessed be the God and Father of our Lord
    Jesus Christ,
    who has blessed us in Christ
    with every spiritual blessing in the
      heavens,
    as he chose us in him, before the foundation
      of the world,
    to be holy and without blemish before him.
In love he destined us for adoption to himself
      through Jesus Christ,
    in accord with the favor of his will,
    for the praise of the glory of his grace
    that he granted us in the beloved.

In him we were also chosen,
    destined in accord with the purpose of the
      One
    who accomplishes all things according to
      the intention of his will,
    so that we might exist for the praise of his
      glory,
    we who first hoped in Christ.

Gospel (cont.)
Matt 1:1-25; L13ABC

After the Babylonian exile,
    Jechoniah became the father of Shealtiel,
    Shealtiel the father of Zerubbabel,
    Zerubbabel the father of Abiud.
Abiud became the father of Eliakim,
    Eliakim the father of Azor,
    Azor the father of Zadok.
Zadok became the father of Achim,
    Achim the father of Eliud,
    Eliud the father of Eleazar.
Eleazar became the father of Matthan,
    Matthan the father of Jacob,
    Jacob the father of Joseph, the husband of Mary.
Of her was born Jesus who is called the Christ.

Thus the total number of generations
    from Abraham to David
    is fourteen generations;
    from David to the Babylonian exile,
    fourteen generations;
    from the Babylonian exile to the Christ,
    fourteen generations.

Now this is how the birth of Jesus Christ came about.

When his mother Mary was betrothed to Joseph,
    but before they lived together,
    she was found with child through the Holy Spirit.
Joseph her husband, since he was a righteous man,
    yet unwilling to expose her to shame,
    decided to divorce her quietly.
Such was his intention when, behold,
    the angel of the Lord appeared to him in a dream and said,
    "Joseph, son of David,
    do not be afraid to take Mary your wife into your home.
For it is through the Holy Spirit
    that this child has been conceived in her.
She will bear a son and you are to name him Jesus,
    because he will save his people from their sins."
All this took place to fulfill
    what the Lord had said through the prophet:
        Behold, the virgin shall conceive and bear a son,
        and they shall name him Emmanuel,
    which means "God is with us."
When Joseph awoke,
    he did as the angel of the Lord had commanded him
    and took his wife into his home.
He had no relations with her until she bore a son,
    and he named him Jesus.

Solemnity of the Blessed Virgin Mary, Mother of God, *January 1, 2004*

FIRST READING
Num 6:22-27

The LORD said to Moses:
    "Speak to Aaron and his sons and tell
        them:
    This is how you shall bless the Israelites.
Say to them:
    The LORD bless you and keep you!
    The LORD let his face shine upon
        you, and be gracious to you!
    The LORD look upon you kindly and
        give you peace!
So shall they invoke my name upon the
        Israelites,
    and I will bless them."

RESPONSORIAL PSALM
Ps 67:2-3, 5, 6, 8

R̝. (2a) May God bless us in his mercy.

May God have pity on us and bless us;
    may he let his face shine upon us.
So may your way be known upon earth;
    among all nations, your salvation.

R̝. May God bless us in his mercy.

May the nations be glad and exult
    because you rule the peoples in equity;
    the nations on the earth you guide.

R̝. May God bless us in his mercy.

May the peoples praise you, O God;
    may all the peoples praise you!
May God bless us,
    and may all the ends of the earth fear him!

R̝. May God bless us in his mercy.

SECOND READING
Gal 4:4-7

Brothers and sisters:
When the fullness of time had come, God sent
    his Son,
    born of a woman, born under the law,
    to ransom those under the law,
    so that we might receive adoption as sons.
As proof that you are sons,
    God sent the Spirit of his Son into our
        hearts,
    crying out, "Abba, Father!"
So you are no longer a slave but a son,
    and if a son then also an heir, through God.

The Epiphany of the Lord, *January 4, 2004*

Gospel (cont.)
Matt 2:1-12; L20ABC

They prostrated themselves and did him homage.
Then they opened their treasures
   and offered him gifts of gold, frankincense, and myrrh.
And having been warned in a dream not to return to Herod,
   they departed for their country by another way.

The Baptism of the Lord, *January 11, 2004*

SECOND READING (cont.)
Titus 2:11-14; 3:4-7

When the kindness and generous love
   of God our savior appeared,
not because of any righteous deeds we had done
   but because of his mercy,
he saved us through the bath of rebirth
   and renewal by the Holy Spirit,
whom he richly poured out on us
   through Jesus Christ our savior,
so that we might be justified by his grace
   and become heirs in hope of eternal life.

Ash Wednesday, *February 25, 2004*

FIRST READING
Joel 2:12-18

Even now, says the LORD,
   return to me with your whole heart,
   with fasting, and weeping, and mourning;
Rend your hearts, not your garments,
   and return to the LORD, your God.
For gracious and merciful is he,
   slow to anger, rich in kindness,
   and relenting in punishment.
Perhaps he will again relent
   and leave behind him a blessing,
Offerings and libations
   for the LORD, your God.

Blow the trumpet in Zion!
   proclaim a fast,
   call an assembly;
Gather the people,
   notify the congregation;
Assemble the elders,
   gather the children
   and the infants at the breast;
Let the bridegroom quit his room
   and the bride her chamber.
Between the porch and the altar
   let the priests, the ministers of the LORD,
      weep,
And say, "Spare, O LORD, your people,
   and make not your heritage a reproach,
   with the nations ruling over them!
Why should they say among the peoples,
   'Where is their God?'"

Then the LORD was stirred to concern for his
      land
   and took pity on his people.

RESPONSORIAL PSALM
Ps 51:3-4, 5-6ab, 12-13, 14, 17

R℟. (see 3a) Be merciful, O Lord, for we have
sinned.

Have mercy on me, O God, in your goodness;
   in the greatness of your compassion wipe
      out my offense.
Thoroughly wash me from my guilt
   and of my sin cleanse me.

R℟. Be merciful, O Lord, for we have sinned.

For I acknowledge my offense,
   and my sin is before me always:
"Against you only have I sinned,
   and done what is evil in your sight."

R℟. Be merciful, O Lord, for we have sinned.

A clean heart create for me, O God,
   and a steadfast spirit renew within me.
Cast me not out from your presence,
   and your Holy Spirit take not from me.

R℟. Be merciful, O Lord, for we have sinned.

Give me back the joy of your salvation,
   and a willing spirit sustain in me.
O Lord, open my lips,
   and my mouth shall proclaim your praise.

R℟. Be merciful, O Lord, for we have sinned.

SECOND READING
2 Cor 5:20–6:2

Brothers and sisters:
We are ambassadors for Christ,
   as if God were appealing through us.
We implore you on behalf of Christ,
   be reconciled to God.
For our sake he made him to be sin who did
      not know sin,
   so that we might become the righteousness
      of God in him.

Working together, then,
   we appeal to you not to receive the grace of
      God in vain.
For he says:

   *In an acceptable time I heard you,
      and on the day of salvation I helped you.*

Behold, now is a very acceptable time;
   behold, now is the day of salvation.

First Sunday of Lent, *February 29, 2004*

SECOND READING
Rom 10:8-13

Brothers and sisters:
What does Scripture say?
The word is near you,
in your mouth and in your heart
—that is, the word of faith that we preach—,
for, if you confess with your mouth that Jesus is Lord
and believe in your heart that God raised him from the dead,
you will be saved.
For one believes with the heart and so is justified,
and one confesses with the mouth and so is saved.
For the Scripture says,
No one who believes in him will be put to shame.
For there is no distinction between Jew and Greek;
the same Lord is Lord of all,
enriching all who call upon him.
For "everyone who calls on the name of the Lord will be saved."

Third Sunday of Lent, *March 14, 2004*

SECOND READING
[1 Cor 10:1-6, 10-12]

I do not want you to be unaware, brothers and sisters,
that our ancestors were all under the cloud
and all passed through the sea,
and all of them were baptized into Moses
in the cloud and in the sea.
All ate the same spiritual food,
and all drank the same spiritual drink,
for they drank from a spiritual rock that followed them,
and the rock was the Christ.
Yet God was not pleased with most of them,
for they were struck down in the desert.

These things happened as examples for us,
so that we might not desire evil things, as they did.
Do not grumble as some of them did,
and suffered death by the destroyer.
These things happened to them as an example,
and they have been written down as a warning to us,
upon whom the end of the ages has come.
Therefore, whoever thinks he is standing secure
should take care not to fall.

St. Joseph, Husband of the Blessed Virgin Mary, *March 19, 2004*

FIRST READING
2 Sam 7:4-5a, 12-14a, 16

The Lord spoke to Nathan and said:
"Go, tell my servant David,
'When your time comes and you rest with
your ancestors,
I will raise up your heir after you, sprung
from your loins,
and I will make his kingdom firm.
It is he who shall build a house for my name.
And I will make his royal throne firm forever.
I will be a father to him,
and he shall be a son to me.
Your house and your kingdom shall endure
forever before me;
your throne shall stand firm forever.'"

RESPONSORIAL PSALM
Ps 89:2-3, 4-5, 27, 29

R̶. (37) The son of David will live forever.

The promises of the LORD I will sing forever,
through all generations my mouth will
proclaim your faithfulness,
for you have said, "My kindness is established
forever";
in heaven you have confirmed your
faithfulness.

R̶. The son of David will live forever.

"I have made a covenant with my chosen one;
I have sworn to David my servant:
forever will I confirm your posterity
and establish your throne for all
generations."

R̶. The son of David will live forever.

"He shall say of me, 'You are my father,
my God, the Rock my savior!'
Forever I will maintain my kindness toward
him,
my covenant with him stands firm."

R̶. The son of David will live forever.

SECOND READING
Rom 4:13, 16-18, 22

Brothers and sisters:
It was not through the law
that the promise was made to Abraham
and his descendants
that he would inherit the world,
but through the righteousness that comes
from faith.
For this reason, it depends on faith,
so that it may be a gift,
and the promise may be guaranteed to all
his descendants,
not to those who only adhere to the law
but to those who follow the faith of
Abraham,
who is the father of all of us, as it is
written,
I have made you father of many nations.
He is our father in the sight of God,
in whom he believed, who gives life to the
dead
and calls into being what does not exist.
He believed, hoping against hope,
that he would become "the father of many
nations,"
according to what was said, "Thus shall
your descendants be."

That is why "it was credited to him as
righteousness."

Gospel (cont.)
Luke 15:1-3, 11-32; L33C

So he got up and went back to his father.
While he was still a long way off,
  his father caught sight of him, and was filled with compassion.
He ran to his son, embraced him and kissed him.
His son said to him,
  'Father, I have sinned against heaven and against you;
  I no longer deserve to be called your son.'
But his father ordered his servants,
  'Quickly bring the finest robe and put it on him;
  put a ring on his finger and sandals on his feet.
Take the fattened calf and slaughter it.
Then let us celebrate with a feast,
  because this son of mine was dead, and has come to life again;
  he was lost, and has been found.'
Then the celebration began.
Now the older son had been out in the field
  and, on his way back, as he neared the house,
  he heard the sound of music and dancing.
He called one of the servants and asked what this might mean.

The servant said to him,
  'Your brother has returned
  and your father has slaughtered the fattened calf
  because he has him back safe and sound.'
He became angry,
  and when he refused to enter the house,
  his father came out and pleaded with him.
He said to his father in reply,
  'Look, all these years I served you
  and not once did I disobey your orders;
  yet you never gave me even a young goat to feast on with my friends.
But when your son returns
  who swallowed up your property with prostitutes,
  for him you slaughter the fattened calf.'
He said to him,
  'My son, you are here with me always;
  everything I have is yours.
But now we must celebrate and rejoice,
  because your brother was dead and has come to life again;
  he was lost and has been found.'"

The Annunciation of the Lord, *March 25, 2004*

FIRST READING
Isa 7:10-14; 8:10

The LORD spoke to Ahaz, saying:
  Ask for a sign from the LORD, your God;
  let it be deep as the netherworld, or high as
    the sky!
But Ahaz answered,
  "I will not ask! I will not tempt the LORD!"
Then Isaiah said:
  Listen, O house of David!
Is it not enough for you to weary people,
  must you also weary my God?
Therefore the Lord himself will give you this
    sign:
  the virgin shall conceive, and bear a son,
  and shall name him Emmanuel,
  which means "God is with us!"

RESPONSORIAL PSALM
Ps 40:7-8, 8-9, 10, 11

R⁄. (8a and 9a) Here am I, Lord; I come to do
your will.

Sacrifice or offering you wished not,
  but ears open to obedience you gave me.
Holocausts and sin-offerings you sought not;
  then said I, "Behold, I come";

R⁄. Here am I, Lord; I come to do your will.

"In the written scroll it is prescribed for me.
To do your will, O God, is my delight,
  and your law is within my heart!"

R⁄. Here am I, Lord; I come to do your will.

I announced your justice in the vast assembly;
  I did not restrain my lips, as you, O LORD,
    know.

R⁄. Here am I, Lord; I come to do your will.

Your justice I kept not hid within my heart;
  your faithfulness and your salvation I have
    spoken of;
I have made no secret of your kindness and
    your truth
  in the vast assembly.

R⁄. Here am I, Lord; I come to do your will.

SECOND READING
Heb 10:4-10

Brothers and sisters:
It is impossible that the blood of bulls and
    goats
  takes away sins.
For this reason, when Christ came into the
    world, he said:
  "Sacrifice and offering you did not desire,
  but a body you prepared for me;
  in holocausts and sin offerings you took no
    delight.
  Then I said, 'As is written of me in the scroll,
  behold, I come to do your will, O God.'"

First Christ says, "Sacrifices and offerings,
  holocausts and sin offerings,
  you neither desired nor delighted in."
These are offered according to the law.
Then he says, "Behold, I come to do your will."
He takes away the first to establish the
  second.
By this "will," we have been consecrated
  through the offering of the body of Jesus
    Christ once for all.

Gospel at Mass
Luke 22:14–23:56; L38C

When the hour came,
  Jesus took his place at table with the apostles.
He said to them,
  "I have eagerly desired to eat this Passover with you before I suffer,
  for, I tell you, I shall not eat it again
  until there is fulfillment in the kingdom of God."
Then he took a cup, gave thanks, and said,
  "Take this and share it among yourselves;
  for I tell you that from this time on
  I shall not drink of the fruit of the vine
  until the kingdom of God comes."
Then he took the bread, said the blessing,
  broke it, and gave it to them, saying,
  "This is my body, which will be given for you;
  do this in memory of me."
And likewise the cup after they had eaten, saying,
  "This cup is the new covenant in my blood,
  which will be shed for you.

"And yet behold, the hand of the one who is to betray me
  is with me on the table;
  for the Son of Man indeed goes as it has been determined;
  but woe to that man by whom he is betrayed."
And they began to debate among themselves
  who among them would do such a deed.

Then an argument broke out among them
  about which of them should be regarded as the greatest.
He said to them,
  "The kings of the Gentiles lord it over them
  and those in authority over them are addressed as 'Benefactors';
  but among you it shall not be so.
Rather, let the greatest among you be as the youngest,
  and the leader as the servant.
For who is greater:
  the one seated at table or the one who serves?
Is it not the one seated at table?
I am among you as the one who serves.
It is you who have stood by me in my trials;
  and I confer a kingdom on you,
  just as my Father has conferred one on me,
  that you may eat and drink at my table in my kingdom;
  and you will sit on thrones
  judging the twelve tribes of Israel.

"Simon, Simon, behold Satan has demanded
  to sift all of you like wheat,
  but I have prayed that your own faith may not fail;
  and once you have turned back,
  you must strengthen your brothers."
He said to him,
  "Lord, I am prepared to go to prison and to die with you."
But he replied,
  "I tell you, Peter, before the cock crows this day,
  you will deny three times that you know me."

He said to them,
  "When I sent you forth without a money bag or a sack or sandals,
  were you in need of anything?"
"No, nothing," they replied.

He said to them,
  "But now one who has a money bag should take it,
  and likewise a sack,
  and one who does not have a sword
  should sell his cloak and buy one.
For I tell you that this Scripture must be fulfilled in me,
  namely, *He was counted among the wicked;*
  and indeed what is written about me is coming to fulfillment."
Then they said,
  "Lord, look, there are two swords here."
But he replied, "It is enough!"

Then going out, he went, as was his custom, to the Mount of Olives,
  and the disciples followed him.
When he arrived at the place he said to them,
  "Pray that you may not undergo the test."
After withdrawing about a stone's throw from them and kneeling,
  he prayed, saying, "Father, if you are willing,
  take this cup away from me;
  still, not my will but yours be done."
And to strengthen him an angel from heaven appeared to him.
He was in such agony and he prayed so fervently
  that his sweat became like drops of blood
  falling on the ground.
When he rose from prayer and returned to his disciples,
  he found them sleeping from grief.
He said to them, "Why are you sleeping?
Get up and pray that you may not undergo the test."

While he was still speaking, a crowd approached
  and in front was one of the Twelve, a man named Judas.
He went up to Jesus to kiss him.
Jesus said to him,
  "Judas, are you betraying the Son of Man with a kiss?"
His disciples realized what was about to happen, and they asked,
  "Lord, shall we strike with a sword?"
And one of them struck the high priest's servant
  and cut off his right ear.
But Jesus said in reply,
  "Stop, no more of this!"
Then he touched the servant's ear and healed him.
And Jesus said to the chief priests and temple guards
  and elders who had come for him,
  "Have you come out as against a robber, with swords and clubs?
Day after day I was with you in the temple area,
  and you did not seize me;
  but this is your hour, the time for the power of darkness."

After arresting him they led him away
  and took him into the house of the high priest;
  Peter was following at a distance.
They lit a fire in the middle of the courtyard and sat around it,
  and Peter sat down with them.
When a maid saw him seated in the light,
  she looked intently at him and said,
  "This man too was with him."
But he denied it saying,
  "Woman, I do not know him."
A short while later someone else saw him and said,
  "You too are one of them";
  but Peter answered, "My friend, I am not."

About an hour later, still another insisted,
   "Assuredly, this man too was with him,
   for he also is a Galilean."
But Peter said,
   "My friend, I do not know what you are talking about."
Just as he was saying this, the cock crowed,
   and the Lord turned and looked at Peter;
   and Peter remembered the word of the Lord,
   how he had said to him,
   "Before the cock crows today, you will deny me three times."
He went out and began to weep bitterly.
The men who held Jesus in custody were ridiculing and beating him.
They blindfolded him and questioned him, saying,
   "Prophesy! Who is it that struck you?"
And they reviled him in saying many other things against him.

When day came the council of elders of the people met,
   both chief priests and scribes,
   and they brought him before their Sanhedrin.
They said, "If you are the Christ, tell us,"
   but he replied to them, "If I tell you, you will not believe,
   and if I question, you will not respond.
But from this time on the Son of Man will be seated
   at the right hand of the power of God."
They all asked, "Are you then the Son of God?"
He replied to them, "You say that I am."
Then they said, "What further need have we for testimony?
We have heard it from his own mouth."

Then the whole assembly of them arose and brought him before Pilate.
They brought charges against him, saying,
   "We found this man misleading our people;
   he opposes the payment of taxes to Caesar
   and maintains that he is the Christ, a king."
Pilate asked him, "Are you the king of the Jews?"
He said to him in reply, "You say so."
Pilate then addressed the chief priests and the crowds,
   "I find this man not guilty."
But they were adamant and said,
   "He is inciting the people with his teaching
      throughout all Judea,
   from Galilee where he began even to here."

On hearing this Pilate asked if the man was a Galilean;
   and upon learning that he was under Herod's jurisdiction,
   he sent him to Herod who was in Jerusalem at that time.
Herod was very glad to see Jesus;
   he had been wanting to see him for a long time,
   for he had heard about him
   and had been hoping to see him perform some sign.
He questioned him at length,
   but he gave him no answer.
The chief priests and scribes, meanwhile,
   stood by accusing him harshly.
Herod and his soldiers treated him contemptuously and mocked him,
   and after clothing him in resplendent garb,
   he sent him back to Pilate.
Herod and Pilate became friends that very day,
   even though they had been enemies formerly.
Pilate then summoned the chief priests, the rulers, and the people
   and said to them, "You brought this man to me
   and accused him of inciting the people to revolt.

I have conducted my investigation in your presence
   and have not found this man guilty
   of the charges you have brought against him,
   nor did Herod, for he sent him back to us.
So no capital crime has been committed by him.
Therefore I shall have him flogged and then release him."

But all together they shouted out,
   "Away with this man!
   Release Barabbas to us."
—Now Barabbas had been imprisoned for a rebellion
   that had taken place in the city and for murder.—
Again Pilate addressed them, still wishing to release Jesus,
   but they continued their shouting,
   "Crucify him! Crucify him!"
Pilate addressed them a third time,
   "What evil has this man done?
   I found him guilty of no capital crime.
Therefore I shall have him flogged and then release him."
With loud shouts, however,
   they persisted in calling for his crucifixion,
   and their voices prevailed.
The verdict of Pilate was that their demand should be granted.
So he released the man who had been imprisoned
   for rebellion and murder, for whom they asked,
   and he handed Jesus over to them to deal with as they wished.

As they led him away
   they took hold of a certain Simon, a Cyrenian,
   who was coming in from the country;
   and after laying the cross on him,
   they made him carry it behind Jesus.
A large crowd of people followed Jesus,
   including many women who mourned and lamented him.
Jesus turned to them and said,
   "Daughters of Jerusalem, do not weep for me;
   weep instead for yourselves and for your children
   for indeed, the days are coming when people will say,
   'Blessed are the barren,
   the wombs that never bore
   and the breasts that never nursed.'
At that time people will say to the mountains,
   'Fall upon us!'
   and to the hills, 'Cover us!'
   for if these things are done when the wood is green
   what will happen when it is dry?"
Now two others, both criminals,
   were led away with him to be executed.

When they came to the place called the Skull,
   they crucified him and the criminals there,
   one on his right, the other on his left.
Then Jesus said,
   "Father, forgive them, they know not what they do."
They divided his garments by casting lots.
The people stood by and watched;
   the rulers, meanwhile, sneered at him and said,
   "He saved others, let him save himself
   if he is the chosen one, the Christ of God."
Even the soldiers jeered at him.
As they approached to offer him wine they called out,
   "If you are King of the Jews, save yourself."

Above him there was an inscription that read,
  "This is the King of the Jews."

Now one of the criminals hanging there reviled Jesus, saying,
  "Are you not the Christ?
  Save yourself and us."
The other, however, rebuking him, said in reply,
  "Have you no fear of God,
  for you are subject to the same condemnation?
And indeed, we have been condemned justly,
  for the sentence we received corresponds to our crimes,
  but this man has done nothing criminal."
Then he said,
  "Jesus, remember me when you come into your kingdom."
He replied to him,
  "Amen, I say to you,
  today you will be with me in Paradise."

It was now about noon and darkness came over the whole land
  until three in the afternoon
  because of an eclipse of the sun.
Then the veil of the temple was torn down the middle.
Jesus cried out in a loud voice,
  "Father, into your hands I commend my spirit";
  and when he had said this he breathed his last.

Here all kneel and pause for a short time.

The centurion who witnessed what had happened glorified God and said,
  "This man was innocent beyond doubt."
When all the people who had gathered for this spectacle
    saw what had happened,
  they returned home beating their breasts;
  but all his acquaintances stood at a distance,
  including the women who had followed him from Galilee
  and saw these events.

Now there was a virtuous and righteous man named Joseph who,
  though he was a member of the council,
  had not consented to their plan of action.
He came from the Jewish town of Arimathea
  and was awaiting the kingdom of God.
He went to Pilate and asked for the body of Jesus.
After he had taken the body down,
  he wrapped it in a linen cloth
  and laid him in a rock-hewn tomb
  in which no one had yet been buried.
It was the day of preparation,
  and the sabbath was about to begin.
The women who had come from Galilee with him followed behind,
  and when they had seen the tomb
  and the way in which his body was laid in it,
  they returned and prepared spices and perfumed oils.
Then they rested on the sabbath according to the commandment.

Gospel (cont.)

John 13:1-15

So when he had washed their feet
and put his garments back on and reclined at table again,
he said to them, "Do you realize what I have done for you?
You call me 'teacher' and 'master,' and rightly so, for indeed I am.
If I, therefore, the master and teacher, have washed your feet,
you ought to wash one another's feet.
I have given you a model to follow,
so that as I have done for you, you should also do."

FIRST READING

Exod 12:1-8, 11-14

The LORD said to Moses and Aaron in the
land of Egypt,
"This month shall stand at the head of
your calendar;
you shall reckon it the first month of the
year.
Tell the whole community of Israel:
On the tenth of this month every one of
your families
must procure for itself a lamb, one apiece
for each household.
If a family is too small for a whole lamb,
it shall join the nearest household in
procuring one
and shall share in the lamb
in proportion to the number of persons
who partake of it.
The lamb must be a year-old male and
without blemish.
You may take it from either the sheep or the
goats.
You shall keep it until the fourteenth day of
this month,
and then, with the whole assembly of Israel
present,
it shall be slaughtered during the evening
twilight.
They shall take some of its blood
and apply it to the two doorposts and the
lintel
of every house in which they partake of
the lamb.
That same night they shall eat its roasted
flesh
with unleavened bread and bitter herbs.

"This is how you are to eat it:
with your loins girt, sandals on your feet
and your staff in hand,
you shall eat like those who are in flight.
It is the Passover of the LORD.
For on this same night I will go through Egypt,
striking down every firstborn of the land,
both man and beast,
and executing judgment on all the gods of
Egypt—I, the LORD!
But the blood will mark the houses where you
are.
Seeing the blood, I will pass over you;
thus, when I strike the land of Egypt,
no destructive blow will come upon you.

"This day shall be a memorial feast for you,
which all your generations shall celebrate
with pilgrimage to the LORD, as a perpetual
institution."

RESPONSORIAL PSALM

Ps 116:12-13, 15-16bc, 17-18

R̶̸. (cf. 1 Corinthians 10:16) Our blessing-cup
is a communion with the Blood of Christ.

How shall I make a return to the LORD
for all the good he has done for me?
The cup of salvation I will take up,
and I will call upon the name of the LORD.

R̶̸. Our blessing-cup is a communion with the
Blood of Christ.

Precious in the eyes of the LORD
is the death of his faithful ones.
I am your servant, the son of your handmaid;
you have loosed my bonds.

R̶̸. Our blessing-cup is a communion with the
Blood of Christ.

To you will I offer sacrifice of thanksgiving,
and I will call upon the name of the LORD.
My vows to the LORD I will pay
in the presence of all his people.

R̶̸. Our blessing-cup is a communion with the
Blood of Christ.

SECOND READING

1 Cor 11:23-26

Brothers and sisters:
I received from the Lord what I also handed
on to you,
that the Lord Jesus, on the night he was
handed over,
took bread, and, after he had given thanks,
broke it and said, "This is my body that is
for you.
Do this in remembrance of me."
In the same way also the cup, after supper,
saying,
"This cup is the new covenant in my blood.
Do this, as often as you drink it, in
remembrance of me."
For as often as you eat this bread and drink
the cup,
you proclaim the death of the Lord until he
comes.

Gospel (cont.)
John 18:1–19:42

So the band of soldiers, the tribune, and the Jewish guards seized Jesus,
    bound him, and brought him to Annas first.
He was the father-in-law of Caiaphas,
    who was high priest that year.
It was Caiaphas who had counseled the Jews
    that it was better that one man should die rather than the people.

Simon Peter and another disciple followed Jesus.
Now the other disciple was known to the high priest,
    and he entered the courtyard of the high priest with Jesus.
But Peter stood at the gate outside.
So the other disciple, the acquaintance of the high priest,
    went out and spoke to the gatekeeper and brought Peter in.
Then the maid who was the gatekeeper said to Peter,
    "You are not one of this man's disciples, are you?"
He said, "I am not."
Now the slaves and the guards were standing around a charcoal fire
    that they had made, because it was cold,
    and were warming themselves.
Peter was also standing there keeping warm.

The high priest questioned Jesus
    about his disciples and about his doctrine.
Jesus answered him,
    "I have spoken publicly to the world.
I have always taught in a synagogue
    or in the temple area where all the Jews gather,
    and in secret I have said nothing. Why ask me?
Ask those who heard me what I said to them.
They know what I said."
When he had said this,
    one of the temple guards standing there struck Jesus and said,
    "Is this the way you answer the high priest?"
Jesus answered him,
    "If I have spoken wrongly, testify to the wrong;
    but if I have spoken rightly, why do you strike me?"
Then Annas sent him bound to Caiaphas the high priest.

Now Simon Peter was standing there keeping warm.
And they said to him,
    "You are not one of his disciples, are you?"
He denied it and said,
    "I am not."
One of the slaves of the high priest,
    a relative of the one whose ear Peter had cut off, said,
    "Didn't I see you in the garden with him?"
Again Peter denied it.
And immediately the cock crowed.

Then they brought Jesus from Caiaphas to the praetorium.
It was morning.
And they themselves did not enter the praetorium,
    in order not to be defiled so that they could eat the Passover.
So Pilate came out to them and said,
    "What charge do you bring against this man?"
They answered and said to him,
    "If he were not a criminal,
    we would not have handed him over to you."
At this, Pilate said to them,
    "Take him yourselves, and judge him according to your law."

The Jews answered him,
    "We do not have the right to execute anyone,"
    in order that the word of Jesus might be fulfilled
    that he said indicating the kind of death he would die.
So Pilate went back into the praetorium
    and summoned Jesus and said to him,
    "Are you the King of the Jews?"
Jesus answered,
    "Do you say this on your own
    or have others told you about me?"
Pilate answered,
    "I am not a Jew, am I?
Your own nation and the chief priests handed you over to me.
What have you done?"
Jesus answered,
    "My kingdom does not belong to this world.
If my kingdom did belong to this world,
    my attendants would be fighting
    to keep me from being handed over to the Jews.
But as it is, my kingdom is not here."
So Pilate said to him,
    "Then you are a king?"
Jesus answered,
    "You say I am a king.
For this I was born and for this I came into the world,
    to testify to the truth.
Everyone who belongs to the truth listens to my voice."
Pilate said to him, "What is truth?"

When he had said this,
    he again went out to the Jews and said to them,
    "I find no guilt in him.
But you have a custom that I release one prisoner to you at Passover.
Do you want me to release to you the King of the Jews?"
They cried out again,
    "Not this one but Barabbas!"
Now Barabbas was a revolutionary.

Then Pilate took Jesus and had him scourged.
And the soldiers wove a crown out of thorns and placed it on his head,
    and clothed him in a purple cloak,
    and they came to him and said,
    "Hail, King of the Jews!"
And they struck him repeatedly.
Once more Pilate went out and said to them,
    "Look, I am bringing him out to you,
    so that you may know that I find no guilt in him."
So Jesus came out,
    wearing the crown of thorns and the purple cloak.
And he said to them, "Behold, the man!"
When the chief priests and the guards saw him they cried out,
    "Crucify him, crucify him!"
Pilate said to them,
    "Take him yourselves and crucify him.
I find no guilt in him."
The Jews answered,
    "We have a law, and according to that law he ought to die,
    because he made himself the Son of God."

Now when Pilate heard this statement,
he became even more afraid,
and went back into the praetorium and said to Jesus,
"Where are you from?"
Jesus did not answer him.
So Pilate said to him,
"Do you not speak to me?
Do you not know that I have power to release you
and I have power to crucify you?"
Jesus answered him,
"You would have no power over me
if it had not been given to you from above.
For this reason the one who handed me over to you
has the greater sin."
Consequently, Pilate tried to release him; but the Jews cried out,
"If you release him, you are not a Friend of Caesar.
Everyone who makes himself a king opposes Caesar."

When Pilate heard these words he brought Jesus out
and seated him on the judge's bench
in the place called Stone Pavement, in Hebrew, Gabbatha.
It was preparation day for Passover, and it was about noon.
And he said to the Jews,
"Behold, your king!"
They cried out,
"Take him away, take him away! Crucify him!"
Pilate said to them,
"Shall I crucify your king?"
The chief priests answered,
"We have no king but Caesar."
Then he handed him over to them to be crucified.
So they took Jesus, and, carrying the cross himself,
he went out to what is called the Place of the Skull,
in Hebrew, Golgotha.
There they crucified him, and with him two others,
one on either side, with Jesus in the middle.
Pilate also had an inscription written and put on the cross.
It read,
"Jesus the Nazarene, the King of the Jews."
Now many of the Jews read this inscription,
because the place where Jesus was crucified was near the city;
and it was written in Hebrew, Latin, and Greek.
So the chief priests of the Jews said to Pilate,
"Do not write 'The King of the Jews,'
but that he said, 'I am the King of the Jews.'"
Pilate answered,
"What I have written, I have written."

When the soldiers had crucified Jesus,
they took his clothes and divided them into four shares,
a share for each soldier.
They also took his tunic, but the tunic was seamless,
woven in one piece from the top down.
So they said to one another,
"Let's not tear it, but cast lots for it to see whose it will be,"
in order that the passage of Scripture might be fulfilled that says:
They divided my garments among them,
and for my vesture they cast lots.

This is what the soldiers did.
Standing by the cross of Jesus were his mother
and his mother's sister, Mary the wife of Clopas,
and Mary of Magdala.
When Jesus saw his mother and the disciple there whom he loved
he said to his mother, "Woman, behold, your son."
Then he said to the disciple,
"Behold, your mother."
And from that hour the disciple took her into his home.

After this, aware that everything was now finished,
in order that the Scripture might be fulfilled,
Jesus said, "I thirst."
There was a vessel filled with common wine.
So they put a sponge soaked in wine on a sprig of hyssop
and put it up to his mouth.
When Jesus had taken the wine, he said,
"It is finished."
And bowing his head, he handed over the spirit.

Here all kneel and pause for a short time.

Now since it was preparation day,
in order that the bodies might not remain
on the cross on the sabbath,
for the sabbath day of that week was a solemn one,
the Jews asked Pilate that their legs be broken
and that they be taken down.
So the soldiers came and broke the legs of the first
and then of the other one who was crucified with Jesus.
But when they came to Jesus and saw that he was already dead,
they did not break his legs,
but one soldier thrust his lance into his side,
and immediately blood and water flowed out.
An eyewitness has testified, and his testimony is true;
he knows that he is speaking the truth,
so that you also may come to believe.
For this happened so that the Scripture passage might be fulfilled:
Not a bone of it will be broken.
And again another passage says:
They will look upon him whom they have pierced.

After this, Joseph of Arimathea,
secretly a disciple of Jesus for fear of the Jews,
asked Pilate if he could remove the body of Jesus.
And Pilate permitted it.
So he came and took his body.
Nicodemus, the one who had first come to him at night,
also came bringing a mixture of myrrh and aloes
weighing about one hundred pounds.
They took the body of Jesus
and bound it with burial cloths along with the spices,
according to the Jewish burial custom.
Now in the place where he had been crucified there was a garden,
and in the garden a new tomb, in which no one had yet been
buried.
So they laid Jesus there because of the Jewish preparation day;
for the tomb was close by.

FIRST READING

Isa 52:13–53:12

See, my servant shall prosper,
   he shall be raised high and greatly exalted.
Even as many were amazed at him—
   so marred was his look beyond human
      semblance
   and his appearance beyond that of the sons
      of man—
so shall he startle many nations,
   because of him kings shall stand speechless;
for those who have not been told shall see,
   those who have not heard shall ponder it.

Who would believe what we have heard?
   To whom has the arm of the Lord been
      revealed?
He grew up like a sapling before him,
   like a shoot from the parched earth;
there was in him no stately bearing to make
      us look at him,
   nor appearance that would attract us to him.
He was spurned and avoided by people,
   a man of suffering, accustomed to infirmity,
one of those from whom people hide their faces,
   spurned, and we held him in no esteem.

Yet it was our infirmities that he bore,
   our sufferings that he endured,
while we thought of him as stricken,
   as one smitten by God and afflicted.
But he was pierced for our offenses,
   crushed for our sins;
upon him was the chastisement that makes us
      whole,
   by his stripes we were healed.
We had all gone astray like sheep,
   each following his own way;
but the Lord laid upon him
   the guilt of us all.

Though he was harshly treated, he submitted
   and opened not his mouth;
like a lamb led to the slaughter
   or a sheep before the shearers,
   he was silent and opened not his mouth.
Oppressed and condemned, he was taken away,
   and who would have thought any more of
      his destiny?
When he was cut off from the land of the living,
   and smitten for the sin of his people,
a grave was assigned him among the wicked
   and a burial place with evildoers,
though he had done no wrong
   nor spoken any falsehood.
But the Lord was pleased
   to crush him in infirmity.

If he gives his life as an offering for sin,
   he shall see his descendants in a long life,
   and the will of the Lord shall be
      accomplished through him.

Because of his affliction
   he shall see the light
      in fullness of days;
through his suffering, my servant shall justify
      many,
   and their guilt he shall bear.
Therefore I will give him his portion among
      the great,
   and he shall divide the spoils with the
      mighty,
because he surrendered himself to death
   and was counted among the wicked;
and he shall take away the sins of many,
   and win pardon for their offenses.

RESPONSORIAL PSALM

Ps 31:2, 6, 12-13, 15-16, 17, 25

R. (Luke 23:46) Father, into your hands I
commend my spirit.

In you, O Lord, I take refuge;
   let me never be put to shame.
In your justice rescue me.
   Into your hands I commend my spirit;
you will redeem me, O Lord, O faithful God.

R. Father, into your hands I commend my
spirit.

For all my foes I am an object of reproach,
   a laughingstock to my neighbors, and a
      dread to my friends;
   they who see me abroad flee from me.
I am forgotten like the unremembered dead;
   I am like a dish that is broken.

R. Father, into your hands I commend my
spirit.

But my trust is in you, O Lord;
   I say, "You are my God.
In your hands is my destiny; rescue me
   from the clutches of my enemies and my
      persecutors."

R. Father, into your hands I commend my
spirit.

Let your face shine upon your servant;
   save me in your kindness.
Take courage and be stouthearted,
   all you who hope in the Lord.

R. Father, into your hands I commend my
spirit.

SECOND READING

Heb 4:14-16; 5:7-9

Brothers and sisters:
Since we have a great high priest who has
      passed through the heavens,
   Jesus, the Son of God,
   let us hold fast to our confession.
For we do not have a high priest
   who is unable to sympathize with our
      weaknesses,
   but one who has similarly been tested in
      every way,
   yet without sin.
So let us confidently approach the throne of
      grace
   to receive mercy and to find grace for
      timely help.

In the days when Christ was in the flesh,
   he offered prayers and supplications with
      loud cries and tears
   to the one who was able to save him from
      death,
   and he was heard because of his reverence.
Son though he was, he learned obedience
      from what he suffered;
   and when he was made perfect,
   he became the source of eternal salvation
      for all who obey him.

FIRST READING
Gen 1:1–2:2

In the beginning, when God created the
heavens and the earth,
the earth was a formless wasteland, and
darkness covered the abyss,
while a mighty wind swept over the waters.

Then God said,
"Let there be light," and there was light.
God saw how good the light was.
God then separated the light from the darkness.
God called the light "day," and the darkness
he called "night."
Thus evening came, and morning followed—
the first day.

Then God said,
"Let there be a dome in the middle of the
waters,
to separate one body of water from the
other."
And so it happened:
God made the dome,
and it separated the water above the dome
from the water below it.
God called the dome "the sky."
Evening came, and morning followed—the
second day.

Then God said,
"Let the water under the sky be gathered
into a single basin,
so that the dry land may appear."
And so it happened:
the water under the sky was gathered into
its basin,
and the dry land appeared.
God called the dry land "the earth,"
and the basin of the water he called "the
sea."
God saw how good it was.
Then God said,
"Let the earth bring forth vegetation:
every kind of plant that bears seed
and every kind of fruit tree on earth
that bears fruit with its seed in it."
And so it happened:
the earth brought forth every kind of plant
that bears seed
and every kind of fruit tree on earth
that bears fruit with its seed in it.
God saw how good it was.
Evening came, and morning followed—the
third day.

Then God said:
"Let there be lights in the dome of the sky,
to separate day from night.
Let them mark the fixed times, the days and
the years,

and serve as luminaries in the dome of the
sky,
to shed light upon the earth."
And so it happened:
God made the two great lights,
the greater one to govern the day,
and the lesser one to govern the night;
and he made the stars.
God set them in the dome of the sky,
to shed light upon the earth,
to govern the day and the night,
and to separate the light from the darkness.
God saw how good it was.
Evening came, and morning followed—the
fourth day.

Then God said,
"Let the water teem with an abundance of
living creatures,
and on the earth let birds fly beneath the
dome of the sky."
And so it happened:
God created the great sea monsters
and all kinds of swimming creatures with
which the water teems,
and all kinds of winged birds.
God saw how good it was, and God blessed
them, saying,
"Be fertile, multiply, and fill the water of
the seas;
and let the birds multiply on the earth."
Evening came, and morning followed—the
fifth day.

Then God said,
"Let the earth bring forth all kinds of
living creatures:
cattle, creeping things, and wild animals of
all kinds."
And so it happened:
God made all kinds of wild animals, all
kinds of cattle,
and all kinds of creeping things of the earth.
God saw how good it was.
Then God said:
"Let us make man in our image, after our
likeness.
Let them have dominion over the fish of the sea,
the birds of the air, and the cattle,
and over all the wild animals
and all the creatures that crawl on the
ground."
God created man in his image;
in the image of God he created him;
male and female he created them.
God blessed them, saying:
"Be fertile and multiply;
fill the earth and subdue it.
Have dominion over the fish of the sea, the
birds of the air,

and all the living things that move on the
earth."
God also said:
"See, I give you every seed-bearing plant all
over the earth
and every tree that has seed-bearing fruit
on it to be your food;
and to all the animals of the land, all the
birds of the air,
and all the living creatures that crawl on
the ground,
I give all the green plants for food."
And so it happened.
God looked at everything he had made, and
he found it very good.
Evening came, and morning followed—the
sixth day.

Thus the heavens and the earth and all their
array were completed.
Since on the seventh day God was finished
with the work he had been doing,
he rested on the seventh day from all the
work he had undertaken.

or

Gen 1:1, 26-31a

In the beginning, when God created the
heavens and the earth,
God said: "Let us make man in our image,
after our likeness.
Let them have dominion over the fish of the sea,
the birds of the air, and the cattle,
and over all the wild animals
and all the creatures that crawl on the
ground.
God created man in his image;
in the image of God he created him;
male and female he created them.
God blessed them, saying:
"Be fertile and multiply;
fill the earth and subdue it.
Have dominion over the fish of the sea, the
birds of the air,
and all the living things that move on the
earth."
God also said:
"See, I give you every seed-bearing plant all
over the earth
and every tree that has seed-bearing fruit
on it to be your food;
and to all the animals of the land, all the
birds of the air,
and all the living creatures that crawl on
the ground,
I give all the green plants for food."
And so it happened.
God looked at everything he had made, and
found it very good.

RESPONSORIAL PSALM

Ps 104:1-2, 5-6, 10, 12, 13-14, 24, 35

R̞. (30) Lord, send out your Spirit, and renew the face of the earth.

Bless the LORD, O my soul!
  O LORD, my God, you are great indeed!
You are clothed with majesty and glory,
  robed in light as with a cloak.

R̞. Lord, send out your Spirit, and renew the face of the earth.

You fixed the earth upon its foundation,
  not to be moved forever;
with the ocean, as with a garment, you
    covered it;
  above the mountains the waters stood.

R̞. Lord, send out your Spirit, and renew the face of the earth.

You send forth springs into the watercourses
  that wind among the mountains.
Beside them the birds of heaven dwell;
  from among the branches they send forth
    their song.

R̞. Lord, send out your Spirit, and renew the face of the earth.

You water the mountains from your palace;
  the earth is replete with the fruit of your
    works.
You raise grass for the cattle,
  and vegetation for man's use,
producing bread from the earth.

R̞. Lord, send out your Spirit, and renew the face of the earth.

How manifold are your works, O LORD!
  In wisdom you have wrought them all—
  the earth is full of your creatures.
Bless the LORD, O my soul!

R̞. Lord, send out your Spirit, and renew the face of the earth.

or

Ps 33:4-5, 6-7, 12-13, 20-22

R̞. (5b) The earth is full of the goodness of the Lord.

Upright is the word of the LORD,
  and all his works are trustworthy.
He loves justice and right;
  of the kindness of the LORD the earth is full.

R̞. The earth is full of the goodness of the Lord.

By the word of the LORD the heavens were
    made;
  by the breath of his mouth all their host.
He gathers the waters of the sea as in a
    flask;
  in cellars he confines the deep.

R̞. The earth is full of the goodness of the Lord.

Blessed the nation whose God is the LORD,
  the people he has chosen for his own
    inheritance.
From heaven the LORD looks down;
  he sees all mankind.

R̞. The earth is full of the goodness of the Lord.

Our soul waits for the LORD,
  who is our help and our shield.
May your kindness, O LORD, be upon us
  who have put our hope in you.

R̞. The earth is full of the goodness of the Lord.

SECOND READING

Gen 22:1-18

God put Abraham to the test.
He called to him, "Abraham!"
"Here I am," he replied.
Then God said:
  "Take your son Isaac, your only one, whom
      you love,
  and go to the land of Moriah.
There you shall offer him up as a holocaust
  on a height that I will point out to you."
Early the next morning Abraham saddled his
    donkey,
  took with him his son Isaac and two of his
    servants as well,
  and with the wood that he had cut for the
    holocaust,
  set out for the place of which God had told
    him.

On the third day Abraham got sight of the
    place from afar.
Then he said to his servants:
  "Both of you stay here with the donkey,
  while the boy and I go on over yonder.
We will worship and then come back to you."
Thereupon Abraham took the wood for the
    holocaust
  and laid it on his son Isaac's shoulders,
  while he himself carried the fire and the
    knife.
As the two walked on together, Isaac spoke to
    his father Abraham:
  "Father!" Isaac said.
"Yes, son," he replied.
Isaac continued, "Here are the fire and the
    wood,
  but where is the sheep for the holocaust?"
"Son," Abraham answered,
  "God himself will provide the sheep for the
    holocaust."
Then the two continued going forward.

When they came to the place of which God
    had told him,

Abraham built an altar there and arranged
    the wood on it.
Next he tied up his son Isaac,
  and put him on top of the wood on the altar.
Then he reached out and took the knife to
    slaughter his son.
But the LORD's messenger called to him from
    heaven,
  "Abraham, Abraham!"
"Here I am," he answered.
"Do not lay your hand on the boy," said the
    messenger.
"Do not do the least thing to him.
I know now how devoted you are to God,
  since you did not withhold from me your
    own beloved son."
As Abraham looked about,
  he spied a ram caught by its horns in the
    thicket.
So he went and took the ram
  and offered it up as a holocaust in place of
    his son.
Abraham named the site Yahweh-yireh;
  hence people now say, "On the mountain
    the LORD will see."

Again the LORD's messenger called to
    Abraham from heaven and said:
  "I swear by myself, declares the LORD,
  that because you acted as you did
  in not withholding from me your beloved
    son,
  I will bless you abundantly
  and make your descendants as countless
  as the stars of the sky and the sands of the
    seashore;
  your descendants shall take possession
  of the gates of their enemies,
  and in your descendants all the nations of
    the earth
    shall find blessing—
  all this because you obeyed my
    command."

or

Gen 22:1-2, 9a, 10-13, 15-18

God put Abraham to the test.
He called to him, "Abraham!"
"Here I am," he replied.
Then God said:
  "Take your son Isaac, your only one, whom
      you love,
  and go to the land of Moriah.
There you shall offer him up as a holocaust
  on a height that I will point out to you."

When they came to the place of which God
    had told him,
  Abraham built an altar there and arranged
    the wood on it.

Then he reached out and took the knife to
    slaughter his son.
But the LORD's messenger called to him from
    heaven,
    "Abraham, Abraham!"
"Here I am," he answered.
"Do not lay your hand on the boy," said the
    messenger.
"Do not do the least thing to him.
I know now how devoted you are to God,
    since you did not withhold from me your
        own beloved son."
As Abraham looked about,
    he spied a ram caught by its horns in the
        thicket.
So he went and took the ram
    and offered it up as a holocaust in place of
        his son.

Again the LORD's messenger called to
    Abraham from heaven and said:
    "I swear by myself, declares the LORD,
    that because you acted as you did
    in not withholding from me your beloved son,
    I will bless you abundantly
    and make your descendants as countless
    as the stars of the sky and the sands of the
        seashore;
    your descendants shall take possession
    of the gates of their enemies,
    and in your descendants all the nations of
        the earth
        shall find blessing—
    all this because you obeyed my command."

RESPONSORIAL PSALM
Ps 16:5, 8, 9-10, 11

R℣. (1) You are my inheritance, O Lord.

O LORD, my allotted portion and my cup,
    you it is who hold fast my lot.
I set the LORD ever before me;
    with him at my right hand I shall not be
        disturbed.

R℣. You are my inheritance, O Lord.

Therefore my heart is glad and my soul rejoices,
    my body, too, abides in confidence;
because you will not abandon my soul to the
    netherworld,
    nor will you suffer your faithful one to
        undergo corruption.

R℣. You are my inheritance, O Lord.

You will show me the path to life,
    fullness of joys in your presence,
    the delights at your right hand forever.

R℣. You are my inheritance, O Lord.

THIRD READING
Exod 14:15–15:1

The LORD said to Moses, "Why are you crying
    out to me?
Tell the Israelites to go forward.
And you, lift up your staff and, with hand
    outstretched over the sea,
    split the sea in two,
    that the Israelites may pass through it on
        dry land.
But I will make the Egyptians so obstinate
    that they will go in after them.
Then I will receive glory through Pharaoh
    and all his army,
    his chariots and charioteers.
The Egyptians shall know that I am the LORD,
    when I receive glory through Pharaoh
    and his chariots and charioteers."

The angel of God, who had been leading
    Israel's camp,
    now moved and went around behind them.
The column of cloud also, leaving the front,
    took up its place behind them,
    so that it came between the camp of the
        Egyptians
    and that of Israel.
But the cloud now became dark, and thus the
    night passed
    without the rival camps coming any closer
        together all night long.
Then Moses stretched out his hand over the
    sea,
    and the LORD swept the sea
    with a strong east wind throughout the night
    and so turned it into dry land.
When the water was thus divided,
    the Israelites marched into the midst of the
        sea on dry land,
    with the water like a wall to their right and
        to their left.

The Egyptians followed in pursuit;
    all Pharaoh's horses and chariots and
        charioteers went after them
    right into the midst of the sea.
In the night watch just before dawn
    the LORD cast through the column of the
        fiery cloud
    upon the Egyptian force a glance that
        threw it into a panic;
    and he so clogged their chariot wheels
    that they could hardly drive.
With that the Egyptians sounded the retreat
    before Israel,
    because the LORD was fighting for them
        against the Egyptians.

Then the LORD told Moses, "Stretch out your
    hand over the sea,
    that the water may flow back upon the
        Egyptians,
    upon their chariots and their charioteers."
So Moses stretched out his hand over the sea,
    and at dawn the sea flowed back to its
        normal depth.
The Egyptians were fleeing head on toward
    the sea,
    when the LORD hurled them into its midst.
As the water flowed back,
    it covered the chariots and the charioteers
    of Pharaoh's whole army
    which had followed the Israelites into the sea.
Not a single one of them escaped.
But the Israelites had marched on dry land
    through the midst of the sea,
    with the water like a wall to their right and
        to their left.
Thus the LORD saved Israel on that day
    from the power of the Egyptians.
When Israel saw the Egyptians lying dead on
    the seashore
    and beheld the great power that the LORD
    had shown against the Egyptians,
    they feared the LORD and believed in him
    and in his servant Moses.

Then Moses and the Israelites sang this song
    to the LORD:
    I will sing to the LORD, for he is gloriously
        triumphant;
    horse and chariot he has cast into the sea.

RESPONSORIAL PSALM
Exod 15:1-2, 3-4, 5-6, 17-18

R℣. (1b) Let us sing to the Lord; he has covered
himself in glory.

I will sing to the LORD, for he is gloriously
    triumphant;
    horse and chariot he has cast into the sea.
My strength and my courage is the LORD,
    and he has been my savior.
He is my God, I praise him;
    the God of my father, I extol him.

R℣. Let us sing to the Lord; he has covered
himself in glory.

The LORD is a warrior,
    LORD is his name!
Pharaoh's chariots and army he hurled into
    the sea;
    the elite of his officers were submerged in
        the Red Sea.

R℣. Let us sing to the Lord; he has covered
himself in glory.

273

The flood waters covered them,
 they sank into the depths like a stone.
Your right hand, O LORD, magnificent in
   power,
 your right hand, O LORD, has shattered the
   enemy.

R̂. Let us sing to the Lord; he has covered
himself in glory.

You brought in the people you redeemed
 and planted them on the mountain of your
   inheritance—
the place where you made your seat, O
 LORD,
 the sanctuary, LORD, which your hands
   established.
The LORD shall reign forever and ever.

R̂. Let us sing to the Lord; he has covered
himself in glory.

FOURTH READING

Isa 54:5-14

The One who has become your husband is
   your Maker;
 his name is the LORD of hosts;
your redeemer is the Holy One of Israel,
 called God of all the earth.
The LORD calls you back,
 like a wife forsaken and grieved in spirit,
 a wife married in youth and then cast off,
   says your God.
For a brief moment I abandoned you,
 but with great tenderness I will take you
   back.
In an outburst of wrath, for a moment
 I hid my face from you;
but with enduring love I take pity on you,
 says the LORD, your redeemer.
This is for me like the days of Noah,
 when I swore that the waters of Noah
 should never again deluge the earth;
so I have sworn not to be angry with you,
 or to rebuke you.
Though the mountains leave their place
 and the hills be shaken,
my love shall never leave you
 nor my covenant of peace be shaken,
 says the LORD, who has mercy on you.
O afflicted one, storm-battered and unconsoled,
 I lay your pavements in carnelians,
 and your foundations in sapphires;
I will make your battlements of rubies,
 your gates of carbuncles,
 and all your walls of precious stones.
All your children shall be taught by the LORD,
 and great shall be the peace of your children.

In justice shall you be established,
 far from the fear of oppression,
 where destruction cannot come near you.

RESPONSORIAL PSALM

Ps 30:2, 4, 5-6, 11-12, 13

R̂. (2a) I will praise you, Lord, for you have
rescued me.

I will extol you, O LORD, for you drew me
   clear
 and did not let my enemies rejoice over me.
O LORD, you brought me up from the
   netherworld;
 you preserved me from among those going
   down into the pit.

R̂. I will praise you, Lord, for you have
rescued me.

Sing praise to the LORD, you his faithful ones,
 and give thanks to his holy name.
For his anger lasts but a moment;
 a lifetime, his good will.
At nightfall, weeping enters in,
 but with the dawn, rejoicing.

R̂. I will praise you, Lord, for you have
rescued me.

Hear, O LORD, and have pity on me;
 O LORD, be my helper.
You changed my mourning into dancing;
 O LORD, my God, forever will I give you
   thanks.

R̂. I will praise you, Lord, for you have
rescued me.

FIFTH READING

Isa 55:1-11

Thus says the LORD:
All you who are thirsty,
 come to the water!
You who have no money,
 come, receive grain and eat;
come, without paying and without cost,
 drink wine and milk!
Why spend your money for what is not bread,
 your wages for what fails to satisfy?
Heed me, and you shall eat well,
 you shall delight in rich fare.
Come to me heedfully,
 listen, that you may have life.
I will renew with you the everlasting
   covenant,
 the benefits assured to David.
As I made him a witness to the peoples,
 a leader and commander of nations,
so shall you summon a nation you knew not,

and nations that knew you not shall run to
   you,
because of the LORD, your God,
 the Holy One of Israel, who has glorified you.

Seek the LORD while he may be found,
 call him while he is near.
Let the scoundrel forsake his way,
 and the wicked man his thoughts;
let him turn to the LORD for mercy;
 to our God, who is generous in forgiving.
For my thoughts are not your thoughts,
 nor are your ways my ways, says the LORD.
As high as the heavens are above the earth,
 so high are my ways above your ways
 and my thoughts above your thoughts.

For just as from the heavens
 the rain and snow come down
and do not return there
 till they have watered the earth,
 making it fertile and fruitful,
giving seed to the one who sows
 and bread to the one who eats,
so shall my word be
 that goes forth from my mouth;
my word shall not return to me void,
 but shall do my will,
 achieving the end for which I sent it.

RESPONSORIAL PSALM

Isa 12:2-3, 4, 5-6

R̂. (3) You will draw water joyfully from the
springs of salvation.

God indeed is my savior;
 I am confident and unafraid.
My strength and my courage is the LORD,
 and he has been my savior.
With joy you will draw water
 at the fountain of salvation.

R̂. You will draw water joyfully from the
springs of salvation.

Give thanks to the LORD, acclaim his name;
 among the nations make known his deeds,
 proclaim how exalted is his name.

R̂. You will draw water joyfully from the
springs of salvation.

Sing praise to the LORD for his glorious
   achievement;
 let this be known throughout all the earth.
Shout with exultation, O city of Zion,
 for great in your midst
 is the Holy One of Israel!

R̂. You will draw water joyfully from the
springs of salvation.

SIXTH READING
Bar 3:9-15, 32—4:4

Hear, O Israel, the commandments of life:
　listen, and know prudence!
How is it, Israel,
　that you are in the land of your foes,
　grown old in a foreign land,
defiled with the dead,
　accounted with those destined for the
　　netherworld?
You have forsaken the fountain of wisdom!
　Had you walked in the way of God,
　you would have dwelt in enduring peace.
Learn where prudence is,
　where strength, where understanding;
that you may know also
　where are length of days, and life,
　where light of the eyes, and peace.
Who has found the place of wisdom,
　who has entered into her treasuries?

The One who knows all things knows her;
　he has probed her by his knowledge—
the One who established the earth for all
　　time,
　and filled it with four-footed beasts;
　he who dismisses the light, and it departs,
　calls it, and it obeys him trembling;
before whom the stars at their posts
　shine and rejoice;
when he calls them, they answer, "Here we
　　are!"
　shining with joy for their Maker.
Such is our God;
　no other is to be compared to him:
he has traced out the whole way of
　　understanding,
　and has given her to Jacob, his servant,
　to Israel, his beloved son.

Since then she has appeared on earth,
　and moved among people.
She is the book of the precepts of God,
　the law that endures forever;
all who cling to her will live,
　but those will die who forsake her.
Turn, O Jacob, and receive her:
　walk by her light toward splendor.
Give not your glory to another,
　your privileges to an alien race.
Blessed are we, O Israel;
　for what pleases God is known to us!

RESPONSORIAL PSALM
Ps 19:8, 9, 10, 11

R℣. (John 6:68c) Lord, you have the words of
everlasting life.

The law of the LORD is perfect,
　refreshing the soul;
the decree of the LORD is trustworthy,
　giving wisdom to the simple.

R℣. Lord, you have the words of everlasting life.

The precepts of the LORD are right,
　rejoicing the heart;
the command of the LORD is clear,
　enlightening the eye.

R℣. Lord, you have the words of everlasting life.

The fear of the LORD is pure,
　enduring forever;
the ordinances of the LORD are true,
　all of them just.

R℣. Lord, you have the words of everlasting life.

They are more precious than gold,
　than a heap of purest gold;
sweeter also than syrup
　or honey from the comb.

R℣. Lord, you have the words of everlasting life.

SEVENTH READING
Ezek 36:16-17a, 18-28

The word of the LORD came to me, saying:
　Son of man, when the house of Israel lived
　　in their land,
　they defiled it by their conduct and deeds.
Therefore I poured out my fury upon them
　because of the blood that they poured out
　　on the ground,
　and because they defiled it with idols.
I scattered them among the nations,
　dispersing them over foreign lands;
　according to their conduct and deeds I
　　judged them.
But when they came among the nations
　　wherever they came,
　they served to profane my holy name,
　because it was said of them: "These are the
　　people of the LORD,
　yet they had to leave their land."
So I have relented because of my holy name
　which the house of Israel profaned
　among the nations where they came.
Therefore say to the house of Israel: Thus
　　says the Lord GOD:
　Not for your sakes do I act, house of Israel,
　but for the sake of my holy name,
　which you profaned among the nations to
　　which you came.
I will prove the holiness of my great name,
　profaned among the nations,
　in whose midst you have profaned it.
Thus the nations shall know that I am the
　　LORD, says the Lord GOD,
　when in their sight I prove my holiness
　　through you.
For I will take you away from among the
　nations,

gather you from all the foreign lands,
　and bring you back to your own land.
I will sprinkle clean water upon you
　to cleanse you from all your impurities,
　and from all your idols I will cleanse you.
I will give you a new heart and place a new
　　spirit within you,
　taking from your bodies your stony hearts
　and giving you natural hearts.
I will put my spirit within you and make you
　　live by my statutes,
　careful to observe my decrees.
You shall live in the land I gave your fathers;
　you shall be my people, and I will be your
　　God.

RESPONSORIAL PSALM
Ps 42:3, 5; 43:3, 4

R℣. (42:2) Like a deer that longs for running
streams, my soul longs for you, my God.

Athirst is my soul for God, the living God.
　When shall I go and behold the face of God?

R℣. Like a deer that longs for running streams,
my soul longs for you, my God.

I went with the throng
　and led them in procession to the house of
　　God,
amid loud cries of joy and thanksgiving,
　with the multitude keeping festival.

R℣. Like a deer that longs for running streams,
my soul longs for you, my God.

Send forth your light and your fidelity;
　they shall lead me on
and bring me to your holy mountain,
　to your dwelling-place.

R℣. Like a deer that longs for running streams,
my soul longs for you, my God.

Then will I go in to the altar of God,
　the God of my gladness and joy;
then will I give you thanks upon the harp,
　O God, my God!

R℣. Like a deer that longs for running streams,
my soul longs for you, my God.

or

Isa 12:2-3, 4bcd, 5-6

R℣. (3) You will draw water joyfully from the
springs of salvation.

God indeed is my savior;
　I am confident and unafraid.
My strength and my courage is the LORD,
　and he has been my savior.
With joy you will draw water
　at the fountain of salvation.

R℣. You will draw water joyfully from the
springs of salvation.

Give thanks to the LORD, acclaim his name;
  among the nations make known his deeds,
  proclaim how exalted is his name.

R7. You will draw water joyfully from the
springs of salvation.

Sing praise to the LORD for his glorious
  achievement;
  let this be known throughout all the earth.
Shout with exultation, O city of Zion,
  for great in your midst
  is the Holy One of Israel!

R7. You will draw water joyfully from the
springs of salvation.

or

Ps 51:12-13, 14-15, 18-19

R7. (12a) Create a clean heart in me, O God.

A clean heart create for me, O God,
  and a steadfast spirit renew within me.
Cast me not out from your presence,
  and your Holy Spirit take not from me.

R7. Create a clean heart in me, O God.

Give me back the joy of your salvation,
  and a willing spirit sustain in me.
I will teach transgressors your ways,
  and sinners shall return to you.

R7. Create a clean heart in me, O God.

For you are not pleased with sacrifices;
  should I offer a holocaust, you would not
  accept it.
My sacrifice, O God, is a contrite spirit;
  a heart contrite and humbled, O God, you
  will not spurn.

R7. Create a clean heart in me, O God.

EPISTLE
Rom 6:3-11

Brothers and sisters:
Are you unaware that we who were baptized
  into Christ Jesus
  were baptized into his death?
We were indeed buried with him through
  baptism into death,
  so that, just as Christ was raised from the
  dead
  by the glory of the Father,
  we too might live in newness of life.

For if we have grown into union with him
  through a death like his,
  we shall also be united with him in the
  resurrection.
We know that our old self was crucified with
  him,
  so that our sinful body might be done away
  with,
  that we might no longer be in slavery to sin.
For a dead person has been absolved from
  sin.
If, then, we have died with Christ,
  we believe that we shall also live with
  him.
We know that Christ, raised from the dead,
  dies no more;
  death no longer has power over him.
As to his death, he died to sin once and for
  all;
  as to his life, he lives for God.
Consequently, you too must think of
  yourselves as being dead to sin
  and living for God in Christ Jesus.

RESPONSORIAL PSALM
Ps 118:1-2, 16-17, 22-23

R7. Alleluia, alleluia, alleluia.

Give thanks to the LORD, for he is good,
  for his mercy endures forever.
Let the house of Israel say,
  "His mercy endures forever."

R7. Alleluia, alleluia, alleluia.

The right hand of the LORD has struck with
  power;
  the right hand of the LORD is exalted.
I shall not die, but live,
  and declare the works of the LORD.

R7. Alleluia, alleluia, alleluia.

The stone which the builders rejected
  has become the cornerstone.
By the LORD has this been done;
  it is wonderful in our eyes.

R7. Alleluia, alleluia, alleluia.

The Mass of Easter Day, *April 11, 2004*

Gospel
Luke 24:1-12; L41ABC

At daybreak on the first day of the week
  the women who had come from Galilee with Jesus
  took the spices they had prepared
  and went to the tomb.
They found the stone rolled away from the tomb;
  but when they entered,
  they did not find the body of the Lord Jesus.
While they were puzzling over this, behold,
  two men in dazzling garments appeared to them.
They were terrified and bowed their faces to the ground.
They said to them,
  "Why do you seek the living one among the dead?
He is not here, but he has been raised.
Remember what he said to you while he was still in Galilee,

that the Son of Man must be handed over to sinners
  and be crucified, and rise on the third day."
And they remembered his words.
Then they returned from the tomb
  and announced all these things to the eleven
  and to all the others.
The women were Mary Magdalene, Joanna, and Mary the mother of
  James;
  the others who accompanied them also told this to the apostles,
  but their story seemed like nonsense
  and they did not believe them.
But Peter got up and ran to the tomb,
  bent down, and saw the burial cloths alone;
  then he went home amazed at what had happened.

or, at an afternoon or evening Mass

Gospel
Luke 24:13-35; L46

That very day, the first day of the week,
   two of Jesus' disciples were going
   to a village seven miles from Jerusalem called Emmaus,
   and they were conversing about all the things that had occurred.
And it happened that while they were conversing and debating,
   Jesus himself drew near and walked with them,
   but their eyes were prevented from recognizing him.
He asked them,
   "What are you discussing as you walk along?"
They stopped, looking downcast.
One of them, named Cleopas, said to him in reply,
   "Are you the only visitor to Jerusalem
   who does not know of the things
   that have taken place there in these days?"
And he replied to them, "What sort of things?"
They said to him,
   "The things that happened to Jesus the Nazarene,
   who was a prophet mighty in deed and word
   before God and all the people,
   how our chief priests and rulers both handed him over
   to a sentence of death and crucified him.
But we were hoping that he would be the one to redeem Israel;
   and besides all this,
   it is now the third day since this took place.
Some women from our group, however, have astounded us:
   they were at the tomb early in the morning
   and did not find his body;
   they came back and reported
   that they had indeed seen a vision of angels
   who announced that he was alive.

Then some of those with us went to the tomb
   and found things just as the women had described,
   but him they did not see."
And he said to them, "Oh, how foolish you are!
How slow of heart to believe all that the prophets spoke!
Was it not necessary that the Christ should suffer these things
   and enter into his glory?"
Then beginning with Moses and all the prophets,
   he interpreted to them what referred to him
   in all the Scriptures.
As they approached the village to which they were going,
   he gave the impression that he was going on farther.
But they urged him, "Stay with us,
   for it is nearly evening and the day is almost over."
So he went in to stay with them.
And it happened that, while he was with them at table,
   he took bread, said the blessing,
   broke it, and gave it to them.
With that their eyes were opened and they recognized him,
   but he vanished from their sight.
Then they said to each other,
   "Were not our hearts burning within us
   while he spoke to us on the way and opened the Scriptures to us?"
So they set out at once and returned to Jerusalem
   where they found gathered together
   the eleven and those with them who were saying,
   "The Lord has truly been raised and has appeared to Simon!"
Then the two recounted
   what had taken place on the way
   and how he was made known to them in the breaking of bread.

FIRST READING
Acts 10:34a, 37-43

Peter proceeded to speak and said:
   "You know what has happened all over
      Judea,
   beginning in Galilee after the baptism
   that John preached,
   how God anointed Jesus of Nazareth
   with the Holy Spirit and power.
He went about doing good
   and healing all those oppressed by the devil,
   for God was with him.
We are witnesses of all that he did
   both in the country of the Jews and in
      Jerusalem.
They put him to death by hanging him on a
      tree.
This man God raised on the third day and
      granted that he be visible,
   not to all the people, but to us,
   the witnesses chosen by God in advance,
   who ate and drank with him after he rose
      from the dead.

He commissioned us to preach to the people
   and testify that he is the one appointed by
      God
   as judge of the living and the dead.
To him all the prophets bear witness,
   that everyone who believes in him
   will receive forgiveness of sins through his
      name.

RESPONSORIAL PSALM
Ps 118:1-2, 16-17, 22-23

R⁊. (24) This is the day the Lord has made; let us rejoice and be glad.
   or:
R⁊. Alleluia.

Give thanks to the LORD, for he is good,
   for his mercy endures forever.
Let the house of Israel say,
   "His mercy endures forever."

R⁊. This is the day the Lord has made; let us rejoice and be glad.
   or:
R⁊. Alleluia.

"The right hand of the LORD has struck with
      power;
   the right hand of the LORD is exalted.
I shall not die, but live,
   and declare the works of the LORD."

R⁊. This is the day the Lord has made; let us rejoice and be glad.
   or:
R⁊. Alleluia.

The stone which the builders rejected
   has become the cornerstone.
By the LORD has this been done;
   it is wonderful in our eyes.

R⁊. This is the day the Lord has made; let us rejoice and be glad.
   or:
R⁊. Alleluia.

SECOND READING
Col 3:1-4

Brothers and sisters:
If then you were raised with Christ, seek
    what is above,
        where Christ is seated at the right hand of
        God.
Think of what is above, not of what is on earth.
For you have died, and your life is hidden
    with Christ in God.
When Christ your life appears,
    then you too will appear with him in glory.

or

1 Cor 5:6b-8

Brothers and sisters:
Do you not know that a little yeast leavens all
    the dough?
Clear out the old yeast,
    so that you may become a fresh batch of
    dough,
    inasmuch as you are unleavened.
For our paschal lamb, Christ, has been
    sacrificed.
Therefore, let us celebrate the feast,
    not with the old yeast, the yeast of malice
    and wickedness,
    but with the unleavened bread of sincerity
    and truth.

SEQUENCE
Victimae paschali laudes

Christians, to the Paschal Victim
    Offer your thankful praises!
A Lamb the sheep redeems;
    Christ, who only is sinless,
    Reconciles sinners to the Father.
Death and life have contended in that combat
    stupendous:
    The Prince of life, who died, reigns
        immortal.
Speak, Mary, declaring
    What you saw, wayfaring.
"The tomb of Christ, who is living,
    The glory of Jesus' resurrection;
Bright angels attesting,
    The shroud and napkin resting.
Yes, Christ my hope is arisen;
    To Galilee he goes before you."
Christ indeed from death is risen, our new life
    obtaining.
    Have mercy, victor King, ever reigning!
    Amen. Alleluia.

Second Sunday of Easter (or Divine Mercy Sunday), *April 18, 2004*

Gospel (cont.)
John 20:19-31; L45C

Then he said to Thomas, "Put your finger here and see my hands,
    and bring your hand and put it into my side,
    and do not be unbelieving, but believe."
Thomas answered and said to him, "My Lord and my God!"
Jesus said to him, "Have you come to believe because you have seen
    me?
Blessed are those who have not seen and have believed."

Now Jesus did many other signs in the presence of his disciples
    that are not written in this book.
But these are written that you may come to believe
    that Jesus is the Christ, the Son of God,
    and that through this belief you may have life in his name.

Third Sunday of Easter, *April 25, 2004*

Gospel (cont.)
John 21:1-19; L48C

Jesus said to them, "Bring some of the fish you just caught."
So Simon Peter went over and dragged the net ashore
  full of one hundred fifty-three large fish.
Even though there were so many, the net was not torn.
Jesus said to them, "Come, have breakfast."
And none of the disciples dared to ask him, "Who are you?"
  because they realized it was the Lord.
Jesus came over and took the bread and gave it to them,
  and in like manner the fish.
This was now the third time Jesus was revealed to his disciples
  after being raised from the dead.

When they had finished breakfast, Jesus said to Simon Peter,
  "Simon, son of John, do you love me more than these?"
Simon Peter answered him, "Yes, Lord, you know that I love you."
Jesus said to him, "Feed my lambs."
He then said to Simon Peter a second time,
  "Simon, son of John, do you love me?"

Simon Peter answered him, "Yes, Lord, you know that I love you."
Jesus said to him, "Tend my sheep."
Jesus said to him the third time,
  "Simon, son of John, do you love me?"
Peter was distressed that Jesus had said to him a third time,
  "Do you love me?" and he said to him,
  "Lord, you know everything; you know that I love you."
Jesus said to him, "Feed my sheep.
Amen, amen, I say to you, when you were younger,
  you used to dress yourself and go where you wanted;
  but when you grow old, you will stretch out your hands,
  and someone else will dress you
  and lead you where you do not want to go."
He said this signifying by what kind of death he would glorify God.
And when he had said this, he said to him, "Follow me."

Fourth Sunday of Easter, *May 2, 2004*

SECOND READING
Rev 7:9, 14b-17

I, John, had a vision of a great multitude,
  which no one could count,
  from every nation, race, people, and tongue.
They stood before the throne and before the
    Lamb,
  wearing white robes and holding palm
    branches in their hands.

Then one of the elders said to me,
  "These are the ones who have survived the
    time of great distress;
  they have washed their robes
  and made them white in the blood of the
    Lamb.

"For this reason they stand before God's
    throne
  and worship him day and night in his
    temple.
The one who sits on the throne will shelter
    them.
They will not hunger or thirst anymore,
  nor will the sun or any heat strike them.
For the Lamb who is in the center of the
    throne
  will shepherd them
  and lead them to springs of life-giving
    water,
  and God will wipe away every tear from
    their eyes."

Sixth Sunday of Easter, *May 16, 2004*

SECOND READING
Rev 21:10-14, 22-23

The angel took me in spirit to a great, high
    mountain
  and showed me the holy city Jerusalem
  coming down out of heaven from God.
It gleamed with the splendor of God.
Its radiance was like that of a precious stone,
  like jasper, clear as crystal.
It had a massive, high wall,
  with twelve gates where twelve angels were
    stationed

and on which names were inscribed,
  the names of the twelve tribes of the
    Israelites.
There were three gates facing east,
  three north, three south, and three west.
The wall of the city had twelve courses of
    stones as its foundation,
  on which were inscribed the twelve names
  of the twelve apostles of the Lamb.

I saw no temple in the city
  for its temple is the Lord God almighty and
    the Lamb.

The city had no need of sun or moon to shine
    on it,
  for the glory of God gave it light,
  and its lamp was the Lamb.

The Ascension of the Lord, *May 20, 2004*

SECOND READING
Eph 1:17-23

Brothers and sisters:
May the God of our Lord Jesus Christ, the
Father of glory,
    give you a Spirit of wisdom and revelation
    resulting in knowledge of him.
May the eyes of your hearts be enlightened,
    that you may know what is the hope that
        belongs to his call,
    what are the riches of glory
    in his inheritance among the holy ones,
    and what is the surpassing greatness of
        his power
    for us who believe,
    in accord with the exercise of his great
        might:
    which he worked in Christ,
    raising him from the dead
    and seating him at his right hand in the
        heavens,
    far above every principality, authority,
        power, and dominion,
    and every name that is named
    not only in this age but also in the one to
        come.

And he put all things beneath his feet
    and gave him as head over all things to the
        church,
    which is his body,
    the fullness of the one who fills all things
        in every way.

or

Heb 9:24-28; 10:19-23

Christ did not enter into a sanctuary made by
    hands,
    a copy of the true one, but heaven itself,
    that he might now appear before God on
        our behalf.
Not that he might offer himself repeatedly,
    as the high priest enters each year into the
        sanctuary
    with blood that is not his own;
    if that were so, he would have had to suffer
        repeatedly
    from the foundation of the world.
But now once for all he has appeared at the
    end of the ages
    to take away sin by his sacrifice.
Just as it is appointed that men and women
    die once,
    and after this the judgment, so also Christ,
    offered once to take away the sins of many,
    will appear a second time, not to take away
        sin
    but to bring salvation to those who eagerly
        await him.

Therefore, brothers and sisters, since through
    the blood of Jesus
we have confidence of entrance into the
    sanctuary
    by the new and living way he opened for us
        through the veil,
    that is, his flesh,
    and since we have "a great priest over the
        house of God,"
    let us approach with a sincere heart and in
        absolute trust,
    with our hearts sprinkled clean from an
        evil conscience
    and our bodies washed in pure water.
Let us hold unwaveringly to our confession
    that gives us hope,
    for he who made the promise is
        trustworthy.

Pentecost Sunday Mass During the Day, *May 30, 2004*

SECOND READING
Rom 8:8-17

Brothers and sisters:
Those who are in the flesh cannot please God.
But you are not in the flesh;
    on the contrary, you are in the spirit,
    if only the Spirit of God dwells in you.
Whoever does not have the Spirit of Christ
    does not belong to him.
But if Christ is in you,
    although the body is dead because of sin,
    the spirit is alive because of righteousness.
If the Spirit of the one who raised Jesus from
    the dead dwells in you,
    the one who raised Christ from the dead
    will give life to your mortal bodies also,
    through his Spirit that dwells in you.
Consequently, brothers and sisters,
    we are not debtors to the flesh,
    to live according to the flesh.
For if you live according to the flesh, you will
    die,
    but if by the Spirit you put to death the
        deeds of the body,
    you will live.

For those who are led by the Spirit of God are
    sons of God.
For you did not receive a spirit of slavery to
    fall back into fear,
    but you received a Spirit of adoption,
    through whom we cry, "Abba, Father!"
The Spirit himself bears witness with our
    spirit
    that we are children of God,
    and if children, then heirs,
    heirs of God and joint heirs with Christ,
    if only we suffer with him
    so that we may also be glorified with him.

SEQUENCE
Veni, Sancte Spiritus

Come, Holy Spirit, come!
And from your celestial home
    Shed a ray of light divine!
Come, Father of the poor!
Come, source of all our store!
    Come, within our bosoms shine.
You, of comforters the best;
You, the soul's most welcome guest;
    Sweet refreshment here below;

In our labor, rest most sweet;
Grateful coolness in the heat;
    Solace in the midst of woe.
O most blessed Light divine,
Shine within these hearts of yours,
    And our inmost being fill!
Where you are not, we have naught,
Nothing good in deed or thought,
    Nothing free from taint of ill.
Heal our wounds, our strength renew;
On our dryness pour your dew;
    Wash the stains of guilt away:
Bend the stubborn heart and will;
Melt the frozen, warm the chill;
    Guide the steps that go astray.
On the faithful, who adore
And confess you, evermore
    In your sevenfold gift descend;
Give them virtue's sure reward;
Give them your salvation, Lord;
    Give them joys that never end. Amen.
    Alleluia.

OPTIONAL SEQUENCE
Lauda Sion

Laud, O Zion, your salvation,
Laud with hymns of exultation,
   Christ, your king and shepherd true:

Bring him all the praise you know,
He is more than you bestow.
   Never can you reach his due.

Special theme for glad thanksgiving
Is the quick'ning and the living
   Bread today before you set:

From his hands of old partaken,
As we know, by faith unshaken,
   Where the Twelve at supper met.

Full and clear ring out your chanting,
Joy nor sweetest grace be wanting,
   From your heart let praises burst:

For today the feast is holden,
When the institution olden
   Of that supper was rehearsed.

Here the new law's new oblation,
By the new king's revelation,
   Ends the form of ancient rite:

Now the new the old effaces,
Truth away the shadow chases,
   Light dispels the gloom of night.

What he did at supper seated,
Christ ordained to be repeated,
   His memorial ne'er to cease:

And his rule for guidance taking,
Bread and wine we hallow, making
   Thus our sacrifice of peace.

This the truth each Christian learns,
Bread into his flesh he turns,
   To his precious blood the wine:

Sight has fail'd, nor thought conceives,
But a dauntless faith believes,
   Resting on a pow'r divine.

Here beneath these signs are hidden
Priceless things to sense forbidden;
   Signs, not things are all we see:

Blood is poured and flesh is broken,
Yet in either wondrous token
   Christ entire we know to be.

Whoso of this food partakes,
Does not rend the Lord nor breaks;
   Christ is whole to all that taste:

Thousands are, as one, receivers,
One, as thousands of believers,
   Eats of him who cannot waste.

Bad and good the feast are sharing,
Of what divers dooms preparing,
   Endless death, or endless life.

Life to these, to those damnation,
See how like participation
   Is with unlike issues rife.

When the sacrament is broken,
Doubt not, but believe 'tis spoken,
   That each sever'd outward token
   Doth the very whole contain.

Nought the precious gift divides,
Breaking but the sign betides
   Jesus still the same abides,
   Still unbroken does remain.

The shorter form of the sequence begins here.

Lo! the angel's food is given
To the pilgrim who has striven;
   See the children's bread from heaven,
   Which on dogs may not be spent.

Truth the ancient types fulfilling,
Isaac bound, a victim willing,
   Paschal lamb, its lifeblood spilling,
   Manna to the fathers sent.

Very bread, good shepherd, tend us,
Jesu, of your love befriend us,
   You refresh us, you defend us,
   Your eternal goodness send us
In the land of life to see.

You who all things can and know,
Who on earth such food bestow,
   Grant us with your saints, though lowest,
   Where the heav'nly feast you show,
Fellow heirs and guests to be. Amen. Alleluia.

FIRST READING

Ezek 34:11-16

Thus says the Lord GOD:
   I myself will look after and tend my sheep.
As a shepherd tends his flock
   when he finds himself among his scattered
      sheep,
   so will I tend my sheep.
I will rescue them from every place where
      they were scattered
   when it was cloudy and dark.
I will lead them out from among the peoples
   and gather them from the foreign lands;
   I will bring them back to their own country
   and pasture them upon the mountains of
      Israel
   in the land's ravines and all its inhabited
      places.
In good pastures will I pasture them,
   and on the mountain heights of Israel
   shall be their grazing ground.
There they shall lie down on good grazing
      ground,
   and in rich pastures shall they be pastured
   on the mountains of Israel.
I myself will pasture my sheep;
   I myself will give them rest, says the Lord
      GOD.
The lost I will seek out,
   the strayed I will bring back,
   the injured I will bind up,
   the sick I will heal,
   but the sleek and the strong I will destroy,
   shepherding them rightly.

RESPONSORIAL PSALM

Ps 23:1-3a, 3b-4, 5, 6

℟. (1) The Lord is my shepherd; there is nothing I shall want.

The LORD is my shepherd; I shall not want.
   In verdant pastures he gives me repose;
beside restful waters he leads me;
   he refreshes my soul.

℟. The Lord is my shepherd; there is nothing
I shall want.

He guides me in right paths
   for his name's sake.
Even though I walk in the dark valley
   I fear no evil; for you are at my side
with your rod and your staff
   that give me courage.

℟. The Lord is my shepherd; there is nothing
I shall want.

You spread the table before me
   in the sight of my foes;
you anoint my head with oil;
   my cup overflows.

℟. The Lord is my shepherd; there is nothing
I shall want.

Only goodness and kindness follow me
   all the days of my life;
and I shall dwell in the house of the LORD
   for years to come.

℟. The Lord is my shepherd; there is nothing
I shall want.

SECOND READING

Rom 5:5b-11

Brothers and sisters:
The love of God has been poured out into our
      hearts
   through the Holy Spirit that has been given
      to us.
For Christ, while we were still helpless,
   died at the appointed time for the ungodly.
Indeed, only with difficulty does one die for a
      just person,
   though perhaps for a good person
   one might even find courage to die.
But God proves his love for us
   in that while we were still sinners Christ
      died for us.
How much more then, since we are now
      justified by his blood,
   will we be saved through him from the
      wrath.
Indeed, if, while we were enemies,
   we were reconciled to God through the
      death of his Son,
   how much more, once reconciled,
   will we be saved by his life.
Not only that,
   but we also boast of God through our Lord
      Jesus Christ,
   through whom we have now received
      reconciliation.

FIRST READING
Isa 49:1-6

Hear me, O coastlands
  listen, O distant peoples.
The LORD called me from birth,
  from my mother's womb he gave me my
    name.
He made of me a sharp-edged sword
  and concealed me in the shadow of his arm.
He made me a polished arrow,
  in his quiver he hid me.
You are my servant, he said to me,
  Israel, through whom I show my glory.

Though I thought I had toiled in vain,
  and for nothing, uselessly, spent my strength,
yet my reward is with the LORD,
  my recompense is with my God.
For now the LORD has spoken
  who formed me as his servant from the
    womb,
that Jacob may be brought back to him
  and Israel gathered to him;
and I am made glorious in the sight of the
    Lord,
  and my God is now my strength!
It is too little, he says, for you to be my servant,
  to raise up the tribes of Jacob,
  and restore the survivors of Israel;
I will make you a light to the nations,
  that my salvation may reach to the ends of
    the earth.

RESPONSORIAL PSALM
Ps 139:1-3, 13-14, 14-15

R̶̸. (14a) I praise you for I am wonderfully
made.

O LORD you have probed me and you know
    me;
  you know when I sit and when I stand;
  you understand my thoughts from afar.
My journeys and my rest you scrutinize,
  with all my ways you are familiar.

R̶̸. I praise you for I am wonderfully made.

Truly you have formed my inmost being;
  you knit me in my mother's womb.
I give you thanks that I am fearfully,
    wonderfully made;
  wonderful are your works.

R̶̸. I praise you for I am wonderfully made.

My soul also you knew full well;
  nor was my frame unknown to you
when I was made in secret,
  when I was fashioned in the depths of the
    earth.

R̶̸. I praise you for I am wonderfully made.

SECOND READING
Acts 13:22-26

In those days, Paul said:
  "God raised up David as their king;
  of him he testified,
  'I have found David, son of Jesse, a man
    after my own heart;
  he will carry out my every wish.'
From this man's descendants God, according
    to his promise,
  has brought to Israel a savior, Jesus.
John heralded his coming by proclaiming a
    baptism of repentance
  to all the people of Israel;
  and as John was completing his course, he
    would say,
  'What do you suppose that I am? I am not he.
Behold, one is coming after me;
  I am not worthy to unfasten the sandals of
    his feet.'

"My brothers, children of the family of
    Abraham,
  and those others among you who are God-
    fearing,
  to us this word of salvation has been sent."

SS. Peter and Paul, Apostles, *June 29, 2004*

FIRST READING
Acts 12:1-11

In those days, King Herod laid hands upon
some members of the church to harm
them.
He had James, the brother of John, killed by
the sword,
and when he saw that this was pleasing to
the Jews
he proceeded to arrest Peter also.
—It was the feast of Unleavened Bread.—
He had him taken into custody and put in
prison
under the guard of four squads of four
soldiers each.
He intended to bring him before the people
after Passover.
Peter thus was being kept in prison,
but prayer by the church was fervently
being made
to God on his behalf.

On the very night before Herod was to bring
him to trial,
Peter, secured by double chains,
was sleeping between two soldiers,
while outside the door guards kept watch
on the prison.
Suddenly the angel of the Lord stood by him
and a light shone in the cell.
He tapped Peter on the side and awakened
him, saying,
"Get up quickly."
The chains fell from his wrists.
The angel said to him, "Put on your belt and
your sandals."
He did so.

Then he said to him, "Put on your cloak and
follow me."
So he followed him out,
not realizing that what was happening
through the angel was real;
he thought he was seeing a vision.
They passed the first guard, then the second,
and came to the iron gate leading out to the
city,
which opened for them by itself.
They emerged and made their way down an
alley,
and suddenly the angel left him.

RESPONSORIAL PSALM
Ps 34:2-3, 4-5, 6-7, 8-9

R̊. (8) The angel of the Lord will rescue those
who fear him.

I will bless the LORD at all times;
his praise shall be ever in my mouth.
Let my soul glory in the LORD;
the lowly will hear me and be glad.

R̊. The angel of the Lord will rescue those
who fear him.

Glorify the LORD with me,
let us together extol his name.
I sought the LORD, and he answered me
and delivered me from all my fears.

R̊. The angel of the Lord will rescue those
who fear him.

Look to him that you may be radiant with joy,
and your faces may not blush with shame.
When the poor one called out, the LORD heard,
and from all his distress he saved him.

R̊. The angel of the Lord will rescue those
who fear him.

The angel of the LORD encamps
around those who fear him, and delivers
them.
Taste and see how good the LORD is;
blessed the man who takes refuge in him.

R̊. The angel of the Lord will rescue those
who fear him.

SECOND READING
2 Tim 4:6-8, 17-18

I, Paul, am already being poured out like a
libation,
and the time of my departure is at hand.
I have competed well; I have finished the race;
I have kept the faith.
From now on the crown of righteousness
awaits me,
which the Lord, the just judge,
will award to me on that day, and not only
to me,
but to all who have longed for his
appearance.

The Lord stood by me and gave me strength,
so that through me the proclamation might
be completed
and all the Gentiles might hear it.
And I was rescued from the lion's mouth.
The Lord will rescue me from every evil
threat
and will bring me safe to his heavenly
kingdom.
To him be glory forever and ever. Amen.

Fourteenth Sunday in Ordinary Time, *July 4, 2004*

Gospel (cont.)
Luke 10:1-12, 17-20; L102C

The seventy-two returned rejoicing, and said,
"Lord, even the demons are subject to us because of your name."
Jesus said, "I have observed Satan fall like lightning from the sky.
Behold, I have given you the power to 'tread upon serpents' and
scorpions
and upon the full force of the enemy and nothing will harm you.
Nevertheless, do not rejoice because the spirits are subject to you,
but rejoice because your names are written in heaven."

Fifteenth Sunday in Ordinary Time, *July 11, 2004*

Gospel (cont.)
Luke 10:25-37; L105C

He approached the victim,
poured oil and wine over his wounds and bandaged them.
Then he lifted him up on his own animal,
took him to an inn, and cared for him.
The next day he took out two silver coins
and gave them to the innkeeper with the instruction,
'Take care of him.
If you spend more than what I have given you,
I shall repay you on my way back.'
Which of these three, in your opinion,
was neighbor to the robbers' victim?"
He answered, "The one who treated him with mercy."
Jesus said to him, "Go and do likewise."

Fifteenth Sunday in Ordinary Time, *July 11, 2004*

RESPONSORIAL PSALM
Ps 19:8, 9, 10, 11

℟. (9a) Your words, Lord, are Spirit and life.

The law of the LORD is perfect,
    refreshing the soul;
the decree of the LORD is trustworthy,
    giving wisdom to the simple.

℟. Your words, Lord, are Spirit and life.

The precepts of the LORD are right,
    rejoicing the heart;
the command of the LORD is clear,
    enlightening the eye.

℟. Your words, Lord, are Spirit and life.

The fear of the LORD is pure,
    enduring forever;
the ordinances of the LORD are true,
    all of them just.

℟. Your words, Lord, are Spirit and life.

They are more precious than gold,
    than a heap of purest gold;
sweeter also than syrup
    or honey from the comb.

℟. Your words, Lord, are Spirit and life.

Seventeenth Sunday in Ordinary Time, *July 25, 2004*

Gospel (cont.)
Luke 11:1-13; L111C

"And I tell you, ask and you will receive;
    seek and you will find;
    knock and the door will be opened to you.
For everyone who asks, receives;
    and the one who seeks, finds;
    and to the one who knocks, the door will be opened.
What father among you would hand his son a snake
    when he asks for a fish?
Or hand him a scorpion when he asks for an egg?
If you then, who are wicked,
    know how to give good gifts to your children,
    how much more will the Father in heaven
    give the Holy Spirit to those who ask him?"

SECOND READING
Col 2:12-14

Brothers and sisters:
You were buried with him in baptism,
    in which you were also raised with him
    through faith in the power of God,
    who raised him from the dead.
And even when you were dead
    in transgressions and the uncircumcision of your flesh,
    he brought you to life along with him,
    having forgiven us all our transgressions;
obliterating the bond against us, with its legal claims,
    which was opposed to us,
    he also removed it from our midst, nailing it to the cross.

Nineteenth Sunday in Ordinary Time, *August 8, 2004*

Gospel (cont.)
Luke 12:32-48; L117C

Then Peter said,
    "Lord, is this parable meant for us or for everyone?"
And the Lord replied,
    "Who, then, is the faithful and prudent steward
    whom the master will put in charge of his servants
    to distribute the food allowance at the proper time?
Blessed is that servant whom his master on arrival finds doing so.
Truly, I say to you, the master will put the servant
    in charge of all his property.
But if that servant says to himself,
    'My master is delayed in coming,'
    and begins to beat the menservants and the maidservants,
    to eat and drink and get drunk,

then that servant's master will come
    on an unexpected day and at an unknown hour
    and will punish the servant severely
    and assign him a place with the unfaithful.
That servant who knew his master's will
    but did not make preparations nor act in accord with his will
    shall be beaten severely;
    and the servant who was ignorant of his master's will
    but acted in a way deserving of a severe beating
    shall be beaten only lightly.
Much will be required of the person entrusted with much,
    and still more will be demanded of the person entrusted with more."

Gospel (cont.)

Luke 1:39-56; L622

> He has cast down the mighty from their thrones,
>   and has lifted up the lowly.
> He has filled the hungry with good things,
>   and the rich he has sent away empty.
> He has come to the help of his servant Israel
>   for he has remembered his promise of mercy,
>   the promise he made to our fathers,
>   to Abraham and his children forever."

Mary remained with her about three months
   and then returned to her home.

Twenty-Fourth Sunday in Ordinary Time, *September 12, 2004*

Gospel (cont.)

Luke 15:1-32; L132C

Then he said,
   "A man had two sons, and the younger son said to his father,
   'Father give me the share of your estate that should come to me.'
So the father divided the property between them.
After a few days, the younger son collected all his belongings
   and set off to a distant country
   where he squandered his inheritance on a life of dissipation.
When he had freely spent everything,
   a severe famine struck that country,
   and he found himself in dire need.
So he hired himself out to one of the local citizens
   who sent him to his farm to tend the swine.
And he longed to eat his fill of the pods on which the swine fed,
   but nobody gave him any.
Coming to his senses he thought,
   'How many of my father's hired workers
   have more than enough food to eat,
   but here am I, dying from hunger.
I shall get up and go to my father and I shall say to him,
   "Father, I have sinned against heaven and against you.
I no longer deserve to be called your son;
   treat me as you would treat one of your hired workers."'
So he got up and went back to his father.
While he was still a long way off,
   his father caught sight of him,
   and was filled with compassion.
He ran to his son, embraced him and kissed him.
His son said to him,
   'Father, I have sinned against heaven and against you;
   I no longer deserve to be called your son.'
But his father ordered his servants,
   'Quickly bring the finest robe and put it on him;
   put a ring on his finger and sandals on his feet.

Take the fattened calf and slaughter it.
Then let us celebrate with a feast,
   because this son of mine was dead, and has come to life again;
   he was lost, and has been found.'
Then the celebration began.
Now the older son had been out in the field
   and, on his way back, as he neared the house,
   he heard the sound of music and dancing.
He called one of the servants and asked what this might mean.
The servant said to him,
   'Your brother has returned
   and your father has slaughtered the fattened calf
   because he has him back safe and sound.'
He became angry,
   and when he refused to enter the house,
   his father came out and pleaded with him.
He said to his father in reply,
   'Look, all these years I served you
   and not once did I disobey your orders;
   yet you never gave me even a young goat to feast on with my
      friends. But when your son returns,
   who swallowed up your property with prostitutes,
   for him you slaughter the fattened calf.'
He said to him,
   'My son, you are here with me always;
   everything I have is yours.
But now we must celebrate and rejoice,
   because your brother was dead and has come to life again;
   he was lost and has been found.'"

Gospel (cont.)
Luke 16:1-13; L135C

"For the children of this world
  are more prudent in dealing with their own generation
    than are the children of light.
I tell you, make friends for yourselves with dishonest wealth,
  so that when it fails, you will be welcomed into eternal dwellings.
The person who is trustworthy in very small matters
  is also trustworthy in great ones;
    and the person who is dishonest in very small matters
      is also dishonest in great ones.
If, therefore, you are not trustworthy with dishonest wealth,
  who will trust you with true wealth?
If you are not trustworthy with what belongs to another,
  who will give you what is yours?
No servant can serve two masters.
He will either hate one and love the other,
  or be devoted to one and despise the other.
You cannot serve both God and mammon."

Gospel (cont.)
Luke 16:19-31; L138C

He said, 'Then I beg you, father,
  send him to my father's house, for I have five brothers,
    so that he may warn them,
      lest they too come to this place of torment.'
But Abraham replied, 'They have Moses and the prophets.
Let them listen to them.'
He said, 'Oh no, father Abraham,
  but if someone from the dead goes to them, they will repent.'
Then Abraham said, 'If they will not listen to Moses and the prophets,
  neither will they be persuaded if someone should rise from the dead.'"

All Saints, *November 1, 2004*

FIRST READING
Rev 7:2-4, 9-14

I, John, saw another angel come up from the
    East,
  holding the seal of the living God.
He cried out in a loud voice to the four angels
  who were given power to damage the land
      and the sea,
  "Do not damage the land or the sea or the
      trees
    until we put the seal on the foreheads of
      the servants of our God."
I heard the number of those who had been
    marked with the seal,
  one hundred and forty-four thousand
      marked
    from every tribe of the Israelites.

After this I had a vision of a great multitude,
  which no one could count,
    from every nation, race, people, and tongue.
They stood before the throne and before the
    Lamb,
  wearing white robes and holding palm
      branches in their hands.
They cried out in a loud voice:
  "Salvation comes from our God,
    who is seated on the throne,
      and from the Lamb."
All the angels stood around the throne
  and around the elders and the four living
      creatures.

They prostrated themselves before the throne,
    worshiped God, and exclaimed:
  "Amen. Blessing and glory, wisdom and
      thanksgiving,
    honor, power, and might
      be to our God forever and ever. Amen."
Then one of the elders spoke up and said to
    me,
  "Who are these wearing white robes, and
      where did they come from?"
I said to him, "My lord, you are the one who
    knows."
He said to me,
  "These are the ones who have survived the
      time of great distress;
    they have washed their robes
      and made them white in the blood of the
        Lamb."

RESPONSORIAL PSALM
Ps 24:1-2, 3-4, 5-6

R℔. (cf. 6) Lord, this is the people that longs to
see your face.

The LORD's are the earth and its fullness;
  the world and those who dwell in it.
For he founded it upon the seas
  and established it upon the rivers.

R℔. Lord, this is the people that longs to see
your face.

Who can ascend the mountain of the LORD?
  or who may stand in his holy place?
One whose hands are sinless, whose heart is
    clean,
  who desires not what is vain.

R℔. Lord, this is the people that longs to see
your face.

He shall receive a blessing from the LORD,
  a reward from God his savior.
Such is the race that seeks for him,
  that seeks the face of the God of Jacob.

R℔. Lord, this is the people that longs to see
your face.

SECOND READING
1 John 3:1-3

Beloved:
See what love the Father has bestowed on us
  that we may be called the children of God.
Yet so we are.
The reason the world does not know us
  is that it did not know him.
Beloved, we are God's children now;
  what we shall be has not yet been revealed.
We do know that when it is revealed we shall
    be like him,
  for we shall see him as he is.
Everyone who has this hope based on him
    makes himself pure,
  as he is pure.

FIRST READING
Job 19:1, 23-27a; L1011.2

Job answered Bildad the Shuhite and said:
Oh, would that my words were written down!
    Would that they were inscribed in a record:
That with an iron chisel and with lead
    they were cut in the rock forever!
But as for me, I know that my Vindicator
        lives,
    and that he will at last stand forth upon the
        dust;
Whom I myself shall see:
    my own eyes, not another's, shall behold
        him;
And from my flesh I shall see God;
    my inmost being is consumed with longing.

RESPONSORIAL PSALM
Ps 143:1-2, 5-6, 7ab and 8ab, 10; L1013.10

℟. (1a) O Lord, hear my prayer.

O LORD, hear my prayer;
    hearken to my pleading in your
        faithfulness;
    in your justice answer me.
And enter not into judgment with your
        servant,
    for before you no living man is just.

℟. O Lord, hear my prayer.

I remember the days of old;
    I meditate on all your doings;
    the works of your hands I ponder.
I stretch out my hands to you;
    my soul thirsts for you like parched land.

℟. O Lord, hear my prayer.

Hasten to answer me, O LORD;
    for my spirit fails me.
At dawn let me hear of your mercy,
    for in you I trust.

℟. O Lord, hear my prayer.

Teach me to do your will,
    for you are my God.
May your good spirit guide me
    on level ground.

℟. O Lord, hear my prayer.

SECOND READING
Rom 8:31b-35, 37-39; L1014.5

Brothers and sisters:
If God is for us, who can be against us?
He did not spare his own Son
    but handed him over for us all,
        will he not also give us everything else
            along with him?
Who will bring a charge against God's chosen
        ones?
It is God who acquits us.
Who will condemn?
It is Christ Jesus who died, rather, was raised,
    who also is at the right hand of God,
    who indeed intercedes for us.
What will separate us from the love of Christ?
Will anguish, or distress or persecution, or
        famine,
    or nakedness, or peril, or the sword?

No, in all these things, we conquer
        overwhelmingly
    through him who loved us.
For I am convinced that neither death, nor life,
    nor angels, nor principalities,
    nor present things, nor future things,
    nor powers, nor height, nor depth,
    nor any other creature will be able to
        separate us
    from the love of God in Christ Jesus our
        Lord.

Thirty-Third Sunday in Ordinary Time, *November 14, 2004*

Gospel (cont.)
Luke 21:5-19; L159C

"Before all this happens, however,
    they will seize and persecute you,
    they will hand you over to the synagogues and to prisons,
    and they will have you led before kings and governors
    because of my name.
It will lead to your giving testimony.
Remember, you are not to prepare your defense beforehand,
    for I myself shall give you a wisdom in speaking
    that all your adversaries will be powerless to resist or refute.
You will even be handed over by parents, brothers, relatives,
    and friends,
    and they will put some of you to death.
You will be hated by all because of my name,
    but not a hair on your head will be destroyed.
By your perseverance you will secure your lives."

FIRST READING
Sir 50:22-24; L943.2

And now, bless the God of all,
   who has done wondrous things on earth;
Who fosters people's growth from their
     mother's womb,
   and fashions them according to his will!
May he grant you joy of heart
   and may peace abide among you;
May his goodness toward us endure in Israel
   to deliver us in our days.

RESPONSORIAL PSALM
Ps 113:1-2, 3-4, 5-6, 7-8; L945.2

℞. (see 2) Blessed be the name of the Lord for
ever.
   or:
℞. Alleluia.

Praise, you servants of the Lord,
   praise the name of the Lord.
Blessed be the name of the Lord
   both now and forever.
℞. Blessed be the name of the Lord for ever.
   or:
℞. Alleluia.

From the rising to the setting of the sun
   is the name of the Lord to be praised.
High above all nations is the Lord;
   above the heavens is his glory.
℞. Blessed be the name of the Lord for ever.
   or:
℞. Alleluia.

Who is like the Lord, our God, who is
     enthroned on high
   and looks upon the heavens and the earth
     below?
℞. Blessed be the name of the Lord for ever.
   or:
℞. Alleluia.

He raises up the lowly from the dust;
   from the dunghill he lifts up the poor.
To seat them with princes,
   with the princes of his own people.
℞. Blessed be the name of the Lord for ever.
   or:
℞. Alleluia.

SECOND READING
1 Cor 1:3-9; L944.1

Brothers and sisters:
Grace to you and peace from God our Father
   and the Lord Jesus Christ.

I give thanks to my God always on your
     account
   for the grace of God bestowed on you in
     Christ Jesus,
   that in him you were enriched in every way,
   with all discourse and all knowledge,
   as the testimony to Christ was confirmed
     among you,
   so that you are not lacking in any spiritual
     gift
   as you wait for the revelation of our Lord
     Jesus Christ.
He will keep you firm to the end,
   irreproachable on the day of our Lord Jesus
     Christ.
God is faithful,
   and by him you were called to fellowship
     with his Son, Jesus Christ our Lord.

Choral Settings for the General Intercessions

Purchasers of this volume may reproduce these choral arrangements for use in their parish or community. The music must be reproduced as given below, with composer's name and copyright line.

ADVENT

CHRISTMAS and EASTER

LENT

SOLEMNITIES

ORDINARY TIME, WEEKS 2-7

ORDINARY TIME, WEEKS 12-20

ORDINARY TIME, WEEKS 21-33

Lectionary Pronunciation Guide

Lectionary Word	Pronunciation
Aaron	EHR-uhn
Abana	AB-uh-nuh
Abednego	uh-BEHD-nee-go
Abel-Keramin	AY-b'l-KEHR-uh-mihn
Abel-meholah	AY-b'l-mee-HO-lah
Abiathar	uh-BAI-uh-ther
Abiel	AY-bee-ehl
Abiezrite	ay-bai-EHZ-rait
Abijah	uh-BAI-dzhuh
Abilene	ab-uh-LEE-neh
Abishai	uh-BIHSH-ay-ai
Abiud	uh-BAI-uhd
Abner	AHB-ner
Abraham	AY-bruh-ham
Abram	AY-br'm
Achaia	uh-KAY-yuh
Achim	AY-kihm
Aeneas	uh-NEE-uhs
Aenon	AY-nuhn
Agrippa	uh-GRIH-puh
Ahaz	AY-haz
Ahijah	uh-HAI-dzhuh
Ai	AY-ee
Alexandria	al-ehg-ZAN-dree-uh
Alexandrian	al-ehg-ZAN-dree-uhn
Alpha	AHL-fuh
Alphaeus	AL-fee-uhs
Amalek	AM-uh-lehk
Amaziah	am-uh-ZAI-uh
Amminadab	ah-MIHN-uh-dab
Ammonites	AM-uh-naitz
Amorites	AM-uh-raits
Amos	AY-muhs
Amoz	AY-muhz
Ampliatus	am-plee-AY-tuhs
Ananias	an-uh-NAI-uhs
Andronicus	an-draw-NAI-kuhs
Annas	AN-uhs
Antioch	AN-tih-ahk
Antiochus	an-TAI-uh-kuhs
Aphiah	uh-FAI-uh
Apollos	uh-PAH-luhs
Appius	AP-ee-uhs
Aquila	uh-KWIHL-uh
Arabah	EHR-uh-buh
Aram	AY-ram
Arameans	ehr-uh-MEE-uhnz
Areopagus	ehr-ee-AH-puh-guhs
Arimathea	ehr-uh-muh-THEE-uh
Aroer	uh-RO-er
Asaph	AY-saf
Asher	ASH-er
Ashpenaz	ASH-pee-naz
Assyria	a-SIHR-ee-uh
Astarte	as-TAHR-tee
Attalia	at-TAH-lee-uh
Augustus	uh-GUHS-tuhs
Azariah	az-uh-RAI-uh
Azor	AY-sawr
Azotus	uh-ZO-tus
Baal-shalishah	BAY-uhl-shuh-LAI-shuh
Baal-Zephon	BAY-uhl-ZEE-fuhn
Babel	BAY-bl
Babylon	BAB-ih-luhn
Babylonian	bab-ih-LO-nih-uhn
Balaam	BAY-lm
Barabbas	beh-REH-buhs
Barak	BEHR-ak
Barnabas	BAHR-nuh-buhs
Barsabbas	BAHR-suh-buhs
Bartholomew	bar-THAHL-uh-myoo
Bartimaeus	bar-tih-MEE-uhs
Baruch	BEHR-ook
Bashan	BAY-shan
Becorath	bee-KO-rath
Beelzebul	bee-EHL-zee-buhl
Beer-sheba	BEE-er-SHEE-buh
Belshazzar	behl-SHAZ-er
Benjamin	BEHN-dzhuh-mihn
Beor	BEE-awr
Bethany	BEHTH-uh-nee
Bethel	BETH-el
Bethesda	beh-THEHZ-duh
Bethlehem	BEHTH-leh-hehm
Bethphage	BEHTH-fuh-dzhee
Bethsaida	behth-SAY-ih-duh
Beth-zur	behth-ZER
Bildad	BIHL-dad
Bithynia	bih-THIHN-ih-uh
Boanerges	bo-uh-NER-dzheez
Boaz	BO-az
Caesar	SEE-zer
Caesarea	zeh-suh-REE-uh
Caiaphas	KAY-uh-fuhs
Cain	kayn
Cana	KAY-nuh
Canaan	KAY-nuhn
Canaanite	KAY-nuh-nait
Canaanites	KAY-nuh-naits
Candace	kan-DAY-see
Capernaum	kuh-PERR-nay-uhm
Cappadocia	kap-ih-DO-shee-u
Carmel	KAHR-muhl
carnelians	kahr-NEEL-yuhnz
Cenchreae	SEHN-kree-ay
Cephas	SEE-fuhs
Chaldeans	kal-DEE-uhnz
Chemosh	KEE-mahsh
Cherubim	TSHEHR-oo-bihm
Chislev	KIHS-lehv
Chloe	KLO-ee
Chorazin	kor-AY-sihn
Cilicia	sih-LIHSH-ee-uh
Cleopas	KLEE-o-pas
Clopas	KLO-pas
Corinth	KAWR-ihnth
Corinthians	kawr-IHN-thee-uhnz
Cornelius	kawr-NEE-lee-uhs
Crete	kreet
Crispus	KRIHS-puhs
Cushite	CUHSH-ait
Cypriot	SIH-pree-at
Cyrene	sai-REE-nee
Cyreneans	sai-REE-nih-uhnz
Cyrenian	sai-REE-nih-uhn
Cyrenians	sai-REE-nih-uhnz
Cyrus	SAI-ruhs
Damaris	DAM-uh-rihs
Damascus	duh-MAS-kuhs
Danites	DAN-aits
Decapolis	duh-KAP-o-lis
Derbe	DER-bee
Deuteronomy	dyoo-ter-AH-num-mee
Didymus	DID-I-mus
Dionysius	dai-o-NIHSH-ih-uhs
Dioscuri	dai-O-sky-ri
Dorcas	DAWR-kuhs
Dothan	DO-thuhn
dromedaries	DRAH-muh-dher-eez
Ebed-melech	EE-behd-MEE-lehk
Eden	EE-dn
Edom	EE-duhm
Elamites	EE-luh-maitz
Eldad	EHL-dad
Eleazar	ehl-ee-AY-zer
Eli	EE-lai
Eli Eli Lema Sabachthani	AY-lee AY-lee luh-MAH sah-BAHK-tah-nee

Lectionary Word	Pronunciation	Lectionary Word	Pronunciation	Lectionary Word	Pronunciation
Eliab	ee-LAI-ab	Gilead	GIHL-ee-uhd	Joppa	DZHAH-puh
Eliakim	ee-LAI-uh-kihm	Gilgal	GIHL-gal	Joram	DZHO-ram
Eliezer	ehl-ih-EE-zer	Golgotha	GAHL-guh-thuh	Jordan	DZHAWR-dn
Elihu	ee-LAI-hyoo	Gomorrah	guh-MAWR-uh	Joseph	DZHO-zf
Elijah	ee-LAI-dzhuh	Goshen	GO-shuhn	Joses	DZHO-seez
Elim	EE-lihm	Habakkuk	huh-BAK-uhk	Joshua	DZHAH-shou-ah
Elimelech	ee-LIHM-eh-lehk	Hadadrimmon	hay-dad-RIHM-uhn	Josiah	dzho-SAI-uh
Elisha	ee-LAI-shuh	Hades	HAY-deez	Jotham	DZHO-thuhm
Eliud	ee-LAI-uhd	Hagar	HAH-gar	Judah	DZHOU-duh
Elizabeth	ee-LIHZ-uh-bth	Hananiah	han-uh-NAI-uh	Judas	DZHOU-duhs
Elkanah	el-KAY-nuh	Hannah	HAN-uh	Judea	dzhou-DEE-uh
Eloi Eloi Lama	AY-lo-ee AY-lo-ee	Haran	HAY-ruhn	Judean	dzhou-DEE-uhn
Sabechthani	LAH-mah sah-	Hebron	HEE-bruhn	Junia	dzhou-nih-uh
	BAHK-tah-nee	Hermes	HER-meez	Justus	DZHUHS-tuhs
Elymais	ehl-ih-MAY-ihs	Herod	HEHR-uhd	Kephas	KEF-uhs
Emmanuel	eh-MAN-yoo-ehl	Herodians	hehr-O-dee-uhnz	Kidron	KIHD-ruhn
Emmaus	eh-MAY-uhs	Herodias	hehr-O-dee-uhs	Kiriatharba	kihr-ee-ath-AHR-buh
Epaenetus	ee-PEE-nee-tuhs	Hezekiah	heh-zeh-KAI-uh	Kish	kihsh
Epaphras	EH-puh-fras	Hezron	HEHZ-ruhn	Laodicea	lay-o-dih-SEE-uh
ephah	EE-fuh	Hilkiah	hihl-KAI-uh	Lateran	LAT-er-uhn
Ephah	EE-fuh	Hittite	HIH-tait	Lazarus	LAZ-er-uhs
Ephesians	eh-FEE-zhuhnz	Hivites	HAI-vaitz	Leah	LEE-uh
Ephesus	EH-fuh-suhs	Hophni	HAHF-nai	Lebanon	LEH-buh-nuhn
Ephphatha	EHF-uh-thuh	Hor	HAWR	Levi	LEE-vai
Ephraim	EE-fray-ihm	Horeb	HAWR-ehb	Levite	LEE-vait
Ephrathah	EHF-ruh-thuh	Hosea	ho-ZEE-uh	Levites	LEE-vaits
Ephron	EE-frawn	Hur	her	Leviticus	leh-VIH-tih-kous
Epiphanes	eh-PIHF-uh-neez	hyssop	HIH-suhp	Lucius	LOO-shih-uhs
Erastus	ee-RAS-tuhs	Iconium	ai-KO-nih-uhm	Lud	luhd
Esau	EE-saw	Isaac	AI-zuhk	Luke	look
Esther	EHS-ter	Isaiah	ai-ZAY-uh	Luz	luhz
Ethanim	EHTH-uh-nihm	Iscariot	ihs-KEHR-ee-uht	Lycaonian	lihk-ay-O-nih-uhn
Ethiopian	ee-thee-O-pee-uhn	Ishmael	ISH-may-ehl	Lydda	LIH-duh
Euphrates	yoo-FRAY-teez	Ishmaelites	ISH-mayehl-aits	Lydia	LIH-dih-uh
Exodus	EHK-so-duhs	Israel	IHZ-ray-ehl	Lysanias	lai-SAY-nih-uhs
Ezekiel	eh-ZEE-kee-uhl	Ituraea	ih-TSHOOR-ree-uh	Lystra	LIHS-truh
Ezra	EHZ-ruh	Jaar	DZHAY-ahr	Maccabees	MAK-uh-beez
frankincense	FRANGK-ihn-sehns	Jabbok	DZHAB-uhk	Macedonia	mas-eh-DO-nih-uh
Gabbatha	GAB-uh-thuh	Jacob	DZHAY-kuhb	Macedonian	mas-eh-DO-nih-uhn
Gabriel	GAY-bree-ul	Jairus	DZH-hr-uhs	Machir	MAY-kih
Gadarenes	GAD-uh-reenz	Javan	DZHAY-van	Machpelah	mak-PEE-luh
Galatian	guh-LAY-shih-uhn	Jebusites	DZHEHB-oo-zaits	Magdala	MAG-duh-luh
Galatians	guh-LAY-shih-uhnz	Jechoniah	dzhehk-o-NAI-uh	Magdalene	MAG-duh-lehn
Galilee	GAL-ih-lee	Jehoiakim	dzhee-HOI-uh-kihm	magi	MAY-dzhai
Gallio	GAL-ih-o	Jehoshaphat	dzhee-HAHSH-uh-fat	Malachi	MAL-uh-kai
Gamaliel	guh-MAY-lih-ehl	Jephthah	DZHEHF-thuh	Malchiah	mal-KAI-uh
Gaza	GAH-zuh	Jeremiah	dzhehr-eh-MAI-uh	Malchus	MAL-kuhz
Gehazi	gee-HAY-zai	Jericho	DZHEHR-ih-ko	Mamre	MAM-ree
Gehenna	geh-HEHN-uh	Jeroham	dzhehr-RO-ham	Manaen	MAN-uh-ehn
Genesis	DZHEHN-uh-sihs	Jerusalem	dzheh-ROU-suh-lehm	Manasseh	man-AS-eh
Gennesaret	gehn-NEHS-uh-reht	Jesse	DZHEH-see	Manoah	muh-NO-uh
Gentiles	DZHEHN-tailz	Jethro	DZHEHTH-ro	Mark	mahrk
Gerasenes	DZHEHR-uh-seenz	Joakim	DZHO-uh-kihm	Mary	MEHR-ee
Gethsemane	gehth-SEHM-uh-ne	Job	DZHOB	Massah	MAH-suh
Gideon	GIHD-ee-uhn	Jonah	DZHO-nuh	Mattathias	mat-uh-THAI-uhs

Lectionary Word	Pronunciation	Lectionary Word	Pronunciation	Lectionary Word	Pronunciation
Matthan	MAT-than	Parmenas	PAHR-mee-nas	Sababth	SAB-uhth
Matthew	MATH-yoo	Parthians	PAHR-thee-uhnz	Sadducees	SAD-dzhoo-seez
Matthias	muh-THAI-uhs	Patmos	PAT-mos	Salem	SAY-lehm
Medad	MEE-dad	Peninnah	pee-NIHN-uh	Salim	SAY-lim
Mede	meed	Pentecost	PEHN-tee-kawst	Salmon	SAL-muhn
Medes	meedz	Penuel	pee-NYOO-ehl	Salome	suh-LO-mee
Megiddo	mee-GIH-do	Perez	PEE-rehz	Salu	SAYL-yoo
Melchizedek	mehl-KIHZ-eh-dehk	Perga	PER-guh	Samaria	suh-MEHR-ih-uh
Mene	MEE-nee	Perizzites	PEHR-ih-zaits	Samaritan	suh-MEHR-ih-tuhn
Meribah	MEHR-ih-bah	Persia	PER-zhuh	Samothrace	SAM-o-thrays
Meshach	MEE-shak	Peter	PEE-ter	Samson	SAM-s'n
Mespotamia	mehs-o-po-TAY-mih-uh	Phanuel	FAN-yoo-ehl	Samuel	SAM-yoo-uhl
Micah	MAI-kuh	Pharaoh	FEHR-o	Sanhedrin	san-HEE-drihn
Midian	MIH-dih-uhn	Pharisees	FEHR-ih-seez	Sarah	SEHR-uh
Milcom	MIHL-kahm	Pharpar	FAHR-pahr	Sarai	SAY-rai
Miletus	mai-LEE-tuhs	Philemon	fih-LEE-muhn	saraph	SAY-raf
Minnith	MIHN-ihth	Philippi	fil-LIH-pai	Sardis	SAHR-dihs
Mishael	MIHSH-ay-ehl	Philippians	fih-LIHP-ih-uhnz	Saul	sawl
Mizpah	MIHZ-puh	Philistines	fih-LIHS-tihnz	Scythian	SIH-thee-uihn
Moreh	MO-reh	Phinehas	FEHN-ee-uhs	Seba	SEE-buh
Moriah	maw-RAI-uh	Phoenicia	fee-NIHSH-ih-uh	Seth	sehth
Mosoch	MAH-sahk	Phrygia	FRIH-dzhih-uh	Shaalim	SHAY-uh-lihm
myrrh	mer	Phrygian	FRIH-dzhih-uhn	Shadrach	SHAY-drak
Mysia	MIH-shih-uh	phylacteries	fih-LAK-ter-eez	Shalishah	shuh-LEE-shuh
Naaman	NAY-uh-muhn	Pi-Hahiroth	pai-huh-HAI-rahth	Shaphat	Shay-fat
Nahshon	NAY-shuhn	Pilate	PAI-luht	Sharon	SHEHR-uhn
Naomi	NAY-o-mai	Pisidia	pih-SIH-dih-uh	Shealtiel	shee-AL-tih-ehl
Naphtali	NAF-tuh-lai	Pithom	PAI-thahm	Sheba	SHEE-buh
Nathan	NAY-thuhn	Pontius	PAHN-shus	Shebna	SHEB-nuh
Nathanael	nuh-THAN-ay-ehl	Pontus	PAHN-tus	Shechem	SHEE-kehm
Nazarene	NAZ-awr-een	Praetorium	pray-TAWR-ih-uhm	shekel	SHEHK-uhl
Nazareth	NAZ-uh-rehth	Priscilla	PRIHS-kill-uh	Shiloh	SHAI-lo
nazirite	NAZ-uh-rait	Prochorus	PRAH-kaw-ruhs	Shinar	SHAI-nahr
Nazorean	naz-aw-REE-uhn	Psalm	Sahm	Shittim	sheh-TEEM
Neapolis	nee-AP-o-lihs	Put	puht	Shuhite	SHOO-ait
Nebuchadnezzar	neh-byoo-kuhd-NEHZ-er	Puteoli	pyoo-TEE-o-lai	Shunammite	SHOO-nam-ait
Negeb	NEH-gehb	Qoheleth	ko-HEHL-ehth	Shunem	SHOO-nehm
Nehemiah	nee-hee-MAI-uh	qorban	KAWR-bahn	Sidon	SAI-duhn
Ner	ner	Quartus	KWAR-tuhs	Silas	SAI-luhs
Nicanor	nai-KAY-nawr	Quirinius	kwai-RIHN-ih-uhs	Siloam	sih-LO-uhm
Nicodemus	nih-ko-DEE-muhs	Raamses	ray-AM-seez	Silvanus	sihl-VAY-nuhs
Niger	NAI-dzher	Rabbi	RAB-ai	Simeon	SIHM-ee-uhn
Nineveh	NIHN-eh-veh	Rabbouni	ra-BO-nai	Simon	SAI-muhn
Noah	NO-uh	Rahab	RAY-hab	Sin (desert)	sihn
Nun	nuhn	Ram	ram	Sinai	SAI-nai
Obed	O-behd	Ramah	RAY-muh	Sirach	SAI-rak
Olivet	AH-lih-veht	Ramathaim	ray-muh-THAY-ihm	Sodom	SAH-duhm
Omega	o-MEE-guh	Raqa	RA-kuh	Solomon	SAH-lo-muhn
Onesimus	o-NEH-sih-muhs	Rebekah	ree-BEHK-uh	Sosthenes	SAHS-thee-neez
Ophir	O-fer	Rehoboam	ree-ho-BO-am	Stachys	STAY-kihs
Orpah	AWR-puh	Rephidim	REHF-ih-dihm	Succoth	SUHK-ahth
Pamphylia	pam-FIHL-ih-uh	Reuben	ROO-b'n	Sychar	SI-kar
Paphos	PAY-fuhs	Revelation	reh-veh-LAY-shuhn	Syene	sai-EE-nee
		Rhegium	REE-dzhee-uhm	Symeon	SIHM-ee-uhn
		Rufus	ROO-fuhs	synagogues	SIHN-uh-gahgz

Lectionary Word	Pronunciation	Lectionary Word	Pronunciation	Lectionary Word	Pronunciation
Syrophoenician	SIHR-o fee-NIHSH-ih-uhn	Timon	TAI-muhn	Zebedee	ZEH-beh-dee
		Titus	TAI-tuhs	Zebulun	ZEH-byoo-luhn
Tabitha	TAB-ih-thuh	Tohu	TO-hyoo	Zechariah	zeh-kuh-RAI-uh
Talitha koum	TAL-ih-thuh-KOOM	Trachonitis	trak-o-NAI-tis	Zedekiah	zeh-duh-KAI-uh
Tamar	TAY-mer	Troas	TRO-ahs	Zephaniah	zeh-fuh-NAI-uh
Tarshish	TAHR-shihsh	Tubal	TYOO-b'l	Zerah	ZEE-ruh
Tarsus	TAHR-suhs	Tyre	TAI-er	Zeror	ZEE-rawr
Tekel	TEH-keel	Ur	er	Zerubbabel	zeh-RUH-buh-behl
Terebinth	TEHR-ee-bihnth	Urbanus	er-BAY-nuhs	Zeus	zyoos
Thaddeus	THAD-dee-uhs	Uriah	you-RAI-uh	Zimri	ZIHM-rai
Theophilus	thee-AH-fih-luhs	Uzziah	yoo-ZAI-uh	Zion	ZAI-uhn
Thessalonians	theh-suh-LO-nih-uhnz	Wadi	WAH-dee	Ziph	zihf
Theudas	THU-duhs	Yahweh-yireh	YAH-weh-yer-AY	Zoar	ZO-er
Thyatira	thai-uh-TAI-ruh	Zacchaeus	zak-KEE-uhs	Zorah	ZAWR-uh
Tiberias	tai-BIHR-ih-uhs	Zadok	ZAY-dahk	Zuphite	ZUHR-ait
Timaeus	tai-MEE-uhs	Zarephath	ZEHR-ee-fath		

INDEX OF LITURGICAL TOPICS

Advent
and redemption, 5
penance service, 9
purple, 219
service music, 5
Announcing the Christmas mystery, 19
Ascension, choice of second reading, 135

Baptisms, parish, 77

Cantor
helping the, Part 1, 211
helping the, Part 2, 215
Change
and liturgy, 239
and liturgical music, 239
Choice of readings (Holy Family), 29
Christ's presence in liturgy, 61
Communion hymn, purpose, 25
Creed and intercessions, 73
Cross, 159
Cup, drinking from the, 153

Discipleship
and victory, 255
liturgical music and growth in, 255

Easter
Sunday, special ritual features, 109
Lectionary, first reading from Acts, 115
Lectionary, hinge Sunday, 123
maintaining festivity, 119
Epiphany themes, 45
Eschatological turning point in Luke's gospel, 203
Eucharist
faithfulness and thankfulness, 227
God's gift asking for response, 119
Eucharist's epiphanies, 45
Eucharistic
mystery, breadth of, 153
word and its fulfillment, 49

Faithfulness, Stewardship and liturgy, 191
Father's Day, 159
First Readings during Lent, 73

Genealogy, Matthew's, 25
Gift of worship, 35
Good Friday
singing the solemn prayers, 105
special ritual features, 105

Hands as sacramental symbol, 123
Holy, Holy, Holy, 219
Holy Saturday, special ritual features, 107
Holy Thursday, special ritual features, 103
Hospitality ministers, 179

Indwelling, God's, 131
Intercessions
Creed and, 73
for the dead at Mass, 127

July 4th, 171

Lamb of God, 235
Lent
First readings during, 73
Year C Lenten gospels, 81
Year A Lenten readings, 81
Liturgical law: enslavement or freedom?, 175
Liturgical music
and growth in discipleship, 255
change and, 239
Liturgy
change and, 239
as prayer, 183, 231
God's prodigality in, 211
stewardship, faithfulness, and, 191
Liturgy of the Word, 53
Liturgy's true focus, 187
"Lord, I am not worthy . . . ," 57
Luke's gospel, eschatological turning point, 203

Mass "trains" us, 65
Ministry
as service, 223
of the assembly, 15, 251
Mother's Day, 127

Parish baptisms, 77
Participation in passion gospels, 97
Passion gospels, participation in, 97
Penitential rite, 9
and confession of sins, 81
Pentecost
readings, 143
birthday of the Church?, 143
Postludes, preludes and, 175
Prayer
as gift of elder community members, 139
intercessory, 207
intimacy of, 139

liturgy as, 183, 231
Praying always, 215
Prefaces, 199
Preludes and postludes, 175
Procession with palms, 97
Processions at Mass, 165

Readings, choosing longer or shorter forms, 171
Repentance, why communal dimension, 93
Responsorial psalm
    choice of, 175
    helping the assembly sing, Part 1, 203
    helping the assembly sing, Part 2, 207
    role of, Part 1, 179
    role of, Part 2, 183
    role of, Part 3, 187
    selecting musical settings, Part 1, 191
    selecting musical settings, Part 2, 199
Resurrection of the dead, 247

Seasonal service music, selecting
    Part 1, 45
    Part 2, 49
    Part 3, 53

Part 4, 57
Part 5, 61
Part 6, 65
Part 7, 159
Part 8, 165
Sequence, singing the, 143
Service music
    changing, 199
    for Ordinary Time, 39
Sign of the Cross, making the, 149
Silences during Mass, 135
Sin
    affects the whole body, 87
    Why communal dimension, 93
Solemnities, Sundays and, 195
Stewardship, faithfulness, and liturgy, 191
Strengthening family life, 29
Sundays and solemnities, 195
". . . sweat became like drops of blood . . .," 97
Symbols of baptism, 39

Veneration of the cross, music during, 105
Vigil readings (Christmas), 25

INDEX OF BIBLICAL TOPICS

Baptism and identity, 37
Barren fig tree, 79
Beatitudes
    in Luke, 59
    moral life flows from, 63
Being fed and feeding others, 117
Book of Glory (John's gospel), 125

Call of Simon Peter, 55
Crisis, act now to avoid, 213

Day is coming (end time), 249
Discipleship
    cost of, 205
    sitting at his feet, 177
Door, the narrow, 197

Faith, 147
    and obedience, 221
Families of Jesus and Samuel, 27
Feeding the 5000, and the kingdom, 151
Forgiveness, and new life, 113

Genealogy of Jesus, 23
Gift of revelation, 33
Good News for Gentiles, 51

High priestly prayer, Jesus', 137
Holy Spirit, New life, 113
Humility and prayer, 233

Infancy and passion, 17
Isaiah and national restoration, 91

Jerusalem, journey to
    Part 1, 163
    Part 2, 225
Jesus
    as Savior, 253
    in the passion according to Luke, 95
    and the Father are one, 121
Journey to Jerusalem
    Part 1, 163
    Part 2, 225

Kingdom
    and feeding the 5000, 151
    of God, 169
    Son of Man and, 189

Love and law, 173
Luke's gospel, major themes conclude, 133

Meals and table fellowship, 201
Mercy, 193
Moral life flows from the Beatitudes, 63

New Jerusalem, 129
New life: Holy Spirit, peace, forgiveness, 113

Obedience, faith and, 221

Passion
    Transfiguration and, 75
    Jesus in, according to Luke, 95
Peace, and new life, 113
Pentecost as fitting conclusion to fifty days, 141
Pharisees, Scribes and, 209
Pierced, look on him whom they have, 157
Poor, rich and, 217
Prayer
    asking confidently, 181
    humility and, 233
Promise/Fulfillment, 3
Prophecy and fulfillment, 47

Repentance/Forgiveness, 7
Repentance
    and relationship with God, 13
    "Coming to his senses," 85
Resurrection, 245
Rich and poor, 217
Riches, wealth and, 185

Savior, Jesus as, 253
Scribes and Pharisees, 209
Signs, 43
Son of Man and the Kingdom of God, 189

Table fellowship, meals and, 201
Tax collectors, Zacchaeus and, 237
Temptations, 71
Transfiguration and passion, 75

Wealth and riches, 185
Widow, persistent, 229

Zacchaeus and tax collectors, 237

Living Liturgy Bulletins

Bulletins that truly are "parish-able"

Food for the soul . . . these are bulletins that you will definitely want to share with your parishioners, who won't be able to put them down once they have them in their hands.

Living Liturgy Bulletins are also practical. They nurture your parishioners. The bulletins share the Sunday gospel reading and a reflection for living the Gospel and send people forth to live it, bringing the liturgy into their homes and meeting places.

The bulletins are divided into major sections offering:

A the Opening Prayer of the Day

B the gospel reading

C commissioned full-color artwork

D a reflection on the reading

E questions that pertain to the Gospel and the reflection

F weekday reading references

G a closing prayer—not shown below, appears after reflection

Together, they all highlight one main point that encourages your parishioners to live the Gospel. Each section provides food for the soul to last throughout the week.

Sunday Bulletins

Four Color, 14 x 8 1/2, printed on one side

25-75	$1.35 net per 25, per week
100-275	$4.95 net per 100, per week
300 or more	$4.68 net per 100, per week

Prices do not include shipping and handling.
Please order in quantities of 25, billed and shipped 13 weeks at a time.

Sunday Inserts

Four Color, 7 x 8 1/2, printed on both sides
$3.95 per 100, per week,
plus shipping and handling
Includes Advent and Lent inserts. Minimum order: 100, order in quantities of 25 over the minimum. Billed and shipped 13 weeks at a time.

Single subscriptions of Sunday Inserts are just $30.00 net per year, billed once and shipped 13 weeks at a time.

SPECIAL OFFER FOR SMALL PARISH GROUPS

These Sunday Inserts can also be used as faith-sharing aids. Small parish groups can receive bulk subscription pricing for inserts. Anyone wishing to order less than 100 sets can order 25 inserts per week for 52 weeks for just $89.00. Includes shipping and handling. Billed once and shipped 13 weeks at a time.

Advent Bulletin Inserts

A0-8146-2559-2
Four Color, 7 x 8 1/2,
printed on both sides
Set of four Advent inserts, $25.00 per 100 sets, plus shipping and handling
Minimum order: 100 sets, order in quantities of 25 sets over the minimum.

Order both Advent and Lent inserts together and receive an additional 5% discount.

Lent Bulletin Inserts

A0-8146-2721-8
Four Color, 7 x 8 1/2, printed on both sides
Set of six Lent inserts, $37.50 per 100 sets, plus shipping and handling
Minimum order: 100 sets, order in quantities of 25 sets over the minimum.

LITURGICAL MINISTRY

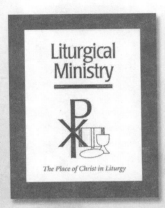

Different from other pastoral liturgical publications, *Liturgical Ministry* grounds its pastoral material in consistent liturgical theology. Both the scholarly research and pastoral materials are included in the same issues as complementary aspects of liturgical renewal.

Scholarly Update—keeps ministers aware of issues of liturgical importance.

Pastoral Focus—addresses the practicalities of liturgy-making. It also concentrates on relevant pastoral implications, sacramentality, spirituality, and issues of Christian living.

Liturgical Notes—by Joyce Ann Zimmerman, C.PP.S., Editor, show how good practice must be grounded in good liturgical theology.

Music Notes—by Kathleen Harmon, S.N.D. de N., focus on developing relevant aspects of a theology of liturgical music.

Bulletin Inserts—build liturgical awareness and tangibly enhance parish worship. Twelve bulletin inserts are included in each issue, one for each week between the four issues.

Subscriptions:	**$30.00, one year (four issues); $53.00, two years**
Foreign:	**$35.00, one year; $63.00, two years**
Libraries:	**$46.00, one year**
Single copy:	**$10.00**

www.litpress.org/mag/litmin.html

"The Lord has truly blessed you with great scholarship and provocative insights. There is a pastoral need for your publication of Liturgical Ministry. *You have made a great contribution to the cause of liturgy with this publication."*
    Most Rev. Donald W. Trautman
    Bishop of Erie

THE LITURGICAL PRESS
St. John's Abbey, P.O. Box 7500
Collegeville, MN 56321-7500
Phone: 1-800-858-5450, ext. 2226

BOOKMARK

Living Liturgy

Individual Use

Each individual who uses *Living Liturgy* will probably develop a process that best suits her or his prayer, reflection, and study. This day-by-day suggestion might help people get started.

MONDAY
- Read reflectively the gospel
- Use the "Assembly & Faith-Sharing Groups" spirituality statements (and the specific liturgical ministry statements if they apply) to help you live the gospel during the day

TUESDAY
- Read the gospel again
- Read and study "Focusing the Word"
- Pray the [alternative] opening prayer

WEDNESDAY
- Read reflectively the first reading
- Read the second reading (during festal seasons)
- Read "Reflecting on the Gospel"
- Consider what further insights into the gospel you have gained

THURSDAY
- Read and study "Living the Paschal Mystery"
- Pray the "Model General Intercessions"

FRIDAY
- Read the responsorial psalm
- Read "Appreciating the Responsorial Psalm"
- Reflect on the connection between first reading and gospel that the responsorial psalm makes
- Pray the responsorial psalm

SATURDAY
- Reread the gospel
- Reflect on how you have been able to live this gospel during the week
- Read the page titled "Catechesis" in order to further your understanding of liturgy
- Pray the "Model Penitential Rite" (outside of Easter time); pray the [alternative] opening prayer (during Easter time)

SUNDAY
- Enter fully into the celebration of Eucharist
- Enjoy a day of rest

BOOKMARK

Living Liturgy

Group Use

Groups using *Living Liturgy* for prayer and faith-sharing might begin with the following general format and then adjust it to fit different occasions.

OPENING PRAYER

- Begin with a hymn
- Pray the "Model Penitential Rite" and/or the [alternative] opening prayer for the Sunday or solemnity

GOD'S WORD

- Proclaim the gospel
- Observe a brief period of silence
- [Proclaim another reading, if time permits]

INDIVIDUAL STUDY, REFLECTION, PRAYER

- Read and consider one or more of the following: "Reflecting on the Gospel," "Living the Paschal Mystery," "Focusing the Word," and/or the page entitled "Catechesis"
- Spend some time in reflection and prayer

FAITH-SHARING

- Use the "Assembly & Faith-Sharing Groups" spirituality statements (and the specific liturgical ministry statements if they apply)
- Consider what ways you are being challenged to *live* the liturgy you will celebrate on Sunday

CONCLUDING PRAYER

- Pray the "Model General Intercessions"
- Pray the Our Father at the end of the intercessions
- Conclude with a hymn

LITURGICAL PRESS
St. John's Abbey, P.O. Box 7500
Collegeville, MN 56321-7500

Phone: **1-800-858-5450**   Fax: **1-800-445-5899**
E-mail: **sales@litpress.org**   Order online: **www.litpress.org**

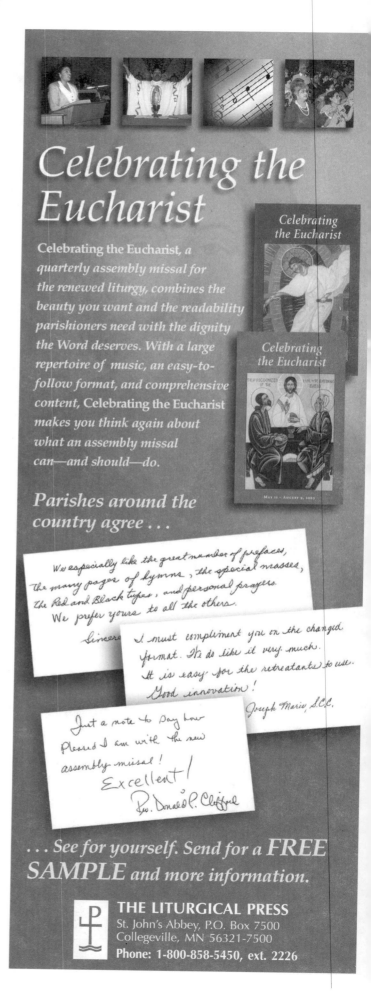